基本
A HANDBOOK
CHARACTERS

基本汉字学习手册
A Handbook for 1,000 Basic Chinese Characters

王国安 主编

Edited by

Wang Guo'an

The Chinese University Press

A Handbook for 1,000 Basic Chinese Characters
   Edited by Wang Guo'an

© **The Chinese University of Hong Kong,** 2006

ISBN 962–996–283–7

THE CHINESE UNIVERSITY PRESS
The Chinese University of Hong Kong
SHA TIN, N.T., HONG KONG
Fax: +852 2603 6692
      +852 2603 7355
E-mail: cup@cuhk.edu.hk
Web-site: www.chineseupress.com

Printed in Hong Kong

Table of Contents

Preface

A Handbook for 1,000 Basic Chinese Characters is designed for foreign learners of the Chinese language. Except for native speakers of Japanese and Korean, where learning Chinese characters is part of their own linguistic heritage, foreign learners of Chinese always find learning Chinese characters a barrier that is hard to overcome. Indeed, the overwhelming number, a complicated stroke pattern, and the multiple meanings and nuances depending on usage are an obvious challenge. It may even reduce the drive and interest to learn the language. This volume should help address the problem.

The salient features of this *Handbook* are as follows:

(1) The choice of characters is based on *The Outline of Graded Chinese Characters* (汉字等级大纲) as promulgated by the Examination Section in the Office of the National Committee for Chinese as a Second Language. These 1,000 characters are chosen from the list.

(2) Each and every character is given its meaning in English together with pronunciation and the equivalent traditional form, if any.

(3) Besides its meanings, each character is given its parts of speech along with its usage.

(4) Each character is attached to its usual collocations and idiomatic usage.

(5) The entire content is expressed bilingually in Chinese and English.

We sincerely believe that frequent consultation of this *Handbook* will enhance the Chinese language proficiency of the Chinese language learner.

While I am the Editor of this *Handbook*, Prof. Tao Lien, Associate Editor, has helped in many ways. We also appreciate the valuable contributions from our fellow language teachers and colleagues at Fudan, namely, Hsu Yuming, Gao Shunquan, Wu Jinli, Wang Xiaoman, Ji Xiaojing and Shen Lan. The English portion of this work has been read and revised by an American alumni of Fudan, Mr. Richard L. Mertl. Dr. Steven K. Luk, Director of the Chinese University Press, has edited the manuscript and provided valuable comments during the process.

We sincerely hope that this volume will provide much needed assistance to the beginning learners of the Chinese language, and are looking forward to their comments, which will be of use when this *Handbook* is revised.

Wang Guo'an
College of International Cultural Exchange, Fudan University
Shanghai, China

Abbreviations

This is a list of commonly used abbreviations in this work:

a.	adjective 形容词
adv.	adverb 副词
conj.	conjunction 连词
measure w.	measure word 量词
n.	noun 名词
num.	number 数词
pol.	polite 表示礼貌
prep.	preposition 介词
pron.	pronoun 代词
sb.	somebody 某人
sth.	something 某事
v.	verb 动词
aux. w.	auxiliary words 助词

汉语拼音索引

　　本索引按照单字的读音，依汉语拼音顺序排序，同音者依笔画数由少至多排序，同笔画者则依页数由小至大排序。多音字根据不同读音多处列出。

　　本索引采繁体与简体并列，繁体字加方括号〔　〕附更其简体字之后。

Index Based on *Hanyu Pinyin*

This index first arranges entries according to their spelling in the *Hanyu Pinyin* phonetic system. Characters that have the same pronunciation are arranged, in ascending order, according to the number of strokes used to write them. When the stroke numbers are also the same, the characters are organized by page number. A character of multlple pronunciations is shown in separate entries.

Both traditional and simplified forms of the characters are shown in this index. The traditional forms are indicated in square brackets [　] next to their respective simplified forms.

笔画数索引

　　本索引按照单字的笔画数由少至多排序，同笔画数者则依页码由少至多排序，同页码者则依汉语拼音顺序排序。繁体字加圆括号（　）以作识别。

Index Based on Stroke Numbers

　　Characters in this index are arranged, in ascending order, according to the number of strokes used to write them. When the stroke numbers are the same, the characters are organized by page numbers. The characters on the same page are then ordered by their *Pinyin* pronunciations. Traditional forms of the characters are indicated in brackets (　).

挨₁ āi   一 亅 扌 扩 护 护 护 挓 挨 挨

释义 Meaning

动词 v.

1. follow a regular order or sequence; do sth. in sequence or by turns: 他一早就挨家挨户送报纸。He goes from house to house delivering the newspaper in the morning.

2. be or get close to; be next to: 我家挨着电影院。My home is next to a cinema.

词语 Words and phrases

| 挨边 | āibiān | keep close to the edge; be close to; be connected with the subject |
| 挨肩 | āijiān | sit or stand shoulder to shoulder. |

熟语 Idioms

| 挨肩擦膀 | āi jiān cā bǎng | go in a jostling crowd; rub shoulders |
| 挨门逐户 | āi mén zhú hù | go from house to house; from door to door |

挨₂ ái   一 亅 扌 扩 护 护 护 挓 挨 挨

释义 Meaning

动词 v.

1. suffer; endure: 我挨了爸爸一记耳光。I got a box on the ear from my father.

2. struggle to pull through (hard times); drag out: 丈夫死后，她挨了三十年苦日子。She suffer day after day for 30 years since her husband died.

3. delay; stall; put off: 下雨了，运动会要挨到下星期了。The sports meeting should be put off till next week because of the rain.

词语 Words and phrases

挨整　　 āizhěng　　be the target of criticism or attack.

矮 ǎi

丿　丿　丿　丿　矢　矢　矢　矣　矫　矫

矮　矮　矮

释义 Meaning

形容词 a.

1. short (of stature): 我比姐姐矮。I'm shorter than my sister.
   反义词 antonym: 高

2. low: 城外有座矮墙。There is a low wall outside the town.
   反义词 antonym: 高

3. low in rank or grade: 跳级以前他比我矮一级。He was a grade lower than I before he skipped a grade. 反义词 antonym: 高

词语 Words and phrases

矮凳　　ǎidèng　　a low stool

矮胖　　ǎipàng　　short and stout; dumpy

矮小　　ǎixiǎo　　short and small; undersized

矮子　　ǎizi　　a short person; dwarf

矮墩墩　ǎidūndūn　pudgy; dumpy; stumpy

熟语 Idioms

矮子里拔　　ǎizi li bá　　choose a general from the
将军　　　　jiāngjūn　　dwarfs; pick the best out
of a mediocre bunch

爱 ài

一　一　一　四　四　严　严　严　爱　爱

(愛

一　一　一　四　四　严　严　恶　恶　恶　愛

愛　愛)

释义 Meaning

动词 v.

1. love: 我爱上那个姑娘了。I have fallen in love with that girl. 反义词 antonym: 恨

2. like; be fond of; be keen on: 他爱跳舞。He is fond of dancing.

3. cherish; treasure; hold dear; take good care of: 我们应该教育孩子从小爱公物。We should teach children to take good care of public property.

4. be apt to; be in the habit of: 妈妈总爱发脾气。Mother is always losing her temper.

词语 Words and phrases

爱戴	àidài	love and esteem
爱国	àiguó	love one's country; be patriotic
爱好	àihào	① take great pleasure in; be keen on ② interest; hobby
爱护	àihù	cherish; treasure; take good care of
爱情	àiqíng	love (between man and woman)
爱人	àirén	① husband or wife ② sweetheart; lover

熟语 Idioms

爱不释手	ài bú shì shǒu	be so delighted with sth. that one will not put it down; be too fond of sth. to let go of it
爱莫能助	ài mò néng zhù	be willing to help but cann't; love but have no ability to render assistance
爱屋及乌	ài wū jí wū	love for a person extends even to the crows on his roof; love one thing on account of another

安 ān   ` ´ ` ` 安 安

释义 Meaning

（一）形容词 a.

1. peaceful; at ease; undisturbed; calm: 吃了这片药，你可以安睡到天亮。You will sleep peacefully until daybreak after you've taken the tablet.

2. safe; secure; in good health: 孩子的病情已经转危为安了。The child's condition has already stablized. 反义词 antonym: 危

（二）动词 v.

1. rest content; be satisfied: 你不应该安于落后。You shouldn't be satisfied with your backward state and not wish to do any better.

2. install; fix; fit: 中国大部分的家庭都安上了电话。Most families in China have installed the telephone.

（三）代词 pron.

1. where: 30年前的老屋如今安在？Where lies the old house of 30 years ago?

2. (used in rhetorical question) how: 我是他的好朋友，安能袖手旁观？I'm his good friend, how can I stand by and do nothing?

词语 Words and phrases

安定	āndìng	① stable; quiet; settled ② stabilize
安家	ānjiā	① settle down ② set up a home
安静	ānjìng	① quiet; peaceful ② calm; undisturbed ③ quiet down
安排	ānpái	arrange (matters); plan the details; dispose
安全	ānquán	safe; secure

安装	ānzhuāng	install; fix; set up
平安	píngān	safe and sound; without mishap
早安	zǎoān	good morning

熟语 Idioms

| 安分守己 | ānfèn shǒujǐ | law-abiding; abide by the status or law and behave oneself accordingly |
| 安居乐业 | ān jū lè yè | enjoy a good and prosperous life; live a good life |

岸 àn   丷 丷 丷 丷 屵 屵 崀 岸

释义 Meaning

名词 n.

bank; shore; coast: 江岸有一排柳树。On the bank of the river stands a row of willow trees.

词语 Words and phrases

| 岸标 | ànbiāo | shore beacon |

按 àn   二 十 扌 扩 扩 扩 按 按 按

释义 Meaning

(一)动词 v.

1. press; push down: 有人在按门铃，去看看是谁。Go to see who is ringing the doorbell.

2. leave aside; shelve: 这事先按下，以后再说。The matter should be put aside for a period of time.

(二)介词 prep.

according to; in accordance with; in the light of: 一切应当按规章制度办。Everything should be done in accordance with the rules and regulations.

词语 Words and phrases

按理	ànlǐ	according to the principle and reason
按摩	ànmó	massage
按时	ànshí	on time; on schedule
按照	ànzhào	according to; in the light of

熟语 Idioms

按部就班	àn bù jiù bān	keep to the schedule for doing things; step by step
按劳分配	àn láo fēnpèi	each according to his work; distribution according to labour
按捺不住	ànnà bú zhù	cannot control oneself; unable to restrain

八 bā　　ノ　八

释义 Meaning

数词 num.

eight: 这个西瓜重八公斤。This watermelon weighs eight kilos.

词语 Words and phrases

八宝饭	bābǎofàn	eight-treasure rice pudding (steamed glutinous rice with bean paste, lotus seeds, preserved fruits, etc.)
八方	bāfāng	the eight points of the compass; all directions
八卦	bāguà	the Eight Trigrams (used in divination in China)
八月	bāyuè	August
八成	bāchéng	① eighty per cent ② most probably; most likely
八辈子	bā bèizi	eight lifetimes; a long time

熟语 Idioms

八面玲珑	bā miàn líng lóng	be a good mixer; be smooth and slick (in establishing social relations)
八九不离十	bā jiǔ bù lí shí	most probably; very close; nine times out of ten
八字没一撇	bā zì méi yì piě	there's not the slightest sign of success yet; things aren't even starting to take shape yet

吧₁ bā ｜ 𠃌 𠄌 𠃌 𠃌 𠃌 吧

释义 Meaning

象声词 onomatopoeia

"吧"的一声，他把一根树枝折断了。With a snap, he broke off a branch.

吧₂ ba ｜ 𠃌 𠄌 𠃌 𠃌 𠃌 吧

释义 Meaning

助词 aux. w.

1. (indicating a suggestion, a request or a mild command): 我们去看电影吧。Let's go to the cinema.

2. (indicating consent or approval): 行，明天上午十点在这儿见面吧。Ok, we'll see each other at 10 o'clock tomorrow morning.

3. (forming a leading question which asks for confirmation of a supposition): 你是广东人吧？You are from Guang Dong, I suppose?

4. (marking a pause after suppositions as alternatives): 去吧，太晚了；不去吧，又不好。If I go, it's too late; If I don't, it's no good.

拔 bá   二 十 扌 扩 扩 扮 拔 拔

释义 Meaning

动词 v.

1. pull out; pull up: 她在田里拔草。She is pulling up weeds in the field.
2. choose; select; pick: 我们没办法，只好矮子里拔将军。We have no choice but to pick the best out of a mediocre bunch.

词语 Words and phrases

拔除	báchú	pull out; remove
拔萃	bácuì	stand out from one's peers; be out of the common run
拔高	bágāo	tug-of-war
拔河	báhé	tug-of-war
拔腿	bátuǐ	① lift the foot (and begin to run) ② leave (one's work); get away; free oneself
选拔	xuǎnbá	select; choose
海拔	hǎibá	elevation; height above sea level

熟语 Idioms

拔苗助长	bá miáo zhù zhǎng	try to help the rice shoots grow by pulling them up; pull up seedlings in the mistaken hope of helping them grow

把 bǎ   二 十 扌 扌 扌 扌 把

释义 Meaning

（一）动词 v.

1. hold; grasp: 小男孩把住栏杆不肯放手。The boy is holding on to the railing tightly without loosening.

2. hold (a baby while it relieves itself): 丈夫在给宝宝把尿。My husband is holding our baby out to let it urinate.

3. guard; watch: 那老头儿把门很严。The old man guards the door closely.

（二）名词 n.

handle (of a pushcart, etc.): 自行车把是黑色的。The handle bars of the bicycle are black.

（三）量词 measure w.

1. for sth. with a handle: 我买了两把扇子。I bought two fans.

2. handful of: 他摘了一把玫瑰给心上人。He plucked a bunch of roses for his beloved.

3. for certain abstract ideas: 我已经一把年纪了，该退休了。I'm getting on in years and should retire.

4. for sth. done with the hand: 拉我一把，我没力气爬了。Please give me a hand, I haven't the strength to keep climbing.

（四）介词 prep.

(used to shift the object before the verb, which must be reduplicated or accompanied by another word or expression): 请你把词典放到书架上。Put the dictionary on the bookshelf please.

词语 Words and phrases

把柄	bǎbǐng	① handle ② an excurse
把关	bǎguān	① guard a pass ② guard against
把守	bǎshǒu	guard
把握	bǎwò	① hold; grasp ② assurance; certainty
把戏	bǎxì	① acrobatics; jugglery ② cheap trick; game

把兄弟　　bǎxiōngdì　　sworn brothers

熟语 Idioms

把水搅浑　　bǎ shuǐ jiǎo hún　　muddy the water; create confusion

爸 bà ＇ ＾ ＾ ＜ ＜ 父 爷 爸 爸

释义 Meaning

名词 n.

pa; dad; father: 我爸是个工程师。My dad is an engineer.

词语 Words and phrases

爸爸　　bàba　　papa; dad; father

白 bái ＇ ｜' 白 白 白

释义 Meaning

（一）形容词 a.

1. white: 妈妈头上已经生出了几根白发。Mother has already had a few white hairs.

2. pure; plain; blank: 借我几张白纸好吗？Would you please loan me a few blank pieces of paper?

（二）副词 adv.

1. in vain; to no purpose; for nothing: 我白跑一趟，什么也没买到。I've made a fruitless trip, for I was unable to buy anything.

2. free of charge; gratis: 为了道歉，餐馆白送我一顿饭。In apology to me, the restaurant gave me a meal for free.

（三）动词 v.

look at sb. with the white of the eye; give sb. a supercilious look; coldly stare at sb.: 她白了我一眼，没说什么。She gave me a supercilious look and said nothing.

词语 Words and phrases

白菜	báicài	Chinese cabbage
白痴	báichī	① idiocy ② idiot
白人	báirén	Caucasian man or woman
白糖	báitáng	(refined) white sugar
白天	báitiān	daytime; day
白眼	báiyǎn	supercilious look
表白	biǎobái	express or state clearly; explain oneself
空白	kòngbái	blank space

熟语 Idioms

白璧无瑕	bái bì wú xiá	flawless white jade; impeccable moral integrity
白手起家	bái shǒu qǐ jiā	start empty-handed; build up from nothing

百 bǎi   一 ア 丁 百 百 百

释义 Meaning

（一）数词 num.

hundred: 差不多有一百人参加这次会议。There were almost one hundred people attending the meeting.

（二）形容词 a.

numerous; all kinds of: 花园里百花盛开。All kinds of flowers come into bloom in the garden.

词语 Words and phrases

百倍	bǎibèi	a hundred times; a hundredfold
百合	bǎihé	lily
百货	bǎihuò	general merchandise
百年	bǎinián	① a hundred years; a century ② life time
百事通	bǎishìtōng	① knowledgeable person ② know-all
百姓	bǎixìng	common people

百叶窗　　bǎiyèchuāng　　shutter; blind; jalousie
百科全书 bǎikē quánshū　encyclopaedia

熟语 Idioms

百读不厌	bǎi dú bú yàn	be worth reading a hundred times; never get tired of reading something
百花齐放	bǎi huā qí fàng	flowers of every kind are in bloom; let a hundred flowers bloom
百无聊赖	bǎi wú liáo lài	bored to death; time hangs heavy on one's hands
百依百顺	bǎi yī bǎi shùn	be obedient in every aspect; all obedience; obey sb. implicitly
百闻不如一见	bǎi wén bù rú yí jiàn	better to see sth. once than to hear about it a hundred times; seeing for oneself is better than hearing from others

摆bǎi 一 十 扌 扌 扩 护 押 押 押 押
捏 摆 摆

(擺 一 十 扌 扌 扩 护 押 押 押 押 护
揹 揹 揹 揹 擺 擺 擺)

释义 Meaning

动词 v.

1. put; place; arrange: 开饭了，快点儿摆好碗筷。Time to eat, set the table quickly.

2. put on; assume: 他总在年轻人面前摆老资格。He's always flaunting his seniority in front of the young people.

3. sway; wave: 她向我摆摆手就走了。She waved to me and then went away.

词语 Words and phrases

摆放	bǎifàng	put; place; lay
摆架子	bǎijiàzi	put on airs; give oneself airs
摆平	bǎipíng	be fair to; be impartial to
摆设	bǎishè	furnish and decorate (a room)
摆脱	bǎituō	shake off; cast off; break away from; free oneself from
摆钟	bǎizhōng	pendulum clock

败 bài 丨 冂 贝 贝 贝 财 败 败

(敗 丨 冂 日 日 目 貝 貝 敗 敗 敗)

释义 Meaning

动词 v.

1. be defeated; lose: 这场足球赛他们败了。They were defeated in this soccer contest. 反义词 antonym: 胜、赢

2. spoil: 这件事情就败在你手里。It's you who spoiled the whole thing. 反义词 antonym: 成

3. decay; wither: 这朵花没开几天就败了。The flower bloomed for a few days and then withered. 反义词 antonym: 开

词语 Words and phrases

败坏	bàihuài	ruin; corrupt; undermine
败家子	bàijiāzǐ	spendthrift; wastrel; prodigal
败类	bàilèi	scum of a community; degenerate
败露	bàilù	(of a plot, etc.) fall through and stand exposed
败兴	bàixìng	have one's spirits dampened; feel dis-

appointed

败仗	bàizhàng	lost battle; defeat
失败	shībài	① be defeated; lose (a war, etc.) ② fail
成败	chéngbài	success or failure

熟语 Idioms

| 败柳残花 | bàiliǔcánhuā | a faded flower and withered willow; fallen women |

拜 bài　一　三　三　手　手　手　手　手　拜

释义 Meaning

动词 v.

1. do obeisance: 奶奶又到庙里去拜佛了。Grandma went to the temple again to worship Buddha.

2. congratulate (on a certain occasion): 我们去给老师拜年吧。Let's go to pay the teacher a new year call.

3. visit; pay a visit: 小张拜亲友去了。Xiao Zhang went to pay a visit to his relatives and friends.

4. acknowledge sb. as one's master, godfather, etc.: 我拜他为师学武术。I became a martial arts student of his.

词语 Words and phrases

拜别	bàibié	*pol.* take leave of
拜读	bàidú	*pol.* read with respect
拜访	bàifǎng	pay a visit; call on
拜见	bàijiàn	① pay a formal visit; call to pay respects ② meet one's senior or superior
拜寿	bàishòu	congratulate an elderly person on his birthday; offer birthday felicitations
拜堂	bàitáng	old (of bride and groom) make ceremonial obeisances; perform the marriage ceremony
拜托	bàituō	*pol.* request sb. to do sth.

拜金主义 bàijīn zhǔyì money worship

班 bān 　一　三　干　王　歪　玐　玐　玣　班　班

释义 Meaning

（一）名词 n.

1. class; team: 我们班有二十个学生。There are 20 students in our class.

2. shift; duty: 我是早上的班。I'm on duty in the morning.

（二）量词 measure w.

1. a group of people: 这班女孩子都很活泼。This bunch of young girls is lively.

2. a trip by bus, boat, etc.: 我乘下一班飞机去北京。I'll take the next plane to Beijing.

（三）形容词 a.

regularly-run; regular; scheduled: 我坐公司班车回家。I always take the regular company bus back home.

词语 Words and phrases

班房	bānfáng	① jail ② classroom
班级	bānjí	classes and grades in school
班长	bānzhǎng	① class monitor ② squad leader ③ (work) team leader
班子	bānzi	① old theatrical ② organized group
班组	bānzǔ	teams and groups (in factories, etc.)
上班	shàngbān	go to work; start work; be on duty
坐班	zuòbān	keep office hours

熟语 Idioms

班门弄斧	bān mén nòng fǔ	show off one's skill with the axe before Lu Ban, the master carpenter; show off before a superior man

搬 bān   一 十 扌 扩 扩 扐 扐 扐 扐 扔 扔 扐 搬 搬

释义 Meaning

动词 v.

1. take away; move; remove: 把电视机搬到柜子上去。
   Put the television on the cabinet.

2. move (house): 他们一个月前搬走了。They moved out
   a month ago.

词语 Words and phrases

搬动	bāndòng	① move; remove; shift ② employ; draw on; dispatch
搬家	bānjiā	move (house); remove
搬迁	bānqiān	move; transfer; remove
搬运	bānyùn	carry; transport
搬运工	bānyùngōng	porter (at a railway station); docker (at a seaport)

熟语 Idioms

搬弄是非	bānnòng shìfēi	sow discord; gossip; make mischief
搬起石头打自己的脚	bān qǐ shítou dǎ zìjǐ de jiǎo	be hoist by one's own petard; pick up a stone only to drop it on one's own feet

板 bǎn   一 十 才 木 杧 杬 板 板

释义 Meaning

（一）名词 n.

1. board; plank; plate: 书桌上压了一块玻璃板。The desk
   has a plate-glass top.

2. an accented beat in traditional Chinese music; time; measure:

她京剧唱得有板有眼的。She sings the Beijing opera with an excellent rhythm.

（二）形容词 a.

1. hard: 好久没下雨了，土都板了。It hadn't rained for so long a time that the ground had become hard.

2. stiff; unnatural: 照片上的表情太板了。The expression in the picture is too stiff.

（三）动词 v.

stop smiling; look serious: 老师板着脸批评我们。The teacher criticized us with a straight face.

词语 Words and phrases

板车	bǎnchē	a flatbed cart
板凳	bǎndèng	wooden bench or stool
板块	bǎnkuài	plate
板球	bǎnqiú	① cricket ② cricket ball
板书	bǎnshū	① write on the blackboard ② words written on the blackboard; blackboard writing
板子	bǎnzi	① board; plank ② bamboo or birch for corporal punishment
黑板	hēibǎn	blackboard
快板	kuàibǎn	allegro

熟语 Idioms

板板六十四	bǎnbǎn liùshísì	unaccommodating; stick to rules strictly
板上钉钉	bǎn shàng dìng dīng	that clinches it; no two ways about it

办 bàn　フ 力 办 办

（辦　ヽ　亠　宀　亠　立　立　辛　刔　勃　勃　剃　剃　剃　辨　辨　辦）

释义 Meaning

动词 v.

1. do; handle; manage; tackle; attend to: 这件事让她一个人去办就行了。She can just handle this matter by herself.

2. set up; run: 她哥哥办了一家乡镇企业。Her brother set up a village and township enterprise.

3. prepare; get sth. ready: 他俩下个月就要办喜事了。They prepare to get married next month.

词语 Words and phrases

办案	bàn'àn	handle a legal case; apprehend (a criminal)
办法	bànfǎ	way; means; measure
办公室	bàngōngshì	office
办货	bànhuò	make purchases for an organization or enterprise; purchase
办理	bànlǐ	handle; conduct; transact
办事处	bànshìchù	office; agency
办学	bànxué	run a school

半 bàn ⼂ ⼝ 兰 兰 半

释义 Meaning

（一）名词 n.

1. half; semi: 他来中国已经半年了。He has been to China for half a year.

2. in the middle; halfway: 他走到半路又回来了。He only walked halfway before turning back.

3. very little; the least bit: 关于这个秘密他半个字也不说。He wouldn't tell a word about the secret.

（二）副词 adv.

partly; about half: 他半开玩笑半认真地说。He says sth.

half jokingly and half seriously.

词语 Words and phrases

半辈子	bànbèizi	half a lifetime
半岛	bàndǎo	peninsula
半决赛	bànjuésài	semifinals (in sports)
半票	bànpiào	half-price ticket; half fare
半球	bànqiú	hemisphere
半数	bànshù	half the number; half
半天	bàntiān	① half of the day ② a long time; quite a while
半夜	bànyè	midnight; in the middle of the night

熟语 Idioms

半工半读	bàn gōng bàn dú	work while studying at school; work-study program
半斤八两	bàn jīn bā liǎng	six of one and half a dozen of the other; as broad as long
半途而废	bàn tú érfèi	give up halfway; stop midway
半新不旧	bàn xīn bú jiù	no longer new; showing signs of wear
半夜三更	bànyè sāngēng	in the depth of night; at midnight

扮 bàn　一　十　扌　扩　扒　扮　扮

释义 Meaning

动词 v.

1. be dressed up as; play the part of; disguise oneself as: 她在这部电影里扮一位中学教师。She plays the part of a middle school teacher in this film.

2. put on (an expression): 儿子对我扮了一个鬼脸。My son grimaced at me.

词语 Words and phrases

扮相	bànxiàng	the appearance of an actor or actress in costume and makeup
扮演	bànyǎn	play the part of; act
扮装	bànzhuāng	(of an actor, etc.) put on makeup; make up

帮 bāng 一 二 三 丰 丰彡 邦 邦 帮 帮

(幫 一 十 土 圭 圭 圭 圭 封 封 封 封 封 封 幇 幇 幫 幫 幫）

释义 Meaning

（一）动词 v.

1. help; assist; aid: 你能帮我搬一下电视机吗？Will you please help me to move the television?

2. be hired: 她在我们家帮佣。She was hired as a servant in our family.

（二）名词 n.

1. side (of a boat, truck, etc.) or upper (of a shoe): 他站在船帮上。He stood at the side of the boat.

2. outer leaf (of cabbage, etc.): 这菜帮可真难吃。This outer leaf of the cabbage is too bad to eat.

3. gang; band; clique: 他们是旧上海滩上的青帮。They belonged to the Qing Gang in old Shanghai.

（三）量词 measure w.

group: 我们公司里来了一帮大学生。A group of university students has come to our company.

词语 Words and phrases

帮会	bānghuì	secret society; underworld gang
帮忙	bāngmáng	help; give (or lend) a hand; do a favour; do a good turn
帮派	bāngpài	faction; clique
帮腔	bāngqiāng	speak in support of sb.; echo sb.; chime in with sb.
帮手	bāngshǒu	helper; assistant
帮凶	bāngxiōng	accomplice; accessary
帮助	bāngzhù	help; assist; aid

包 bāo   ノ 勹 勹 勹 包

释义 Meaning

（一）动词 v.

1. wrap: 用报纸把这本书包起来。Please wrap up the book in a sheet of newspaper.

2. surround; encircle; envelop: 烟雾包住了整个房子。The house was shrouded in a thick smoke.

3. undertake the whole thing: 买票的事包在我身上。Just leave it all to me to buy the tickets.

4. assure; guarantee: 放心吧，这儿的一切包你满意。You can set your mind at rest, I assure you that everything here will be all right.

5. hire; charter: 他们结婚的时候包了30桌酒席。They reserved thirty banquet tables when they got married.

（二）名词 n.

1. bag; sack: 这个商店出售各种各样的包。The shop has all kinds of bags to sell.

2. protuberance; swelling; lump: 我的腿上被蚊子咬了一个包。My leg swelled where the mosquito bit me.

（三）量词 measure w.

package; bundle: 我们家一个月要吃两包大米。Our family consumes two sacks of rice every month.

词语 Words and phrases

包庇	bāobì	shield; harbour; cover up
包打听	bāodǎtīng	① detective ② nosy parker; snooper
包袱	bāofu	① cloth-wrapper ② a bundle wrapped in cloth ③ millstone round one's neck; load; weight; burden
包含	bāohán	contain; embody; include
包括	bāokuò	include; consist of; comprise; incorporate
包围	bāowéi	surround; encircle
包扎	bāozhā	wrap up; bind up; pack
包装	bāozhuāng	pack (commodities); package

熟语 Idioms

包办代替	bāobàn dàitì	do everything on behalf of; run things all by oneself without consulting others
包罗万象	bāoluó wànxiàng	cover and contain everything; all inclusive

宝 bǎo `丶丷宀宀宀宇宝宝`

（寶 `丶丷宀宁宁宇宝宯宲宲宲宲寳寳寳寳寳寶寶`）

释义 Meaning

（一）名词 n.

treasure: 钻石是宝中之宝。Diamond is the treasure among treasures.

（二）形容词 a.

1. precious; treasured: 这把宝刀是我家祖传的。This precious sword is handed down from our ancestors.

2. *honor; your*: 我要借你们宝地一用。I want to borrow your place.

词语 Words and phrases

宝宝	bǎobo	(a pet name for a child) darling; baby
宝贝	bǎobèi	① treasured object; treasure ② darling; baby (used ironically) good-for-nothing or queer character
宝贵	bǎoguì	① valuable; precious ② value; treasure; set store by
宝石	bǎoshí	precious stone; gem
宝藏	bǎozàng	precious (mineral) deposits
宝座	bǎozuò	throne

熟语 Idioms

宝刀不老	bǎodāo bù lǎo	the man is old, but not his sword; he is still at the height of his powers

饱bǎo ノ 亻 亻 亻 饣 饣 饣 饣 饱

(飽 ノ 𠂉 𠂉 今 今 含 食 食 食 飠 飠 飠 飽)

释义 Meaning

（一）动词 v.

1. have eaten one's fill; be full: 你吃饱了吗？Are you full? 反义词antonym: 饿

2. satisfy: 这次旅行真饱眼福了。We have feasted our eyes on this trip.

（二）形容词 a.

full; plump: 今年的谷粒都很饱。The grains are quite plump this year. 反义词 antonym: 瘪

（三）副词 adv.

fully; to the full: 妈妈的眼里饱含着激动的泪水。Mother's eyes are filled with tears of excitement.

词语 Words and phrases

饱餐	bǎocān	eat to one's heart's content
饱和	bǎohé	saturation; saturated
饱满	bǎomǎn	full; plump
饱受	bǎoshòu	suffer enough from; have one's fill of

熟语 Idioms

饱汉不知饿汉饥	bǎo hàn bù zhī è hàn jī	the well-fed doesn't know how the starving suffer
饱经沧桑	bǎo jīng cāngsāng	have experienced many vicissitudes of life

报 bào 一 十 扌 扌 扩 扚 报 报

（報 一 十 士 去 去 幸 幸 幸 幸 幸 報 報 報 ）

释义 Meaning

（一）动词 v.

1. report; announce; declare: 这个议案我们还要报上级批准。We should report the proposal to the higher authorities for approval.

2. reply; respond; reciprocate: 观众对她的表演报以热烈的掌声。Spectators responded with warm applause to her performance.

3. revenge: 杀父之仇我一定要报。I will certainly take revenge against the one who killed my father.

（二）名词 n.

1. recompense; requite: 你帮我这么大的忙，我简直无以为报。You help me so much, I'm quite unable to repay the kindness at all.

2. newspaper: 快来看报！今天有重要新闻。Come to read the newspaper quickly! It has important news today.

词语 Words and phrases

报案	bào'àn	report a case to security authorities
报酬	bàochou	reward; remuneration; pay
报到	bàodào	report for duty; check in; register
报复	bàofù	make reprisals; retaliate
报告	bàogào	① report; make known ② report; speech; talk; lecture
报警	bàojǐng	report (an incident) to the police
报名	bàomíng	enter one's name; sign up
报社	bàoshè	general office of a newspaper; newspaper office
报纸	bàozhǐ	newspaper
画报	huàbào	illustrated magazine or newspaper; pictorial
电报	diànbào	telegram; cable

熟语 Idioms

报仇雪恨	bàochóu xuěhèn	get even with a hated enemy; take revenge
报喜不报忧	bào xǐ bú bào yōu	report only what is good while concealing what is unpleasant

抱 bào　一　十　扌　扩　扨　拘　抱　抱

释义 Meaning

动词 v.

1. hold or carry in the arms; embrace; hug: 街上人太多，把孩子抱起来吧。The street is too crowded, take the child in your arms.

2. have one's first child or grandchild: 老张家抱了一个孙子。Lao Zhang's family has already had their first grandson.

3. adopt (a child): 二十年前抱的孩子已经长大了。The child who was adopted twenty years ago has grown up.

4. cherish; harbour: 我对考大学不抱希望。I cherish no hope of passing the college entrance examination.

词语 Words and phrases

抱不平	bàobùpíng	be outraged by an injustice (done to sb. else)
抱负	bàofù	aspiration; ambition
抱歉	bàoqiàn	be sorry; feel apologetic; regret
抱怨	bàoyuàn	complain; grumble

熟语 Idioms

抱头鼠窜	bào tóu shǔ cuàn	be frightened away; cover one's face and creep away
抱头痛哭	bào tóu tòng kū	weep in each other's arms; hang on sb's neck and weep out

杯bēi 一 十 才 木 杧 杧 杯 杯

释义 Meaning

（一）量词 measure w.

cup: 妈妈给客人倒了一杯茶。Mother pours a cup of tea for the guest.

（二）名词　n.

1. (alcoholic) drink: 咱们俩去喝一杯吧。Let's go to have a drink.
2. (prize) cup; trophy: 女足又拿到了世界杯冠军。The women's soccer team has won the World Cup again.

词语 Words and phrases

杯中物	bēizhōngwù	wine
杯子	bēizi	cup; glass

熟语 Idioms

杯弓蛇影	bēi gōng shé yǐng	mistaking the reflection of a bow in the cup for a snake; be suspicious of intrigue
杯盘狼藉	bēi pán lángjí	the cups, bowls and dishes lie about in disorder
杯水车薪	bēi shuǐ chē xīn	trying to put out a blazing cartload of faggots with a cup of water; a useless attempt

北 běi　丨　十　丬　北′　北

释义 Meaning

名词　n.

north: 我们去城北那家餐厅吃饭吧。We go to the restaurant north of the city to eat.

词语 Words and phrases

北半球	běibànqiú	the Northern Hemisphere
北边	běibiān	① north; the northern side ② same as 北方
北方	běifāng	north; the northern part of the country, esp. the area north of the Yellow River; the North

北风	běifēng	north wind
北极	běijí	① North Pole; Arctic Pole ② north magnetic pole
北面	běimiàn	① face north; be a subject or vassal ② north; the northern side
北纬	běiwěi	northern latitude

背₁ bēi　丨　丁　ヨ　ヨ′　ヨ゛　北　背　背　背

释义 Meaning

1. carry on the back: 孩子病了，我背他去医院。The child is sick, I carry him on my back to the hospital.

2. bear; shoulder: 我背不起这么大的责任。I can't shoulder such a heavy responsibility.

词语 Words and phrases

背包	bēibāo	① knapsack; rucksack; infantry (or field) pack; backpack ② blanket roll
背包袱	bēi bāofu	carry baggage; have a weight (or load) on one's mind
背黑锅	bēi hēiguō	be made a scapegoat; be unjustly blamed
背债	bēi zhài	be in debt; be saddled with debts

背₂ bèi　丨　丁　ヨ　ヨ′　ヨ゛　北　背　背　背

释义 Meaning

（一）名词 n.

1. the back of the body: 我背上好痒啊！My back itches so much!

2. the back of an object: 爸爸的衣服在椅背上放着呢！Father's clothes are lyingt on the back of the chair!

（二）动词 v.

1. with the back towards: 这个房间是背着太阳的。The

room faces away from the sun.

2. turn away: 她背过脸哭起来了。She turns her face away and begins to cry.

3. hide sth. from; do sth. behind sb.'s back: 她总喜欢背着人说坏话。She likes to speak ill of others behind the back.

4. recite from memory; learn by heart (or by rote): 这些生词你都背出来了吗？Have you already learnt these new words by heart?

词语 Words and phrases

背地里	bèidìli	behind sb's back; privately; on the sly
背后	bèihòu	① behind; at the back; in the rear ② behind sb's back
背景	bèijǐng	background; backdrop
背面	bèimiàn	the back; the reverse side; the wrong side
背叛	bèipàn	betray; forsake
背诵	bèisòng	recite; repeat from memory
背心	bèixīn	a sleeveless garment; vest
背影	bèiyǐng	a view of sb's back; a figure viewed from behind:

熟语 Idioms

背道而驰	bèi dào ér chí	be diametrically opposed to; diverging
背井离乡	bèi jǐng lí xiāng	leave one's hometown; be far away from home
背水一战	bèi shuǐ yí zhàn	fight with one's back to the river; fight to win or die

倍 bèi   ノ 亻 亻 广 广 佇 倅 倅 倍 倍

释义 Meaning

（一）名词 n.

times; -fold: 今年的留学生比去年增加了五倍。The number of foreign students this year has increased by five times that of last year.

（二）副词 adv.

double; twice as much: 他的鼓励使我勇气倍增。His encouragement made me do everything with redoubled courage.

词语 Words and phrases

倍儿	bèir	awfully; terribly
倍数	bèirshù	multiple
倍增器	bèizēngqì	Multiplier

本 běn   一 十 才 木 本

释义 Meaning

（一）名词 n.

1. foundation; basis; origin: 水是生命之本。Water is the foundation of life.
2. book: 答案都写在笔记本上。The answer is written in the notebook.

（二）代词 pron.

1. one's own; native: 有问题请与本人联系。Please get in touch with me if you have any question.
2. current; this; present: 运动会将在本周举行。The sports meeting will be held this week.

（三）副词 adv.

originally; at first: 我本想考完试以后再说这件事的。Originally I didn't want to talk about the matter untill the examination had finished.

（四）量词 measure.w.

(for books, parts of a serial, etc.): 我借了一本汉英词典给他。I lent a Chinese-English dictionary to him.

词语 Words and phrases

本地	běndì	this locality; local
本分	běnfèn	① one's duty ② honest; decent ③ humble
本行	běnháng	one's line; one's own profession
本家	běnjiā	a member of the same clan; a distant relative with the same family name
本科	běnkē	(take as a major subject in college)
本来	běnlái	① original ② originally; at first ③ it goes without saying; of course
本领	běnlǐng	skill; ability; capability
本质	běnzhì	essence; nature; innate character

熟语 Idioms

本末倒置	běnmò dào zhì	take the branch for the root; confuse cause and effect
本性难移	běnxìng nán yí	it is difficult to alter one's character; the leopard can't change his spots

笨bèn   丿 ㇏ ㇏ ㇏ ㅆ ㅆ ㅆ 笁 竺 竺 笨 笨

释义 Meaning

形容词 a.

1. stupid; dull; foolish: 你真笨！You are so stupid!

2. clumsy; awkward: 我的手太笨，不会打毛衣。I'm all thumbs and not good at knitting a sweater.

词语 Words and phrases

笨伯	bènbó	*formal* a stupid person
笨蛋	bèndàn	*offens.* fool; idiot
笨重	bènzhòng	heavy; cumbersome; unwieldy
笨拙	bènzhuō	clumsy; awkward; stupid

熟语 Idioms

笨口拙舌	bèn kǒu zhuō shé	awkward in speech; inarticulate
笨鸟先飞	bèn niǎo xiān fēi	a slow sparrow should make an early start; the slow need to start early (self-depreciating)
笨手笨脚	bèn shǒu bèn jiǎo	clumsy; havea hand like a foot

逼 bī   一 厂 тт ਗ਼ 戸 畐 畐 畐 畐 ʻ畐 逼 逼

释义 Meaning

动词 v.

1. force; compel; press: 他逼她说出了实情。He forced her to tell the truth.

2. press on towards; press up to; close in on: 敌军已直逼城下。The enemy troops have already pressed on to the city wall.

词语 Words and phrases

逼供	bīgòng	extort a confession
逼近	bījìn	press on towards; close in on
逼迫	bīpò	force; compel; coerce
逼债	bizhài	press for payment of debts
逼真	bīzhēn	lifelike; true to life

熟语 Idioms

逼上梁山　　bī shàng liángshān　be driven to join the Liangshan rebels; be driven to revolt

鼻 bí　　ˊ ㇗ ㇆ 自 自 自 臭 臭 畠 畠 畠 畠 鼻 鼻

释义 Meaning

名词 n.

nose: 五官是指眼、耳、口、鼻、舌吗？Do the five sense organs refer to eye, ear, lip, nose and tongue?

词语 Words and phrases

鼻尖	bíjiān	tip of the nose
鼻孔	bíkǒng	nostril
鼻梁	bíliáng	bridge of the nose
鼻涕	bítì	nasal mucus; snivel
鼻炎	bíyán	rhinitis
鼻音	bíyīn	nasal sound
鼻子	bízi	nose

熟语 Idioms

鼻青脸肿　　bí qīng liǎn zhǒng　a bloody nose and a swollen face; get a bloody nose

比 bǐ　　一 上 上 比

释义 Meaning

（一）动词 v.

1. compare; contrast: 你的成绩能跟她比吗？Can your grades compare with hers?

2. emulate; compete; match: 这家商店的服务质量比不上那家。This shop can't match that one for good service.

3. draw an analogy; liken to; compare to: 儿童常常被比作花朵。Children are often likened to flowers.

（二）介词 prep.

1. to (in a score): 他们三比一赢了对手。They beat the opponent by a score of three to one.

2. than: 我比她早来十分钟。I came ten minutes earlier than she did.

词语 Words and phrases

比方	bǐfāng	① analogy; instance ② suppose
比分	bǐfēn	score
比画	bǐhuà	gesture; gesticulate
比较	bǐjiào	① compare; contrast ② prep. (used to compare a difference degree) ③ adv. fairly; comparatively; relatively; quite; rather
比例	bǐlì	① proportion ② scale
比率	bǐlǜ	ratio; rate
比如	bǐrú	for example; for instance; such as
比赛	bǐsài	match; competition
比喻	bǐyù	metaphor; analogy; figure of speech
比重	bǐzhòng	① Specific Gravity ② proportion

熟语 Idioms

| 比比皆是 | bǐbǐjiē shì | can be found everywhere; meet the eye everywhere |
| 比上不足，比下有余 | bǐ shàng bù zú, bǐ xià yǒu yú | not up to those above, but above those below; middling; passable; tolerable |

笔 bǐ   ⼃ ⼃ ⼃ ⼃ 竹 竹 竻 竻 竿 笔

（筆 ノ ト ⺮ ⺮ ⺮ ⺮ 竺 竺 竺 筆 筆 筆）

释义 Meaning

（一）名词 n.

1. pen; pencil or writing brush: 我喜欢用毛笔写字。I like to write with a brush.

2. stroke; touch: 这个字少了一笔。The character lacks one stroke.

（二）量词 measure w.

1. (for sums of money, financial accounts, debts, etc.): 我有一笔钱存在银行里。I have a sum of money deposited in the bank.

2. (for skill in calligraphy or painting): 他年纪虽小，却写得一笔好字。Although he is young, he can write a good hand.

词语 Words and phrases

笔调	bǐdiào	(of writing) tone; style
笔记	bǐjì	① take down (in writing) ② notes
笔迹	bǐjì	a person's handwriting; hand
笔录	bǐlù	① put down (in writing); take down ② notes; record
笔试	bǐshì	written examination
笔顺	bǐshùn	order of strokes observed in calligraphy
笔挺	bǐtǐng	① standing very straight; straight as a ramrod; bolt upright ② well-ironed; trim
笔者	bǐzhě	the present writer; the author
笔直	bǐzhí	perfectly straight; straight as a ramrod; bolt upright

| 文笔 | wénbǐ | style of writing |

熟语 Idioms

| 笔底生花 | bǐ dǐ shēng huā | flowers blooming under the brush; write like an angel |
| 笔墨官司 | bǐmò guānsī | written polemics; controversy in writing |

币 bì　　二 厂 币 币

(幣　` 丷 广 片 尚 尚 尚 尚 尚 尚 敝
敝 幣 幣)

释义 Meaning

名词 n.

money; currency: 请找我硬币好吗？Give me coins for change, all right?

词语 Words and phrases

| 币值 | bìzhí | currency value |
| 币制 | bìzhì | currency (or monetary) system |

必 bì　　丶 心 心 必 必

释义 Meaning

副词 adv.

1. certainly; surely; necessarily: 你放心，明天上午八点我必到。Set your mind at rest, I'll definitely be here at eight o'clock tomorrow morning.

2. must; have to: 这些都是必修课。These are required courses.

词语 Words and phrases

必得	bìděi	must; have to
必定	bìdìng	① must; have to ② be bound to; be sure to
必然	bìrán	① inevitable; certain ② be bound to; be sure to ③ necessity
必然规律	bìránguīlǜ	inexorable law
必须	bìxū	must; have to
必需	bìxū	essential; indispensable
必要	bìyào	necessary; essential; indispensable

熟语 Idioms

必不可少	bì bù kě shǎo	absolutely necessary; essential
必由之路	bì yóu zhī lù	inevitable course; the only way

边biān

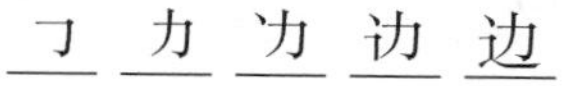

(邊

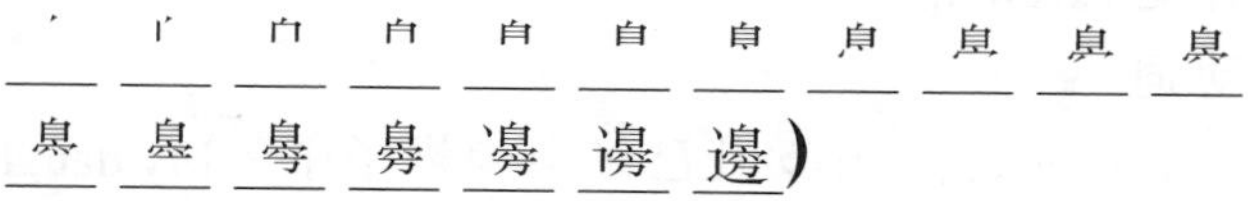

)

释义 Meaning

名词 n

1. side; margin; edge; brim; rim: 街道两边都是商店。Both sides of the street are lined with shops.
2. limit; bound: 这玩笑开得太没边了。This joke is just too absurd.
3. the place next to a person or thing: 老人身边一个亲人也没有。The old man has had no family member at his side.

词语 Words and phrases

边防	biānfáng	frontier (or border) defence

边关	biānguān	frontier pass
边际	biānjì	limit; bound; boundary; marginal
边疆	biānjiāng	border area; borderland; frontier
边界	biānjiè	boundary; border
边境	biānjìng	border; frontier
边缘	biānyuán	① edge; fringe; verge; brink; periphery ② marginal; borderline
边远	biānyuǎn	far from the centre; remote; outlying
旁边	pángbiān	side

编 biān ⁄ 乡 纟 纟 纟` 纩 纩 绗 绐 绢 绢 编 编

(編 ⁄ 乡 幺 乡 乡 糸 糸` 紆 紆 紵 紵 絹 絹 編 編)

释义 Meaning

动词 v.

1. weave; plait: 女儿已经会编辫子了。My daughter has already learned to plait her hair.

2. organize; group; arrange: 新来的学生被编到了A班。New students are grouped into A class.

3. edit; compile: 这几天我正忙着编教材。I have been busy compiling teaching materials these severals days.

4. write; compose: 作家又编了一个新剧本。The writer has written another new play.

5. fabricate; invent; make up; cook up: 我不信，这一定是你编出来的。I don't believe it; it must be made up by you.

词语 Words and phrases

编导	biāndǎo	① write and direct (a play, film, etc.) ② playwright-director
编辑	biānjí	① edit; compile ② editor
编剧	biānjù	① write a play, scenario, etc. ② playwright ③ screenwriter; scenarist
编年史	biānniánshǐ	annalistic history; annals; chronicle
编写	biānxiě	① compile ② write; compose
编造	biānzào	① compile; draw up; work out ② fabricate; invent; concoct; make up; cook up
编者	biānzhě	editor; compiler
编织	biānzhī	weave; knit; plait; braid
编著	biānzhù	compile; write

变 biàn 丶 亠 广 立 亦 亦 变 变

(變 丶 亠 ㄠ 글 产 言 言 纩 结 结 结 结 结 结 綜 綜 綜 綜 綜 綜 綜 綜 變 變)

释义 Meaning

动词 v.

1. become different; change: 几年不见，你变了样儿了。 You look quite different now from how you looked several years ago when we last met.

2. change into; become: 春天到了，天气变暖和了。 Spring is coming, and the weather becomes warmer.

3. transform; change; alter: 我们得想一些变废为宝的主意。 We should think out some ideas that can change waste materials into things of value.

词语 Words and phrases

变成	biànchéng	change into; turn into; become; transform into
变动	biàndòng	alteration; change
变革	biàngé	transform; change
变化	biànhuà	change; vary
变色龙	biànsèlóng	① chameleon ② a changeable or fickle person (esp. in politics)
变态	biàntài	① metamorphosis ② abnormal; anomalous
变心	biànxīn	cease to be faithful; change loyalties; break faith
变形	biànxíng	be out of shape; become deformed
变质	biànzhì	go bad; deteriorate

熟语 Idioms

变本加厉	biàn běn jiā lì	aggravate; with ever-increasing intensify
变化无常	biànhuà wúcháng	constantly changing; capricious

遍 biàn   丶 亠 亠 户 户 肖 肖 肩 扁 扁 编 编 遍

释义 Meaning

（一）形容词 a.

all over; everywhere: 为了买这本书，我找遍了所有书店。I looked through every bookshop in order to buy this book.

（二）量词 measure w.

(for actions) once through; a time: 这本小说我读过好几遍。I've read this novel many times.

词语 Words and phrases

遍布	biànbù	be found everywhere; spread all over
遍地	biàndì	all over the place; everywhere
遍及	biànjí	extend (or spread) all over

熟语 Idioms

| 遍地开花 | biàn dì kāi huā | be a mass of flowers; spring up all over the place |
| 遍体鳞伤 | biàn tǐ lín shāng | be covered all over with cuts and bruises; black and blue all over |

表 biǎo   二 三 丰 圭 声 表 表 表

释义 Meaning

（一）名词 n.

1. surface; outside; external: 今天地表的温度达到了45度。 Today the earth's surface has reached a temperature of 45 degrees centigrade.

2. the relationship between the children or grandchildren of a brother and a sister or of sisters: 我表姐是个医生。 My elder female cousin is a doctor.

3. table; form; list: 请你先填一下这张表。 Please fill the form first.

4. (表) watch (a timepiece): 你的表几点了？ What's the time by your watch?

（二）动词 v.

show; express (or declare) one's determination 我对你的遭遇深表同情。 I show deep sympathy for your misfortune.

词语 Words and phrases

| 表达 | biǎodá | express; convey; voice |
| 表决 | biǎojué | decide by vote; vote |

表面	biǎomiàn	surface; face; outside; appearance
表明	biǎomíng	make known; make clear; state clearly; indicate
表情	biǎoqíng	① express one's feelings ② expression
表示	biǎoshì	① show; express; indicate ② expression; indication
表现	biǎoxiàn	① show; display; manifest ② expression; manifestation; display ③ behavior; performance ④ show off
表演	biǎoyǎn	① perform; act; play ② performance; exhibition ③ demonstrate
表扬	biǎoyáng	praise; commend

熟语 Idioms

| 表里如一 | biǎo lǐ rú yī | be the same outside and inside; think and act in one and the same way |
| 表面文章 | biǎomiàn wénzhāng | specious writing; ostentation |

别 bié   ⺀ ⼝ ⼝ 别 别 别 别

释义 Meaning

（一）代词 pron.

other; another: 你到别的地方去买吧。You can buy it at another place.

（二）名词 n.

difference; distinction: 你不知道男女有别吗？Don't you know that there is distinction between the sexes?

（三）动词 v.

fasten with a pin or clip: 请把这几份试卷别在一起。Please pin these few examination papers together.

（四）副词 adv.

(used in giving commands or advice) don't; had better not: 明天别忘了早点起床。Don't forget to get up earlier tomorrow.

词语 Words and phrases

别离	biélí	take leave of; leave
别人	biérén	other people; others; people
别墅	biéshù	villa
别样	biéyàng	other; different; a different style
别针	biézhēn	safety pin; pin brooch
别致	biézhì	unique; unconventional
告别	gàobié	leave; part from; bid farewell to; say goodbye to (also used in a funeral)
区别	qūbié	distinguish; differentiate; make a distinction between

熟语 Idioms

别出心裁	bié chū xīn cái	adopt an original approach; an out-of-the-ordinary idea
别具一格	bié jù yì gé	be a class by itself; have a unique style
别开生面	bié kāi shēng miàn	start sth. new (or original); in a novel way
别来无恙	bié lái wú yàng	you have been well, I trust, since we parted?
别有用心	bié yǒu yòngxīn	have another motive; have an axe to grind

冰 bīng 丶 冫 冫 沭 冰 冰

释义 Meaning

（一）名词 n.

ice: 气温在零度以下，水就会结成冰。Water freezes when the temperature reaches 0 ℃.

(二) 动词 v.

put on the ice; ice: 把这些啤酒冰一下。Ice these bottles of beer.

词语 Words and phrases

冰场	bīngchǎng	skating (or ice) rink; ice stadium; ice arena
冰川	bīngchuān	glacier
冰灯	bīngdēng	ice lantern
冰棍儿	bīnggùnr	ice-lolly; popsicle; ice-sucker; frozen sucker
冰凉	bīngliáng	ice-cold
冰山	bīngshān	① an icy mountain ② iceberg ③ an individual or a group not to be relied upon for long
冰释	bīngshì	(of misgivings, misunderstanding, etc.) disappear; vanish; be dispelled
冰糖	bīngtáng	crystal sugar; rock candy
冰箱	bīngxiāng	icebox; refrigerator

熟语 Idioms

冰冻三尺，非一日之寒	bīng dòng sān chǐ, fēi yí rì zhī hán	ice three feet thick is not due to one cold day; the trouble has been brewing for quite some time
冰清玉洁	bīng qīng yù jié	as pure as jade and as clean as ice; pure and noble
冰天雪地	bīng tiān xuě dì	a world of ice and snow; covered all over with ice and snow

兵 bīng 一 厂 F 斤 乒 乒 兵

释义 Meaning

名词 n.

1. weapons; arms: 敌人有坚兵利甲，我们赢不了他们。
   As the enemies have strong armour and sharp weapons, we
   will not be able to defeat them.

2. soldier: 我弟弟明年就要当兵了。My young brother will
   be a soldier next year.

词语 Words and phrases

兵变	bīngbiàn	mutiny
兵法	bīngfǎ	art of war; military strategy and tactics
兵工厂	bīnggōngchǎng	munitions (or ordnance) factory; arsenal
兵力	bīnglì	military strength; armed forces
兵器	bīngqì	weaponry; weapons; arms
兵权	bīngquán	military leadership; military power
兵役	bīngyì	military service
兵营	bīngyíng	military camp; barracks

熟语 Idioms

兵荒马乱	bīng huāng mǎ luàn	the turmoil and chaos of war; chaotic war
兵来将挡，水来土淹	bīng lái jiàng dǎng, shuǐ lái tǔ yān	confront soldiers with generals and stem water with earth; give tit for tat

饼bǐng 丿 亻 仁 仁 仁 饣 饣 饣 饼

(餠 丿 亻 亼 亼 亼 亼 貪 貪 貪 貪
　　　 餠 餠 餠 餅)

释义 Meaning

名词 n.

1. a round flat cake: 你爱吃月饼吗？Do you like to eat moon cakes?
2. sth. shaped like a cake: 她是个铁饼运动员。She is a discus throw athlete.

词语 Words and phrases

| 饼干 | bǐnggān | biscuit; cracker |
| 饼子 | bǐngzi | (maize or millet) pancake |

病bìng　　丶　亠　广　广　疒　疒　疒　疒　病　病

释义 Meaning

（一）名词 n.

disease; illness; sickness: 听说他的病已经好了。I hear that he is well again.

（二）动词 v.

ill; sick: 我不知道她病了。I didn't know that she is ill.

词语 Words and phrases

病倒	bìngdǎo	be down with an illness; be laid up
病毒	bìngdú	virus
病房	bìngfáng	ward (of a hospital); sickroom
病故	bìnggù	die of illness
病号	bìnghào	sick personnel; person on the sick list; patient
病句	bìngjù	a faulty sentence (grammatically or logically)
病历	bìnglì	medical record; case history
病情	bìngqíng	state of an illness; patient's condition
病人	bìngrén	① a sick person; invalid ② patient
病因	bìngyīn	cause of disease; pathogeny

| 病愈 | bìngyù | recover (from an illness) |
| 病征 | bìngzhēng | symptom (of a disease) |

熟语 Idioms

| 病急乱投医 | bìng jí luàn tóu yī | consult anybody when in a desperate plight; men in a desperate plight will try anything |
| 病入膏肓 | bìng rù gāohuāng | the disease has attacked the vitals; be hopelessly ill |

薄₁ báo 一 十 艹 艹 芦 芦 芦 芦 芦 芦 蒲 蒲 蒲 蓮 薄 薄

释义 Meaning

形容词 a.

1. thin; flimsy: 这张纸太薄了，不能写字。This paper is too thin to write on. 反义词 antonym: 厚

2. lacking in warmth; cold: 我对她不薄呀，她怎么能这样！How can she do like that! I treat her quite well.

词语 Words and phrases

薄饼	báobǐng	thin pancake
薄脆	báocuì	crisp fritter
薄页纸	báoyèzhǐ	① tissue paper ② flimsy

薄₂ bó 一 十 艹 艹 芦 芦 芦 芦 芦 芦 蒲 蒲 蒲 蓮 薄 薄

释义 Meaning

形容词 a.

slight; meagre; small: 这点薄礼你就收下吧。Please accept my small gift. 反义词 antonym: 厚

词语 Words and phrases

薄待	bódài	treat sb. ungenerously
薄地	bódì	unfertile land
薄利	bólì	small profits
薄命	bómìng	(usu. of women) born under an unlucky star; born unlucky
薄情	bóqíng	inconstant in love; fickle
薄弱	bóruò	weak; frail

补 bǔ ` ㇇ 礻 礻 礻 补 补

(補 ` ㇇ 礻 礻 礻 礻 衤 衤 袹 補 補)

释义 Meaning

动词 v.

1. mend; patch; repair: 衣服破了，得补一下。The clothes are worn-out and should be patched.

2. fill; supply; make up for: 下星期老师要给我们补课。The teacher will help us make up the lesson we missed.

3. nourish: 你这两天太累了，应该补一补身体。You are too tired these a few days, and should build up your health.

词语 Words and phrases

补偿	bǔcháng	compensate; make up
补充	bǔchōng	① replenish; supplement; complement; add ② additional; complementary; supplementary
补丁	bǔdīng	patch
补救	bǔjiù	remedy
补考	bǔkǎo	make-up examination
补品	bǔpǐn	tonic

补习	bǔxí	take lessons after school or work; take a make-up course
补牙	bǔyá	fill a tooth; have a tooth filled
补助	bǔzhù	help financially; subsidize; subsidy; allowance

不 bù   二 丆 丆 不

释义 Meaning

副词 adv.

1. (used before verbs, adjectives, and other adverbs; never before 有) not; won't; not want to: 我今晚不参加晚会了。 I won't attend the party tonight.

2. (used before certain nouns to form an adjective) un-; in-: 不法行为终究会被取缔的。 Unlawful practices will be banned finally.

3. (used by itself or with a particle in responses) not so; no: 你是日本人吗？—不，我是中国人。 Are you Japanese? —No, I'm Chinese. 反义词 antonym: 是

4. (used between a verb and its complement) cannot: 这么贵的衣服我买不起。 I cannot afford to buy such expensive clothing

词语 Words and phrases

不安	bù'ān	① intranquil; unpeaceful; unstable ② uneasy; disturbed; restless ③ sorry
不必	búbì	need not; do not have to
不错	búcuò	① correct; right ② not bad; pretty good
不但	búdàn	(used correlatively with 而且，并且，也 or 还) not only
不得了	bùdéliǎo	① no way out; no end of trouble ② (used after 得 as a complement) extremely; exceedingly

不断	búduàn	unceasing; uninterrupted
不顾	búgù	in spite of; regardless of
不过	búguò	① (used as an intensifier after an adjective) ② only; merely; no more than ③ but; however
不见得	bújiànde	not necessarily; not likely
不仅	bùjǐn	① not the only one ② not only
不久	bùjiǔ	① soon; before long ② not long after; soon after
不满	bùmǎn	resentful; discontented; dissatisfied
不然	bùrán	① not so ② (used at the beginning of a sentence to express disagreement) no ③ or else; otherwise; if not
不同	bù tóng	not alike; different; distinct
不幸	búxìng	① misfortune; adversity ② unfortunate; sad ③ unfortunately
不足	bùzú	① not enough; insufficient; inadequate ② not worth ③ cannot; should not

熟语 Idioms

不出所料	bù chū suǒ liào	it happens jus as expected; not surprising
不到长城非好汉	bú dào cháng chéng fēi hǎohàn	if you fail to reach the Great Wall you are not a real man; not to stop until one's aim is attained
不干不淨	bù gān bú jìng	unclean; filthy
不堪一击	bù kān yì jī	cannot withstand a single blow; be finished off at one blow
不毛之地	bù máo zhī dì	barren land; desert
不三不四	bù sān bú sì	half-and-half; shady; neither one thing nor the other

不识抬举	bù shí tái jǔ	fail to appreciate sb's. kindness; show no appreciation of a favor from sb.
不屑一顾	búxiè yí gù	cock a snook at; shrug off; deign to take a glance
不以为然	bù yǐ wéi rán	not to accept as right; take exception to
不知不觉	bù zhī bù jué	unconsciously; unaware

布 bù   二 𠂇 𠂇 右 布

释义 Meaning

（一）名词 n.

cotton cloth; cloth: 买一块布做窗帘吧。How about buying a piece of cotton cloth to make a window curtain.

（二）动词 v.

1. declare; announce; publish; proclaim: 把这个消息公布给大家。Release the news to everybody.

2. spread; disseminate: 佛教很早就在中国传布开来了。Buddhism spread throughout China long time ago.

词语 Words and phrases

布店	bùdiàn	cloth store; draper's; piece-goods store
布告	bùgào	notice; bulletin; proclamation
布谷鸟	bùgǔniǎo	cuckoo
布景	bùjǐng	① composition (of a painting) ② setting
布局	bùjú	① overall arrangement; layout; distribution ② composition (of a picture, piece of writing, etc.) ③ position (of pieces on a chessboard)
布匹	bùpǐ	cloth; piece goods
布鞋	bùxié	cloth shoes

| 布置 | bùzhì | ① fix up; arrange; decorate ② assign; make arrangements for; give instructions about |

步bù

丨 ㅏ 止 ᅪ 牛 牛 步

释义 Meaning

名词 n.

1. step; pace: 往前走几步就到邮局了。Just a few steps ahead you will find the post office.

2. stage; step: 下一步就该收集资金了。The next step is to collect the funds.

3. condition; situation; state: 你们的关系怎么会发展到这一步？How did your relations get into such a state?

词语 Words and phrases

步兵	bùbīng	① infantry; ② infantry man; foot soldier
步伐	bùfá	step; pace
步枪	bùqiāng	rifle
步行	bùxíng	go on foot; walk
步骤	bùzhòu	step; move; measure

熟语 Idioms

| 步调一致 | bùdiào yí zhì | march in step; take concerted action |
| 步人后尘 | bù rén hòu chén | follow sb's track; step into sb's shoes; a copycat |

擦cā

一 十 扌 扩 扩 扩 扩 扩 护 护 护 护 护 掠 掠 擦 擦 擦

释义 Meaning

动词 v.

1. rub: 他摔了一跤，擦破了点皮。He had a fall and got

a scratch.

2. wipe: 你出了这么多汗，擦一下吧。You sweat a lot, have it wiped.

3. apply or spread sth. on: 你的伤口一天要擦三次药。 You need to apply medicinal ointment to your wound three times a day.

词语 Words and phrases

擦背	cābèi	rub one's back with a towel while bathing
擦边球	cābiānqiú	edge ball; touch ball
擦亮眼睛	cāliàng yǎnjīng	remove the scales from one's eyes; sharpen one's vigilance
擦屁股	cā pìgu	clear up the mess left by sb. else
擦拭	cāshì	wipe clean; cleanse
擦澡	cāzǎo	rub oneself down with a wet towel

才₁ cái 二 十 才

释义 Meaning

名词 n.

ability; talent: 这小夥子有才有貌。The young man has both look and talent.

才₂ cái 二 十 才

(**纔** ⺰ 纟 幺 幺 幺 纟)

副词 adv.

1. a moment ago; just: 她大学才毕业就结婚了。She had just graduated when she got married.

2. (preceded by an expression of time) not until: 八点钟考试，可他九点才来。The test started at eight, but he didn't come until nine.

3. (follow by a numerical expression) only: 这孩子才十岁就会说英语了。The child is only ten, and he can speak English.

4. (used in an assertion or contradiction, emphasizing what comes before 才, usu. with 呢 at the end of the sentence) actually; really: 他爱骗人，我才不相信他呢！He likes to lie, I really don't believe him.

词语 Words and phrases

才干	cáigàn	ability; competence
才华	cáihuá	literary or artistic talent
才能	cáinéng	ability; capability
才学	cáixué	talent and learning; scholarship
才子	cáizǐ	a talented scholar

熟语 Idioms

| 才貌双全 | cái mào shuāng quán | be as wise as fair; be endowed with both beauty and talent |
| 才子佳人 | cáizǐ jiārén | gifted scholars and beautiful ladies; the wit and beauty |

采 cǎi　一　丷　丷　亚　平　采　采

释义 Meaning

动词 v.

1. pick, pluck or gather: 妈妈上山采茶去了。Mother went up the hill to pick tea.

2. mine; extract: 这个油田每天能采二百吨油。Two hundred tons of oil can be extracted from this oilfield every day.

词语 Words and phrases

采伐	cǎifá	cut timber; lumber
采访	cǎifǎng	① hunt for and collect ② gather news; cover
采购	cǎigòu	make purchases for an organization or enterprise; purchase
采集	cǎijí	gather; collect
采矿	cǎikuàng	mining
采纳	cǎinà	accept (opinions, suggestions, requests, etc.); adopt
采取	cǎiqǔ	adopt; assume or take
采用	cǎiyòng	select and use; adopt
采摘	cǎizhāi	pick (fruit, flowers, leaves, etc.); pluck

彩 cǎi   一 亠 亠 肀 亚 平 平 采 采 彩 彩

释义 Meaning

名词 n.

1. colour: 五彩缤纷的气球飞上了蓝天。Colourful balloons are rising into the sky.

2. variety; brilliance; splendour: 你们的业余生活真是丰富多彩呀！Your spare-time activities are so rich and varied.

3. coloured silk; variegated silk: 老李家张灯结彩，准备
办喜事。Lao Li's home is decorated with lanterns and
coloured streamers getting ready for the wedding.

词语 Words and phrases

彩笔	cǎibǐ	colour pencil; crayon
彩车	cǎichē	① float (in a parade) ② bridal car
彩灯	cǎidēng	coloured lights
彩电	cǎidiàn	① colour television (broadcasting) ② colour television set; colour TV
彩虹	cǎihóng	rainbow
彩礼	cǎilǐ	betrothal gifts (from the bridegroom to the bride's family); bride-price
彩排	cǎipái	dress rehearsal
彩票	cǎipiào	lottery ticket
彩色	cǎisè	multicolour; with colour
彩头	cǎitóu	good luck in business, contests or lotteries

菜 cài 　一 艹 艹 艾 苹 芋 苹 茎 苹 苹 菜

释义 Meaning

名词　n.

1. vegetable; greens: 我家后院种了一些菜。We grow some
vegetables in the back yard of our house.

2. (non-staple) food: 妈妈上超市买菜去了。Mother went
to the supermarket to buy groceries.

3. dish; course: 我们点了三个菜，一个汤。We ordered
a soup and three courses.

词语 Words and phrases

菜场	càichǎng	food market

菜单	càidān	menu; bill of fare
菜地	càidì	vegetable plot
菜篮子	càilánzi	① shopping basket (for food); food basket ② food supply
菜谱	càipǔ	① menu; bill of fare ② cookery book
菜肴	càiyáo	cooked dishes (usu. meat dishes)
菜园	càiyuán	vegetable garden; vegetable farm

藏₁ cáng 二 艹 艹 芦 芦 芦 芦 芦 芦 芦 芦 芦 萨 藏 藏 藏

释义 Meaning

动词 v.

1. hide; conceal: 你把我的眼镜藏哪儿去了？Where did you hide my glasses?

2. store; lay by: 地下室里藏了许多过冬的蔬菜。We stored a lot of vegetables for winter in the basement.

词语 Words and phrases

藏身	cángshēn	hide oneself; go into hiding
藏书	cángshū	① collect books ② a collection of books; library
藏拙	cángzhuō	hide one's inadequacy by keeping quiet

熟语 Idioms

| 藏污纳垢 | cáng wū nà gòu | shelter evil people and countenance evil practices; harbour criminals |
| 藏龙卧虎 | cáng lóng wò hǔ | a place where dragons and tigers are hiding; great men living anonymously |

藏₂ zàng 二 艹 艹 芦 芦 芦 芦 芦 芦 芦 芦 芦 萨 藏 藏 藏

释义 Meaning

名词 n.

1. storing place; depository: 海洋中有无数宝藏等待人们去发现。There are innumerable precious deposits in the oceans that are awaiting people to discover.

2. the Zang nationality; Tibetan: 他妻子是藏族人。His wife is Tibetan.

词语 Words and phrases

藏蓝	zànglán	purplish blue
藏青	zàngqīng	dark blue
藏族	zàngzú	the Zang (Tibetan) nationality, or the Zangs (Tibetans) , distributed over the Xizang Autonomous Region, Qinghai, Sichuan, Gansu and Yunnan Provinces in China

操 cāo 一 十 扌 扩 扩 护 护 护 护 捛 捛 捛 撮 撺 操 操

释义 Meaning

动词 v.

1. grasp; hold: 他操起一根棍子就向贼打过去。He grabbed a stick and struck out at the thief.

2. speak (a language or dialect): 他操一口地道的北京话。He speaks with a pure Beijing dialect.

词语 Words and phrases

操办	cāobàn	manage affairs; make preparations or arrangements for
操场	cāochǎng	playground; sports ground; drill ground
操劳	cāoláo	① work hard ② take care; look after

操练	cāoliàn	drill; train
操心	cāoxīn	worry; take trouble; take pains
操纵	cāozòng	① operate; control ② manipulate
操作	cāozuò	operate; manipulate

熟语 Idioms

| 操之过急 | cāo zhī guò jí | too hasty; act with undue haste |

草 cǎo   二 节 艹 芢 节 苎 苴 苴 草

释义 Meaning

（一）名词 n.

grass: 牛在山坡上吃草。The cattle are grazing on the hillside.

（二）形容词 a.

careless; rough: 你的字写得太草了，我认不出来。Your characters are written in such a sloppy hand that I can't read.

词语 Words and phrases

草包	cǎobāo	① straw bag; straw sack ② an unsophisticated person
草场	cǎochǎng	meadow; pasture; grassland
草创	cǎochuàng	start (an enterprise, etc.) from scratch
草地	cǎodì	① grassland; meadow; pasture ② lawn
草稿	cǎogǎo	rough draft; preliminary draft
草帽	cǎomào	straw hat
草莓	cǎoméi	strawberry (the plant or the fruit)
草率	cǎoshuài	sloppy; careless; slapdash; perfunctory
草药	cǎoyào	herbal medicine
草原	cǎoyuán	grasslands; prairie

熟语 Idioms

| 草草收场 | cǎocǎo shōuchǎng | hastily wind up a matter |

| 草菅人命 | cǎo jiān rénmìng | look upon human lives as if they were grass; act with utter disregard for human life |
| 草木皆兵 | cǎo mù jiē bīng | grass and trees mistaken for enemy troops; a state of extreme suspicion and fear |

层 céng 　一　ニ　尸　尸　尸　层　层

(層 　一　ニ　尸　尸　尸　尸　尸　屄　屄　屟　屟　屟　層　層　層)

释义 Meaning
量词 measure w.

1. storey; floor: 这是一幢十五层的大楼。This is a fifteen-storey building.
2. a component part in a sequence: 他说的话有两层意思。What he said has two implications.
3. layer; stratum: 她脸上涂了一层厚厚的粉。Her face is covered with a thick layer of powder.

词语 Words and phrases

层层	céngcéng	layer upon layer; ring upon ring
层次	céngcì	① presentation of ideas (in writing or speech) ② administrative levels ③ *photog.* gradation
层迭	céndié	one on top of another

熟语 Idioms

| 层出不穷 | céng chū bù qióng | emerge endlessly; emerge in endless succession |
| 层峦迭嶂 | céng luán dié zhàng | peaks rising one upon another; multiple ranges of hills |

茶 chá　二 十 艹 艹 艾 艾 苯 苯 茶 茶

释义 Meaning

名词 n.

1. tea (the plant or it's leaves): 我的家乡产茶。My hometown produces tea.

2. tea (the drink): 这杯茶太浓了。This cup of tea is too strong.

3. certain kinds of drink or liquid food: 请尝尝这杯杏仁茶。Please have a taste of the almond paste.

词语 Words and phrases

茶杯	chábēi	teacup
茶馆	cháguǎn	teahouse
茶壶	cháhú	teapot
茶话会	cháhuàhuì	a tea party at which the participants chat or give talks
茶几	chájī	tea table; side table
茶水	cháshuǐ	tea or plain boiled water (for drinking)
茶叶	cháyè	tea leaves; tea
茶园	cháyuán	① tea plantation ② a place where tea and soft drinks are served; tea garden

熟语 Idioms

茶余饭后	chá yú fàn hòu	over a cup of tea or after a meal; in one's leisure hours

查 chá　二 十 才 木 木 杏 杏 查 查

释义 Meaning

动词 v.

1. check; examine: 今天领导要来查卫生。Today the officer will make a public health and sanitation check.

2. look into; investigate: 你去查一下事故的原因。Go to find out the cause of the accident.

3. look up; consult: 这个词我得查一下词典。I should look up this expression in a dictionary.

词语 Words and phrases

查处	cháchǔ	investigate and prosecute
查封	cháfēng	seal up; close down
查户口	chá hùkǒu	check residence cards; check on house-hold occupants
查禁	chájìn	ban; prohibit; suppress; censor
查看	chákàn	look over; examine
查询	cháxún	inquire about
查夜	cháyè	① go the rounds at night ② night patrol
查帐	cházhàng	check (or audit) accounts
检查	jiǎnchá	① check up; inspect; examine ② self-criticism

差₁ chā ` ⺌ ⺌ ⺍ ⺍ ⺷ 差 差 差

释义 Meaning

名词 n.

difference; dissimilarity: 他们夫妻的年龄之差达二十岁。The disparity in age between the husband and his wife is 20 years.

词语 Words and phrases

差别	chābié	difference; disparity
差错	chācuò	① mistake; error; slip ② mishap; accident
差距	chājù	① gap; disparity ② difference
差异	chāyì	difference; divergence; discrepancy; diversity

熟语 Idioms

| 差强人意 | chā qiáng rén yì | just passable; barely satisfactory |
| 差之毫厘，失之千里 | chā zhī háo lí, shī zhī qiān lǐ | a slight discrepancy leads to a gigantic error; the breath of a single hair can lead to a thousand *li* astray |

差₂ chà ㇏ ㆍㅀ 兰 兰 兰 差 差 差 差

释义 Meaning

（一）动词 v.

1. differ from; fall short of: 这点钱离买房子还差得远。This little money still falls far short of buying a house.

2. be less than; be short of: 这个婴儿是零点差一分出生的。The baby was born just one minute before midnight.

（二）形容词 a.

not up to standard; poor: 这孩子成绩太差了。The child's scores are too poor.

词语 Words and phrases

差不多	chàbùduō	① about the same; similar ② just about right; just about enough; not bad ③ almost; nearly
差点儿	chàdiǎnr	① not quite up to the mark ② almost; nearly; on the verge of
差劲	chàjìn	(of quality, ability, etc.) no good; disappointing

差₃ chāi ㇏ ㆍㅀ 兰 兰 兰 差 差 差 差

释义 Meaning

动词 v.

send on an errand; dispatch: 你不用来了，我差人给你送

去。You needn't come; I'll dispatch someone to bring it to you.

词语 Words and phrases

差遣	chāiqiǎn	send sb. on an errand or mission; dispatch; assign
差事	chāishi	① errand; assignment ② official post; billet; commission; job
出差	chūchāi	go or be away on an official business; go or be on a business trip

拆 chāi 一 十 扌 扩 扩 扩 折 拆

释义 Meaning

动词 v.

1. tear open; take apart: 快点拆信！看看有什么消息。Hurry, open the letter! Let's see what news there is.

2. pull down; dismantle: 她家的房子被人拆了。Her house had been pulled down.

词语 Words and phrases

拆除	chāichú	dismantle; tear down; demolish
拆开	chāikāi	take apart; open; separate
拆迁	chāiqiān	have an old building pulled down and its occupants moved elsewhere
拆墙角	chāi qiángjiǎo	undermine; pull away a prop
拆散	chāisàn	break up (a marriage, family, group, etc.)
拆台	chāitái	cut the ground from under sb.'s feet; pull away a prop
拆线	chāixiàn	take out stitches (in surgery)

熟语 Idioms

| 拆穿西洋镜 | chāichuān xī yángjìng | nail a lie; expose sb's tricks |
| 拆东墙，补西墙 | chāi dōng qiáng, bǔ xī qiáng | repair the west wall by tearing down the east; rob Peter to pay Paul |

产 chǎn ` 亠 宀 产 产 产

(**產** ` 亠 宀 产 产 产 产 产 产 產 產）

释义 Meaning

动词 v.

1. give birth to; be delivered of: 这头猪产了十二只猪崽。 This sow has delivered twelve piglets.
2. produce; yield: 这种茶叶主要产在南方。 This kind of tea is grown chiefly in the south.

词语 Words and phrases

产地	chǎndì	place of production (or origin); producing area
产妇	chǎnfù	a pregnant woman; a woman in childbirth
产量	chǎnliàng	output; yield
产卵	chǎnluǎn	(of birds) lay eggs; (of fishes, frogs, etc.) spawn; (of insects) oviposit
产品	chǎnpǐn	product; produce
产生	chǎnshēng	(used with immaterial things) give rise to; bring about; evolve; emerge; come into being
产物	chǎnwù	outcome; result; product
产业	chǎnyè	① estate; property ② industry

长₁ cháng ˊ ˴ ⺄ 长

(長 ⼀ ⼚ ⼫ ⼫ ⼳ ⼴ ⼵ 長)

释义 Meaning

（一）形容词 a.

(of space or time) long: 她的腿真长啊！Her legs are so long! 反义词 antonym: 短

（二）名词 n.

1. length: 这座大桥全长六千七百七十二米。The over-all length of the bridge is 6,772 metres.

2. strong point; forte: 你应该取长补短。You should over-come your shortcomings by learning from other's strong points. 反义词 antonym: 短

（三）动词 v.

be good at: 她长于书法。She is good at calligraphy.

词语 Words and phrases

长处	chángchù	good qualities; strong points
长度	chángdù	length
长年	chángnián	all the year round
长期	chángqī	over a long period of time; long-term; long-lasting
长寿	chángshòu	a long life; longevity
长途	chángtú	① a long distance ② short for 长途电话
长远	chángyuǎn	long-term; long-range

熟语 Idioms

长话短说	cháng huà duǎn shuō	to make a long story short; make short of long
长年累月	cháng nián lěi yuè	year in year out; for months and years

长生不老　　chángshēng bù lǎo　live forever and never grow old; ever-living

长₂ zhǎng　ノ 一 上 长

（長 一 厂 厂 匚 巨 戸 長 長）

释义 Meaning

（一）形容词 a.

older; elder; senior: 姐姐比我长两岁。My sister is two years older than I. 反义词antonym: 小、幼

（二）名词 n.

chief; head: 你是一家之长，你决定吧。You are the head of the family, you decide.

（三）动词 v.

1. grow; develop: 田里的庄稼长得很好。The crops in the field are growing very well.

2. come into being; begin to grow; form: 我儿子已经长了十颗牙了。My son has already had ten teeth.

词语 Words and phrases

长辈	zhǎngbèi	elder member of a family; elder; senior
长大	zhǎngdà	grow up; be brought up
长进	zhǎngjìn	progress
长相	zhǎngxiàng	looks; features; appearance
长子	zhǎngzǐ	eldest son

尝 cháng　丶 丷 丷 丷 丿 尚 尚 尝 尝

（嘗 丶 丷 丷 丷 尚 尚 尚 尚 尚 嘗 嘗 嘗 嘗 嘗）

释义 Meaning

动词 v.

taste; try the flavour of: 你尝尝这个汤的味道怎么样？
Try the soup and see if it tastes all right?

词语 Words and phrases

尝试	chángshì	attempt; try
尝鲜	chángxiān	have a taste of a delicacy; have a taste of what is just in season
尝新	chángxīn	have a taste of what is just in season

常 cháng

释义 Meaning

（一）形容词 a.

1. ordinary; common; normal: 这是常理，谁都知道。This is a general rule, everyone knows it.
2. constant; invariable: 祝你青春常在！Wish you eternal youth!

（二）副词 adv.

frequently; often; usually: 我们常去听音乐会。We go to concerts quite often.

词语 Words and phrases

常常	chángcháng	frequently; often; many a time; more often than not
常规	chángguī	conventional; common practice; routine
常见	chángjiàn	be common
常年	chángnián	① throughout the year; year in year out ② an average year
常识	chángshí	① general knowledge; elementary knowledge ② common sense

| 常态 | chángtài | normal behaviour or conditions; normality; normalcy |
| 常用 | chángyòng | in common use |

厂 chǎng　一 厂

(廠　丶 一 广 广 广 广 庁 庁 庁 庿 庿 庿 廄 廄 廠)

释义 Meaning

名词 n.

factory, mill; plant; works: 她在一家鞋厂工作。She works in a shoe factory.

词语 Words and phrases

厂家	chǎngjiā	factory; mill
厂商	chǎngshāng	① factory owner ② factories and stores
厂休	chǎngxiū	a factory's day of rest (usu. on a weekday)
厂长	chǎngzhǎng	factory director
厂址	chǎngzhǐ	the site (or location) of a factory
厂主	chǎngzhǔ	factory owner; millowner

场 chǎng　一 十 土 圬 场 场

(場　一 十 土 圤 圹 圹 圹 坍 坍 埸 場 場)

释义 Meaning

（一）名词 n.

a large place used for a particular purpose: 郊区有家很大的养鸡场。There is a big chicken farm in the suburb.

（二）量词 measure w.

(for recreational or sports activities)：今晚有场足球赛。
There is a football game tonight.

词语 Words and phrases

场次	chǎngcì	the number of showings of a film, play, etc.
场地	chǎngdì	space; place; site
场合	chǎnghé	occasion; situation
场面	chǎngmiàn	① scene (in drama, fiction, etc.); spectacle ② occasion; scene
场所	chǎngsuǒ	place; arena

唱 chàng   丨 刂 刂 ㅁ 匚 吖 吜 唱 唱 唱
唱 唱

释义 Meaning

动词 v.

sing：你给大家唱首歌吧！Would you please sing a song for everybody!

词语 Words and phrases

唱白脸	chàng báiliǎn	wear the white mask of the villain; play the villain; pretend to be harsh and severe
唱对台戏	chàng duìtáixì	put on a rival show; enter into rivalry with sb.
唱高调	chàng gāodiào	high-sounding words; say fine-sounding things; affect a high moral tone
唱歌	chànggē	sing (a song)
唱红脸	chàng hóngliǎn	wear the red mask of the hero; play the hero; pretend to be generous and kind

唱片	chàngpiān	phonograph (or gramophone) record; disc
唱腔	chàngqiāng	vocal music in a Chinese opera
唱双簧	chàng shuānghuáng	① give a two-man comic show (with one speaking or singing while hiding behind the other who gesticulates) ② collaborate with each other
唱戏	chàngxì	sing and act in a traditional opera

抄₁ chāo 二 十 扌 扌 扚 抄 抄

释义 Meaning

动词 v.

1. copy; transcribe: 请你把这篇文章抄一下。Please make a fair copy of the article.

2. plagiarize; lift: 你怎么抄别人的作业？How can you copy other's written work?

词语 Words and Phrases

抄本	chāoběn	hand-copied manuscript; transcript
抄件	chāojiàn	duplicate; copy
抄录	chāolù	make a handwritten copy of; copy
抄袭	chāoxí	① plagiarize; lift ② borrow indiscriminately from other people's experience
抄写	chāoxiě	copy (by hand); transcribe

抄₂ chāo 二 十 扌 扌 扚 抄 抄

释义 Meaning

动词 v.

1. search and confiscate; make a raid upon: 他们家被土匪

给抄了。Their house was destroyed by the bandits.

2. take a short cut: 我们抄近路赶到他们前面去。Let's take a shortcut to outstrip them.

3. grab; take up: 他抄起桌上的菜刀就向她砍去。He grabed the kitchen knife on the table and struck out at her.

词语 Words and Phrases

抄道	chāodào	① take a shortcut ② shortcut
抄家	chāojiā	search sb's house and confiscate his property (usually by the government)
抄袭	chāoxí	launch a surprise attack on the enemy by making a detour

超 chāo   一　十　土　耂　耂　赱　走　起　起
起　超　超

释义 Meaning

动词 v.

1. exceed; surpass; overtake: 你的孩子身高已经超标了。Your child's height has already surpassed the standard.

2. ultra; super; extra: 她今天真是超水平地发挥！She gave the play to extra level today!

3. transcend; go beyond: 这是一部超现实主义的小说。This is a surrealistic novel.

词语 Words and Phrases

超常	chāocháng	be above average; be above the common run
超出	chāochū	overstep; go beyond; exceed
超短裙	chāoduǎnqún	miniskirt
超过	chāoguò	outstrip; surpass; exceed
超级	chāojí	super
超群	chāoqún	head and shoulders above all others;

		pre-eminent
超人	chāorén	① be out of the common run ② superman
超脱	chāotuō	① unconventional; original ② be detached; stand (or hold, keep) aloof
超越	chāoyuè	surmount; overstep; transcend; surpass

熟语 Idioms

超尘拔俗	chāo chén bá sú	avoid earthly concerns and hold oneself aloof from the vulgar; above the average

朝₁ cháo 　一　十　广　古　古　古　直　卓　卓

朝　朝　朝

释义 Meaning

（一）名词 n.

1. royal court; government: 官员们都上朝了。Officials have all gone to court.

2. dynasty: 康熙是清朝的皇帝。Kangxi is an Emperor in the Qing Dynasty.

（二）介词 prep.

facing; towards: 这几个房间全是朝南的。These several rooms are all facing south.

词语 Words and Phrases

朝代	cháodài	dynasty
朝见	cháojiàn	have an audience with a sovereign
朝廷	cháotíng	① royal or imperial court ② royal or imperial government
朝向	cháoxiàng	turn towards; face
朝政	cháozhèng	(in imperial times) court administration; affairs of state

熟语 Idioms

| 朝中有人
好做官 | cháo zhōng yǒu rén
hǎo zuò guān | it's easy to be an official
if you have friends at the
court (to protect you when
you are in trouble). |

朝₂ zhāo   一　十　广　古　古　古　直　卓　朝
朝　朝　朝

释义 Meaning

名词 n.

early morning; morning: 我们上班时间一直是朝九晚五。
Our work hours are always from nine a.m. to five p.m. 反义
词 antonym: 暮，夕

词语 Words and Phrases

朝气	zhāoqì	youthful spirit; vigour; vitality
朝霞	zhāoxiá	rosy clouds of dawn; rosy dawn
朝阳	zhāoyáng	the rising sun; the morning sun

熟语 Idioms

朝不保夕	zhāo bù bǎo xī	may fall at any moment; not know at dawn what may happen by dusk
朝气蓬勃	zhāo qì péng bó	full of youthful spirit; fresh and vigorous
朝三暮四	zhāo sān mù sì	blow hot and cold; change one's mind frequently

吵 chǎo   丨　丨丨　口　叩　叫　吵　吵

释义 Meaning

动词 v.

1. make a noise: 别吵！孩子在睡觉。Don't make so much
   noise! The baby is sleeping.

2. quarrel; wrangle; squabble: 你们俩怎么一见面就吵呀？Why do you two quarrel with each other as soon as you meet?

词语 Words and Phrases

吵架	chǎojià	quarrel; have a row; wrangle
吵闹	chǎonào	① wrangle; kick up a row ② harass; disturb
吵嚷	chǎorǎng	make a racket; shout in confusion; clamour
吵嘴	chǎo zuǐ	quarrel; bicker

车 chē 一 𠂉 𠃋 车

(車 一 厂 𠃍 百 亘 亘 車)

释义 Meaning

(一) 名词 n.

1. vehicle: 我们坐公共汽车去吧。Let's go by bus.
2. a wheeled instrument: 这种布是用纺车织出来的。This kind of cloth is woven by a spinning wheel.

(二) 动词 v.

1. operate a lathe: 我的工作就是车零件。My job is turning the machine parts on the lathe.
2. lift water by waterwheel: 今年干旱，又得把水车到田里去。It's dry this year; we had to lift water into the fields again.

词语 Words and Phrases

车道	chēdào	(traffic) lane; roadway
车队	chēduì	motorcade
车祸	chēhuò	traffic accident; road accident
车间	chējiān	workshop (in a factory)

车辆	chēliàng	vehicles
车轮	chēlún	wheel (of a vehicle)
车票	chēpiào	train or bus ticket; ticket
车厢	chēxiāng	railway carriage; railroad car
车站	chēzhàn	station; depot; stop

熟语 Idioms

| 车到山前
必有路 | chē dào shān qián
bì yǒu lù | the cart will find its way round the hill when it gets there; we'll cross that bridge when we get to it; things will eventually sort themselves out |
| 车水马龙 | chē shuǐ mǎ lóng | be crowded with people and vehicles; traffic is heavy |

晨 chén ⎿ ⎛ ⎓ ⎓ ⎓ ⎓ ⎓ ⎓ ⎓ 晨 晨

释义 Meaning

名词 n.

morning: 今晨有大雾。It will be very foggy this morning.

反义词 antonym: 暮，昏

词语 Words and Phrases

晨操	chéncāo	morning exercise
晨光	chénguāng	the light of the early morning sun; dawn
晨曦	chénxī	the first rays of the morning sun

熟语 Idioms

| 晨钟暮鼓 | chén zhōng mù gǔ | the morning bell and the evening drum (in a monastery); exhortations to virtue and purity |

称₁ chèn 一 二 千 千 禾 禾 秆 秆 称 称

(稱 一 二 千 千 禾 禾 秆 秆 秆 秆 稻 稻 稱 稱)

释义 Meaning

动词 v.

fit; match; suit: 这件上衣很称你的皮肤。This coat fits the colour of your skin very well.

词语 Words and Phrases

称身	chènshēn	(of a garment) fit
称愿	chènyuàn	be gratified (esp. at the misfortune of a rival)
称职	chènzhí	prove oneself competent at one's job; fill a post with credit; be well qualified for a post

熟语 Idioms

称心如意	chènxīn rúyì	be well-satisfied; very gratifying and satisfactory

称₂ chēng 一 二 千 千 禾 禾 秆 秆 称 称

(稱 一 二 千 千 禾 禾 秆 秆 秆 秆 稻 稻 稱 稱)

释义 Meaning

(一) 动词 v.

1. call: 我们称她什么好呢？How should we address her?

2. say; state: 一曲听罢，人人称好。After hearing the music,

everyone say it was good.

(二) 名词 n.

name: 香港素有「东方之珠」之称。Hong Kong has long been known as "the Pearl of the Orient".

词语 Words and Phrases

称病	chēngbìng	claim to be ill; offer illness as an excuse; plead illness
称道	chēngdào	speak approvingly of; praise; acclaim
称号	chēnghào	title; name; designation
称呼	chēnghu	① call; address ② a form of address
称谓	chēngwèi	appellation; title
称赞	chēngzàn	praise; acclaim; commend

熟语 Idioms

称王称霸	chēng wáng chēng bà	act like an overlord; rule supreme; domineering
称兄道弟	chēng xiōng dào dì	think of sb. as one's own brother; be on intimate terms with

称₃ **chēng**　一 二 千 千 禾 禾 称 称 称 称

(稱　一 二 千 千 禾 禾 称 称 称 称 稻 稻 稱 稱**)**

释义 Meaning

动词 v.

weigh: 请给我称两斤桃子。I'd like one kilo of peaches, please.

词语 Words and Phrases

| 称量 | chēngliáng | weigh |

熟语 Idioms

称斤掂两　chēng jīn diān liǎng　engage in petty calculation; be calculating in small matters

成 chéng　二 厂 厃 成 成 成

释义 Meaning

（一）动词 v.

1. accomplish; succeed: 事成之后，我一定会报答你。I will repay you after this is achieved. 反义词 antonym: 败

2. become; turn into: 他们一见面就成了好朋友。They became good friends as soon as they met.

（二）名词 n.

achievement; result: 他什么也不做，只想坐享其成。He won't do anything, only sit idle and expect to enjoy the fruits of other's work.

（三）形容词 a.

fully developed or fully grown: 过了十八岁，就是成人了。A person becomes an adult at the age of eighteen.

（四）量词 measure w.

one tenth: 这次考试我有九成的把握。I feel 90 percent confident of passing the examination.

词语 Words and Phrases

成本	chéngběn	cost
成分	chéngfèn	① composition; component part; ingredient ② one's class status; one's profession or economic status
成功	chénggōng	succeed; be a success

成婚	chénghūn	get married
成绩	chéngjì	result (of work or study); achievement; success
成就	chéngjiù	① achievement; success; attainment; accomplishment ② achieve; accomplish
成立	chénglì	① found; establish; set up ② be tenable
成品	chéngpǐn	end product; finished product
成熟	chéngshú	ripe; mature
成为	chéngwéi	become; turn into
成问题	chéng wèntí	be a problem; be open to question (or doubt, objection)
成语	chéngyǔ	set phrase (usu. composed of four characters); idiom
成员	chéngyuán	member (of a group or family)

熟语 Idioms

成家立业	chéngjiālìyè	marry and embark on a career; get married and settle down to a job
成年累月	chéng nián lěi yuè	year in year out; for months and years
成千上万	chéng qiān shàng wàn	thousands and tens of thousands; tens of thousands of
成事不足，败事有余	chéng shì bù zú, bài shì yǒu yú	unable to accomplish anything but liable to spoil everything; spoil rather than accomplish things

城 chéng   一 十 土 圹 圹 坂 城 城 城

释义 Meaning

名词 n.

1. city wall; wall: 我去城外办点事。 I want to handle some

affairs outside the city.

2. city: 我家住东城。 I live in the eastern part of the city.

词语 Words and Phrases

城堡	chéngbǎo	castle
城府	chéngfǔ	a mind hard to fathom; subtle thinking
城隍	chénghuáng	city god (in Taoist legend); god of the city
城楼	chénglóu	a tower over a city gate; gate tower
城市	chéngshì	town or city
城乡	chéngxiāng	town and country; urban and rural areas; the city and the countryside
城镇	chéngzhèn	cities and towns

熟语 Idioms

城门失火，殃及池鱼	chéng mén shī huǒ, yāng jí chí yú	when the city gate catches fire, the fish in the moat comes to grief; innocent people suffering from what happens to others

乘 chéng ⼀ ⼆ 千 千 千 千 乖 乖 乘 乘

释义 Meaning

动词 v.

1. ride: 我打算乘飞机去旅行。 I intend to travel by plane.

2. take advantage of; avail oneself of: 乘现在还凉快，我们早点出发吧。 Let's start earlier; while it's still cool.

3. multiply: 八乘五等于四十。 Eight multiplied by five is forty.

词语 Words and Phrases

乘便	chéngbiàn	when it is convenient; at one's conven-

ience

乘方	chéngfāng	(in math) ① involution ② power
乘客	chéngkè	passenger
乘凉	chéngliáng	enjoy the cool; relax in a cool place
乘务员	chéngwùyuán	attendant on a train; bus conductor
乘兴	chéngxìng	while one is in high spirits

熟语 Idioms

乘龙快婿	chéng lóng kuài xù	an ideal son-in-law
乘人之危	chéng rén zhī wēi	utilize sb's disasters
乘虚而入	chéngxū ér rù	act when one's opponent is off guard; exploit one's opponent's weakness

吃 chī 　 丨　丨　卩　卩′　吒　吃

释义 Meaning

动词 v.

1. eat; take: 你要吃苹果吗？Do you want to have an apple?

2. live on (or off): 你这么大了还吃父母呀？At your age, you're still supported by your parents?

3. annihilate; wipe out: 这场战斗我们吃掉了敌人一个师。We annihilate an enemy division in this battle.

4. absorb; soak up: 这种纸不吃水。This kind of paper does not absorb water.

5. suffer; bear; incur: 她结婚以后吃了不少苦。She has suffered a great deal since she got married.

词语 Words and Phrases

吃白食	chī báishí	eat food that isn't earned; not an honest living; live off others
吃不开	chī bùkāi	be unpopular
吃不消	chī bùxiāo	be unable to stand (exertion, fatigue,

etc.)

吃醋	chī cù	be jealous (usu. of a rival in love)
吃豆腐	chī dòufǔ	① flirt with a woman ② crack a joke ③ visit the bereaved to offer one's condolences (old custom)
吃饭	chī fàn	① eat; have a meal ② keep alive; make a living
吃回扣	chī huíkòu	get by graft; kickback
吃惊	chījīng	be startled; be shocked; be amazed; be taken aback
吃亏	chī kuī	① suffer losses; come to grief; get the worst of it ② be at a disadvantage; be in an unfavourable situation
吃力	chī lì	① entail strenuous effort; be a strain ② tired; fatigued
吃闲饭	chī xiánfàn	lead an idle life; be a loafer or sponger
吃香	chī xiāng	be very popular; be much sought after; be well-liked
吃斋	chī zhāi	practise abstinence from meat (as a religious exercise); be a vegetarian for religious reasons

熟语 Idioms

吃不了 兜着走	chī bùliǎo dōu zhe zǒu	be in for it; land oneself in serious trouble
吃喝玩乐	chī hē wán lè	eat, drink and be merry; feasting and reveling
吃软 不吃硬	chī ruǎn bù chī yìng	be open to persuasion, but not to coercion
吃一堑， 长一智	chī yí qiàn, zhǎng yí zhì	a fall into the pit, a gain in your wit; learn by experience

迟 chí　　フ　ユ　尸　尺　迟　迟　迟

(遲 一 ㄱ 尸 尸 戸 戸 戸 屍 屍 屋 犀
犀 犀 遲 遲)

释义 Meaning

形容词 a.

late: 对不起，我来迟了。I'm sorry; I'm late. 反义词
antonym: 早

词语 Words and Phrases

迟到	chídào	be (or come, arrive) late
迟钝	chídùn	slow (in thought or action); obtuse
迟缓	chíhuǎn	slow; tardy; sluggish
迟暮	chímù	① dusk; twilight ② past one's prime; late in one's life
迟疑	chíyí	hesitate
迟早	chízǎo	sooner or later

持 chí　一 十 扌 扩 扩 拃 持 持

释义 Meaning

动词 v.

hold; grasp: 对这个问题，我持相反意见。I hold a contrary opinion on this problem.

词语 Words and Phrases

持家	chíjiā	run one's home; keep house
持久	chíjiǔ	lasting; enduring; protracted
持平	chípíng	unbiased; fair; balanced
持续	chíxù	continue; sustain
持有	chíyǒu	hold; own

熟语 Idioms

| 持之以恒 | chí zhī yǐ héng | persevere; keep up |

尺 chǐ ㄱ ㄱ 尸 尺

释义 Meaning

名词 n.

ruler: 这条裤子的长度，得用尺量一下。The length of the trousers should be measured by a ruler.

量词 measure w.

a traditional unit of length: 一尺等于0.333米。One *chi* is equivalent to 0.333 metre.

词语 Words and Phrases

尺寸	chǐcùn	① measurement; dimensions; size ② proper limits for speech or action; sense of propriety
尺度	chǐdù	yardstick; measure; scale
尺码	chǐmǎ	size; measures
尺子	chǐzi	rule; ruler

熟语 Idioms

尺有所短，寸有所长	chǐ yǒu suǒ duǎn, cùn yǒu suǒ cháng	sometimes a foot may prove short while an inch may prove long; everyone has his strong and weak points

冲₁ chōng 丶 冫 冫 冲 冲 冲

(衝 丶 彳 彳 彳 彳 行 行 行 徍 徍 徍 衝 衝 衝)

释义 Meaning

动词 v.

1. charge; rush; dash: 他冲进大火，救出了女儿。He dashed into the fire and rescued his daughter.

2. pour boiling water on: 我给你冲一杯咖啡吧。Let me make a cup of coffee for you.

3. rinse; flush: 请把这些盘子冲一下。Have these plates rinsed please.

4. develop: 冲一卷胶卷要多少钱？How much does it cost to develop a roll of film?

词语 Words and Phrases

冲刺	chōngcì	spurt; sprint
冲动	chōngdòng	① impulsive ② get excited; be impetuous
冲锋	chōngfēng	charge; assault
冲击	chōngjī	① lash; pound ② charge; assault
冲破	chōngpò	break through; breach
冲刷	chōngshuā	① wash and brush; wash down ② erode; wash away
冲突	chōngtū	conflict; clash
冲撞	chōngzhuàng	① collide; bump; ram ② give offence; offend

熟语 Idioms

冲昏头脑	chōnghūn tóunǎo	turn sb's head; get dizzy with; overwhelmed (by sth.)

虫 chóng 丨 冂 口 中 虫 虫

(蟲 丨 冂 口 中 虫 虫 虫 虫 虫 虫 虫 虫 虫 蟲 蟲 蟲 蟲 蟲 蟲）

释义 Meaning

名词 n.

insect or worm: 有一条虫在地上爬。There is a worm creeping on the ground.

词语 Words and Phrases

虫害	chónghài	pest
虫牙	chóngyá	decayed tooth
虫灾	chóngzāi	a plague of insects
虫子	chóngzi	insect or worm

抽 chōu 一 十 扌 扣 扣 扣 抽 抽

释义 Meaning
动词 v.

1. take out (from in between): 他从书包里抽出了一张纸。He took a piece of paper out of the satchel.

2. take (a part from a whole): 抽几个学生去参加演讲比赛。Release several students from their study to attend the oratorical contest.

3. obtain by drawing, etc.: 医生给我抽了二百毫升血。I had 200cc blood drawn by the doctor.

4. lash; whip; thrash: 他在马背上抽了一鞭子。He whipped the horse on its back.

词语 Words and Phrases

抽查	chōuchá	carry out selective examination; make spot checks; spot-check
抽动	chōudòng	twitch; have a spasm; jerk spasmodically
抽风	chōufēng	pump air
抽空	chōukòng	manage to find time
抽签	chōuqiān	draw (or cast) lots
抽屉	chōuti	drawer
抽象	chōuxiàng	① abstract ② form a general idea from particular instances

抽烟　　chōuyān　　smoke (a cigarette or a pipe)

抽样　　chōuyàng　　sampling (in statistics and research)

愁 chóu　一　二　千　禾　禾　禾　禾′　秒　秋　秋　愁　愁　愁

释义 Meaning

动词 v.

worry; be anxious: 你这么有钱还愁什么？You are so rich, what do you have to worry about?

词语 Words and Phrases

愁苦　　chóukǔ　　anxiety; distress

愁闷　　chóumèn　　feel gloomy; be in low spirits; be depressed

愁容　　chóuróng　　worried look; anxious expression

愁思　　chóusī　　sad thoughts; feelings of anxiety

愁云　　chóuyún　　gloomy clouds; gloom; melancholy

熟语 Idioms

愁眉苦脸　　chóu méi kǔ liǎn　　wear a worried look; a gloomy face

臭 chòu　′　厂　宀　白　自　自　自　臭　臭　臭

释义 Meaning

（一）形容词 a.

1. smelly; foul; stinking: 这个鸡蛋臭了。This egg stinks.
   反义词 antonym: 香

2. disgusting; disgraceful: 他的名声很臭。He is in disgrace.

（二）副词 adv.

severely: 我被他臭骂了一顿。I got a tongue-lashing from him.

词语 Words and Phrases

臭虫	chòu chóng	bedbug
臭烘烘	chòuhōnghōng	stinking; foul-smelling; smelly
臭美	chòuměi	show off shamelessly; be disgustingly smug
臭钱	chòuqián	stinking money; filthy money
臭球	chòuqiú	a lousy pass, stroke, or shot in a ball game; a lousy game or match

熟语 Idioms

臭名远播	chòu míng yuǎn yáng	notorious; bad repute
臭味相投	chòu wèi xiāng tóu	be birds of a feather; be two of a kind

出₁ chū 亠 ⼐ 屮 出 出

释义 Meaning

动词 v.

1. go or come out: 出了站向右拐就是邮局。If you come out of the station and turn right you will come to the post office. 反义词antonym: 进

2. exceed; go beyond: 他们结婚不出三年就离了。They divorced within three years after gettirg married.

3. issue; put out: 你帮我出个主意好吗？Can you throw out any idea for me?

4. produce; turn out: 这个小城里出了不少人才。This little town has produced a lot of outstanding talents.

5. arise; happen: 高架桥上出事故了。There was an accident on the flyover.

出₂ chū 亠 ⼐ 屮 出 出

（齣　　⺊　⺊　⺊　⺊　⺊　⺊　⺊　⺊　⺊
　⺊　⺊　齒　齒　齣　齣　齣　齣　齣）

释义 Meaning

量词 measure w.

(for operas or plays): 我看完这出戏就回家。I will go back home after seeing the play.

词语 Words and Phrases

出版	chūbǎn	come off the press; publish; put out or come out
出差	chūchāi	go or be away on a business trip
出错	chūcuò	make a mistake
出发	chūfā	① set out; start off ② take...as a starting point in consideration; proceed from
出风头	chūfēngtou	seeking or be in the limelight
出汗	chūhàn	perspire; sweat
出嫁	chūjià	(of a woman) get married; marry
出力	chūlì	put forth one's strength; exert oneself
出门	chūmén	① go out ② leave home; go on a journey ③ (of a woman) get married; marry
出名	chūmíng	① be famous; be well known ② lend one's name; use the name of
出色	chūsè	outstanding; remarkable; splendid
出世	chūshì	① come into the world; be born; come into being ② renounce the world ③ rise high above the world
出席	chūxí	be present (at a meeting, social gathering, etc.); attend
出现	chūxiàn	appear; arise; emerge
出洋相	chūyángxiàng	make an exhibition of oneself; make a spectacle of oneself (usu. negative)

出租	chūzū	hire out; rent; let

熟语 Idioms

出口成章	chū kǒu chéng zhāng	toss off smart remarks; well-versed in literature
出类拔萃	chū lèi bá cuì	be distinguished from one's kind; be out of the common run
出人头地	chū rén tóu dì	rise head and shoulders above others; excel most men
出人意料	chū rén yìliào	exceeding all expectations; surprising

除 chú　⻖ ⻖ ⻖ ⻖ ⻖ ⻖ 阼 除 除

释义 Meaning

（一）动词 v.

1. ret rid of; eliminate; remove: 你把院子里的草除一下。Have the weeds in the yard removed.

2. divide: 十除以二等于五。Ten divided by two is five.

（二）介词 prep.

1. except: 除小李以外，所有的人都去了。Everyone has gone except Xiao Li.

2. besides: 除西瓜外，我还买了香蕉、葡萄等。Besides watermelons, I also bought bananas, grapes, ets.

词语 Words and Phrases

除法	chúfǎ	division
除非	chúfēi	① only if; only when ② (not)...unless ③ must needs; necessarily
除名	chúmíng	remove sb's name from the rolls; strike sb's name off the rolls
除霜	chúshuāng	defrost

| 除夕 | chúxī | New Year's Eve (of the Chinese lunar calender) |

熟语 Idioms

| 除暴安良 | chú bào ān liáng | get rid of the bullies and bring peace to the good people; champion the good and kill the tyrants |
| 除旧布新 | chú jiù bù xīn | get rid of the old to make way for the new; do away with the old and set up the new |

处₁ chǔ ノ ク 夂 处 处

（處 ＇ ⺊ ⺊ 广 广 虍 虍 虘 虑 處 處）

释义 Meaning

动词 v.

1. get along (with sb.): 这个人不容易跟他相处。 It is not easy to get along with this person.

2. be situated in; be in a certain condition: 这些孩子正处于生长发育阶段。 These children are in their puperty stage.

3. punish; sentence: 犯人被处以十年徒刑。 The prisoner is sentenced to a ten year jail term.

词语 Words and Phrases

处罚	chǔfá	punish; penalize
处方	chǔfāng	① write out a prescription; prescribe ② prescription; recipe
处分	chǔfèn	① take disciplinary action against; punish ② handle; manage; deal with
处境	chǔjìng	unfavourable situation; plight
处理	chǔlǐ	① handle; deal with; dispose of ② treat

(a work piece or product) by a special process ③ sell at reduced price

处女	chǔnǚ	virgin; maiden
处事	chǔshì	handle affairs; deal with matters
处置	chǔzhì	① handle; deal with; manage; dispose of ② punish

熟语 Idioms

| 处心积虑 | chǔ xīn jī lǜ | seek by all means; consantly scheming |

处₂ chù ノ ク 夂 处 处

(處 一 ト ⼾ ⼴ 广 ⼾ ⼾ 虍 虍 虙 處 處)

释义 Meaning

（一）名词 n.

1. place: 那儿有一个停车处。There is a parking lot over there.

2. point; part: department; office: 你们的观点有相同之处。The opinions of you both have something in common.

（二）量词 measure w.

(for places or for occurrences or activities in different places): 这篇文章里有几处错误。There are several mistakes in the article.

词语 Words and Phrases

处处	chùchù	everywhere; in all respects
处所	chùsuǒ	place; location
处长	chùzhǎng	the head of a department or office; section chief

穿 chuān 、 ﹀ ﹁ 宀 宊 空 空 穽 穿 穿

释义 Meaning

动词 v.

1. pierce through; penetrate: 我的衣服穿了一个洞。There is a hole on my clothing.

2. pass through; cross: 火车在这条线上要穿三十几个洞。The train will pass through thirty odd caves along this railway line.

3. wear; put on; be dressed in: 她今天穿了一条红裙子。She is dressed in a red skirt today. 反义词 antonym: 脱

词语 Words and Phrases

穿戴	chuāndài	apparel; dress
穿过	chuānguò	go across or through; cross; penetrate
穿孔	chuānkǒng	① bore (or punch) a hole; perforate ② perforation
穿梭	chuānsuō	shuttle back and forth
穿小鞋	chuān xiǎoxié	give sb. tight shoes to wear; make things hard for sb. by abusing one's power; make it hot for sb.
穿着	chuānzhe	dress; apparel

熟语 Idioms

穿凿附会	chuānzáo fùhuì	give strained interpretations and draw farfetched analogies; far-fetched
穿针引线	chuānzhēn yǐnxiàn	act as a go-between; make a match of it

传₁ chuán ノ 亻 仁 仨 传 传

（**傳** ノ 亻 仁 仁 俨 俨 俥 傅 傅 傳 傳 傳）

释义 Meaning

动词 v.

1. pass; pass on: 请将试卷一个一个地往下传。Please pass over these examination papers one by one.

2. hand down: 这幅画是我家祖上传下来的。This painting has been down from my ancestors.

3. pass on (knowledge, skill, etc.); impart; teach: 我师傅把他的厨艺全传给我了。My instructer passed all his cooking skills on to me.

4. spread: 这个消息是他传出去的。He is the one who spread the news.

5. infect; be contagious: 我们孩子传上了流感。Our child has caught the flu.

词语 Words and Phrases

传播	chuánbō	① disseminate; propagate; spread ② phys. propagation
传达	chuándá	① pass on (information, etc.); transmit; relay; communicate ② reception and registration of callers at a public establishment ③ janitor
传单	chuándān	leaflet; handbill
传递	chuándì	transmit; deliver; transfer
传家宝	chuánjiābǎo	① family treasure ② a cherished tradition or heritage
传染	chuánrǎn	infect; be contagious
传世	chuánshì	be handed down from ancient times
传说	chuánshuō	① pass from mouth to mouth; it is said; they say ② legend; tradition
传统	chuántǒng	tradition

| 传闻 | chuánwén | ① it is said; they say ② hearsay; rumour; talk |
| 传真 | chuánzhēn | ① portraiture ② facsimile; fax |

熟语 Idioms

| 传宗接代 | chuán zōng jiē dài | produce a male heir to continue the family line |

传₂ chuán　ノ　亻　仁　仨　传　传

(傳　ノ　亻　仁　仁　伫　俥　伃　俥　俥　俥　傅　傳　傳)

释义 Meaning

名词 n.

1. commentaries on classics: 你读过《左传》吗？Have you read The *Zuo Commentary* (on *The Spring and Autumn Annals*)?

2. biography: 我很爱读名人传。I like to read biographies of famous people very much.

3. story or novel (usu. used in titles): 你最喜欢《水浒传》里的哪一位英雄？Which hero do you like the best in *Water Margin*?

词语 Words and Phrases

| 传记 | zhuànjì | biography |
| 传略 | zhuànlüè | brief biography; biographical sketch |

船 chuán　′　丿　几　舟　舟　舟　舟　船　船　船　船

释义 Meaning

名词 n.

boat; ship: 从重庆到上海坐船需要三天。It takes three days from Chongqing to Shanghai by boat.

词语 Words and Phrases

船舶	chuánbó	shipping; boats and ships
船舱	chuáncāng	① ship's hold ② cabin
船家	chuánjiā	one who owns a boat and makes a living as a boatman; boatman
船老大	chuánlǎodà	① the chief crewman of a wooden boat ② boatman
船身	chuánshēn	hull (of a ship)
船位	chuánwèi	① accommodation on a ship ② ship's position (at sea); a seat reservation in a ship
船员	chuányuán	(ship's) crew
船长	chuánzhǎng	captain; skipper

熟语 Idioms

船到江心补漏迟	chuán dào jiāng xīn bǔ lòu chí	repair a leak in mid stream is too late to avoid a disaster

窗 chuāng   丶 丶 宀 宀 宀 空 空 宀 窗 窗 窗 窗 窗

释义 Meaning

名词 n.

window: 开窗换换空气。Open the window and air the room.

词语 Words and Phrases

窗玻璃	chuāngbōlí	windowpane
窗户	chuānghu	window; casement

窗口	chuāngkǒu	window
窗帘	chuānglián	curtain
窗台	chuāngtái	windowsill
窗子	chuāngzi	window

熟语 Idioms

窗明几净	chuāng míng jī jìng	with bright windows and clean tables; clean and peaceful

床 chuáng `丶 亠 广 广 庄 庄 床`

释义 Meaning

（一）名词 n.

1. bed: 她躺在床上看书。She lies in the bed to read.

2. sth. shaped like a bed: 河水干涸了，河床都露出来了。The river is dry and the riverbed is exposed.

（二）量词 measure w.

(for bedding): 得给孩子买一床小被子。We had to buy a small quilt for our child.

词语 Words and Phrases

床单	chuángdān	sheet
床垫	chuángdiàn	mattress
床头柜	chuángtóuguì	bedside cupboard
床位	chuángwèi	berth; bunk; bed
床罩	chuángzhào	bedspread; counterpane

吹 chuī `丨 冂 口 ㅁ 吥 吩 吹`

释义 Meaning

动词 v.

1. blow; puff: 一阵风把蜡烛给吹灭了。A blast of wind blows out the candle.

2. play (wind instruments): 他很会吹小号。He is good at playing trumpet.

3. boast; brag: 你别吹了，谁信你呀！Don't brag; no one will believe you!

4. break off; break up; fall through: 听说他们俩吹了。It's said that the couple has broken up.

词语 Words and Phrases

吹风	chuīfēng	① be in a draught; catch a chill ② dry (hair, etc.) with a blower; blow-dry ③ let sb. in on sth. in advance
吹拂	chuīfú	① (of a breeze) sway; stir ② praise and recommend sb.
吹鼓手	chuīgǔshǒu	① music makers at old-time weddings or funerals ② eulogist
吹牛	chuīniú	boast; brag; talk big
吹捧	chuīpěng	flatter; laud to the skies; lavish praise on
吹嘘	chuīxū	lavish praise on oneself or others; boast

熟语 Idioms

吹吹拍拍	chuī chuī pāi pāi	boasting and toadying
吹胡子瞪眼	chuī húzi dèng yǎn	blow a fuse; fume with anger
吹毛求疵	chuī máo qiú cī	find fault; be very fastidious; nit-picking

春 chūn 一 二 三 声 夫 夫 春 春 春

释义 Meaning

名词 n.

1. spring: 昆明四季如春。In Kungming it's like spring all the year round.

2. love; lust: 十八岁正是怀春的年纪。Eighteen is the age to harbour thoughts of love.

词语 Words and Phrases

春风	chūnfēng	① spring breeze ② a kindly and pleasant countenance
春光	chūnguāng	sights and sounds of spring; spring scenery
春季	chūnjì	spring; springtime
春节	chūnjié	Spring Festival (Lunar New Year)
春联	chūnlián	Spring Festival couplets (pasted on gateposts or door panels conveying one's best wishes for the year); New Year couplets
春色	chūnsè	① spring's colours; spring scenery ② joyful look; wineflushed face
春心	chūnxīn	thoughts of love; stirrings of love; budding love

熟语 Idioms

| 春风得意 | chūnfēngdé yì | be flushed with success; look triumphant |
| 春意盎然 | chūnyì àngrán | spring is in the air |

词 cí 　 ` 讠 订 订 词 词 词

(詞 　 ` 亠 亠 ⺩ 訁 言 言 訂 訂 詞 詞 詞)

释义 Meaning

名词 n.

1. word; term: 这个词是什么意思？What's the meaning of this word?

2. a kind of Chinese poetry written to certain tunes with

strict tonal patterns and rhyme schemes, in fixed numbers of lines and words, originated in the Tang Dynasty (618-907) and fully developed in the Song Dynasty (960-1279): 我最喜欢李清照的词。I like Li Qingzhao's *ci* the best.

词语 Words and Phrases

词典	cídiǎn	dictionary
词汇	cíhuì	vocabulary; words and phrases
词句	cíjù	words and phrases; expressions
词牌	cípái	names of the tunes to which *ci* poems are composed
词性	cíxìng	syntactical functions and morphological features that help to determine a part of speech
词义	cíyì	the meaning (or sense) of a word
词语	cíyǔ	words and expressions; terms
词组	cízǔ	word group; phrase

熟语 Idioms

词不达意	cí bù dá yì	the words fail to convey the idea; the expression does not convey the actual meaning

此 cǐ ｜ ⼘ ⼐ 止 ⽌ 此

释义 Meaning

代词 pron.

1. this: 我不喜欢此人。I don't like this person.
2. here and now: 从此以后，我和他成了好朋友。From that time on, we became good friends.

词语 Words and Phrases

此地	cǐdì	this place; here

此后	cǐhòu	after this; hereafter; henceforth
此刻	cǐkè	this moment; now; at present
此生	cǐshēng	this life
此外	cǐwài	besides; in addition; moreover
此致	cǐzhì	I hereby communicate (used at the close of an official report or a business letter)

熟语 Idioms

| 此地无银
三百两 | cǐ dì wú yín
sānbǎi liǎng | no 300 taels of silver is buried here; a clumsy denial resulting in self- exposure |
| 此起彼伏 | cǐ qǐ bǐ fú | here rising there falling; arise in succession |

次 cì　　丶 冫 冫 冫 冫 次

释义 Meaning

(一) 形容词 a.

1. second; next: 介绍一下，这是我的次子。Let me introduce, this is my second son.

2. second-rate; inferior: 这些产品可真够次的。These products are really inferior.

(二) 量词 measure w.

occurrence; time: 我去过三次北京。I have been to Beijing three times.

词语 Words and Phrases

次等	cìděng	second-class; second-rate; inferior
次品	cìpǐn	substandard products; defective goods
次日	cìrì	the next day
次数	cìshù	number of times; frequency
次序	cìxù	order; sequence

| 次要 | cìyào | less important; secondary; subordinate; minor |

从 cóng 丿 人 丛 从

(從 ´ ˊ 彳 彳 彳 彳 彳 彳 彳 從 從)

释义 Meaning

(一)动词 v.

follow; comply with; obey: 父亲的丧事还是从简吧！The funeral arrangements of father had better conform to the principle of simplicity.

(二)形容词 a.

secondary; accessary: 他们俩谁主谁从，我很清楚。Of the two, I know clearly who is the principal and who is the subordinate.

(三)介词 prep.

1. in a certain manner; according to a certain principle: 他还是个孩子，你就从轻发落吧！He is still a child, you should deal with him leniently.

2. from (a time, a place, or a point of view): 从现在开始，一切都要听我的！From now on, everything should be under my command.

3. via, through, or past (a place): 我们从小路上走近一点。It will be closer if we take a backstreet.

(四)副词 adv.

(followed by a negative) ever: 我从不抽烟。I never smoke.

词语 Words and Phrases

| 从此 | cóngcǐ | from this time on; from now on; from then on; henceforth; thereupon |
| 从犯 | cóngfàn | accessary criminal; accessary |

从军	cóngjūn	join the army; enlist
从命	cóngmìng	do sb's bidding; comply with sb's wish; obey an order
从前	cóngqián	before; formerly; in the past
从师	cóngshī	follow a teacher or a master
从事	cóngshì	① go in for; be engaged in ② deal with
从政	cóngzhèng	go into politics; take up a government post

熟语 Idioms

| 从容不迫 | cóngróng bú pò | calm and unhurried; take it easy |
| 从一而终 | cóng yī ér zhōng | be faithful to one's master to the end; marry one husband in her life |

粗 cū   ` ˋ ˊ 丷 ᄼ ᄼ ᄽ 米 籶 籵 粗 粗 粗

释义 Meaning

形容词 a.

1. wide (in diameter); thick: 这根绳不够粗。The rope is not thick enough. 反义词 antonym: 细

2. coarse; crude; rough: 现在很难买到粗盐。It's not easy to buy the crude salt now. 反义词 antonym: 细

3. gruff; husky: 他天生一副粗嗓子。He was born with a husky voice.

4. careless; negligent: 你的心也太粗了！You are too careless! 反义词 antonym: 细

5. rude; unrefined; vulgar: 别说粗话！Don't speak vulgar language!

词语 Words and Phrases

粗暴	cūbào	rude; rough; crude; brutal
粗糙	cūcāo	① coarse; rough ② crude
粗犷	cūguǎng	① rough; rude; boorish ② straightforward and uninhibited; bold and unconstrained; rugged
粗粮	cūliáng	coarse food grain (e.g. maize, sorghum, millet, etc. as distinct from wheat flour and rice)
粗浅	cūqiǎn	superficial; shallow; simple
粗人	cūrén	① a rough fellow; a rash person ② an unrefined person; boor
粗俗	cūsú	vulgar; coarse
粗心	cūxīn	careless; thoughtless
粗壮	cūzhuàng	① sturdy; thickset; brawny ② thick and strong ③ deep and resonant

熟语 Idioms

粗茶淡饭	cū chá dàn fàn	plain tea and simple food; homely fare; cheap and simple meal
粗枝大叶	cū zhī dà yè	crude and careless; in a cursory fashion; slapdash

村 cūn   一 十 才 木 朴 村 村

释义 Meaning

名词 n.

village; hamlet: 海边有一个小渔村。There is a little fishing village at the seaside.

词语 Words and Phrases

村口	cūnkǒu	entrance to a village
村落	cūnluò	village; hamlet

村民	cūnmín	villager; village people
村野	cūnyě	① villages; countryside ② rustic; coun-trified
村庄	cūnzhuāng	village; hamlet
村子	cūnzi	village; hamlet

存 cún 　一 ナ 疒 产 存 存

释义 Meaning

动词 v.

1. store; keep: 明天停水，今晚得存一些水。There would be no water service tomorrow, so we had better store some water tonight.

2. deposit: 钱存在银行里很保险。Money deposited in the bank is quite safe.

3. leave with; check: 存自行车要多少钱？How much is it to leave the bicycle in a bicycle park.

4. cherish; harbour: 你别对他存任何幻想。You'd better not harbour any illusions about him.

词语 Words and Phrases

存单	cúndān	deposit receipt
存放	cúnfàng	① leave with; leave in sb's care ② deposit (money)
存活	cúnhuó	survive
存款	cúnkuǎn	① deposit money (in a bank) ② deposit; bank savings
存亡	cúnwáng	live or die; survive or perish; stand or fall
存心	cúnxīn	① cherish certain intentions ② intentionally; deliberately; on purpose
存在	cúnzài	exist; be

存折　　　cúnzhé　　　deposit book; passbook

寸 cùn　二　十　寸

释义 Meaning

（一）量词 measure w.

a traditional unit of length; 1/10 *chi*：请把我的头发剪短一寸。I want to have my hair cut for one *cun* please.

（二）形容词 a.

very little; very short; small：这点礼物聊表寸心。This little gift is as a small token of my feelings.

词语 Words and Phrases

寸步	cùnbù	a tiny step; a single step
寸功	cùngōng	a minor achievement (or contribution)
寸铁	cùntiě	a small weapon
寸头	cùntóu	crew cut

熟语 Idioms

寸步难行	cùn bù nán xíng	be unable to move even a single step; it is difficult to move a step
寸草不留	cùn cǎo bù liú	leave not even a blade of grass; complete devastation (of the land)
寸金难买 寸光阴	cùn jīn nán mǎi cùn guāng yīn	money can't buy time; an inch of gold will not buy an inch of time
寸土必争	cùn tǔ bì zhēng	fight for every inch of land; advance under advesre circumstances

错 cuò　丿　𠂉　𠂉　钅　钅　钅　钅　钅　错　错　错　错

(错 丿 𠂉 𠂔 𠂓 牟 牟 钅 金 釒 釒 錯 錯 錯 錯 错 **)**

释义 Meaning

（一）形容词 a.

wrong; mistake; erroneous: 我错了，你能原谅我吗？I'm wrong, can you please forgive me? 反义词 antonym: 对

（二）名词 n.

fault; demerit: 都是我的错，不怪他。It's my fault, he is not to blame.

（三）动词 v.

alternate; stagger: 你把时间错一下，不就能参加这个会了吗？If you only staggered the time, wouldn't you be able to attend the meeting?

词语 Words and Phrases

错别字	cuòbiézì	wrongly written or mispronounced characters
错过	cuòguò	miss; let slip
错觉	cuòjué	illusion; misconception; wrong impression
错误	cuòwù	① wrong; be mistaken; erroneous ② mistake; error; blunder

熟语 Idioms

错落有致	cuò luò yǒu zhì	in picturesque disorder
错综复杂	cuòzōng fùzá	be intricate and complex

达 dá 一 ナ 大 犬 达 达

(達 一 十 去 去 去 去 查 查 坴 幸 幸 達 達 **)**

释义 Meaning

动词 v.

1. extend: 这趟列车直达北京。This is a nonstop train to Beijing.
2. reach; attain; amount to: 今年的留学生人数达一千个。The number of foreign students has reached 1,000 this year.

词语 Words and Phrases

达标	dábiāo	reach a set standard
达成	dáchéng	reach (agreement)
达到	dádào	achieve; attain; reach
达观	dáguān	take things philosophically
达意	dáyì	express (or convey) one's ideas

熟语 Idioms

达官贵人	dáguānguìrén	high officials and noble lords; VIPs; magnates

答 dá ノ ＾ ＾ ＾ ＾ ＾ ＾ ＾ ＾ 答 答 答

释义 Meaning

动词 v.

answer; reply; respond: 老师的问题我答不出来。I couldn't answer the teacher's question. 反义词antonym: 问

词语 Words and Phrases

答案	dá'àn	answer; solution; key
答辩	dábiàn	reply (to a charge, query or an argument)
答复	dáfù	answer; reply
答谢	dáxiè	express appreciation (for sb's kindness or hospitality); acknowledge

| 答疑 | dáyí | answer question (from a teacher, speaker, etc.) |

熟语 Idioms

| 答非所问 | dá fēi suǒ wèn | give an irrelevant answer; answer what is not asked |

打 dǎ 　 一 十 扌 扩 打

释义 Meaning

（一）动词 v.

1. break; smash: 我打了一个杯子。I broke a cup.

2. beat; fight; attack: 他们俩又打起来了。The couple came to blows again.

3. make (articles of daily use or food): 这些家具全是我自己打的。This furniture is of my own making.

4. hold up; hoist; raise: 那个打伞的女孩是我妹妹。That girl holding up an umbrella is my sister.

5. send; dispatch; project: 我一到家就给你打电话。I'll call you as soon as I have gotten home.

6. buy: 你去打一瓶酱油。Go to buy a bottle of soy sauce.

7. play: 我们打蓝球去吧。Let's go to play basketball.

8. go through (some physical action): 他向我打了一个"胜利"的手势。He made a gesture of "victory" to me.

（二）介词 prep.

from; since: 我打小就喜欢音乐。I've liked music since my childhood.

词语 Words and Phrases

| 打扮 | dǎbàn | ① dress up; make up; deck out ② way or style of dressing |
| 打倒 | dǎdǎo | overthrow |

打的	dǎdí	go by taxi; take a taxi
打工	dǎgōng	do manual work; work
打官司	dǎ guānsī	① go to court (or law); engage in a lawsuit ② squabble
打击	dǎjī	hit; strike; attack
打架	dǎjià	come to blows; fight; scuffle
打交道	dǎ jiāodào	come into (or make) contact with; have dealings with
打瞌睡	dǎ kēshuì	doze off; nod
打扫	dǎsǎo	sweep; clean
打算	dǎsuàn	① plan; intend ② idea; intention
打听	dǎtīng	ask about; inquire about
打仗	dǎzhàng	fight; go to war; make war
打招呼	dǎ zhāohu	①greet sb.; say hello ② notify; let sb. know ③ warn; remind
打折扣	dǎ zhékòu	① sell at a discount; give a discount ② fall short of a requirement or promise
打针	dǎzhēn	give or have an injection
打主意	dǎ zhǔyì	① think of a plan; evolve an idea ② try to obtain; seek
打字	dǎzì	typewrite; type

熟语 Idioms

打抱不平	dǎ bàobùpíng	a champion of the weak; defend sb. against an injustice; be the champion of the oppressed
打草惊蛇	dǎ cǎo jīng shé	beat the grass and startle the snake; act rashly and alert the enemy
打肿脸充胖子	dǎ zhǒng liǎn chōng pàngzi	keep up unnecessary appearances; puff oneself up at one's own cost

大 dà 一 ナ 大

释义 Meaning

(一) 形容词 a.

1. big; large; great: 我出生在一座大城市。I was born in a big city. 反义词 antonym: 小

2. heavy (rain, etc.); strong (wind, etc.): 雨下得很大，等一会儿再走。The rain is falling heavily, stay a while longer before you leave. 反义词 antonym: 小

3. loud: 把电视机的声音开大一点。Turn the television up a bit louder. 反义词 antonym: 小

(二) 名词 n.

size: 你穿多大的衣服？What size of clothes do you wear?

(三) 副词 adv.

1. greatly; fully: 听完这个故事，所有的人都大笑起来。Everyone laughed heartily after hearing the story.

2. in a big way; on a big (or large) scale; with all-out efforts; vigorously: 老师对我的文章大删大改。The teacher did a thorough job in revising my article.

词语 Words and Phrases

大大	dàdà	greatly; enormously
大胆	dàdǎn	bold; daring; audacious
大道理	dàdàolǐ	major principle; general principle; great truth
大地	dàdì	earth; mother earth
大都	dàdū	for the most part; mostly
大方	dàfāng	① generous; liberal ② natural and poised; easy; unaffected ③ in good taste; tasteful
大概	dàgài	① general idea; broad outline ② general; rough; approximate ③ probably; most

		likely; presumably
大话	dàhuà	big (or tall) talk; boast; bragging
大家	dàjiā	all; everybody
大款	dàkuǎn	tycoon; moneybags
大力士	dàlìshì	a man of unusual strength, esp. a weight-lifter
大量	dàliàng	① a large number; a great quantity ② generous; magnanimous
大陆	dàlù	continent; mainland; the Chinese Mainland
大肆	dàsì	without restraint; wantonly
大王	dàwáng	① king; magnate ② a person of the highest class or skill in sth.; ace
大型	dàxíng	large-scale; large
大学	dàxué	university; college
大约	dàyuē	① approximately; about ② probably
大致	dàzhì	roughly; approximately; more or less
大众	dàzhòng	the masses; the people; the public; the broad masses of the people

熟语 Idioms

大吃一惊	dà chī yìjīng	be greatly surprised; be quite taken aback
大腹便便	dà fù piánpián	potbellied; a fat and heavy belly; pregnant
大同小异	dà tóng xiǎo yì	much the same but with minor differences; alike except for slight differences; much the same
大智若愚	dà zhì ruò yú	a man of great wisdom but pretending to be slow-witted; a great man looks dull; great wisdom appears stupid

呆 dāi   `丨 冂 卩 므 早 呆 呆`

释义 Meaning

（一）形容词 a.

1. slow-witted; dull: 他家的儿子有点呆。His son is a little slow-witted.

2. blank; wooden: 孩子被恐怖片吓呆了。The child was stupefied after seeing the horror film.

（二）动词 v.

stay: 我在中国已经呆了三年了。I have stayed in China for three years.

词语 Words and Phrases

呆板	dāibǎn	stiff and awkward; rigid; not natural; inflexible
呆帐	dāizhàng	bad debt
呆滞	dāizhì	① dull ② idle
呆子	dāizi	idiot; simpleton; blockhead

熟语 Idioms

呆若木鸡	dāi ruò mù jī	stand motionless like a statue; be stupefied
呆头呆脑	dāi tóu dāi nǎo	stupid-looking; idiotic

代 dài   `丿 亻 仁 代 代`

释义 Meaning

（一）动词 v.

take the place of; be in place of: 老李病了，我代他值班。Lao Li is ill; I'm on duty to take his place.

（二）名词 n.

1. historical period: 故事发生在唐代。The story took place during the Tang Dynasty.

2. generation: 我们家有四代人。There are four generations
   in our family.

词语 Words and Phrases

代表	dàibiǎo	① deputy; delegate; representative ② represent; stand for
代沟	dàigōu	generation gap
代价	dàijià	price; cost; opportunity cost
代劳	dàiláo	do sth. for sb.; take trouble on sb.'s behalf
代理	dàilǐ	① act on behalf of sb. in a responsible position ② act as agent (or proxy, procurator)
代替	dàitì	replace; substitute for; take the place of
代用品	dàiyòngpǐn	substitute

熟语 Idioms

代人受过	dài rén shòu guò	suffer for the faults of another; bear the blame for sb. else;

带 dài 　一 十 卅 卅 卅 世 芾 芾 带

（帯　一 十 卅 卅 卅 世 芾 芾 带 带）

释义 Meaning

（一）动词 v.

1. take; bring; carry: 考试时可以带词典吗？Is it permitted
   to bring a dictionary to the test?

2. do sth. incidentally: 你上街时顺便带一点菜回来。When
   you go out, bring some food back.

3. bear; have: 她的脸上带着幸福的笑容。Her face wears
   a smile of happiness.

4. lead; head: 王教授带了几个研究生？How many post-
   graduates did Professor Wang supervise?

5. look after; bring up; raise: 我妈帮我带孩子。My mother looks after the children for me.

（二）名词 n.

1. belt; girdle; ribbon; band; tape: 找根带子把这些旧报纸捆起来。Find a band to bundle these old newspapers up.

2. zone; area; belt: 江南一带空气湿润。The air is moist around the area of south of the Yangzi River.

词语 Words and Phrases

带病	dàibìng	in spite of illness
带动	dàidòng	drive; spur on; bring along
带劲	dàijìn	① energetic; forceful ② interesting; exciting; wonderful
带领	dàilǐng	lead; guide
带路	dàilù	show (or lead) the way; act as a guide
带头	dàitóu	take the lead; be the first; take the initiative; set an example
带孝	dàixiào	wear mourning for a parent or close relative; be in mourning
带信儿	dài xìnr	take or bring a message

袋 dài ㇒ 亻 仁 代 代 代 伐 袋 袋 袋 袋

释义 Meaning

（一）名词 n.

bag; sack; pocket; pouch: 她背了个旅行袋出门了。She went out carrying a travelling bag on her back.

（二）量词 measure w.

(for bags, sacks, etc.): 一袋大米有五十斤。A sack of rice weights fifty *jin*.

词语 Words and Phrases

袋泡茶	dàipàochá	teabag
袋鼠	dàishǔ	kangaroo
袋装	dàizhuāng	in bags
袋子	dàizi	sack; bag

戴 dài 一 十 吉 产 吉 青 青 直 直 直 直 直 直 裏 戴 戴 戴

释义 Meaning

动词 v.

put on; wear: 她戴了一顶漂亮的帽子。She put on a pretty hat.

词语 Words and Phrases

戴高帽子	dài gāomàozi	① flatter; ② wear a tall paper hat (as a mark of shame)；wear a dunce cap
戴帽子	dài màozi	be branded as; be labelled
爱戴	àidài	love and esteem (by subordinates)

熟语 Idioms

戴罪立功	dài zuì lì gōng	make up for the mistake one had committed; redeem oneself by good work

单 dān 丶 丷 丷 丷 单 单 单 单

(單 丨 冂 冃 冃 冃 冃 冃 罒 罒 單 單 單 單 單)

释义 Meaning

（一）形容词 a.

1. one; single: 我要买一张单人床。I want to buy a single bed.

2. unlined (clothing): 这么冷的天，你怎么还穿单衣呀？ It's so cold, why do you still wear an unlined garment.

（二）副词 adv.

only; alone: 我单看见她一个人从那个门里出来。I only saw her going out of that door.

词语 Words and Phrases

单薄	dānbó	① (of clothing) thin ② thin and weak; frail ③ insubstantial; flimsy; thin
单纯	dānchún	① simple; pure ② alone; purely; merely
单单	dāndān	only; alone
单调	dāndiào	monotonous; dull; drab
单独	dāndú	alone; by oneself; on one's own; single-handed; independent
单人房	dānrénfáng	single-bed room
单身	dānshēn	① unmarried; single ② not be with one's family; live alone
单位	dānwèi	① unit (as a standard of measurement) ② unit (as an organization, department, division, section, etc.)
单相思	dānxiāngsī	unrequited love
单一	dānyī	single; unitary
简单	jiǎndān	① simple; uncomplicated ② (usu. used in the negative) commonplace; ordinary ③ oversimplified; casual
床单	chuángdān	sheet
名单	míngdān	name list

熟语 Idioms

单刀直入	dān dāo zhí rù	come directly to the point;

		speak out without beating about the bush
单枪匹马	dān qiāng pǐ mǎ	single-handed; all by oneself

担$_1$ dān 一 十 扌 扌 扣 扣 担 担

(擔 一 十 扌 扌 扌 扌 扌 扌 扌 扌 扌 扌 扌 擔 擔 擔)

释义 Meaning

动词 v.

1. carry on a shoulder pole: 村民们吃水都是到河里担的。The villagers' drinking water is all carried on a shoulder pole from the river.
2. take on; undertake: 我们作这个决定是要担风险的。We will be taking some risks in choosing this alternative.

词语 Words and Phrases

担保	dānbǎo	assure; guarantee; vouch for
担当	dāndāng	take on; undertake; assume
担负	dānfù	bear; shoulder; take on; be charged with
担架	dānjià	stretcher; litter
担任	dānrèn	assume the office of; hold the post of
担心	dānxīn	worry; feel anxious
担忧	dānyōu	worry; be anxious

熟语 Idioms

担惊受怕	dān jīng shòu pà	be in a state of anxiety; be afraid and on the edge of

担$_2$ dàn 一 十 扌 扌 扣 扣 担 担

(擔 一 十 扌 扩 扩 扩 扩 扩 扩 扩 扩 扩 扩 扩 擔 擔 擔）

释义 Meaning

（一）名词 n.

burden (on shoulder): 全家的重担压在他一个人肩上。The burden of supporting the entire family falls on his shoulders alone.

（二）量词 measure w.

1. a unit of weight (= 50 kilograms): 一担米有五十公斤重。A *dan* of rice weights 50 kilograms.

2. shoulder-pole load: 他挑着一担水仍走得飞快。He can walk at lightning speed even when he is carrying two buckets of water.

词语 Words and Phrases

担担面	dàndànmiàn	a kind of Sichuan flavour noodles with peppery sauce only
担子	dànzi	① a carrying (or shoulder) pole and the loads on it; load; burden ② task

但 dàn ノ 亻 亻 佢 但 但 但

释义 Meaning

（一）连词 conj.

but; yet; still; nevertheless: 他很聪明，但不用功。He is very intelligent but not very hard working.

（二）副词 adv.

only; merely: 我不求有功，但求无过。I don't seek to have performed a meritorious service but seek only to avoid blame.

词语 Words and Phrases

但凡	dànfán	in every case; without exception; as long as
但是	dànshì	but; yet; still; nevertheless
但愿	dànyuàn	if only; I wish

熟语 Idioms

但愿如此	dànyuàn rúcǐ	I wish it were true; I hope so

淡 dàn ` ` 冫 冫 沪 沙 沙 沙 沙 泌 淡

释义 Meaning

形容词 a.

1. bland; tasteless; weak; without enough salt: 这道菜味道淡了一点。This course is a little bit bland. 反义词 antonym: 浓

2. (of colour) light; pale: 那块淡紫色的布怎么样？How about that piece of light purple cloth? 反义词 antonym: 深

词语 Words and Phrases

淡泊	dànbó	do not seek fame and wealth
淡薄	dànbó	① thin; light ② tasteless; weak ③ become indifferent ④ faint; dim; hazy
淡淡	dàndàn	① thin; light; pale ② indifferent; cool ③ (of ripples) undulatingly gentle
淡化	dànhuà	desalinate; dilute; de-emphasise
淡季	dànjì	slack (or dull, off) season
淡漠	dànmò	① indifferent; apathetic; nonchalant ② faint; dim; hazy
淡忘	dànwàng	fade from one's memory

| 淡雅 | dànyǎ | simple but elegant; quietly elegant; un-adorned and in good taste |

熟语 Idioms

| 淡泊明志 | dànbó míng zhì | live a simple and honest life; show high ideals by simple living |
| 淡然处之 | dànrán chǔ zhī | take things coolly; regard coolly |

蛋 dàn　一 丁 丆 疋 疋 疋 蛋 蛋 蛋 蛋 蛋

释义 Meaning

名词 n.

1. egg; hen's egg: 我买十二个蛋。 I bought 12 eggs.

2. an egg-shaped thing: 孩子们在玩儿泥蛋儿。 The children are playing with mud balls.

词语 Words and Phrases

蛋白	dànbái	① egg white; albumen ② protein
蛋糕	dàngāo	cake
蛋黄	dànhuáng	yolk
蛋壳	dànké	eggshell
蛋青	dànqīng	pale blue
蛋子	dànzi	an egg-shaped thing

当 dāng　丨 丷 丷 当 当 当

(當　丨 丷 丷 丷 尚 尚 常 常 常 當 當 當 當)

释义 Meaning

（一）动词 v.

1. work as; serve as; be: 他以前当过老师。He worked as a teacher before.

2. bear; accept; deserve: 男子汉大丈夫敢做敢当。A real man dares to act and to take take up responsibilities.

（二）介词 prep.

1. in sb.'s presence; to sb.'s face: 我敢当他的面批评他。I dare to criticize him to his face.

2. just at (a time or place): 当他只有三岁的时候，就会写字了。When only three, he could write characters.

（三）助动词 aux. v.

ought to; should; must: 这种事当断就得断。For matters of this sort, it is imperative to act when action is called for.

词语 Words and Phrases

当初	dāngchū	originally; at the outset; in the first place; at that time
当代	dāngdài	the present age; the contemporary era
当地	dāngdì	at the place in question; in the locality; local
当家	dāngjiā	manage (household) affairs
当今	dāngjīn	① now; at present; nowadays ② the reigning emperor
当面	dāngmiàn	to sb.'s face; in sb.'s presence
当年	dāngnián	① in those years (or days) ② the prime of life
当前	dāngqián	① before one; facing one ② present; current
当然	dāngrán	①without doubt; certainly; of course; to be sure ② natural ③ ex officio

当时	dāngshí	then; at that time
当心	dāngxīn	take care; be careful; look out
当中	dāngzhōng	① in the middle; in the centre ② among

熟语 Idioms

当机立断	dāngjī lì duàn	decide quickly; make a prompt decision
当务之急	dāng wù zhī jí	a pressing matter of the moment; a top priority task; urgent matter
当之无愧	dāng zhī wú kuì	fully deserve (a title, an honor, etc.); be worthy of (a certain title or honor)

党 dǎng 丶 丶 丷 丷 丷 丷 丷 丵 丵 党

(黨 丶 丶 丷 丷 丷 丷 丷 丷 丷 丷 丷 丷 丷 丷 丷 丷 丷 丷 黨)

释义 Meaning

名词 n.

1. political party; party: 你支援哪个党？Which political party do you support?

2. the Party (the Communist Party of China): 你入党了吗？ Have you joined the Communist Party (of China)?

词语 Words and Phrases

党风	dǎngfēng	a party's work style; party members' conduct
党纪	dǎngjì	party discipline
党籍	dǎngjí	party membership
党龄	dǎnglíng	party standing; party seniority

党派	dǎngpài	political parties and groups; party groupings
党委	dǎngwěi	party committee
党员	dǎngyuán	party member
党组	dǎngzǔ	leading Party members' group (in a state organ, of ministerial level)

熟语 Idioms

| 党同伐异 | dǎng tóng fá yì | side with one's group against those who differ in opinion; cliquish |

刀 dāo 丁 刀

释义 Meaning

（一）名词 n.

1. knife; sword: 你拿着刀干什么？Why are you holding a knife?

2. sth. shaped like a knife: 小心！别让冰刀伤着你。Look out! Don't let the ice skates injure you.

（二）量词 measure w.

one hundred sheets (of paper): 家里纸没有了，你去买两刀吧。There's no paper in the house, go to buy two hundred sheets.

词语 Words and Phrases

刀叉	dāochā	knife and fork
刀功	dāogōng	(in preparing food) cutting and slicing skill
刀口	dāokǒu	① the edge of a knife ② where a thing can be put to best use; the crucial point; the right spot ③ cut; incision

| 刀刃 | dāorèn | ① the edge of a knife ② where a thing can be put to best use; the crucial point |
| 刀子 | dāozi | small knife; pocketknife |

熟语 Idioms

| 刀光剑影 | dāo guāng jiàn yǐng | the glint and flash of daggers and swords; flashing with knives and swords |
| 刀山火海 | dāo shān huǒ hǎi | a mountain of swords and a sea of flames – extremely dangerous places; most severe trials |

导 dǎo ⁻ ⁻ 彐 彐 导 导

(導 ` ` ⺌ ⺌ ⺥ 首 首 首 首 ` 首 道

道 道 導 導)

释义 Meaning

动词 v.

1. lead; guide: 他们挖了一条沟，要把河里的水导入田里。 They dug a ditch to channel water from the river into the field.

2. transmit; conduct: 木棍导不导电呀？ Does a wooden stick conduct electricity?

词语 Words and Phrases

导弹	dǎodàn	guided missile
导电	dǎodiàn	transmit electric current; conduct electricity
导航	dǎoháng	navigation
导火线	dǎohuǒxiàn	① (blasting) fuse ② a small incident that touches off a crisis

导师	dǎoshī	① tutor; teacher ② guide of a great cause; teacher
导演	dǎoyǎn	① direct (a film, play, etc.) ② director
导游	dǎoyóu	① conduct a sightseeing tour ② tourist guide ③ guidebook
导致	dǎozhì	lead to; bring about; result in; cause

倒₁ dǎo ノ イ イ 任 任 伒 侄 侄 倒 倒

释义 Meaning

动词 v.

1. fall; topple: 大风把树吹倒了。 The strong wind uprooted the tree.

2. close down; go bankrupt; go out of business: 那家商店开了两个月就倒了。 That shop opened only two months and then closed down.

3. change; exchange: 下车以后倒11路车，乘三站就到了。 Get off the bus to change to the No.11 Bus, you will arrive at the third station.

词语 Words and Phrases

倒班	dǎobān	change shifts; work in shifts; work by turns
倒闭	dǎobì	close down; go bankrupt; go into liquidation
倒车	dǎochē	go to opposite direction
倒卖	dǎomài	resell at a profit; scalp
倒霉	dǎoméi	have bad luck; be out of luck; be down on one's luck
倒塌	dǎotā	collapse; topple down
倒台	dǎotái	fall from power; downfall
倒胃口	dǎo wèikǒu	spoil one's appetite

| 倒运 | dǎoyùn | have bad luck; be out of luck; be down on one's luck |

倒₂ dào ノ 亻 亻 仁 仵 仵 佮 佮 佮 倒 倒

释义 Meaning

（一）动词 v.

1. move backwards; turn upside down: 快让开，我要倒车了。Quick, get out of the way, I want to back the car.

2. pour; tip: 给客人倒一杯茶。Pour a cup of tea for the guest.

（二）形容词 a.

upside down; inverted; inverse; reverse: 那幅画挂倒了。The picture was hung upside down.

（三）副词 adv.

1. (indicating sth. unexpected): 没想到，你倒比我先来。It's unexpected that you came earlier than I did.

2. (indicating contrast): 他长得倒很高大，可是一点力气也没有。He is tall and big, but has no strength at all.

3. (indicating concession): 这件衣服好倒是好，就是太贵了。This piece of clothing is good all right, but it's too expensive.

词语 Words and Phrases

倒插门	dàochāmén	(of a man) marry into the wife's family
倒立	dàolì	① stand upside down ② handstand
倒数	dàoshǔ	count from bottom to top or from rear to front; count backwards
倒退	dàotuì	go backwards; fall back
倒影	dàoyǐng	inverted image; inverted reflection in water

熟语 Idioms

| 倒打一耙 | dào dǎ yì pá | lay the blame on others while oneself is at fault; put the blame on one's victim; |
| 倒行逆施 | dào xíng nì shī | go against the trend of the times; push a reactionary policy; perverse acts; go against the tide of history |

到 dào 　一　匸　云　즉　至　至　到　到

释义 Meaning

（一）动词 v.

1. arrive; reach: 再过一个小时我们就到家了。We will be home in one hour.

2. go to; leave for: 你到哪儿去？Where are you leaving for?

3. (used as a verb complement to show the result of an action): 我终于找到了我的钱包。I finally found my wallet.

（二）介词 prep.

up until; up to: 我们从星期一到星期五上班。We work from Monday to Friday.

词语 Words and Phrases

到处	dàochù	at all places; everywhere
到达	dàodá	arrive; get to; reach
到底	dàodǐ	① to the end ② at last; in the end; finally ③ (used in a question for emphasis) ④ after all; in the final analysis
到点	dàodiǎn	it's time to do sth.; time is up
到家	dàojiā	reach a very high level; be perfect; be excellent

| 到期 | dàoqī | become due; mature; expire |
| 到手 | dàoshǒu | in one's hands; in one's possession |

道 dào ` ` ` ` ` ` ` ` ` ` ` 首 首 首 首 道 道 道

释义 Meaning

(一) 名词 n.

1. road; way; path: 远处有一条乡间小道。There is a country path way off in the distance.

2. way; method: 你挺懂养生之道的。You really understand how to care for life.

3. line: 谁在我的书上画这么多道呀？Who drew so many lines on my book?

(二) 量词 measure w.

1. (for long and narrow objects): 窗户只开了一道缝儿。The window opened only a crack.

2. (for doors, walls, etc.): 进故宫要过好几道门。You must pass through quite a few successive doors to get into the Imperial Palace.

3. (for orders, questions, etc.): 父亲下了一道命令。Father had given an order.

4. (for courses in a meal, stages in a procedure, etc.): 这四道菜都是他拿手的。He has a special kanck for these four courses.

(三) 动词 v.

1. say; talk; speak: 她的男朋友能说会道。Her boyfriend has a ready and eloquent tongue.

2. say (the words quoted): 她惊奇地说道："你怎么认识我？"She said with surprise: "How do you know me?"

词语 Words and Phrases

道白	dàobái	spoken parts in an opera
道别	dàobié	bid farewell; say goodbye
道德	dàodé	morals; morality; ethics
道教	dàojiào	the Taoist religion; Taoism
道具	dàojù	stage property; equipment
道理	dàolǐ	① principle; truth; hows and whys ② reason; argument; sense
道路	dàolù	road; way; path
道歉	dàoqiàn	apologize; make an apology
道谢	dàoxiè	express one's thanks; thank
道义	dàoyì	morality and justice

熟语 Idioms

| 道貌岸然 | dàomào ànrán | pose as a person of high morals; look gentlemanly; pretend to be a moralist |
| 道听途说 | dào tīng tú shuō | second-hand information; hearsay; gossip |

得₁ dé　´ ⺄ 亻 亻 ⺈ 彳 彳 但 但 得 得

释义 Meaning

动词 v.

1. get; obtain; gain: 这次考试我得了第一名。I got a first in this examination.

2. (of a calculation) result in: 三三得九。Three times three is nine.

3. be finished; be ready: 饭得了，来吃吧。The dinner is ready, please come!

4. (expressing approval or prohibition): 得了，我们见面

再聊吧。 All right! Let's talk next time we meet.

词语 Words and Phrases

得病	débìng	fall ill; contract a disease
得到	dédào	get; obtain; gain; receive
得奖	déjiǎng	win (or be awarded) a prize
得救	déjiù	be saved (or rescued)
得胜	déshèng	win a victory; triumph
得失	déshī	① gain and loss; success and failure ② advantages and disadvantages; merits and demerits
得势	déshì	① be in power ② get the upper hand be in the ascendant
得意	déyì	proud of oneself; pleased with oneself; complacent
得知	dézhī	have learned of sth.; have heard of sth.
得罪	dézuì	offend; displease

熟语 Idioms

得心应手	dé xīn yìng shǒu	with great facility; with high proficiency; handy
得意忘形	dé yì wàng xíng	grow dizzy with success; forget oneself in the excitement

得₂ de　ʼ ʼ 彳 彳 彳 彳 彳 得 得 得 得

释义 Meaning

助词 aux. w.

1. (used after a verb or an adjective to express possibility or capability): 你怎么批评不得呀？Why can't you be criticized?

2. (inserted between a verb and its complement to express possibility or capability): 这个包太重了，你拿得动吗？ The bag is heavy, can you carry it?

3. (used to link a verb or an adjective to a complement which describes the manner or degree): 她汉语说得很好。She can speak Chinese very well.

得₃ děi ′ ′ 亻 亻 彳 彳 彳 彳 得 得

释义 Meaning

助动词 aux. v.

1. need: 这个任务得三个星期才能完成。This task will take three weeks to complete.

2. must; have to: 公民都得遵守法律。Citizen must abide by the law.

3. certainly will: 再不走，我们就得迟到了。We'll be late if we still don't go.

的 de ′ 亻 白 白 白 白 的 的

释义 Meaning

助词 aux. w.

1. (used after an attribute): 参加会议的人都到齐了吗？ Have all the people who attend the meeting arrived?

2. (used to form a noun phrase or nominal expression): 我太太是个教书的。My wife is a teacher.

3. (used after a verb or between a verb and its object to stress an element of the sentence): 这些书是谁买的？Who bought these books?

4. (used at the end of a declarative sentence for emphasis): 这

孩子真够调皮的。The child is really naughty.

词语 Words and Phrases

的话   dehuà   (used to express a condition)

灯 dēng ｀ ´ ⺀ 火 灯 灯

（**燈** ｀ ´ ⺀ 火 灯 灯 灯 灯 燈 燈 燈
燈 燈 燈 燈 燈 ）

释义 Meaning

名词 n.

lamp; lantern; light: 宿舍11点熄灯。The lights go out at eleven in our dormitory.

词语 Words and Phrases

灯光   dēngguāng   ① the light of a lamp; lamplight
                             ② (stage) lighting

灯笼   dēnglóng   lantern

灯谜   dēngmí   riddles written on lanterns; lantern riddles

灯泡   dēngpào   (electric) bulb; light bulb

灯塔   dēngtǎ   lighthouse; beacon

熟语 Idioms

灯红酒绿   dēng hóng jiǔ lù   red lanterns and green wine—scene of feasting and festivity

登 dēng ⁊ ⁊ ⁊ ⁊ 癶 癶 癶 登 登 登
登 登

释义 Meaning

动词 v.

1. ascend; mount; scale (a height): 运动员终于登上了峰顶。The mountaineer reached the summit at last.

2. publish; record; enter: 很多报纸都登了这个广告。The advertisement was carried in many newspapers.

3. press down with the foot; pedal; treadle: 他顶着风，吃力地登着三轮车。He is pedaling a tricycle against the wind.

词语 Words and Phrases

登报	dēngbào	publish in a newspaper
登场	dēngchǎng	appear on stage
登机	dēngjī	board a plane
登记	dēngjì	register; check in; enter one's name
登山	dēngshān	mountain-climbing; mountaineering
登台	dēngtái	mount a platform; go up on the stage
登载	dēngzǎi	publish (in newspaper or magazines); carry

熟语 Idioms

登峰造极	dēng fēng zào jí	reach the peak of perfection; attain a level never known before; reach the summit

等 děng ⼀ ⼂ ⼃ ⼄ 竹 竺 竿 竺 笁 笁 笁 等 等

释义 Meaning

（一）名词 n.

1. class; grade; rank: 我们班学生的成绩可以分成三等。The results of students in our class could be classified into three levels.

2. kind; sort: 这等人我才看不起呢！I look down on this kind of person.

（二）动词 v.

1. wait; await: 等爸爸回来再开饭。Wait for father for dinner.

2. when; till: 等我写完这封信再走。Stay till I finish writing this letter.

（三）助词aux. w.

1. and so on; and so forth; etc.: 爷爷买了苹果、香蕉等水果。Grandpa bought some fruits such as apples, bananas and so on.

2. (indicating the end of an enumeration): 这次参赛的有江苏、湖北、广东、浙江等四个队。There are four teams namely, Jiangsu, Hubei, Guangdong, and Zhejiang attending this match.

词语 Words and Phrases

等次	děngcì	place in a series; grade
等待	děngdài	wait; await
等候	děnghòu	wait; await; expect
等级	děngjí	① grade; rank ② order and degree; social estate; social stratum
等同	děngtóng	equate; be equal
等于	děngyú	① equal to; equivalent to ② amount to; be tantamount to
等着瞧	děngzheqiáo	wait and see

熟语 Idioms

等闲视之	děngxián shì zhī	regard as a matter of small importance; treat lightly

低dī　ノ　亻　亻　仠　仹　低　低

释义 Meaning

（一）形容词 a.

low: 你的声音太低，我听不见。Your voice is too low for me to hear. 反义词antonym: 高

（二）动词 v.

let drop; hang down: 他不好意思地低下了头。He hung his head down feeling embarrassed.

词语 Words and Phrases

低沉	dī chén	① overcast; lowering ② (of voice) low and deep ③ low-spirited; downcast
低档	dī dàng	① low gear ② low grade
低估	dī gū	underestimate; underrate
低级	dī jí	① elementary; rudimentary; lower ② vulgar; low
低劣	dī liè	inferior; low-grade
低能	dī néng	mental deficiency; feeblemindedness
低下	dī xià	(of status or living standards) low; lowly

熟语 Idioms

| 低三下四 | dī sān xià sì | low and menial; be the lowest of the low; servile |
| 低声下气 | dī shēng xià qì | speak humbly and in a low voice; be meek and sub-servient; with soft talk |

滴 dī   ` ` 氵 氵 汸 汸 浐 浐 渧 渧 滴 滴 滴 滴

释义 Meaning

（一）动词 v.

drip: 他脸上的汗不停地往下滴。The sweats kept drip

ping from his face.

（二）量词 measure w.

drop: 桌子上弄到一滴墨水。There was a drop of ink on the table.

词语 Words and Phrases

滴答	dīdā	tick; ticktack; ticktock
滴漏	dīlòu	water clock; clepsydra; hourglass

熟语 Idioms

滴水穿石	dī shuǐ chuān shí	constant dripping water wears through rock; little strokes fell great oaks

底 dǐ   ` 亠 广 广 庀 庐 底 底

释义 Meaning

名词 n.

1. bottom; base: 他是个井底之蛙。He is like a frog at the bottom of a well. 反义词 antonym: 顶

2. a copy kept as a record: 这封信得留个底儿。A copy of his letter should be kept on file.

3. end of a year or month: 我月底一定还你钱。I'll pay you back at the end of the month. 反义词 antonym: 初

4. ground; background; foundation: 我喜欢那块蓝底白花的布。I like that piece of cloth with white flowers on a blue background.

词语 Words and Phrases

底层	dǐcéng	① (British) ground floor; (American) first floor ② bottom; the lowest level
底稿	dǐgǎo	draft; manuscript
底价	dǐjià	base price

底牌	dǐpái	cards in one's hand; hand
底片	dǐpiàn	photographic plate; negative
底数	dǐshù	① the truth or root of a matter; how a matter actually stands ② base number
底细	dǐxì	ins and outs; exact details
底下	dǐxià	① under; below; beneath ② next; later; afterwards
底子	dǐzi	① bottom; base ② foundation ③ rough draft or sketch ④ a copy kept as a record remnant ⑤ ground; background; foundation

地 dì   一 十 土 圠 圠 地

释义 Meaning

名词 n.

1. fields: 他妻子在地里干活。His wife is working in the fields.

2. ground; floor: 过去我们家铺的都是水泥地。Our house was paved with a cement floor in the past.

3. place; locality: 他每到一地都会给我写信。He writes to me from wherever he is.

4. distance travelled (measured in *li* 里 or stops 站): 我家离学校只有两站地。My home is only a couple of bus stops from the school.

词语 Words and Phrases

地板	dìbǎn	① floor board ② floor
地步	dìbù	① condition; plight ② extent ③ room for action
地道	dìdào	① from the place noted for the product; genuine ② pure; typical ③ well-done; thorough

地点	dìdiǎn	place; site; locale
地方	dìfāng	① place; space; room ② part; respect
地理	dìlǐ	① geographical features of a place ② geography
地区	dìqū	① area; district; region ② prefecture
地毯	dìtǎn	carpet; rug
地位	dìwèi	① position; standing; place; status ② place (as occupied by a person or thing)
地域	dìyù	region; district
地震	dìzhèn	earthquake; seism
地址	dìzhǐ	address

熟语 Idioms

地大物博	dì dà wù bó	wide in area and abundant in products; a vast land with rich resource; a big country abounding in natural wealth
地地道道	dìdìdàodào	out-and-out; in no less sense; hundred-percent
地老天荒	dì lǎo tiān huāng	be of the remote past; till the end of the world; far back

弟 dì   `  ` `  ` `  ` ` 弟 弟

释义 Meaning

名词 n.

younger brother: 那个戴眼镜的人是我弟弟。The man with glasses is my younger brother.

词语 Words and Phrases

| 弟弟 | dìdì | younger brother; brother |

弟妹	dìmèi	① younger brother and sister ② younger brother's wife; sister-in-law
弟子	dìzǐ	disciple; pupil; follower

递 dì 丶 丷 䒑 当 肖 弟 弟 辶弟 递 递

(遞 一 厂 𠂆 𠂆 戶 戶 虍 虒 虒 虒 辶虒 遞 遞**)**

释义 Meaning

动词 v.

Hand over; pass; give: 把信递给我。Hand me the letter please.

词语 Words and Phrases

递交	dìjiāo	hand over; present; submit
递进	dìjìn	① go forward one by one ② increase progressively; increase by degrees
递送	dìsòng	send; deliver
递眼色	dì yǎnsè	tip sb. the wink; wink at sb.
递增	dìzēng	increase progressively; increase by degrees

第 dì 丿 𠂉 ⺮ ⺮ ⺮ ⺮ 竺 竺 笃 第 第

释义 Meaning

前缀 pref.

(used before numerals to form ordinal numbers): 我在家里排行第三。I am the third child of my family.

词语 Words and Phrases

第二次世界大战	dì'èr cì shìjiè dàzhàn	the Second World War (1939-1945); World War II

第三产业	dìsān chǎnyè	tertiary industry; the service sector
第三世界	dìsān shìjiè	the Third World
第三者	dìsānzhě	a third party (in disputes, divorce proceedings, etc.)
第一	dìyī	first; primary; foremost
第一把手	dìyībǎshǒu	first in command; number one man; a person holding primary responsibility
第一手	dìyīshǒu	firsthand
第一线	dìyīxiàn	forefront; front line; first line

点 diǎn ｜ 卜 广 占 占 卢 占 点 点

(點 ｜ 冂 冂 冃 冃 甲 里 里 里 黑 黑 黑 黙 黙 點 點)

释义 Meaning

（一）名词 n.

1. spot; dot; speck: 你的裙子上有两个墨水点。There are two ink spots on your skirt.

2. decimal point; point: 这个房间有十八点五平方米。This room has a floor space of eighteen point five sq. m.

3. aspect; feature: 从这点上看，他还是有良心的。Viewed from this aspect, he still has a conscience.

4. o'clock: 现在九点了。It's nine o'clock now.

（二）动词 v.

1. put a dot: 老师在这个句子下面点了几个点。The teacher put several dots under this sentence.

2. drip: 奶奶该点眼药水了！It's time to drip the eye drops, grandma!

3. check one by one: 你把这些钱仔细地点一下。Please check the money carefully and see if it is right.

4. select; choose: 你想点什么菜？What dishes do you want to order?

5. light; burn; kindle: 停电了，把蜡烛点起来吧。The power is out, light the candles.

（三）量词 measure w.

1. a little; a bit; some: 妈妈，给我点钱好吗？Mum, please give me some money, won't you?

2. (for items): 我们给领导提了几点意见。We expressed our opinions to the leadership.

词语 Words and Phrases

点播	diǎnbō	request a programme from a radio station
点滴	diǎndī	① a bit ② intravenous drip
点名	diǎnmíng	① call the roll ② mention sb. by name
点明	diǎnmíng	point out; put one's finger on
点燃	diǎnrán	light; kindle; ignite
点头	diǎntóu	nod one's head; nod
点心	diǎnxīn	light refreshment; pastry
点缀	diǎnzhuì	① embellish; ornament; adorn ② use sth. merely for show
点子	diǎnzi	① key point ② idea; pointer

熟语 Idioms

点石成金	diǎn shí chéngjīn	touch a stone and turn it into gold; turn a crude essay into a literary gem
点头哈腰	diǎn tóu hā yāo	nod and bow; bow and scrape

电 diàn 丨 冂 日 日 电

(電 一 厂 厅 而 而 而 雨 雨 雨 雪 雪 雪 雷 電)

释义 Meaning

(一) 名词 n.

1. electricity: 电是一种很重要的能源。Electricity is a very important kind of energy.

2. telegram; cable: 这个问题得致电上级请示一下。This problem should be telegraphed to the higher authorities for instructions.

(二) 动词 v.

give or get an electric shock: 我修灯的时候被电了一下。I got a shock when I was repairing the lighting.

词语 Words and Phrases

电报	diànbào	telegram; cable
电车	diànchē	① tram; cablecar; streetcar ② trolley-bus; trolley
电池	diànchí	(electric) cell; battery
电灯	diàndēng	electric lamp; electric light
电动	diàndòng	motor-driven; power-driven; power-operated; electric
电话	diànhuà	① telephone; phone ② phone call
电力	diànlì	electric power; power
电脑	diànnǎo	electronic computer
电器	diànqì	electrical equipment (or appliance)
电视	diànshì	television; TV
电梯	diàntī	lift; elevator

| 电影 | diànyǐng | film; movie; motion picture |
| 电子 | diànzi | electron; electronic |

店 diàn ` 亠 广 广 庐 庐 店 店

释义 Meaning

名词 n.

1. shop; store: 那家店什么都卖。That shop sells everything you can think of.

2. inn: 我们到镇上找家店住下吧！Let's find an inn to stay in the town.

词语 Words and Phrases

店铺	diànpū	shop; store
店小二	diànxiǎo'èr	waiter; attendant
店员	diànyuán	shop assistant; salesclerk; clerk; salesman or saleswoman

调₁ diào ` 讠 讥 讱 讱 调 调 调 调

（調 ` 亠 亠 亖 言 言 言 訂 訂 訶 調

調 調 調 調）

释义 Meaning

（一）动词 v.

transfer; shift; move: 我爱人调到北京去工作了。My husband was transferred to Beijing to work.

（二）名词 n.

1. accent: 他说话怎么南腔北调的？Why does he speak with a mixture of accents?

2. key: 这个调太高，我唱不来。The key is too high for me to sing.

词语 Words and Phrases

调查	diàochá	investigate; inquire into; look into; survey
调动	diàodòng	① transfer; shift ② move (troops); manoeuvre; muster ③ bring into play; arouse; mobilize
调令	diàolìng	transfer order
调遣	diàoqiǎn	dispatch; assign
调研	diàoyán	investigation and research; survey and study
调运	diàoyùn	allocate and transport
调子	diàozi	① tune; melody ② tone (of speech); note

熟语 Idioms

调兵遣将	diàobīngqiǎnjiàng	move troops and dispatch generals; deploy forces; muster and organize manpower
调虎离山	diào hǔ lí shān	lure the tiger out of the mountains; make the opponent leave his advantageous position

调₂tiáo ˋ 讠 讠 讠 讠 讠 讠 调 调 调

(調 ˋ 亠 亠 言 言 言 訂 訂 訂 調 調 調 調 調)

释义 Meaning

动词 v.

mix; adjust: 你在牛奶里加点蜂蜜调一下。Mix some honey into the milk.

词语 Words and Phrases

调和	tiáohé	① be in harmonious proportion ② mediate; reconcile ③ (usu. used in the negative) compromise; make concessions
调价	tiáojià	readjust (or modify) prices
调节	tiáojié	regulate; adjust
调侃	tiáokǎn	ridicule; jeer at; deride
调料	tiáoliào	condiment; seasoning; flavouring
调皮	tiáopí	① naughty; mischievous ② unruly; tricky ③ insincere; scheming
调味品	tiáowèipǐn	condiment; seasoning; flavouring
调养	tiáoyǎng	take good care of oneself (as in poor health or after an illness); build up one's health by rest and by taking nourishing food; be nursed back to health
调整	tiáozhěng	adjust; regulate; revise

掉 diào 　一　十　扌　扩　扩　扩　挓　挓　挿　挿 掉

释义 Meaning

动词 v.

1. fall; drop; shed; come off: 这本小说让我掉了不少眼泪。I have shed a lot of tears over this novel.

2. fall behind: 士兵中有一个掉在后面了。One of the soldiers lagged behind.

3. lose; be missing: 我的钱包掉了。My wallet was lost.

4. reduce; drop: 锻炼一星期以后我掉了五公斤。I lost 5 kilograms after exercising for one week.

5. turn: 他把枪口掉过来对着我。He turns the gun around

and pointed it at me.

6. (used after certain verbs to indicate removal): 把黑板上
的字全擦掉！Wipe all the characters off the blackboard!

词语 Words and Phrases

掉包	diàobāo	stealthily substitute one thing for another
掉膘	diàobiāo	(of a domestic animal) lose flesh
掉队	diàoduì	drop out (or off); fall behind
掉价	diàojià	fall (or drop) in price; go down in price
掉书袋	diàoshūdài	a walking satchel; a person who lards his speech with quotations and allusions
掉头	diàotóu	turn round; turn about

熟语 Idioms

掉以轻心	diào yǐ qīng xīn	lower one's guard; casual attitude; treat sth. lightly

顶 dǐng 　一　丁　厂　厂　厂　顷　顶　顶

(頂 一　丁　厂　厂　厂　顶　顶　頂　頂　頂　頂)

释义 Meaning

(一) 名词 n.

top: 看！楼顶上站着一个人！Look! A person is standing at the top of the building.

(二) 动词 v.

1. carry on the head: 他头上顶着一篮蔬菜。He is carrying a basket of vegetable on his head.

2. go against: 农民顶着烈日收割庄稼。The peasants are reaping rice under the scorching sun.

3. retort; turn down: 你怎么敢跟领导顶呀？How dare you talk to the leader in retort?

4. cope with; stand up to: 这个工作太辛苦，我顶不住了。
The work is so hard that I can't cope with it.

5. equal; be equivalent to: 他一个人顶两个人的饭量。
He has the appetite of two persons.

（三）量词 measure w.

(for things which have a top): 这顶帽子好看吗？Is this cap good-looking?

（四）副词 adv.

very; most; extremely: 我顶喜欢吃西餐。I like to eat Western style food very much.

词语 Words and Phrases

顶点	dǐngdiǎn	① apex; zenith; acme; pinnacle ② vertex; apex ③ the most expensive kind of dim sum in a restaurant
顶端	dǐngduān	① top; peak; apex ② end
顶峰	dǐngfēng	peak; summit; pinnacle
顶梁柱	dǐngliángzhù	pillar; backbone
顶替	dǐngtì	① take sb.'s place; replace ② get a job at one parent place of work when the parent retires or dies
顶头上司	dǐngtóu shàngsi	one's immediate (or direct) superior
顶用	dǐngyòng	be of use (or help); serve the purpose
顶撞	dǐngzhuàng	contradict (one's elder or superior)
顶嘴	dǐngzuǐ	reply defiantly (usu. to one's elder or superior); answer back; talk back

熟语 Idioms

顶风冒雨	dǐng fēng mào yǔ	be undeterred by wind and rain; in spite of wind and rain
顶天立地	dǐng tiān lì dì	most respectable; of gigantic stature; of indomitable spirit and morals

定 dìng ` ´ ⺌ ⺌ 宁 宇 定 定

释义 Meaning

（一）动词 v.

1. decide; fix; set: 会议时间定在下星期三上午。The meeting is scheduled for next Wednesday morning.

2. subscribe to (a newspaper, etc.); book (seats, tickets, etc.); order (merchandise, etc.): 船票定了吗？Is the cruise ticket booked?

（二）形容词 a.

calm; stable: 结果没出来，我心里不定。I can't be calm until the result is known.

（三）副词 adv.

surely; certainly; definitely: 这场比赛我们定能取胜！We'll be sure to win this match.

词语 Words and Phrases

定单	dìngdān	order for goods; order form
定额	dìng'é	quota; norm
定婚	dìnghūn	be engaged (to be married); be betrothed
定价	dìngjià	① fix a price ② list price
定居	dìngjū	settle down
定论	dìnglùn	final conclusion
定期	dìngqī	① fix (or set) a date ② regular; at regular intervals; periodical
定心丸	dìngxīnwán	sth. capable of setting sb.'s mind at ease
定义	dìngyì	definition
定员	dìngyuán	fixed number of staff members or passengers
定罪	dìngzuì	declare sb. guilty; convict sb. (of a crime)

丢 diū　一　二　千　壬　丢　丢

释义 Meaning

动词 v.

1. lose; mislay: 我丢了三百块钱。I've lost three hundred yuan.
2. throw; cast; toss: 快把这脏东西丢掉！Throw the dirty thing away quickly!
3. put (or lay) aside: 我说的话你全丢到脑后去了。You completely ignore all of what I said.

词语 Words and Phrases

丢丑	diūchǒu	lose face; be disgraced
丢脸	diūliǎn	lose face; be disgraced
丢弃	diūqì	abandon; discard; give up
丢失	diūshī	lose
丢眼色	diū yǎnsè	wink at sb.; tip sb. the wink

熟语 Idioms

丢人现眼	diūrén-xiànyǎn	make a fool of oneself; make a spectacle of oneself
丢三落四	diū sān là sì	missing this and that; be always forgetting things

东 dōng　二　ㄊ　车　东　东

(東　二　厂　冂　百　亘　宙　東　東)

释义 Meaning

名词 n.

1. east: 这房间窗户是朝东的。The window of the room faces east.
2. host: 今天是谁的东？Who will be the host today?

词语 Words and Phrases

东半球	dōngbànqiú	the Eastern Hemisphere
东道	dōngdào	one who treats sb. to a meal; host
东方	dōngfāng	① east ② the East; the Orient ③ a two-character surname
东风	dōngfēng	① east wind; spring wind ② driving force of revolution
东家	dōngjiā	a form of address formerly used by an employee to his employer or a tenant-peasant to his landlord; master; boss
东西	dōngxi	thing (referring to a person or animal) thing; creature

熟语 Idioms

东奔西跑	dōng bēn xī pǎo	run to and fro; bustle about; rush around
东拉西扯	dōng lā xī chě	drag in irrelevant matters; talk incoherently
东山再起	dōng shān zài qǐ	make a comeback; resume one's former position
东张西望	dōng zhāng xī wàng	peer around; glance this way and that; gaze right and left

冬 dōng ノ ク 久 冬 冬

释义 Meaning

名词 n.

winter: 我喜欢雪，但不喜欢冬的寒冷。I like snow, but I don't like the winter cold.

词语 Words and Phrases

冬瓜	dōngguā	wax gourd; winter melon
冬烘	dōnghōng	shallow but pedantic
冬季	dōngjì	winter

冬眠	dōngmián	winter sleep; hibernation
冬天	dōngtiān	winter
冬泳	dōngyǒng	winter outdoor swimming

懂 dǒng 　丶丶丨忄忙忙忙忙忙忙忙懂懂懂懂

释义 Meaning

动词 v.

understand; know: 听说他懂好几门外语。It's said that he knows quite a few foreign languages.

词语 Words and Phrases

懂得	dǒngdé	understand; know; grasp
懂行	dǒngháng	(dial.) know the business; know the ropes
懂事	dǒngshì	sensible; intelligent

动 dòng 　一二云云动动

(動 　一二千千千重重重動動)

释义 Meaning

动词 v.

1. move; stir: 你怎么站在那儿不动啊？How can you stand there and not move a step? 反义词 antonym: 静

2. act; get moving: 大家都动起来，别闲着！Everyone gets moving! Don't stand idle!

3. change; alter: 这篇文章只要动一两个地方就行了。This article will be all right with just a couple of minor changes.

4. use: 你动脑筋想想吧！Use your head to think about it!

5. touch (one's heart); arouse: 她对那小伙子动了感情。

She has been swept away by that young man.

词语 Words and Phrases

动不动	dòngbúdòng	easily; frequently; at every turn
动机	dòngjī	motive; intention; motivation
动静	dòngjìng	① the sound of sth. astir ② movement; activity
动力	dònglì	① power ② motive (or driving) force; impetus
动人	dòngrén	moving; touching
动身	dòngshēn	go (or set out) on a journey; leave (for a distant place)
动听	dòngtīng	interesting or pleasing to the ears
动物	dòngwù	animal
动摇	dòngyáo	shake; vacillate; waver
动员	dòngyuán	mobilize; arouse
动作	dòngzuò	① movement; motion; action ② act; start moving

释语 Idioms

动手动脚	dòng shǒu dòng jiǎo	be fresh with sb.; put out hand and foot
动弹不得	dòngtán bù dé	cannot move; incapable of moving

冻 dòng ` 冫 厂 产 冻 冻 冻

(凍 ` 冫 厂 厂 沪 沪 沪 沪 涑 凍 凍)

释义 Meaning

动词 v.

1. freeze: 把肉放冰箱里冷冻起来。Put the meat into the refrigerator to freeze.

2. feel very cold; freeze; be frostbitten: 天太冷了，她冻得

全身发抖。She was shivering from head to toe with cold.

词语 Words and Phrases

冻疮	dòngchuāng	chilblain
冻僵	dòngjiāng	frozen stiff; numb with cold
冻结	dòngjié	freeze; congeal (of wages, prices, etc.)
冻死	dòngsǐ	freeze to death; freeze and perish; die of frost
肉冻	ròudòng	meat jelly; aspic
果冻	guǒdòng	jelly

洞 dòng　丶　丶　氵　汩　汩　泂　洞　洞　洞

释义 Meaning

名词 n.

hole; cavity: 你的衬衣破了一个洞。There is a hole in your shirt.

词语 Words and Phrases

洞察	dòngchá	see clearly; have an insight into
洞穿	dòngchuān	① pierce ② have an insight into; understand fully
洞房	dòngfáng	bridal (or nuptial) chamber; wedding
洞开	dòngkāi	(of doors, windows, etc.) be wide open
洞悉	dòngxī	know clearly; understand thoroughly
洞晓	dòngxiǎo	have a clear knowledge of
洞穴	dòngxué	cave; cavern

熟语 Idioms

洞房花烛	dòngfáng huā zhú	wedding festivities; wedding
洞若观火	dòng ruò guān huǒ	plain as a pikestaff; see sth. as clearly as a blazing fire

洞天福地　　　dòngtiān fúdì　　　cave heaven and blessed region; the land of fairies

都₁ dōu 一 十 土 耂 耂 者 者 者 都 都

释义 Meaning

副词 adv.

1. all; both: 我们都穿着黑衣服。We are all dressed in black.

2. already: 都十一点了，你怎么还不睡？It's already eleven o'clock, why don't you go to bed?

3. even: 她连一句话都不跟我说。She never said even a word to me.

4. all (referring to reasons): 对不起，都是我的错。I'm sorry. It' all my fault.

词语 Words and Phrases

都是　　　dōushì　　　all (giving explanation)

都₂ dū 一 十 土 耂 耂 者 者 者 都 都

释义 Meaning

名词 n.

1. capital: 北京是中国的首都。Beijing is the capital of China.

2. big city; metropolis: 徐州是我国的煤都。Xuzhou is the coal metropolis of China.

词语 Words and Phrases

都城	dūchéng	capital
都会	dūhuì	chief city
都市	dūshì	city; big city
首都	shǒudū	capital

豆 dòu 一 厂 戸 戸 戸 豆 豆

释义 Meaning
名词 n.

beans; peas: 种瓜得瓜，种豆得豆。If you plant melons, you'll get melons; If you sow beans, you'll get beans. You reap what you have sown.

词语 Words and Phrases

豆腐	dòufu	bean curd
豆浆	dòujiāng	soya-bean milk
豆芽儿	dòuyár	bean sprouts
豆油	dòuyóu	soya-bean oil
豆汁	dòuzhī	soya-bean milk
豆子	dòuzi	beans or peas
大豆	dàdòu	soybean
黄豆	huángdòu	soybean
绿豆	lùdòu	mung bean

熟语 Idioms

豆蔻年华	dòu kòu nián huá	used to call 13-14 years old girls.

读₁ dòu　乀 讠 讠 讠 讠 讠 讠 讠 读 读

（讀　乀 亠 亠 亠 言 言 言 訁 訁 讀 讀 訁 訁 訁 訁 讀 讀 讀 讀 讀 讀 讀）

释义 Meaning
名词 n.

a slight pause in reading

词语 Words and Phrases

句读	jùdòu	the period and the comma; sentences and phrases

读₂ dú ` 讠 讠 讠 讠 讠 讠 读 读

(讀 ` ˊ ˊ ˊ 言 言 言 言 言 言 言 言 讀 讀 讀 讀 讀 讀 讀 讀 讀 讀)

释义 Meaning

动词 v.

1. read: 他正在读信。He is reading a letter.

2. read aloud: 学生们正在读课文。The students are reading the text aloud.

3. go to school or college: 他不想在上海读书。He doesn't want to study in Shanghai.

词语 Words and Phrases

读本	dúběn	reader; textbook
读书	dúshū	① read; study; ② go to school
读物	dúwù	reading material
读音	dúyīn	pronunciation
读者	dúzhě	reader
朗读	lǎngdú	read aloud

度 dù ` 亠 广 广 广 庐 庐 庐 度

释义 Meaning

（一）名词 n.

1. a unit of measurement for temperature, angles etc.; degree: 水的沸点是摄氏100度。The boiling point of water is 100 degrees Centigrade.

2. limit; degree; extent: 他劳累过度了。He's been overworked.

3. tolerance; magnanimity: 他很大度。He is very magnanimous

4. consideration: 她早已把自己的生死置之度外。She gave no thought to her own safety.

（二）量词 measure w.

time; occasion: 欢迎再度光临。Welcome to come again.

（三）动词 v.

spend; pass: 这个周末我是在农村度过的。I spent this weekend in the countryside.

词语 Words and Phrases

度假	dùjià	spend one's holidays
度量	dùliàng	tolerance; magnanimity
度日	dùrì	subsist (in hardship); do for a living
度数	dùshù	number of degrees

熟语 Idioms

| 度日如年 | dù rì rú nián | one day seems like a year; time passes slowly |

端 duān 丶 亠 亠 亠 立 立' 立ㅛ 立ㅛ 立ㅛ 立ㅛ 立ㅛ 端 端 端

释义 Meaning

（一）名词 n.

1. end; extremity: 我住在岛的西端。I live at the west end of this island.

2. beginning: 开端不错。The beginning is good. 反义词 antonym: 尾；终

3. reason; cause: 她总是无端地指责我。She always reproaches me without reason.

（二）形容词 a.

upright; proper: 学生们都端坐在他们的座位上。All students are sitting straight in their seats.

（三）动词 v.

carry; hold sth. level with both hands: 请给我端杯茶来。
Please bring me a cup of tea.

词语 Words and Phrases

端量	duānliàng	look sb. up and down
端午节	duānwǔjié	Dragon Boat Festival (the 5th day of the 5th lunar month)
端详	duānxiáng	① details ② dignified and serene
端详	duānxiáng	look sb. up and down
端正	duānzhèng	① upright; regular ② proper ③ correct
端庄	duānzhuāng	dignified (esp. women); sedate

熟语 Idioms

首鼠两端	shǒu shǔ liǎng duān	be in two minds; shilly-shally

短 duǎn ノ ⺅ ⺉ 乍 矢 矢 矩 矩 矩 矩 短 短

释义 Meaning

（一）形容词 a.

short; brief: 这条棍子太短了。The stick is too short. 反义词 antonym: 长

（二）动词 v.

1. lack; be short of: 就短了一个人。Only one person is absent.

2. owe: 我还短她一块钱呢。I still owe her one yuan.

（三）名词 n.

fault; weak point: 请不要揭别人的短。Please don't pick on other's weakness. 反义词 antonym: 长

词语 Words and Phrases

短波	duǎnbō	short wave
短处	duǎnchù	shortcoming; weakness; fault
短促	duǎncù	short; very brief
短见	duǎnjiàn	① suicide ② shortsighted view
短期	duǎnqī	short-term; short period
短浅	duǎnqiǎn	narrow and shallow
短缺	duǎnquē	shortage; deficiency
短小	duǎnxiǎo	short and small
短暂	duǎnzàn	brief; of short duration

熟语 Idioms

短兵相接	duǎn bīng xiāng jiē	fight hand-in-hand
短篇小说	duǎnpiān xiǎo shuō	short story
短小精悍	duǎn xiǎo jīng hàn	short and pithy; short but well-built

段 duàn 一 厂 厂 斤 斤 段 段 段 段

释义 Meaning

（一）量词 measure w.

section; part: 我刚买了一段衣料。I've just bought a length of dress material.

（二）名词 n.

paragraph; passage: 我能背诵这段文章。I can recite this passage.

词语 Words and Phrases

段落	duànluò	paragraph; phase; stage
工段	gōngduàn	workshop section; a section of a construction project
手段	shǒuduàn	① means; method; medium; measure ② trick

断 duàn ` ˊ ˋ ⺦ ⺶ 米 迷 迷ˊ 断 断
断

（斷 ′ ⼳ ⼳ ⼳ ⼳ 丝 毕 毕 毕 毕
毕 毕 豳 豳 斷 斷 斷）

释义 Meaning

（一）动词 v.

1. break; cut; snap: 这座桥断了。The bridge is broken.

2. give up: 我无法断烟。I can not give up smoking.

3. decide; judge: 遇事要当机立断。You must make a prompt decision when you get into trouble.

（二）副词 adv.

(used only in negative sentences) absolutely; decidely: 此事断不可信。This thing is absolutely incredible.

词语 Words and Phrases

断层	duàncéng	fault; broken
断肠	duàncháng	heartbroken
断炊	duànchuī	run out of food and fuel; go hungry
断定	duàndìng	decide; conclude; form a judgment
断绝	duànjué	break off; cut off; sever
断气	duànqì	① breathe one's last; die ② cut off the gas
断然	duànrán	① absolutely; flatly ② resolute; drastic
断送	duànsòng	ruin; foreit (one's life, futurn, etc.)
断言	duànyán	affirm; assert; say with certainty

熟语 Idioms

断垣残壁	duàn yuán cán bì	debris; broken walls
断章取义	duàn zhāng qǔ yì	quote out of context; garble a statement, etc.

| 断子绝孙 | duàn zǐ jué sūn | the last of the male line |
| 当机立断 | dāng jī lì duàn | make a prompt decision; resolute |

堆 duī 一 十 土 圠 圢 圹 圹 垆 垆 堆 堆

释义 Meaning

（一）动词 v.

pile up; stack: 我的书桌上堆满了书。My desk was piled with books.

（二）名词 n.

pile; heap; stack: 这儿有个草堆。Here is a haystack.

（三）量词 measure w.

pile; heap; crowd: 房间里有一大堆人。There is a crowd in the room.

词语 Words and Phrases

堆放	duīfàng	pile up; heap; stack
堆积	duījī	heap up; pile up
堆砌	duīqì	① write in a florid language ② pile up (stones, rocks, etc. to build sth.)
土堆	tǔduī	mound
草堆	cǎoduī	haystack

队 duì 了 阝 队 队

(隊 了 阝 阝 阝 阼 阼 阼 阽 阽 隊)

释义 Meaning

（一）名词 n.

1. team; group: 我们学校有一支篮球队。There is a basketball team in our school.

2. line; a row of people: 学生们站成了四队。The students fall into four lines.

（二）量词 measure w.

　　a row of; a line of: 那儿有一队小学生。There is a row of pupils over there.

词语 Words and Phrases

队列	duìliè	formation
队旗	duìqí	team pennant
队伍	duìwǔ	① troops ② ranks
队形	duìxíng	formation
队员	duìyuán	team member
队长	duìzhǎng	team leader
排队	páiduì	form a line; queue up; line up
游击队	yóujīduì	guerrilla forces

对 duì 　フ　又　ヌ　对　对

（對　丨　刂　刂ㅣ　业ㅣ　业　业　业　茔　堇　堇　堇
　　堇　對　對）

释义 Meaning

（一）动词 v.

1. answer; reply: 我无言以对。I have nothing to say in reply.

2. treat; against; cope with: 她妈妈对我不错。Her mother treats me well.

3. be directed at; face: 把我们的枪口对准敌人。Aim our gun at the enemy.

4. check; identify; compare: 我来对一下号码。Let me check the numbers.

5. agree; suit; get along: 中国菜很对我的胃口。Chinese

food suits my taste very well.

6. set; adjust fit one into the other: 出发时别忘了对一下表。Don't forget to set your watch when you leave.

7. add; mix: 请在我的咖啡里对点儿牛奶。Add some milk to my coffee, please.

（二）形容词 a.

right; correct: 你说得很对。What you said is right. 反义词antonym: 错

（三）量词 measure w.

pair; couple: 一对夫妻一个孩儿。One married couple, one child.

（四）介词 prep.

她对成功抱有信心。She feels confident of success.

词语 Words and Phrases

对白	duìbái	dialogue (in a novel, film or play)
对比	duìbǐ	① contrast; compare ② ratio
对不起	duìbùqǐ	① I'm sorry; excuse me ② be unfair to sb.
对策	duìcè	countermeasure
对称	duìchèn	symmetry
对答	duìdá	answer; reply
对待	duìdài	treat; approach
对方	duìfāng	opposite side; the other party
对付	duìfù	deal with; cope with; do with
对话	duìhuà	dialogue
对抗	duìkàng	① antagonism ② resist; oppose
对立	duìlì	oppose; set sth. against
对面	duìmiàn	① opposite ② face to face ③ right in front
对手	duìshǒu	① match ② adversary; opponent

| 对象 | duìxiàng | ① object; target ② boy or girl friend |
| 对照 | duìzhào | compare; collate |

熟语 Idioms

| 对牛弹琴 | duì niú tán qín | Cast pearls before a swine |
| 对症下药 | duì zhèng xià yào | suit the medicine to the illness; suit the remedy to the case |

顿 dùn 一 匚 口 屯 屯 屯 屯 顿 顿 顿

(頓 一 匚 口 屯 屯 屯 屯 頓 頓 頓 頓 頓 頓)

释义 Meaning

(一) 动词 v.

1. pause: 他看着我，顿了顿，又继续说了下去。He paused; looked at me, then continued.

2. touch the ground (with one's head) or stamp (one's foot): 他伤心得捶胸顿足。He was so sad that he beat his breast and stamped his foot.

(二) 量词 measure w.

我今天只吃了一顿饭。I've only had one meal today.

词语 Words and Phrases

顿号	dùnhào	a slight-pause mark used in punctuation to set off items in a series (、)
顿时	dùnshí	immediately; at once
顿悟	dùnwù	suddenly realize the truth, etc., attain enlightenment

熟语 Idioms

| 顿足捶胸 | dùn zú chuí xiōng | stamp one's foot and beat one's breast |

| 茅塞顿开 | máo sè dùn kāi | suddenly see the light |
| 抑扬顿挫 | yìyáng dùncuò | cadence |

多 duō　ノ　ク　タ　タ　多　多

释义 Meaning

（一）形容词 a.

1. many; much; more: 教室里有那么多学生。There are so many students in the classroom. 反义词antonym: 少

2. over; more; odd: 她妈妈已经八十多岁了。Her mother is over eighty years old.

3. excessive; too many; too much: 这句话里多了几个字。There are a few words too many in this sentence. 反义词 antonym: 少

4. far more; much more: 小王觉得今天好多了。Xiao Wang feels much better today.

（二）副词 adv.

(indicating degree, extent, etc.): 你爸爸多大年纪了？How old is your father?

词语 Words and Phrases

多半	duōbàn	① most; the greater part ② probably
多变	duōbiàn	varied; changeable
多次	duōcì	many times; repeatedly; on many occasions
多方	duōfāng	in every way; in many ways
多亏	duōkuī	luckily; thanks to
多么	duōme	(indicating degree, etc.) how; what
多情	duōqíng	susceptible; full of tenderness or affection (for a person of the opposite sex)
多少	duōshǎo	① number; amount ② somewhat; more or less

多少		how many; how much; (also used to indicate an uncertain quantity)
多时	duōshí	a long time
多事	duōshì	① meddlesome ② eventful
多数	duōshù	most; majority
多谢	duōxiè	thanks a lot
多心	duōxīn	over sensitive; suspicious
多余	duōyú	extra; unneccessary; superfluous
多云	duōyún	cloudy

熟语 Idioms

多才多艺	duō cái duō yì	versatility; gifted in many ways
多愁善感	duō chóu shàn gǎn	sensitivity; sentimental
多此一举	duō cǐ yì jǔ	hold a candle to the sun
多多益善	duō duō yì shàn	the more the better
多种多样	duō zhǒng duō yàng	multiplicity; manifold

夺 duó 一 ナ 六 产 夺 夺

(奪 一 ナ 六 术 术 衣 衣 奋 畬 奮 奮 奪 奪 奪)

释义 Meaning

动词 v.

1. seize; wrest; take by force: 我从他的手中把刀子夺了过来。I wrested the knife out of his hands.

2. win; strive for; contend for: 我们一定要夺得这场比赛的胜利。We must win the match.

3. force one's way: 她伤心已极，眼泪夺眶而出。She was so sad that tears rolled from her eyes.

词语 Words and Phrases

夺目	duómù	dazzle the eyes
夺取	duóqǔ	① seize; wrest; capture ② strive for
夺权	duóquán	seize power; take over power
定夺	dìngduó	decide; make a final decision
掠夺	lüèduó	rob; plunder; pillage
抢夺	qiǎngduó	seize; grab
争夺	zhēngduó	fight for; contend for

熟语 Idioms

光彩夺目	guāng cǎi duó mù	brilliant; dazzling

躲 duǒ 丿 冖 甪 甪 身 身 身 躯 躯 躯 躲 躲 躲

释义 Meaning

动词 v.

avoid; dodge; hide (oneself): 学生们总是想法躲开他们的英语老师。The students always try to avoid their English teacher.

词语 Words and Phrases

躲避	duǒbì	① hide (oneself) ② avoid; dodge; elude
躲藏	duǒcáng	hide oneself; conceal oneself; go into hiding
躲懒	duǒlǎn	shirk; shy away from work
躲闪	duǒshǎn	evade; dodge
躲债	duǒzhài	avoid a crediter

熟语 Idioms

明枪易躲，暗箭难防	míng qiāng yì duǒ, àn jiàn nán fáng	easy to dodge a spear in the open, but difficult to dodge an arrow shot from hiding

饿è 　ノ 𠂉 饣 饣 饣 饣 饣 饿 饿 饿

(餓 　ノ 𠆢 𠆢 𠂉 𠂉 𠂉 𠂉 食 食 飠 飠 飠 飠 飠 餓 餓)

释义 Meaning

（一）形容词 a.

　hungry: 我很饿。I'm very hungry. 反义词antonym: 饱

（二）动词 v.

　starve: 他说宁愿饿死也不愿乞讨。He said he would starve to death rather than beg for food.

词语 Words and Phrases

饿死	èsǐ	starve to death
挨饿	ái'è	go hungry
饥饿	jī'è	hunger; starvation

熟语 Idioms

| 饿虎扑食 | è hǔ pū shí | (do sth.) like a hungry tiger pouncing on its prey |
| 饿殍遍野 | è piǎo biàn yě | strewn with bodies of the starved everywhere; times of starvation |

儿ér 　丿 儿

(兒 　⺊ 𠂉 臼 臼 臼 臼 臼 兒)

释义 Meaning

（一）名词 n.

　1. son: 她有一儿一女。She has one son and one daughter.

　2. child: 我们都很喜欢少儿读物。We all like children books.

　3. youth; yougster: 退休了，可还得为儿辈的事儿操心。

I still worry about the younger generation even though I'm retired.

（二）后缀 suff.

楼里有点儿亮儿。There's a dim light in the building.

词语 Words and Phrases

儿歌	érgē	children song; nursery rhymes
儿化	érhuà	a phonetic phenomenon the retroflex ending 'r'
儿科	érkē	paediatrics
儿女	érnǚ	① children; sons and daughters ② youth
儿孙	érsūn	children and grandchildren; posterity
儿童	értóng	children
儿子	érzi	son
花儿	huār	flower

熟语 Idioms

| 儿女情长 | érnǚ qíng cháng | be immersed in romantic love |

耳 ěr   二 丆 丌 圧 耳 耳

释义 Meaning

（一）名词 n.

ear; any ear-like thing: 他的左耳比右耳大。His left ear is bigger than the right one.

（二）形容词 a.

side; flanking; on both sides: 他家有两间耳房。There are two side rooms in his house. 反义词antonym: 正

词语 Words and Phrases

| 耳朵 | ěrduo | ear |
| 耳目 | ěrmù | ① ears and eyes ② what one sees and hears |

耳生	ěrshēng	unfamiliar to the ear; strange-sounding
耳熟	ěrshú	familiar to the ear
耳闻	ěrwén	hear about (of)
耳语	ěryǔ	whisper (in sb. 's ear)

熟语 Idioms

耳聪目明	ěr cōng mù míng	can see and hear well
耳目一新	ěr mù yì xīn	find everything new and fresh
耳濡目染	ěr rú mù rǎn	be imperceptibly influenced by what one constantly sees and hears
耳闻目睹	ěrwén mùdǔ	what one sees and hears

二 èr   二 二

释义 Meaning

(一) 数词 num.

two: 他女朋友今年22岁。His girl friend is twenty-two years old.

(二) 形容词 a.

different: 他对妻子忠心不二。He is loyal to his wife.

词语 Words and Phrases

二等	èrděng	second-rate; second class
二胡	èrhú	a two-stringed bowed instrument
二话	èrhuà	demur; objection
二十	èrshí	twenty
二心	èrxīn	disloyalty; half-heartedness
二月	èryuè	February
第二	dì`èr	second

熟语 Idioms

| 三心二意 | sān xīn èr yì | be of two minds; half- |

hearted

独一无二　　dú yī wú èr　　unique; in a class by one-self

发₁ fā　亠　广　乡　发　发

（**發**　フ　ヲ　ヺ　ヺ　癶　癶　癶　發　發　發　發　發）

释义 Meaning

（一）动词 v.

1. issue; deliver; distribute; send out: 我刚刚发了一个通知。I've just issued a notice. 反义词antonym: 收

2. express; utter: 有十位老师在会上发了言。Ten teacheres spoke at the meeting.

3. occur; come (or bring) into existence: 去年发了大水。A flood occurred last year.

4. emit; expose: 食品发出阵阵香味。The food emits a nice smell.

5. come or bring into existance: 他的旧病又复发了。He has a recurrence of an old illness.

6. become; get into a certain state: 纸张已经开始发黄了。The paper is begining to turn yellow.

7. feel; have a feeling: 我觉得有点儿发冷。I feel a bit chilly.

8. start; set out: 早上5点发车。The bus sets off at five o'clock in the morning.

（二）量词 measure w.

(for ammunition) 士兵们丢了几发子弹。The soldiers lost a few cartridges.

词语 Words and Phrases

发表　　fābiǎo　　publish; issue

发布	fābù	issue; release
发财	fācái	get rich; make fortune
发愁	fāchóu	worry; be anxious
发出	fāchū	issue; send out; give off
发达	fādá	developed; flourishing
发动	fādòng	① start; launch ② mobilize; arouse; call into action
发抖	fādǒu	tremble; shiver; shake
发放	fāfàng	provide; grant
发疯	fāfēng	go mad; go crazy; be out of one's mind
发挥	fāhuī	① bring into play; give play to ② elaborate
发火	fāhuǒ	lose one s temper; get angry
发觉	fājué	find; discover
发明	fāmíng	① invent ② invention
发胖	fā pàng	get fat; gain weight
发脾气	fāpíqi	get angry; lose one's temper
发票	fāpiào	recept; bill
发起	fāqǐ	① initiate; sponsor ② start; launch
发球	fāqiú	serve a ball
发烧	fāshāo	have a fever
发射	fāshè	fire; shoot; launch; project
发生	fāshēng	happen; occur; take place
发誓	fāshì	vow; swear; pledge
发现	fāxiàn	discover; find
发泄	fāxiè	let off; give vent to
发行	fāxíng	publish; distribute; (of currency, etc.) issue
发扬	fāyáng	① develop; carry on ② make the most of
发音	fāyīn	pronunciation
发育	fāyù	growth; development

发展　　fāzhǎn　　① develop; grow; expand ② recruit

熟语 Idioms

发号施令　　fā hào shī lìng　　issue orders; order people about

发人深省　　fā rén shēn xǐng　　set people thinking

发₂ fà　　乁　屶　屶　发　发

(發　乁　屶　屶　屶　屶　屶　屶　屶　屶　屶

發**)**

释义 Meaning

名词 n.

hair: 金发好漂亮啊！Blonde hair is so beautiful!

词语 Words and Phrases

发型　　fàxíng　　hair style

理发　　lǐfà　　haircut

熟语 Idioms

令人发指　　lìng rén fà zhǐ　　make one's hair bristle with anger

法 fǎ　　丶　丶　氵　氵　汁　泔　法　法

释义 Meaning

名词 n.

1. law: 法律不允许我们做这样的事。The law doesn't allow us to do this.

2. way; method: 他正在研究教学法。He is researching on teaching methods.

词语 Words and Phrases

法办　　fǎbàn　　deal with according to law; punish by law

法定	fǎdìng	legal; statutory
法官	fǎguān	judge; justice
法规	fǎguī	rules; laws and regulations
法令	fǎlìng	decree; laws and decrees
法律	fǎlǜ	law
法庭	fǎtíng	court; tribunal
法学	fǎxué	legal studies
法院	fǎyuàn	court; law court; court of justice
法治	fǎzhì	rule by law
法制	fǎzhì	legality; legal system
办法	bànfǎ	method; way

熟语 Idioms

| 目无法纪 | mù wú fǎ jǐ | disregard for law and discipline |
| 奉公守法 | fèng gōng shǒu fǎ | law-abiding; observe the law |

翻 fān   一 ⺁ ⺁ 立 平 平 采 采 番 番
番 番 畨 畨 畨 翻 翻 翻

释义 Meaning

动词 v.

1. turn over; turn up: 这辆轿车翻了。The car turned over.

2. translate: 他把这本小说翻成了英文。He translated this story into English.

3. cross; get over: 小偷翻墙而逃。The thief climbed over the wall and got away.

4. rummage; search: 我翻遍了所有的抽屉，但什么也没找到。I rummaged all the drawers, but found nothing.

5. reverse: 他已经把案翻过来了。He's already reversed the verdict.

6. multiply; double: 学生的人数翻了一番。The number of students has doubled.

7. fall out; break up: 他们夫妇俩闹翻了。The couple fell out.

词语 Words and Phrases

翻案	fānàn	reverse a verdict
翻滚	fāngǔn	roll; tumble; toss
翻脸	fānliǎn	fall out; turn hostile
翻然	fānrán	(change) quickly and completely
翻身	fānshēn	① turn over ② free oneself; stand up
翻新	fānxīn	recondition; renovate; make over
翻修	fānxiū	rebuild
翻译	fānyì	① translate ② translator
翻阅	fānyuè	browse; glance over; look over

熟语 Idioms

翻来覆去	fān lái fù qù	① toss from side to side; ② repeatedly
翻然悔悟	fānrán huǐwù	quickly wake up to one's error
翻山越岭	fān shān yuè lǐng	cross over mountain after mountain
翻天覆地	fān tiān fù dì	world-shaking

烦 fán 丶 丶 丬 火 灯 灯 灯 炬 烦 烦

（煩 丶 丶 丬 火 灯 灯 灯 炬 煩 煩 煩 煩 煩）

释义 Meaning

（一）形容词 a.

1. vexed; annoyed; irritated: 我觉得很烦。I feel vexed.

2. prolix; superfluous and confusing: 他讲话的内容太烦
了。His speech is very prolix. 反义词antonym: 简

（二）动词 v.

1. be tired of: 老读这种书，我已经烦透了。I'm tired of
reading such books.

2. trouble; bother: 烦将此信交给王先生，好吗？May I
trouble you to take the letter to Mr. Wang?

词语 Words and Phrases

烦劳	fánláo	bother; trouble
烦闷	fánmèn	worried; unhappy
烦恼	fánnǎo	vexed; worried
烦扰	fánrǎo	① bother; disturb ② feel disturbed
烦琐	fánsuǒ	loaded down with trivial details
烦躁	fánzào	irritable; fidgety; agitated

熟语 Idioms

自寻烦恼	zì xún fánnǎo	worry oneself for nothing
要言不烦	yào yán bù fán	giving the essentials in simple language

反 fǎn 二 厂 反 反

释义 Meaning

（一）动词 v.

1. turn over: 此事易如反掌。It's as easy as turning over
my palm.

2. rebel; revolt; oppose: 他们总是反其道而行之。They
always act in a diametrically opposite way.

（二）副词 adv.

1. in revers; inside out; in an opposite direction: 他被反绑着
双手。His hands were tied behind his back.

2. instead; on the contrary: 如此非但无益，反会弄得更糟。 This will not do much good; on the contrary, it will make things even worse.

词语 Words and Phrases

反常	fǎncháng	unusual; abnormal
反动	fǎndòng	① reactionary ② reaction
反对	fǎnduì	oppose; fight; combat; be against
反而	fǎnér	instead; on the contrary
反复	fǎnfù	① repeatedly; again and again ② reversal; relapse
反感	fǎngǎn	dislike; repugnant; disgusted with
反悔	fǎnhuǐ	go back to one's word (or promise)
反抗	fǎnkàng	resist; revolt
反面	fǎnmiàn	① back; reverse side; wrong side ② opposite; negative side
反射	fǎnshè	① reflection ② reflex
反问	fǎnwèn	ask in retort; counter with a question
反省	fǎnxǐng	self-examination; introspection
反应	fǎnyìng	① reaction ② react; respond
反映	fǎnyìng	① reflect; depict; mirror ② report; make known
反正	fǎnzhèng	anyway; anyhow; in any case

熟语 Idioms

反败为胜	fǎn bài wéi shèng	win instead of lose; turn defeat into victory
反客为主	fǎn kè wéi zhǔ	reverse the positions of the host and the guest; take initiative
反咬一口	fǎnyǎo yì kǒu	trump up a counterchgarge against one's accuser
易如反掌	yì rú fǎn zhǎng	as easy as turning one's palm over

| 适得其反 | shì dé qí fǎn | just the opposite to what one wishes |

犯 fàn ´ ㄅ ㄅ ㄅ 犯

释义 Meaning

（一）动词 v.

1. attack; invade; assail: 人不犯我，我不犯人。We'll not attack unless we are attacked.

2. have an attack of (an old illness); revert to (a bad habit): 他又犯脾气了。He's got angry again.

3. violate; offend (against law, etc.): 学生们常常会犯纪律。The students always violated school discipline.

4. commit (a mistake, etc.): 你这样做会犯错误的。You'll make a mistake if you do it like this.

（二）名词 n.

criminal: 他是个杀人犯。He is a murderer.

词语 Words and Phrases

犯病	fànbìng	have an attack of one's old illness
犯愁	fànchóu	worry; be anxious
犯法	fànfǎ	break (or violate) the law
犯规	fànguī	break the rules; foul
犯人	fànrén	prisoner; convict
犯罪	fànzuì	commit a crime (or an offence)
犯不着	fànbùzháo	not worthwhile
犯得着	fàndezháo	(in rhetorical question) worthwhile

饭 fàn ´ ㄅ ㄅ ㄅ 饣 饭 饭

（饭 ´ ㄅ ㄅ ㄅ 今 今 今 食 食 食 飰 飯 飯）

释义 Meaning

名词 n.

cooked rice; meal: 我不喜欢米饭。I don't like rice.

词语 Words and Phrases

饭菜	fàncài	meal; repast; dishes to go with rice, steamed buns, etc.
饭店	fàndiàn	hotel; restaurant
饭馆	fànguǎn	restaurant
饭票	fànpiào	meal ticket
饭厅	fàntīng	dining hall; dining room
饭桶	fàntǒng	① rice bucket ② big eater ③ fathead; good-for-nothing
饭碗	fànwǎn	① rice bowl ② job
晚饭	wǎnfàn	dinner; supper
午饭	wǔfàn	lunch
早饭	zǎofàn	breakfast

方 fāng ㇏ 亠 亅 方

释义 Meaning

(一) 名词 n.

1. direction; place; region: 他自远方而来。He comes from a faraway place.

2. side; party: 这将对双方都有好处。This will be of benefit to both sides.

3. way; method: 我们一定会想方法去做好这项工作。We'll try every means possible to do it better.

4. prescription: 您给我开个什么药方？What do you prescribe for my illness?

(二) 形容词 a.

square: 屋子里只有一张方桌。There is only one square

table in the room. 反义词antonym: 圆

（三）副词 adv.

just: 她今年年方十八。She is just eighteen years old.

（四）量词 measure w.

for square objects; short for square metre or cubic metre: 我们的新房子铺了50方地板。We lay 50 square metres of wooden floor in our new house.

词语 Words and Phrases

方案	fāng'àn	scheme; programme; plan
方便	fāngbiàn	① convenient; proper ② go to the restroom ③ have money to spare or lend
方才	fāngcái	just now
方法	fāngfǎ	way; method; means
方面	fāngmiàn	side; aspect; respect
方式	fāngshì	way; pattern; fashion
方位	fāngwèi	direction; position
方向	fāngxiàng	direction; orientation
方言	fāngyán	dialect
方圆	fāngyuán	① circumference ② neighbourhood

熟语 Idioms

方兴未艾	fāng xīng wèi ài	be just unfolding
千方百计	qiān fāng bǎi jì	leave no stone unturned
四面八方	sìmiàn bā fāng	in all direction

防 fáng ⻖ ⻖ ⻖ ⻖ 防 防

释义 Meaning

（一）动词 v.

prevent; guard against: 我们应该准备好，以防万一。We must be ready for every eventuality.

（二）名词 n.

defence: 国防需要大量的金钱。Much money must be spent on national defence.

词语 Words and Phrases

防备	fángbèi	guard against; take precautions against
防范	fángfàn	keep a lookout; be on guard
防护	fánghù	protect; shelter
防火	fánghuǒ	fireproof; prevent fire
防守	fángshǒu	guard; defend
防卫	fángwèi	defend
防止	fángzhǐ	avoid; prevent; guard against
防治	fángzhì	prevention and cure
国防	guófáng	national defence
预防	yùfáng	take precautions; prevent sth. (usu. undesirable) from happening

熟语 Idioms

防不胜防	fáng bù shèng fáng	impossible to put up an all-round effective defense
防患未然	fáng huàn wèi rán	to provide against possible trouble
防微杜渐	fáng wēi dù jiàn	A stitch in time saves nine
以防万一	yǐ fáng wànyī	be prepared for all eventualities

房 fáng 　 丶 亠 亠 户 户 户 房 房

释义 Meaning

（一）名词 n.

1. house: 学校旁边有一排平房。There is a single-storey house near the school.

2. room: 病房里请勿喧哗。Please keep quiet in the sickward.

3. a house-like structure: 蜂房很小。The beehive is very small.

（二）量词 measure w.

for branches of a family: 他的两房儿媳妇都很贤惠。His two doughters-in-law are very virtuous.

词语 Words and Phrases

房产	fángchǎn	house property
房顶	fángdǐng	roof
房东	fángdōng	the owner of the house one lives in
房基	fángjī	foundations (of a building)
房间	fángjiān	room
房客	fángkè	lodger; tenant (of a room or a house)
房事	fángshì	sexual intercourse
房屋	fángwū	building; house
房主	fángzhǔ	house-owner
房子	fángzi	building; house; room
客房	kèfáng	guest room
书房	shūfáng	study

访 fǎng ` 讠 讠 讠 访 访

（訪 ` 亠 亠 亖 言 言 言 訁 訪 訪 訪）

释义 Meaning

动词 v.

1. visit; call on: 今天下午我要去访一位朋友。 I'll visit a friend this afternoon.

2. try to get; seek by inquiry or search: 他常常下乡去访民乐。He always goes to the countryside to search for folk songs.

词语 Words and Phrases

访问	fǎngwèn	visit; interview; call on
拜访	bàifǎng	visit; call on
采访	cǎifǎng	cover; (of a reporter) gather material
互访	hùfǎng	exchange visits
探访	tànfǎng	① go in search of ② pay a call on

熟语 Idioms

| 访亲问友 | fǎng qīn wèn yǒu | call on friends and relatives |

放 fàng 丶 亠 方 方 方 方 放 放

释义 Meaning

动词 v.

1. release; let go; set free: 把浴盆里的水放掉。Let the water out of the bathtub.

2. let oneself go; give way to: 他伤心地放声大哭。He cried loudly and bitterly.

3. put; place; add: 把书放到书包里去。Put the book into your schoolbag.

4. let off; give out: 孩子们正在放焰火。The children are setting off fireworks.

5. blossom; open: 公园里百花齐放，漂亮极了。The flowers in the park are all blooming in multitudes; it's very beautiful.

6. put out to pasture: 放牛是他的职业。To put cattle out to pasture is his job.

7. expand; let out; make larger, longer, etc.: 把我的裤腰放大一厘米。Let my trousers out one centimetre at the waist.

8. leave alone; lay aside: 此事先放一放吧。Let's lay it aside

for the moment.

9. show; play (film, radio, etc.): 他在放录音呢。He is playing a tape recording.

10. lend money for interest: 他靠放债为生。He depends on the interest of lending money for a living.

词语 Words and Phrases

放大	fàngdà	enlarge; amplify; magnify
放荡	fàngdàng	① dissolute; dissipated ② unconventional
放风	fàngfēng	① let in fresh air ② spread news or rumours ③ let prisoners out for exercise
放过	fàngguò	let off; let slip
放假	fàngjià	have a holiday or vacation
放空炮	fàng kōng pào	talk big; spout hot air
放屁	fàngpì	① fart; break wind ② talk nonsense
放晴	fàngqíng	(after rain) clear up
放任	fàngrèn	① let alone; not interfere ② no interference; ③ *laissez-faire*
放射	fàngshè	radiate
放手	fàngshǒu	① let go; release one's hold ② have a free hand; go all out
放肆	fàngsì	wanton; unbridled
放松	fàngsōng	relax; loosen; slacken
放心	fàngxīn	be at ease; set one's mind at rest; feel relieved
放学	fàngxué	class dismissed
放映	fàngyìng	show; project; play (film, etc.)
放置	fàngzhì	lay up; lay aside
放纵	fàngzòng	indulge; connive at; let sb. have his own way

熟语 Idioms

放荡不羁	fàngdàng bùjī	to show one's wild oats
放任自流	fàngrèn zìliú	surrender oneself to
放之四海 而皆准	fàng zhīsìhǎi ér jiē zhǔn	valid everywhere

飞 fēi　乁 飞 飞

(飛　乁 飞 飞 飞 飞 飛 飛 飛 飛)

释义 Meaning

（一）动词 v.

fly; flit: 蜜蜂在鲜花丛中飞来飞去。Bees are flitting from flower to flower.

（二）副词 adv.

swiftly: 我们沿着大街飞奔。We flew down the street.

词语 Words and Phrases

飞驰	fēichí	speed along
飞虫	fēichóng	winged insect
飞船	fēichuán	airship; dirigible
飞碟	fēidié	UFO
飞机	fēijī	plane; aeroplane; aircraft
飞快	fēikuài	① very fast; at lightning speed ② extremely sharp
飞速	fēisù	at full speed
飞舞	fēiwǔ	flutter; dance in the air
飞翔	fēixiáng	hover; circle in the air
飞行	fēixíng	flying; flight
飞跃	fēiyuè	leap
飞涨	fēizhǎng	(of prices, etc.) soar; skyrocket; shoot up

熟语 Idioms

飞黄腾达	fēihuáng téng dá	come into one's kingdom; rise in the world
飞禽走兽	fēiqín zǒushòu	birds and beasts
飞檐走壁	fēi yán zǒu bì	leap onto roofs and vault over walls

非 fēi　丨 丨 丬 丬 非 非 非 非

释义 Meaning

（一）形容词 a.

un-, non-, etc.: 我们不能做这种非正义的事。We cann't do it because it is unjust.

（二）副词 adv.

simply must; insist on; have to: 我非要试一试。I simply must have a try.

（三）名词 n.

1. wrong; evildoing: 你们一定要分清是非。You must distinguish between right and wrong. 反义词 antonym: 是

2. short for Africa: 亚非拉的大多数国家都属于第三世界。Most countries in Asia, Africa and Latin America belong to the Third World.

（四）动词 v.

not; no: 他们总是答非所问。They always give an irrelevant answer.

词语 Words and Phrases

非常	fēicháng	① very; extremely; highly ② unusual; extraordinary; special
非得	fēiděi	must; have got to
非法	fēifǎ	illegal; unlawful
非凡	fēifán	uncommon; outstanding; extraordinary

非礼	fēilǐ	rude
非难	fēinàn	reproach; blame; censure
非人	fēirén	① inhuman ② not the right person
非正式	fēizhèngshì	informal; unonfficial
非洲	fēizhōu	Africa
是非	shìfēi	right and wrong

熟语 Idioms

非同小可	fēi tóng xiǎo kě	no small matter
答非所问	dá fēi suǒ wèn	give irrelevant answers
为非作歹	wéi fēi zuò dǎi	commit crimes
无可非议	wú kě fēi yì	beyond reproach; above reproach
混淆是非	hùnxiáo shìfēi	confound right and wrong

肥 féi　丿 刀 刀 月 肝 肥 肥 肥

释义 Meaning

(一) 形容词 a.

1. fat: 这块肉太肥了。The piece of meat is too fat. 反义词 antonym: 瘦

2. loose; wide: 他穿着一件很肥的外套。He wears a loose garment. 反义词 antonym: 瘦

3. (of land, soil, etc.) fertile; rich: 这块土地很肥。The soil is very fertile. 反义词 antonym: 薄；瘦

(二) 名词 n.

manure; fertilizer: 请使用农家肥。Please use farmyard manure.

词语 Words and Phrases

肥大	féidà	① large; loose ② fat; plump; corpulent
肥料	féiliào	fertilizer; manure
肥胖	féipàng	fat; corpulent

肥硕	féishuò	① (of fruit) big and fleshy ② (of limbs and body) large and firm-fleshed
肥沃	féiwò	fertile; rich (soil)
肥皂	féizào	soap
肥壮	féizhuàng	stout and strong
化肥	huàféi	chemical fertilizer

费 fèi　一　二　三　弗　弗　弗　弗　费　费

(費 一　二　三　弗　弗　弗　弗　弗　費　費　費)

释义 Meaning

（一）名词 n.

fee; charge; dues; expenses: 我必须自己付学费。I must pay my tuition fees by myself.

（二）动词 v.

1. cost; spend; expend: 买这台电脑费了我们不少钱。This computer costs us a lot of money.

2. consuming too much, expending sth. too quickly: 空调太费电了。The air conditioner consumes too much eletricity.

反义词antonym: 省

词语 Words and Phrases

费工	fèigōng	take a lot of work; require a lot of labour
费解	fèijiě	obscure; unintelligible; hard to understand
费劲	fèijìn	be strenuous; need great effort
费力	fèilì	be strenuous; need great effort
费时	fèishí	take time; be time-consuming
费事	fèishì	take (or give) a lot of trouble
费心	fèixīn	take a lot of trouble; need a lot of care

费用	fèiyòng	cost; expenses
免费	miǎnfèi	free of charge
学费	xuéfèi	tuition; tuition fees

熟语 Idioms

| 费尽心机 | fèi jìn xīn jī | leave no stone unturned to do sth. |

分₁ fēn ㇒ ㇔ 分 分

释义 Meaning

（一）动词 v.

1. divide; part; separate: 一年分为四季。One year is divided into four seasons. 反义词antonym: 合

2. assign; distribute; allot: 电影票都已经分完了。The movie tickets have been distributed.

3. distinquish; tell one from another: 我分不清她们姐妹俩。I cann't tell her from her sister.

（二）名词 n.

1. branch: 我们在上海有一家分公司。We have a branch company in Shanghai.

2. point; mark: 我们队又得了一分。Our team scores another point.

3. fraction: 三分之一。one-third.

4. one-tenth; 10 per cent: 四分成绩，六分错误。40 per cent achievments, 60 per cent mistakes.

（三）量词 measure w.

1. of time (1/60 of an hour): 现在八点差五分。It's five to eight.

2. of money in China (1/100 of yuan): 我花了两块四毛八分钱。I have spent 2.48 yuan RMB.

3. of weight (1/2 of a gram): 它重3两6钱6分。It weighs 3.66 *liang*.

4. of area (66.666 square metres): 他一共只有一亩三分地。He has only 13 *fen* of land.

5. of length (1/3 of a centimetre): 我一分也不比他矮。I'm not shorter than he by any means.

6. of degree (1/60 of a degree): 此地位于东经108度12分。It's situated at longitude 108 degrees 12 minutes East.

词语 Words and Phrases

分辨	fēnbiàn	distinguish; differentiate
分辩	fēnbiàn	defend oneself (against a charge); offer an explanation
分别	fēnbié	① part; leave each other ② difference ③ separately; respectively
分寸	fēncùn	sense of propriety; proper limits for speech or action
分担	fēndān	share responsibility for
分发	fēnfā	issue; distribute; hand out
分工	fēn gōng	division of labour; divide the work
分管	fēn guǎn	be put in charge of; be assigned personal responsibility for
分化	fēnhuà	become divided; split up; break up
分家	fēnjiā	break up the family and live apart
分界线	fēnjièxiàn	boundary; line of demarcation
分居	fēnjū	(wife and husband) live apart; separate
分开	fēnkāi	separate; part
分类	fēnlèi	classify
分离	fēnlí	separate; sever
分裂	fēnliè	sever; split; divide; break up
分娩	fēnwǎn	childbirth; parturition
分明	fēnmíng	① clearly; plainly; evidently ② distinct;

		clearly demarcated
分配	fēnpèi	① assign; distribute; allot ② distribution
分歧	fēnqí	difference; divergence
分散	fēnsàn	disperse; scatter; decentralize
分手	fēnshǒu	say good-bye; part company
分数	fēnshù	① mark; grade ② fraction
分水岭	fēn shuǐ lǐng	① divide; watershed ② line of demarcation
分头	fēntóu	severally; separately
分析	fēnxī	analyse
分享	fēnxiǎng	share (joy, rights, etc.); partake of
分心	fēnxīn	divert one's attention
分忧	fēnyōu	share sb.'s cares and burdens; help sb. to get over a difficulty
分组	fēnzǔ	divide into groups

熟语 Idioms

分道扬镳	fēn dào yáng biāo	separate and go one's own way
分门别类	fēn mén bié lèi	classify
分秒必争	fēn miǎo bì zhēng	not even a second is to be lost
争分夺秒	zhēng fēn duó miǎo	seize every minute and second; not a second is to be lost

分₂ fèn ノ 八 分 分

释义 Meaning

名词 n.

1. component: 海水的盐分很高。Salt content of sea water is very high.

2. what is within the scope of one's rights or obligations: 你

的要求过分了。Your demands are excessive.

词语 Words and Phrases

分量	fènliang	weight; share
分内	fènnèi	one's job; one's duty
分外	fènwài	① not one's duty ② especially; particularly
分子	fènzǐ	member; element
本分	běnfèn	one's duty; contented with one's lot
过分	guòfèn	excessive; going too far; exceeding what is proper

粉 fěn ` ˊ ⺌ ⺼ ⺧ ⺧ ⺧ ⺧ 粉 粉

释义 Meaning

（一）名词 n.

powder: 我买了一袋奶粉。I've bought a bag of powdered milk.

（二）形容词 a.

pink: 她喜欢粉色的衣服。She like pink clothes.

词语 Words and Phrases

粉笔	fěnbǐ	chalk
粉红	fěnhóng	pink
粉饰	fěnshì	whitewash; gloss over
粉刷	fěnshuā	whitewash; plaster
粉丝	fěnsī	vermicelli made from bean starch, etc.
粉碎	fěnsuì	smash; crush; shatter; broken into pieces
粉条	fěntiáo	noodles made from bean or sweet potato starch

熟语 Idioms

粉身碎骨	fěn shēn suì gǔ	have one's body smashed into pieces

份 fèn ノ 亻 亻 仍 份 份

释义 Meaning

（一）名词 n.

share; portion: 公司也有我的一份。I've some shares in this company.

（二）量词 mearsur w.

of gift, newspaper, food, etc.: 生日时，她送给我一份礼物。She gave me a gift in my birthday.

词语 Words and Phrases

份额	fèn'é	share; portion
份子	fènzi	one's share for a joint untertaking
股份	gǔfèn	stock; share

风 fēng ノ 几 凡 风

（風 ノ 几 凡 凡 凬 凬 凬 凬 凬 凬）

释义 Meaning

名词 n.

1. wind: 他们每天都忙得风里来，雨里去的。Everyday they carry out that tasks even in the teeth of wind and rain.

2. style; custom; practice: 我们必须纠正不正之风。We have to correct unhealthy tendencies.

3. news; information: 你听到什么风了吗？Have you got any news?

词语 Words and Phrases

风暴	fēngbào	storm; windstorm
风波	fēngbō	disturbance
风采	fēngcǎi	charisma; graceful bearing

风车	fēngchē	① windmill ② pinwheel
风尘	fēngchén	travel fatigue
风度	fēngdù	demeanour; elegant manners
风格	fēnggé	style
风光	fēngguāng	view; scene; sight
风寒	fēnghán	cold; chill
风景	fēngjǐng	landscape; scenery;
风力	fēnglì	① wind power ② wind force
风流	fēngliú	① talented and meritorious ② gifted; romantic ③ dissolute
风貌	fēngmào	① style and features ② view; scene
风靡	fēngmǐ	fashionable
风气	fēngqì	atmosphere; general mood; common practice
风情	fēngqíng	amorous feelings; firtatious expressions
风趣	fēngqù	hummour; wit
风沙	fēngshā	dust storm; sand blown by the wind
风声	fēngshēng	rumour; news
风水	fēngshuǐ	geomantic omen
风俗	fēngsú	social customs
风味	fēngwèi	special flavour; local flavour; local colour
风险	fēngxiǎn	risk; hazard
风雨	fēngyǔ	wind and rain; trials and hardships
风云	fēngyún	wind and cloud; a fast-changing situation
风筝	fēngzheng	kite
风姿	fēngzī	charisma; charm

熟语 Idioms

风尘仆仆	fēng chén púpú	endure the hardships of a long journey

风驰电掣	fēng chí diàn chè	swift as wind and quick as lightning
风吹草动	fēng chuī cǎo dòng	a sign of trouble or disturbance
风平浪静	fēng píng làng jìng	calm; uneventful
风调雨顺	fēng tiáo yǔ shùn	good weather for the crops
风土人情	fēngtǔ rénqíng	natural conditions and social customs of a place
风言风语	fēngyán fēng yǔ	groundless talk
风雨无阻	fēngyǔ wúzǔ	in all weathers
风云人物	fēngyún rénwù	influential man; man of the time
风烛残年	fēngzhú cánnián	have one foot in the grave

封 fēng 一 十 土 圭 丰 圭 丰 封 封

释义 Meaning

（一）动词 v.

1. seal: 他封好信并寄了出去。He sealed the letter and mailed it out. 反义词 antonym: 开

2. confer (a title, teritory, etc.) on: 皇帝封他为亲王。The emperor made him a prince.

（二）名词 n.

seal; envelope: 女儿寄来的包裹还没拆封呢。The parcel from my daughter is still sealed.

（三）量词 measure w.

of letter, etc: 我刚收到女朋友的一封信。I've just received a letter from my girl friend.

词语 Words and Phrases

封闭	fēngbì	seal; close; sheltered
封底	fēngdǐ	back cover of a book
封建	fēngjiàn	feudal

封口	fēngkǒu	seal; say nothing
封面	fēngmiàn	front (or back) cover of a book
封锁	fēngsuǒ	block; blockade; seal off
封条	fēngtiáo	a strip of paper used for sealing doors, drawers, etc.
信封	xìnfēn	envelope

熟语 Idioms

| 封山育林 | fēng shān yù lín | seal a mountain pass to facilitate afforestation |
| 故步自封 | gù bù zì fēng | complacent and conservative |

佛 fó ノ 亻 仁 仁 佛 佛 佛

释义 Meaning

名词 n.

1. Buddha: 佛在心中。Buddha is in your heart.

2. Buddhism: 他妈妈信佛。His mother believes in Buddhism.

3. statue of Buddha: 我奶奶请了一尊铜佛。My grandmother bought a bronze statue of Buddha.

词语 Words and Phrases

佛教	fójiào	Buddhism
佛经	fójīng	Buddhist Scripture; Buddhist Sutra
佛堂	fótáng	hall for worshipping Buddha
佛像	fóxiàng	statue (figure, or image) of Buddha
佛学	fóxué	Buddhism
佛教徒	fójiàotú	Buddhist
佛门弟子	fómén dìzǐ	Buddhists; followers of Buddhism

熟语 Idioms

| 吃斋念佛 | chīzhāi niànfó | practise abstinence from meat and chant the name of Buddha |

扶 fú　 一 十 扌 扩 抃 抾 扶

释义 Meaning

动词 v.

1. support with the hand: 上楼时扶好栏杆。Keep a hand on the banisters as you go upstairs.
2. help; relieve; straighten sth. up: 人人都应扶危济困。 Everyone should help the old and the weak.

词语 Words and Phrases

扶持	fúchí	help; support
扶手	fúshǒu	handrail; banisters; armrest
扶梯	fútī	staircase
扶植	fúzhí	foster; pop up
扶助	fúzhù	help; support; assist

熟语 Idioms

扶老携幼	fúlǎo xié yòu	bring along the young and the old
扶摇直上	fúyáo zhí shàng	skyrocket; rise steeply
救死扶伤	jiù sǐ fú shāng	heal the wounded and save the dying

服 fú　 丿 刀 月 月 朋 朋 服 服

释义 Meaning

（一）名词 n.

clothes; dress: 小学生穿着校服去上学。The pupils go to school in school uniform.

（二）动词 v.

1. obey; be convinced: 他的话有理，我服了。His words are reasonable, I'm convinced.

2. serve: 有些国家人人都要服兵役。In some contries, everyone must serve in the army.

3. take (medicine, etc.): 日服两次，每次四粒。To be taken two times a day, four tablets each time.

4. be accustomed to: 在上海时，我有点儿水土不服。I was not accustomed to the climate when I was in Shanghai.

词语 Words and Phrases

服从	fúcóng	obey; submit to; be subordinated to
服毒	fúdú	take poison
服气	fúqì	be convinced
服式	fúshì	style of clothes
服侍	fúshì	attend; wait upon
服饰	fúshì	dress; dress and personal adornment
服输	fúshū	admit defeat; acknowledge defeat
服务	fúwù	serve; give service to
服装	fúzhuāng	dress; costume; clothes
工作服	gōngzuòfú	work clothes
和服	héfú	kimono
礼服	lǐfú	ceremonial robe or dress; full dress
西服	xīfú	Western-style clothes
衣服	yīfu	dress; clothes
制服	zhìfú	① uniform ② subdue; check; bring under control

福 fú ` ㇒ ㇇ ㇇ ㇇ 衤 衤 衤 衤 福 福 福 福

释义 Meaning

名词 n.

happiness; blessing; good fortune: 你真有福气。 You have good fortune. 反义词 antonym: 祸

词语 Words and Phrases

福利	fúlì	welfare; material benefits; well-being
福气	fúqì	good fortune; happy lot
福星	fúxīng	mascot; lucky star
福音	fúyīn	Gospel; glad tidings
幸福	xìngfú	happy; happiness; well-being

父 fù ㇒ ㇒ ㇒ 父

释义 Meaning

名词 n.

father: 我父母都七十岁了。 Both my father and mother are 70 years old.

词语 Words and Phrases

父老	fùlǎo	elders of a county or district
父母	fùmǔ	parents; father and mother
父亲	fù'qīn	father
父系	fùxì	paternal line; the father's side of the family
父兄	fùxiōng	father and elder brothers
伯父	bófù	uncle (father's elder brother)
祖父	zǔfù	grandfather (father's father)

付 fù ㇒ 亻 仁 什 付

释义 Meaning

动词 v.

1. pay: 学生应该付学费。The students must pay their tution fees.

2. entrust; hand over to; commit to: 他将信件都付之一炬。He burnt his letters.

词语 Words and Phrases

付出	fùchū	pay; extend
付款	fùkuǎn	pay a sum of money
付清	fùqīng	pay off; clear a bill
付印	fùyìn	send to the press
付帐	fùzhàng	pay a bill
交付	jiāofù	hand over to; commit to
托付	tuōfù	entrust

熟语 Idioms

付之一炬	fù zhī yí jù	hand over to the flames
付之一笑	fù zhī yí xiào	dismiss with a laugh
付诸实施	fù zhū shí shī	bring into effect; put into practice

负 fù ／ ㇀ 亻 乍 乊 负

(負 ／ ㇀ 亻 乍 乍 负 负 負 負)

释义 Meaning

(一) 动词 v.

1. bear; carry on the back or the shoulder: 他肩负重任。He shouldered heavy responsibilities.

2. suffer: 战士们负伤了。The soldiers were wounded.

3. owe: 我常常负债。I am always in debt.

4. lose (a game, match, battle, etc.); be defeated: 我们球队
以1：2负于对手。Our ball team lost the game 1：2. 反义
词antonym: 赢；胜

5. betray; fail in one's duty or obligation: 他是个忘恩负义
的家伙。He is an ungrateful guy.

（二）名词 n.

minus; negative: "-"是负号的标志。"-" is the negative
sigh. 反义词antonym: 正

词语 Words and Phrases

负担	fùdàn	should; bear; load; burden
负数	fùshù	negative number
负责	fùzé	conscientious; be in charge of; be responsible for
担负	dānfù	shoulder; bear; take on
肩负	jiānfù	shoulder; bear; undertake; take on

熟语 Idioms

负隅顽抗	fù yú wánkàng	put up a desperate struggle
忘恩负义	wàng ēn fù yì	be ungrateful
不分胜负	bù fēn shèngfù	end in a tie; end in a draw; break even
如释重负	rú shì zhòng fù	feel greatly relieved; feel as if relieved of a heavy load

复₁ fù ノ 一 一 一 一 一 一 复 复

（復 ノ ノ イ イ 犷 彳 彳 彳 彳 彳 復
復）

释义 Meaning

（一）动词 v.

1. reply; answer: 请速复信。Please reply to the letter immediately.

2. recover; resume: 他已经复职了。He's alredy resumed his work.

（二）副词 adv.

again: 时光一去不复返。One cannot relive the past.

复₂ fù ´ ⺈ ⼌ ⼌ ⼌ ⼌ ⼌ 复 复

（複 ` ⼂ ⼀ ⼀ ⼀ ⼀ 衤 衤 衤 複 複 複 複 複）

释义 Meaning

形容词 a.

complex; compound: 司马是个复姓。Sima is a comound surname. 反义词antonym: 单

词语 Words and Phrases

复仇	fùchóu	revenge; retaliate; avenge
复发	fùfā	recur; have a relapse
复工	fùgōng	return to work
复古	fùgǔ	return to the old times; restore ancient ways
复活	fùhuó	① revive; bring back to life ② Resurrection
复句	fùjù	a sentence of more clauses, compond sentence
复述	fùshù	① repeat ② retell
复苏	fùsū	① recovery ② resusciate; come back to life or consciousness

复习	fùxí	review; revise
复信	fùxìn	① reply; letter in reply ② write a letter in reply
复兴	fùxīng	revive; resurge; rejuvenate
复印	fùyìn	duplicate; copy
复原	fùyuán	① restore; rehabilitate ② recover from an illness
复杂	fùzá	complex; complicated
复制	fùzhì	reproduce; duplicate; copy
报复	bàofù	retaliate; revenge
重复	chóngfù	repeat; duplicate
答复	dáfù	reply; answer
回复	huífù	reply

熟语 Idioms

| 周而复始 | zhōu ér fù shǐ | go round and round; begin again and again |

副 fù   一   下   下   百   戸   盲   畐   畐   畐   副   副

释义 Meaning

（一）形容词 a.

1. vice; deputy; assistant: 她丈夫是副校长。Her husband is the vice president of the university. 反义词antonym: 正

2. secondary; subsidiary; substandard: 我从不买副品。I've never bought substandard goods. 反义词antonym: 正

（二）动词 v.

fit; correspond to: 他是个名不副实的家伙。He is a guy whose name falls short of the reality.

（三）量词 measure w.

1. of facial expression: 尽管很伤心，他还是装出一副笑

脸。Although he was very sad, he assumed a smiling face.

2. pair: 我刚买了一副新眼镜。I've just bought a pair of new glasses.

词语 Words and Phrases

副本	fùběn	copy; duplicate; transcript
副标题	fùbiāo tí	subtitle; subheading
副产品	fùchǎnpǐn	by-product
副词	fùcí	adverb; adverbial word
副刊	fùkān	supplement; literary supplement
副品	fùpǐn	substandard goods; seconds
副食	fùshí	non-staple food
副手	fùshǒu	assistant
副业	fùyè	sideline; side occupation
副职	fùzhí	the position of a deputy to the chief of a department, office, etc.
副作用	fùzuóyòng	side effect; secondary action

熟语 Idioms

名副其实	míng fù qí shí	the name corresponds to the reality
名不副实	míng bú fù shí	the name falls short of the reality

富 fù 丶 丷 宀 宀 宀 宀 宀 宀 富 富 富 富

释义 Meaning

形容词 a.

rich; weathy; abundant: 学生们都很富。All the students are very rich. 反义词 antonym: 贫; 穷

词语 Words and Phrases

富贵	fùguì	wealth and in high official rank; riches

		and honour
富强	fùqiáng	prosperous and powerful
富饶	fùráo	abundant; fertile; richly endowed
富翁	fùwēng	wealthy man
富有	fùyǒu	① rich; wealthy ② full of; rich in
富裕	fùyù	prosperous; well-off; well-to-do
富余	fùyú	have more than needed
富足	fùzú	abundant; plentiful; rich
财富	cáifù	fortune; wealth

熟语 Idioms

| 富国强兵 | fù guó qiáng bīng | make the country rich and build up its military power |
| 富丽堂皇 | fùlì tánghuáng | magnificence; splendid; gorgeous |

该 gāi `丶 讠 讠 讠 讠 讠 该 该

（該 `丶 亠 亠 亖 言 言 言 訁 訁 訁 該 該 該）

释义 Meaning

（一）动词 v.

1. be one's turn to do sth.: 这次该我了。It's my turn this time.

2. owe: 我该他100块钱。I owe him 100 yuan RMB.

（二）助动词 aux. v.

should; ought to: 该吃午饭了。It's time for lunch.

（三）代词 pron.

it; this; that: 该生学习非常努力。This student studies very hard.

(四) 副词 adv.

used for emphasis: 你要是嫁给我该有多好啊！How nice it would be if you were to marry me.

词语 Words and Phrases

该当	gāidāng	should; deserve
该死	gāisǐ	damn; damn it all
应该	yīnggāi	should; ought to

改 gǎi   ⊐ ⊐ 卫 卫 卫 改 改

释义 Meaning

动词 v.

1. change; transform: 这家公司刚改了名字。The company has just changed its name.

2. correct; rectify; put right: 老师正在改我们的家庭作业。 The teacher is correcting our homework.

词语 Words and Phrases

改编	gǎibiān	① rewrite; adapt reorganize
改变	gǎibiàn	change; transform; alter
改道	gǎidào	change one's route (of a river) change its course
改掉	gǎidiào	give up
改动	gǎidòng	change; modify
改革	gǎigé	reform
改行	gǎiháng	change one's profession (trade, occupation, etc.)
改换	gǎihuàn	replace; change
改嫁	gǎijià	(of a woman) remarry
改进	gǎijìn	improve; make better
改良	gǎiliáng	improve; ameliorate reform

改期	gǎiqī	change the date
改善	gǎishàn	improve; ameliorate; make better
改写	gǎixiě	rewrite; revise
改选	gǎixuǎn	re-elect
改造	gǎizào	reform; transform; remould
改正	gǎizhèng	correct; amend; put right
改组	gǎizǔ	reorganize; reshuffle

熟语 Idioms

改过自新	gǎiguò zìxīn	start with a clean slate
改头换面	gǎi tóu huàn miàn	change the new appearance but not the substance
改邪归正	gǎi xié guī zhèng	give up evil and return to good

盖 gài   丶 丷 丷 兰 羊 羊 羊 盖 盖 盖 盖

释义 Meaning

（一）动词 v.

1. cover: 大雪覆盖了地面。Heavy snow covered the ground.

2. build: 新房盖好了。The new house has been built. 反义词antonym: 拆

3. overwhelm; top; surpass: 学生们的欢呼声盖过了老师的喊叫。The joyful sounds of students drowned their teacher's shouting.

（二）名词 n.

1. lid; cover: 我的水壶盖给弄丢了。The lid of my kettle has been lost.

2. shell (of a crab, tortoise, etc.): 每只螃蟹都有个硬盖。Every crab has a hard shell.

词语 Words and Phrases

盖浇饭	gàijiāofàn	rice served with meat and vegetables on top
盖世	gàishì	matchless; unparalleled; peerless
盖章	gàizhāng	seal; stamp; affix one's seal
盖子	gàizi	lid; cover; top; cap

熟语 Idioms

盖棺定论	gài guān dìng lùn	final judgment on a person when he is dead

干₁ gān 二 三 干

(乾 一 十 广 古 古 直 直 卓 卓 乾 乾)

释义 Meaning

（一）形容词 a.

1. dry; dried: 这木头很干。This wood is very dry. 反义词 antonym: 湿

2. empty: 水壶已经干了。The teapot is already empty. 反义词 antonym: 满

3. relatives not linked by blood: 她是我干女儿。She is my adopted daughter.

（二）副词 adv.

futilely; without result; (do sth.) for nothing: 早上我干等了你好久。This morning I wasted a lot of time waiting for you.

（三）名词 n.

relation; be concerned with: 此处与她何干？What's it to do with her?

词语 Words and Phrases

干巴巴	gābābā	insipid; wizened; dried-up; dull and dry
干杯	gānbēi	cheers; drink a toast
干草	gāncǎo	dry hay
干脆	gāncuì	simply; just; altogether straightforward
干旱	gānhàn	dry; arid
干涸	gānhé	dry up; run dry
干净	gānjìng	clean totally; completely
干枯	gānkū	dried-up; withered; wizened
干扰	gānrǎo	disturb; obstruct; interfere
干涉	gānshè	interfere; intervene; meddle; be related to
干燥	gānzào	dry; arid dull; uninteresting

熟语 Idioms

干打雷， 不下雨	gān dǎ léi, bú xià yǔ	only thunder but no rain; noisy but no action

干₂ gàn 二 三 干

（幹 一 十 十 古 古 古 直 卓 卓 乾 乾 乾 幹）

释义 Meaning

（一）动词 v.

do; work: 你让我干什么都行。I can do anything you want me to do.

（二）名词 n.

1. trunk; main part: 树干很高。The tree-trunk is very high.
2. official; cadre: 他爸爸是高干。His father is a senior official.

词语 Words and Phrases

干部	gànbù	official; cadre
干掉	gàndiào	kill; get rid of
干活	gànhuó	work; do one's job
干将	gànjiàng	go-getter; capable person
干劲	gànjìn	vigour; drive; enthusiasm
干吗	gànmá	why; whatever for what to do
干什么	gànshénme	why; what to do
干事	gànshi	secretary; clerical worker
干线	gànxiàn	artery; main line; trunk line
高干	gāogàn	senior official
骨干	gúgàn	backbone

赶 gǎn 一 十 土 キ キ キ 走 走 赶 赶 赶

(趕 一 十 土 キ キ キ 走 赶 赶 赶 趕
趕 趕 趕**)**

释义 Meaning

(一) 动词 v.

1. overtake; catch up with: 我们将尽力赶上世界先进水平。We'll do our best to catch up with the most advanced world standards.

2. take; catch; rush for; make a dash for: 我们必须赶头班车。We must catch the first bus.

3. hurry through; rush through: 他在赶任务呢。He is rushing through his job.

4. drive; expel; drive away: 男孩正在把山羊赶上山。The boy is driving the goats up the hill.

5. happen to; find oneself in (a situation): 我到他家时，正

赶上他去学校了。When I arrived at his home, he happened to be away at school.

（二）介词 prep.

till; until; up to (the time when): 赶母亲死后他才离开。He lived at home until his mother's death.

词语 Words and Phrases

赶紧	gǎnjǐn	hasten; lose no time
赶快	gǎnkuài	quickly; at once
赶路	gǎnlù	hurry on one's way
赶忙	gǎnmáng	hasten; hurry; rush
赶巧	gǎnqiǎo	happen to
追赶	zhuīgǎn	run after
赶时髦	gǎnshímáo	follow the fashion

熟语 Idioms

赶尽杀绝	gǎn jìn shā jué	be ruthless; spare none

敢 gǎn 一 一 亇 亇 亓 亓 亘 亘 敢 敢 敢

释义 Meaning

动词 v.

1. dare: 我从不敢问老师问题。I've never dared to ask questions of my teachers.

2. be certain; be sure; have the confidence to: 我不敢说他何时能来。I'm not sure when he will come.

词语 Words and Phrases

敢于	gǎnyú	dare to; have the courage to
果敢	guǒgǎn	courageous and resolute
勇敢	yǒnggǎn	brave; courageous

熟语 Idioms

敢怒	gǎn nù	choke with silent fury but
而不敢言	ér bù gǎn yán	dare not utter a word

刚 gāng 丨 冂 刀 冈 刚 刚

（**剛** 丨 冂 冂 冏 冏 冏 岡 岡 剛 剛）

释义 Meaning

（一）形容词 a.

hard; firm; strong: 他的性子刚得很。He has a strong will.

反义词 antonym: 柔

（二）副词 adv.

1. just; exactly: 这件衣服我穿着刚好。This coat is just the right size for me.

2. barely; only just; no more than: 我女儿上小学时刚满6岁。When my daughter entered primary school, she was barely 6 years old.

3. just; only a short while ago: 我们刚下课。Our class has just ended.

4. just; only at this moment: 我刚要走他就来了。He came just when I was about to leave.

词语 Words and Phrases

刚才	gāngcái	just now; a while (moment) ago；
刚刚	gānggāng	just; exactly; only; just now; a while (moment) ago
刚好	gānghǎo	just; exactly; happen to
刚健	gāngjiàn	robust; forceful; bold; energetic
刚强	gāngqiáng	firm; unyielding; staunch
刚巧	gāngqiǎo	just; exactly; happen to
刚毅	gāngyì	resolute and steadfast

| 刚直 | gāngzhí | upright and outspoken |

熟语 Idioms

| 刚愎自用 | gāngbì zìyòng | self-willed; perversity |
| 刚正不阿 | gāngzhèng bù ē | upright; principled and never stooping to flattery |

钢 gāng ノ ／ ﾆ ﾆ 钅 钅 钅 钢 钢

(鋼 ノ ／ ﾆ ﾆ ﾆ 午 牟 金 金 鈤 釘 釕 釕 鋼 鋼 鋼 鋼)

释义 Meaning

名词 n.

steel: 钢铁厂在市郊。The steelworks factory is in the suburb of the city.

词语 Words and Phrases

钢笔	gāngbǐ	pen
钢材	gāngcái	steel products
钢管	gāngguǎn	steel tube
钢琴	gāngqín	piano
钢丝	gāngsī	steel wire
钢铁	gāngtiě	steel and iron
炼钢	liàn gāng	steelmaking
不锈钢	bùxiùgāng	stainless steel

高 gāo ﾞ ﾗ ﾗ ﾗ 亖 亖 宫 高 高 高

释义 Meaning

(一)形容词 a.

1. tall; high: 他比我高。He is taller than I. 反义词 antonym: 矮

2. of a high level or degree; above the average: 你的主意真
高！How brilliant your idea is!

（二）名词 n.

height: 这棵树有4米高。The tree is 4 metres in height.

词语 Words and Phrases

高矮	gāo'ǎi	height
高傲	gāo'ào	haughty; supercilious; arrogant
高产	gāochǎn	high productivity; high yield
高超	gāochāo	superb; excellent
高潮	gāocháo	high tide; high water; climax; orgasm
高大	gāodà	tall; tall and big; lofty
高档	gāodàng	high quality; top grade
高等	gāoděng	higher (education)
高低	gāodī	height; diference in
高度	gāodù	height; altitude highly; to a high degree
高尔夫球	gāo'ěrfūqiú	golf; golf ball
高峰	gāofēng	peak; height; summit
高贵	gāoguì	noble; high; elitist; highly privileged
高级	gāojí	senior; high-level; high-quality; high-grade
高空	gāo kōng	upper air; high altitude
高帽子	gāomàozi	tall paper hat; flattery
高明	gāomíng	wise; brilliant
高强	gāoqiáng	excel in; be master of; be skilled in
高尚	gāoshàng	lofty; noble
高速	gāosù	high speed
高温	gāowēn	high temperature
高兴	gāoxìng	happy; glad; cheerful; pleased
高血压	gāoxuèyā	hypertension; high blood pressure

高姿态　　gāo zītài　　loft stance; high handed

熟语 Idioms

高不可攀	gāo bù kě pān	too high (of one's social position) to reach
高高在上	gāo gāo zài shàng	stand high above the masses
高楼大厦	gāo lóu dà shà	high building and large mansion
高谈阔论	gāo tán kuò lùn	spout; harangue; empty talk
高瞻远瞩	gāo zhān yuǎn zhǔ	stand high and see far; show great foresight
高枕无忧	gāozhěn wú yōu	shake up the pillow and have a good sleep; rest easy; have no worries

搞 gǎo　 一 十 扌 扩 扩 扩 护 护 护 搞
　　　　搞 搞 搞

释义 Meaning

动词 v.

1. do; make; produce; work out: 他们搞了那么多菜。They made so many dishes.

2. arrange; organize; build; set up: 学生们搞了一个生日晚会。The students arranged a birthday party.

3. get; buy; get hold of: 请给我搞点儿喝的东西。Please get me something to drink.

词语 Words and Phrases

搞好	gǎohǎo	do well; make a good job
搞鬼	gǎoguǐ	play tricks; be up to some mischief
乱搞	luàngǎo	do carelessly; carry on an affair with sb.; be promiscuous

告 gào ノ 一 ヒ 生 生 告 告

释义 Meaning

动词 v.

1. tell; notify; inform: 何时抵沪，盼告。Please inform me of your arrival time at Shanghai.

2. request; ask for: 她从来也没告过假。She's never asked for leave.

3. declare; proclaim; announce: 此事暂告一段落。It's come to the end of a phase.

4. accuse; bring an action against: 他们告他犯了盗窃罪。They accused him of theft.

词语 Words and Phrases

告别	gàobié	leave; part from; say good-bye to;
告辞	gàocí	take leave of one's host
告发	gàofā	inform against sb. to the police
告急	gàojí	ask for emergency help; be in an emergency
告假	gàojià	ask for leave
告诫	gàojiè	warn; admonish
告密	gàomì	inform against sb.
告示	gàoshì	official notice
告诉	gàosù	tell; let know
报告	bàogào	report; make known; lecture; speech
控告	kònggào	accuse; charge; complain

熟语 Idioms

自告奋勇	zì gào fèn yǒng	come forward; volunteer to do sth.
大功告成	dà gōng gàochéng	success

哥 gē 一 厂 哥 哥 哥 哥 哥 哥 哥 哥

释义 Meaning

名词 n.

elder brother: 我哥是个汉语老师。My elder brother is a Chinese teacher.

词语 Words and Phrases

哥哥	gēge	elder brother
哥儿们	gērmen	brothers; pals; buddies

歌 gē 一 厂 哥 哥 哥 哥 哥 哥 哥 哥 哥 哥 歌 歌

释义 Meaning

（一）名词 n.

song: 这首歌非常优美动听。The song is very beautiful.

（二）动词 v.

sing: 她正在纵情高歌。She is singing loudly without constraint.

词语 Words and Phrases

歌唱	gēchàng	sing
歌词	gēcí	lyrics of a song
歌剧	gējù	opera
歌谱	gēpǔ	music of a song
歌曲	gēqū	song
歌手	gēshǒu	singer; vocalist
歌颂	gēsòng	extol; eulogize; sing the praises of
歌舞	gēwǔ	song and dance
歌谣	gēyáo	folk song; nursery rhyme
歌咏	gēyǒng	singing

熟语 Idioms

歌功颂德   gē gōng sòng dé   praise one's virtues and achievements

格 gé   二 十 才 木 术 杦 柊 柊 格 格

释义 Meaning

名词 n.

1. check; squares: 我喜欢那块方格的桌布。I like that check tablecloth.

2. division: 我的书架有很多格。My bookcase has many shelves.

3. style; standard; pattern: 这顶帽子真是别具一格。This cap has a style of its own.

词语 Words and Phrases

格调	gédiào	style
格局	géjú	pattern; structure; setup
格式	géshì	form; pattern
格外	géwài	especially; exceptionally
格言	géyán	motto; maxim
格子	gézi	check; squares formed by crossed lines
风格	fēnggé	style
人格	réngé	character; personality; moral quality

熟语 Idioms

格格不入   gé gé bú rù   against the grain; out of one's element

个 gè   丿 个 个

(個 丿 亻 仜 仴 個 個 個 個 個 個)

释义 Meaning
量词 measure w.

1. used before nouns which have no special measure words of their own: 我是两个星期前来的。I came here two weeks ago.
2. used between a verb and its object: 我必须要洗个澡。I have to take a bath.
3. used before a verb and its complement: 这孩子哭个不停。The baby cried on and on.

词语 Words and Phrases

个别	gèbié	individual; specific very few; one or two
个个	gègè	all; every one; each one
个儿	gèr	height; size; stature;
个人	gèrén	individual; I
个体	gètǐ	individual
个性	gèxìng	individuality; personality; individual character
个子	gèzi	height; size; stature;

各 gè ノ　ク　久　冬　各　各

释义 Meaning
代词 pron.

each; every; different; various: 她们的衣着各不相同。Their clothes have nothing in common with each other.

词语 Words and Phrases

各别	gèbié	different; distinct
各个	gègè	each; every
各级	gèjí	all levels; different levels
各界	gèjiè	all circles; all walks of life
各自	gèzì	each

熟语 Idioms

各奔前程	gè bèn qián chéng	everyone goes his own way
各持己见	gè chí jǐ jiàn	everyone sticks to his own view
各得其所	gè dé qí suǒ	everyone has a role to play
各取所需	gè qǔ suǒ xū	everyone takes what he needs
各抒己见	gè shū jǐ jiàn	everyone express his own view
各行其是	gè xíng qí shì	everyone does what he thinks is right
各有所长	gè yǒu suǒ cháng	everyone has his own strong points
各有所好	gè yǒu suǒ hǎo	everyone has his own hobby
各执一词	gè zhí yì cí	everyone sticks to his own version or argument
各自为政	gè zì wéi zhèng	everyone does things by himself
各人自扫门前雪，哪管他人瓦上霜。	gè rén zì sǎo mén qián xuě nǎ guǎn tā rén wǎ shàng shuāng	Every one sweeps the snow on his own doorstep and doesn't bother about the frost on other's rooftop; selfish

给 gěi ⟨笔顺⟩

(給 ⟨笔顺⟩ 給）

释义 Meaning

（一）动词 v.

1. give: 我把笔当作礼物给了他。I gave him a pen as a

present.

  2. let: 给我看看。Let me have a look.

（二）介词 prep.

  1. to; for: 我们给老师们唱了一首歌。We sang a song for our teachers.

  2. as a passive indicator: 我的T恤衫都给汗水浸透了。My T-shirt was soaked with sweat.

（三）助词 aux. w.

  used with 叫，让，or 把 for emphasis: 他把我的字典给拿走了。He took my dictionary away.

词语 Words and Phrases

给以   gěiyǐ   give

根 gēn 一 十 扌 才 木 杆 杆 杆 柜 柜 根

释义 Meaning

（一）名词 n.

  1. root; foot; base: 他在我们学校里没什么根。He has no roots in our university.

  2. cause; origin; source: 愚昧是贫穷之根。Ignorance is the root of poverty.

（二）副词 adv.

  completely; thoroughly: 我们必须根除一切形式的欺诈。We must eradicate all forms of cheating.

（三）量词 measure w.

  used of long and thin objects: 我带了一根小绳子。I've brought a piece of string with me.

词语 Words and Phrases

根本   gēnběn   basic; essential ; foundamental; simply; at all

根除	gēnchú	eradicate; root out; thoroughly do away with
根据	gēnjù	basis; foundation; according to; on the basis of
根绝	gēnjué	eradicate; exterminate; stamp out
根由	gēnyóu	reason; cause; origin
根源	gēnyuán	root; origin; source
根子	gēnzi	root; source; origin

熟语 Idioms

| 根深蒂固 | gēn shēn dì gù | rootedness; ingrained |

跟 gēn ｜ 冂 冂 뮤 뮤 뮤 뮤 딛 딛 딛 趵 跟 跟

释义 Meaning

（一）名词 n.

heel: 她的鞋跟很高。The heels of her shoes are very high.

（二）动词 v.

follow: 请跟我读。Please read after me.

（三）连词 conj.

and; with: 我跟她都买了一本汉语词典。Both she and I bought a Chinese dictionary.

（二）介词 prep.

to; towards: 跟我们说说你的女朋友。Tell us something about your girlfriend.

词语 Words and Phrases

跟前	gēnqián	near; in front of; close to
跟上	gēnshàng	catch up with; keep pace with
跟随	gēnsuí	follow
跟头	gēntou	somersault fall

| 跟踪 | gēnzōng | follow the tracks of |

更₁ gēng 一 厂 厂 戸 戸 更 更

释义 Meaning

动词 v.

change; alter; replace: 请您更衣。Change your clothes, please.

词语 Words and Phrases

更迭	gēngdié	change; alternate
更动	gēngdòng	alter; change
更改	gēnggǎi	change; alter
更换	gēnghuàn	replace; change
更替	gēngtì	replace
更新	gēngxīn	renew; replace
更正	gēngzhèng	correct
变更	biàngēng	alter; change; modify

熟语 Idioms

| 万象更新 | wàn xiàng gēng xīn | everything takes on a new look (referring to New Year) |
| 自力更生 | zì lì gēng shēng | self-dependence; self-reliance |

更₂ gèng 一 厂 厂 戸 戸 更 更

释义 Meaning

副词 adv.

even; further; more: 她比你女朋友更漂亮。She is even more beautiful than your girlfriend.

词语 Words and Phrases

| 更加 | gèngjiā | more; even; further; still more |

工 gōng 一 丁 工

释义 Meaning

（一）名词 n.

1. worker; the working class: 他父亲是位矿工。His father is a miner.

2. work; labour: 我们每天都要去上工。Everyday we have to go to work.

3. (contruction) project: 这项工程将于下周完工。This project will be completed next week.

4. industry: 化工是很重要的。The chemical industry is very important.

（二）形容词 a.

be versed in; be good at: 我们老师工于书画。Our teacher is well versed in painting and calligraphy.

词语 Words and Phrases

工厂	gōngchǎng	factory; plant; works
工程	gōngchéng	project; engineering
工地	gōngdì	building site
工夫	gōngfu	time; effort; work; skill; art
工会	gōnghuì	labour union; trade union
工具	gōngjù	tool; instrument
工科	gōngkē	engineering course
工农兵	gōngnóngbīng	workers, peasants and soldiers
工期	gōngqī	time limit for a project
工钱	gōngqián	salary; wages charge for a service
工人	gōngrén	worker
工商业	gōngshāngyè	industry and commerce
工业	gōngyè	industry
工艺	gōngyì	craft; technology

工整	gōngzhěng	careful and neat
工资	gōngzī	wages; salary
工作	gōngzuò	work; job
工作者	gōngzuòzhě	worker
竣工	jùngōng	complete a project

公 gōng ノ 八 公 公

释义 Meaning

（一）形容词 a.

1. public; collective; state-owned: 人人都应爱护公物。Everyone should take good care of public property. 反义词 antonym: 私

2. just; fair; impartial: 他们办事不公。They are unjust in handling public affairs.

3. male (animal): 今天早上我买了一只公鸡。I bought a cock this morning. 反义词 antonym: 母

（二）名词 n.

1. official business; public affair: 他因公外出了。He has been away on official business.

2. husband's father: 我妻子的公婆就是我的父母。My parents are my wife's parents-in-law.

（三）动词 v.

make public: 我们将把此事公之于众。We'll reveal it to the public.

词语 Words and Phrases

公安	gōng'ān	public security; police; policeman
公报	gōngbào	bulletin; communique
公布	gōngbù	announce; make public
公费	gōngfèi	public expense

公告	gōnggào	announce; announcement
公共	gōnggòng	public; common
公公	gōnggong	husband's father
公害	gōnghài	environmental pollution
公家	gōngjiā	the state; the public
公斤	gōngjīn	kilogram
公开	gōngkāi	open; public; make public
公款	gōngkuǎn	public fund
公里	gōnglǐ	kilometre
公理	gōnglǐ	axiom; universally accepted truth
公路	gōnglù	highway
公民	gōngmín	citizen
公平	gōngpíng	fair; just; equitable; impartial
公认	gōngrèn	generally recognized; universally acknowledged
公式	gōngshì	formula
公事	gōngshì	public affairs; official business
公司	gōngsī	firm; company; corporation
公益	gōngyì	public welfare
公用	gōngyòng	communal; for public use
公约	gōngyuē	pact; convention; joint pledge
公允	gōngyǔn	fair and proper
公正	gōngzhèng	fair; just; impartial
公众	gōngzhòng	the public
公主	gōngzhǔ	princess
老公	lǎogōng	husband
公证人	gōng zhèngrén	notary; notary public

狗 gǒu ⼁ ⺈ ⺉ ⺊ 狗 狗 狗 狗

释义 Meaning

名词 n.

dog: 一条狗正站在那儿。A dog is standing there.

词语 Words and Phrases

狗屁	gǒupì	rubbish; horseshit; nonsense
狗窝	gǒuwō	doghouse; kennel
狗熊	gǒuxióng	black bear; coward

熟语 Idioms

狗屎堆	gǒushǐduī	a heap of dog dung
狗腿子	gǒutuǐzi	henchman; "running dog"
狗胆包天	gǒu dǎn bāo tiān	monstrous audacity
狗急跳墙	gǒu jí tiào qiáng	a cornered beast will do everything desperate
狗仗人势	gǒu zhàng rén shì	be a bully under the protection of a powerful man
狗眼看人低	gǒu yǎn kàn rén dī	do everything like a snob
狗嘴里吐不出象牙	gǒu zuǐ lǐ tǔbùchū xiàng yá	"Don't look for ivory in a dog's mouth"; a filthy mouth can't utter decent language

古 gǔ　　二 十 古 古 古

释义 Meaning

形容词 a.

ancient; old: 我昨天买了一幅古画。I bought an ancient painting yesterday. 反义词antonym: 今

词语 Words and Phrases

古板	gǔbǎn	old-fasioned and inflexible
古代	gǔdài	ancient times
古典	gǔdiǎn	classical; classical allusion

古都	gǔdū	ancient capital
古怪	gǔguài	strange; eccentric; odd
古迹	gǔjì	historic site
古老	gǔlǎo	ancient; age-old
古朴	gǔpǔ	(of art, etc.) simple and unsophisticated
古人	gǔrén	the ancient people; the deceased
古书	gǔshū	ancient books
古文	gǔwén	ancient prose; classical-styled prose
古稀	gǔxī	seventy years of age

熟语 Idioms

古色古香	gǔ sè gǔ xiāng	classical decor
古往今来	gǔ wǎng jīn lái	of all ages; from ancient times to the present

鼓 gǔ   一 十 士 吉 吉 吉 壴 壴 壹 壴 壴 鼓 鼓

释义 Meaning

(一) 名词 n.

drum: 他在敲鼓呢。He is beating a drum.

(二) 动词 v.

1. rouse; instigate; pluck up: 他终于鼓起勇气，站了起来。He finally plucked up his courage and stood up.

2. bulge; swell: 她鼓着嘴，一句话也不说。She pouted and said nothing.

词语 Words and Phrases

鼓吹	gǔchuī	preach; play up; advocate
鼓动	gǔdòng	instigate; incite; agitate; arouse
鼓励	gǔlì	encourage; urge
鼓舞	gǔwǔ	inspire; hearten

鼓掌　　gǔzhǎng　　applaud; clap one's hands

熟语 Idioms

鼓足干劲　　gǔ zú gàn jìn　　go all out

一鼓作气　　yì gǔ zuò qì　　at one fling

顾 gù 　 一 厂 厂 后 厄 厄 厢 顾 顾 顾

（顧 　 丶 ヽ ゛ 户 户 疒 疒 疒 雇 雇 雇

雇 雇 雇 雇 顧 顧 顧 顧 顧 顧）

释义 Meaning

动词 v.

1. turn round and look at: 他环顾了一下四周，但什么也没看见。He looked around but saw nothing.

2. attend to; give consideration to: 我们要顾大局。We must take the whole situation into consideration.

词语 Words and Phrases

顾忌	gùjì	scruple; misgivings
顾客	gùkè	customer; client
顾虑	gùlǜ	misgivings; worry; apprehension
顾盼	gùpàn	look around
顾全	gùquán	show consideration for
顾问	gùwèn	adviser; consultant
回顾	huígù	review; look back
照顾	zhàogù	look after; attend to; give consideration to

熟语 Idioms

顾此失彼	gù cǐ shī bǐ	attend to one thing and lose another
顾名思义	gù míng sī yì	just as its name implies
顾影自怜	gù yǐng zì lián	lament one's own lonelin-

ess; admire oneself

顾前不顾后　　gù qián bú gù hòu　drive ahead without considering the consequences

瓜 guā　　一　厂　瓜　瓜　瓜

释义 Meaning

名词 n.

melon; gourd: 瓜儿离不开秧。The melon clings to the stem.

词语 Words and Phrases

瓜分	guāfēn	partition; carve up
瓜葛	guāgé	connection; involvement
瓜子	guāzǐ	melon seeds
冬瓜	dōngguā	white gourd; winter melon
黄瓜	huángguā	cucumber
南瓜	nánguā	pumpkin
西瓜	xīguā	watermelon

熟语 Idioms

瓜熟蒂落　　guā shú dì luò　things will be easily settled in due course

挂 guà　　一　十　扌　扩　扩　挂　挂　挂

释义 Meaning

（一）动词 v.

1. hang; put up: 墙上挂着一幅画儿。A painting is hanging on the wall.

2. hitch; get caught: 他的夹克让钉子给挂住了。His jacket got caught on a nail.

3. call; ring up: 我明天给你挂电话。I'll call you tomorrow.

4. hang up: 她把电话给挂了。She has hung up (the phone).

5. register (at a hospital): 我要挂外科。I want to register for surgery.

（二）量词 measure w.

(for things in strings): 我刚买了几挂鞭炮。I've just bought a few strings of firecrackers.

词语 Words and Phrases

挂彩	guàcǎi	be decorate for festive occasions
挂钩	guàgōu	link up with; contact with; get in touch with
挂号	guàhào	register
挂名	guàmíng	nominal; only in name
挂念	guàniàn	miss; worry about
挂失	guàshī	report the loss of sth.
挂钟	guàzhōng	wall clock

熟语 Idioms

挂一漏万	guà yī lòu wàn	the work is far from complete
挂羊头卖狗肉	guà yángtóu mài gǒuròu	hang up a sheep's head but selling dog's meat; try to palm off sth. inferior to what it purports to be

拐 guǎi 一 十 扌 扩 护 护 拐 拐

释义 Meaning

（一）动词 v.

1. turn: 一直往前走，然后向右拐。Go ahead and turn to the right.

2. limp: 他一拐一拐地走着。He is walking with a limp.

3. swindle; abduct; make off with: 他拐走了朋友的不少钱。He's swindled some money out of his friends.

（二）名词 n.

crutch; walking stick: 他拄着拐走路。He walked with a crutch.

词语 Words and Phrases

拐棍	guǎigùn	crutch; walking stick
拐角	guǎijiǎo	turning; corner
拐骗	guǎipiàn	swindle; abduct
拐弯	guǎiwān	turn; turn a corner; turn round; pursue a new course
拐杖	guǎizhàng	crutch; walking stick
拐子	guǎizi	cripple; abductor; swindler

熟语 Idioms

| 拐弯抹角 | guǎi wān mò jiǎo | ambages; talk in a round-about way |

怪 guài ′ 丶 忄 忊 忆 怿 怪 怪

释义 Meaning

（一）形容词 a.

strange; unusual; queer: 我听到一个很怪的声音。I heard a strange noise.

（二）名词 n.

demon; monster; ghost; goblin: 恶怪会在夜晚出现。The goblins will appear at night.

（三）动词 v.

blame: 失败时她常怪父母。She often blames her parents for her failure.

（四）副词 adv.

quite; rather; very: 你女儿怪可爱的。Your daughter is quite lovely.

词语 Words and Phrases

怪不得	guàibùdé	no wonder; so that's why; not to blame
怪话	guàihuà	complaint; grumble; cynical remark
怪物	guàiwù	demon; monster; an eccentric person
怪异	guàiyì	unusual; strange
怪罪	guàizuì	blame
奇怪	qíguài	strange; surprising
责怪	zéguài	blame

熟语 Idioms

怪模怪样　　guài mó guài yàng　bizarre; grotesque

关 guān 　`　ⸯ　兰　兰　关　关

（關　｜　厂　阝　阝　阝　門　門　門　門　門　門
門　閗　閗　閗　關　關　關　關）

释义 Meaning

（一）动词 v.

1. close; shut: 请把门关上。Close the door, please. 反义词 antonym: 开

2. turn off: 请关上灯。Please turn off the light. 反义词 antonym: 开

3. close down: 我把店给关了。I closed my shop. 反义词 antonym: 开

4. shut in; lock up: 他给关进监狱了。He was locked up in the prison. 反义词 antonym: 放

5. concern; affect; involve: 这不关我的事。It doesn't concern me.

（二）名词 n.

pass; check; barrier: 我过关了。I passed (the checkpoint).

词语 Words and Phrases

关闭	guānbì	close; shut close down; shut down
关怀	guānhuái	be concerned about; show loving care for
关键	guānjiàn	key; hinge; crux
关口	guānkǒu	juncture strategic pass
关联	guānlián	be related; be connected
关门	guānmén	close; shut refuse to accept different views
关切	guānqiè	be deeply concerned
关税	guānshuì	customs duty
关系	guānxì	relation ties; connection bearing concern; involve
关心	guānxīn	care for; be concerned with; pay attention to
关于	guānyú	about; on; concerning; with regard to
关照	guānzhào	look after; care for tell (sb. to do sth.)
关注	guānzhù	pay attention to; be interested in
海关	hǎiguān	customs; customhouse
难关	nánguān	difficulty; crisis

熟语 Idioms

关起门来 打狗	guān qǐ mén lái dǎ gǒu	close the door and beat the dog; block the enemy's retreat and destroy them

观 guān 　丿　又　刅　刅冂　观　观

（觀　一　十　艹　芒　芦　芦　芒　芒　芌　苩
　萨　萨　萨　萑　萑　萑　雚　雚　雚　雚　雚
　觀　觀）

释义 Meaning

（一）名词 n.

1. sight; view: 三峡是世界上的一道奇观。The Three Gorges is one of the rare wonders of the world.

2. idea; viewpoint; outlook; concept: 他的人生观很狭隘。He is a man with a narrow outlook in life.

（二）动词 v.

see; watch; observe; look at: 明天我要去海边观日出。I'll go to the seaside to watch the sunrise tomorrow.

词语 Words and Phrases

观测	guāncè	observe and survey
观察	guānchá	observe; watch; examine
观点	guāndiǎn	viewpoint; standpoint; point of view
观光	guānguāng	visit; tour; sightseeing
观看	guānkàn	watch; look at
观念	guānniàn	idea; concept
观赏	guānshǎng	view and admire; watch and enjoy; enjoy the sight of
观望	guānwàng	wait-and-see; look around
观众	guānzhòng	audience; viewer; spectator
悲观	bēiguān	pessimistic
可观	kěguān	considerable; sizable; impressive
客观	kèguān	objective
乐观	lèguān	optimistic; hopeful
奇观	qíguān	wonder; wonderful sight; marvellous spectacle
世界观	shìjièguān	world outlook; world view; outlook on life
主观	zhǔguān	subjective
壮观	zhuàngguān	splendor; magnificent sight

馆 guǎn ⺊ ⺀ ⺈ ⺈ ⺈ 𫠠 𫠠 𫠠 𫠠 馆 馆

(館 ⺊ ⺀ ⺈ ⺈ ⺈ ⺈ 食 食 食 食 館 館 館 館 館 館)

释义 Meaning

名词 n.

house; hall; shop; a place for cultural activities: 我明天去大使馆。 Tomorrow I'll go to the Embassy.

词语 Words and Phrases

馆子	guǎnzi	restaurant
博物馆	bówùguǎn	museum
宾馆	bīnguǎn	questhouse; hotel
茶馆	cháguǎn	teahouse
饭馆	fànguǎn	restaurant
酒馆	jiǔguǎn	wineshop; restaurant; public house
旅馆	lǚguǎn	hotel; inn
美术馆	měishùguǎn	art gallery
体育馆	tǐyùguǎn	gymnasium
图书馆	túshūguǎn	library
文化馆	wénhuàguǎn	cultural centre
展览馆	zhǎnlǎnguǎn	exhibition hall

管 guǎn ⺊ ⺀ ⺈ ⺈ ⺈ ⺈ ⺈ 竺 竺 管 管 管 管 管

释义 Meaning

(一)名词 n.

tube; pipe: 煤气管爆裂了。 The gas-pipes burst.

（二）量词 measure w.

(used of tube-shaped things): 我刚买了一管牙膏。I've just bought a tube of toothpaste.

（三）介词 prep.

(in conjunction with): 我们管她叫小猫。We call her "Little Kitten".

（四）动词 v.

1. run; manage; be in charge of; be responsible for: 我妈妈管伙食。My mother is in charge of the meals.

2. control; care for: 谁来管这个孩子？Who will care of this baby?

3. mind; bother about; attend to: 别管我！Don't bother about me!

4. provide: 我会管你住的。I'll provide accommodation for you.

词语 Words and Phrases

管保	guǎnbǎo	assure; guarantee; certainly; surely
管教	guǎnjiào	subject sb. to discipline; take sb. in hand
管理	guǎnlǐ	manage; run; administer
管事	guǎnshì	effective; of use; be in charge of
管束	guǎnshù	control; restrain
管制	guǎnzhì	control; under surveillance
管子	guǎnzi	tube; pipe

光 guāng `丶 丷 止 止 光 光`

释义 Meaning

（一）名词 n.

1. light; ray: 月光朦胧。The moonlight is dim.

2. brightness; lustre: 她的耳环闪闪发光。Her ear-rings have
   a fine lustre.

3. glory; honour: 他在奥运会上为国争了光。He won an
   honour for his country in the Olympic Games.

（二）形容词 a.

1. glossy; smooth; polished: 冰块又光又滑。The piece of
   ice is smooth and shiny.

2. naked; bare: 我们房后有一棵光树。There is a bare tree
   behind our house.

3. nothing left; used up: 钱都用光了。The money's used
   up.

（三）副词 adv.

only; alone; merely; solely: 光有好主意是不够的。It's not
enough to have good ideas alone.

词语 Words and Phrases

光彩	guāngcǎi	lustre; brilliance; splendour; glorious; honourable
光顾	guānggù	welcome to our store, shop, etc.
光棍	guānggùn	ruffian; unmarried man
光滑	guānghuá	smooth; glossy
光辉	guānghuī	glory; brilliance; glorious; brilliant
光景	guāngjǐng	scene; conditions; around; about
光亮	guāngliàng	shiny; bright
光临	guānglín	presence
光溜溜	guāngliūliū	smooth; slippery; naked; bare
光明	guāngmíng	light; bright; promising; open-hearted
光荣	guāngróng	glory; honour; credit; glorious
光头	guāngtóu	bareheaded;
光秃秃	guāngtūtū	naked; bare

光线	guāngxiàn	ray; light
光阴	guāngyīn	time
光泽	guāngzé	gloss; lustre; sheen

熟语 Idioms

| 光明磊落 | guāng míng lěi luò | aboveboard; open and frank |

广 guǎng ` ﾠ广

(廣 ` ﾠ广 广 广 广 广 庐 庐 廣 庐 廣 廣)

释义 Meaning

（一）形容词 a.

broad; wide; extensive; numerous: 这是我第一次在大庭广众面前演讲。It's the first time for me to make a speech in the public. 反义词antonym: 狭；窄

（二）动词 v.

spread; broaden; expand: 她为广流传而把故事告诉了每一个人。She told her story to everybody so that it may spread far and wide.

词语 Words and Phrases

广播	guǎngbō	broadcast
广博	guǎngbó	(of knowledge) extensive; wide
广场	guǎngchǎng	(public) square
广大	guǎngdà	wide; vast; widespread
广度	guǎngdù	scope; range
广泛	guǎngfàn	extensive; widespread; wide-ranging
广告	guǎnggào	advertisment
广寒宫	guǎnghángōng	the Moon Palace

| 广阔 | guǎngkuò | wide; broad; vast |
| 推广 | tuīguǎng | popularize |

熟语 Idioms

| 广开言路 | guǎng kāi yán lù | encourage the airing of views |

鬼 guǐ ＇ 「 宀 宀 甶 甶 尹 鬼 鬼 鬼

释义 Meaning

（一）名词 n.

1. ghost; devil; spirit: 他不信鬼。He does not believe in ghosts.

2. (address of a person with evil habit): 你是个胆小鬼。You are a coward.

3. dirty trick; sinister plot: 我想你心里一定有鬼。I think you must have a quilty conscience.

（二）形容词 a.

1. clever; quick; smart: 你真鬼！How clever you are! 反义词antonym: 笨

2. damnable: 这鬼地方！What a damnable place!

词语 Words and Phrases

鬼把戏	guǐbǎxì	sinister plot; underhand trick
鬼怪	guǐguài	ghosts and monsters; monsters of all kinds
鬼话	guǐhuà	lie; damned lie
鬼魂	guǐhún	spirit; ghost; apparition
鬼混	guǐhùn	lead an aimless or irregular existence
鬼神	guǐshén	ghosts and gods
酒鬼	jiǔ guǐ	drunkard; alcoholic
胆小鬼	dǎnxiǎoguǐ	coward
懒鬼	lǎnguǐ	lazy bone

做鬼脸　　zuòguǐliǎn　　make faces; make grimaces

熟语 Idioms

鬼鬼祟祟　　guǐguǐ suìsuì　　stealthy; furtive
心怀鬼胎　　xīn huái guǐtāi　　have evil intentions

贵 guì

一 丨 口 曰 虫 虫 串 带 贵 贵

(貴

一 丨 口 曰 虫 虫 串 串 贵 貴 貴 貴 貴)

释义 Meaning

形容词 a.

1. expensive; costly: 这顶帽子不贵。The cap is not expensive. 反义词 antonym: 贱

2. valuable; precious; highly valued: 人贵有自知之明。Self-knowledge is wisdom.

3. your: 请问您贵姓？May I ask your family name?

4. noble; honoured; of high rank: 您是我们的贵客。You are our guest of honour.

词语 Words and Phrases

贵宾　　guìbīn　　guest of honour; distinguished guest
贵重　　guìzhòng　　valuable; precious
贵族　　guìzú　　noble; aristocracy
宝贵　　bǎoguì　　precious; value; treasure

滚 gǔn

丶 丶 氵 沪 沪 广 汻 汻 涿 滂 滂 滂 滚

释义 Meaning

动词 v.

1. roll: 历史的车轮滚滚不息。The wheel of history rolls on.

2. get away: 你给我滚出去！Get out!

3. boil: 水滚了。The water is boilling.

词语 Words and Phrases

滚动	gǔndòng	roll; trundle
滚圆	gǔnyuán	round as a ball
圆滚滚	yuángǔngǔn	round as a ball

熟语 Idioms

| 滚瓜烂熟 | gǔn guā làn shú | (read, recite, etc.) fluently; well-rehearsed; well-cooked |

国 guó 丨 冂 冂 冃 冐 国 国 国

(國 丨 冂 冂 冃 冋 冋 冋 國 國 國 國)

释义 Meaning

(一) 名词 n.

country; nation; state: 我要回国去了。I have to return to my own country.

(二) 形容词 a.

national; Chinese; of the state: 我非常喜欢国画。I like traditional Chinese paintings very much.

词语 Words and Phrases

国产	guóchǎn	made in China; made in one's own country
国防	guófáng	national defence
国歌	guógē	national anthem
国会	guóhuì	parliament; Congress
国籍	guójí	nationality
国际	guójì	international
国家	guójiā	country; nation; state

国民	guómín	national
国旗	guóqí	national flag
国情	guóqíng	national conditions
国庆	guóqìng	National Day
国事	guóshì	state affairs
国王	guówáng	king
国债	guózhài	national debt
国务院	guówùyuàn	the State Council; the State Department
中国	zhōngguó	China

果 guǒ 丨 冂 冃 日 旦 里 果 果

释义 Meaning

（一）名词 n.

1. fruit: 各种水果我都很喜欢。I like all kinds of fruits.

2. result; consequence: 种好因必得好果。Sow that you can reap. 反义词 antonym: 因

（二）副词 adv.

really; sure enough; as expected: 事情果不出我们所料。The result is just as we expected.

词语 Words and Phrases

果断	guǒduàn	resolute; decisive
果敢	guǒgǎn	resolute and courageous
果酱	guǒjiàng	jam
果然	guǒrán	really; sure enough; as expected
果实	guǒshí	fruit; gains
果树	guǒshù	fruit tree
果园	guǒyuán	orchard
果真	guǒzhēn	really; truly; if indeed; if really
果汁	guǒzhī	fruit juice
结果	jiéguǒ	result; outcom; finish off

如果	rúguǒ	if
水果	shuǐguǒ	fruit
效果	xiàoguǒ	effect; result

熟语 Idioms

自食其果　　zì shí qí guǒ　　　　reap as one has sown

过 guò 　一 十 寸 寸 讨 过

(過 ⎺ ⎕ ⎕ 尸 凸 呙 咼 咼 渦 渦 過)

释义 Meaning

（一）动词 v.

1. cross; pass: 一匹马正在过河。A horse is crossing the river.

2. spend (time; life): 周末过得怎么样？How did you spend your weekend?

3. go through; go over: 我们把课文再过一遍。Let's go over the text once again.

4. exceed; go beyond: 冬天这儿雪深过膝。The snow will be more than knee-deep here in winter.

（二）名词 n.

fault; error; mistake: 你应该勇于改过。You should be bold in correcting your mistakes. 反义词antonym: 功

（三）副词 adv.

excessively; unduly; too: 她过早地恋爱了。She fell in love too early.

（四）助词 aux. w.

indicating completion of an action as an experience: 我看过这本小说。I've read this novel.

词语 Words and Phrases

过不去　　guòbúqù　　cannot get through; find fault with; be

		hard on; feel sorry
过程	guòchéng	process; course
过错	guòcuò	fault; error; mistake
过得去	guòdequ	can get through; passable; so-so; not too bad
过度	guòdù	excessively; unduly; too
过渡	guòdù	transition
过分	guòfèn	excessively; unduly; over
过关	guòguān	pass a barrier; pass a test; reach a standard; be approved
过后	guòhòu	later; afterwards
过火	guòhuǒ	overdo; carry things too far
过奖	guòjiǎng	overpraise
过节	guòjié	celebrate a festival
过来	guòlái	come over; come up
过目	guòmù	look over (for check or approval)
过年	guònián	spend the new year
过期	guòqī	expire; be overdue
过去	guòqù	past; former; previous
过去	guòqu	go over; pass by
过人	guòrén	surpass; excel
过剩	guòshèng	excess; surplus
过失	guòshī	fault; error; slip
过时	guòshí	out-of-date; out-of-fashion
过头	guòtóu	overdo; go beyond the limit
过问	guòwèn	concern oneself with; take an interest in
过夜	guòyè	spend the night; stay overnight
过于	guòyú	too; excessively; unduly

熟语 Idioms

| 过日子 | guò rìzi | to live |

过河拆桥	guò hé chāi qiáo	pull down the bridge after crossing the river; burn your bridges
过意不去	guò yì bú qù	be sorry; feel apologetic

还₁ hái 一 丁 不 不 还 还

(還 ' 丨 冂 冂 罒 罒 罒 严 罪 罪 罘 罘 罘 罘 罘 還 還 還)

释义 Meaning

副词 adv.

1. still; yet: 老师还没来。The teacher is not here yet.

2. also; too; as well: 我们去了北京，还去了上海。We went to Shanghai as well as Beijing.

3. even more; still more: 你做的比老师做的还好。What you did is even better than what our teacher did.

4. rather; fairly; passably: 我觉得还可以。I feel just so-so.

词语 Words and Phrases

还好	háihǎo	① so-so; passable; not bad ② fortunately
还是	háishì	① or ② still; nevertheless; all the same ③ had better

还₂ huán 一 丁 不 不 还 还

(還 ' 丨 冂 冂 罒 罒 罒 严 罪 罪 罘 罘 罘 罘 還 還)

释义 Meaning

动词 v.

1. come back; go back: 还家的路是那么漫长。Going back home is a long distance. 反义词 antonym: 离

2. return; repay; give back: 请把钥匙还给我。Give the key back to me, please. 反义词antonym: 借

词语 Words and Phrases

还本	huánběn	repayment of principal (or capital)
还击	huánjī	fight back; return fire
还价	huánjià	bargain; counter-offer; counter-bid
还手	huánshǒu	hit back; strike back
还原	huányuán	restore; return to the original shape or condition
还债	huánzhài	repay a debt; pay one's debt
偿还	chánghuán	pay back
归还	guīhuán	return; give back

孩hái 乛 了 孑 孑 孑 孩 孩 孩 孩

释义 Meaning

名词 n.

child: 一对夫妻一个小孩。One couple, and one child.

词语 Words and Phrases

孩童	háitóng	child
孩子	háizi	child
孩子气	háiziqì	childish; childishness
男孩	nánhái	boy
女孩	nǚhái	girl
小孩	xiǎohái	child

海hǎi 丶 丶 氵 汁 汇 汇 海 海 海 海

释义 Meaning

（一）名词 n.

1. sea or big lake: 海比洋小。A sea is smaller than an ocean.

2. many people or things coming together: 那儿真是人山人海。There are huge crowds of people.

(二) 形容词 a.

extra large; of great capacity: 他吃了一大碗饭。He had a very big bowl of rice. 反义词 antonym: 小

词语 Words and Phrases

海岸	hǎi'àn	coast; seacoast; seashore
海拔	hǎibá	height above sea level
海报	hǎibào	poster; playbill
海滨	hǎibīn	seaside; seashore
海底	hǎidǐ	seabed; sea floor; the bottom of the sea
海港	hǎigǎng	harbour; seaport
海关	hǎiguān	customs; customs house
海军	hǎijūn	navy
海内	hǎinèi	thoughout the country (China); within the seas
海外	hǎiwài	overseas; abroad; outside China
海峡	hǎixiá	strait; channel
海洋	hǎiyáng	ocean; seas and oceans
海员	hǎiyuán	sailor; seaman

熟语 Idioms

海枯石烂	hǎi kū shí làn	the seas dry and the rocks crumble; a long time
海阔天空	hǎi kuò tiān kōng	as boundless as sky and sea; a vast area
海誓山盟	hǎi shì shān méng	vow eternal love; swear an oath of eternal fidelity

害 hài ` ゛ 宀 宀 宀 宔 丰 害 害

释义 Meaning

（一）名词 n.

evil; harm; calamity: 此事害多利少。This does more harm than good. 反义词 antonym: 益；利

（二）形容词 a.

harmful; injurious; destructive: 这是一只害鸟。It's a harmfull bird. 反义词 antonym: 益

（三）动词 v.

1. kill; murder: 他是在办公室里被害的。He was murdered in his office.

2. impair; do harm to; cause trouble to: 吸烟真是害人。Smoking does people great harm.

3. suffer from: 他妈妈去年害了一场大病。His mother had a serious attack of illness last year.

4. feel (afraid, ashamed, etc.): 她从不害羞。She's never shy.

词语 Words and Phrases

害处	hàichù	harm
害怕	hàipà	fear; be afraid
害羞	hàixiū	be shy; be bashful
利害	lìhài	gains and losses
伤害	shānghài	hurt; harm; injure
损害	sǔnhài	damage; harm; injure
危害	wēihài	endanger; harm; jeopardize

熟语 Idioms

害群之马　　hài qún zhī mǎ　　a black sheep

喊 hǎn　丨　丨丨　丨丨　丨丆　叮　叮　叮　咸　咸　喊　喊　喊

释义 Meaning

动词 v.

1. shout; yell; cry out: 他们正在喊口号。They are shouting slogans.

2. call (a person): 别忘了喊我一声。Don't forget to give me a yell.

词语 Words and Phrases

喊话	hǎnhuà	① communicate by tele-equipment; ② propaganda directed to the enemy at the front line
喊叫	hǎnjiào	shout; cry out
呼喊	hūhǎn	shout; call out
叫喊	jiàohǎn	yell; shout; howl

熟语 Idioms

| 大喊大叫 | dà hǎn dà jiào | howl; yell; shout |
| 贼喊捉贼 | zéi hǎn zhuō zéi | a thief shouting 'Stop thief!' |

汉 hàn `  ` 氵 汊 汉

(漢 `  ` 氵 汇 汇 浐 浐 浐 滹 滹 漌 漌 漢 漢)

释义 Meaning

名词 n.

1. the Han Dynasty (206 B.C–220 A.D): 汉是中国历史上最繁荣的朝代之一。The Han Dynasty is one of most prosperous dynasties in Chinese history.

2. the Han nationality: 汉族是中国最大的民族。The Han is the main nationality in China.

3. Chinese language: 我刚买了一本汉英词典。I've just bought a Chinese-English dictionary.

4. man: 我认识这个老汉。I know this old man.

词语 Words and Phrases

汉学	hànxué	Sinology
汉语	hànyǔ	Chinese language
汉字	hànzì	Chinese character
汉子	hànzi	① man; fellow ② husband
汉族	hànzú	the Han nationality
好汉	hǎohàn	hero; true man

好₁ hǎo ㄑ ㄐ ㄐ ㄐˊ ㄐ 好

释义 Meaning

（一）形容词 a.

1. good; nice; fine: 多好的姑娘啊！What a nice girl! 反义词antonym: 坏；差

2. kind; friendly: 你对我真是太好了！It's very kind of you to help me. 反义词antonym: 凶

3. (be) in good health; (get) well: 现在他的病好了。He's well now.

4. to indicate the completion of an action (used after a verb): 我们准备好了。We are ready now.

（二）副词 adv.

1. easy (to do); convenient: 此事不太好做。This is not easy to do. 反义词antonym: 难

2. very; quite; so: 你今天好漂亮！How beautiful you are today!

3. so that; so as to: 说得清楚点儿好让我弄懂你的意思。Speak clearly so that I can catch your meaning.

词语 Words and Phrases

好比	hǎobǐ	like; can be compared to

好不	hǎobù	very; quite; so
好不容易	hǎo bù róng yì	not easy (to do); with great difficulty
好吃	hǎochī	delicious; nice
好处	hǎochù	① benefit; advantage ② profit; gain
好感	hǎogǎn	good impression; good opinion
好过	hǎoguò	① be in good circumstances ② feel well
好好儿	hǎohāor	① all out; to one's heart's content ② in good condition
好话	hǎohuà	good word; word of praise
好看	hǎokàn	① good looking; beautiful ② interesting
好日子	hǎorìzi	① good days; happy life ② wedding day
好容易	hǎoróngyì	not easy (to do); with great difficulty
好事	hǎoshì	① good turn ② good works
好受	hǎoshòu	feel better
好似	hǎosì	like; seem
好听	hǎotīng	pleasant to hear
好玩儿	hǎowánr	interesting; amusing
好象	hǎoxiàng	like; seem
好笑	hǎoxiào	funny; ridiculous
好心	hǎoxīn	good intention
好意思	hǎoyìsi	have the nerve; have the cheek

熟语 Idioms

| 好好先生 | hǎohǎo-xiān sheng | one who tries not to offend anyone |

| 好事多磨 | hǎoshì duō mó | the road to happiness is full of hardships |

好₂ hào ㄑ ㄠ ㄠ ㄠˊ 奵 好

释义 Meaning

动词 v.

1. love; like; be fond of; be eager to: 他真是虚心好学。He is modest and eager to learn. 反义词 antonym: 恶

2. be liable to: 他妈妈好晕船。His mother is liable to seasickness.

词语 Words and Phrases

好客	hàokè	be hospitable
好奇	hàoqí	be curious
好强	hàoqiáng	eager to do well in everything
好胜	hàoshèng	eager to compete
好事	hàoshì	officious; meddlesome
好战	hàozhàn	warlike; bellicose

熟语 Idioms

好吃懒做	hào chī lǎn zuò	be fond of eating but averse to work
好大喜功	hào dà xǐ gōng	crave for greatness and success
好高骛远	hào gāo wù yuǎn	aim too high
好逸恶劳	hào yì è láo	indolence; love comfort and easy but hate hard work

号 hào 丨 口 口 므 号

(號 丨 口 口 므 号 号 虓 虓 號 號 號 號 號)

释义 Meaning

名词 n.

1. name; assumed name; alternative name: 我有个外号。I have a nickname.

2. mark; sign; signal: "？"是问号。"？" is a question mark.

3. size; number: 我住在8号楼。I live in Building No. 8.

4. order: 老师们总是发号施令。The teachers always issue orders.

5. date: 今天几号？What date is it today?

6. instruments such as bugle, trumpet, etc.: 他是位号手。He is a bugler.

7. anything used as a horn: 我妹妹很喜欢螺号。My sister likes conch-shell trumpet.

8. business house: 这是我们公司的一间分号。This is one branch of our firm.

（二）量词 measure w.

used in the number of people: 我们村有一万多号人。There are over ten thousands people in my village.

词语 Words and Phrases

号角	hàojiǎo	① horn; bugle ② bugle call
号令	hàolìng	order
号码	hàomǎ	number
号外	hàowài	extra (of a newspaper)
号召	hàozhào	call; appeal
记号	jìhào	mark; signal; sign
口号	kǒuhào	slogan; watchword

喝₁ hē 丨 刂 刂 刂ˊ 刂ㄱ 刂ㄇ 刂日 呾 呫 喝 喝 喝

释义 Meaning

动词 v.

drink; drink alcoholic liquor: 他喝多了。He was drunk.

词语 Words and Phrases

喝酒 　hējiǔ　　drink alcoholic liquor

熟语 Idioms

喝西北风　hē xīběifēng　　to drink the northwest wind; have nothing to eat

喝₂ hè 丨 刂 刂 刂ˊ 刂ㄱ 刂ㄇ 刂日 呾 呫 喝 喝 喝

释义 Meaning

动词 v.

yell; shout loudly: 他突然大喝一声。He gave a loud shout suddenly.

词语 Words and Phrases

喝彩	hècǎi	cheer; acclaim
喝令	hèlìng	shout an order
喝问	hèwèn	shout a question
喝倒彩	hè dào cǎi	hoot; boo; make catcalls

合 hé 丿 人 스 全 合 合

释义 Meaning

（一）动词 v.

1. close; shut: 请把书合起来。Close your books, please.

反义词antonym: 开

2. suit; agree: 你的话正合我意。Your words suit me fine. 反义词antonym: 违

3. combine; join: 我们必须合力而为。We must make a joint effort to do that. 反义词antonym: 分

4. add up to; be equal to: 一公里合三千尺。One Km is equal to 3000 *chi* .

（二）形容词 a.

whole: 合家团聚是我们的期望。The reunion of the whole family is our expectation.

词语 Words and Phrases

合并	hébìng	combine; merge
合唱	héchàng	chorus
合成	héchéng	① compose; compound ② synthesize
合法	héfǎ	legal; lawful; rightful
合格	hégé	qualified; up to standard
合伙	héhuǒ	form a partnership
合理	hélǐ	reasonable; rational; equitable
合力	hélì	make a joint effort; combined strength
合拍	hépāi	in step; in time; in harmony
合身	héshēn	fit
合适	héshì	suitable; right; appropriate
合同	hétóng	contract
合影	héyǐng	group picture
合作	hézuò	cooperate; work together
符合	fúhé	in accord with; conform to
会合	huìhé	meet; converge; assemble
适合	shìhé	suit; fit

熟语 Idioms

| 合二而一 | hé èr ér yī | two combine into one |

和 hé ⼀ ⼆ ⼲ ⽲ ⽲ 和 和 和

释义 Meaning

（一）名词 n.

1. peace: 他们讲和了。They have made peace. 反义词 antonym: 战

2. sum: 10是4与6之和。10 is the sum of 4 and 6.

（二）形容词 a.

1. gentle; kind; mild: 他们和风细雨般地互相批评。They criticize each other in a gentle manner.

2. harmonious; on good terms: 他们俩感情不和。They are on bad terms.

3. draw; tie: 这盘棋和了。The game of Chinese chess ended in a draw.

（三）副词 adv.

together with: 他常常和衣而卧。He often sleeps with his clothes on.

（四）介词 prep.

denoting relations, comparison, etc.: 他和女朋友一样高。He's the same height as his girlfriend.

（五）连词 conj.

and: 我和妻子都喜欢。Both my wife and I like it.

词语 Words and Phrases

和好	héhǎo	become reconciled
和缓	héhuǎn	① gentle; mild ② relax; ease up
和解	héjiě	become reconciled
和睦	hémù	harmony; amity; concord
和平	hépíng	① peace ② mild
和气	héqì	gentle; polite; kind
和善	héshàn	genial; gentle and kind

和尚	héshang	Buddhist monk
和谈	hétán	peace talks
和谐	héxié	harmonious
和约	héyuē	peace treaty
饱和	bǎohé	saturation
缓和	huǎnhé	relax; mitigate; ease up; calm down
温和	wēnhé	mild; temperate; gental

熟语 Idioms

和事老	héshìlǎo	peacemaker
和蔼可亲	héǎi kěqīn	affability; kindness; clemency
和盘托出	hé pán tuō chū	empty the bag; reveal everything
和颜悦色	hé yán yuè sè	with a kind and pleasant countenance
心平气和	xīn píng qì hé	at ease; calm and good-natured

盒 hé ノ 人 人 个 合 合 合 含 盒 盒 盒

释义 Meaning

（一）名词 n.

box; case: 我刚给女儿买了一个铅笔盒。I've just bought a pencil box for my daughter.

（二）量词 measure w.

a box of: 桌子上放着一盒火柴。There is a box of matches on the table.

词语 Words and Phrases

盒子	hézi	box; case

黑 hēi 丨 冂 冂 冂 回 甲 里 里 黒 黑 黑 黑

释义 Meaning

形容词 a.

1. black: 请看黑板。Please look at the blackboard. 反义词 antonym: 白

2. dark: 天要黑了。It's getting dark. 反义词 antonym: 亮；明

3. secret; clandestine; shady; wicked; sick: 他们在开黑会。They are having a clandestine meeting. 反义词 antonym: 明

词语 Words and Phrases

黑暗	hēiàn	dark
黑板	hēibǎn	blackboard
黑店	hēidiàn	shop, restaurant, etc. run by gangs
黑海	hēihǎi	the Black Sea
黑话	hēihuà	① (bandits') argot ② doubletalk
黑色	hēisè	black
黑市	hēishì	black market
黑心	hēixīn	black heart; evil mind

熟语 Idioms

黑洞洞	hēidòngdòng	pitch-dark
黑名单	hēimíngdān	blacklist
黑压压	hēiyāyā	a dark mass of
黑油油	hēiyóuyóu	shiny black
黑白分明	hēibáifēnmíng	with black and white; clear
黑灯瞎火	hēidēng-xiāhuǒ	unlighted; very dark

很 hěn ⺅ ⺅ 彳 彳 彳 彳 衧 很 很

释义 Meaning

副词 adv.

> very; quite: 你很聪明。You are very clever.

恨hèn ＇ ＇ 忄 忄 忄 忄 恨 恨 恨

释义 Meaning

（一）动词 v.

> hate: 我恨你。I hate you. 反义词antonym: 爱

（二）名词 n.

> enmity; regret: 难忘民族之恨。It's difficult to forget the national enmity.

词语 Words and Phrases

仇恨	chóuhèn	hatred; hostility
愤恨	fènhèn	detest; indignantly; resent

红hóng ＜ ＜ ＜ 红 红 红

（红 ＜ ＜ ＜ ＜ ＜ ＜ 紅 紅 紅）

释义 Meaning

（一）形容词 a.

> 1. red: 她买了件红外套。She bought a red jacket.
> 2. revolutionary: 他死于红五月。He died in the red month of May.

（二）名词 n.

> 1. symbol of success: 我希望能来个开门红。I hope I can get off to a good start.
> 2. bonus; dividend: 公司每年分红。The company distributes dividends every year.

词语 Words and Phrases

红茶	hóngchá	black tea
红尘	hóngchén	human society
红利	hónglì	bonus; dividend
红绿灯	hónglǜdēng	traffic light (signal)
红旗	hóngqí	red flag
红人	hóngrén	a rising star; a favourite with sb. in power
红润	hóngrùn	rosy; ruddy
红色	hóngsè	① red ② revolutionary
红十字会	hóngshízìhuì	the Red Cross

熟语 Idioms

红光满面	hóngguāng mǎnmiàn	glowing with health

后 hòu 一 厂 广 戶 后 后

(後 一 彳 彳 彳 彳 徉 徉 後)

释义 Meaning

（一）名词 n.

1. offspring: 他是名人之后。He is an offspring of a famous person.
2. behind; rear; back: 房后有两排树。There are two rows of trees behind the house. 反义词 antonym: 前

词语 Words and Phrases

后备	hòubèi	reserve
后代	hòudài	offspring; later generations
后果	hòuguǒ	aftermath; consequence
后悔	hòuhuǐ	regret; repent
后来	hòulái	later; afterwards
后路	hòulù	① a way of escape ② route of retreat

后门	hòumén	① back gate ② backdoor influence
后面	hòumiàn	① back; behind ② later
后天	hòutiān	① postnatal; acquired ② the day after tomorrow
后退	hòutuì	retreat; draw back
后卫	hòuwèi	guard; rear guard
后遗症	hòuyízhèng	sequelae

熟语 Idioms

后继无人	hòujì wú rén	nobody to carry on the work
后来居上	hòu lái jū shàng	the new comers surpass the old ones
后起之秀	hòuqǐ zhī xiù	an up-and-coming generation
后生可畏	hòushēng kě wèi	the young will earn our respect

厚hòu　二 厂 厂 厈 厊 厍 厚 厚 厚

释义 Meaning

形容词 a.

1. thick: 木板很厚。The plank is very thick. 反义词antonym: 薄

2. deep; profound: 他们俩情深意厚。They have profound friendship. 反义词antonym: 薄；浅

3. large; generous: 他收到了一些厚礼。He received some generous gifts. 反义词antonym: 薄

词语 Words and Phrases

厚道	hòudào	honest and kind
厚度	hòudù	thickness
厚意	hòuyì	kindness; kind thought
浓厚	nónghòu	① dense; thick ② (of colour, interest,

etc.) strong

| 深厚 | shēnhòu | ① deep; profound ② solid; deep-seated |
| 忠厚 | zhōnghòu | honest and loyal |

熟语 Idioms

| 厚脸皮 | hòu liǎnpí | thick-skinned; shameless; brass |
| 厚颜无耻 | hòuyán wúchǐ | shameless; effrontery; bold as brass |

候 hòu　ノ　亻　仁　仁　仁　伊　伊　伊　候　候

释义 Meaning

动词 v.

wait; await: 请稍候。Wait a minute, plese.

词语 Words and Phrases

等候	děnghòu	wait; await
时候	shí hou	time; moment
问候	wènhòu	send one's regards to; extend greetings to

呼 hū　丨　丬　丬　叮　呀　呀　呀　呼

释义 Meaning

（一）动词 v.

1. exhale; breathe out: 我呼了一口气。I exhaled once. 反义词 antonym: 吸

2. shout; cry out: 他们高呼着："毛主席万岁"。They were shouting : "Long live Chairman Mao!"

3. call: 有人在呼救。Someone is calling for help.

（二）象声词 onomatopoeia

used for wind: 西北风呼呼地吹着。The northwest wind is whistling.

词语 Words and Phrases

呼喊	hū hǎn	shout; call out
呼号	hū hào	cry out in distress
呼唤	hū huàn	call; shout to
呼叫	hūjiào	shout; call out
呼救	hūjiù	call for help
呼吸	hūxī	breathe
呼应	hūyìng	echo; work in concert with
呼吁	hūyù	appeal; call on
欢呼	huānhū	cheer; shout joyfully

熟语 Idioms

呼风唤雨	hū fēng huàn yǔ	summon wind and rain; (a person) of unusual abilities or power

湖 hú 　` ｀ ｀ 氵 氵 汁 汁 沽 沽 湖 湖 湖 湖

释义 Meaning

名词 n.

lake: 这儿有许多湖。There are many lakes here.

词语 Words and Phrases

湖滨	húbīn	lakeside
湖畔	húpàn	lakeside
湖泊	húpō	lakes
湖心亭	húxīntíng	a pavilion in the middle of a lake

虎 hǔ 　` ｜ ⺊ 广 庐 虍 虎 虎

释义 Meaning

（一）名词 n.

tiger: 小虎也很可爱。The tiger cub is lovely too.

（二）形容词 a.

brave; vigorous: 真是一员虎将。What a brave gengeral!

词语 Words and Phrases

虎劲	hǔjìn	dash; dauntless drive
虎口	hǔkǒu	① tiger's mouth ② part of the hand between the thumb and the index finger ③ a place of danger
虎穴	hǔxuè	tiger's den
老虎	lǎohǔ	tiger

熟语 Idioms

纸老虎	zhǐ lǎo hǔ	paper tiger
虎视耽耽	hǔ shì dān dān	glare as a tiger watching its prey
虎头蛇尾	hǔ tóu shé wěi	anticlimax; fine start but poor finish

互 hù 　　一　丌　互　互

释义 Meaning

副词 adv.

each other: 我们应该互学互助。We should learn and help each other.

词语 Words and Phrases

互访	hùfǎng	exchange visits
互换	hùhuàn	exchange
互相	hùxiāng	mutual; each other
互助	hùzhù	help each other
相互	xiānghù	mutual; each other

熟语 Idioms

| 互惠互利 | hùhuì hùlì | mutually beneficial |
| 互通有无 | hùtōng yǒuwú | supply each other (what the other needs) |

户 hù　　`　亠　彐　户

释义 Meaning

名词 n.

1. door: 我非常喜欢户外活动。I like outdoor activities very much.

2. family; household: 我们村差不多有一百户。There are about a hundred households in our village.

词语 Words and Phrases

户籍	hùjí	① household register ② registered permanent residence
户口	hùkǒu	① number of households and total population ② registered permanent residence
户头	hùtóu	bank account
户主	hùzhǔ	head of a household
窗户	chuānghù	window
门户	ménhù	door
帐户	zhànghù	bank account

护 hù　　一　十　扌　扩`　护　护　护

(護 `　亠　亠　亖　訁　訁　訁　訁　訁　詁　詁　詁　詁　詁　諀　諀　護　護）

释义 Meaning

动词 v.

1. guard; protect; shield: 护林是他的工作。His job is to protect the forest.

2. be partial to; shield from censure: 他总是护着自己的孩子。He is always most partial to his own children.

词语 Words and Phrases

护城河	hùchénghé	city moat
护理	hùlǐ	nurse; tend
护身符	hùshēnfú	① amulet; talisman ② shield
护士	hùshi	nurse
护送	hùsòng	escort; convoy
护照	hùzhào	passport
爱护	àihù	protect; cherish; take good care of
保护	bǎohù	protect; safeguard
看护	kānhù	nurse; look after
维护	wéihù	defend; safeguard; uphold

花 huā　二 十 艹 艹 艹 艻 花

释义 Meaning

（一）名词 n.

1. flower; blossom: 他给女朋友买了一束花儿。He bought a bunch of flowers for his girlfriend.

2. anything resembling a flower: 雪花在空中飞舞着。The snowflakes are dancing in the sky.

3. pattern; design: 她裙子上的花很雅致。The design on her skirt is quite elegant.

（二）动词 v.

spend; expend: 去上海花了我不少时间。It took me a lot of time to get to Shanghai. 反义词 antonym: 省

（三）形容词 a.

1. coloured; multicoloured; variegated: 她喜欢那些花衣服。She likes those bright-coloured clothes.

2. flowery; fancy; blurred: 他的字很花。His handwriting is very fancy.

词语 Words and Phrases

花白	huābái	(of hair) grey; grizzled
花茶	huāchá	scented tea; jasmine tea
花朵	huāduǒ	flower
花费	huāfèi	spend; expenses
花甲	huājiǎ	a cycle of sixty years
花匠	huājiàng	gardener
花瓶	huāpíng	vase; flower vase
花色	huāsè	① design and colour ② variety of designs, colours, sizes, etc.
花生	huāshēng	peanut; groundnut
花样	huāyàng	① pattern; variety ② trick
花园	huāyuán	garden
火花	huǒhuā	spark

熟语 Idioms

花花公子	huāhuā-gōngzi	dandy; clubman; coxcomb; playboy
花花绿绿	huāhuā-lǜlǜ	colorful
花言巧语	huā yán qiǎo yǔ	sweet words; double talk

滑 huá   `  ` 氵 氵 沪 沪 沪 沪 沪 滑
滑 滑

释义 Meaning

（一）动词 v.

slide; slip: 他在路上滑倒而且摔断了左腿。He slied on the road and broke his left leg.

（二）形容词 a.

smooth; slippery: 路太滑了。The road is too slippery. 反

义词antonym: 涩

词语 Words and Phrases

滑冰	huábīng	skate; ice-skating
滑稽	huájī	funny; amusing; ridiculous
滑头	huátóu	① slippery; shifty ② sly; slippery fellow
滑行	huáxíng	slide; coast
滑雪	huáxuě	skiing

化 huà ノ 亻 化 化

释义 Meaning

（一）动词 v.

1. turn; change; transform: 我们尽力争取化害为利。We do our best to turn harm into good.

2. melt; dissolve; get rid of: 雪已经化了。The snow has already melted.

（二）后缀 suff.

added to a noun or an adjective to form a verb: 你们应该将手续简化。You should simplify the procedures.

词语 Words and Phrases

化工	huàgōng	chemical industry
化身	huàshēn	incarnation
化学	huàxué	chemistry; chemical
化验	huàyàn	chemical examination; laboratory test
变化	biànhuà	change; turn

划 huà 二 七 戈 戈 划 划

（劃 一 一 一 一 聿 聿 聿 書 書 書 書 書 畫 畫 劃）

释义 Meaning

（一）动词 v.

1. delimit; differentiate; draw: 他们为两国划了界。They've delimited the boundary between the two countries.

2. assign; transfer; appropriate: 这笔款子将由银行划给。The money will be transfered through the bank.

（二）名词 n.

stroke (of a Chinese character): "人"字共有两划。The character 人 is made up of two strokes.

词语 Words and Phrases

划拨	huàbō	assign; trransfer; appropriate
划分	huàfēn	① divide ② differentiate
划归	huàguī	put under (sb.'s administration)
划清	huàqīng	make a clear distinction
策划	cèhuà	plan; plot
计划	jìhuà	① plan; programme ② plan; map out

熟语 Idioms

| 划时代 | huáshídài | epoch-making |
| 整齐划一 | zhěng jì huáyī | trim; uniform; in order |

画 huà　二 厂 厂 匚 而 田 画 画

（**畫** 一 十 卉 圭 聿 聿 書 書 書 畫 畫 畫 畫）

释义 Meaning

（一）名词 n.

1. painting; picture; drawing: 这幅油画真美。How beautiful this oil painting is!

2. stroke (of a Chinese character): "正"字共有五画。The character 正 is made up of five strokes.

（二）动词 v.

draw; paint: 他正在画画儿。He is drawing a picture.

词语 Words and Phrases

画报	huàbào	pictorial; illustrated newspaper (or magazine)
画册	huàcè	album
画家	huàjiā	painter; artist
画廊	huàláng	① (picture) gallery ② painted corridor
画面	huàmiàn	① frame ② tableau; general appearance of a picture
画室	huàshì	a painter's studio
画展	huàzhǎn	exhibition of paintings; art exhibition

熟语 Idioms

| 画龙点睛 | huà lóng diǎn jīng | bring the painted dragon to life by putting in the pupils of it's eyes; make the finishing touch |
| 画蛇添足 | huà shé tiān zú | draw a snake and add feet to it; perform an unnecessary act to show off |

话 huà ` 讠 讠 讠 讦 讦 话 话

（話 ` ˊ ˊ ˊ ˊ 言 言 言 言 訂 訂 話 話）

释义 Meaning

（一）名词 n.

word; remark: 请给我说句话。Say some words to me, please.

（二）动词 v.

say; talk about: 他没给我们话别就走了。He left without saying good-bye to us.

词语 Words and Phrases

话别	huàbié	say good-bye; say some parting words
话剧	huàjù	stage play; modern drama
话题	huàtí	topic of conversation; subject of a talk
话筒	huàtǒng	① microphone ② telephone transmitter
废话	fèihuà	nonsense; superfluous words
说话	shuōhuà	① say; speak; talk ② chat ③ criticize

熟语 Idioms

话里有话	huà lǐ yǒu huà	it means more than the word

坏 huài 一 十 土 扩 圹 坏 坏

（**壤** 一 十 土 扩 扩 扩 护 护 护 护 护 护 护 埒 壕 壕 壕 壤）

释义 Meaning

（一）形容词 a.

bad: 他是个坏孩子。He is a bad boy. 反义词 antonym: 好

（二）副词 adv.

badly; awfully; very: 他乐坏了。He is wild with joy.

（三）动词 v.

ruin; spoil; go bad: 肉已经坏了。The meat has already gone bad.

（四）名词 n.

evil idea; dirty trick: 他总是给老师使坏。He always plays dirty tricks on his teacher.

词语 Words and Phrases

坏处	huàichù	harm; disadvantage
坏蛋	huàidàn	bastard; scoundrel; bad egg

坏东西	huàidōngxi	scoundrel; evildoer; bad person
坏话	huàihuà	① unpleasant words ② vicious talk; malicious remarks
坏人	huàirén	scoundrel; evildoer; bad person
坏事	huàishì	① bad thing; evil deed ② make things worse; ruin sth.
坏心眼儿	huài xīnyǎnr	ill will; evil intention
破坏	pòhuài	destroy; wreck

环 huán 一 二 干 王 王 环 环 环

(環 一 二 干 王 王 环 环 环 严 严 严 严 環 環 環 環 環)

释义 Meaning

（一）名词 n.

1. ring; hoop: 他给妻子买了只耳环。He bought a pair of earrings for his wife.

2. link: 每一环都很重要。Each link is very important.

（二）动词 v.

surround; encircle: 小湖四面环山。The small lake is surrounded by mountains.

词语 Words and Phrases

环保	huánbǎo	environmental protection
环抱	huánbào	surround; encircle; hem in
环顾	huán gù	look round
环节	huánjié	① link ② segment
环境	huánjìng	environment; surroundings; circumstances

环绕	huánrào	surround; encircle; revolve around
环行	huánxíng	going in a ring
耳环	ěrhuán	earring
光环	guānghuán	halo
循环	xúnhuán	cycle; circulate

换 huàn 一 十 扌 扩 扩 护 挡 挡 换 换

释义 Meaning

动词 v.

1. change: 他正在换衣服。He is changing his clothes.
2. exchange; trade; barter: 他和妻子换了个位子。He exchanged seats with his wife.

词语 Words and Phrases

换钱	huànqián	change money
换取	huànqǔ	exchange sth. for; get in return
换算	huànsuàn	conversion
兑换	duìhuàn	exchange; convert
交换	jiāohuàn	exchange; barter

熟语 Idioms

| 换汤 | huàn tāng | change in form but not |
| 不换药 | bú huàn yào | in substance |

黄 huáng 一 十 艹 昔 芌 苊 苗 苗 甴 黄 黄

释义 Meaning

形容词 a.

yellow; sallow: 他的上衣是黄的。His coat is yellow.

词语 Words and Phrases

| 黄澄澄 | huángdèngdèng | glistening yellow |

黄豆	huángdòu	soybean; soya bean
黄瓜	huángguā	cucumber
黄河	huánghé	the Yellow River
黄昏	huánghūn	dusk
黄金	huángjīn	gold
黄酒	huángjiǔ	yellow rice wine
黄牛	huángniú	ox
黄色	huángsè	① yellow ② decadent; obscene; pronographic
黄土	huángtǔ	loess
黄油	huángyóu	butter
金黄	jīnhuáng	golden yellow

熟语 Idioms

| 黄粱美梦 | huángliángměimèng | pipe dream; a fool's paradise |

挥huī 一 十 扌 扌 扌 扩 护 挥 挥 挥

（揮 一 十 扌 扌 扌 扩 护 护 捎 捎 揎 揮）

释义 Meaning

动词 v.

1. wave; wield: 他正在挥着双手。He is waving his hands.

2. wipe off: 她挥泪而别。She wiped her tears and said goodbye.

3. scatter; disperse: 花花公子常常都是挥金如土。A dandy always wastes money.

词语 Words and Phrases

| 挥动 | huīdòng | wave; brandish |
| 挥发 | huīfā | volatilize; evaporate |

挥手	huīshǒu	wave one's hand
挥舞	huīwǔ	wave; wield; brandish
发挥	fāhuī	① give play to; bring into play ② develop (an idea, a theme, etc.)
指挥	zhǐhuī	① command; direct; conduct ② commander; director

熟语 Idioms

挥金如土	huī jīn rú tǔ	squander money; spend money like water

回 huí ｜ 冂 冂 冈 回 回

释义 Meaning

(一) 动词 v.

1. return; come (go) back: 下课后我就回家。 I'll return home after class. 反义词 antonym: 去

2. circle; turn round: 她回过身来，愤怒地看着我。 She turned round and looked at me with anger.

3. reply; answer: 他终于给我回了封信。 He's finally sent me a letter in reply.

(二) 量词 measure w.

1. time: 这儿我来过三回了。 I've been here three times.

2. chapter: 这部小说共有八十回。 The novel has 80 chapters.

词语 Words and Phrases

回报	huíbào	① repay; requite; reciprocate ② retaliate ③ report back
回避	huíbì	evade; dodge; avoid (metting sb.)
回答	huídá	reply; answer; response
回访	huífǎng	pay a return visit (or call)
回复	huífù	reply
回顾	huígù	review; look back

回见	huíjiàn	see you later; good-bye
回绝	huíjué	refuse; decline
回来	huílái	return; be back; come back
回去	huíqù	return; be back; go back
回声	huíshēng	echo
回首	huíshǒu	① recollect; look back ② turn one's head; turn round
回头	huítóu	① repent ② later ③ turn round; turn one's head
回味	huíwèi	① aftertaste ② call sth. to mind and ponder over it
回想	huíxiǎng	recall; recollect; think back
回信	huíxìn	reply; write back
回忆	huíyì	recall; recollect; call to mind
回音	huíyīn	echo; reply

熟语 Idioms

回心转意   huí xīn zhuǎn yì   come around to the right way of thinking

会 huì ノ 人 人 스 쇼 会

(會 ノ 人 人 个 숙 命 命 命 命 命 會 會 會)

释义 Meaning

(一) 动词 v.

1. meet; see; get together: 我星期天去会她。I'll meet her on Sunday.

2. grasp; understand: 你会错了我的意。You misunderstood my intentions.

3. be good at; be skillful in: 他很会玩电脑游戏。He's skillful in playing computer games.

（二）助动词 aux. v.

can; be able to: 我不会说中文。I can't speak Chinese.

1. be going to; be sure to; be likely to: 我会再来看你的。
I'll come to see you again.

（三）名词 n.

meeting; party; gathering: 晚上有个欢迎会。There's going to be a welcoming party tonight.

词语 Words and Phrases

会餐	huìcān	dine together; have a dinner party
会场	huìchǎng	meeting-place; conference hall
会费	huìfèi	membership dues
会合	huìhé	meet; join; assemble; converge
会话	huìhuà	dialogue; conversation
会见	huìjiàn	meet with
会客	huìkè	receive a guest (or a visitor)
会面	huìmiàn	meet
会谈	huìtán	talks
会心	huìxīn	knowing; understanding
会议	huìyì	meeting
会意	huìyì	knowing; understanding;
会员	huìyuán	member of a society, association, etc.
帮会	bānghuì	secret society
都会	dūhuì	capital; chief city
机会	jīhuì	chance; occasion; opportunity
开会	kāihuì	hold (attend) a meeting
省会	shěnghuì	provincial capital
一会儿	yíhuìr	moment; a little while

昏 hūn   一 厂 厂 氏 氏 昏 昏 昏

释义 Meaning

（一）名词 n.

dusk: 这老妇人晨昏都来公园锻炼。The old woman comes to the park to do exercise at dawn and dusk. 反义词antonym: 晨

（二）形容词 a.

1. dark; dim: 我喜欢坐在昏黑的灯光里思考。I like to sit and think in the dim light. 反义词antonym: 亮

2. confused; muddled; fatuous: 昏君被人民推翻了。The fatuous ruler was overthrown by the people. 反义词antonym: 明

（三）动词 v.

lose consciousness: 病人昏了过去。The patient fell into a coma.

词语 Words and Phrases

昏暗	hūn'àn	dusky; dim
昏沉沉	hūn'chénchén	① murky ② dazed; befuddled
昏花	hūnhuā	blurred; dim-sighted
昏黄	hūnhuáng	faint; yellow; dim
昏乱	hūnluàn	befuddled; dazed and confused
昏迷	hūnmí	coma; stupor
昏睡	hūnshuì	lethargy; a deep slumber
昏眩	hūnxuàn	dizzy; giddy

熟语 Idioms

昏天黑地	hūn tiān hēi dì	① dizzy; ② pitch-dark; ③ chaos
天昏地暗	tiān hūn dì àn	① in a state of chaos and darkness; ② dark all round
利令智昏	lì lìng zhì hūn	be blinded by lust for money

活 huó   丶 丶 氵 氵 汗 汗 汗 活 活

释义 Meaning

（一）动词 v.

live: 他活在幻想之中。He lives in an illusion. 反义词 antonym: 死

（二）名词 n.

1. work: 年轻人应该干重活儿。A youth should do heavy work.

2. product: 这批活儿做得不错。This batch of products is well made.

（三）形容词 a.

1. living; alive: 那些敌人被活捉了。Those enemies were captured alive. 反义词 antonym: 死

2. vivid; lively; moving: 你脑子很活。You have a quick mind. 反义词 antonym: 死

（四）副词 adv.

exactly; simply: 这孩子活像他爸爸。The child looks exactly like his dad.

词语 Words and Phrases

活动	huódòng	① activity; manoeuvre ② exercise ③ mobile ④ shaky; unsteady
活该	huógāi	serve sb. right
活力	huólì	vigour; vitality; energy
活泼	huópo	lively; vivid; vivacious
活期	huóqī	current; no fixed duration
活页	huóyè	loose-leaf
活跃	huóyuè	① active; brisk; dynamic ② enliven; animate

熟语 Idioms

活受罪	huóshòuzuì	living death; have a hell of a life
活灵活现	huó líng huó xiàn	vivid; lifelike; come alive
生动活泼	shēngdòng huópo	vivid; lively; vivacious

火 huǒ　丶　丷　少　火

释义 Meaning

（一）名词 n.

1. fire: 姐姐正在生火。My sister is making a fire.

2. anger; temper: 他发火了。He's lost his temper.

（二）形容词 a.

1. firy; flaming: 火红的太阳高挂空中。The flaming sun is up in the sky.

2. urgent; pressing: 火速回电。Call me immediately.

（三）动词 v.

anger; flare; make angery: 一听她的话，他就火了。He flared up when he heard her words.

词语 Words and Phrases

火把	huǒbǎ	torch
火柴	huǒchái	match
火车	huǒchē	train
火红	huǒhóng	fiery; flaming; red as fire
火急	huǒjí	urgent; pressing
火箭	huǒjiàn	rocket
火警	huǒjǐng	fire alarm
火炬	huǒjù	torch
火辣辣	huǒlàlà	burning
火腿	huǒtuǐ	ham
火灾	huǒzāi	conflagration; fire (as a disaster)

熟语 Idioms

火上加油　　huǒ shàng jiā yóu　　pour oil on the flames

或 huò 　 二 厂 下 戸 豆 式 或 或

释义 Meaning

（一）副词 adv.

maybe; perhaps; probably: 我们明年或可访沪。Maybe we can visit Shanghai next year.

（二）连词 conj.

or; either-or-: 请把词典交给玛丽或她的同屋。Please give this dictionary to Mary or her roommate.

词语 Words and Phrases

或许　　huòxǔ　　maybe; perhaps; probably

或者　　huòzhě　　or; either-or-

获 huò 　 二 节 节 芹 芹 芹 莽 莽 获 获

（獲 ʼ 犭 犭 犭 犭 犷 犷 犷 犷 犷 犷 犷 犷 犷 犷 犷 獲 獲）

释义 Meaning

动词 v.

1. obtain; win; reap; get in: 他在演讲比赛中获了一等奖。He won first prize in the speech contest. 反义词 antonym: 失

2. catch; capture: 是我抓获了他。It's me who captured him.

词语 Words and Phrases

获得　　huòdé　　obtain; gain; win; acquire; achieve

获胜　　huòshèng　　win; triumph; be victorious

获悉　　huòxī　　learn; know

捕获	bǔhuò	capture; catch
俘获	fúhuò	capture
收获	shōuhuò	① harvest ② gain; results

几₁ jī 丿 几

释义 Meaning

（一）名词 n.

a small table: 请把杯子放在茶几上。Please put your cup on the tea table.

词语 Words and Phrases

| 几乎 | jīhū | almost; nearly; practically |
| 茶几 | chájī | tea table |

几₂ jī 丿 几

（幾 ´ ⸗ ⸗ ⸗ ⸗ ⸗ ⸗ ⸗ ⸗ 幾 幾 幾）

释义 Meaning

代词 pron.

1. how many: 你家有几口人？How many persons are there in your family?

2. some; several; a few: 我过几天来看你。I'll come to see you in a couple of days.

词语 Words and Phrases

几分	jǐfēn	rather; somewhat; a bit
几何	jǐhé	① geometry ② how many; how much
几时	jǐshí	when; what time
几许	jǐxǔ	how many; how much

机 jī 一 十 才 木 机 机

(機 一 十 才 木 杧 杧 椕 椕 椕 椕 椕 椕 椕 機 機 機)

释义 Meaning

（一）名词 n.

1. machine; engine: 她房间里有一架缝纫机。There is a sewing machine in her room.

2. plane; aeroplane; aircraft: 我将乘机前往。I'll go there by aeroplane.

3. chance; opportunity; occasion: 我最好寻机告诉她。I'd better to find an opportunity to tell her.

（二）形容词 a.

1. flexible; quickwitted: 这姑娘很机敏。The girl is very clever.

2. organic: 他在复旦大学学习无机化学。He studies inorganic chemistry at Fudan University.

词语 Words and Phrases

机场	jīchǎng	airport; airfield
机动	jīdòng	① motorized; power-driven ② mobile; flexible ③ in reserve
机构	jīgòu	① organization; setup ② mechanism
机关	jīguān	① office; organ ② ; mechanism; gear ③ intrigue
机会	jīhuì	chance; opportunity; occasion
机密	jīmì	secret; confidential
机器	jīqì	machine; machinery; apparatus
机械	jīxiè	① machinery; machine ② mechanical; rigid

| 机遇 | jīyù | opportunity; good fortune |
| 机智 | jīzhì | resourceful; quick-witted |

熟语 Idioms

| 随机应变 | suí jī yìng biàn | play to the score |

鸡 jī ┐ ㄡ ㄡˊ ㄡˊ ㄡˊ 鸡 鸡

(雞 一 ㇐ ㇐ ㇐ ㇐ ㇐ ㇐ ㇐ ㇐ ㇐ ㇐
雞 雞 雞 雞 雞 雞 雞)

释义 Meaning

名词 n.

chicken: 炸鸡并非美味。The fried chicken is really not so delicious.

词语 Words and Phrases

鸡蛋	jīdàn	egg
鸡肋	jīlèi	① chicken ribs ② things of little value or interest
鸡尾酒	jīwěijiǔ	cocktail
公鸡	gōngjī	cock; rooster
母鸡	mǔjī	hen
小鸡	xiǎojī	chick; chicken

熟语 Idioms

鸡飞蛋打	jī fēi dàn dǎ	"the chickens have flown and the eggs are smashed"; all is lost
鸡毛蒜皮	jīmáo suànpí	trifles; fragment; chicken feathers and garlic skins
鸡犬不宁	jī quǎn bù níng	general turmoil

级 jí　ㄥ ㄠ ㄠ ㄠ ㄠ 级 级

(級 ㄥ ㄠ ㄠ ㄠ ㄠ ㄠ ㄠ 級 級)

释义 Meaning

(一)名词 n.

level; rank; grade; class: 这些是一级品。 These are first-class products.

(二)量词 measure w.

step; stage: 共有39级台阶。 There are 39 steps in all.

词语 Words and Phrases

级别	jíbié	level; rank; grade; scale
等级	děngjí	① grade; rank ② order and degree
低级	dījí	① lower; elementary; rudimentary ② vulgar; low
高级	gāojí	① senior; high-ranking; high-level ② advanced; high-quality
阶级	jiējí	(social) class

极 jí　二 十 才 木 朾 极 极

(極 二 十 才 木 朾 朾 朾 柯 柯 極 極 極)

释义 Meaning

(一)名词 n.

1. extremity; utmost: 你真是愚蠢之极。 You are the height of folly.

2. Poles: 他上星期到了南极。 He arrived at the South Pole last week.

（二）**副词** adv.

most; extremely; exceedingly: 女孩高兴极了。The girl is extremely happy.

词语 Words and Phrases

极地	jídì	polar region
极点	jídiǎn	extremity; the limit; the utmost point
极度	jídù	extreme; exceeding
极端	jíduān	① extreme ② exceeding
极力	jílì	do one's utmost
极目	jímù	look as far as the eyes can see
极品	jípǐn	best quality; highest grade
极其	jíqí	most; extremely; exceedingly
极限	jíxiàn	the limit; the maximum

熟语 Idioms

极乐世界	jílè shìjiè	Elysium; Pure Land
乐极生悲	lè jí shēng bēi	extreme joy begets sadness

急 jí ⺍ ⺈ ⺈ ⼓ ⼓ ⼓ 急 急 急

释义 Meaning
形容词 a.

1. anxious; impatient; eager: 他急着要去上海。He needs to visit Shanghai immediately. 反义词 antonym: 慢

2. irritated; angered; nettled; annoyed: 他太容易急了。He is easily irritated.

3. fast; rapid; violent: 雨下得很急。It's raining hard. 反义词 antonym: 缓

4. urgent; pressing: 我刚收到一封急电。I've just received an urgent telegram. 反义词 antonym: 慢

词语 Words and Phrases

急促	jícù	① hurried; rapid ② (of time) short
急救	jíjiù	emergency treatment; first aid
急剧	jíjù	rapid; sharp; sudden
急忙	jímáng	hurriedly; hastily; in a hurry; in haste
急切	jíqiè	① eager; anxious; impatient ② in a hurry; in haste
急速	jísù	rapidly; fast; at high speed
急性子	jíxìngzi	① quick-tempered; of impatient disposition ② an impetuous person
急需	jíxū	① urgent need ② be badly in need of
急于	jíyú	eager; anxious; impatient
着急	zháojí	feel worried

熟语 Idioms

急功近利	jí gōng jìn lì	crave instant success and benefit
急起直追	jí qǐ zhí zhuī	wake oneself to catch up
急中生智	jí zhōng shēng zhì	show wisdom in an emergency

集 jí   ノ 亻 亻 亻 亻 亻 隹 隹 隹 隹
隹 集

释义 Meaning

(一) 动词 v.

gather; assemble; collect: 孩子们都喜欢集邮。The children like to collect stamps.

(二) 名词 n.

1. market; fair: 我下午要去赶集。I'll go to the country fair this afternoon.

2. collection; anthology; album: 我的诗文集出版了。My anthology has been published.

（三）量词 measure w.

　　volume; part: 他的诗文集将分五集出版。His anthology will be published in five volumes.

词语 Words and Phrases

集合	jíhé	gather; assemble; call together
集会	jíhuì	meeting; gathering; assembly; rally
集权	jíquán	centralization of power
集体	jítǐ	collective
集团	jítuán	group; circle; clique
集中	jízhōng	centralize; concentrate; focus; gather together
聚集	jùjí	gather; collect; assemble; get together
收集	shōují	collect; gather

挤 jǐ 一 亅 扌 扩 扩 护 挤 挤 挤

（挤 一 亅 扌 扩 扩 扩 扩 扩 扩 扩 扩 扩 挤 挤 挤）

释义 Meaning

动词 v.

1. press; squeeze: 请把水分挤干。Please squeeze the water out.

2. crowd; cram; pack: 我房间里挤不下这么多人。It's impossible to pack so many people into my room.

3. jostle; push against: 我们让他们挤来挤去的。We were jostled by them.

词语 Words and Phrases

挤奶	jǐnǎi	milk (a cow, etc.)
挤压	jǐyā	press; extrude
拥挤	yōngjǐ	crowd; be crowded; be packed

熟语 Idioms

挤牙膏	jǐ yágāo	① squeeze tooth paste out of a tube; ② be forced to tell sth. bit by bit
挤眉弄眼	jǐ méi nòng yǎn	wink; blink; make eyes

计 jì　　`　亠　亠　计

(計　`　亠　亠　言　言　言　言　計)

释义 Meaning

（一）动词 v.

count; calculate; compute; estimate: 男女教师计十人。The teachers, male and female, numbered ten in all.

（二）名词 n.

1. idea; plan; ruse: 真是妙计。That's a good idea.
2. meter; gauge: 温度计很有用。A thermometer is useful.

词语 Words and Phrases

计策	jìcè	plan; stratagem
计划	jìhuà	① plan; project; programme ② plan, map out
计较	jìjiào	① argue; dispute ② plan; think over ③ haggle over
计量	jìliàng	measure; estimate; calculate
计谋	jìmóu	stratagem; scheme
计算	jìsuàn	① count; calculate; compute ② consideration; planning
计算机	jìsuànjī	computer
计算器	jìsuànqì	calculator
计议	jìyì	consult; deliberate; talk over
会计	kuàijì	accounting; accountant; bookkeeper

记 jì   `ı ı⁷ ı⁷ 记

(記 ` ˊ ˋ ˈ ˈ 言 言 言 訂 訂 記)

释义 Meaning

（一）动词 v.

1. record; write down: 把号码记在纸上。Write the number down on a piece of paper.

2. remember; bear in mind: 我记不起来了。I can't remember it. 反义词antonym: 忘

（二）名词 n.

1. notes; record: 学生们上课时记了许多笔记。The students take many notes during class.

2. sign; mark; birthmark: 他脸上有块记。There's a birthmark on his face.

（三）量词 measure w.

(for slap): 我给了他一记耳光。I gave him a slap on his face.

词语 Words and Phrases

记得	jìde	remember
记号	jìhào	mark; sign
记录	jìlù	① record ② notes; minutes ③ take notes ④ notetaker
记性	jìxìng	memory
记叙	jìxù	narrate
记忆	jìyì	① recall; remember ② memory
记载	jìzǎi	① account; record ② put down in writing
记者	jìzhě	journalist; reporter; correspondent
笔记	bǐjì	① notes ② take down in writing

日记	rìjì	diary
忘记	wàngjì	forget
游记	yóujì	travelogue; travel notes

熟语 Idioms

| 记忆犹新 | jìyì yóu xīn | remain fresh in one's memory |

技 jì　一 十 扌 扩 扩 抟 技

释义 Meaning

名词 n.

skill; trick; ability: 他从父亲那儿学到了一项绝技。He's learnt a unique skill from his father.

词语 Words and Phrases

技工	jìgōng	① technician; mechanic ② skilled worker
技能	jìnéng	skill; technique
技巧	jìqiǎo	skill; finesse; sleight; craftsmanship
技术	jìshù	technology; skill; technique
技艺	jìyì	skill; feat; artistry
杂技	zájì	acrobatics

熟语 Idioms

| 一技之长 | yí jì zhī cháng | one type of skill; what one is skilled in |

季 jì　一 二 千 禾 禾 禾 季 季

释义 Meaning

名词 n.

season: 一年有四季。There are four seasons in a year.

词语 Words and Phrases

| 季度 | jìdù | quarter (of a year) |

季节	jìjié	season
四季	sìjì	four seasons; whole year

寄 jì ` ` ` 宀 宀 宁 宇 宎 宎 客 客 客 寄

释义 Meaning

动词 v.

1. send; mail; post: 她男朋友每周给她寄一封信。Her boy-friend posts her a letter every week.

2. lodge; depend on; attach oneself to: 孩提时代，他不得不在叔父家过着寄人篱下的生活。

   When he was a boy, he had to depend on his uncle for a living.

3. deposit; entrust; place: 我只能寄希望于女儿了。I can only place my hopes on my daughter.

词语 Words and Phrases

寄存	jìcún	deposit; check; leave with
寄放	jìfàng	leave with; leave in the care of
寄居	jìjū	sojourn
寄生虫	jìshēngchóng	parasite
寄宿	jìsù	① lodge ② (of students) board
寄托	jìtuō	① leave with sb. ② place (hope, etc.) on
寄养	jìyǎng	entrust one's baby to the care of sb.
寄予	jìyǔ	① show; express ② place (hope, etc.) on
寄语	jìyǔ	send word to

熟语 Idioms

寄人篱下　　jì rén lí xià　　depend on sb. for a living; live under sb's. roof

加 jiā　　乛　力　加　加　加

释义 Meaning

动词 v.

1. plus: 一加一等于二。One plus one makes two. 反义词 antonym: 减

2. add; append; put in: 给课文加上注解。Add explanatory notes to the text. 反义词 antonym: 减

3. increase; augment: 老板给我们加了工资。The boss has increased our wages. 反义词 antonym: 减

词语 Words and Phrases

加班	jiābān	work overtime
加倍	jiābèi	double; redouble
加工	jiāgōng	① process ② working; machining
加害	jiāhài	injure; do harm to
加紧	jiājǐn	intensify; step up; speed up
加剧	jiājù	aggravate; exacerbate; exasperation
加快	jiākuài	quicken; accelerate; expedite; speed up
加宽	jiākuān	widen; broaden
加强	jiāqiáng	intensify; reinforce; enhance; strengthen; fortify
加热	jiārè	heat up
加入	jiārù	① add; mix; put in ② join; interpolate; go into
加深	jiāshēn	deepen
加速	jiāsù	quicken; expedite; accelerate; speed up
加以	jiāyǐ	moreover; in addition

加油	jiāyóu	① oil; lubricate ② refuel ③ make an extra effort
加重	jiāzhòng	① aggravate; make heavier ② make (become) more serious
更加	gèngjiā	more; even more; still more
增加	zēngjiā	add; enhance; increase; raise

夹 jiā 　 一 一 厂 厸 厸 夷 夹

释义 Meaning

（一）名词 n.

clamp; clip; folder: 你的发夹很漂亮。Your hairpin is very beautiful.

（二）动词 v.

1. place in between; press from both sides: 把书签夹在书里。Put the bookmark in between the pages.

2. mix; mingle; intersperse: 他们夹在人群里。They mingled with the crowd.

词语 Words and Phrases

夹板	jiābǎn	① splint ② boards for pressing sth. together
夹道	jiādào	① passageway; a narrow lane ② line both sides of street
夹缝	jiāfèng	crack; crevice; a narrow space between two adjacent things
夹攻	jiāgōng	attack from both sides; pincer attack; converging attack
夹击	jiājī	attack from both sides; pincer attack; converging attack
夹心	jiāxīn	with filling
夹杂	jiāzá	be mingled with; be mixed up with
夹子	jiāzi	clamp; clip; folder

发夹	fàjiā	hairpin

熟语 Idioms

夹生饭	jiāshēngfàn	half-cooked rice

家 jiā 　 丶 丷 宀 宀 宀 宀 家 家 家 家

释义 Meaning

（一）名词 n.

1. family; household: 他家有三口人。There are three people in his family.

2. home: 我要回家了。I'll go home.

3. a specialist in a certain field: 她爸爸是个科学家。Her father is a scientist.

4. a person or family engaged in a certain trade: 她生于渔家。She was born into a fishman's family.

（二）形容词 a.

1. my; our: 家父已七十岁了。My father is 70 years old.

2. domestic; tame: 马是家畜。The horse is a domestic animal.
   反义词antonym: 野

（三）量词 measure w.

used to count the number of families, shops, etc.: 这家电影院不错。This is a good cinema.

词语 Words and Phrases

家常	jiācháng	domestic trivia; the daily life of a family
家伙	jiāhuo	① fellow; guy ② tool; weapon
家教	jiājiào	upbringing; family education
家境	jiājìng	family circumstances; family financial situation
家具	jiājù	furniture
家谱	jiāpǔ	family tree

家属	jiāshǔ	family members; family dependents
家庭	jiātíng	family; household
家务	jiāwù	household duties
家乡	jiāxiāng	hometown; native place
家园	jiāyuán	home; homeland
家长	jiāzhǎng	① patriarch; the head of a family ② the parent of a child
家族	jiāzú	clan; family

熟语 Idioms

家常便饭	jiācháng biànfàn	home cooking
家家户户	jiājiā hùhù	each family
家破人亡	jiāpò rénwáng	family broken up and some dead
家喻户晓	jiā yù hù xiǎo	known to every household

假₁ jiǎ   ノ 亻 亻' 亻' 亻' 亻' 亻' 亻' 亻' 假 假

释义 Meaning
名词 n.

（一）形容词 a.

false; fake; sham; phoney; artificial: 这是一枚假牙。This is a false tooth. 反义词 antonym: 真

（二）连词 conj.

if: 假若下雨，我就不来了。If it rains, I won't come.

词语 Words and Phrases

假扮	jiǎbàn	disguise oneself as; dress up as
假冒	jiǎmào	pass oneself off as; palm off
假如	jiǎrú	if; in case
假设	jiǎshè	① suppose; assume; grant ② hypothesis

假使	jiǎshǐ	if; in case; in the event that
假想	jiǎxiǎng	① imagination; supposition ② hypothetical; fictitious
假装	jiǎzhuāng	pretend; simulate; feign; make believe

假₂ jià ╱ 亻 亻 亻 亻 亻 亻 亻 亻 亻 假

释义 Meaning

名词 n.

holiday; vacation; furlough: 暑假我要去北京。I'll go to Beijing during summer vacation.

词语 Words and Phrases

假期	jiàqī	vacation; period of leave
假日	jiàrì	holiday
病假	bìngjià	sick leave
请假	qǐngjià	ask for leave

价 jià ╱ 亻 亻 亻 价 价

(價 ╱ 亻 亻 亻 亻 價 價 價 價 價 價 價 價 價 價)

释义 Meaning

名词 n.

1. price: 批发价比零售价低。The wholesale price is lower than the retail price.

2. value: 他们给我的房子估了价。They have estimated the value of my house.

词语 Words and Phrases

| 价格 | jiàgé | price |

价目	jiàmù	price; marked price
价钱	jiàqián	price
价值	jiàzhí	value

熟语 Idioms

| 价值连城 | jiàzhí liánchéng | priceless; invaluable |
| 等价交换 | děngjià jiāohuàn | equipollence; equivalence |

架 jià 　フ　力　加　加　加　朾　枈　架　架

释义 Meaning

（一）名词 n.

1. shelf; frame; rack; stand: 他自己做了个书架。He made a bookshelf by himself.

2. fight; quarrel: 他在劝架呢。He is trying to stop them from the fighting.

（二）动词 v.

1. erect; put up: 我们在长江上架起一座桥。We put up a bridge over the Yangtze River. 反义词 antonym: 拆

2. withstand; fend off; ward off: 我架开了他的一击。I fended off his blow.

3. help; support; prop: 他架着双拐。He is walking on crutches.

4. kidnap; take sb. away forcibly: 我们硬把他架走了。We carried him away by force.

（三）量词 measure w.

used for a radio, TV set, etc.: 我想买架电视机。I want to buy a TV set.

词语 Words and Phrases

| 架空 | jiàkōng | ① built on stilts ② make sb. a mere figurehead |

架设	jiàshè	erect; put up; set up
架子	jiàzi	① shelf; frame ② skeleton; outline ③ posture ④ haughty manner
打架	dǎjià	fight; come to blows; engage in a brawl

尖 jiān　丨 丷 ⺌ 亚 尖 尖

释义 Meaning

（一）名词 n.

point; top; tip：鸟蹲在塔尖上。A bird is sitting on the pointed top of the tower.

（二）形容词 a.

1. pointed; tapering：他长着个尖下巴。He has a pointed chin. 反义词 antonym：平

2. sharp：你耳朵真尖。You have sharp ears.

词语 Words and Phrases

尖端	jiānduān	① peak; pointed end ② most advanced
尖刻	jiānkè	acrimonious; caustic; biting
尖利	jiānlì	① sharp; keen ② shrill; piercing
尖锐	jiānruì	① sharp; intense ② keen; incisive ③ shrill; piercing ④ sharp-pointed
拔尖儿	bá jiānr	① tiptop; top-notch ② pick the best

熟语 Idioms

| 尖酸刻薄 | jiānsuān kèbó | verjuice; caustic; tart |

间₁ jiān　丶 厂 门 门 冂 间 间

（間　丨 厂 ⺋ 尸 尸 門 門 門 門 問 間 間）

释义 Meaning

（一）名词 n.

1. room: 孩子在洗澡间。The child is in the bathroom.
2. a definite time or space: 我晚间从不喝咖啡。I never drink coffee in the evening.

（二）量词 measure w.

for room, etc.: 这套公寓有两间卧室。There are two bed-rooms in this apartment.

词语 Words and Phrases

房间	fángjiān	room
空间	kōngjiān	space
时间	shíjiān	time

熟语 Idioms

间不容发	jiān bù róng fā	even a hair cannot be put in between; be in imminent danger

间₂ jiàn 丶 亠 门 门 问 间 间

（間 丨 丨 丬 丬 丬 門 門 門 門 問 問 間）

释义 Meaning

（一）名词 n.

space in between: 他们俩亲密无间。They are closely united.

（二）动词 v.

separate: T恤衫的花色是黑白相间的。The designs of the T-shirt are chequered with black and white.

词语 Words and Phrases

间谍	jiàndié	spy

间断	jiànduàn	interrupted; disconnected; interruption
间隔	jiàngé	interval; intermission
间接	jiànjiē	indirect; secondhand
间隙	jiànxì	interval; space; gap
离间	líjiàn	sow discord; drive a wedge between

熟语 Idioms

亲密无间	qīnmì wú jiàn	as thick as thieves; on intimate terms

肩 jiān　丶 亠 ⺈ 户 户 肩 肩 肩

释义 Meaning

（一）名词 n.

shoulder: 我们并肩而行。We walk shoulder to shoulder.

（二）动词 v.

undertake; shoulder; bear; take on: 年轻人将身肩重任。The youth will shoulder heavy responsibilities.

词语 Words and Phrases

肩膀	jiānbǎng	shoulder
肩负	jiānfù	undertake; shoulder; bear; take on
并肩	bìngjiān	shoulder to shoulder; side by side

捡 jiǎn　一 十 扌 扌 扒 抡 抡 拾 捡 捡

(撿　一 十 扌 扌 扒 抡 抡 拾 拾 捡 拾 捡 撿 撿 撿 撿)

释义 Meaning

动词 v.

collect; gather; pick up: 孩子们正在海边捡贝壳。The children are collecting sea-shells on the seashore.

词语 Words and Phrases

捡拾	jiǎnshí	pick up
捡破烂	jiǎn pòlàn	pick odds and ends from refuse heaps

熟语 Idioms

捡了芝麻，丢了西瓜	jiǎn le zhīma, diū le xīguā	pick up the sesame, throw away the watermelons; penny wise and pound foolish

减 jiǎn ` 冫 冫 厂 厈 厈 厈 沥 沥 减 减 减

释义 Meaning

动词 v.

1. minus; subtract: 八减四等于四。Eight minus four is four. 反义词 antonym: 加

2. reduce; decrease; cut: 电视机减价出售。TV sets are being sold at a reduced price. 反义词 antonym: 涨

词语 Words and Phrases

减低	jiǎndī	lower; reduce; cut; bring down
减法	jiǎnfǎ	subtraction
减价	jiǎnjià	reduce the price; mark down
减免	jiǎnmiǎn	① reduce or remit (taxation, etc.) ② mitigate or annul (a punishment)
减轻	jiǎnqīng	lighten; mitigate; ease; alleviate
减弱	jiǎnruò	weaken; abate
减色	jiǎnsè	lose lustre; impair the excellence of
减少	jiǎnshǎo	decrease; reduce; lessen; cut down
减速	jiǎnsù	decelerate; slow down
减缩	jiǎnsuō	reduce; cut down
减退	jiǎntuì	drop; go down

剪 jiǎn　、　丷　屵　产　产　前　前　前　前　前 前

剪

释义 Meaning

动词 v.

cut (with scissors): 她有剪报的习惯。 He has a habit of clipping from newspapers.

词语 Words and Phrases

剪报	jiǎnbào	newspaper cutting
剪彩	jiǎncǎi	cut the ribbon at an opening ceremony
剪刀	jiǎndāo	scissors; shears
剪辑	jiǎnjí	montage; film editing
剪贴	jiǎntiē	clip and paste
剪贴簿	jiǎntiēbù	scrapbook
剪纸	jiǎnzhǐ	paper-cut
剪子	jiǎnzi	scissors; clippers

见 jiàn　丨　冂　贝　见

（见　丨　冂　冃　且　目　助　見）

释义 Meaning

（一）动词 v.

1. see; catch sight of: 我见他从这个门出去的。I saw him going out from this door.

2. meet with; be exposed to: 这样的好天气真是难得一见。Such a fine day is really rare.

3. meet; call on: 好久不见，最近怎么样？Haven't seen you for quite a long time, how are you these days?

（二）名词 n.

opinion; view: 依我之见，我们还是拒绝他们为好。In

my opinion, we'd better refuse them.

词语 Words and Phrases

见不得	jiànbùdé	① can't be exposed to ② I don't think so
见怪	jiànguài	mind; take offense
见鬼	jiànguǐ	① absurd; fantastic ② go to hell
见解	jiànjiě	opinion; idea
见面	jiànmiàn	① meet; ② contact
见识	jiànshí	① experience; knowledge ② widen one's knowledge; enrich one's experience
见外	jiànwài	regard sb. as an outsider
见闻	jiànwén	what one sees and hears; information
见习	jiànxí	be on probation
见效	jiànxiào	become effective
见笑	jiànxiào	laugh at (me/us)
见证	jiànzhèng	testimony; witness

熟语 Idioms

见多识广	jiàn duō shí guǎng	with rich experience and extensive knowledge; be up to a thing or two
见风使舵	jiàn fēng shǐ duò	trim one's sails; sail with the wind
见缝插针	jiàn fèng chā zhēn	stick in a pin wherever there's room; make use of every single space or second
见怪不怪	jiàn guài bú guài	become used to the unusual
见利忘义	jiàn lì wàng yì	forget all moral principles at the sight of profit
见仁见智	jiàn rén jiàn zhì	different people have different views
见世面	jiàn shìmiàn	face the world; enrich

one's experience

见死不救	jiàn sǐ bú jiù	bear to see someone die without trying to rescue
见义勇为	jiàn yì yǒng wéi	never hesitate to do what is right
见异思迁	jiàn yì sī qiān	change one's mind the moment one sees something new

件 jiàn　 ノ　亻　亻　仁　仨　件

释义 Meaning

量词 measure w.

a piece of (upper garment, work, thing, matter, etc.) 今天他穿了一件棕色夹克。He is wearing a brown jacket today.

词语 Words and Phrases

案件	ànjiàn	law case
部件	bùjiàn	components; parts
附件	fùjiàn	appendex; enclosure
稿件	gǎojiàn	manuscript; contribution
零件	língjiàn	spare parts; spares
配件	pèijiàn	fittings (of a machine, etc.)
事件	shìjiàn	event; incident
文件	wénjiàn	documents; file
信件	xìnjiàn	letters; mail
邮件	yóujiàn	postal matter
证件	zhèngjiàn	certificate; credentials

建 jiàn　 ⁻　⁻　彐　⁻　彐　聿　建　建

释义 Meaning

动词 v.

1. establish; set up: 这是一所新建的学校。This is a newly

built school.

2. build; construct: 这座大桥将在年内建成。This bridge will be built within a year.

词语 Words and Phrases

建交	jiànjiāo	establish diplomatic relations
建立	jiànlì	build; establish; set up; found
建设	jiànshè	build; construct
建议	jiànyì	① propose; suggest ② proposal; suggestion
建造	jiànzào	build; construct; make
建制	jiànzhì	organizational system
建筑	jiànzhù	① build; construct; erect ② buildings; structure

江 jiāng 丶 丶 氵 氵 汀 江

释义 Meaning

名词 n.

1. the Changjiang (Yangtze) river: 他的家乡是一座秀丽的江南小镇。His hometown is a small beautiful town at the south of the Changjiang River.

2. river: 我们从小就在江中游泳。We swam in the river from childhood.

词语 Words and Phrases

| 江湖 | jiānghú | ① rivers and lakes ② all corners of the country |
| 江山 | jiāngshān | ① rivers and mountains; landscape ② country; state power |

熟语 Idioms

| 江郎才尽 | jiāngláng cái jìn | at the end of one's resources; have used up one's talent and energy |

| 江山易改，
　本性难移 | jiāngshān yì gǎi,
　běnxìng nán yí | the wolf may lose his teeth,
but never his nature |
| 江洋大盗 | jiāngyáng dàdào | a noted pirate; an infamous
robber |

将₁ jiāng 　丶　丬　丬　丬　丬　丬　丬　将　将

(將 　丨　丬　丬　丬　丬　丬　丬　丬　丬　將　將)

释义 Meaning

(一) 副词 adv.

will; shall; be about to; be going to: 本届电视节将于下月8号到15号举行。The TV festival will be held from the 8th to the 15th of next month.

(二) 介词 prep.

with; by: 他将手中的本子递给了我。He handed me the notebook in his hand.

词语 Words and Phrases

将近	jiāngjìn	nearly; close to
将就	jiāngjiu	make do with; make the best of
将军	jiāngjūn	① general ② check (in a chest game) ③ put sb. on the spot; embarrass
将来	jiānglái	future
将要	jiāngyào	be going to; will; shall

熟语 Idioms

将错就错	jiāng cuò jiù cuò	make the best of a mistake
将功补过	jiānggōng bǔ guò	amend for one's faults by good deeds
将计就计	jiāng jì jiù jì	beat sb. at his own game; turn sb.'s trick against him
将心比心	jiāng xīn bǐ xīn	feel for others; judge other people's feelings by one's own

将信将疑　　jiāng xìn jiāng yí　　half believing, half doubting; half seriously and half sceptically

将₂ jiàng 　丶 丬 爿 爿 爿 爿 爿 将 将

(將 丨 爿 爿 爿 爿 爿 爿 爿 爿 將 將)

释义 Meaning
名词 n.

general; commander: 张飞是一名人人皆知的猛将。Zhang Fei was a well-known valiant general.

词语 Words and Phrases
将领　　jiànglǐng　　general; high-ranking military officer
将士　　jiàngshì　　officers and men

熟语 Idioms
将在外，君命有所不受　　jiàng zài wài, jūn mìng yǒu suǒ bú shòu　　a field commander may defy even against imperial orders

讲 jiǎng 　丶 讠 讠 讲 讲 讲

(講 丶 亠 言 言 言 言 言 言 言 詳 詳 詳 講 講 講 講)

释义 Meaning

1. speak; say; tell: 妈妈每晚给宝宝讲童话故事。Mum tells fariy tales to her baby every night.
2. explain; make clear: 你越讲我越糊涂。The more you explain, the more confused I become.
3. discuss; negotiate: 开始工作前我们先把报酬讲清楚。Let's make the pay clear before we start to work.

4. lay emphasis on; pay special attention to: 他从不讲卫生。He never pays attetion to hygiene.

5. as far as sth. is concerned; with regard to: 讲能力，我不如你。As to ability, I am not your match.

词语 Words and Phrases

讲稿	jiǎnggǎo	draft for a speech or lecture
讲和	jiǎnghé	make pease; become reconciled
讲话	jiǎnghuà	speak; give a speech
讲解	jiǎngjiě	explain; interpret
讲究	jiǎngjiū	① be particular about; pay attention to ② exquisite; elegant
讲课	jiǎngkè	teach; lecture
讲理	jiǎnglǐ	① reason with sb.; argue ② be reasonable
讲评	jiǎngpíng	comment on and appraise
讲情	jiǎngqíng	plead for sb.; intercede
讲求	jiǎngqiú	strive for; be particular about
讲师	jiǎngshī	lecturer
讲授	jiǎngshòu	lecture; teach
讲台	jiǎngtái	platform; rostrum
讲演	jiǎngyǎn	lecture; speech
讲义	jiǎngyì	teaching materials
讲座	jiǎngzuò	a course of lectures

熟语 Idioms

| 讲排场 | jiǎng páichǎng | go for showy display; hanker after vainglory |

奖 jiǎng ＼ ＞ ㅓ ㅛ ㅆ ㅄ 씈 奖 奖 奖

（奖 ㄴ ㄐ ㄐ ㅒ ㅒ ㅒ ㅒ ㅒ ㅒ 將 將

奖 奖 奖 **）**

释义 Meaning

（一）名词 n.

award; prize: 李明获得书法比赛的一等奖。Li Ming won the first prize in this calligraphy competition.

（二）动词 v.

reward; encourage: 学校奖给考试成绩优秀的学生每人一本词典。All the students who did excellent scores on the test were awarded a dictionary by the school. 反义词 antonym: 罚，惩

词语 Words and Phrases

奖杯	jiǎngbēi	cup (as a prize)
奖惩	jiǎngchéng	rewards and punishments
奖金	jiǎngjīn	money award; bonus
奖励	jiǎnglì	encourage and reward; award
奖牌	jiǎngpái	medal
奖品	jiǎngpǐn	prize; trophy
奖学金	jiǎngxuéjīn	scholarship
奖状	jiǎngzhuàng	certificate of merit; certificate of award

交 jiāo　　丶　亠　宀　六　产　交

释义 Meaning

（一）动词 v.

1. hand in; hand over: 这作业明天要交吗？Shall the homework be handed in tomorrow?

2. associate with: 他在国外旅行的时候交了好多朋友。He made a lot of friends while he was travelling abroad.

3. meet; reach: 祝你交好运！Wish you good luck!

（二）名词 n.

1. relationship; friendship: 你下次再这样我就和你绝交。
   I will break off the friendship with you if you do that again.
2. fall: 他脚下滑摔了一交。He slipped and fell down.

词语 Words and Phrases

交班	jiāobān	hand over to the next shift; turn over one's duty
交叉	jiāochā	① crisscross; intersect ② alternatively
交差	jiāochāi	report on one's mission; report on the fulfillment of one's duty
交错	jiāocuò	interlock; crisscross
交代	jiāodài	① tell; leave words ② explain; account for ③ confess
交底	jiāodǐ	put all one's cards on the table; tell the real intentions
交锋	jiāofēng	cross swords; engage in a battle or contest
交付	jiāofù	① pay ② turn over; hand over
交换	jiāohuàn	exchange; interchange
交货	jiāohuò	deliver (orderd goods)
交际	jiāojì	social intercourse; communication
交界	jiāojiè	have a common boundary
交流	jiāoliú	exchange; interchange
交情	jiāoqíng	friendship
交手	jiāoshǒu	fight hand to hand; match
交替	jiāotì	replace alternatively
交通	jiāotōng	traffic
交往	jiāowǎng	association; contact
交响乐	jiāoxiǎngyuè	symphony
交易	jiāoyì	deal; business
交战	jiāozhàn	be at war; fight

教₁ jiāo

一 十 土 耂 耂 孝 孝 孝 孝 教 教

释义 Meaning

动词 v.

teach: 我在中学教了二十年英语。I have taught English for twenty years in high school. 反义词 antonym: 学

词语 Words and Phrases

教书	jiāoshū	teach school

教₂ jiào

一 十 土 耂 耂 孝 孝 孝 孝 教 教

释义 Meaning

（一）动词 v.

teach; instruct: 父亲的言传身教给了我很大的影响。I was greatly influenced by my father's words and deeds.

（二）名词 n.

religion: 我不信教，但我尊重所有信教的人。I don't believe in any religion, but I respect all belivers of any religion.

词语 Words and Phrases

教材	jiàocái	teaching material
教导	jiàodǎo	① ② guidance; teaching
教父	jiàofù	god-father
教皇	jiàohuáng	Pope
教会	jiàohuì	church
教诲	jiàohuì	teaching; instruction
教练	jiàoliàn	coach; instructor
教母	jiàomǔ	god-mother
教师	jiàoshī	teacher

教室	jiàoshì	classroom
教授	jiàoshòu	① professor ② teach; instruct
教唆	jiàosuō	instigate; put sb. up to sth.
教堂	jiàotáng	church; cathedral
教条	jiàotiáo	doctrine; dogma
教徒	jiàotú	believer or follower of a religion
教训	jiàoxùn	① lesson; moral ② teach sb. a lesson
教育	jiàoyù	① education ② teach; educate
教子	jiàozǐ	god-son

熟语 Idioms

| 教学相长 | jiào xué xiāng zhǎng | Learning while teaching others |

角₁ jiǎo ⼃ ⺈ ⼴ ⻆ ⻆ 角 角

释义 Meaning

（一）名词 n.

1. horn: 这是一枚用牛角做的印章。This is a seal made of ox horn.

2. corner: 他站在墙角的阴影里。He stood in the shadows at the corner of the wall.

3. angle: 两条线直角相交。Two lines intersect at a right angle.

（二）量词 measure w.

a fractional unit of money in China, 1/10 yuan: 你还有一角的硬币吗？Have you any coins of one *jiao*?

词语 Words and Phrases

角度	jiǎodù	① angle ② point of view; angle
角落	jiǎoluò	corner; nook
角球	jiǎoqiú	corner kick
角铁	jiǎotiě	angle iron

角₂ jué ╱ ╱ ╱ ⺈ 角 角 角

释义 Meaning

名词 n.

1. role; character: 她在这部电影中又演主角。She acts the leading role again in this film.

2. actor; actress: 这场演出汇聚了许多戏剧名角。A lot of famous theatere actors and actresses participated in this performance.

词语 Words and Phrases

角斗	juédòu	wrestle
角色	juésè	role; part
角逐	juézhú	contest; enter into rivalry

较 jiào 一 ㇓ 车 车 车 车 轩 轩 较 较

(較 一 厂 ㅜ 百 百 亘 車 車 軒 軒 軒 軒 較)

释义 Meaning

(一) 介词 prep.

compare; in comparison with: 今年的利润较去年增加了百分之十五。This year's profits have increased by fifiteen percent as compared to that in last year.

(二) 副词 adv.

comparatively; fairly; quite: 他在我们班里是个子较高的一个。He is one of the taller guys in our class.

词语 Words and Phrases

| 较量 | jiàoliàng | measure one's strength with; have a contest |

脚 jiǎo   丿 刀 刀 月 尸 肚 肚 脐 胠 脚 脚

释义 Meaning

名词 n.

1. foot: 他冬天也赤着脚。He goes bare foot even in the winter.

2. base; foot: 村子就在山脚下。The village was located at the foot of the hill.

词语 Words and Phrases

脚本	jiǎoběn	script; scenario
脚步	jiǎobù	step; pace
脚底	jiǎodǐ	sole
脚跟	jiǎogēn	heel
脚尖	jiǎojiān	tiptoe
脚气	jiǎoqì	athlete's foot
脚手架	jiǎoshǒujià	scaffold; falsework
脚印	jiǎoyìn	footprint; footmark
脚趾	jiǎozhǐ	toe
脚注	jiǎozhù	footnote

熟语 Idioms

脚踏两只船	jiǎo tà liǎng zhī chuán	straddle two boats; be a fence-sitter
脚踏实地	jiǎo tā shí dì	have one's feet planted on solid ground; in a well-grounded way

叫 jiào   丨 刂 口 叫 叫

释义 Meaning

（一）动词 v.

1. name; call: 我们都叫她小猫咪。We all call her "kitten".

2. call; greet: 楼下有人在叫你。Someone downstairs is calling you.

3. order; hire: 我给你叫了饺子和鸡蛋汤。I ordered dumplings and an egg soup for you.

4. ask; order: 我叫你过来，你再过来。Wait till I call you to come.

5. shout; cry: 你在走廊里大叫什么？What makes you cry aloud in the corridor?

（二）介词 prep.

by: 我忘在桌上的书叫人拿走了。The book I left on the desk was taken away by someone.

词语 Words and Phrases

叫喊	jiàohǎn	shout; yell
叫好	jiàohǎo	applaud; shout "well done"
叫苦	jiàokǔ	moan and groan; complain of hardship or suffering
叫骂	jiàomà	shout curses
叫卖	jiàomài	cry one's wares
叫座	jiàozuò	draw a large audience
叫作	jiàozuò	be called; be known as

熟语 Idioms

叫苦连天	jiào kǔ lián tiān	complain to high heaven; acutely hurt or feels unfair

接 jiē 　一　十　扌　扩　扩　护　护　挍　接　接　接

释义 Meaning

动词 v.

1. connect; join: 他把水管接在水龙头上。He connected a hose to the tap.

2. take hold of; receive: 我好久没有接到他的信了。I haven't received his letters for quite a long time.

3. meet; welcome: 我一定去机场接你。I will certainly go to the airport to meet you. 反义词 antonym: 送

词语 Words and Phrases

接班	jiēbān	take one's turn on duty; take over from
接班人	jiēbānrén	successor
接触	jiēchù	contact; get in touch with
接待	jiēdài	receive; admit
接风	jiēfēng	give a reception for a guest from afar
接见	jiējiàn	receive sb. ; grant an interview to
接近	jiējìn	be close to; near
接口	jiēkǒu	interface
接力	jiēlì	relay
接连	jiēlián	in succession; on end
接纳	jiēnà	admit; take in
接收	jiēshōu	receive; admit
接受	jiēshòu	accept
接替	jiētì	take over; replace
接头	jiētóu	① connect; joint ② contact; get in touch with
接吻	jiēwěn	kiss
接线员	jiēxiànyuán	(telephone) operator
接着	jiēzhe	follow; go on with
接种	jiēzhǒng	have an inoculation

熟语 Idioms

接二连三　　 jiē èr lián sān 　　 one after another; consecutive

街 jiē ⼃ ⼃ ⼃ ⼃ ⼃ ⼃ ⼃ ⼃ ⼃ ⼃ ⼃ 街

释义 Meaning

名词 n.

street: 街上人多车也多。The street is filled with people and vehicles.

词语 Words and Phrases

街道　　 jiēdào 　　 ① street ② neighbourhood
街头　　 jiētóu 　　 street; street corner

熟语 Idioms

街谈巷议　　 jiē tánxiàng yì 　　 street gossip; town talk
街头巷尾　　 jiē tóu xiàng wěi 　　 every street and alley

节 jié ⼀ ⼀ ⼀ ⼀ 节

(節 ⼃ ⼃ ⼃ ⼃ ⼃ ⼃ ⼃ ⼃ ⼃ ⼃ ⼃ 節 節)

释义 Meaning

(一)名词 n.

1. joint; knot: 绳子被打了个死结，我解不开。 I can't untie the cord because there is a fast knot on it.

2. festival; holiday: 中国人过春节的时候都要走亲访友。 Chinese people like to visit their relatives and friends during the Spring Festival.

（二）动词 v.

save; economize: 采用了新技术，一天能节水四吨。After adopting a new technology, we can save four tons of water daily.

（三）量词 measure w.

section; period: 小说最精彩的是第四节。The most wonderful part of the novel is the fourth section.

词语 Words and Phrases

节俭	jiéjiǎn	thrifty; frugal
节目	jiémù	programme; item (on a play-bill)
节日	jiérì	festival; holiday
节省	jiéshěng	use sparingly; cut down on
节约	jiéyuē	save; practise thrift
节制	jiézhì	control; be moderate in
节奏	jiézòu	rhythm

熟语 Idioms

| 节外生枝 | jiéwài shēng zhī | side issues crop up unexpectedly; raise obstacles |
| 节衣缩食 | jié yī suō shí | save on food and clothing; live frugally |

结₁ jié 乚 纟 纟 纟 纩 纩 结 结 结

（結 乚 纟 纟 纟 糸 糸 紅 紆 結 結 結 結 ）

释义 Meaning

动词 v.

bear (fruit); form (seed): 花儿已经结子了。The flowers have gone to seed already.

词语 Words and Phrases

结巴	jiēba	① stammer; stutter ② stammerer; stutterer
结实	jiēshi	solid; strong

结₂ jié 乙 幺 纟 纟 纠 纩 结 结 结

(結 乙 幺 幺 幺 糸 糸 紅 紆 結 結 結 結 **)**

释义 Meaning

（一）名词 n.

knot: 小女孩头上打了一个漂亮的蝴蝶结。The girl wears a beautiful bow in her hair.

（二）动词 v.

1. tie; knit; knot; weave: 蜘蛛在墙角结了一张大网。A spider wove a big web at the cornor of the wall.

2. congeal; form: 河水已经结冰了。The river water has already frozen.

3. settle; conclude: 离开的时候请去那个柜台结账。Please settle your accounts at that counter when you leave.

词语 Words and Phrases

结冰	jiébīng	freeze; ice up
结构	jiégòu	structure; construction
结果	jiéguǒ	① result; outcome ② at last; finally
结合	jiéhé	① combine; unite; link ② marry; be tied in wedlock
结婚	jiéhūn	marry; get married
结交	jiéjiāo	make friend with; associated with

结晶	jiéjīng	① crystallize ② crystal ③ crystallization; quintessence; fruit
结局	jiéjú	final result; outcome
结论	jiélùn	conclusion
结盟	jiéméng	form an alliance; ally
结石	jiéshí	stone, turn into stone
结识	jiéshí	get acquainted with sb.; get to know sb.
结束	jiéshù	end; finish
结算	jiésuàn	settle accounts
结尾	jiéwěi	ending
结业	jiéyè	complete a course
结账	jiézhàng	settle accounts

姐 jiě　　乚 女 女 如 如 姐 姐 姐

释义 Meaning

名词 n.

elder sister: 他大姐是个医生。His eldest sister is a doctor.

词语 Words and Phrases

姐夫	jiěfu	elder sister's husband
姐姐	jiějie	elder sister
姐妹	jiěmèi	sisters

解 jiě　　⼃ ⺈ ⼴ 勹 角 角 角 觧 觧 解 觧 解 解

释义 Meaning

动词 v.

1. untie; undo: 扣子都没解开，你怎么脱衣服？How can you take off the coat before you undo the buttons?

2. allay; dismiss: 这种药有解热镇痛的作用。This medicine can allay fever and ease pain.

3. explain; solve: 为解这个方程，我花了两个小时。I spent two hours on solving the equation.

4. understand; comprehend: 他的做法有些令人不解。His practice is a little bit incomprehensible.

词语 Words and Phrases

解除	jiěchú	remove; get rid of
解答	jiědá	answer; explain
解冻	jiědòng	① unfreeze ② thaw
解放	jiěfàng	liberate; emancipate
解雇	jiěgù	discharge; fire
解恨	jiěhèn	vent one's hatred
解决	jiějué	solve; settle
解渴	jiěkě	quench one's thirst
解闷	jiěmèn	divert oneself from boredom
解剖	jiěpōu	dissect
解散	jiěsàn	dismiss; dissolve
解释	jiěshì	explain; interpret
解手	jiěshǒu	go to the toilet
解说	jiěshuō	explain orally; comment
解体	jiětǐ	disintegrate; break up

熟语 Idioms

解铃系铃	jiě líng xì líng	one's fault should be amended by oneself

借₁ jiè ⼂ 亻 仁 什 什 併 併 借 借 借

释义 Meaning

动词 v.

1. borrow: 我向他借了二百块钱。I borrowed two hundred yuan from him. 反义词 antonym: 还

2. lend: 他不肯把书借给别人。He is not willing to lend his books to others. 反义词 antonym: 还

词语 Words and Phrases

借调	jièdiào	temporarily transfer; be on loan
借读	jièdú	study at a school on temporary basis
借故	jiègù	find an excuse
借光	jièguāng	excuse me
借鉴	jièjiàn	use for reference; draw lessons from
借口	jièkǒu	① use sth. as an excuse; on the excuse of ② excuse; pretext
借条	jiètiáo	receipt for a loan; IOU
借用	jièyòng	① borrow; have the loan of ② use sth. for another purpose
借助	jièzhù	have the aid of; with the help of

熟语 Idioms

借刀杀人	jiè dāo shā rén	murder with a borrowed knife; kill sb. by another's hand
借古讽今	jiè gǔ fěng jīn	use ancient things to satirize the present
借花献佛	jiè huā xiàn fó	present Buddha with borrowed flowers; give a present provided by somebody else
借题发挥	jiè tí fā huī	make use of a subject as a pretext for one's drawn-out talks

借₂ jiè 丿 亻 亻 什 件 借 借 借 借

(藉 一 艹 艹 艹 艹 萨 萨 萨 萨 萨 藉 藉 藉 藉 藉 藉)

释义 Meaning

动词 v.

make use of; take advantage of: 他借着路灯的光亮看书。
He read under the street lamp.

斤 jīn 二 厂 斤 斤

释义 Meaning

量词 measure w.

a unit of weight, 1/2 kilogram: 你出生的时候才四斤二
两。You were only 4.2 *jin* when you were born.

词语 Words and Phrases

斤两　　　jīnliǎng　　　weight

熟语 Idioms

斤斤计较　　jīnjīn jìjiào　　haggle over every ounce;
be calculating

金 jīn 丿 𠆢 𠆢 𠆢 全 全 金 金

释义 Meaning

名词 n.

1. gold: 老板手上戴满了金戒指。The boss has gold rings
on each finger.
2. golden: 他喜欢金发女郎。He is fond of blondes.

词语 Words and Phrases

金杯　　jīnbēi　　golden cup
金笔　　jīnbǐ　　fountain pen (with a gold nib)

金币	jīnbì	gold coin
金刚	jīngāng	Buddha's warrior attendant
金牌	jīnpái	gold medal
金钱	jīnqián	money
金融	jīnróng	finance; banking
金色	jīnsè	golden
金属	jīnshǔ	metal
金子	jīnzi	gold

熟语 Idioms

金碧辉煌	jīnbì-huīhuáng	looking splendid in green and gold; shine with gold and jade; colourful
金蝉脱壳	jīnchán tuō ké	slip out of a predicament like a cicada sloughing its skin; slime away
金鸡独立	jīn jī dú lì	standing on one foot as a cock does
金科玉律	jīn kē yù lù	golden rule and precious precept; infallible law
金口玉言	jīn kǒu yù yán	oracular words; words of wisdom
金石丝竹	jīnshí-sīzhú	all kinds of traditional Chinese musical struments
金屋藏娇	jīn wū cáng jiāo	keep a mistress in a love nest; take a concubine
金银财宝	jīn yín cái bǎo	treasures

紧 jǐn　　丨 丬 丬 臤 臤 堅 臤 紧 紧 紧

(緊　一 ｢ 丂 臣 臣 臣 臤 臤 堅 堅 緊 緊 緊)

释义 Meaning

（一）形容词 a.

1. tight; taut; close: 这双鞋我穿太紧了。This pair of shoes is too tight for me. 反义词 antonym: 松

2. urgent; pressing; tense: 时间很紧，大家快行动吧。Time is pressing, let's do it at once.

3. short of money; hard up: 快到月底了，心头有点儿紧。It's close to the end of the month, I am hard up.

（二）副词 adv.

closely: 那家就是白天也是门窗紧闭。The doors and windows of that family are closely shut even in the daytime.

词语 Words and Phrases

紧凑	jǐncòu	compact; well-knit; tight
紧急	jǐnjí	urgent; emergent; critical
紧紧	jǐnjǐn	closely; firmly
紧密	jǐnmì	close together
紧迫	jǐnpò	pressing; urgent; imminent
紧身	jǐnshēn	close-fitting (garment)
紧张	jǐnzhāng	① nervous; keyed up ② tense ③ in short supply

熟语 Idioms

紧锣密鼓	jǐn luó mì gǔ	an intense publicity campaign in preparation for an important undertaking

尽₁ jǐn ⁻ ⁼ 尸 尺 尽 尽

（盡 ⁻ ⁺ ⁼ 聿 聿 聿 肀 肃 肃 肃 盡
　　 盡 盡 盡）

释义 Meaning

副词 adv.

1. to the greatest extent: 我尽可能早些到。I'll try my best to come a little bit earlier.

2. keep on doing sth.: 这些日子尽下雨。It rains all these days.

词语 Words and Phrases

尽管	jǐnguǎn	① though; in spite of ② not hesitate to; feel free to
尽可能	jǐn kěnéng	as far as possible; to the best of one's ability
尽快	jǐnkuài	as quick/soon/early as possible
尽量	jǐnliàng	to the best of one's ability; as far as possible

尽₂ jìn ㄱ ㄱ 尸 尺 尽 尽

(盡 ㄱ ㄱ ㅋ 圭 圭 圭 圭 聿 聿 聿 畫

盡 盡 盡)

释义 Meaning

(一) 动词 v.

1. exhausted; to the limit: 自然资源不是用之不尽的。Natural resources are not endlessly available for human utilization.

2. use up; try one's best: 我一定尽力把这件事情办好。I will try my best to settle the matter.

(二) 副词 adv.

all; completely: 鬼神之事，不可不信，不可尽信。As for ghosts and spirits, one can't entirely dismiss their existance, yet one mustn't believe every spooky story one hears either.

词语 Words and Phrases

尽力	jìnlì	do all one can; try one's best
尽情	jìnqíng	to one's heart's content; as much as one likes
尽是	jìnshì	full of; without exception
尽头	jìntóu	end
尽心	jìnxīn	put one's heart and soul into
尽兴	jìnxìng	to one's heart's content; enjoy oneself to the full
尽早	jìnzǎo	with the least delay; at one's earliest convenience
尽职	jìnzhí	fulfill one's duty

熟语 Idioms

尽其所能	jìn qí suǒ néng	do it to the best of one's ability
尽人皆知	jìn rén jiē zhī	be known to everyone
尽善尽美	jìn shàn jìn měi	perfect; beau ideal
尽释前嫌	jìn shì qián xián	forget all the old grudges

近 jìn 　一　厂　斤　斤　斤　近　近

释义 Meaning

形容词 a.

1. near; close: 这儿离公司很近。This place is very close to the company. 反义词 antonym: 远

2. close to; approximately: 有近八万人观看了比赛。About eighty thousand people watched the match.

3. intimate; closely related: 她们两家的关系一直很近。The two families are on intimate terms all the time.

词语 Words and Phrases

| 近代 | jìndài | modern times |

近况	jìnkuàng	recent developments
近来	jìnlái	recently; lately
近期	jìnqī	in the near future; short-term
近亲	jìnqīn	close relative
近日	jìnrì	① in the past few days; recently ② within the next few days
近视	jìnshì	shortsightedness; myopia
近似	jìnsì	similar; approximate

熟语 Idioms

| 近水楼台
先得月 | jìn shuǐ lóutái
xiān dé yuè | a waterfront pavilion gets the moonlight first; have the advantage of being in a favorable position |
| 近朱者赤，
近墨者黑 | jìn zhū zhě chì,
jìn mò zhě hēi | one who stays near vermilion gets stained red, and one who stays near ink gets stained black; one takes on the color of one's company |

进 jìn　一 二 圭 井 讲 讲 进

(進 ノ 亻 亻 广 产 产 隹 隹 淮 進)

释义 Meaning

动词 v.

1. move forward; advance: 逆水行舟，不进则退。A boat sailing against the current must forge ahead or it will be driven back. 反义词 antonym: 退

2. enter; come into: 他十五岁就进大学读书了。He entered college when he was fifteen. 反义词 antonym: 出

3. eat; drink; take: 能赏光与我共进晚餐吗？May I have the honour of having dinner with you?

词语 Words and Phrases

进步	jìnbù	① advance; improve ② progressive
进场	jìnchǎng	enter the field
进程	jìnchéng	course; process
进出	jìnchū	① get in and out ② receipts and payments; turnover
进出口	jìnchūkǒu	① imports and exports ② entrances and exits
进度	jìndù	rate of progress
进而	jìnér	and then; proceed to the next step
进攻	jìngōng	attack; offensive
进化	jìnhuà	evolution
进货	jìnhuò	order merchandise for sale
进军	jìnjūn	march; move an army
进来	jìnlái	come in; enter
进去	jìnqù	go in; enter
进入	jìnrù	enter; get into
进行	jìnxíng	① be in progress; go on ② carry on; carry out
进修	jìnxiū	take a refresher course; engage in advanced studies
进一步	jìnyíbù	go a step further
进展	jìnzhǎn	make progress; make headway

景 jǐng   丨 冂 日 旦 旱 昙 景 景 景 景 景

释义 Meaning

名词 n.

scenery; view: 我们欣赏了西湖的美景。We enjoyed the enchanting scenery of the West Lake.

词语 Words and Phrases

景点	jǐngdiǎn	scenic spot
景观	jǐngguān	landscape
景气	jǐngqì	prosperity; boom
景色	jǐngsè	scenery; view; landscape
景泰蓝	jǐngtàilán	cloisonne enamel;
景物	jǐngwù	scenery
景致	jǐngzhì	view; scenery; scene

静 jìng 一 二 キ 主 丰 青 青 青 青 青 靜 静 静 静

释义 Meaning

形容词 a.

1. quiet; silent: 大家都静静地等待着最后的结果。Everybody is waiting in silence for the final result.

2. still; motionless: 除了睡觉，这孩子没有静的时候。The kid keeps on moving all the time except when he is sleeping.

词语 Words and Phrases

静电	jìngdiàn	static electricity
静脉	jìngmài	vein
静悄悄	jìngqiāoqiāo	very quiet
静止	jìngzhǐ	static; motionless
静坐	jìngzuò	sit-in

镜 jìng 丿 广 丘 丘 钅 钅 钅 铲 铲 铲 铲 铲 铲 镜 镜 镜

(镜 ノ ㇒ ㇒ ㇒ 牟 牟 金 金 釒 釒 釒
釒 釒 釒 鋕 鏡 鏡 鏡 鏡)

释义 Meaning

名词 n.

1. mirror; looking glass: 他简直认不出镜中的自己。He could hardly recognize himself in the mirror.

2. any kind of optical instruments: 他用天文望远镜观察月亮。He observed the moon with an astronomical telescope.

词语 Words and Phrases

镜框	jìngkuāng	① picture frame ② spectacle frame
镜片	jìngpiàn	lens
镜头	jìngtóu	① lens; camera ② shot; scene
镜子	jìngzi	mirror

熟语 Idioms

| 镜花水月 | jìng huā shuǐ yuè | flowers in a mirror and the moon in the water; an illusion |

九 jiǔ   丿 九

释义 Meaning

数词 num.

nine: 我家住在九楼。My home is on the ninth floor.

词语 Words and Phrases

| 九月 | jiǔyuè | September |
| 第九 | dì-jiǔ | ninth |

熟语 Idioms

| 九牛二虎之力 | jiǔ niú èr hǔ zhī lì | the strength of nine bulls and two tigers; tremendous effort |

九牛一毛	jiǔ niú yì máo	a single hair out of nine oxes; a drop in the ocean
九死一生	jiǔ sǐ yì shēng	a narrow escape of one's life
九霄云外	jiǔ xiāo yún wài	beyond the highest heavens; far, far away

久 jiǔ 　 丿　 勹　 久

释义 Meaning

(一)形容词 a.

long; for a long time: 故事发生在很久很久以前。The story happened a long time ago.

(二)名词 n.

of a specific duration: 你来香港已经多久了？How long have you been in Hong Kong?

词语 Words and Phrases

久久	jiǔjiǔ	for a long, long time
久违	jiǔwéi	haven't meet for a long time
久仰	jiǔyǎng	I've long been looking forward to meeting with you; I have long desired to know you

熟语 Idioms

久别重逢	jiǔ bié chóng féng	meet again after a long separation
久病成良医	jiǔ bìng chéng liáng yī	prolonged illness makes a patient into a good doctor
久而久之	jiǔ ér jiǔ zhī	in the course of time; as time passes
久旱逢甘霖	jiǔ hàn féng gānlín	have a welcome rain after a long drought; have a long-felt need satisfied
久经考验	jiǔ jīng kǎo yàn	long-tested; well-steeled

久闻大名　　　jiǔ wén dàmíng　　　I've long known of your great reputation

酒 jiǔ 　`　`　氵　氵　汀　汀　洒　洒　酒

释义 Meaning

名词 n.

alcoholic drink; wine; liquor: 邢老汉除了喝两口酒，再没有别的爱好了。The old Xing hasn't had any other hobbies besides sipping spirits.

词语 Words and Phrases

酒吧	jiǔbā	bar
酒杯	jiǔbēi	wine glass
酒馆	jiǔguǎn	tavern; public house
酒鬼	jiǔguǐ	alcoholic; tippler
酒壶	jiǔhú	wine pot; flagon
酒家	jiǔjiā	wineshop; restaurant
酒精	jiǔjīng	ethyl alcohol
酒量	jiǔliàng	capacity for liquor
酒酿	jiǔniàng	fermented glutinous rice
酒席	jiǔxí	feast
酒糟鼻	jiǔzāobí	acne rosacea; brandy nose
黄酒	huángjiǔ	yellow wine; rice wine
白酒	báijiǔ	white spirit
啤酒	píjiǔ	beer
葡萄酒	pútáojiǔ	wine
鸡尾酒	jīwěijiǔ	cocktail

熟语 Idioms

酒不醉	jiǔ bú zuì	it's not the wine that intoxicates but the drinker who gets himself drunk
人人自醉	rén rén zì zuì	

酒逢知己 千杯少	jiǔ féng zhī jǐ qiān bēi shǎo	a thousand glasses of wine are not enough when drinking with close friends
酒后吐真言	jiǔ hòu tǔ zhēn yán	in wine there is truth
酒囊饭袋	jiǔ náng fàn dài	a useless person good only for feasting and drinking

旧 jiù 丨 刂 旧 旧 旧

（舊 一 ナ 艹 艹 艹 艹 芢 芢 萑 萑 萑 萑 萑 舊 舊 舊 舊）

释义 Meaning

形容词 a.

1. old; past; bygone: 你年纪轻轻，可旧思想却不少。There are a lot of old ideas in your young body. 反义词 antonym: 新

2. used; worn; secondhand: 他房间里的彩电、冰箱都是旧的。Both the color TV set and the refrigerator in his room are old. 反义词 antonym: 新

词语 Words and Phrases

旧货	jiùhuò	secondhand goods; junk
旧居	jiùjū	old residence; old home
旧框框	jiùkuāngkuang	conventional; traditional
旧诗	jiùshī	old-style poetry; classical poetry
旧式	jiùshì	old type
《旧约》	jiùyuē	the *Old Testament*
旧址	jiùzhǐ	former site; former address

熟语 Idioms

| 旧调重弹 | jiù diào chóng tán | play an old tune; dwell repeatedly on the same topic |

| 旧梦重温 | jiù mèng chóng wēn | renew one's old romance; recall the past sweet dream |
| 酒瓶装新酒 | jiǔpíngzhuāngxīnjiǔ | new wine in an old bottle; new content in old format |

救 jiù　二　十　寸　才　求　求　求　求　求　救　救

释义 Meaning

动词 v.

1. save; rescue: 他把孩子从水中救了出来。He saved the child from drowning.

2. help; relieve: 大水刚退，村民们就开始了生产自救。Everyone turned their hands to pulling the village back together as soon as the flood receeded.

词语 Words and Phrases

救兵	jiùbīng	relief troops; reinforcement
救护	jiùhù	relieve a sick or injured person; rescue
救火	jiùhuǒ	fire fighting
救急	jiùjí	help sb. to cope with an emergency; help sb. to meet an urgent need
救济	jiùjì	relieve
救命	jiùmìng	① save sb.'s life ② Help!
救生	jiùshēng	lifesaving
救世主	jiùshìzhǔ	the Savior; the Redeemer
救星	jiùxīng	liberator; emancipator
救灾	jiùzāi	provide disaster relief; relieve the victims of a disaster

熟语 Idioms

| 救苦救难 | jiù kǔ jiù nàn | help the needy and relieve the distressed |

救死扶伤	jiù sǐ fú shāng	heal the wounded and rescue the dying

就 jiù
丶 亠 广 古 古 亨 亨 京 京 就 就 就

释义 Meaning

（一）副词 adv.

1. at once; in a moment: 你别走，我就来。Wait a moment, I'm coming right away.

2. as early as; already: 他早上六点就走了。He left at six this morning.

3. only; merely: 我们就去了两个地方。We went to just two places.

4. as many as; as much as: 他一个月的电费就是两百多块。He has to pay more than 200 *yuan* for electricity each month.

5. as soon as; right after: 你一提起他我就想起来了。I remembered him as soon as you mentioned him.

6. exactly; precisely: 我就要你手上的那一个。What I want is just the one in your hand.

（二）介词 prep.

with regard to; in the light of; as far as: 大家还就共同关心的问题进行了热烈的讨论。Everyone addressed the questions of common interest through a warm discussion.

词语 Words and Phrases

就地	jiùdì	on the spot
就近	jiùjìn	without having to go far; in the neighbourhood
就任	jiùrèn	take up one's post; take office
就是	jiùshì	① quite right; exactly ② even if; even

就是说	jiùshìshuō	that is to say; in other words
就算	jiùsuàn	even if; granted that
就要	jiùyào	be about to; be going to
就业	jiùyè	obtain employment; get a job
就义	jiùyì	die a martyr; be executed for championing a just cause
就座	jiùzuò	take one's seat; be seated

熟语 Idioms

| 就事论事 | jiù shì lùn shì | judge the case as it stands; consider the matter in isolation |

居 jū 一 ㄱ 尸 尸 尸 尸 居 居

释义 Meaning

动词 v.

1. be located at; occupy (a place): 这座古庙位居山腰。
   The ancient temple was located on the mountain side.
2. reside; dwell: 久居都市的人向往农村。Those who have lived in cities for a long time yearn for the countryside.

词语 Words and Phrases

居留	jūliú	reside
居民	jūmín	resident; inhabitant
居心	jūxīn	harbour (evil) intentions
居住	jūzhù	reside; dwell

熟语 Idioms

| 居安思危 | jū ān sī wēi | be prepared for danger in times of peace; think of danger in time of safety |
| 居高临下 | jū gāo lín xià | look down from a height; occupy a commanding position |

居功自傲　　　jū gōng zì ào　　claim credit for oneself and become arrogant

局 jú　　コ　ユ　尸　尸　局　局　局

释义 Meaning

名词 n.

1. bureau; office: 他是我们局新来的局长。He is the new head of our bureau.

2. game; set: 他输了前两局，但赢了最后三局。He lost the first two games, but won the last three.

3. situation; state of affairs: 我们还有扭转败局的机会。We still have the opportunity to turn back the tide of defeat.

词语 Words and Phrases

局部	júbù	in part
局促	júcù	① narrow ② short ③ feel or show constraint
局面	júmiàn	situation; prospects; phase
局势	júshì	situation; trends
局外人	júwàirén	outsider
局限	júxiàn	confine; limitation

举 jǔ　　丶　丷　丷　丷　严　兴　兴　兴　举

（擧　丿　丆　F　F　F　臼　臼　臼　臼　臼　與
與　與　與　擧　擧）

释义 Meaning

（一）动词 v.

1. lift; raise; hold up: 它太重了，我举不动它。It's too heavy to lift for me.

2. enumerate; cite: 他举了许多例子来说明这个道理。He

gave a lot of examples to illustrate the argument.

（二）名词 n.

act; deed; move: 他的壮举感动了在场的每一个人。Everyone on the spot was touched by his heroic undertaking.

词语 Words and Phrases

举办	jǔbàn	hold; conduct; run
举动	jǔdòng	movement; act
举国	jǔguó	whole nation; throughout the country
举例	jǔlì	cite an instance; give an example
举世	jǔshì	all over the world
举手	jǔshǒu	raise one's hands
举行	jǔxíng	hold; stage
举止	jǔzhǐ	bearing; manner; mien
举重	jǔzhòng	weight lifting

熟语 Idioms

举棋不定	jǔ qí bú dìng	hesitate about what move to make; be in two minds
举一反三	jǔ yī fǎn sān	draw inferences about other cases from one instance; witty
举足轻重	jǔ zú qīng zhòng	play a decisive role; carry big weight

句 jù   ノ 勹 勺 句 句

释义 Meaning

（一）名词 n.

sentence: 在阅读中遇到难句，我就向老师请教。Whenever I come across with difficult sentences while reading, I go to consult the teacher.

(二)量词 measure word

used for a sentence (a line of poetry, a proverb, etc.): 他坐在那儿，一句话也不说。He sat there, not saying a word.

词语 Words and Phrases

句号	jùhào	full stop; period
句子	jùzi	sentence
警句	jǐngjù	aphorism; epigram

剧 jù　一　ㄱ　尸　尸　尸　尸　居　居　屇　剧

(劇　丶　亠　产　卢　卢　卢　卢　虍　虐　虏　虏　虏　虏　豦　劇)

释义 Meaning

(一)名词 n.

drama; play; opera: 他在剧中演一个医生。He plays a doctor in the play.

(二)形容词 a.

severe; fierce; acute: 他感到头部一阵剧痛。He felt a severe pain in his head.

词语 Words and Phrases

剧本	jùběn	script
剧场	jùchǎng	theater
剧烈	jùliè	violent; acute; severe
剧情	jùqíng	the story of a play or opera; curtain
剧作家	jùzuòjiā	playwright; dramatist
剧终	jùzhōng	the end of a play or opera
电视剧	diànshìjù	TV play
京剧	jīngjù	Peking Opera
话剧	huàjù	modern drama; stage play

| 喜剧 | xǐjù | comedy |
| 悲剧 | bēijù | tragedy |

据 jù 一 十 扌 扩 扩 护 护 护 护 据 据

（據 一 十 扌 扩 扩 扩 扩 护 护 护 护 据 据 据 据 据）

释义 Meaning

（一）动词 v.

occupy; seize: 他常常把别人的东西据为己有。He often takes forcible possession of others' things.

（二）介词 prep.

according to; on the ground of: 据我所知，他是个很正直的人。As far as I know, he is a very honest man.

（三）名词 n.

evidence; certificate: 以此为据，我们可证明他有罪。We can use this evidence to prove his guilt.

词语 Words and Phrases

据说	jùshuō	allegedly; it is said; other people say
论据	lùnjù	ground of argument; argument
收据	shōujù	receipt

熟语 Idioms

| 据理力争 | jù lǐ lì zhēng | argue strongly on just grounds |
| 真凭实据 | zhēnpíng shíjù | factual evidence; conclusive evidence |

卷₁ juǎn 丶 丷 严 兰 关 关 卷 卷

(捲 一 十 扌 扩 扩 扩 捄 捄 捊 捲)

释义 Meaning

（一）动词 v.

1. roll up: 把那幅画卷起来。Roll up that painting, please.
2. sweep off; carry along: 一辆汽车开过去，卷起一阵尘土。A car went past, raising a cloud of dust.

（二）形容词 a.

curly; wavy: 她的头发很卷。Her hair is very curly.

（三）量词 measure w.

roll; reel; spool: 我买一卷手纸。I bought a roll of toilet paper.

词语 Words and Phrases

卷尺	juǎnchǐ	tape measure; band tape
卷心菜	juǎnxīncài	cabbage
卷筒纸	juǎntǒngzhǐ	a roll of paper
春卷	chūnjuǎn	spring roll (a thin sheet of dough, rolled, stuffed and fried)
胶卷	jiāojuǎn	a roll of film; film

熟语 Idioms

卷土重来　　juǎn tǔ chóng lái　　stage a comeback

卷₂ juàn ⺊ ⺋ 丷 丷 半 关 关 卷 卷

释义 Meaning

（一）名词 n.

1. book: 他总是手不释卷。He always has a book in his hand.
2. examination paper: 每次考试，他都是第一个交卷。In every exam he is the first to hand in the exam paper.

（二）量词 measure w.

volume: 俗话说，"读书破万卷，下笔如有神"。As the saying goes, "if you have read numerous volumes of books, you can write very well".

词语 Words and Phrases

卷子	juànzǐ	exam paper
答卷	dájuàn	answer sheet of an exam; answer exam questions in the exam paper

熟语 Idioms

开卷有益	kāi juàn yǒu yì	Reading is very benificial.

觉₁ jué 、 ＂ ＂ ′′ ″ ″ ″ ′′ ″ ″
（覺 ′ ′ ′ ′ ′ ′ ′ ′ ′ ′ ′
′ ′ ′ ′ ′ ′ ′ ′ ′）

释义 Meaning

（一）动词 v.

become aware; feel: 这房间一到晚上就觉出冷来了。As soon as night falls, this room begins to feel chilly.

（二）名词 n.

feeling; sense: 这样会给人造成错觉。This will give people a false impression.

词语 Words and Phrases

觉察	juéchá	detect; perceive
觉得	juéde	feel; sense; think
觉悟	juéwù	consciousness; awareness

熟语 Idioms

先知先觉	xiān zhī xiān jué	having foresight

觉₂ jiào ` `` `` ``` ``` ``` ``` 觉 觉

（覺 ` ⺁ ⺁ ⺁ ⺁ ⺁ ⺁ ⺁ ⺁ ⺁ ⺁

⺁ 與 學 學 學 學 覺 覺 覺）

释义 Meaning

名词 n.

sleep: 祝你睡个好觉。Have a good sleep!

词语 Words and Phrases

睡觉	shuìjiào	sleep; go to bed
午觉	wǔjiào	mid-day nap

军 jūn ` ` `` `` 军 军 军

（軍 ` ` `` `` 冖 冖 冟 冟 軍）

释义 Meaning

名词 n.

army; troops: 高中一毕业，他就参军了。As soon as he graduated from high school, he joined the army.

词语 Words and Phrases

军队	jūnduì	armed forces; army;
军官	jūnguān	officer
军火	jūnhuǒ	munitions; arms and ammunition
军人	jūnrén	armyman; serviceman
军事	jūnshì	military affairs
军训	jūnxùn	military training

开 kāi ` `` 一 开

(開 ⌐ 厂 厂 厂 戸 門 門 門 閂 閂 開 開)

释义 Meaning

动词 v.

1. open: 孩子不给陌生人开门。The child didn't open the door for the stranger. 反义词：关

2. blossom; open out: 玫瑰花什么时候开？When do roses blossom? 反义词：谢

3. start; operate: 火车下午四点开。The train will leave at four this afternoon.

4. set up; run: 他打算开一家小商店。He is going to set up a small shop.

5. hold (a meeting, exhibition, etc): 学校明天开运动会。The school athletic meet is going to be held tomorrow.

6. write out; make a list of: 麻烦您给我开个介绍信。May I trouble you to write me a letter of introduction?

7. (used after a verb,) indicates the meaning of departure or separation: 请打开窗。Please open the window.

8. (used after a verb,) indicates the meaning of capacity: 这客厅太小，跳舞跳不开。The drawing room is too small for dancing.

词语 Words and Phrases

开车	kāichē	start or drive a car, train, etc.
开除	kāichú	discharge; expel
开发	kāifā	exploit; develop
开关	kāiguān	switch (of lamp, machine, etc.)
开放	kāifàng	come into bloom; be open (to the public), open up

开口	kāikǒu	open one's mouth; start to talk
开朗	kāilǎng	optimistic; sanguine
开始	kāishǐ	begin; start
开玩笑	kāi wánxiào	play a joke; make fun of
开心	kāixīn	feel happy; rejoice
开演	kāiyǎn	(a play, drama, movie, etc.) begin

熟语 Idioms

| 开天辟地 | kāi tiān bì dì | the creation of the world; since the beginning of history |
| 异想天开 | yì xiǎng tiān kāi | indulge in an absurd fantasy; have a very fantastic idea |

看₁ kān 一 二 三 壬 壬 看 看 看 看

释义 Meaning

动词 v.

1. tend; look after: 她退休后帮别人看孩子。Since she retired, she looks after children for others.

2. keep under surveillance: 看住这个家伙，别让他跑了！Keep an eye on this rascal in case he runs away.

词语 Words and Phrases

看护	kānhù	nurse
看家	kānjiā	look after the house
看门	kānmén	guard the entrance; act as doorkeeper

看₂ kàn 一 二 三 壬 壬 看 看 看 看

释义 Meaning

动词 v.

1. look at; see; read; watch: 我很喜欢看电影。I like watching

movies

2. think; consider: 你对他的做法怎么看？What do you think of his behavior?

3. regard; look upon: 我把她看成我最好的朋友。I regard her as my best friend.

4. visit; call on: 他常去看爷爷。He often goes to see his grandfather.

5. (used after a reduplicated form of a verb or verb structure) to indicate trying to do something: 让我尝尝看。Let me just taste it.

词语 Words and Phrases

看病	kànbìng	(of a patient) see a doctor; (of a doctor) treat a patient
看不起	kànbùqǐ	look down upon; despise
看待	kàndài	treat; regard
看法	kànfǎ	view; a way of looking at a thing
看见	kànjiàn	see; catch sight of
看上	kànshàng	take a fancy to; settle on
看望	kànwàng	visit; call on; see
看重	kànzhòng	value; regard as important

熟语 Idioms

看风使舵	kàn fēng shǐ tuó	trim one's sails; change one's opinion opportunistically

抗 kàng 　一　十　扌　扩　扩　扩　抗

释义 Meaning

动词 v.

resist; combat; fight: 这是一种新型抗病毒药品。This is a newly developed anti-viral medicine.

词语 Words and Phrases

抗旱	kànghàn	fight a drought
抗洪	kànghóng	fight a flood
抗拒	kàngjù	resist; defy
抗灾	kàngzāi	fight a disaster
抵抗	dǐkàng	resist; stand up to
违抗	wéikàng	disobey; defy

考 kǎo   一　十　土　耂　考　考

释义 Meaning

（一）动词 v.

1. give or take an examination: 弟弟考上了名牌大学。
   My younger brother was admitted to a famous university.

2. raise questions and let the opposite side answer: 我来考考
   你。Let me quiz you.

（二）名词 n.

1. examination: 下个月我们有中考。Next month we will
   have mid-term exams.

词语 Words and Phrases

考查	kǎochá	examine; check
考场	kǎochǎng	examination hall or room
考究	kǎojiū	particular; exquisite
考卷	kǎojuàn	examination paper
考虑	kǎolù	think over; consider
考试	kǎoshì	examination; test
考验	kǎoyàn	test; trial

烤 kǎo   丶　丷　少　火　灯　灶　烂　烤　烤　烤

释义 Meaning

动词 v.

roast; bake; toast: 他喜欢吃妈妈烤的面包。He loves to eat the bread his mother bakes.

词语 Words and Phrases

烤火	kǎohuǒ	warm oneself by a fire
烤炉	kǎolú	oven
烤肉	kǎoròu	roast meat; roast
烤鸭	kǎoyā	roast duck

靠 kào ′ 二 牛 告 告 告 告 靠 靠 靠 靠 靠 靠 靠 靠

释义 Meaning

动词 v.

1. lean against; lean on: 他们俩背靠背坐着。They sat back to back.
2. keep to; get near; come up to: 请靠右边走。Please keep to the right.
3. near; by: 我家靠海边。My home is by the sea.
4. depend on; rely on: 他能取得这么好的成绩，全靠自己的努力。That he could make such great achievements depended entirely on his own efforts.
5. trust: 他是个靠得住的人。He is a trustworthy man.

词语 Words and Phrases

靠岸	kào'àn	pull in to shore (boat)
靠边	kàobiān	keep to the side
靠不住	kàobúzhù	unreliable; untrustworthy
靠近	kàojìn	near; close to; by
靠山	kàoshān	backer; backing; patron

| 可靠 | kěkào | reliable; trustworthy |
| 依靠 | yīkào | depend on; rely on |

熟语 Idioms

| 靠山吃山，
靠水吃水 | kào shān chī shān,
kào shuǐ chī shuǐ | make use of local
resources |

楼 kē 一 十 才 木 朴 朾 柙 栶 桿 桿
桿 楼

释义 Meaning

量词 measure w.

used for plants like trees, grass, etc.: 院子里长着一棵大树。A tall tree is growing in the courtyard.

颗 kē 丨 冂 冃 日 旦 甲 里 果 果 果
颗 颗 颗 颗

（颗 丨 冂 冃 日 旦 甲 里 果 果 果 果
颗 颗 颗 颗 颗 颗）

释义 Meaning

量词 measure word

used for small and roundish objects like stars, pearls, diamonds, etc.: 她有一颗善良的心。She has a very kind heart.

熟语 Idioms

| 颗粒无收 | kē lì wú shōu | gather in no grain |
| 颗粒归仓 | kē lì guī cāng | every grain to the grainary |

可 kě 一 丆 冂 叮 可

释义 Meaning

（一）副词 adv.

used to strengthen the tone: 这件事很重要，你可别忘记啊。This matter is very important, so don't forget it!

（二）连词 conj.

but; yet: 我告诉他那里很危险，可他还是坚持要去。I told him that it was very dangerous there, but he still insisted on going.

（三）能愿动词 modal verb

may; can: 这次活动不是很重要，可参加可不参加。This activity is not that important, so you can either attend or not.

词语 Words and Phrases

可爱	kěài	lovely; lovable
可悲	kěbēi	sad; lamentable
可观	kěguān	considerable; impressive
可贵	kěguì	valuable; commendable
可见	kějiàn	it is thus clear that; evidently
可口	kěkǒu	tasty; delicious; palatable
可怜	kělián	pitiful; pitiable; poor
可能	kěnéng	maybe; probably; possible; probable
可是	kěshì	but; yet; however
可惜	kěxī	it's a pity; it's too bad
可笑	kěxiào	fuuny; ridiculous; laughable
可以	kěyǐ	can; may; not bad; pretty good

熟语 Idioms

可望而不可即	kě wàng ér bù kě jí	beyond one's reach; reach; unattainable
模棱两可	mó léng liǎng kě	in an ambiguous way; equivocal

渴kě

丶 丶 氵 氵 氵 氵 氵 氵 渴 渴 渴 渴

释义 Meaning

形容词 a.

thirsty: 渴了就喝茶吧。Have a drink of tea if you're thirsty.

词语 Words and Phrases

渴求	kěqiú	desire; yearn for
渴望	kěwàng	yearn for; long for; thirst for
解渴	jiěkě	quench one's thirst
口渴	kǒukě	thirsty

刻kè

丶 亠 亠 亥 亥 亥 刻 刻

释义 Meaning

(一) 名词 n.

1. a quarter (of an hour): 他每天六点三刻起床。He gets up at 6:45 a. m. every day.
2. moment: 他永远忘不了那激动人心的一刻。He can never forget that exciting moment.

(二) 动词 v.

carve; cut; engrave: 这件工艺品是用木头刻的。This handicraft is a woodcut.

词语 Words and Phrases

刻薄	kèbó	mean; harsh; unkind
刻画	kèhuà	depict; portray
刻苦	kèkǔ	hardworking; diligent; painstaking
刻意	kèyì	purposely
刻字	kèzì	carve characters on a seal, etc.
深刻	shēnkè	deep; profound

熟语 Idioms

刻不容缓	kè bù róng huǎn	very urgent; demand immediate attention
刻骨铭心	kè gú míng xīn	remember all one's life
刻舟求剑	kè zhōu qiú jiàn	act without regard to changes in circumstances

客 kè ` ` 宀 宀 灾 宠 宓 客 客

释义 Meaning

名词 n.

1. visitor; guest: 家里来客了。 A guest came to visit us.
2. customer: 这家饭店生意很好，常常客满。 The business of this restaurant is booming and the seats are often filled.

词语 Words and Phrases

客车	kèchē	passenger train; bus
客房	kèfáng	guest room
客气	kèqì	polite; courteous
客人	kèrén	guest; visitor
乘客	chéngkè	passenger
顾客	gùkè	customer; shopper
游客	yóukè	tourist; sightseer; visitor
旅客	lǚkè	passenger; traveler
作客	zuòkè	be a guest

课 kè ` i i i i i 评 课 课

(課 ` ` ` ` 言 言 言 訁 訶 詚 誯 課 課)

释义 Meaning

（一）名词 n.

1. course; subject: 我很喜欢上历史课。I like history classes very much.

2. class: 今天下午我没有课。I have no class this afternoon.

（二）量词 measure w.

lesson: 这本教科书共有二十课。This textbook contains twenty lessons.

词语 Words and Phrases

课本	kèběn	textbook
课程	kèchéng	course; curriculum
课堂	kètáng	classroom; schoolroom
课外	kèwài	exracurricular; outside class
课文	kèwén	text
课余	kèyú	after school; after class
功课	gōngkè	school work; homework
选修课	xuǎnxiūkè	elective course
必修课	bìxiūkè	required course

肯 kěn ⎜ ⊢ ⊢ ⊢ ⊢ 肯 肯 肯

释义 Meaning

动词 v.

be willing to; be ready to: 你肯不肯一个人做这项工作？
Are you willing to do this work alone?

词语 Words and Phrases

肯定	kěn dìng	certainly; definitely; undoubtedly; positive; affirmative; definite; sure
肯干	kěn gàn	be ready to do hard work

空₁ kōng ⎜ ⎝ 宀 宀 穴 空 空 空

释义 Meaning

（一）形容词 a.

empty; hollow; void: 箱子里是空的。The box is empty.

反义词：满

（二）名词 n.

sky; air: 空中飘着几朵白云。There are some clouds floating in the sky.

（三）副词 ad.

for nothing; in vain: 他的话让我空欢喜一场。What he said gave me a burst of false hope.

词语 Words and phrases

空荡荡	kōngdàngdàng	empty; deserted
空话	kōnghuà	empty talk; hollow words
空间	kōngjiān	space
空军	kōngjūn	air force
空旷	kōngkuàng	open; spacious
空气	kōngqì	air; atmosphere
空前	kōngqián	unprecedented
空手	kōngshǒu	empty-handed
空谈	kōngtán	indulge in empty talk; empty talk
空虚	kōngxū	hollow; void
天空	tiānkōng	the sky; the heavens

熟语 Idioms

空空如也	kōngkōng rú yě	have nothing inside
空口无凭	kōng kǒu wú píng	a mere verbal statement is of no proof
空前绝后	kōng qián jué hòu	unprecedented
空中楼阁	kōng zhōng lóu gé	illusions that can't be realized; castle in the air

空₂ kòng　丶　丶　宀　宀　穴　空　空　空

释义 Meaning

（一）动词 v.

leave empty or blank: 请把第一排座位空出来。Please leave the first row of seats vacant.

（二）形容词 a.

unoccupied; vacant: 客厅很大，但家俱很少，所以显得很空。The big drawing room with a few pieces of furniture looks very empty. 反义词：挤

（三）名词 n.

1. empty space: 每个字之间留一点空儿。Leave a little space between each character.

2. free time; spare time: 今晚我没空。I have no time tonight.

词语 Words and phrases

空白	kòngbái	blank space
空格	kònggé	empty space in a form
空暇	kòngxiá	free time; leisure
空闲	kòngxián	idle; free time; spare time

熟语 Idioms

钻空子	zuān kòngzi	avail oneself to loopholes (in law, contract, etc.); exploit an advantage

口 kǒu　丨　冂　口

释义 Meaning

（一）名词 n.

1. mouth: 我们要注意饮食卫生，因为病从口入。We should pay attention to dietary hygiene, for many deseases are transmitted orally.

2. opening; entrance; mouth: 瓶子口 太小了。 The mouth of the bottle is too small.

3. cut; hole: 茶杯缺了个口儿。 The rim of the cup is chipped.

（二）量词 measure word

used for family members, well, knife, etc.: 你家有几口人？ How many people are there in your family?

词语 Words and phrases

口才	kǒucái	eloquence
口袋	kǒudài	pocket
口号	kǒuhào	slogan; watchword
口渴	kǒukě	thirsty
口试	kǒushì	oral examination; oral test
口述	kǒushù	oral account
口头	kǒutóu	orally
口味	kǒuwèi	a person's taste; the flavour of food
口译	kǒuyì	oral interpretation
口音	kǒuyīn	accent; voice

熟语 Idioms

口蜜腹剑	kǒu mì fù jiàn	honey on one's lips and murder in one's heart
口若悬河	kǒu ruò xuán hé	be eloquent

哭 kū ｜ 冂 口 吅 吅 吅 罒 罘 哭 哭

释义 Meaning

动词 v.

cry; weep: 这孩子夜里好哭。 The child likes to cry at night.

反义词：笑

词语 Words and Phrases

哭鼻子	kū bízi	snivel

| 哭泣 | kūqì | cry; weep; sob |

熟语 Idioms

| 哭笑不得 | kūxiào bù dé | make people feel sth. both funny and annoying |

苦 kǔ   一 艹 艹 艹 芋 芋 苦 苦

释义 Meaning

（一）形容词 a.

bitter: 有的蔬菜味道很苦。Some of the vegetables taste bitter. 反义词：甜

（二）名词 n.

hardship; suffering; pain: 他从小吃了很多苦。He suffered a bitter childhood.

（三）动词 v.

cause sb. suffering; give sb. a hard time: 这事可苦了他了。This matter really gave him a hard time.

（四）副词 ad.

doing one's utmost; painstakingly: 母亲苦苦地劝儿子回家，可儿子不答应。The mother earnestly persuaded her son to go home, but he refused.

词语 Words and Phrases

苦干	kǔgàn	work hard
苦功	kǔgōng	painstaking effort; hard work
苦海	kǔhǎi	sea of bitterness; abyss of misery
苦难	kǔnàn	suffering; misery; distress
苦恼	kǔnǎo	vexed; worried
苦头	kǔtóu	suffering
苦心	kǔxīn	trouble taken; pains
苦衷	kǔzhōng	pain or hardships that one is reluctant to mention or discuss

熟语 Idioms

苦尽甘来	kǔ jìn-gān lái	happiness comes after bitterness
苦口婆心	kǔ kǒu pó xīn	urge sb. patiently and earnestly with good intentions
苦思冥想	kǔ sī míng xiǎng	rack one's brains to think

裤kù ` ﹀ 衤 衤 衤 衤 衤 衤 衤 衤 裤 裤

(褲 ` ﹀ 衤 衤 衤 衤 衤 衤 衤 褃 褃 褃 褃 褲)

释义 Meaning

名词 n.

trousers; pants: 他新买了一条裤子。He has just bought a pair of new trousers.

词语 Words and Phrases

裤腿	kùtuǐ	trouser legs
短裤	duǎnkù	shorts
毛裤	máokù	woolen trousers
棉裤	miánkù	cotton-padded trousers
牛仔裤	niúzǎikù	close-fitting trousers; jeans

块kuài 一 十 土 圡 坮 垆 块

(塊 一 十 土 圡 圹 垆 垆 坤 坤 塊 塊 塊)

释义 Meaning

（一）名词 n.

1. piece; lump; chunk: 把土豆切成块儿。Please cut the potato into cubes.

（二）量词 measure w.

1. used of a slice or chunk of sth: 我送他一块蛋糕作礼物。I gave him a piece of cake as a gift.

2. *yuan*, the basic unit of money in China: 我只有十块钱了。I have only ten *yuan* with me now.

词语 Words and Phrases

方块字　　fāngkuàizì　Chinese characters

快 kuài 　 丶 丶 忄 忄 忙 快 快

释义 Meaning

（一）形容词 a.

1. fast; quick; rapid: 请不要说得这么快。Please don't speak so fast. 反义词：慢

2. quick-witted; clever: 他脑子不快，但很用功。Though not quick-witted, he is very diligent. 反义词：笨

3. sharp: 这把水果刀很快，你要小心手。This fruit knife is very sharp, so be careful of your finger. 反义词：钝

（二）副词 ad.

1. hurry up; hastily: 快走，时间来不及了。Hurry up, there is no time left.

2. soon; before long; nearly: 我学汉语快两年了。I have been learning Chinese for nearly two years.

词语 Words and Phrases

快餐　　kuàcān　　　fast food
快车　　kuàichē　　　express train or bus

快活	kuàihuo	happy; merry
快件	kuàijiàn	express mail
快乐	kuàilè	happy; cheerful; joyful
赶快	gǎnkuài	at once; make haste
尽快	jìnkuài	as soon as possible
凉快	liángkuài	nice and cool

熟语 Idioms

| 快马加鞭 | kuài mǎ jiā biān | spur on the flying horse to full speed |
| 大快人心 | dà kuài rén xīn | to the greatest satisfaction of all |

筷 kuài ㇒ ㇒ ㇒ ㇒ 竹 竹 竹 竹 竿 竿 筒 筷 筷

释义 Meaning

名词 n.

chopsticks: 她正在帮妈妈收拾碗筷。She is helping mum to clear away the bowls and chopsticks .

词语 Words and phrases

| 筷子 | kuài zi | chopsticks |

宽 kuān ㇔ ㇔ 宀 宀 宀 宀 宀 宿 宽 宽

（宽 ㇔ ㇔ 宀 宀 宀 宀 宀 宿 宿 宿 宽 宽 宽）

释义 Meaning

（一）形容词 a.

1. wide; broad: 这条小河很宽。This river is very wide. 反义词：窄

2. well-off; comfortably off: 最近他手头不太宽。He has

not been very well-off recently. 反义词：紧

3. generous; lenient: 我们应该宽以带人，严以律己。One should be lenient with others and be strict with oneself. 反义词：严

（二）名词 n.

width; breadth: 卧室有四米宽。The bedroom is four metres wide.

（三）动词 v.

relax; relieve: 得知孩子已经脱险，他的心就宽多了。He was greatly relieved to learn that the child was out of danger.

词语 Words and Phrases

宽敞	kuānchǎng	spacious; roomy
宽度	kuāndù	width; breadth
宽广	kuānguǎng	broad; extensive; vast
宽厚	kuānhòu	generous
宽容	kuānróng	tolerant; lenient
宽恕	kuānshù	forgive
宽裕	kuānyù	well-to-do; ample; comfortably off

熟语 Idioms

宽宏大量	kuānhóng dàliàng	broad-minded; magnanimous

拉 lā   一 十 扌 扩 扩 扩 拉 拉

释义 Meaning

动词 v.

1. pull; draw; drag: 马在拉很重的车。The horse is pulling a heavy cart.

2. transport by vehicle; haul: 这车只能拉人，不拉货。

This car only carries people, not goods.

3. play (bowed stringed instruments): 他小提琴拉得很好。
He plays the violin very well.

4. give a helping hand; help: 朋友有困难的时候，应该拉一把。We must give a helping hand when our friends are in need.

词语 Words and Phrases

拉倒	lādǎo	(orally) forget about it; drop it
拉拢	lālǒng	draw sb. over to one's side; rope in
拉手	lāshǒu	handle (of a door, window, drawer, etc); hold hands

熟语 Idioms

| 拉关系 | lā guānxi | try to establish a relationship with sb.; cotton up to |
| 拉下水 | lā xià shuǐ | drag sb. into the mire; corrupt sb. |

来 lái   一 广 䒑 平 来 来

(來   一 广 䒑 夾 來 來 來)

释义 Meaning

（一）动词 v.

1. come, approach; crop up: 一场暴风雨就要来了。A storm is coming up soon. 反义词：去；离开

2. used before a verb to indicate going to do sth.: 我来自我介绍一下。Let me introduce myself.

3. used together with "得" or "不"，to indicate possibility or impossibility to do sth.: 唱歌我唱得来，但跳舞我跳不来。I can sing, but I can't dance.

4. used to take place of the verb of concrete meaning: 先生，来一瓶啤酒。Waiter, bring me one bottle of beer, please.

5. used between two verb structures indicating the aim of doing sth.: 你打算用什么方法来帮助他呢？How are you going to help him?

6. used after a verb to indicate coming to do sth.: 我向你们告别来了。I am here to say goodbye to you.

7. used after a verb as a complement to indicate that the action is moving toward the speaker: 明天请把词典带来。Please bring your dictionary here tomorrow.

8. used after a verb to indicate the result of the action: 一觉醒来，已是下午两点。 Waking after a sound sleep, the time was already 2:00 p.m..

（二）助词 auxiliary word

1. used after numerals to indicate an approximate number: 他看上去五十来岁。He appears to be in his fifties.

2. ever since: 几个月来，他一直都很忙。He has been very busy for these past few months.

3. used after numerals to enumerate reasons: 我这次去北京，一来是旅游，二来是看看老同学。My trip to Beijing this time is for two reasons: one is sightseeing, the other is to visit my old classmates.

词语 Words and Phrases

来宾	láibīn	guest; visitor
来不及	láibùjí	there's not enough time (to do sth.); it's too late (to do sth.)
来得及	láidejí	there's still time; be able to do sth. in time
来访	láifǎng	come to visit; come to call
来历	láilì	origin; source; past history; background
来年	lái nián	next year; the coming year

来往	láiwǎng	① come and go
		② dealings; contact; intercourse
来信	láixìn	incoming letter; send a letter here
来源	láiyuán	① origin; source ② stem from; originate
从来	cónglái	always; at all times
向来	xiànglái	all along; always
原来	yuánlái	original; former

熟语 Idioms

来龙去脉	lái lóng qù mò	cause and result; the whole story of (an event)
来日方长	láirì fāng cháng	there will be ample time for doing something
来之不易	lái zhī bú yì	be not easy to get

拦 lán 一 十 扌 扩 扩 扩 拦 拦

(攔 一 十 扌 扌 扩 扩 扩 扩 押 押 押 押 押 押 攔 攔 攔 攔 攔)

释义 Meaning

动词 v.

hold back; bar: 别拦他，让他去吧。Don't stop him, just let him go.

词语 Words and Phrases

拦路	lánlù	block the way
拦腰	lányāo	by the waist; round the middle
遮拦	zhēlán	obstruct; block
阻拦	zǔlán	bar the way; stop

熟语 Idioms

| 拦路虎 | lánlùhǔ | (sb. is a) obstacle; stumbling block |

蓝 lán
一 十 艹 艹 艹 芷 芷 芷 苂 苂
苂 蓝 蓝

(藍
一 十 艹 艹 艹 艹 芍 芍 莇 莇 藍
莇 莇 蓙 藍 藍 藍)

释义 Meaning

（一）形容词 a.

blue: 天空蓝蓝的。The sky is blue.

（二）名词 n.

blue color: 这只猫的眼睛绿中带蓝。This cat's eyes are green with a tinge of blue.

词语 Words and Phrases

蓝宝石	lánbǎoshí	sapphire
蓝图	lántú	blueprint
碧蓝	bìlán	dark blue
景泰蓝	jǐngtàilán	enamel
天蓝	tiānlán	sky blue
蔚蓝	wèilán	azure

熟语 Idioms

青出于蓝	qīng chū yú lán	(analogy) the pupil learns from the master and surpasses the master

懒 lǎn
丶 丷 忄 忄 忄 忄 忄 忄 怀 悚
悚 悚 懒 懒 懒 懒

释义 Meaning

形容词 a.

lazy; slothful: 他是个很懒的人。He is a lazy man. 反义词：勤劳

词语 Words and Phrases

懒得	lǎnde	not feel like (doing sth.); not be in the mood to
懒惰	lǎnduò	lazy
懒骨头	lǎngútou	lazy-bones
懒洋洋	lǎnyángyáng	languid; listless
偷懒	tōulǎn	be lazy; loaf on the job

熟语 Idioms

| 心灰意懒 | xīn huī yì lǎn | be downhearted; be discouraged |

狼 láng ´ ⺅ ⺅ ⺅ ⺅ ⺅ ⺅ 狼 狼 狼

释义 Meaning

名词 n.

wolf: 这座山上有很多狼。There are many wolves on this mountain.

词语 Words and Phrases

| 狼狗 | lánggǒu | wolfhound; German shepard |
| 狼藉 | lángjí | in disorder; scatter about in a mess |

熟语 Idioms

狼狈为奸	lángbèi wéi jiān	collude in doing evil; act in collusion with each other
狼吞虎咽	láng tūn hǔ yān	gobble up; wolf down
狼心狗肺	láng xīn gǒu fèi	ungrateful

浪 làng ` ` ⺡ ⺡ ⺡ ⺡ ⺡ 浪 浪 浪

释义 Meaning

名词 n.

wave; billow: 海上浪很大。The waves on the sea are huge.

词语 Words and Phrases

浪费	làngfèi	waste; squander
浪花	lànghuā	spray; spindrift
浪漫	làngmàn	romantic
风浪	fēnglàng	stormy waves; storm
流浪	liúlàng	roam about; lead a vagrant life

熟语 Idioms

浪子回头	làngzǐ huí tóu	good change of a prodigal son
长江后浪推前浪	cháng jiāng hòulàng tuī qiánlàng	each generation excels the previous one
无风不起浪	wú fēng bù qǐ làng	no smoke without fire

捞lāo 一 十 扌 扩 扩 扩 扩 捞 捞 捞

(捞 一 十 扌 扌 扩 扩 扩 扩 扩 扩 扩 扩 扨 捞 捞)

释义 Meaning

动词 v.

1. drag for; fish for: 孩子们在河边捞鱼。The children are netting fish near the river.

2. get by improper means: 他从这里捞到了不少好处。 He got a lot of good from this.

词语 Words and Phrases

捞着	lāozháo	get the opportunity of doing sth.
捕捞	bǔlāo	fish for (aquatic animals and plants)
打捞	dǎlāo	get out of the water; salvage

熟语 Idioms

| 捞稻草 | lāo dàocǎo | try to take advantage of sth. |

老lǎo 　 一 　 十 　 土 　 尹 　 考 　 老

释义 Meaning

（一）形容词 a.

1. old; aged: 他看上去比实际年龄老。He appears older than his actual age. 反义词：小

2. old; of long standing: 我们是老朋友了。We are old friends. 反义词：新

3. outdated: 这种机器太老了。This type of machine is out of date. 反义词：新

4. tough; overgrown: 这鸡肉太老了。The chicken meat tastes too tough. 反义词：嫩

（二）名词 n.

old people; the aged: 年轻人应该尊老：爱老。The young should respect and cherish for the elderly.

（三）副词 ad.

1. very: 他从老远的地方赶来。He rushed here from far away.

2. always: 你怎么上班老迟到？Why are you always late for work?

词语 Words and Phrases

老百姓	lǎobǎixìng	common people; civilians
老板	lǎobǎn	boss
老伴	lǎobàn	(of an old married couple) husband or wife
老规矩	lǎo guīju	old rules and regulations; conventions
老虎	lǎohǔ	tiger
老家	lǎojiā	native place; old home
老年	lǎonián	old age
老婆	lǎopo	(orally) wife

老人	lǎorén	old people
老师	lǎoshī	teacher
老实	lǎoshi	honest; frank
老手	lǎoshǒu	old hand; veteran
老鼠	lǎoshǔ	mouse
古老	gǔlǎo	ancient
月老	yuèlǎo	the god who unites persons in marriage; matchmaker

熟语 Idioms

老大难	lǎodànán	long standing and difficult problem
老当益壮	lǎo dāng yì zhuàng	old but full of vigor
老虎屁股 摸不得	lǎohǔ pìgu mō bù dé	(like a tiger whose back side) sthg. no one dares to intervene
老骥伏枥， 志在千里	lǎo jì fú lì, zhì zài qiān lǐr	old people with high aspiration
老马识途	lǎo mǎ shí tú	an old hand is a good guide; an experience person knows the ropes
老谋深算	lǎo móu shēn suàn	experienced and astute (plot something evil)

乐₁ lè 二 仁 乐 乐 乐

(樂 ' 亻 亅 白 白 㿥 纠 纠 綿 綿 綿 樂 樂 樂 樂)

释义 Meaning

动词 v.

1. happy; joyfull: 他心里乐开了花。His heart was filled with joy.

2. laugh; be amused: 你在乐什么呀？What are you laugh-

ing at?

词语 Words and Phrases

乐观	lèguān	optimistic
乐趣	lèqù	pleasure; delight
乐土	lètǔ	merry land; paradise
乐于	lèyú	be glad to; take delight in
乐园	lèyuán	paradise
欢乐	huānlè	happy; joyful
取乐	qǔlè	amuse oneself; seek pleasure
娱乐	yúlè	entertainment; amusement

熟语 Idioms

乐不可支	lè bù kě zhī	overjoyed
乐不思蜀	lè bù sī shǔ	indulge in pleasure and forget what one should do
乐此不疲	lè cǐ bù pí	never be tired of doing it
乐极生悲	lè jí shēng bēi	extreme joy precedes sorrow

乐₂ yuè 一 ㄷ 乐 乐 乐

（樂 ' ⺊ ⺊ 白 白 ⺉白 纠 纠 纲 樂 樂 樂 樂 樂 樂）

释义 Meaning

名词 n.

music: 他的音乐感很强。He has strong sense of music.

词语 Words and Phrases

乐队	yuèduì	orchestra; band
乐器	yuèqì	musical instrument
乐曲	yuèqǔ	musical compositon
交响乐	jiāoxiǎngyuè	symphony

| 音乐 | yīnyuè | music |
| 奏乐 | zòuyuè | strike up a tune; play music |

雷 léi

一 厂 一 一 一 一 一 一 一 雪 雪
雪 雷 雷

释义 Meaning

名词 n.

thunder: 好像要打雷了。Thunder seems likely.

词语 Words and Phrases

雷达	léidá	radar
雷声	léishēng	thunderclap
雷同	léitóng	echoing what others have said; duplicate; similar
雷阵雨	léizhènyǔ	shower with thunder

熟语 Idioms

雷打不动	léi dǎ bú dòng	unshakable; stick to something
雷厉风行	léi lì fēng xíng	do something vigorously and speedily
雷声大，雨点小	léishēng dà, yǔdiǎn xiǎo	loud thunder but small rain drops; much said but little done

泪 lèi

丶 丶 氵 氵 汩 汩 汩 泪

释义 Meaning

名词 n.

tear; teardrop: 她满脸都是泪。Her face was bathed in tears.

词语 Words and Phrases

| 泪花 | lèihuā | tears in one's eyes |
| 泪水 | lèishuǐ | tear |

泪汪汪	lèiwāngwāng	(eyes) brimming with tears
泪珠	lèizhū	teardrop
眼泪	yǎnlèi	tears

熟语 Idioms

| 鳄鱼眼泪 | èyú yǎnlèi | crocodile tears |

类 lèi ` ` ⺍ 半 半 米 米 米 类 类

（類 ` ` ⺍ 米 米 米 米 米 米 类 類 類 類 類 類 類 類 類）

释义 Meaning

（一）名词 n.

kind; category: 他们属于同一类人。They are the same kind of people.

（二）动词 v.

be similar to: 这个故事听上去类乎神话。The story sounds like a fairy tale.

词语 Words and Phrases

类别	lèibié	classification
类似	lèisì	similar
类推	lèituī	analogize
类型	lèixíng	type
分类	fēnlèi	classify
同类	tónglèi	be of a kind
种类	zhǒnglèi	type; variety

熟语 Idioms

| 不伦不类 | bù lún bú lèi | neither fish nor fowl |
| 画虎类犬 | huà hǔ lèi quǎn | attempt something too ambitious and end in failure |

物以类聚 wù yǐ lèi jù like attracts like

累$_1$ lèi 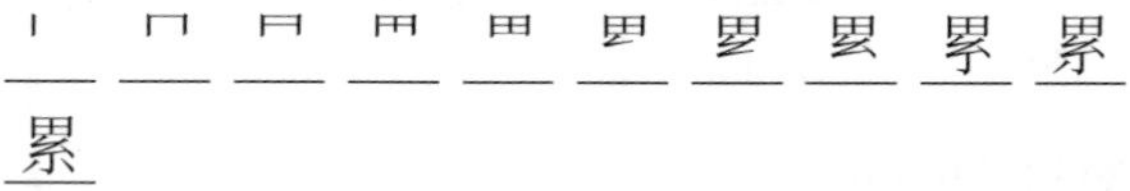

释义 Meaning

（一）形容词 a.

tired: 我今天累坏了。I'm worn out today.

（二）动词 v.

1. tire; wear out: 长时间坐在电脑前工作，很累眼睛。Working before a computer for a long time strains the eyes.
2. work hard: 你累了一天了，该休息了。You've been working hard all day, so you need a rest.

词语 Words and Phrases

累人	lèirén	tiring
劳累	láolèi	overworked
受累	shòulèi	be put to much trouble

累$_2$ léi 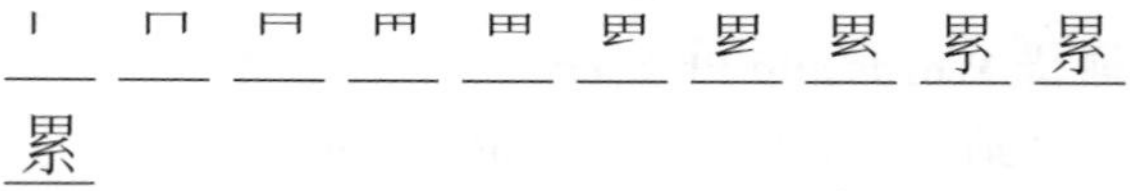

(纍 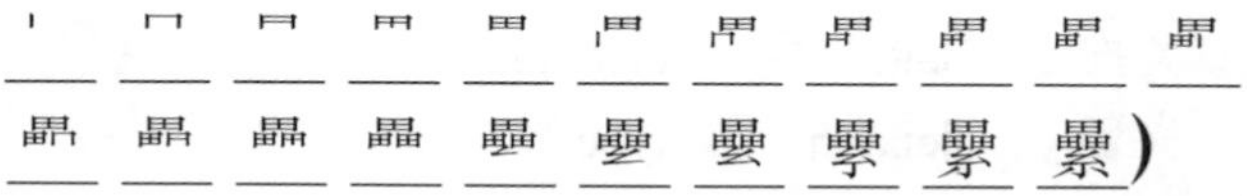**)**

词语 Words and Phrases

累累	léiléi	clusters of; heaps of
累赘	léizhui	① burdensome ② nuisance; burden

累$_3$ lěi 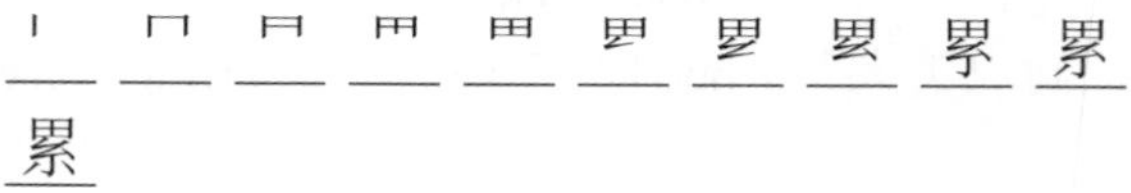

(纍 ' 冂 冃 冊 罒 罒 罒 罒 罒 罍 罍 罍 罍 罍 罍 纍 纍 纍 纍 纍 纍）

释义 Meaning

动词 v.

accumulate; pile up: 日积月累，他收集了大量的资料。
He has accumulated a wealth of data over a long period.

词语 Words and Phrases

累积	lěijī	accumulate
累及	lěijí	involve; drag in
累计	lěijì	① add up
		② grand total
连累	liánlěi	get sb. into trouble; implicate
牵累	qiānlěi	① tie down
		② implicate; involve (in trouble)

冷lěng ` 冫 冫 冫 冷 冷 冷

释义 Meaning

形容词 a.

1. cold: 外面很冷。It's very cold outside. 反义词：热
2. cold in manner: 他待人很冷。He is very cold to others.
3. discouraged: 听到他的回答，我的心冷了半截。I was quite discouraged at his answer.

词语 Words and Phrases

冷冰冰	lěngbīngbīng	icy; frosty
冷餐	lěngcān	buffet
冷淡	lěngdàn	indifferent
冷冻	lěngdòng	freezing
冷静	lěngjìng	calm; sober
冷酷	lěngkù	unfeeling; grim

冷落	lěngluò	treat coldly; leave out in the cold
冷漠	lěngmò	cold and detached; indifferent
冷暖	lěngnuǎn	changes in temperature; ups and downs (in one's life)
冷清	lěngqīng	desolate; deserted
冰冷	bīnglěng	ice-cold
寒冷	hánlěng	frigid

熟语 Idioms

冷若冰霜	lěng ruò bīng shuāng	cold in manner
冷言冷语	lěng yán lěng yǔ	sarcastic remarks
冷眼旁观	lěng yǎn páng guān	look on coldly

梨lí

一 二 千 禾 禾 利 利 利 犁 梨 梨

释义 Meaning

名词 n.

pear: 你喜欢吃梨子吗？Do you like eating pears?

词语 Words and Phrases

| 梨膏 | lígāo | pear syrup (for the relief of cough) |
| 鸭梨 | yālí | a kind of pear grown in Hebei province in China |

离lí

丶 亠 亠 文 这 卤 卤 卨 离 离

（離

丶 亠 亠 文 这 卤 卨 卨 离 离 离

斎 斎 斎 斎 斎 離 離）

释义 Meaning

（一）动词 v.

1. leave; be away from: 他离家已经有十年了。He has been away from home for ten years.

2. (live) without; independent of: 人离不了空气。Man can't
live without air.

（二）介词 prep.

off; away: 离新年只有十天了。The New Year is only ten
days away.

词语 Words and Phrases

离别	líbié	part (for a long period)
离婚	líhūn	divorce
离境	líjìng	leave a country or a place
离开	líkāi	leave; depart from
离奇	líqí	odd; fantastic
离职	lízhí	leave office
分离	fēnlí	separate
距离	jùlí	① distance ② be away from
脱离	tuōlí	separate onself from; break away from

熟语 Idioms

不即不离	bù jí bù lí	be neither too close nor too distant
貌合神离	mào hé shén lí	(of two persons) seemingly in harmony but actually at odds
形影不离	xíng yǐng bù lí	always together as body and shadow
若即若离	ruò jí ruò lí	be neither friendly nor frosty; keep a lukewarm relationship

礼 lǐ ` ㇀ 礻 礻 礼

（禮 ` ㇀ 礻 礻 礻 礻 礻 禮 禮 禮 禮 禮 禮 禮 禮）

释义 Meaning

名词 n.

1. ceremony: 婚礼举行得很隆重。It was a grand wedding.

2. manners; courtesy: 士兵向上校敬了个礼。The soldier gave a salute to the captain.

3. gift: 俗话说，千里送鹅毛，礼轻情意重。As the saying goes, the gift itself may be light as a goose feather, but, sent from afar, it conveys a deep feeling.

词语 Words and Phrases

礼拜	lǐbài	week; day of the week; church service
礼节	lǐjié	etiquette; courtesy
礼貌	lǐmào	politeness; manners
礼品	lǐpǐn	gift
礼堂	lǐtáng	auditorium
礼物	lǐwù	gift; present
礼仪	lǐyí	rite; protocol
典礼	diǎnlǐ	ceremony
回礼	huílǐ	send a gift in return
赔礼	péilǐ	make an apology
失礼	shīlǐ	breach of etiquette; impoliteness
送礼	sònglǐ	present a gift to sb.
见面礼	jiànmiànlǐ	a gift given to sb. on first meeting

熟语 Idioms

| 礼尚往来 | lǐ shàng wǎng lái | treat others in the way they treat you |

里 lǐ ⼁ 冂 ⽇ 日 甲 里 里

(裏 ⼀ ⼇ 广 亠 立 亠 审 审 車 東 褁 褁 褁 裏)

释义 Meaning

名词 n.

inside; in: 房间里没人。There is nobody in the room. 反义词：外

measure of distance: 你要走一英里。you have to walk one (British) mile.

词语 Words and Phrases

里边	lǐbian	inside; within
里程碑	lǐchéngbēi	milestone
里面	lǐmiàn	inside; interior
公里	gōnglǐ	kilometer (km.)
邻里	línlǐ	neighbourhood
那里	nàlǐ	there
这里	zhèlǐ	here

熟语 Idioms

里应外合	lǐ yīng wài hé	act from inside in coordination with forces from outside
鹏程万里	péng chéng wàn lǐ	make a roc's flight of ten thousand *li*—have a bright future
十万八千里	shíwàn bāqiān lǐ	a long distance; be widely separated
一日千里	yí rì qiān lǐ	one thousand *li* a day; at a tremendous pace

理 lǐ   一 三 千 王 王 珥 珥 珥 理 理 理

释义 Meaning

（一）名词 n.

1. reason; logic; truth: 俗话说，有理走遍天下，无理寸

步难行。As the saying goes, with justice on your side, you can go anywhere; without it, you can't move even one step.

2. natural science: 你学文还是学理？Do you study the arts or the sciences? 反义词：文

（二）动词 v.

1. tidy up; put in order: 他在理书架上的书。He is rearranging the books on the bookshelf.

2. pay attention to; acknowledge (usually used in negative sentices): 他生我气了，所以不理我。Because he got angry at me, he didn't acknowledge me at all.

词语 Words and Phrases

理睬	lǐcǎi	pay attention to; show interest in
理会	lǐhuì	take notice of; pay attention to
理解	lǐjiě	understand; comprehend
理科	lǐkē	natural sciences (as a school subject); science departments in a college
理论	lǐlùn	theory
理想	lǐxiǎng	ideal
理由	lǐyóu	reason; ground
理智	lǐzhì	reason; sense
道理	dàolǐ	reason; argument
管理	guǎnlǐ	manage; administer
合理	hélǐ	reasonable; rational
经理	jīnglǐ	manager
条理	tiáolǐ	orderliness; proper arrangement or presentation
物理	wùlǐ	physics
心理	xīnlǐ	physchology
整理	zhěnglǐ	put in order; tidy up

助理　　　zhùlǐ　　　　assistant

熟语 Idioms

理屈词穷	lǐ qū cí qióng	be unable to argue further when running out of reason
理所当然	lǐ suǒ dāng rán	right and natural
理直气壮	lǐ zhí qì zhuàng	be bold and confident with justice on one's side

力 lì　　　乛 力

释义 Meaning

（一）名词 n.

1. power; ability: 他的理解力很强。He has a good understanding.

2. physical strength: 我感到全身无力。My body feels weak.

（二）动词 v.

try one's best; do all one can: 他力劝我回国。He did his best to persuade me to go back to my country.

词语 Words and Phrases

力量	lìliàng	power; force
力气	lìqì	physical strength; effort
力求	lìqiú	make every effort to; strive to
力争	lìzhēng	work hard for; do all one can to
脑力	nǎolì	mental power
能力	nénglì	ability
体力	tǐlì	physical power
吸引力	xīyǐnlì	appeal; attraction

熟语 Idioms

| 力不从心 | lì bù cóng xīn | ability falls short of one's desires |

力所能及　　lì suǒ néng jí　　　within one's ability

立lì　　`　亠　亠　立　立

释义 Meaning

（一）动词 v.

1. erect; set up: 把梯子立起来。Set up the ladder, please.

2. establish; found; set up: 请立个字据。Please sign a written pledge.

（二）副词 adv.

immediately: 立侯回音。Awaiting your prompt reply.

词语 Words and Phrases

立场	lìchǎng	standpoint; position
立即	lìjí	immediately
立刻	lìkè	at once; promptly
立志	lìzhì	resolve; be determined
立足	lìzú	have a foothold somewhere
成立	chénglì	found; establish
独立	dúlì	independence
建立	jiànlì	build; set up
树立	shùlì	establish
自立	zìlì	earn one's own living

熟语 Idioms

立竿见影	lì gān jiàn yǐng	get results instantly
立于不败之地	lì yú bú bài zhī dì	remain victorious and no one can conquer
势不两立	shì bù liǎng lì	irreconcilable; absolutely hostile
亭亭玉立	tíng tíng yù lì	(of a young woman) slim and graceful

利lì　　`　亠　千　利　利　利　利

释义 Meaning

（一）形容词 a.

favorable: 形势对我们很不利。The situation is unfavourable to us.

（二）名词 n.

1. advantage: 这么做利大于弊。The advantages in dong this are more than the disadvantages. 反义词：弊

2. profit; interest: 他连本带利都赔了。He lost both the principal and the interest.

（三）动词 v.

do good to; benefit: 积极储蓄，利国利民。To save is beneficial to the country as well as to the people themselves.

反义词：害

词语 Words and Phrases

利弊	lìbì	advantages and disadvantages
利率	lìlǜ	interest rate
利润	lìrùn	profit
利用	lìyòng	use; utilize
锋利	fēnglì	sharp
吉利	jílì	auspicious
流利	liúlì	fluent
权利	quánlì	right
胜利	shènglì	victory; triumph

熟语 Idioms

利令智昏	lì lìng zhì hūn	be blinded by one's desire for gain
利欲熏心	lì yù xūn xīn	be obsessed with avarice
急功近利	jí gōng jìn lì	be eager for instant success and benefit

连 lián　一　𠂇　𠂇　车　车　连　连

（**連**　一　厂　厈　𠧋　亘　亘　車　車　連　連）

释义 Meaning

（一）动词 v.

link; connect: 大家只要心连心，就一定能战胜困难。
We will certainly overcome the difficulties so long as we
stand united.

（二）副词 ad.

one after another; repeatedly: 我连写了三封信给他。I wrote
three letters to him in succession.

（三）连词 conj.

even: 这个道理连孩子也懂。Even a child understands the
reason.

（四）介词 prep.

including: 连他在内，一共八个人。There are altogether
eight persons including himself.

词语 Words and Phrases

连接	liánjiē	join; link
连连	liánlián	again and again
连忙	liánmáng	at once; in a hurry
连日	liánrì	for days
连续	liánxù	continuous; successive
接连	jiēlián	in succession; on end

熟语 Idioms

藕断丝连	ǒu duàn sī lián	(between lovers) apparently apart, actually still connected

脸 liǎn 丿 刀 月 月 肝 肸 肸 胎 脸 脸
脸

(臉 丿 刀 月 月 肝 肸 肸 胎 脸 脸 脸
脸 脸 脸 脸 臉 臉 **)**

释义 Meaning

face: 她长着一张圆圆的脸。She has a round face.

词语 Words and Phrases

脸蛋儿	liǎndànr	cheeks (referring to children)
脸红	liǎnhóng	blush with anger; blush with shame
脸面	liǎnmiàn	face; self-respect
脸色	liǎnsè	look; facial expression
丢脸	diūliǎn	lose face
鬼脸	guǐliǎn	funny face; grimace
笑脸	xiàoliǎn	smiling face

熟语 Idioms

脸红脖子粗	liǎn hóng bó zi cū	the face becomes red with agitation
愁眉苦脸	chóu méi kǔ liǎn	have a distressed expression
嬉皮笑脸	xī pí xiào liǎn	grin cheekily

练 liàn 乚 纟 纟 红 纩 练 练 练

(練 乚 纟 纟 纟 纟 纟 纟 紅 紅 紜 絧 絧
絧 紳 練 練 **)**

释义 Meaning

动词 v.

practise; train: 他每天都练画画儿。He practises drawing
every day.

词语 Words and Phrases

练功	liàngōng	do exercise in gymnastics; practise one's skill; practise martial arts
练习	liànxí	exercise; practise
操练	cāoliàn	drill; practise
老练	lǎoliàn	experienced and assured
锻炼	duànliàn	① take exercise; have physical training ② temper; steel
排练	páiliàn	rehearse
熟练	shúliàn	proficient; skilled
训练	xùnliàn	train

凉 liáng ` 冫 冫 广 广 庐 庐 凉 凉 凉

释义 Meaning

形容词 a.

1. cool; cold: 菜凉了，快吃吧。The dishes are getting cold, so let's hurry to eat. 反义词：热

2. discouraged: 听了他的话，我的心凉了。I was discouraged by his words.

词语 Words and Phrases

凉菜	liángcài	cold dish
凉快	liángkuai	pleasantly cool
凉爽	liángshuǎng	nice and cool
凉台	liángtái	balcony
荒凉	huāngliáng	bleak and desolate
清凉	qīngliáng	cool and refreshing
着凉	zháoliáng	catch cold

熟语 Idioms

世态炎凉	shì tài yán liáng	inconstancy of human relationships

两 liǎng 二 厂 丙 两 两 两

（**兩** 二 厂 丙 兩 兩 兩 兩）

释义 Meaning

（一）数词 numeral

1. two (used before measure word and "half", "thousand" "ten thousand" etc.): 离考试还有两个星期。There are two weeks before the exam.

2. a few; some: 我来说两句。I'd like to say a few words.

（二）名词 n.

both sides; either side: 学习工作两不误。Carry on both study and work without neglecting either.

（三）量词 measure word

liang, a unit of weight for silver: 一斤等于十两。One *jin* equals to ten *liang* .

词语 Words and Phrases

两边	liǎng biān	both sides; both directions
两可	liǎngkě	either will do
两口子	liǎngkǒuzi	(used in oral speech) couple
两面	liǎngmiàn	two sides; both sides
两头	liǎngtóu	both ends; either end
两样	liǎngyàng	different

熟语 Idioms

两耳不闻窗外事	liǎng ěr bù wén chuāngwài shì	be unaware of the outside world
两面三刀	liǎng miàn sān dāo	double-faced
两全其美	liǎng quán qí měi	be satisfactory to both sides
半斤八两	bàn jīn bā liǎng	of equal strength

| 此地无银三百两* | cǐ dì wú yín sānbǎi liǎng | a guilty person gives himself away by conspicuously protesting his innocence |

亮 liàng ` 亠 广 产 亨 产 亨 亨 亮

释义 Meaning

（一）形容词 a.

1. bright: 天亮了。It's light already. 反义词：黑；暗

2. loud and clear: 他的嗓子很亮。He has a resonant voice.

3. be enlightened: 他这么一说，我的心里亮了许多。My mind was greatly enlightened by his remarks. 反义词：暗

（二）动词 v.

1. shine: 教室里亮着灯光。Lights are shining in the classroom.

2. show: 他亮了一下身份证就进去了。He showed his identity card and went in.

词语 Words and Phrases

亮光	liàngguāng	light
亮晶晶	liàngjīngjīng	glittering; sparkling
亮堂	liàngtáng	light; enlightened
洪亮	hóngliàng	loud and clear; sonorous
明亮	míngliàng	bright
漂亮	piàoliang	pretty; beautiful
响亮	xiǎngliàng	sonorous; resonant
月亮	yuèliang	moon

---

* In a folk tale, a man tries to hide his money by putting up a sign " The 300 taels are not here" on the spot when he buried the coins.

熟语 Idioms

心明眼亮   xīn míng yǎn liàng   be sharp-eyed and clear-minded

辆 liàng   一   仁   车   车   轩   轩   轫   轫   辆   辆
辆

(輛   一   厂   币   同   百   亘   車   軒   軒   軒   輌
輌   輌   輛   輛)

释义 Meaning

量词 measure word

used for vehicles: 我买了一辆小汽车。I bought a small car.

量₁ liáng   丨   冂   曰   曰   昌   昌   昌   昌   昌
量   量   量

释义 Meaning

动词 v.

measure: 医生给我量了量体温。The doctor took my temperature.

词语 words and Phrases

比量	bǐliang	take rough measurements (with the hand, a stick, etc.)
打量	dǎliang	look up and down; look over
估量	gūliáng	estimate; assess
衡量	héngliáng	measure; weigh; evaluate
商量	shāngliang	discuss; talk over
思量	sīliang	turn sth. over in one's mind; consider
丈量	zhàngliáng	measure (land)

量₂ liàng ⌐ ⌐ ⌐ ⌐ ⌐ ⌐ ⌐ ⌐ ⌐ ⌐ 昌 昌 昌 量 量 量

释义 Meaning

（一）名词 n.

1. amount; volume: 今天的工作量很大。Today's work load is great.

2. capacity: 他的饭量很小。He is a light eater.

（二）动词 v.

estimate; measure: 我们凡事应该量力而行。We should act according to our capability in all things.

词语 words and phrases

产量	chǎnliàng	output
大量	dàliàng	a large number of
胆量	dǎnliàng	guts; courage
海量	hǎiliàng	great capacity for liquor
尽量	jìnliàng	to the best of one's ability
质量	zhìliàng	quality
重量	zhòngliàng	weight

熟语 Idioms

量入为出	liàng rù wéi chū	live within one's income
量体裁衣	liàng tǐ cái yī	act according to actual situation

聊 liáo ⌐ ⌐ ⌐ ⌐ ⌐ ⌐ ⌐ 耵 聊 聊 聊

释义 Meaning

动词 v.

chat: 我想和你聊聊。I want to have a chat with you.

词语 Words and Phrases

聊天	liáotiān	chat
无聊	wúliáo	bored; senseless
闲聊	xiánliáo	chat

熟语 Idioms

| 聊胜于无 | liáo shèng yú wú | a little is better than nothing |
| 聊以自慰 | liáo yǐ zì wèi | just to comfort oneself |

了₁ liǎo 一 了

释义 Meaning

动词 v.

1. end; settle: 他一开口就没完没了。He won't stop once he opens his mouth.

2. (used with "得" or "不" together after a verb) indicates possiblity: 这么多菜我一个人吃不了。I can't eat so many dishes alone.

词语 Words and Phrases

了不得	liǎobude	① terrific; extraordinary ② terrible; awful
了不起	liǎobuqǐ	amazing; wonderful
了解	liǎojiě	① understand; comprehend ② know; acquaint oneself with; find out
了事	liǎoshì	dispose of a matter; get sth. over
明了	míngliǎo	① understand; be clear about ② clear; plain
不得了	bùdéliǎo	(used after " " as compliment) extremely; exceedingly
免不了	miǎnbuliǎo	be unavoidable

熟语 Idioms

　　了如指掌　　liǎo rú zhǐ zhǎng　　know sth. thoroughly

了₂ le　　⺕ 了

释义 Meaning

助词 auxiliary. word

1. used after a verb or adjective to indicate completion of work: 他下了课就走了。He left right after the class.

2. used in the end of a sentence or at a pause in a sentence to indicate confirmation, the appearance of new situation or dissuasion: 又下雨了！It rains again!

料 liào　　丶 丷 丷 半 半 米 米 米 料 料

释义 Meaning

（一）动词 v.

　　expect: 我没料到他会这么做。I didn't expect him to behave like this.

（二）名词 n.

　　material; stuff: 料备足了没有？Have we got enough materials?

词语 Words and Phrases

料理	liàolǐ	manage; attend to; (Japanese) food
料想	liàoxiǎng	expect; presume
不料	búliào	to one's surprise
材料	cáiliào	material; stuff
预料	yùliào	expect; predict
原料	yuánliào	raw material
资料	zīliào	data; material

熟语 Idioms

料事如神	liào shì rú shén	predict with miraculous accuracy
出人意料	chū rén yì liào	beyond everyone's expectations

邻 lín 　ノ　㇒　㇏　今　令　邻　邻

(鄰 　丶　丷　丷　⺍　米　米　米　粦　粦　粦　粦
粦　鄰　鄰)

释义 Meaning

(一) 名词 n.

neighbour: 常言说，远亲不如近邻。As the saying goes, neighbours are dearer than distant relatives.

(二) 形容词 a.

neighbouring; adjacent: 日本是我们的邻国。Japan is our neighbouring country.

词语 Words and Phrases

邻邦	línbāng	neighbouring country
邻近	línjìn	close to; adjacent to
邻居	línjū	neighbour
邻座	línzuò	adjacent seat
四邻	sìlín	near neighbours

林 lín 　一　十　才　木　杧　杧　材　林

释义 Meaning

名词 n.

forest; woods: 这是一片竹林。This is a bamboo grove.

词语 Words and Phrases

林海	línhǎi	immense forest

林立	línlì	stand in great numbers (like trees in a forest)
林子	línzi	woods; grove
丛林	cónglín	jungle; forest
森林	sēnlín	forest
树林	shùlín	woods
艺林	yìlín	art circles
园林	yuánlín	gardens

熟语 Idioms

| 独木不成林 | dú mù bù chéng lín | one tree doesn't make a forest; one person alone can't accomplish a great cause |

铃 líng ㇒ ㇇ ㇏ ㇏ 钅 钅 钅 钅 铃 铃

(鈴 ㇒ ㇇ ㇏ ㇏ 仐 仐 仐 金 鈩 鈩 鈩 鈐 鈴)

释义 Meaning

名词 n.

bell: 电话铃响了。The telephone is ringing.

词语 Words and Phrases

铃铛	língdang	small bell
风铃	fēnglíng	aeolian bells
门铃	ménlíng	door bell
哑铃	yǎlíng	dumb bell

熟语 Idioms

| 解铃还须系铃人 | jiě líng hái xū xì líng rén | let him who tied the bell on [the tiger] take it off; whoever started the trouble should end it |

掩耳盗铃　　　yǎn ěr dào líng　　　bury one's head in the sand

零 líng 　一　广　产　币　币　币　币　币　号　乘
乘　零　零

释义 Meaning

（一）数词 numerals

1. zero sign: 我住306号房间。I live in Room 306.
2. nil: 比赛结果零比一。The score of the game was one-nil.

（二）连词 conj.

used between two numeral-classifier compounds indicating that there is a smaller quantity under a bigger quantity: 找您三十块零五毛。Here is your change of thirty *yuan* and fifty *fen*.

词语 Words and Phrases

零度	língdù	zero degree
零花钱	línghuā qián	incidental expenses
零钱	língqián	small change; pocket money
零散	língsǎn	scattered
零食	língshí	snacks; between-meal nibbles
零碎	língsuì	scrappy; fragmentary
零星	língxīng	piecemeal; odd
凋零	diāolíng	withered, fallen and scattered about

领 líng 　丿　个　今　今　令　令　𬎆　𬎆　领　领
领

(領 丿　个　今　今　令　令　𬎆　𬎆　領　領　領
領　領　領)

释义 Meaning

（一）名词 n.

collar: 衣服领有点儿脏。The collar is a little dirty.

（二）动词 v.

1. lead: 他领我们参观了校园。He showed us around the campus.

2. draw; receive: 我们什么时候领工资？When shall we draw our pay?

词语 Words and Phrases

领带	lǐngdài	necktie
领导	lǐngdǎo	① lead; exercise leadership ② leader; leadership
领会	lǐnghuì	comprehend; grasp
领路	lǐnglù	lead the way
领取	lǐngqǔ	draw; receive
领事	lǐngshì	consul
领土	lǐngtǔ	territory
领先	lǐngxiān	be in the lead; lead
领袖	lǐngxiù	leader
领域	lǐngyù	realm; field
本领	běnlǐng	skill; ability
带领	dàilǐng	lead; guide
占领	zhànlǐng	occupy; seize

熟语 Idioms

| 心领神会 | xīn lǐng shén huì | understand or take a hint tacitly |

令 lìng 　 ノ　人　〈　今　令

释义 Meaning

（一）动词 v.

1. make: 他的行为令我十分吃惊。I was taken aback by what he did.

2. command; order: 军官命令士兵们前进。The officer commanded his soldiers to go forward.

（二）名词 n.

order; decree: 军人必须做到有令必行，有禁必止。Military men should strictly enforce orders and prohibitions.

词语 Words and Phrases

令爱	lìngài	(respectful address) your daughter
令堂	lìngtáng	(respectful address) your mother
令尊	lìngzūn	(respectful address) your father
酒令	jiǔlìng	drinker's wager game
命令	mìnglìng	order; command
绕口令	ràokǒulìng	tongue twister

另 lìng 丨 冂 冂 吕 另

释义 Meaning

副词 adv.

another; separate: 这个办法不行，只有另想办法了。If this way isn't available, we have to find some other way.

词语 Words and Phrases

另外	lìngwài	in addition; moreover

熟语 Idioms

另眼相看	lìng yǎn xiāng kàn	view sb. in a special favor

流 liú 丶 丶 氵 氵 汸 浐 浐 浐 流 流

释义 Meaning

（一）动词 v.

    flow: 这条小河向南流。The river flows south.

（二）名词 n.

    1. stream of water: 这一段是长江的中流。This is a mid-stream section of the Yangtze River.

    2. class; rate: 他的医术是一流的。His medical skill is of the first-class.

词语 Words and Phrases

流畅	liúchàng	easy and smooth
流传	liúchuán	spread; circulate
流动	liúdòng	flow; going from place to place
流泪	liúlèi	shed tears
流利	liúlì	fluent; smooth
流水	liúshuǐ	running water
流行	liúxíng	prevalent; popular
流言	liúyán	gossip; rumour
河流	héliú	river
暖流	nuǎnliú	warm current
气流	qìliú	air current

熟语 Idioms

流芳百世	liú fāng bǎi shì	leave a good reputation for centuries
流连忘返	liú lián wàng fǎn	enjoy oneself so much that one forgets to go home
随波逐流	suí bō zhú liú	drift with the current

留 liú   ⼂ ⼃ ⼄ ⼅ ⼆ ⼇ 留 留 留 留

释义 Meaning

动词 v.

1. stay: 我还要在这里留几天。 I am going to stay here for a few more days.

2. detain: 他把孩子留在家里。 He kept the child at home.

3. reserve; keep: 请给我留个座位。 Please reserve a seat for me.

4. let grow; wear: 我打算留短头发。 I am going to wear my hair short.

5. leave: 他给我留下了深刻的印象。 He made a deep impression on me.

词语 Words and Phrases

留恋	liúliàn	be reluctant to leave; recall with nostalgia
留念	liúniàn	accept or keep as a souvenir
留神	liúshén	be careful
留心	liúxīn	take care; be careful
留学	liúxué	study abroad
留言	liúyán	leave a message
留意	liúyì	look out; keep one's eyes open
留影	liúyǐng	a photo as a memento
保留	bǎoliú	continue to have; reserve
久留	jiǔliú	stay for a long time
居留	jūliú	reside
停留	tíngliú	stay for a time; stop

熟语 Idioms

留得青山在， 不怕没柴烧*	liú dé qīng shān zài, bú pà méi chái shāo	preserve one's strength/prestige for a later day.

---

* "As long as the green mountains are there, there is no need to worry about running out of firewood;"

龙 lóng　一 十 尢 龙 龙

(龍　` ー ゙ ゙ 立 产 产 产 音 育 育 育

育 能 龍 龍 龍)

释义 Meaning

名词 n.

dragon: 中国人很喜欢龙。Chinese like dragons.

词语 Words and Phrases

龙井	lóngjǐng	kind of famous green tea produced in Hangzhou
龙虾	lóngxiā	lobster
龙王	lóngwáng	the Dragon King (the god of the sea in Chinese mythology)
龙舟	lóngzhōu	dragon boat
恐龙	kǒnglóng	dinosaur
沙龙	shālóng	saloon

熟语 Idioms

龙飞凤舞	lóng fēi fèng wǔ	(of calligraphy) lively and vigorous
龙腾虎跃	lóng téng hǔyuè	dragons rising and tigers leaping; with vigor and enthusiasm
龙争虎斗	lóng zhēng hǔ dòu	a fierce struggle between a dragon and a tiger; two evenly matched opponents
变色龙	biàn sè lóng	chameleon
车水马龙	chē shuǐ mǎ lóng	an endless stream of horses and carriages; bustling traffic
叶公好龙	yè gōng hào lóng	Lord Ye's love of dragons; professed love of what one fears in reality

楼 lóu　一　十　才　才　才　术　栏　栏　栏　栏
楼　楼　楼

（樓 一　十　才　才　术　栌　栌　栌　栌　桿　楒
椹　楻　樓　樓）

释义 Meaning

名词 n.

1. a storied building: 这幢高楼就是我的学校。This tall building is my school.
2. storey; floor: 我家住在一楼。My home is on the first floor.

词语 Words and Phrases

楼房	lóufáng	a building
楼上	lóushàng	upstairs
楼梯	lóutī	stairs
楼下	lóuxià	downstairs
阁楼	gélóu	attic; loft

熟语 Idioms

海市蜃楼　　hǎi shì shèn lóu　　mirage

陆 lù　𠃌　阝　阝　阞　阹　陆　陆

（陸 𠃌　阝　阝　阽　陆　陸　陕　陸　陸　陸）

释义 Meaning

名词 n.

land: 据说台风即将登陆。It is said that a typhoon is going to hit the coast.

词语 Words and Phrases

陆地	lùdì	dry land
陆军	lùjūn	ground force; land force; army
陆续	lùxù	one after another; in succession
大陆	dàlù	mainland; continent; (Chinese) Mainland
内陆	nèilù	inland; interior
水陆	shuǐlù	land and water
着陆	zhuólù	land; touch down

露₁ lù 一 厂 戶 币 币 示 示 示 示 示 示 示 示 示 示 示 示 示 示 示 示 示 示 露 露

释义 Meaning

动词 v.

reveal; show: 她一笑，露出一口洁白的牙齿。She reveals her white teeth whenever she smiles.

词语 Words and Phrases

露水	lùshuǐ	dew
露天	lùtiān	in the open air
露珠	lùzhū	dewdrop
暴露	bàolù	expose; lay bear
果子露	guǒzǐlù	fruit syrup
揭露	jiēlù	expose; unmask
流露	liúlù	reveal; show unintentionally
显露	xiǎnlù	appear; manifest itself

露₂ lòu 一 厂 戶 币 币 示 示 示 示 示 示 示 示 示 示 示 示 示 示 示 示 示 示 露 露

释义 Meaning

动词 v.

> (orally uses) reveal; show: 他想装成好人，可时间一长，就露出了马脚。 He pretended to be a good person, but after a while he gave himself away.

词语 Words and Phrases

露脸	lòuliǎn	look good as a result of receiving honour or praise
露面	lòumiàn	make an appearance
露头	lòutóu	show one's head; emerge
露馅儿	lòuxiànér	let the cat out of the bag; spill the beans
露一手	lòuyìshǒu	make an exhibition of one's ability or skills (negative implication)

录 lù

一 ⺆ ⺕ 寻 寻 录 录 录

(錄

／ ⺈ ⺌ ⺍ ⺉ 牟 余 金 金 釒 釒 釒 釠 釠 銯 錄 錄)

释义 Meaning

(一) 动词 v.

> tape-record: 这首歌我很喜欢，要把它录下来。 I like this song very much, so I want to tape it.

(二) 名词 n.

> record; collection: 他的名字已经进入了名人录。 His name has been selected for inclusion in the collection of celebrities.

词语 Words and Phrases

录取	lùqǔ	enroll; admit
录像	lùxiàng	video recording
录音	lùyīn	sound recording
录用	lùyòng	employ; take sb. on the staff

记录	jìlù	① take notes ② notes; minutes
目录	mùlù	catalogue; list
语录	yǔlù	quotation; a book of quotations
备忘录	bèiwànglù	memorandum
回忆录	huíyìlù	memoirs; reminiscences

路 lù

一 丨 口 口 甲 早 趵 趴 趴 趵 路
路 路 路

释义 Meaning

名词 n.

1. road; path: 这条路很宽。This road is very wide.

2. distance; journey: 还有二十里路就到了。We are still 20 *li* away from there.

3. means; way: 他已经无路可走了。He already has no way out.

4. route: 坐 36 路公共汽车可以到博物馆。You can take the No. 36 bus to the museum.

词语 Words and Phrases

路程	lùchéng	distance; journey
路灯	lùdēng	street lamp
路费	lùfèi	traveling expenses
路过	lùguò	pass by or through (a place)
半路	bànlù	on the way; halfway
出路	chūlù	way out; outlet; prospect (a job)
门路	ménlù	knack; social connections (for securing a job etc.)
迷路	mílù	lose one's way
顺路	shùnlù	on the way
思路	sīlù	train of thought; way of thinking
铁路	tiělù	railway

熟语 Idioms

路不拾遗	lù bù shí yí	not to pick up things lost by others on the road; good law and order
路遥知马力	lù yáo zhī mǎ lì	a long journey tests a horse's strength; time can test a person's quality
走投无路	zǒuo tóu wú lù	find no way out; at the end of one's wit

绿 lǜ
ˊ ˪ ˪ 纟 纟 纟 纾 纾 绿 绿
绿

(綠
ˊ ˪ ˪ ˪ ˪ ˪ 纟 纟 纟 紵 紵
紵 綠 綠)

释义 Meaning

形容词 a.

green: 树叶绿绿的。 The leaves are green.

词语 Words and Phrases

绿茶	lǜchá	green tea
绿豆	lǜdòu	mung bean
绿化	lǜhuà	make green by planting trees, flowers, etc.; afforest
绿洲	lǜzhōu	oasis
碧绿	bìlǜ	dark green
草绿	cǎolǜ	grass green
嫩绿	nènlǜ	light green

熟语 Idioms

灯红酒绿	dēng hóng jiǔ lǜ	a scene of debauchery with red lanterns and green wines

乱 luàn 一 二 千 千 舌 舌 乱

(亂 一 一 一 一 四 四 严 𦥯 𦥯 𦥯 𠭯 𠭯 亂）

释义 Meaning

（一）形容词 a.

1. in a mess; in disorder: 房间里很乱。The room is in a mess. 反义词：整齐

2. confused (state of mind): 我心里很乱。My mind is in a turmoil. 反义词：平静

（二）副词 adv.

1. indiscriminately; randomly: 小孩子不要乱说话！Children can't be unruly in speech.

2. mix up; jumble: 那孩子的书和玩具都乱放在桌子上。That child's books and toys are jumbled up together on the desk.

词语 Words and Phrases

乱哄哄	luànhōnghōng	in noisy disorder; in an uproar
乱蓬蓬	luànpéngpéng	jumbled; tangled
乱糟糟	luànzāozāo	in a mess; confused; perturbed
慌乱	huāngluàn	alarmed and bewildered; flurried
混乱	hùnluàn	chaos; confusion
忙乱	mángluàn	be in a rush and muddle
内乱	nèiluàn	civil strife; internal disorder
杂乱	záluàn	in a jumble; in a muddle
战乱	zhànluàn	chaos caused by war

熟语 Idioms

乱七八糟	luàn qī bā zāo	at sixes and sevens; in a mess

乱弹琴	luàn tán qín	act or talk like a fool; talk nonsense
手忙脚乱	shǒu máng jiǎo luàn	in disorderly haste; be thrown into confusion
眼花缭乱	yǎn huā liáo luàn	be dazzled

落₁ là 一 艹 艹 艹 艹 茾 茾 莎 菠 菠 落 落

释义 Meaning
动词 v.

1. be missing; leave out: 在这个句子里你落了一个字。You missed one word in this sentence.

2. forget to bring: 我把钥匙落在家里了。I left my key at home.

3. lag behind: 我因为生病落了两天的课。I was two days behind with my lessons because of the illness.

落₂ luò 一 艹 艹 艹 艹 茾 茾 莎 菠 菠 落 落

释义 Meaning
动词 v.

1. fall; drop: 树上的苹果熟了，都落到了地上。The apples in the trees are ripe, and have all fallen on the ground.

2. set; go down: 潮水落了。The tide has set. 反义词：涨

3. decline; come down: 他怎么会落到这种地步？How could he come to such a situation?

4. fall behind: 他总是不甘心落在别人后面。He is never content to lag behind others.

5. fall onto; rest with: 父亲死后，家庭的重担就落到了他的肩上。The heavy family burden fell on him after his father's death.

词语 Words and Phrases

落后	luòhòu	fall behind; less developed
落实	luòshí	① fix in advance; make sure ② fulfil; carry out
落伍	luòwǔ	fall behind the ranks; drop out
落叶	luòyè	fallen leaves
部落	bùluò	tribe
村落	cūnluò	village
降落	jiàngluò	descend; land
角落	jiǎoluò	corner; nook
失落	shīluò	lose
下落	xiàluò	whereabouts

熟语 Idioms

落花流水	luò huā liú shuǐ	irretrievable as fallen flowers carried away by water; helplessness
落井下石	luò jǐng xià shí	throw rocks in when a person has fallen into a well; take advantage of somebody's misfortune
落落大方	luòluò dà fāng	natural and self-confident
落汤鸡	luòtāngjī	like a drenched chicken; all wet through
瓜熟蒂落	guā shú dì luò	when a melon is ripe, it falls by itself; problems will be easily resolved when conditions are ripe

妈 mā　ㄥ　女　女　奵　妈　妈

（媽　ㄥ　女　女　奵　奵　妒　娾　媽　媽　媽　媽　媽）

释义 Meaning

名词 n.

ma; mum; mother: 我妈是教师。My mother is a teacher.

词语 Words and Phrases

妈妈	māma	mummy; mother
姑妈	gūmā	paternal aunt
后妈	hòumā	stepmother
舅妈	jiùmā	wife of mother's brother
姨妈	yímā	maternal aunt

麻má ` 一 广 广 广 广 庁 麻 麻 麻 麻
麻

释义 Meaning

（一）名词 n.

hemp; flax: 我的心里乱如麻。My mind was confused like flax.

（二）形容词 a.

1. rough; coarse: 这种纸一面光，一面麻。This paper is smooth on one side and rough on the other.

2. have pins and needles; tingle: 坐久了，我的腿很麻。I have pins and needles in my legs after sitting for a while.

词语 Words and Phrases

麻痹	mábì	be numb; lull
麻烦	máfan	① troublesome; inconvenient ② put sb. to trouble; bother
麻利	máli	quick and neat; dexterous
麻木	mámù	numb; apathetic
麻雀	máquè	sparrow

麻醉	mázuì	① anaesthesia; narcosis
		② anaesthetize
芝麻	zhīma	sesame

熟语 Idioms

| 快刀斩 | kuài dāo | cut the Gordian knot |
| 乱麻 | zhǎn luàn má | |

马 mǎ ㄱ 马 马

(馬 一 厂 厂 厍 馬 馬 馬 馬 馬)

释义 Meaning

名词 n.

horse: 他骑着一匹马。He is riding a horse.

词语 Words and Phrases

马车	mǎchē	carriage
马虎	mǎhu	careless; casual
马路	mǎlù	avenue; road
马上	mǎshàng	at once; straight away
马戏	mǎxì	circus
赛马	sàimǎ	horse race
上马	shàngmǎ	① mount a horse
		② start (a project, etc.)

熟语 Idioms

马不停蹄	mǎ bù tíng tí	without a stop
马到成功	mǎ dào chéng gōng	be victorious immediately on arrival
塞翁失马	sài wēng shī mǎ	a loss may happen to be a gain
走马观花	zǒu mǎ guān huā	look at flowers while riding on horse back; make a cursory investigation of the situation

| 指鹿为马 | zhǐ lù wéi mǎ | call a stag a horse; call white black |

骂 mà ｜ 冂 口 叩 叩 叩 骂 骂 骂

(罵 ｜ 冂 口 叩 叩 叩 咒 严 严 严 罵 罵 罵 罵 罵 罵**)**

释义 Meaning

动词 v.

1. abuse; curse: 骂人是很不好的行为。 Swearing is a very bad behavior.

2. rebuke; scold: 爸爸骂了儿子一顿。 The father gave his son a scolding.

词语 Words and Phrases

骂街	màjiē	shout abuses in the street; call people names in public
咒骂	zhòumà	curse; swear
破口大骂	pò kǒu dàmà	let loose a torrent of abuse

吗₁ má ｜ 冂 口 叮 吗 吗

(嗎 ｜ 冂 口 叮 叮 呼 咛 呼 嗎 嗎 嗎 嗎 嗎**)**

释义 Meaning

助词 auxiliary word

what: 你在干吗？ What are you doing?

吗₂ ma ｜ 冂 口 叮 吗 吗

（嗎 丨 丨丨 丨丨 叮 叮 吓 吓 哐 嗎 嗎 嗎
嗎 嗎）

释义 Meaning

助词 auxiliary word

(uses in the end of a sentence) indicates questioning: 你是学生吗？Are you a student?

埋₁ mái 一 十 土 丑 护 护 坦 坢 埋 埋

释义 Meaning

动词 v.

bury; cover up: 他把金子埋在土里。He buried the gold in the ground.

词语 Words and Phrases

埋藏	máicáng	lie hidden in the earth; bury
埋没	máimò	① bury; cover up ② stifle; neglect
埋头	máitóu	immerse oneself in; be engrossed in
埋怨	máiyuàn	complain; blame
埋葬	máizàng	bury

熟语 Idioms

隐姓埋名　yǐn xìng mái míng　conceal one's real name

埋₂ mán 一 十 土 丑 护 护 坦 坢 埋 埋

词语 Words and Phrases

| 埋怨 | mányuàn | complain; blame |

买 mǎi 一 乛 乛 三 买 买

(買 一 冂 冂 冂 罒 罒 罒 罝 罝 罝 買 買)

释义 Meaning

动词 v.

buy: 我要去商店买东西。I am going to buy some things in the store. 反义词：卖

词语 Words and Phrases

买卖	mǎimài	buying and selling; business
买不起	mǎibuqǐ	can't afford
买得起	mǎideqǐ	can afford
购买	gòumǎi	purchase; buy
收买	shōumǎi	buy over; bribe

卖 mài 二 十 士 去 去 去 卖 卖

(賣 二 十 士 产 声 高 高 高 声 亭 亭 亭 亭 亭 賣)

释义 Meaning

动词 v.

1. sell: 他以卖水果为生。He makes a living by selling fruit. 反义词：买

2. exert to the utmost; not spare: 他做事很卖力气。He exerts all his strength in doing everything.

词语 Words and Phrases

卖国	màiguó	traitor of one's country
卖劲儿	màijìnr	exert all strength; spare no effort
卖力	màilì	do all one can; exert oneself to the utmost
卖命	màimìng	work oneself to the bone for sb.; die (unworthly) for

卖艺	màiyì	make a living as a performer
出卖	chūmài	betray; sell out
拍卖	pāimài	auction

满 mǎn `  ` 氵 汇 汇 泔 泔 洴 满 满 满 满 满

(滿 `  ` 氵 汇 汇 泔 泔 洴 满 滿 滿 滿 滿 滿)

释义 Meaning

（一）形容词 a.

1. full; filled: 房间里坐满了人。The room was packed with people.

2. satisfied: 他对此感到很不满。He was very dissatisfied with this.

（二）动词 v.

expire; reach the limit: 我工作刚满一年。It's just one year since I began to work.

（三）副词 adv.

completely; entirely: 我满以为他会来的。I had thought for sure that he would come.

词语 Words and Phrases

满分	mǎnfēn	full marks
满面	mǎnmiàn	have one's face covered with
满身	mǎnshēn	(covered) from head to toe
满意	mǎnyì	satisfied
满足	mǎnzú	① content; contented ② satisfy
充满	chōngmǎn	full of; imbued with

丰满	fēngmǎn	full-grown; full and round
美满	měimǎn	perfectly satisfactory; happy
圆满	yuánmǎn	satisfactory
自满	zìmǎn	complacent

熟语 Idioms

满不在乎	mǎn bú zàihu	not care in the least
满城风雨	mǎn chéng fēng yǔ	like a storm over the whole city
满载而归	mǎn zài ér guī	return fully-loaded
满招损， 谦受益	mǎn zhāo sǔn, qiān shòu yì	self-satisfaction will incur losses, modesty will receive benefit

慢 màn ⺗ ⺗ 忄 忄 忄 忄 忄 忄 悍 悍 悒 悒 慢 慢

释义 Meaning

形容词 a.

1. slow: 我的表慢五分钟。My watch is five minutes slow. 反义词：快

2. postpone; defer: 这件事你先慢点儿告诉他。Don't tell him about this yet. 反义词：早

词语 Words and Phrases

慢车	mànchē	slow train
慢腾腾	màntēngtēng	unhurriedly; at a leisurely pace
慢性子	mànxìngzi	slow-coach; phlegmatic temperament
慢走	mànzǒu	① (used when seeing a visitor out) good-bye ② don't go yet; wait a minute
傲慢	àomàn	arrogant; haughty
缓慢	huǎnmàn	slow

快慢　　kuàimàn　　speed

熟语 Idioms

慢条斯理　　màn tiáo sī lǐ　　unhurriedly and unper-turbedly

忙 máng　　丶 丶 忄 忄 忙 忙

释义 Meaning

（一）形容词 a.

busy: 最近我很忙。I have been very busy recently. 反义词：空

（二）副词 adv.

hasten; make haste: 先别忙着走，想想有没有忘带什么东西。Don't hasten to leave before thinking whether we have forgotten to bring something.

词语 Words and Phrases

忙碌　　mánglù　　be busy; bustle about

忙乱　　mángluàn　　be in a rush and a muddle

忙人　　mángrén　　busy person

帮忙　　bāngmáng　　help; do a favor

匆忙　　cōngmáng　　in a hurry; hastily

繁忙　　fánmáng　　busy

急忙　　jímáng　　hurriedly; in haste

熟语 Idioms

忙里偷闲　　mánglǐ tōu xián　　snatch leisure from a busy life

猫 māo　　丿 犭 犭 犭 犷 犿 猫 猫 猫 猫

释义 Meaning

名词 n.

cat: 这只猫很漂亮。This cat is very pretty.

词语 Words and Phrases

猫叫	māojiào	mewing; purring
猫头鹰	māotóuyīng	owl
小猫	xiǎomāo	kitten

毛máo 一 二 三 毛

释义 Meaning

（一）名词 n.

1. hair; feather: 那只猫身上的毛是白色的。The cat's hair is white.

2. mildew: 多雨的季节，东西放久了容易长毛。During rainy season, things will become mildewed after being layed up long.

（二）形容词 a.

1. woollen: 这件衣服的料子是毛的。This clothing's material is wool.

2. scared; panicky: 那部电影很恐怖，看得我心里直发毛。That film was so terrifying that it made my hair stand on end.

（三）量词 measure w.

mao, a fractional unit of money in China: 找您一块五毛钱。Here is your change of one and a half *yuan*.

词语 Words and Phrases

毛笔	máobǐ	writing brush
毛病	máobìng	trouble; mistake
毛巾	máojīn	towel

毛裤	máokù	long woolen underwear
毛衣	máoyī	woolen sweater
毛毯	máotǎn	woolen blanket
毛重	máozhòng	gross weight

熟语 Idioms

| 毛骨悚然 | máo gǔ sǒngrán | make somebody's blood run cold; absolutely terrified |
| 毛遂自荐 | máo suí zì jiàn | offer one's services as Mao Sui (of the Warring States Period) did; volunteer to do something (usually of negative connotation) |

冒 mào 丨 冂 冂 冃 冃 冒 冒 冒 冒

释义 Meaning

动词 v.

1. emit; give off: 一股水气从地下冒出来。A spray of water is gushing from the ground.

2. risk; brave: 他冒着大雨赶来。He rushed here, braving the heavy rain.

3. falsely (claim, etc.); fraudulently: 他冒称自己是记者。He falsely claimed to be a journalist.

词语 Words and Phrases

冒充	màochōng	pretend to be (sb. or sth. else); pass sb. or sth. off as
冒犯	màofàn	offend; affront
冒火	màohuǒ	burn with anger; flare up
冒昧	màomèi	make bold; take the liberty
冒名	màomíng	go under sb. else's name; assume another's name
冒险	màoxiǎn	take a risk

| 感冒 | gǎnmào | catch a cold |
| 假冒 | jiǎmào | palm off (a fake as genuine) |

熟语 Idioms

| 冒天下之
大不韪 | mào tiānxià zhī
dà bù wěi | defy the universal will of
the people; risk universal
condemnation |

帽 mào 丨 冂 巾 帄 帄 帄 帄 帄 帽 帽
帽 帽

释义 Meaning

名词 n.

1. hat; cap; headgear: 我有一顶红帽子。I have a red hat.

2. cap-like cover for sth.: 我的钢笔帽儿怎么找不到了？
   Why can't I find the cap for my pen?

词语 Words and Phrases

帽子	màozi	hat; cap; headgear
草帽	cǎomào	straw hat
礼帽	lǐmào	a hat that goes with formal dress

没₁ méi 丶 丶 氵 氵 氿 没 没

释义 Meaning

副词 adv.

1. not have; there is no; be without: 房间里没人。Nobody
   is in the room. 反义词：有

2. the negative form for an action already happened: 我没带
   钱包。I didn't bring my wallet with me.

3. not so... as: 他没我高。He is not as tall as I. 反义词：有

词语 Words and Phrases

| 没关系 | méiguānxi | doesn't matter; it's nothing; that's all
right |

没门儿	méiménr	no go; nothing doing
没趣	méiqù	feel snubbed; feel put out
没什么	méi shénme	it's nothing; never mind
没有	méiyǒu	do not have; be without; not so... as; less than

没₂ mò　　丶　丶　氵　氵　氿　殳　没

释义 Meaning

动词 v.

1. submerge; sink: 潜水艇很快就没入水中。 It was not long before the submarine submerged.

2. rise beyond; overflow: 洪水没过了农田。 The flood overflowed the farm land.

词语 Words and Phrases

没落	mò luò	decline; wane
没世	mòshì	till the end of one's life
没收	mò shōu	confiscate
出没	chūmò	come and go
沉没	chénmò	sink
淹没	yānmò	submerge; drown

熟语 Idioms

| 没齿难忘 | mò chǐ nán wàng | will never forget |
| 神出鬼没 | shén chū guǐ mò | come and go mysteriously like a ghost |

煤 méi　　丶　丶　火　火　灯　炉　炉　炉　炉　炉　煤　煤　煤

释义 Meaning

名词 n.

coal: 这个地方出产煤。 This place produces coal.

词语 Words and Phrases

煤矿	méikuàng	coal mine
煤气	méiqì	coal gas
煤田	méitián	coalfield
煤烟	méiyān	smoke from burning coal
块煤	kuàiméi	lump of coal

每 měi ノ 宀 宀 勹 匃 每 每

释义 Meaning

形容词 a.

every; each; per: 我每星期去看一次电影。I go to see a film once a week.

词语 Words and Phrases

每当	měi dāng	whenever; every time
每每	měiměi	often

熟语 Idioms

| 每逢佳节倍思亲 | měi féng jiā jié bèi sī qīn | people miss their close relatives on festival occassions. |
| 每况愈下 | měi kuàng yù xià | worse and worse; be on the down grade |

美 měi 丶 丷 丷 丷 半 羊 差 美 美

释义 Meaning

形容词 a.

1. beautiful; pretty: 那地方的风景很美。The scenery there is very beautiful. 反义词：丑

2. very satisfactory; good: 他们的日子过得挺美。They live quite happily.

词语 Words and Phrases

美称	měichēng	laudatory title; good name
美德	měidé	virtue; moral excellence
美观	měiguān	pleasing to the eye; artistic
美国	měiguó	the United States of America
美好	měihǎo	fine; happy
美化	měihuà	beautify; embellish
美丽	měilì	beautiful
美满	měimǎn	happy; perfectly satisfactory
美妙	měimiào	splendid; wonderful
美容	měiróng	cosmetology; improve one's looks
美味	měiwèi	① delicious food; delicacy ② delicious, dainty
美元	měiyuán	U.S. dollar
美洲	měizhōu	America
健美	jiànměi	vigorous and graceful; strong and handsome
精美	jīngměi	exquisite; elegant
完美	wánměi	perfect; flawless
赞美	zànměi	praise

熟语 Idioms

美不胜收	měi bú shèng shōu	too beautiful to be absorbed all at once
美中不足	měi zhōng bù zú	something lacking in perfection; a blemish in an otherwise perfect thing

妹 mèi ㇒ 女 女 女 妒 妒 妹 妹

释义 Meaning

名词 n.

younger sister: 我有个妹妹。I have a younger sister.

词语 Words and Phrases

妹夫	mèifu	younger sister's husband; brother-in-law
弟妹	dìmèi	younger brother and sister; younger brother's wife
姐妹	jiěmèi	brothers and sisters; sisters

门 mén 丶 亠 门

（門 丨 冂 冃 冃 冐 門 門 門 ）

释义 Meaning

（一）名词 n.

door: 请把门打开。Please open the door.

（二）量词 measure w.

used for things like subject, artillery, etc.: 我还有两门功课要做。I still have two subjects to finish.

词语 Words and Phrases

门道	méndào	way to do sth; knack
门口	ménkǒu	entrance; doorway
门类	ménlèi	class; category
门路	ménlù	① knack; way ② social connections (for securing jobs, etc.)
门牌	ménpái	house number plate
部门	bùmén	department; branch
出门	chūmén	be away from home
关门	guānmén	close the door
窍门	qiàomén	knack
热门	rèmén	popular; in great demand
入门	rùmén	① learn the rudiments of a subject; cross the threshold ② elementary course

熟语 Idioms

门当户对	mén dāng hù duì	be well-matched in social and economic status for marriage
门庭若市	mén tíng ruò shì	the courtyard is as crowded as a marketplace; swarming with visitors

们 men ノ 亻 仆 们 们

(們 ノ 亻 亻 仴 仴 伊 押 們 們 們)

释义 Meaning

名词 n.

used at the end of pronouns and nouns for persons indicating the plural form: 学生们都来了。 All the students have come.

词语 Words and Phrases

你们	nǐ men	you (second person plural)
他们	tāmen	they
它们	tāmen	they (referring to non-people); those (things)
我们	wǒmen	we

梦 mèng 一 十 才 木 杧 杧 材 林 林 梦 梦

(夢 一 艹 艹 芢 芭 苩 苗 苗 莒 莒 夢 夢 夢)

释义 Meaning

名词 n.

dream: 我昨天做了一个梦。 I had a dream yesterday.

词语 Words and Phrases

梦幻	mènghuàn	illusion; dream
梦见	mèngjiàn	see in a dream; dream about
梦境	mèngjìng	dreamland; dreamworld
梦乡	mèngxiāng	dreamland
梦想	mèngxiǎng	earnest wish; fond dream
睡梦	shuìmèng	slumber; sleep

熟语 Idioms

梦寐以求	mèngmèi yǐ qiú	crave sth. even in one's dreams; long for sth. day and night

米 mǐ 丶 丷 兰 半 米 米

释义 Meaning

（一）名词 n.

1. rice: 南方人喜欢吃米，北方人喜欢吃面。The people from the south like to eat rice and those from the north like noodles.

2. shelled or husked seed: 他买了一斤花生米。He bought one *jin* of shelled peanuts.

（二）量词 measure w.

metre: 他有一米七高。He is one point seven metres tall.

词语 Words and Phrases

米饭	mǐfàn	cooked rice
米粒	mǐlì	grain of rice
米色	mǐsè	cream-coloured
大米	dàmǐ	husked rice
玉米	yùmǐ	corn

蜜 mì
丶 丶 宀 宀 忘 宓 宓 宓 宻 宻 宻 宻 蜜 蜜

释义 Meaning

名词 n.

honey: 他的心里像吃了蜜一样甜。 He felt as sweet as if he had had honey.

词语 Words and Phrases

蜜蜂	mìfēng	honeybee
蜜橘	mìjú	tangerine
蜜月	mìyuè	honeymoon
蜂蜜	fēngmì	honey
甜蜜	tiánmì	sweet; happy

面₁ miàn
二 二 厂 百 而 而 而 面 面

释义 Meaning

(一) 名词 n.

1. face: 她总是面带微笑。 There is always a gentle smile on her face.

2. surface; top: 桌子面儿上有很多灰尘。 There is a lot of dust on the top of the table.

3. aspect; side: 看问题不能只看一面。 We can't only look at one side of the question.

4. range; scope; extent: 他的知识面很广。 He has had a wide range of knowledge.

5. side: 我家的东北面是一所学校。 On the northeast side of my house is a school.

(二) 动词 v.

face (a certain direction): 这所房子面南向北。 The house faces south, with it's back to the north.

（三）副词 adv.

directly; personally: 这封信请你一定要面交给他。You
must hand this letter to him personally.

（四）量词 measure w.

used in flat objects: 湖水平得像一面镜子。The surface
of the lake is as flat as a mirror.

词语 Words and Phrases

面对	miànduì	face; confront
面积	miànjī	area
面貌	miànmào	appearance (of people or thing); face
面前	miànqián	in front of: in the face of
面容	miànróng	face; facial features
面熟	miànshú	look familiar
面谈	miàntán	speak to sb. face to face
面向	miànxiàng	① turn one's face to; face ② be geared to the needs of
表面	biǎomiàn	surface; outside; appearance; super-ficial
当面	dāngmiàn	to sb's face; in sb's present
封面	fēngmiàn	front cover

熟语 Idioms

面红耳赤	miànhóng-ěrchì	blush up to the ears
面面俱圆	miànmiàn jù yuán	cover everything; attend to all aspects of a matter
面如土色	miàn rú tǔsè	tallow-faced; turn pale

面₂ miàn 一 ア 厂 百 百 而 面 面 面

（**麺** 一 十 オ オ 朩 朩 夾 夾 夾 麦 麦

麦 麦 麺 麺 麺 麺 麺 麺 麺）

释义 Meaning

名词 n.

wheat flour; flour: 馒头是用面做的。The steamed bread is made of flour.

词语 Words and Phrases

面包	miànbāo	bread
面食	miànshí	cooked wheaten food
面条	miàntiáo	wheat noodles

秒 miǎo ⼀ ⼆ 千 千 禾 利 利 秒 秒

释义 Meaning

量词 measure w.

second: 一分钟等于六十秒。A minute is equal to sixty seconds

词语 Words and Phrases

秒针	miǎozhēn	second hand of a watch or clock

熟语 Idioms

分秒必争	fēn miǎo bì zhēng	not a second is to be lost; seize every moment

灭 miè ⼆ ⼀ ⺧ 夕 灭

(滅 ⼀ ⼀ ⼑ ⼳ 汇 汇 沪 沪 沪 泝 泝 滅 滅 滅)

释义 Meaning

动词 v.

1. (of a light, fire, etc.) go out: 灯突然灭了。All of a sudden the lights went out. 反义词：亮

2. extinguish; put out: 他们正在紧张地灭火。They are in-

tensely working to put out the fire. 反义词：点

3. destory; exterminate: 他怎么能长别人的志气，灭自己的威风？How could he enhance the morale of others and discourage himself?

词语 Words and Phrases

灭顶	mièdǐng	be drowned
灭亡	mièwáng	be destroyed; die out
毁灭	huǐmiè	destroy; exterminate
破灭	pòmiè	be shattered; evaporate
消灭	xiāomiè	die out; eliminate; wipe out

熟语 Idioms

自生自灭	zì shēng zì miè	(of a thing) flourishes by itself and perishes by itself; let alone

民 mín   ⼀ ⼆ ⼸ ⼸ 民

释义 Meaning

名词 n.

1. the people: 当官就应该为民办事。Government officials should work for the people.

2. civilian: 军爱民，民拥军。Military men defend the civilians and civilians support military men. 反义词：军

词语 Words and Phrases

民歌	míngē	folk song
民航	mínháng	civil aviation
民间	mínjiān	among the people; folk
民警	mínjǐng	people's policeman
民俗	mínsú	folk custom; folkways
民乐	mínyuè	folk music
民主	mínzhǔ	democratic rights; democratic

民族	mínzú	nation; nationality
公民	gōngmín	citizen
回民	huímín	members of Hui nationality (mostly Muslims)
农民	nóngmín	peasant
市民	shìmín	residents in a city
渔民	yúmín	fisherman

熟语 Idioms

| 民不聊生 | mín bù liáo shēng | the people are deprived of their means of survival; the masses live in dire poverty |

名 míng ノ ク タ 夕 名 名

释义 Meaning

（一）名词 n.

1. name: 这种水果名为芒果。The name of this fruit is mango.

2. given name: 他姓王名海。His surname is Wang and his given name is Hai.

3. fame; reputation: 他这么努力工作，不为名，不为利。That he works so hard is neither for the sake of fame nor money.

（二）形容词 a.

famous; noted: 他是位名作家。He is a well-known writer.

（三）量词 measure w.

used for people: 他在比赛中得了第一名。He got first place in the competition.

词语 Words and Phrases

名称　　míngchēng　name (of a thing or an organization)

名单	míngdān	name list; roll
名贵	míngguì	famous and precious; rare
名牌	míngpái	famous brand
名片	míngpiàn	visiting card; calling card
名气	míngqì	reputation; fame
名人	míngrén	famous person; eminent person
名胜	míngshèng	a place famous for its scenery or historical relics
名望	míngwàng	fame and prestige
名誉	míngyù	reputation; honorary
名字	míngzì	name
姓名	xìngmíng	full name

熟语 Idioms

名不副实	míng bú fù shí	the title doesn't correspond to the reality; be unworthy of the name or title
名不虚传	míng bù xū chuán	deserve the reputation one enjoys; true to tradition
名列前茅	míng liè qiánmáo	stand first in the list; be among the best of the successful candidates
名落孙山	míng luò sūn shān	fall behind Sun Shan (who was last on the list of candidates); fail in an examination
名正言顺	míngzhèngyánshùn	with right titles and proper words; be perfectly justified

明 míng 丨 冂 日 日 旳 明 明 明

释义 Meaning

形容词 a.

1. bright; light: 天已微明。Day is breaking. 反义词：暗

2. clear; distinct: 他的去向至今不明。His whereabouts are still unknown.

词语 Words and Phrases

明白	míngbái	① clear; plain ② understand; realize; know
明代	míngdài	Ming Dynasty
明亮	míngliàng	light; bright; shining
明年	míngnián	next year
明确	míngquè	① clear and definite; explicit ② make clear
明天	míngtiān	tomorrow
明显	míngxiǎn	obvious; evident
明月	míngyuè	a bright moon
明智	míngzhì	wise; sensible
失明	shīmíng	be blind

熟语 Idioms

明察秋毫	míng chá qiū háo	be perceptive to the minutest detail
明知故问	míng zhī gù wèn	knowingly ask the question
眼明手快	yǎn míng shǒu kuài	sharp-eyed and quick action

命 mìng 　丿 人 人 介 佥 佥 佥 命 命

释义 Meaning

名词 n.

1. life: 医生又救活了一条命。The doctor saved a life again.

2. fate; destiny: 他总说自己命很苦。He always said that he had a cruel fate.

词语 Words and Phrases

命令	mìnglìng	order; command

命名	mìngmíng	name (sb. or sth.)
命题	mìngtí	assign a topic; set a question
命运	mìngyùn	destiny; lot
革命	gémìng	revolution
拼命	pīnmìng	exerting the utmost strength; with all one's might
生命	shēngmìng	life
寿命	shòumìng	life-span
遵命	zūnmìng	obey order

熟语 Idioms

相依为命	xiāng yī wéi mìng	be interdependent; depend on each other for survival

摸mō 一 十 扌 扩 扩 扩 扩 护 措 措 摸 摸 摸

释义 Meaning

动词 v.

1. feel; touch: 妈妈轻轻地摸了摸孩子的头。The mother gently stroked the child's head.

2. feel for; fumble: 他摸着黑赶路。He groped his way in the dark.

3. try to find out; sound out: 我摸不透他是怎么想的。I was unable to find out what he thought.

词语 Words and Phrases

摸底	mōdǐ	try to find out the real situation or intention; sound sb. out
摸索	mōsuǒ	① feel about; fumble ② try to find out
估摸	gūmo	(in oral speech) reckon; guess
捉摸	zhuōmo	(in negative sentences) fathom; ascertain

母mǔ　⺃ 𠃊 毋 母 母

释义 Meaning

(一) 名词 n.

mother: 失败是成功之母。Failure is the mother of success.

(二) 形容词 a.

female (animal): 这只狗是公的还是母的？Is this dog male or female?

词语 Words and Phrases

母爱	mǔ'ài	motherly love; maternal love
母鸡	mǔjī	hen
母亲	mǔqīn	mother
母系	mǔxì	matriarchal; maternal side
母语	mǔyǔ	mother tongue
伯母	bómǔ	aunt
父母	fùmǔ	parent
字母	zìmǔ	letters of an alphabet
祖母	zǔmǔ	grandmother

木mù　一 十 才 木

释义 Meaning

(一) 名词 n.

1. tree: 俗话说，独木不成林。As the saying goes, one tree doesn't make a forest.
2. wooden: 这是一家木制品商店。This is a shop selling wooden products.

(二) 形容词 a.

numb; wooden: 太冷了，两只手都冻木了。It's so cold that both hands are numb.

词语 Words and Phrases

木板	mùbǎn	board; plank
木材	mùcái	wood; timber
木匠	mùjiàng	carpenter
木偶	mù'ǒu	puppet
木头	mùtou	wood; log
木屋	mùwū	log cabin
花木	huāmù	flowers and trees (in parks and gardens)
积木	jīmù	toy bricks; building blocks

熟语 Idioms

行将就木	xíng jiāng jiù mù	to be on the threshold of the grave (derogatory)

目 mù 丨 冂 门 月 目

释义 Meaning

（一）名词 n.

eye: 他简直是目中无人。He simply considered everyone beneath his notice.

词语 Words and Phrases

夺目	duómù	dazzle the eyes
节目	jiémù	programme; item
盲目	mángmù	blindly
数目	shùmù	amount; number
醒目	xǐngmù	(of written words or pictures) catch the eye; be striking

熟语 Idioms

目不暇接	mù bù xiá jiē	too many things to be seen with one's eyes
目不转睛	mù bù zhuǎn jīng	watch with unblinking eyes; look with utmost concentration

| 目瞪口呆 | mù dèng kǒu dāi | dumb-founded; stand aghast |
| 目空一切 | mù kōng yí qiè | with one's nose in the air |

拿ná ノ 𠂉 𠂇 𠂉 𠆢 合 合 拿 拿 拿 拿

释义 Meaning

（一）动词 v.

1. hold; take: 他手里拿着一本书。He is holding a book in his hand.

2. be able to do; be sure of: 这件事我拿不准。I feel uncertain about this matter.

（二）介词 prep.

1. used before the tools, manner, material, etc.: 你们应该拿事实来证明自己的清白。You should prove your innocence with facts.

2. used before the object being dealt with: 我简直拿他没有办法。I simply can't do anything with him.

词语 Words and Phrases

拿不出手	nábùchū shǒu	not be able to pay
拿手	náshǒu	expert; good at
拿主意	ná zhǔyì	make a decision
捉拿	zhuōná	arrest; catch

哪nǎ 丨 丨丨 丨丨 叮 叿 叿 哪 哪 哪

释义 Meaning

代词 pron.

1. which; what: 请问，哪一位是王先生？Excuse me, which one is Mr. Wang?

2. how, indicate a rhetorical question: 不试试哪能知道结果怎样？How can you know the result until you have tried?

词语 Words and Phrases

哪个	nǎge	which one
哪里	nǎlǐ	① where; wherever ② used in a rhetorical question to indicate negative
哪怕	nǎpà	even; even if; no matter how
哪儿	nǎr	where
哪些	nǎxiē	which; what; who
哪样	nǎyàng	in what way

那nà   丁 彐 彐 厾 那 那

释义 Meaning

（一）代词 pron.

that: 那姑娘是我哥哥的女朋友。That girl is my brother's girl friend. 反义词 antonym: 这 this.

（二）连词 conj.

then: 没有什么事的话，那我们就先走了。If there isn't anything to do, then we will leave first.

in that case: 那我就不多说了。In that case, I won't say any more.

词语 Words and Phrases

那个	nàgè	that (one)
那里	nàlǐ	there; that place
那么	nàme	in that way; then
那些	nàxiē	those
那样	nàyàng	like that; such; so

奶nǎi   く 女 女 奶 奶

释义 Meaning

名词 n.

milk: 他不喜欢喝奶。He doesn't like milk.

词语 Words and Phrases

奶粉	nǎifěn	dried milk; milk powder
奶酪	nǎilào	cheese
奶奶	nǎinai	grandmother; grandma
奶水	nǎishuǐ	milk
奶油	nǎiyóu	cream

男 nán　丨　冂　戸　冊　田　畀　男

释义 Meaning

形容词 a.

man; male: 她打扮得像个男人。She dressed up like a man.

反义词 antonym: 女 woman, female.

词语 Words and Phrases

男厕所	nán cèsuǒ	men's lavatory
男护士	nán hùshì	male nurse
男人	nánrén	man; menfolk
男生	nánshēng	boy student; schoolboy; man
男士	nánshì	gentleman
男性	nánxìng	the male sex
男子汉	nánzǐhàn	a manly man, a masculine fellow

南 nán　二　十　广　古　古　南　南　南　南

释义 Meaning

名词 n.

south: 广州在中国南方。Guangzhou is in the south of China.

反义词 antonym: 北 north

词语 Words and Phrases

南半球	nán bànqiú	the Southern Hemisphere
南边	nánbiān	the southern side

南方	nánfāng	the southern part of the country
南极	nánjí	the South Pole
南面	nánmiàn	the southern side
南味儿	nánwèir	food of southern taste anf flavour

熟语 Idioms

| 南腔北调 | nán qiāng běi diào | (speak with) a mixed accent |
| 南辕北辙 | nán yuán běi zhé | act in a way that defeats one's purpose |

难₁ nán ㇆ ㇈ ㇈ ㇈ ㇈ ㇈ ㇈ 难 难

（難 一 十 廾 廾 廾 芇 芇 茧 莗 堇 堇
堇 堇 堇 堇 堇 難 難）

释义 Meaning

形容词 a.

hard: 今天的考试太难了。The exam today is too hard.
他很难相处。He is a difficult man to get on with. 反义词
antonym: 容易 easy

词语 Words and Phrases

难保	nánbǎo	can not say for sure
难处	nánchù	difficulties, trouble
难得	nándé	rare, hard to come by
难度	nándù	degree of difficulty
难怪	nánguài	no wonder; understandable
难过	nánguò	feel sorry, feel bad
难受	nánshòu	feel unwell, feel unhappy
难说	nánshuō	hard to say

熟语 Idioms

| 难言之隐 | nán yán zhī yǐn | a painful topic |

难₂ nàn

(難 一 十 卄 卄 艹 芑 苎 苫 茞 茣 堇 茣
茣 菓 菓 菓 難 難 難 難)

释义 Meaning

名词 n.

calamity; trouble: 朋友有难，我一定会帮助。If my friend is in trouble, I will surely help him out.

词语 Words and Phrases

难民	nànmín	refugee
海难	hǎinàn	perils at sea
空难	kōngnàn	air disaster

脑nǎo 丿 刀 月 月 刖 扩 扩 朡 脑 脑

(腦 丿 刀 月 月 胙 胙 胙 腦 腦 腦 腦
腦 腦)

释义 Meaning

名词 n.

head: 动动脑子，想一个好办法。Use your head to find the best way.

brain: 他最近用脑过度。He has overtaxed his brain recently.

词语 Words and Phrases.

脑袋	nǎodài	head, brain
脑瓜儿	nǎoguār	head
脑海	nǎohǎi	mind
脑筋	nǎojīn	mind
脑力	nǎolì	mental power

脑子	nǎozi	brain, mind
首脑	shǒunǎo	leadership
头脑	tóunǎo	mental capacity

熟语 Idioms

| 鬼头鬼脑 | guǐ tóu guǐ nǎo | thievish, stealthy. |

闹nào ` ⼂ ⼌ ⼃ ⾨ ⾨ 闩 闹

(鬧 ⼁ ⼐ ⼐ ⼐ ⼐ ⼐ ⼐ ⼐ ⼐ 鬥 鬥 鬥 鬥 鬧 鬧)

释义 Meaning

动词 v.

make noise; give vent 孩子们又哭又闹，幼儿园的老师也没办法。The children fussed and cried so hard that it left their kindergarten teacher at a complete loss.

词语 Words and Phrases

闹别扭	nào bièniu	be at odds with sb.
闹肚子	nào dùzi	have diarrhea
闹剧	nàojù	farce
闹情绪	nào qíngxù	be disgruntled
闹市	nàoshì	busy street
闹事	nàoshì	make trouble
闹笑话	nào xiàohua	make a stupid mistake
闹钟	nàozhōng	alarm clock

呢ne ⼁ ⼐ ⼝ ⼝⼂ ⼝⼂ 呢 呢 呢

释义 Meaning

语气词 part.

1. used at the end of a question. 你说他会不会来呢？Can

you tell me whether he will come? 我要一杯牛奶，你呢？I want a glass of milk, what about you?

2. used at the end of a declarative sentence to reinforce the assertion: 我还没准备好呢。I'm not ready yet.

3. used to mark a pause: 这个问题呢，我们还在研究。As for this problem, we are still researching on it.

内 nèi 丨 冂 内 内

释义 Meaning

名词 n.

inner; inside: 一星期内必须交作业。The assignment must be handed in within one week.

词语 Words and Phrases

内部	nèibù	inside; interior; internal
内地	nèidì	inland; interior; Chinese Mainland
内弟	nèidì	wife's younger brother; brother-in-law
内行	nèiháng	expert; adept
内科	nèikē	(department of) internal medicine
内容	nèiróng	content; substance
内外	nèiwài	inside and outside
内向	nèixiàng	introversion
国内	guónèi	home; domestic; inside China
以内	yǐnèi	within; less than

熟语 Idioms

| 内忧外患 | nèi yōu wài huàn | internal revolt and foreign invasion |

能 néng 乚 厶 彳 自 自 自 自 能 能 能

释义 Meaning

（一）形容词 a.

able: 俗话说，"能者多劳"。As the saying goes: "the abler a man is, the busier he gets."

（二）情态动词 aux. v.

can: 你能帮我一个忙吗？Could you help me?

词语 Words and Phrases

能干	nénggàn	capable; competent
能够	nénggòu	can; be able to
能见度	néngjiàndù	visibility
能力	nénglì	ability; capability
能量	néngliàng	energy
能耐	néngnài	ability
能人	néngrén	able person
能手	néngshǒu	expert
能源	néngyuán	energy; energy sources

熟语 Idioms

能说会道	néng shuō huì dào	be a glib talker
能者多劳	néng zhě duō láo	Able people should do more work.
能工巧匠	néng gōng qiǎo jiàng	skilled craftsman

泥ní 丶 丶 氵 汀 汨 沪 沪 泥

释义 Meaning.

名词 n.

mud; mire: 刚下过雨，路上有很多泥水。After the rain, the road is covered with mud.

词语 Words and Phrases

| 泥巴 | níbā | mud |

泥工	nígōng	bricklayer
泥人	nírén	clay figurine
泥沙	níshā	silt
泥土	nítǔ	clay

熟语 Idioms

| 泥牛入海 | ní niú rù hǎi | gone forever |
| 泥菩萨过河， 自身难保 | ní púsà guò hé, zìshēn nán bǎo | One hardly can save one-self, like a clay idol crossing a river. |

你 nǐ   ノ 亻 仃 仃 佲 你 你

释义 Meaning

代词 pronoun.

you: 你好！How are you!

词语 Words and Phrases

| 你们 | nǐ men | you (second person plural) |

熟语 Idioms

| 你死我活 | nǐ sǐ wǒ huó | a life-or-death struggle |

年 nián   ノ 亡 仨 仨 缶 年

释义 Meaning

名词 n.

year: 我学了一年普通话。I have studied Mandarin Chinese for a year.

yearly: 我每年回老家看爷爷一次。I go to my hometown to see my grandfather yearly.

词语 Words and Phrases

| 年代 | niándài | years, a decade of a century |
| 年会 | niánhuì | annual meeting |

年级	niánjí	grade; year
年纪	niánjì	age
年龄	niánlíng	age
年轻	niánqīng	young

熟语 Idioms

| 年富力强 | nián fù lì qiáng | be in the full vigor of life |

念 niàn　乀 ㇒ ㇒ 今 今 念 念 念

释义 Meaning

动词 v.

1. read: 老师让我念课文。The teacher asked me to read the text.
2. attend school 他没念过大学。He has not been to university.

词语 Words and Phrases

念佛	niànfó	pray to Buddha
念旧	niànjiù	remember old friends.
念书	niànshū	study
念头	niàntou	idea

熟语 Idioms

| 念念不忘 | niàn niàn bú wàng | bear in mind constantly |

娘 niáng　㇍ 女 女 女` 女¯ 女¯ 女¹ 娘 娘 娘

释义 Meaning

名词 n.

mother: 有些北方人把妈妈叫"娘"。Some of the northerners call their mother "niang".

词语 Words and Phrases

| 娘家 | niángjiā | parents' home of married women |

娘儿们　　niángrmen　　the womenfolk
娘娘　　　niángniáng　　emperor's wife

鸟 niǎo ´ ㄅ ㄅ 鸟 鸟

(鳥 ´ 冂 冂 户 户 阜 鸟 鳥 鳥 鳥 鳥)

释义 Meaning

名词 n.

bird: 孩子们都喜欢鸟。All children like birds.

词语 Words and Phrases

鸟瞰　　niǎokàn　　get a bird's-eye view
鸟类　　niǎolèi　　birds

熟语 Idioms

鸟语花香　　niǎo yǔ huā xiāng　　birds sing and flowers give forth their fragrance; spring time

您 nín ´ ㄅ ㄏ 伫 伫 你 你 你 您 您 您

释义 Meaning

代词 pron.

you (honor.) 王先生，您早！Good morning, Mr. Wang!

牛 niú ´ ㄏ 乍 牛

释义 Meaning

名词 n.

cattle: 农民最喜欢的动物是牛，不是狗。The peasants' favorite animal aren't dogs but cattle.

词语 Words and Phrases

牛奶	niúnǎi	milk
牛排	niúpái	beefsteak
牛皮	niúpí	bragging
牛脾气	niúpíqì	stubbornness.
牛气	niúqì	arrogant
牛肉	niúròu	beef
牛蛙	niúwā	bullfrog
牛仔裤	niúzǎikù	jeans
公牛	gōngniú	bull
母牛	mǔniú	cow

熟语 Idioms

牛头马面	niú tóu mǎ miàn	devils in animal forms
牛郎织女	niúláng zhīnǚ	the Herd-boy and the Weaving-girl who meet only once a year; husband and wife living in different cities.

农nóng ＇ ＇ ゲ ゲ 农 农

(農 ＇ 口 曰 曲 曲 曲 農 農 農 農 農)

释义 Meaning

名词 n.

agriculture: 他哥哥在老家务农。His old brother is engaged in agriculture in his hometown.

词语 Words and Phrases

农场	nóngchǎng	farm
农村	nóngcūn	countryside

农历	nónglì	the lunar calendar
农民	nóngmín	peasant
农药	nóngyào	agricultural chemical
农业	nóngyè	agriculture
农作物	nóng zuò wù	crops

浓 nóng   `ㄝ 氵 氵 氵 氵 沪 沪 浓 浓

(濃   `ㄝ 氵 氵 氵 氵 汇 浐 浐 浐 浐 浐
浐 浐 濃 濃 濃)

释义 Meaning

形容词 a.

1. heavy: 这花的香气真浓。The flowers give off a heavy fragrance
2. strong: 我喜欢喝浓咖啡。I like to drink strong coffee.
   反义词 antonym: 淡 weak; light

词语 Words and Phrases

浓度	nóngdù	density
浓厚	nónghòu	thick; strong
浓烈	nóngliè	thick, heavy, strong
浓缩	nóngsuō	concentrate
浓妆	nóngzhuāng	heavily made-up

熟语 Idioms

| 浓妆艳抹 | nóngzhuāng-yànmǒ | put on gay clothing and powder one's face; heavily made-up |

怒 nù   ㄥ ㄗ ㄠ ㄠ ㄠ 奴 奴 怒 怒 怒

释义 Meaning

anger 老板发怒了。The boss got angry.

词语 Words and Phrases

怒斥	nùchì	angrily rebuke
怒汹汹	nùxiōngxiōng	in a rage
怒号	nùháo	howl
怒吼	nùhǒu	roar; howl
怒火	nùhuǒ	flames of fury
怒气	nùqì	fury
怒视	nùshì	glare at

熟语 Idioms

怒不可遏	nù bù kě è	be unable to contain one's anger

女 nǔ 　　乚 乜 女

释义 Meaning

形容词 a.

1. woman 她是这个乡村第一个女教师。She is the first woman teacher of this village. 反义词 antonym: 男 man
2. daughter 他有一儿一女。He has a son and a daugher.

词语 Words and Phrases

女厕所	nǔ cèsuǒ	women's lavatory.
女朋友	nǔ péngyou	girl friend
女人	nǔrén	woman;
女神	nǔshén	goddess
女生	nǔshēng	girl student; schoolgirl; woman
女士	nǔshì	lady
女性	nǔxìng	the female sex
女主人	nǔ zhǔrén	hostess

熟语 Idioms

女扮男装	nǔ bàn nán zhuāng	a woman disguised as a man

暖 nuǎn ｜
暖 暖 暖

释义 Meaning

形容词 a.

warm: 朝南的教室很暖和，朝北的很冷。Classrooms facing the south are warm and the ones facing the north are cold.

反义词 antonym: 冷cold

词语 Words and Phrases

暖和	nuǎnhuo	nice and warm
暖流	nuǎnliú	warm feeling (current)
暖气	nuǎnqì	heating equipment
暖色	nuǎnsè	warm colours

爬 pá ˊ 厂 爪 爪 爬 爬 爬 爬

释义 Meaning

动词 v.

crawl: 小孩子们都喜欢爬来爬去。All babies like crawling around.

climb: 狗不会爬树。Dogs can't climb trees.

词语 Words and Phrases

爬高	págāo	climb up
爬升	páshēng	gain altitude
爬行	páxíng	crawl
爬行动物	pá xíng dòng wù	reptile

怕 pà ˊ ˋ 忄 忄 忄 怕 怕 怕

释义 Meaning

动词 v.

1. be afraid of: 小孩子怕黑。The little children are afraid of darkness.
2. worry: 父母怕孩子交上坏朋友。The parents worry that their children might make friends with bad people.

词语 Words and Phrases

怕老婆	pàlǎopó	be henpecked
怕人	pàrén	dread to meet people
怕是	pàshi	perhaps
怕事	pàshi	be afraid of getting into trouble
怕羞	pàxiū	shy; bashful

拍pāi ⟍ 扌 扌 扌′ 扌′ 拍 拍 拍

释义 Meaning

动词 v.

1. pat: 老板拍了拍他的肩膀。The boss gave him a pat on the back.
2. shoot, make (a film, TV play) 他的小说都已经拍成电视剧了。All of his novels have been made into TV plays.

词语 Words and Phrases

拍板	pāibǎn	have the final say
拍马（屁）	pāimǎ(pì)	lick sb.'s boots
拍卖	päimài	auction
拍摄	pāishè	take (a picture)
拍手	pāishǒu	clap one's hands
拍戏	pāixì	make a movie
拍照	pāizhào	take a picture

熟语 Idioms

拍手称快　　pāi shǒu chēng kuài　　clap and cheer

排₁ pái 一 亅 扌 扌 扎 扫 扫 扫 排 排 排 排

释义 Meaning

（一）动词 v.

put in order: 孩子们，把桌子和椅子排好。Children, put the desks and chairs in order！

（二）量词 Meadure word

row: 院子里有五排树。There are five rows of trees in the yard.

（三）名词 n.

line: 您的座位在第一排。Your seat is in the first row.

词语 Words and Phrases

排场	páichǎng	ostentation and extravagance
排队	páiduì	queue up
排骨	páigǔ	spareribs
排练	páiliàn	rehearse
排列	páiliè	arrange
排球	páiqiú	volleyball

排₂ pái 一 亅 扌 扌 扎 扫 扫 扫 排 排 排 排

释义 Meaning

动词 v.

exclude; discharge; drain

词语 Words and Phrases

排斥	páichì	repel
排除	páichú	get rid of, remove
排水	páishuǐ	drain away water
排外	páiwài	antiforeign

熟语 Idioms

排忧解难	pái yōu jiě nàn	exclude the difficulty and anxiety
排山倒海	pái shān dǎo hǎi	topple the mountains and overturn the seas; overwhelming

牌 pái   丿 丿' 爿 片 片' 爿' 爿' 牌 牌 牌 牌 牌

释义 Meaning

名词 n.

1. brand: 年轻人买衣服看重的是牌子，不是名牌不买。
   Young shoppers value the brand very much and buy clothes of well-known brands only.

2. cards: 你喜欢打牌吗？ Do you like to play cards?

词语 Words and Phrases

牌匾	páibiǎn	an inscribed board
牌价	páijià	(market) quotation
牌楼	páilóu	temporary ceremonial scaffold
牌照	páizhào	license
牌子	páizi	brand

派 pài   丶 丶 氵 氵 汇 沪 沪 派 派 派

释义 Meaning

（一）动词 v.

send: 公司派我到美国谈生意。I was sent to America on business.

（二）名词 n.

(political) group; school (of thought or art) 王教授不属于这一派。Professor Wang does not belong to this school.

词语 Words and Phrases

派别	pàibié	group; school
派出所	pàichūsuǒ	local police station
派遣	pàiqiǎn	dispatch
派生	pàishēng	derive
派头	pàitóu	style
派系	pàixì	group; clique
派用场	pàiyòngchǎng	turn to account

盘 pán　 ′ 丿 刀 月 舟 舟 舟 舟 盘 盘 盘

（**盤**　 ′ 丿 刀 月 舟 舟 舟 舟 般 般 般 盤 盤 盤 盤）

释义 Meaning

（一）名词 n.

plate: 洗盘子是大学生打工时常做的工作。College students often take washing plates as their part-time job.

（二）量词 Measure word

plate: 我要一盘牛肉。I want a plate of beef.

词语 Words and Phrases

盘查	pánchá	interrogate and examine

盘踞	pánjù	be entrenched
盘绕	pánrào	twine
盘算	pánsuàn	calculate; figure
盘问	pánwèn	interrogate
盘旋	pánxuán	spiral around
盘子	pánzi	plate; dish

熟语 Idioms

盘根错节	pán gēn cuò jié	with twisted roots and gnarled branches; well entrenched

胖pàng 丿 刀 刀 月 月 肜 肜 肜 胖

释义 Meaning

形容词 a.

1. fat: 他太胖了。He is too fat.

2. put on weight: 去年我胖了五公斤。I put on 5 kilos last year. 反义词 antonym: 瘦 thin

词语 Words and Phrases

胖墩儿	pàngdūnr	fatty child, chubby child
胖子	pàngzi	a fat person

跑pǎo 丨 冂 口 甲 甲 足 足 趵 趵 跑 跑

释义 Meaning

动词 v.

1. run: 我每天早上跑步。I go running every morning.

2. run about doing sth. 我跑了好几家书店，才买到那本书。I had to run around to several bookstores to get that book.

词语 Words and Phrases

跑步	pǎobù	run; jog
跑道	pǎodào	runway (on an airfield)
跑龙套	pǎo lóng tào	play a minor role
跑生意	pǎoshēngyì	be a commercial traveler
跑腿儿	pǎotuǐr	do legwork
跑鞋	pǎoxié	track shoes

熟语 Idioms

跑得了和尚 跑不了庙	pǎo dé liǎo héshang pǎo bù liǎo miào	the monk may run away, but the temple can't run with him; can be traced

陪 péi   了 阝 阝` 阝⁻ 阝⁻ 阝⁻ 阝 陪 陪

释义 Meaning

动词 v.

accompany: 我明天要陪朋友参观农村。I will accompany
my friends on a visit to the rural area tomorrow.

词语 Words and Phrases

陪伴	péibàn	accompany
陪衬	péichèn	serve as a contrast or foil
陪嫁	péijià	dowry
陪审	péishěn	serve on a jury
陪同	péitóng	accompany (on a visit)
陪同团	péitóngtuán	hosting team

赔 péi   l 冂 贝 贝 贝` 贝⁻ 贝⁻ 贝⁻ 赔 赔
     赔 赔

(赔   l 冂 日 日 目 目 贝 贝 贝` 贝⁻ 贝⁻ 贝⁻
     贝⁻ 贝⁻ 赔 赔)

释义 Meaning

动词 v.

1. pay for: 杯子是我打碎的，当然由我赔。I smashed the glass, certainly it's up to me to pay for it.

2. lost money in business 他的公司去年赔了一大笔钱。His company lost a large sum of money last year. 反义词 antonym: 赚 make a profit; earn money.

词语 Words and Phrases

赔本	péiběn	sustain losses in business
赔不是	péibúshi	apologize
赔偿	péicháng	compensate
赔礼	péilǐ	make an apology
赔钱	péiqián	lose money in business
赔笑	péixiào	smile obsequiously
赔罪	péizuì	ask forgiveness for one's wrongdoing

熟语 Idioms

| 赔了夫人
又折兵 | péi le fūrén
yòu zhé bīng | give away one's wife and also got defeated in the battlefield, to pay a double penalty |

朋 péng 丿 刀 月 月 朋 朋 朋 朋

释义 Meaning

名词 n.

friend: 谁都有亲朋好友。Everybody has his relatives and friends.

词语 Words and Phrases

| 朋友 | péngyou | friend |

熟语 Idioms

朋比为奸　　péng bǐ wéi jiān　　gang up (for evil doing)

捧 pěng 一 十 扌 扩 扩 扩 护 挟 捀 捀 捧

释义 Meaning

动词 v.

1. hold or carry in both hands: 他捧着一本书，一看就是半天。Once he begins reading, he may go on for a long time.

2. boost: 别把他捧得太高了。Don't praise him to the skies.

词语 Words and Phrases

捧读　　pěngdú　　reading seriously.

捧场　　pěngchǎng　　sing the praises of; in support of

熟语 Idioms

捧腹大笑　　pěng fù dà xiào　　be convulsed with laughters

碰 pèng 一 厂 石 石 矿 矿 矿 矿 碰 碰 碰 碰

释义 Meaning

动词 v.

1. touch: 这是开水，你可别碰。This is boiled water, you'd best not touch.

2. run into: 我在街上碰到一个朋友。I ran into a friend in the street.

词语 Words and Phrases

碰杯　　pèngbēi　　clink glasses

碰钉子	pèngdīngzi	meet with a rebuff
碰见	pèngjiàn	run into
碰碰船	pèngpèngchuán	bumper boat
碰巧	pèngqiǎo	by chance
碰头	pèngtóu	meet and discuss
碰运气	pèngyùnqi	try one's luck
碰撞	pèngzhuàng	impact

批 pī 二 十 扌 扩 批 扯 批

释义 Meaning

（一）动词 v.

1. criticize: 这是谬论，应该批倒。This is rediculous and it should be criticized.

（二）量词 Meadure word

batch: 商店刚进了一批货。This shop has just replenished stock with a new batch of goods.

词语 Words and Phrases

批驳	pībó	refute
批发	pīfā	wholesale
批复	pīfù	give a written official reply to an organization at a lower level
批改	pīgǎi	correct
批量	pīliàng	in batches
批评	pīpíng	criticize
批示	pīshì	comments on a report submitted by a subordinate.
批准	pīzhǔn	approve

皮 pí 二 厂 广 皮 皮

释义 Meaning

(一) 名词 n.

skin; leather: 把香蕉皮扔到垃圾箱里。Please throw the banana peel into the garbage.

(二) 形容词 a.

naughty: 这男孩真皮！What a naughty boy he is!

词语 Words and Phrases

皮包	píbāo	leather handbag
皮带	pídài	leather belt
皮肤	pífū	skin
皮肤病	pífūbìng	skin disease
皮肤科	pífūkē	dermatology
皮箱	píxiāng	leather suitcase
皮鞋	píxié	leather shoes
皮衣	píyī	leather clothing

熟语 Idioms

皮笑肉不笑　pí xiào ròu bú xiào　　put on a false smile

偏 piān ノ 亻 亻 亻 亻 亻 伫 偏 偏 偏 偏

释义 Meaning

(一) 形容词 a.

slanting: 南京在上海的正西偏北方向。Nanjing is to the west by north of Shanghai.

(二) 副词 adv.

wilfully, insistently 我不明白他为什么偏要那么做。I don't see why must he do it that way.

词语 Words and Phrases

偏爱	piān'ài	show favouritism to sb. or sth.
偏方	piānfāng	folk prescription
偏护	piānhù	be partial to and side with
偏激	piānjī	extreme
偏见	piānjiàn	prejudice
偏离	piānlí	deviate
偏旁	piānpáng	components of Chinese characters
偏偏	piānpiān	wilfully; contrary to expectations
偏袒	piāntǎn	be partial to and side with
偏向	piānxiàng	be partial to
偏心	piānxīn	partiality
偏远	piānyuǎn	remote

篇 piān   ′ ′ ′ ′ ′ ′ ′ ′ ′ ′ ′ ′ 竺 竺 竺 篞 篇 篇

释义 Meaning

量词 Meadure word

sheet; piece: 这篇文章写得很好。This is an excellent article.

词语 Words and Phrases

篇幅	piānfu	length;
篇目	piānmù	contents
篇章	piān zhāng	sections and chapters

片 piàn   ノ ノ′ ノ′ 片

释义 Meaning

（一）名词 n.

1. piece, slice: 地上有很多玻璃片。There are many bits and pieces of glass on the ground.

（二）量词 Meadure word

slice; pieces: 我早饭只吃了二片面包。I only had two slices of bread for breakfast.

词语 Words and Phrases

片段	piànduàn	part, passage
片刻	piànkè	a moment
片面	piànmiàn	one-sided
片头	piàntóu	titles

熟语 Idioms

片甲不留	piàn jiǎ bù liú	(be) completely wipe out
片言只语	piàn yán zhī yǔ	with a few words

骗 piàn　乛 马 马 马' 驴 驴 驴 驴 骗 骗 骗 骗

(骗　一 厂 F F 馬 馬 馬 馬 馬 馬' 馬' 馬' 驴 驴 骗 骗 骗 骗)

释义 Meaning

动词 v.

deceive; cheat: 你想骗我！ You want to cheat me!

词语 Words and Phrases

骗局	piànjú	fraud
骗取	piànqǔ	gain sth. by cheating
骗人	piànrén	cheat sb. out of sth.
骗术	piànshù	ruse
骗子	piànzi	swindler

飘 piāo　一 厂 亓 西 西 西 西 酉 覀 覀 票 票 飘 飘 飘

（飘 一 厂 厂 丙 西 西 覀 覀 栗 票 票 票 飘 飘 飘 飘 飘 飘 飘 飘 飘 ）

释义 Meaning

动词 v.

float in the air; flutter: 春天来了，花香随风飘散。Spring is coming and the delicate scent of the flowers is wafted everywhere along by the breeze.

词语 Words and Phrases

飘带	piāodài	ribbon
飘荡	piāodàng	drift, float
飘动	piāodòng	float
飘流	piāoliú	drift about
飘洒	piāosǎ	float in the air
飘舞	piāowǔ	wave in the wind
飘扬	piāoyáng	flutter
漂移	piāoyí	drift

熟语 Idioms

飘洋过海　　piāo yáng guò hǎi　　leave home and go abroad

票piào 一 厂 厂 丙 西 西 覀 覀 栗 票 票

释义 Meaning

名词 n.

ticket: 火车票很便宜。The railway ticket is very cheap.

词语 Words and Phrases

票房	piàofáng	box office
票根	piàogēn	stub (of a ticket)
票价	piàojià	the price of a ticket

| 票据 | piàojù | note; bill |
| 票面 | piàomiàn | face value |

拼 pīn 　一 丁 扌 扩 扩 拌 拌 拼 拼

释义 Meaning

动词 v.

1. join together: 请把这两张图拼起来，你会得到答案。
   Put the two pictures together, then you will find the answer.

2. go all out in work: 比赛的时候一定要拼才会赢。One
   must go all out to win the match.

词语 Words and Phrases

拼搏	pīnbó	struggle hard
拼凑	pīncòu	piece together
拼命	pīnmìng	risk one's life
拼盘	pīnpán	cold dishes
拼写	pīnxiě	spell
拼音	pīnyīn	phoneticize
拼装	pīnzhuāng	assemble

品 pǐn 　丨 冂 口 戶 叺 吕 品 品 品

释义 Meaning

（一）动词 v.

character; sample: 喝茶要慢慢喝，这样才能品出味。If
you want to savor the flavor of tea, you must sip it slowly.

（二）名词 n.

product; grade: 龙井茶是茶叶里的上品。*Longjing* is the
highest-grade tea.

词语 Words and Phrases

| 品尝 | pǐncháng | taste |

品德	pǐndé	moral character
品级	pǐnjí	grade
品名	pǐnmíng	the name or description of a commodity
品位	pǐnwèi	grade
品味	pǐnwèi	taste
品行	pǐnxíng	behaviour
品质	pǐnzhì	quality
品种	pǐnzhǒng	breed; variety

平 píng 一 一 平 平 平

释义 Meaning

形容词 a.

1. flat: 这条新修的马路路面很平。The surface of this new road is very flat.

2. equal: 双方最后打成三比三平。 The two teams tied at 3-3.

词语 Words and Phrases

平安	píng'ān	safe and sound
平常	píngcháng	common
平淡	píngdàn	insipid
平等	píngděng	equality
平凡	píngfán	ordinary
平衡	pínghéng	balance
平局	píngjú	draw
平均	píngjūn	average
平时	píngshí	at ordinary times
平稳	píngwěn	smooth; balanced
平行	píngxíng	parallel

熟语 Idioms

平易近人　　　píng yì jìn rén　　　easily approachable

评 píng 　`　讠　讠　评　评　评　评

(評 　`　亠　亠　亖　言　言　言　訂　訂　評　評　評)

释义 Meaning

动词 v.

comment; judge: 请你来评评谁说得有道理。 Please judge who speaks in the right.

词语 Words and Phrases

评比	píngbǐ	compare and assess
评定	píngdìng	evaluate
评分	píngfēn	score
评价	píngjià	evaluate
评论	pínglùn	comment on
评判	píngpàn	judge
评审	píngshěn	examine and appraise
评书	píngshū	storytelling
评选	píngxuǎn	choose
评语	píngyǔ	comment, remark

熟语 Idioms

评头论足　　　píng tóu lùn zú　　　be over critical

瓶 píng 　`　丷　丷　兰　羊　并　并　瓶　瓶　瓶

释义 Meaning

名词 n.

bottle; vase: 他一次能喝二十瓶啤酒。 He can drink twenty

bottles of beer at one sitting.

词语 Words and Phrases

瓶装	píngzhuāng	bottled
瓶子	píngzi	bottle; vase

破 pò 一 厂 丆 石 石 矿 矿 矿 破 破

释义 Meaning

形容词 a.

1. broken; damaged: 那个杯子是破的。That glass is broken.
2. lousy: 别老是拿这些破事儿烦我。Don't always bother me with these lousy things.

词语 Words and Phrases

破案	pò'àn	solve a case
破财	pòcái	lose money
破产	pòchǎn	bankruptcy
破除	pòchú	do away with
破费	pòfèi	spend money
破格	pògé	make an exception
破坏	pòhuài	destroy
破旧	pòjiù	old and shabby
破裂	pòliè	broken
破灭	pòmiè	be shattered
破土	pòtǔ	break ground
破译	pòyì	decode
破绽	pòzhàn	weak point

熟语 Idioms

破天荒	pò tiān huāng	occur for the first time
破绽百出	pò zhàn bǎi chū	full of flaws

扑 pū 一 十 扌 扑 扑

(撲 一 十 扌 扌' 扌" 扩 扩 扩 扩 扩 扩 扩 撲 撲)

释义 Meaning

动词 v.

1. throw oneself on/at/into; attack: 那个女孩哭着扑进了妈妈的怀里。The girl cried and threw herself in her mother's arms.

2. throw oneself into (work, etc.): 他一心扑在工作上。He devotes himself heart and soul to his work.

词语 Words and Phrases

扑鼻	pūbí	assail the nostrils (e.g., scent)
扑救	pūjiù	put out a fire
扑克	pūkè	poker
扑空	pūkōng	fail to get/find
扑灭	pūmiè	put out
扑通	pūtōng	the sound of sth. heavy droping

熟语 Idioms

扑朔迷离	pū shuò mí lí	complicated and confusing

七 qī 一 七

释义 Meaning

数词

seven: 一年级一共有七个班。There are seven classes in Grade One.

词语 Words and Phrases

七夕	qīxī	the seventh evening of the seveth month

七月	qīyuè	July; the seventh moon

熟语 Idioms

七拼八凑	qī pīn bā còu	scrape together
七上八下	qīshàng-bāxià	be agitated
七嘴八舌	qī zuǐ bā shé	with seven mouths and eight tongues; all at once speaking out

妻 qī　　二　丁　三　三　丰　妻　妻　妻

释义 Meaning

名词 n.

wife: 他的妻子是个医生。His wife is a doctor.

词语 Words and Phrases

妻儿	qī ér	wife and children
妻子	qīzi	wife

熟语 Idioms

妻离子散	qī lí zǐ sàn	breaking up of one's family

期 qī　　一　十　廿　廿　廿　甘　其　其　期　期　期　期

释义 Meaning

名词 n.

1. stage; phase: 这所大学每年都有暑期班。This university runs summer holiday classes every year.

2. scheduled time 我的贷款快到期了。My loan will expire soon.

词语 Words and Phrases

期待	qīdài	look forward to

期货	qīhuò	futures
期间	qījiān	period
期刊	qīkān	periodical
期盼	qīpàn	look forward to; expect
期望	qīwàng	ardently hope
期限	qīxiàn	time limit; deadline

欺 qī

一 十 卄 卄 卄 亜 其 其 其 欺′ 欺′ 欺

释义 Meaning

动词 v.

1. deceive: 别自欺欺人了。Don't deceive yourself as well as others.

2. bully, take advantage of sb.: 不要认为她软弱可欺。Don't think that she is weak and easy to bully.

词语 Words and Phrases

欺负	qīfù	bully
欺骗	qīpiàn	deceive
欺生	qīshēng	cheat strangers
欺压	qīyā	ride roughshod over
欺诈	qīzhà	swindle

熟语 Idioms

欺人太甚	qī rén tài shèn	push people too hard
欺软怕硬	qī ruǎn pà yìng	bully the weak and fear the strong
欺上瞒下	qī shàng mán xià	deceive the superiors and delude the subordinates
欺世盗名	qī shì dào míng	gain fame by deceiving the public

齐 qí ⟍ 一 亠 文 齐 齐

(齊 ⟍ 一 亠 文 文 齊 齊 齊 齊 齊 齊 齊)

释义 Meaning

形容词 a.

1. neat, uniforn: 把椅子排齐。Arrange the chairs in good order, please.

2. all ready; all preset: 学生都到齐了。All the students have arrived.

词语 Words and Phrases

齐唱	qíchàng	unison
齐全	qíquán	complete; all in readiness
齐声	qíshēng	in chorus
齐奏	qízòu	playing in unison
齐心	qíxīn	be of one mind

熟语 Idioms

齐心协力	qíxīnxiélì	work as one man

其 qí 一 十 廿 甘 甘 苴 其 其

释义 Meaning

代词 pron.

his (her/its/their); "听其言，观其行"这句话是孔子说的。Confucius said "one should judge people by their deeds as well as by their words."

拍马屁要投其所好。If you want to flatter someone, you must cater to his pleasure.

词语 Words and Phrases

其次	qícì	next; then
其后	qíhòu	later
其实	qíshí	actually; in fact
其他	qítā	other
其余	qíyú	the rest
其中	qízhōng	among them, in it

熟语 Idioms

其貌不扬	qí mào bù yáng	have rather common features; nothing attractive about one's appearance; ugly looking

奇 qí   一　ナ　大　本　夲　夻　夻　奇

释义 Meaning

形容词 a.

strange: 这可真是一件奇事。It is truly a strange affair.

词语 Words and Phrases

奇怪	qíguài	strange; odd
奇观	qíguān	marvelous spectacle
奇迹	qíjì	marvel
奇妙	qímiào	marvelous
奇缺	qíquē	in great shortage
奇特	qítè	peculiar
奇异	qíyì	unusual

熟语 Idioms

奇形怪状	qí xíng guài zhuàng	grotesque or fantastic in shape or appearance
奇装异服	qí zhuāng yì fú	outlandish dress

骑 qí ㄱ 马 马 马 驴 驴 骑 骑 骑 骑 骑

(騎 一 厂 F F 馬 馬 馬 馬 馬 馬 駈 騎 騎 騎 騎 騎 騎)

释义 Meaning

动词 v.

ride: 你会骑自行车吗？Can you ride a bike?

词语 Words and Phrases

骑马	qímǎ	ride a horse
骑墙	qíqiáng	sit on the fence
骑手	qíshǒu	horseman
骑术	qíshù	horsemanship

熟语 Idioms

骑虎难下　qí hǔ nán xià　　ride a tiger and find it hard to dismount

起 qǐ 二 十 土 キ キ 走 走 起 起 起

释义 Meaning

动词 v.

1. rise; appear; start 早睡早起是个好习惯。Early to bed and early to rise is a good habit.

2. v-up: 他拿起笔，又放了下来。He took up the pen, but put it down again.

词语 Words and Phrases

起步	qǐbù	start
起草	qǐcǎo	draft
起程	qǐchéng	set out

起初	qǐchū	at first
起床	qǐchuáng	get up
起动	qǐdòng	start
起劲儿	qǐjìnr	energetic
起来	qǐlái	sit up
起立	qǐlì	stand up
起码	qǐmǎ	at least
起因	qǐyīn	cause

熟语 Idioms

起死回生	qǐ sǐ huí shēng	(of a doctor's skill) bring the dying back to life; survive after a disaster

气 qì ╱ ╰ ╰ 气

(氣 ╱ ╰ ╰ 气 气 气 氢 氣 氣 氣)

释义 Meaning

（一）名词 n.

1. air; spirit: 这个篮球气不足。The basketball lacks air.

2. breath: 让我停下来歇口气。Let me stop and have a breath.

（二）动词 v.

be engaged; make angry: 你想故意气我，对不对？You purposely wanted to rile me, didn't you?

词语 Words and Phrases

气氛	qìfēn	atmosphere
气愤	qìfèn	indignant
气候	qìhòu	climate
气量	qìliàng	tolerance
气恼	qìnǎo	get angry
气色	qìsè	complexion

气势	qìshì	imposing manner
气味	qìwèi	smell
气温	qìwēn	temperature
气质	qìzhì	temperament

熟语 Idioms

| 气不打
一处来 | qìbùdǎ
yáchùlái | be filled with anger |
| 气势汹汹 | qìshìxiōngxiōng | overbearing |

汽 qì　　丶丶丿丿丿汽汽汽

释义 Meaning

名词 n.

steam; vapour: 最早的火车使用的是蒸汽发动机。The earliest railroad engines used steam engines.

词语 Words and Phrases

汽车	qìchē	automobile; car
汽笛	qìdí	siren
汽水	qìshuǐ	soda drink
汽艇	qìtǐng	motorboat
汽油	qìyóu	petrol; gas

器 qì　　丨丬丬丬丬丬吕吕哭哭
哭哭哭器器器

释义 Meaning

名词 n.

implement; utensil: 电冰箱是家用电器的一种。The re-frigerator is one of the household appliances.

词语 Words and Phrases

| 器材 | qìcái | equipment |

器官	qìguān	organ
器件	qìjiàn	parts of an appliance
器具	qìjù	utensil
器量	qìliàng	tolerance
器械	qìxiè	apparatus instrument
器重	qìzhòng	regard highly

千 qiān　一　二　千

释义 Meaning

数词

thousand; a great number of: 那家电影院有一千个座位。That cinema can sit a thousand people.

词语 Words and Phrases

千金	qiānjīn	daughter (other than one's own)
千卡	qiānkǎ	kilocalorie
千克	qiānkè	kilogram
千米	qiānmǐ	kilometre
千万	qiānwàn	must

熟语 Idioms

千方百计	qiān fāng bǎi jì	do everything possible to
千篇一律	qiān piān yī lù	follow the same pattern
千言万语	qiān yán wàn yǔ	thousands of words
千真万确	qiān zhēn wàn què	absolutely true

前 qián　丶　丷　丷　宀　宀　前　前　前

释义 Meaning

名词 n.

1. front; forward: 我家门前是一条大马路。There is a big road running in front of my house gate. 反义词 antonym:

后 behind; back; after

2. ago; before: 三天前我就来过这儿。I was here three days ago.

词语 Words and Phrases

前边	qiánbiān	in the front
前程	qiánchéng	future
前后	qiánhòu	around a certain time
前进	qiánjìn	go forward
前景	qiánjǐng	prospect
前期	qiánqī	former time; previously
前天	qiántiān	the day before yesterday
前途	qiántú	future
前言	qiányán	preface

熟语 Idioms

前前后后	qián qián hòu hòu	the ins and outs
前怕狼，后怕虎	qián pà láng, hòu pà hǔ	be full of fears; indecisive

钱 qián ⼁ ⼂ ⼃ ⼄ 钅 钅 钅 钱 钱 钱

(錢 ⼁ ⼂ ⼃ ⼄ 牟 余 金 金 釒 釒 釒 鈞 錢 錢 錢 錢)

释义 Meaning

名词 n.

1. money: 苹果多少钱一斤？How much are the apples?
2. found: 这笔钱是专门作为奖学金用的。The fund will be specially used for scholarship.

词语 Words and Phrases

钱包	qiánbāo	wallet

钱财 qiáncái wealth

熟语 Idioms

钱能通神 qián néng tōng shén Money can move the gods

浅 qiǎn ` ˋ 氵 氵 氵 浅 浅 浅

(淺 ` ˋ 氵 氵 浐 浐 浅 浅 淺 淺)

释义 Meaning

形容词 a.

1. shallow: 附近的那条河水很浅。The river nearby is very shallow.

2. simple: 这篇课文内容很浅，一看就明白。This lesson is so simple that a glance is enough to understand it.

词语 Words and Phrases

浅薄 qiǎnbó superficial

浅见 qiǎnjiàn humble opinion

浅色 qiǎnsè light colour

浅显 qiǎnxiǎn plain

浅易 qiǎnyì simple and easy

熟语 Idioms

浅尝辄止 qiǎn cháng zhé zhǐ stop after gaining a little knowledge of a subject

欠 qiàn ´ ⺈ 欠 欠

释义 Meaning

动词 v.

1. owe; lacking: 那家公司欠银行三十万。That company owes the bank three hundred thousand yuan.

2. not enough: 他经常说话欠考虑。He is often too free with his tongue.

词语 Words and Phrases

欠安	qiàn'ān	feeling unwell
欠佳	qiànjiā	not good enough
欠款	qiànkuǎn	money that is owed
欠缺	qiànquē	be short of
欠条	qiàntiáo	a bill signed of as debt; IOU
欠妥	qiàntuǒ	not proper
欠债	qiànzhài	owe a debt

枪 qiāng 一 十 十 木 朳 朴 枪 枪

(槍 一 十 十 木 朳 朴 朴 柃 槍 槍 槍 槍 槍 槍)

释义 Meaning

名词 n.

gun; firearm: 警察不一定都有枪。Not all policemen have firearms.

词语 Words and Phrases

枪毙	qiāngbì	execute by shooting
枪法	qiāngfǎ	marksmanship
枪伤	qiāngshāng	bullet wound
枪声	qiāngshēng	gunshot sound
枪手	qiāngshǒu	gunner
枪子儿	qiāngzǐr	bullet

熟语 Idioms

枪林弹雨	qiāng lín dàn yǔ	under heavy gun fire

强₁ qiáng 一 一 弓 弜 弨 弨 弨 弨 弨 弨 弨 强 强

释义 Meaning

形容词 a.

1. strong: 我们经理工作能力很强。Our manager is a capable person.
2. better: 这方面他比我强。He surpasses me in this respect.

   反义词 antonym: 弱 weak; inferior

词语 Words and Phrases

强暴	qiángbào	violent
强大	qiángdà	powerful
强调	qiángdiào	emphasize
强化	qiánghuà	strengthen
强奸	qiángjiān	rape
强烈	qiángliè	strong
强权	qiángquán	might
强行	qiángxíng	force

强₂ qiǎng ７ ７ 弓 弓' 弓'' 弓'' 弓'' 弜 弜 弹 强 强

动词 v.

force: 不要强迫别人同意你的意见。Don't force others to agree with you.

词语 Words and Phrases

强逼	qiǎngbī	force
强迫	qiǎngpò	compel
强求	qiǎngqiú	impose

熟语 Idioms

强词夺理	qiǎng cí duó lǐ	use lame arguments and perverted logic

| 强人所难 | qiǎng rén suǒ nán | try to make sb. to do what he is unwilling or unable to do |

墙 qiáng 一 十 土 圹 圹 圹 圹 塘 墙 墙 墙 墙 墙

(墙 一 十 土 圹 圹 圹 圹 圹 圹 塘 塘 墙 墙 墙 墙 墙)

释义 Meaning

名词 n.

wall: 停下来，前面就是墙了。Stop! there is a wall ahead.

词语 Words and Phrases

| 墙壁 | qiángbì | wall |
| 墙纸 | qiángzhǐ | wallpaper |

熟语 Idioms

| 墙倒众人推 | qiáng dǎo zhòng rén tuī | everybody hits a person when has fallen down |

抢 qiǎng 一 十 扌 扩 扩 抡 抢

(搶 一 十 扌 扩 扩 扩 扴 拎 搶 搶 搶 搶)

释义 Meaning

动词 v.

rob: 那个姑娘的钱包被抢了。The girl was robbed of her wallet.

词语 Words and Phrases

| 抢答 | qiǎngdá | race to be the first to answer a question |

抢夺	qiǎngduó	snatch
抢购	qiǎnggòu	rush to purchase
抢劫	qiǎngjié	rob
抢救	qiǎngjiù	rescue
抢先	qiǎngxiān	forestall
抢险	qiǎngxiǎn	rush to deal with an emergency
抢修	qiǎngxiū	rush to repair

敲 qiāo ` ⼀ ⼴ ⼀ ⼀ ⼀ ⾼ ⾼ ⾼ ⾼ ⾼ ⾼ 敲 敲

释义 Meaning

动词 v.

knock: 有人敲门。 Someone is knocking at the door.

词语 Words and Phrases

敲边鼓	qiāo biān gǔ	back sb. up
敲打	qiāodǎ	beat
敲警钟	qiāo jǐng zhōng	sound a warning
敲门砖	qiāo mén zhuān	a stepping-stone to success
敲诈	qiāozhà	blackmail
敲竹杠	qiāozhúgàng	fleece sb.

熟语 Idioms

| 敲诈勒索 | qiāo zhà lè suǒ | extort and racketeer |

桥 qiáo ⼀ ⼗ ⼤ 木 柠 柠 柠 柠 桥 桥

（橋 ⼀ ⼗ ⼤ 木 柠 柠 柠 柠 柠 橋 橋 橋 橋 橋 橋 橋）

释义 Meaning

名词 n.

bridge: 上海有两座有名的桥。There are two famous bridges in Shanghai.

词语 Words and Phrases

桥洞	qiáodòng	bridge opening
桥梁	qiáoliáng	bridge
桥牌	qiáopái	bridge (card game)
桥头	qiáotóu	either end of a bridge

巧 qiǎo   一 丁 工 工 巧

释义 Meaning

形容词 a.

1. skilful: 她的手真巧！How dexterous she is!

2. coincidental: 太巧了，这个饭店的老板是我中学同学。
   What a coincidence! The boss of this restaurant is my school-mate from middle school.

词语 Words and Phrases

巧合	qiǎohé	coincidence
巧克力	qiǎokèlì	chocolate
巧妙	qiǎomiào	ingenious
巧手	qiǎoshǒu	dexterity
巧遇	qiǎoyù	encounter by chance

熟语 Idioms

巧妇难为 无米之炊	qiǎofù nán wéi wú mǐ zhī chuī	one can't make bricks without straw
巧立名目	qiǎo lì míng mù	invent all kinds of names (as pretexts for)

切 qiē   一 土 切 切

释义 Meaning

动词 v.

cut; slice: 学做菜先得学会切菜。To learn cooking, you should learn cutting up vegetables first.

词语 Words and Phrases

切磋	qiēcuō	learn from each other
切断	qiēduàn	cut off
切片	qiēpiàn	section; slice
切线	qiēxiàn	tangent (line); cut in to another lane (driving)
切纸机	qiēzhǐjī	paper cutter

亲qīn ⎯ ⎯ ⎯ ⎯ ⎯ ⎯ ⎯ ⎯ 亲

(親 ⎯ ⎯ ⎯ ⎯ ⎯ ⎯ ⎯ ⎯ ⎯ ⎯ ⎯ ⎯ ⎯ ⎯ ⎯ ⎯ 親)

释义 Meaning

(一) 名词 n.

relative; in person: 他们两个是亲兄弟。The two are blood brothers.

(二) 动词 v.

kiss: 他亲了女儿一下。He kissed his daughter on the cheek.

词语 Words and Phrases

亲爱	qīn'ài	dear
亲近	qīnjìn	be close to
亲口	qīnkǒu	say sth. personally
亲密	qīnmì	intimate
亲朋	qīnpéng	relatives and friends
亲热	qīnrè	affectionate
亲人	qīnrén	family members

亲手	qīnshǒu	with one's own hand
亲眼	qīnyǎn	with one's own eyes
亲自	qīnzì	personally

熟语 Idioms

亲如手足	qīn rú shǒu zú	close as brothers

青 qīng 　二　三　丰　圭　青　青　青　青

释义 Meaning

形容词 a.

blue or green: 这个地方山青水秀。There is beautiful scenery in this place.

词语 Words and Phrases

青菜	qīngcài	general name for vegetable
青草	qīngcǎo	green grass
青春	qīngchūn	youth
青椒	qīngjiāo	green pepper
青睐	qīnglài	good graces
青霉素	qīngméisù	penicillin
青年	qīngnián	youth
青少年	qīngshàonián	teenagers
青山	qīngshān	green hills

熟语 Idioms

青出于蓝	qīngchūyúlán	the pupil surpasses the master

轻 qīng 　二　圡　车　车　轻　轻　轻　轻　轻

（輕 　一　厂　亣　亩　盲　亘　車　軒　軒　輕　輕　輕　輕　輕）

释义 Meaning

形容词 a.

1. light: 这个袋子比那个轻。This bag is ligher than that one. 反义词 antonym: 重 heavy

2. gentle: 这些药要轻拿轻放。These medicines should be handled gently.

词语 Words and Phrases

轻便	qīngbiàn	light; easy and convenient
轻敌	qīngdí	take the enemy lightly
轻活	qīnghuó	light work
轻看	qīngkàn	belittle
轻快	qīngkuài	spry
轻巧	qīngqiǎo	simple
轻生	qīngshēng	suicide
轻率	qīngshuài	rash
轻松	qīngsōng	relaxed
轻信	qīngxìn	readily believe
轻易	qīngyì	rashly
轻音乐	qīngyīnyuè	light music

熟语 Idioms

轻车熟路	qīng chē shú lù	do sth. one knows well and can manage with ease
轻举妄动	qīng jǔ wàng dòng	act rashly

清 qīng ` 丶 氵 汀 汀 浐 浐 浐 清 清 清

释义 Meaning

形容词 a.

clear; distinct: 这儿的水很清。The water here is quite clean.

词语 Words and Phrases

清除	qīngchú	clear away
清楚	qīngchǔ	clear; understand
清点	qīngdiǎn	check thoroughly
清洁	qīngjié	clean
清淨	qīngjìng	peace and quiet
清理	qīnglǐ	put in order
清扫	qīngsǎo	clean up
清晰	qīngxī	clear; distinct
清洗	qīngxǐ	wash
清醒	qīngxǐng	sober
清早	qīngzǎo	early morning

熟语 Idioms

清规戒律	qīng guī jiè lǜ	taboos and regulations (in Buddhist monasteries)

情 qíng 丶 丶 忄 忄 忄 忄 忄 忄 情 情 情

释义 Meaning

名词 n.

1. sentiment; favour: 我欠你一个情。 I owe you a debt of gratitude.
2. situation: 情况怎么样？ How are things going?

词语 Words and Phrases

情报	qíngbào	information
情敌	qíngdí	rival in love
情调	qíngdiào	sentiment
情感	qínggǎn	emotion
情节	qíngjié	plot

情景	qíngjǐng	scene
情况	qíngkuàng	situation
情理	qínglǐ	reason
情面	qíngmiàn	feeling
情人	qíngrén	lover
情绪	qíngxù	feeling
情义	qíngyì	friendship
情愿	qíngyuàn	be willing to

熟语 Idioms

情有可原　　qíng yǒu kě yuán　　excusable

晴 qíng 丨 刂 川 川 旷 旷 呀 昨 睅 晴 晴 晴

释义 Meaning

动词 v.

fine: 天晴了，太阳出来了。The skying is cleaning up and the sun is coming out.

词语 Words and Phrases

晴朗	qínglǎng	sunny
晴天	qíngtiān	fine day
晴雨表	qíng yǔ biǎo	weather glass

熟语 Idioms

| 晴空万里 | qíng kōng wàn lǐ | a boundless sky |
| 晴空霹雳 | qíng kōng pī lì | a bolt from the blue |

请 qǐng 丶 讠 订 汀 汫 诿 请 请 请

(請 丶 亠 言 言 言 言 言 訪 諸 諸 請 請)

释义 Meaning

动词 v.

1. ask 请他给我打个电话。Ask him to call me.
2. invite: 我们想请王教授给我们讲课。We want to invite Professor Wang to give us a lecture.
3. please: 请进。Come in please.

词语 Words and Phrases

请便	qǐngbiàn	do as you wish
请假	qǐngjià	ask for leave
请柬	qǐngjiǎn	invitation card
请教	qǐngjiào	ask for advice
请客	qǐngkè	entertain guests
请求	qǐngqiú	ask
请示	qǐngshì	ask for instruction
请问	qǐngwèn	excuse me
请愿	qǐngyuàn	petition

熟语 Idioms

| 请君入瓮 | qǐng jūn rù wèng | have a taste of what you intended for others |

穷 qióng ` ` 宀 宀 穴 穷 穷

(窮 ` ` 宀 宀 穴 宀 宀 宀 宀 宀 宀 宀 宀 宀 窮)

释义 Meaning

形容词 a.

1. poor: 这个地方的人很穷。The people here are very poor.
   反义词 antonym: 富 rich
2. limit: 知识的力量是无穷的。The power of knowledge

is unlimited.

词语 Words and Phrases

穷尽	qióngjìn	limit
穷开心	qióng kāixīn	enjoy oneself despite poverty
穷困	qióngkùn	poverty-stricken
穷人	qióngrén	the poor
穷日子	qióngrìzi	days of poverty

熟语 Idioms

穷家富路	qióng jiā fù lù	be thrifty at home and spend liberally while traveling
穷凶极恶	qióng xiōng jí è	utterly evil
穷则思变	qióng zé sī biàn	poverty gives rise to the desire for change

秋 qiū　一　二　千　千　禾　禾　利　秒　秋

释义 Meaning

名词 n.

Autumn: 一年有四个季节：春、夏、秋、冬。There are four seasons in a year: spring, summer, autumn and winter.

词语 Words and Phrases

秋波	qiūbō	make eyes
秋风	qiūfēng	autumn wind
秋季	qiūjì	autumn
秋千	qiūqiān	swing
秋天	qiūtiān	autumn
秋色	qiūsè	autumn scenery
秋游	qiūyóu	autumn outing

熟语 Idioms

秋高气爽	qiūgāoqìshuǎng	the autumn sky is clear and the air is bracing

求 qiú   二 十 寸 才 求 求 求

释义 Meaning

动词 v.

1. beg; request: 求你一件事，行吗？May I ask you a favour?
2. seek: 不求名利的人很少。Few seek neither personal fame nor gain.

词语 Words and Phrases

求爱	qiú'ài	court
求和	qiúhé	sue for peace
求婚	qiúhūn	make an offer of marriage
求见	qiújiàn	ask to see; beg for an audience
求救	qiújiù	ask for help
求签	qiúqiān	divine in a temple
求情	qiúqíng	plead
求生	qiúshēng	seek survival
求医	qiúyī	see a doctor
求雨	qiúyǔ	pray for rain
求援	qiúyuán	seek help
求助	qiúzhù	seek help

熟语 Idioms

求同存异	qiútóngcúnyì	seek common ground while allowing for differences
求之不得	qiúzhībùdé	most welcome

球 qiú　一 二 三 干 王 尹 玎 玎 珨 玞 球 球

释义 Meaning

名词 n.

globle ball; ball game: 你喜欢打什么球？ What ball games do you like?

词语 Words and Phrases

球场	qiúchǎng	a ground or field where ball games are played
球队	qiúduì	ball team
球门	qiúmén	goal
球迷	qiúmí	ball game fan
球拍	qiúpāi	racket bat
球星	qiúxīng	ball game star, sport star

区 qū　一 丁 ㄡ 区

(區　一 一 一 一 一 一 一 一 一 一 區)

释义 Meaning

（一）名词 n.

area: 他住在上海市虹口区。He lives at the Hongkou District of Shanghai.

（二）动词 v.

classify: 区分外地人和本地人很容易。It is very easy to distinguish between the locals and the others.

词语 Words and Phrases

区别	qūbié	distinguish
区分	qūfēn	differentiate
区区	qūqū	trifling

| 区域 | qūyù | region |
| 区长 | qūzhǎng | head of a district in a city |

取 qǔ　一　厂　FF　耳　耳　取　取

释义 Meaning

动词 v.

take; fetch: 他去取行李了。He has gone to fetch the baggage.
我去银行取钱。I'm going to the bank for money.

词语 Words and Phrases

取材	qǔcái	draw materials
取代	qǔdài	replace
取得	qǔdé	obtain
取缔	qǔdì	ban
取名	qǔmíng	give a name to
取舍	qǔshě	make choice
取胜	qǔshèng	win victory
取消	qǔxiāo	cancel; abolish
取笑	qǔxiào	ridicule
取证	qǔzhèng	collect evidence

熟语 Idioms

| 取长补短 | qǔ cháng bǔ duǎn | learn others' strong points to offset one's own weaknesses |

去 qù　一　十　土　去　去

释义 Meaning

动词 v.

1. go: 他已经去公司了。He has already gone to the office.
2. send (there): 我已经给他去了五封信。I have sent him five letters.

3. used after or before verbs phrase: 他去图书馆借书去
了。He has gone to the library for some books.

词语 Words and Phrases

去处	qùchù	place to go
去火	qùhuǒ	reduce internal "heat" (as used in Chinese medicine)
去留	qùliú	go or stay
去年	qùnián	last year
去世	qùshì	die
去向	qùxiàng	the direction in which sb. is going

熟语 Idioms

去粗取精	qù cū qǔ jīng	choose what is best
去伪存真	qù wěi cúnzhēn	discard the false and retain the true

全 quán ⺈ ⼇ ⼈ ⼈ 全 全

释义 Meaning

形容词 a.

1. complete: 这家大超市商品品种很全。This supermarket has a complete selection of goods.
2. whole: 这件事传遍了全城。The affair spread throughout the whole city.

词语 Words and Phrases

全部	quánbù	whole; total
全程	quánchéng	full course
全都	quándōu	all
全国	quánguó	the whole country
全局	quánjú	the overall situation

全面	quánmiàn	overall
全年	quánnián	entire year
全权	quánquán	full authority
全球	quánqiú	the whole world
全身	quánshēn	the whole body
全体	quántǐ	entirely

熟语 Idioms

| 全心全意 | quán xīn quán yì | wholeheartedly |

劝 quàn 乛 又 劝 劝

（**勸** 一 十 艹 艹 艹 莳 莳 苗 苗 萠 萠 萠 萠 蓳 蓳 蓳 蓳 勸 勸）

释义 Meaning

动词 v.

1. advise, persuade: 妻子一直劝他戒酒。His wife has been advising him to give up drinking.

2. comfort: 孩子正伤心呢，你去劝劝吧。The child is feeling bad, please go and say a few words to comfort him.

词语 Words and Phrases

劝导	quàndǎo	advise
劝告	quàngào	advise, advice
劝解	quànjiě	mediate
劝酒	quànjiǔ	urge sb. to drink
劝说	quànshuō	persuade
劝阻	quànzǔ	advise sb. not do sth.

缺 quē 丿 上 上 午 缶 缶 缸 缸 缺 缺

释义 Meaning

动词 v.

1. lack: 高原地区缺氧。Plateau areas lack adequate oxygen.
2. be absent: 我们的人还缺三个。Three of us are absent.

词语 Words and Phrases

缺德	quēdé	wicked; immoral
缺点	quēdiǎn	shortcoming
缺乏	quēfá	lack
缺课	quēkè	miss class
缺少	quēshǎo	be short of
缺席	quēxí	absent
缺陷	quēxiàn	defect
缺心眼儿	quēxīnyǎnr	dull-witted

熟语 Idioms

缺斤短两	quējīnduǎnliǎng	give short weight

裙 qún ` ⁊ 衤 衤 衤 衤 衤 衤 衤 裙 裙 裙

释义 Meaning

名词 n.

skirt: 你看这条裙子怎么样？What do you think of this skirt?

词语 Words and Phrases

裙带	qúndài	connected through one's female relatives
裙子	qúnzi	skirt

群 qún ⁊ ⁊ ⁊ 尹 尹 君 君 君 君′ 群 群 群 群

释义 Meaning

量词 Meaure word

crowd; group: 前面走过来一群中学生。A group of middle school students are coming.

词语 Words and Phrases

群岛	qúndǎo	archipelago
群居	qúnjū	living in groups
群情	qúnqíng	public sentiment
群体	qúntǐ	colony; group
群众	qúnzhòng	the masses

熟语 Idioms

| 群龙无首 | qún lóng wú shǒu | a group of people in a common cause without a leader |
| 群起而攻之 | qún qǐ ér gōng zhī | all rise against sb. |

然 rán ノ ク タ ㄅ ㄅ 夗 肰 肰 肰 然 然 然

释义 Meaning

连词 conj.

but: 他在上海住了三年，然 (而) 还没习惯那儿的生活。 He has stayed in Shanghai for three years, but has not accustomed himself to the life there yet.

词语 Words and Phrases

| 然而 | rán'ér | but, however |
| 然后 | ránhòu | then, after that |

让 ràng ` 讠 计 让 让

(讓 ` ˊ ˏ ˋ ˈ ˌ ˌ ˌ ˌ ˌ ˌ
ˌ ˌ ˌ ˌ ˌ ˌ ˌ 讓 讓 讓 讓
讓 讓)

释义 Meaning

（一）动词 v.

let: 让我看看。Let me see.

对不起，请让一下。 Excuse me.

（二）介词 prep.

by: 他的钱包让小偷偷走了。His wallet was stolen by the pick pocket.

词语 Words and Phrases

让步	ràngbù	give way, compromise
让开	ràngkāi	get out of the way
让路	rànglù	give way
让球	ràngqiú	concede points (in a ball game)
让贤	ràngxián	relinquish one's post in favour of sb. better qualified.
让座	ràngzuò	offer one's seat to sb.

绕ráo ˊ ˊ ˊ 纟 纟 线 线 线 绕

(繞 ˊ ˊ ˊ ˊ 纟 纟 纟 红 纟 纟 纟
纟 纟 纟 纟 纟 纟 繞)

释义 Meaning

动词 v.

1. revolve: 月亮绕着地球转。The moon revolves round the earth.

2. go round: 前方修路，车辆绕行。Vehicles should make

a detour at the road construction ahead.

词语 Words and Phrases

绕道	ràodào	make a detour
绕口令	ràokǒulìng	tongue twister
绕圈子	rào quānzi	circle
绕弯子	rào wānzi	talk in a roundabout way
绕行	ràoxíng	make a detour

热 rè 一 亅 扌 打 执 执 执 热 热 热

(熱 一 十 土 产 夫 去 杢 圶 刲 執 執

執 熱 熱 熱 **)**

释义 Meaning

（一）形容词 a.

1. heat, hot: 他每天都用热水洗脚。He bathes his feet in hot water everyday.

2. fever: 这孩子正发热呢。The child is having a fever.

（二）后缀 uffix.

craze: 去年兴起了旅游热。The travel craze rose last year.

词语 Words and Phrases

热爱	rè'ài	ardently love
热潮	rècháo	upsurge
热带	rèdài	the tropics
热点	rèdiǎn	hot spot
热狗	règǒu	hot dog
热泪	rèlèi	hot tears
热烈	rèliè	warm
热门	rèmén	popular
热闹	rènào	lively, bustling

热情	rèqíng	zeal
热心	rèxīn	warmhearted

熟语 Idioms

热情洋溢	rè qíng yáng yì	permeated with warm feelings

人 rén   丿 人

释义 Meaning

名词 n.

1. human being; person; people: 人是最聪明的动物。Man is the cleverest among animals.
2. used as a suffix: 他是个工人。He is a worker.

词语 Words and Phrases

人才	réncái	talent
人格	réngé	personality; human dignity
人工	réngōng	artificial
人和	rénhé	harmonious relations
人际关系	rénjìguānxì	interpersonal relationship
人家	rénjiā	a person(s) other than the speaker or hearer
人间	rénjiān	the world
人口	rénkǒu	population
人类	rénlèi	mankind
人民	rénmín	the people
人品	rénpǐn	moral quality
人情	rénqíng	① human feelings ② favour; gift
人权	rénquán	human rights
人生	rénshēng	life
人为	rénwéi	man-made
人物	rénwù	personage

人员　　　rényuán　　staff

熟语 Idioms

人所共知	rén suǒ gòng zhī	be known to all
人言可畏	rén yán kě wèi	gossip is a fearful thing

认 rèn 　丶 讠 认 认

（認 丶 讠 讠 讠 言 言 言 訂 訒 訒 訒 認 認 認**）**

释义 Meaning

动词 v.

1. recognize; know: 这个村庄有很多人不认识字。Many people don't know how to read in this village.

2. admit: 我认输。I adimt defeat.

3. resigned oneself to: 这次吃亏了，但我认了。I've resigned myself to losing out this time.

词语 Words and Phrases

认错	rèncuò	admit a fault
认得	rènde	know
认定	rèndìng	firmly believe
认可	rènkě	approve
认领	rènlíng	claim
认命	rènmìng	accept fate
认识	rènshi	know
认生	ènshēng	be shy with strangers
认为	rènwéi	think; conside
认帐	rènzhàng	acknowledge a debt
认真	rènzhēn	conscientious
认罪	rènzuì	plead guilty

熟语 Idioms

认贼作父　　rèn zéi zuò fù　　embraced the thieves as kith and kin

扔rēng　一　十　才　扒　扔

释义 Meaning

动词 v.

throw; throw away: 把这些垃圾扔掉。Throw the rubbish away, please.

词语 Words and Phrases

扔掉　　rēngdiào　　throw away

扔下　　rēngxià　　put aside

仍réng　ノ　亻　仍　仍

释义 Meaning

副词adv.

still, yet: 我到北京半年了，仍不习惯这里的气候。I've been in Beijing for half a year; however, I haven't got used to the climate yet.

词语 Words and Phrases

仍旧　　réngjiù　　still yet

仍然　　réngrán　　still, yet

日rì　丨　冂　日　日

释义 Meaning

名词 n.

1. sun, day: 1997年7月1日，香港回归了。Hongkong was returned to China on July 1, 1997.

2. daily: 我常常看中国日报。I often read the *China Daily*.

词语 Words and Phrases

日报	rìbào	daily paper
日本	rìběn	Japan
日常	rìcháng	daily
日程	rìchéng	schedule
日光	rìguāng	sunlight
日后	rìhòu	in the future
日记	rìjì	diary
日历	rìlì	calendar
日期	rìqī	date
日夜	rìyè	day and night
日用	rìyòng	daily use
日子	rìzi	day

熟语 Idioms

日新月异	rì xīn yuè yì	change with each passing day

肉 ròu   丨 冂 内 内 肉 肉

释义 Meaning

名词 n.

meat; flesh: 她不吃肉。She does not eat meat.

词语 Words and Phrases

肉包子	ròu bāozi	steamed meat bun
肉丁	ròudīng	diced meat
肉麻	ròumá	sickening
肉色	ròusè	flesh-tinted
肉丝	ròusī	shredded meat
肉体	ròutǐ	the human body; carnal
肉丸子	ròu wánzi	meatball

肉眼	ròuyǎn	naked eye
肉欲	ròuyù	carnal desire

如 rú　　ㄥ　女　女　如　如　如

释义 Meaning

（一）动词 v.

　1. as; like: 人生如梦。Life is like a dream.

　2. such as: 香港有很多歌星，如张学友、刘德华、郭富城等。 There are many pop stars in Hongkong, such as Zhang Xueyou, Liu Dehua and Guo Fucheng.

（二）连词 conj.

　if; in case of: 那家商店的老板说，他们的东西如假包换。 The proprietor of the shop said, "if you bought false goods from us, we will exchange them."

词语 Words and Phrases

如此	rúcǐ	like that; such
如果	rúguǒ	if; in case of
如何	rúhé	how; what
如今	rújīn	nowadays
如来	rúlái	Tathagata
如期	rúqī	on schedule
如上	rúshàng	as above
如实	rúshí	go strictly by the facts
如同	rútóng	like, as
如下	rúxià	as follows
如意	rúyì	be gratified

熟语 Idioms

如饥似渴	rú jī sì kě	with great eagerness
如梦初醒	rú mèng chū xǐng	wake up as if from a deep sleep

入rù   ノ 入

释义 Meaning

动词 v.

1. enter: 闲人免入。No admittance except on business.
2. join: 他已经入党了。He has already joined the Party.

词语 Words and Phrases

入场	rùchǎng	admission
入股	rùgǔ	become a shareholder
入会	rùhuì	join a society
入籍	rùjí	be naturalized
入境	rùjìng	enter a country
入口	rùkǒu	entrance
入门	rùmén	learn the rudiments; ABC
入迷	rùmí	be fascinated
入侵	rùqīn	invade
入手	rùshǒu	begin with
入睡	rùshuì	fall into sleep
入土	rùtǔ	be buried
入学	rùxué	enter a school
入狱	rùyù	be put in prison
入座	rùzuò	take one's seat

熟语 Idioms

入不敷出	rù bù fū chū	income falling short of expenditure

软ruǎn   一 ナ 车 车 轫 轫 软 软

(軟 一 厂 冇 百 亘 亘 車 車 軒 軒 軟)

释义 Meaning

形容词 a.

1. soft; mild: 草地很软。The lawn is very soft. 反义词 antonym: 硬 hard; stiff

2. moved: 听到孩子的哭声，她的心软了。She was moved by the cry of the baby.

词语 Words and Phrases

软膏	ruǎngāo	ointment
软骨头	ruǎngútou	weak-kneed person
软化	ruǎnhuà	soften
软件	ruǎnjiàn	software
软禁	ruǎnjìn	put sb. under house arrest
软绵绵	ruǎnmiánmián	soft; weak
软弱	ruǎnruò	weak
软水	ruǎnshuǐ	soft water
软糖	ruǎntáng	soft sweets, soft candy
软语	ruǎnyǔ	soft words

熟语 Idioms

软弱无能	ruǎn ruò wú néng	weak and incompetent
软硬不吃	ruǎn yìng bù chī	yield neither to persuasion nor to coercion
软硬兼施	ruǎn yìng jiān shī	resort to the use of both hard and soft measures

弱 ruò　　一　一　弓　弓　弓　弓'　弓'　弱　弱　弱

释义 Meaning

形容词 a.

1. weak: 这孩子身体很弱。This child is weak.
2. inferior; feeble: 我们的防守比对方弱。Our defence is

feebler than our opponent's. 反义词 antonym: 强 strong; better

词语 Words and Phrases

弱点	ruòdiǎn	weak point
弱视	ruòshì	weak-sighted
弱小	ruòxiǎo	weak and small
弱智	ruòzhì	retarded, learning impaired

熟语 Idioms

| 弱不禁风 | ruò bù jīn fēng | too frail to stand a gust of wind |

赛 sài `ㆍ宀宀宀宀宀宀宀宀宀宀寒寒赛赛

(賽 `ㆍ宀宀宀宀宀宀宀宀宀寒寒寨寨賽賽)

释义 Meaning

动词 v.

match; competition: 他喜欢看足球赛。 He likes watching a football game.

词语 Words and Phrases

赛车	sàichē	cycle race; auto race vehicle
赛马	sàimǎ	horse race
赛跑	sàipǎo	race

三 sān 一 三 三

释义 Meaning

数词 num.

1. three: 这孩子今年三岁了。 This child is three years old.

2. more than two; many: 这个问题我三番五次地跟他说
过。I have told him over and over again this problem.

词语 Words and Phrases

三分	sānfēn	30%; somewhat
三伏	sānfú	the three hottest periods of the year
三明治	sānmíngzhì	sandwich
三角	sānjiǎo	triangle
三思	sānsī	think carefullly
三月	sānyuè	March
三只手	sānzhīshǒu	pickpocket

熟语 Idioms

三长两短	sānchángliǎngduǎn	sth. unfortunate (esp. death)
三令五申	sān lìng wǔ shēn	repeatedly
三心二意	sān xīn èr yì	be of two minds

伞 sǎn 　ノ 　人 　𠆢 　介 　仐 　伞

(傘 　ノ 　人 　𠆢 　𠆢 　夵 　夵 　夵 　夵 　夵 　夵 　傘)

释义 Meaning

名词 n.

umbrella: 别忘了带伞。Don't forget to bring an umbrella.

词语 Words and Phrases

伞兵	sǎnbīng	paratrooper
雨伞	yǔsǎn	umbrella

散₁ sǎn 　一 　十 　艹 　艹 　苫 　昔 　昔 　昔 　昔 　昔 　散 　散

释义 Meaning

形容词 a.

1. come loose: 我的鞋带散了。My shoelace has come loose.
2. scattered: 这所大学的老师住得很散。The teachers of this university live rather far apart from one another.

词语 Words and Phrases

散货	sǎnhuò	bulk cargo
散乱	sǎnluàn	in disorder
散漫	sǎnmàn	slack
散文	sǎnwén	prose
散装	sǎnzhuāng	in bulk

熟语 Idioms

散兵游勇	sǎnbīng-yóuyǒng	stragglers and disbanded soldiers; a disorganized group

散 2 **sàn** 一 十 艹 艹 芏 昔 昔 昔 昔 昔 散 散

释义 Meaning

动词 v.

1. break up: 现在散会。The meeting is over.
2. let out: 请打开门散散烟气。Please open the door to let in fresh air.

词语 Words and Phrases

散布	sànbù	spread, be scattered
散步	sànbù	take a walk
散发	sànfā	send out
散会	sànhuì	meeting is over
散心	sànxīn	relieve boredom

扫 sǎo 一 丁 扌 扫 扫 扫

(掃 一 丁 扌 扩 扫 护 护 护 掃 掃)

释义 Meaning

动词 v.

sweep: 你扫地，我擦桌子。You sweep the floor and I wipe the table.

词语 Words and Phrases

扫除	sǎochú	cleaning
扫地	sǎodì	sweep the floor
扫描	sǎomiáo	scanning
扫视	sǎoshì	sweep
扫尾	sǎowěi	round off
扫兴	sǎoxìng	feeling disappointed

熟语 Idioms

扫地出门	sǎo dì chū mén	sweep the garbage out; drive out

色 sè 丿 ⺈ ⺈ 名 兔 色

释义 Meaning

名词 n.

colour: 黄色属于暖色。Yellow is a warm colour.

词语 Words and Phrases

色彩	sècǎi	colour
色胆	sèdǎn	the lust for sex
色调	sèdiào	tones
色鬼	sèguǐ	lecher
色狼	sèláng	lecher
色盲	sèmáng	colour blindness

色情	sèqíng	erotic
色素	sèsù	pigment
色艺	sèyì	looks and skills
色泽	sèzé	colour and lustre

熟语 Idioms

| 色厉内荏 | sè lì nèi rěn | threatening in manner but coward at heart |

森 sēn 一 十 才 木 杢 本 杰 杰 森 森 森

释义 Meaning

名词 n.

forest: 很多地方的森林被破坏了。In many places the forests have been destroyed.

词语 Words and Phrases

| 森林 | sēnlín | forest |
| 森严 | sēnyán | stern; strict |

杀 shā 丿 乂 杀 杀 杀 杀

(殺 丿 乂 杀 杀 杀 杀 杀 杀 殺)

释义 Meaning

动词 v.

1. kill: 那个罪犯杀过三个人。That criminal has murdered three people.
2. reduce: 买东西要会杀价。You should bargain when you buy things.

词语 Words and Phrases

| 杀害 | shāhài | kill; slaughter |

杀价	shājià	bargain the price down
杀戒	shājiè	prohibition against taking life
杀菌	shājūn	sterilize
杀人	shārén	kill a person
杀伤	shāshāng	kill and wound
杀手	shāshǒu	killer

熟语 Idioms

| 杀鸡警猴 | shā jī jǐng hóu | punish someone as a warning to others |
| 杀身成仁 | shā shēn chéng rén | die to achieve virtue; die for a just cause |

傻 shǎ ⼃ ⼁ ⼁ ⼁ ⼁ ⼁ ⼁ ⼁ ⼁ ⼁ ⼁ ⼁ ⼁

释义 Meaning

形容词 a.

stupid; fool: 你太傻了，这种话也相信。How stupid you are to believe this kind of talk.

词语 Words and Phrases

傻瓜	shǎguā	fool
傻呼呼	shǎhūhū	silly
傻话	shǎhuà	foolish words
傻冒儿	shǎmàor	fool
傻眼	shǎyǎn	be stunned
傻子	shǎzi	fool

熟语 Idioms

| 傻头傻脑 | shǎ tóu shǎ nǎo | foolish-looking |

晒 shài ⼁ ⼁ ⽇ ⽇ ⽇ ⽇ ⽇ ⽇ ⽇ ⽇

(曬)

释义 Meaning

动词 v.

shine upon; dry in the sun: 冬天应该多晒晒太阳。You'd better bask yourself in the sunshine whenever you can during the winter.

词语 Words and Phrases

晒台	shàitái	flat roof
晒太阳	shàitàiyáng	bathe in the sun
晒图	shàitú	blueprint

山 shān 丨 山 山

释义 Meaning

名词 n.

1. mountain: 中国南方有很多山。There are lots of mountains in the south of China.
2. hill: 我们村后有一座小山。There is a hill behind our village.

词语 Words and Phrases

山城	shānchéng	mountain city; the city of Chongqing
山村	shāncūn	mountain village
山川	shānchuān	landscape
山地	shāndì	hilly area
山顶	shāndǐng	top of a mountain
山谷	shāngǔ	ravine
山洪	shānhóng	mountain torrents

山口	shānkǒu	mountain pass
山林	shānlín	mountain forest
山坡	shānpō	mountain slope
山区	shānqū	mountain area
山水	shānshuǐ	mountains and rivers; landscape (e.g. painting)
山庄	shānzhuāng	mountain villa

熟语 Idioms

山清水秀	shān qīng shuǐ xiù	picturesque scenery
山穷水尽	shān qióng shuǐ jìn	be at the end of one's rope
山外有山	shān wài yǒu shān	there are better sceneries than the one you have seen
山珍海味	shān zhēn hǎi wèi	delicacies from the land and the sea

扇 shàn   丶 亠 亠 户 户 户 启 扇 扇 扇

释义 Meaning

（一）名词 n.

fan: 他收藏了很多折扇、绢扇。He collected a lot of folding fans and silk fans.

（二）动词 v.

wave (with a pan): 天太热了，扇出的风也是热的。It is so hot that the wind coming out of the fan is hot too.

（三）量词 measure w.

for doors and windows: 整个小房间只有一扇窗。The small room has just one window.

词语 Words and Phrases

| 扇骨 | shàngǔ | the ribs of a fan |
| 扇面 | shànmiàn | the covering of a fan |

扇形	shànxíng	① fan-shaped ② sector
扇子	shànzi	fan
电扇	diànshàn	electric fan
排风扇	páifēngshàn	draft fan
羽毛扇	yǔmáoshàn	feather fan

伤shāng 丿 亻 亻 亻 仂 伤

(傷 丿 亻 亻 亻 亻 亻 亻 亻 亻 亻 傷 傷 傷)

释义 Meaning

(一) 名词 n.

wound; injury: 再过一星期，你的伤就能好了。Your wound should be healed after another week.

(二) 动词 v.

hurt; injury: 我们不要再彼此伤对方的感情了。We don't want to hurt each other's feelings any more.

词语 Words and Phrases

伤疤	shāngbā	scar
伤兵	shāngbīng	wounded soldier
伤风	shāngfēng	catch cold; a cold or flu
伤感	shānggǎn	sick at heart; sentimental
伤害	shānghài	injure; harm; hurt
伤痕	shānghén	scar; hack
伤口	shāngkǒu	wound; cut
伤势	shāngshì	the condition of an injury
伤亡	shāngwáng	injuries and deaths; casualties
伤心	shāngxīn	sad; broken-hearted
伤员	shāngyuán	wounded personnel; the wounded

熟语 Idioms

伤风败俗	shāng fēngbài sú	offend public decency; corrupt public morals
伤筋动骨	shāng jīn dòng gǔ	be injured in the tendons and bones; have a fracture
伤脑筋	shāng nǎo jīn	be a nuisance; troublesome
伤天害理	shāngtiān hài lǐ	do things against Nature and reason; be cruel and heartless

商 shāng

丶 亠 产 产 产 产 产 商 商 商

释义 Meaning

（一）动词 v.

discuss; consult: 代表们汇聚一堂，共商国家大事。All the representatives gathered together to discuss national affairs.

（二）名词 n.

trade; commerce; business: 两年前，他弃政从商。He shifted from politics to business two years ago.

词语 Words and Phrases

商场	shāngchǎng	market; bazaar
商店	shāngdiàn	shop; store
商定	shāngdìng	decide through consultation; agree
商贩	shāngfàn	pedler; small retailer
商行	shānghángtrading company; commercial firm
商会	shānghuì	chamber of commerce
商量	shāngliang	consult; discuss; talk over
商品	shāngpǐn	commodity; goods; merchandise
商人	shāngrén	businessman; merchant; trader

商谈	shāngtán	exchange views; confer; discuss
商讨	shāngtǎo	discuss; deliberate over
商务	shāngwù	commercial affairs; business affairs
商业	shāngyè	commerce; trade; business
商议	shāng yì	confer; discuss

上 shàng 丨 上 上

释义 Meaning

（一）名词 n.

1. up; upper; upward: 我们一起往上爬。We climb upward together. 反义词 antonym: 下

2. previous; superior: 我上星期还见过他。I saw him last week. 反义词 antonym: 下

3. (used after a noun) in; on; at: 杯子上有你的指纹。Your fingerprints are on the cup.

（二）动词 v.

1. go up; get on: 快上车，我送你去。Get in the car, I will drive you there. 反义词 antonym: 下

2. go to; leave for: 星期天我喜欢上电影院。I like to go to the cinema on Sunday.

3. be engaged in; start to do: 今晚我要上夜校。I will go to night school tonight.

4. apply; supply: 还要再上一遍油漆。It still needs one coat of paint.

5. up to; as many as: 学校里有上百人得了感冒。There were as many as a hundred people who caught cold in the school.

6. used after a verb, indicating that some kind of result has be made by the action: 走的时候别忘了把门锁上。Don't forget to lock the door when you leave.

词语 Words and Phrases

上班	shàngbān	go to work; start work
上场	shàngchǎng	① appear on the stage ② enter the court or field
上当	shàngdàng	be taken in; be fooled
上帝	shàngdì	God
上风	shàngfēng	① windward ② advantage; superior position
上钩	shànggōu	rise to the bait; get hooked
上级	shàngjí	higher level; higher authorities
上街	shàngjiē	go into the street; go shopping; demonstrate against
上进	shàngjìn	go forward; make progress
上课	shàngkè	① attend class ② give a lesson
上来	shànglái	come up
上路	shànglù	set out on a journey; start off
上门	shàngmén	come to sb.'s home; drop in
上面	shàngmiàn	on the surface of; on the top of; above; over
上去	shàngqù	go up
上任	shàngrèn	take up an official post; assume office
上市	shàngshì	appear on the market; list (on stock exchange)
上述	shàngshù	above-mentioned; aforementioned
上司	shàngsī	superior; boss
上算	shàngsuàn	paying; worthwhile
上台	shàngtái	① go up onto the platform ② assume power; come to power
上午	shàngwǔ	morning; forenoon
上学	shàngxué	go to school; attend school
上演	shàngyǎn	put on the stage; perform

上瘾	shàngyǐn	be addicted to; get into the habit of
上映	shàngyìng	show (of a film); be on
上游	shàngyóu	① upper reaches ② advanced position
上涨	shàngzhǎng	rise; go up
上阵	shàngzhèn	go into battle; pitch into the work

熟语 Idioms

上轨道	shàng guǐdào	go on the right track; begin to work smoothly
上梁不正 下梁歪	shàng liáng bú zhèng xià liáng wāi	if the upper beam is not straight, the lower ones will go slant; fish begins to stink at the head
上气不接 下气	shàng qì bù jiē xià qì	gasp for air; be out of breath
上天无路， 入地无门	shàng tiān wú lù, rù dì wú mén	there is no road to heaven and no door into the earth; be up against the walls
上无片瓦， 下无寸土	shàng wú piàn wǎ, xià wú cùn tǔ	have neither a tile over one's head nor an inch of land under one's feet; in complete poverty
上行下效	shàng xíng xià xiào	those below follow the (usu. bad) examples of those above

烧 shāo ′ ′ 丬 火 火 灶 烂 烧 烧 烧

(燒 ′ ′ 丬 火 灯 灯 灯 焯 焯 烽 烽 焠 熪 熪 燒 燒)

释义 Meaning

动词 v.

1. burn: 现在农村也不再烧柴了。Now wood is not used to make fire any more in the countryside.

2. cook: 他太太很会烧菜。His wife is a good cook

3. run a fever; have a fever: 他昨天烧到39度。He had a fever of 39 ℃ yesterday.

词语 Words and Phrases

烧荒	shāohuāng	burn the grass on the waste land
烧毁	shāohuǐ	burn down; over burning
烧伤	shāoshāng	suffer from burn
烧香	shāoxiāng	① burn joss sticks ② give sb. a present for special attention

少₁ shǎo 丨 丿 小 少

释义 Meaning

(一)形容词 a.

few; little; less: 你应该少吃一点儿油炸的食品。You should eat less fried food. 反义词 antonym: 多

(二)动词 v.

1. be short; lack: 我们球队少一个好的守门员。Our team lacks a good goalkeeper. 反义词 antonym: 多

2. be missing; lose: 我钱包里少了十块钱。I lost ten *yuan* from my wallet.

词语 Words and Phrases

少不得	shǎobudé	cannot do without; cannot dispense with
少量	shǎoliàng	a small amount
少数	shǎoshù	minority; small number
少有	shǎoyǒu	rare; seldom

熟语 Idioms

少见多怪	shǎo jiàn duō guài	the less a man has seen the more he has to wonder at
少吃多餐	shǎo chī duō cān	have many meals a day but less food at each

少₂ shào 丨 丿 小 少

释义 Meaning

（一）形容词 a.

young: 请你原谅我的年少无知。Please forgive me for my naive ignorance. 反义词 antonym: 老

词语 Words and Phrases

少妇	shàofù	young married woman
少年	shàonián	early youth; juvenile
少女	shàonǚ	young girl
少爷	shàoye	young master (of the house)
少壮	shàozhuàng	the young and vigorous

熟语 Idioms

| 少不更事 | shào bú gēng shì | young and inexperienced; as green as grass |
| 少年老成 | shàonián lǎo chéng | young but prudent and capable; precocious |

舌 shé 一 二 千 千 舌 舌

释义 Meaning

名词 n.

tongue: 食蚁兽用它的长舌进食。The anteater takes food with it's long tongue.

词语 Words and Phrases

舌尖	shéjiān	tip of tongue
舌头	shétou	tongue
舌战	shézhàn	have a verbal battle with; argue heartedly
喉舌	hóushé	mouthpiece
火舌	huǒshé	tongues of fire

帽舌	màoshé	peak (of a cap); visor
鞋舌	xiéshé	tongue of a shoe
学舌	xuéshé	repeat other people's words; gossipy

熟语 Idioms

| 唇枪舌剑 | chún qiāng shé jiàn | cross verbal swords; engage in a battle of words |

蛇 shé ｜ 冂 口 虫 虫 虫 虫 虫 虫 蛇 蛇

释义 Meaning

名词 n.

snake; serpent: 蛇是一种分布很广的动物。Snakes have a widespread distribution on the planet.

词语 Words and Phrases

蛇毒	shédú	snake venom
蛇药	shéyào	antidote for snake-bites
蛇足	shézú	feet added to a snake; sth. superfluous

伸 shēn ノ 亻 仁 仁 伫 伸 伸

释义 Meaning

动词 v.

stretch; extend: 列车行使时不要把手伸出车窗外。Don't stick your arm out of the window while the train is in motion.
反义词 antonym: 缩

词语 Words and Phrases

伸长	shēncháng	elongation
伸手	shēnshǒu	① stretch out one's hand ② ask for help, etc.
伸缩	shēnsuō	stretch out and draw back

| 伸展 | shēnzhǎn | spread; extend; stretch |
| 伸张 | shēnzhāng | uphold; prompt |

身 shēn ˊ ˊ 勹 勹 钅 身 身

释义 Meaning

（一）名词 n.

1. body: 他身高一米七五。He is 1.75m. in height.

2. life: 他具有为事业献身的精神。He is willing to devote his life to this career.

3. the main part of a structure: 车身上画满了广告。The body of bus is covered with advertising posters.

（二）量词 measure w.

suit: 她今天穿了一身新衣服。She is wearing a suit of new clothes today.

词语 Words and Phrases

身边	shēnbiān	at one's side
身材	shēncái	stature; figure
身份	shēnfèn	① identity; status; capacity ② dignity
身后	shēnhòu	after one's death
身价	shēnjià	① social status ② the value (of a football player, etc.)
身上	shēnshàng	① on one's body ② (have sth.) on one
身世	shēnshì	one's life experience; one's lot
身手	shēnshǒu	skill; talent
身体	shēntǐ	① body ② health
身心	shēnxīn	body and mind
身孕	shēnyùn	pregnancy
身子	shēnzi	① body ② pregnancy

熟语 Idioms

| 身败名裂 | shēn bài míng liè | lose all standings and |

		reputations; be utterly dis-credited
身不由己	shēn bù yóu jǐ	involuntarily; not of one's own freewill
身经百战	shēn jīng bǎi zhàn	have fought numerous battles; experienced
身临其境	shēn lín qí jìng	be on the spot in person
身强力壮	shēn qiáng lì zhuàng	healthy and strong; tough and sturdy
身体力行	shēn tǐ lì xíng	practise what one preaches
身无分文	shēn wú fēn wén	be stone-broken; without a penny in one's purse
身先士卒	shēn xiān shì zú	fight at the head of one's men
身在福中不知福	shēn zài fú zhōng bù zhī fú	not appreciate the happy life one is enjoying

深 shēn `　`　氵　氵　氵　氵　氵　氵　氵　深　深

释义 Meaning

形容词 a.

1. deep: 这口井很深。The well is quite deep. 反义词 antonym: 浅

2. dark; deep: 她喜欢穿深色的衣服。She likes to wear dark clothes. 反义词 antonym: 浅，淡

3. profound; penetrating: 她给我留下了很深的印象。She left a deep impression on me.

4. late: 深秋的香山，满是红叶。Xiangshan in late autumn is covered with red leaves. 反义词 antonym: 初

5. deeply; greatly: 她的话使听众深受感动。The audience was deeply moved by her words.

词语 Words and Phrases

深奥	shēn'ào	abstruse; profound
深长	shēncháng	profound
深沉	shēnchén	① dark; deep ② dull; ③ concealing one's real feelings
深处	shēnchù	depths; recesses
深度	shēndù	depth; degree of depth
深厚	shēnhòu	① deep; profound ② solid; deep seated
深化	shēnhuà	deepen
深刻	shēnkè	profound
深浅	shēnqiǎn	① depth ② proper limit (of speech or action)
深情	shēnqíng	deep feeling; deep love
深入	shēnrù	go deep into; penetrate into
深深	shēnshēn	deeply; profoundly
深思	shēnsī	think deeply about; ponder deeply over
深夜	shēnyè	late at night
深渊	shēnyuān	abyss
深远	shēnyuǎn	profound and lasting; far-reaching
深造	shēnzào	take up advanced studies

熟语 Idioms

深仇大恨	shēn chóu dà hèn	bitter and deep-seated hatred
深更半夜	shēngēng-bànyè	in the middle of the night; in the depth of night
深居简出	shēn jū jiǎn chū	lead a secluded life; domesticity
深谋远虑	shēn móu yuǎn lǜ	think deeply and plan carefully; be farsighted and pruden
深入浅出	shēn rù qiǎn chū	explain the profound in

		simple terms
深山老林	shēnshān lǎolín	remote, thickly forested mountains
深恶痛绝	shēn wù tòng jué	have a deep-rooted hatred; hold in abhorrence

神 shén ` 亠 礻 礻 礻 礻 礻 礻 神

释义 Meaning

（一）形容词 a.

supernatural; magical: 这药真神，我一吃就好了。It's really a miracle! I felt better as soon as I had had the medicine.

（二）名词 n.

1. spirit; mind: 爷爷坐在椅子上闭目养神。Grandpa was sitting in the chair reposing himself with his eyes closed.

2. god; deity; divinity: 维纳斯是罗马神话中的爱神和美神。Venus is the goddess of love and beauty in Roman mythology.

词语 Words and Phrases

神话	shénhuà	fairy tale; myth; mythology
神经	shénjīng	nerve
神秘	shénmì	mysterious; mystical
神奇	shénqí	magical; mystical; miraculous
神气	shénqì	① expression; manner ② vigorous; spirited ③ putting on airs; cocky
神情	shénqíng	expression; look
神色	shénsè	expression; look
神圣	shénshèng	sacred; holy
神通	shéntōng	remarkable ability; magical power
神童	shéntóng	child prodigy
神往	shénwǎng	be charmed: be carried away

神仙	shénxiān	immortal; supernatural being
神像	shénxiàng	picture or statue of a god or Buddha
神志	shénzhì	consciousness; senses; mind

熟语 Idioms

神不知， 鬼不觉	shén bù zhī, guǐ bù jué	unknown to either god or ghost; in complete secrecy
神出鬼没	shén chū guǐ mò	come and go like a shadow; appear and disappear mysteriously
神机妙算	shén jī miào suàn	crafty plan; wonderful foresight
神气活现	shénqì huó xiàn	look truculent; as proud as a peacock
神圣不可 侵犯	shénshèng bù kě qīnfàn	holy and inviolable

升 shēng 丿 二 升 升

释义 Meaning

（一）动词 v.

1. rise; ascend; go up: 天刚发白，太阳还没有升起来。The day was just dawning, the sun had not yet risen. 反义词 antonym: 落

2. promote: 他上个月刚升总经理。He was promoted to general menager just last month. 反义词 antonym: 降

（二）量词 measure w.

liter: 这个桶能装五十升。The capacity of this barrel is 50 liters.

词语 Words and Phrases

| 升高 | shēnggāo | go up; raise; ascend |
| 升华 | shēnghuá | ① sublimation ② raising to a higher level; distillation |

升级	shēngjí	go up (a grade); upgrade
升旗	shēngqí	hoist a flag; raise a flag
升学	shēngxué	attend a school of a higher grade
升值	shēngzhí	rise in value

生 shēng ノ 一 ヒ 生 生

释义 Meaning

(一) 动词 v.

1. give birth to; be born: 她生了一个女孩。She bore a baby girl.

2. grow: 柳枝插在土里就会生根。A willow branch may take roots if it is planted into the ground.

3. make; get: 孩子手上都生冻疮了。The child got chilblains on his hands.

(二) 形容词 a.

1. unripe; uncooked; unprocessed: 她喜欢吃生鸡蛋。She likes to eat raw eggs. 反义词 antonym: 熟

2. unfamiliar; strange: 好久没练了，觉得有点儿手生了。I felt a little bit strange because I haven't practised for quite a long times.

(三) 名词 n.

1. life: 是人难免会贪生怕死。It is natural for man to prefer life to death. 反义词 antonym: 死

2. pupil; student: 我们班男生女生一样多。The number of boy students in our class is the same as the number of girl students.

词语 Words and Phrases

| 生病 | shēngbìng | fall ill; be sick |
| 生菜 | shēngcài | romaine lettuce; lettuce |

生产	shēngchǎn	produce; manufacture
生词	shēngcí	new word; vocabulary
生存	shēngcún	exist; live; subsist
生动	shēngdòng	vivid; lively
生活	shēnghuó	① live ② livelihood
生火	shēnghuǒ	make fire; light a fire
生姜	shēngjiāng	ginger
生理	shēnglǐ	physiology
生路	shēnglù	means of livelihood; way out
生命	shēngmìng	life
生怕	shēngpà	for fear that; so as not to; lest
生平	shēngpíng	all one's life
生气	shēngqì	① get angry; take offense ② vitality
生前	shēngqián	during one's lifetime
生日	shēngrì	birthday
生疏	shēngshū	unfamiliar
生死	shēngsǐ	life and death
生态	shēngtài	ecology
生物	shēngwù	living things; organisms
生效	shēngxiào	go into effect; become effective
生锈	shēngxiù	get rusty
生意	shēngyì	① business; trade ② vitality; tendency to grow
生硬	shēngyìng	stiff; rigid; harsh
生育	shēngyù	give birth to; bear
生长	shēngzhǎng	① grow ② be brought up; grow up
生殖器	shēngzhíqì	reproductive organs

熟语 Idioms

生搬硬套	shēng bān yìng tào	copy mechanically and apply indiscriminately

生离死别	shēng lí sǐ bié	part for ever; death
生灵涂炭	shēnglíng tútàn	plunge the people into misery and suffering
生龙活虎	shēng lóng huó hǔ	full of vim and vigor like dragons and tigers
生米煮成熟饭	shēng mǐ zhǔ chéng shú fàn	the rice is already cooked; what is done can't be un-done
生吞活剥	shēng tūn huó bō	swallow sth. raw and whole; take over sth. uncritically
生于忧患，死于安乐	shēng yú yōuhuàn, sǐ yú ānlè	be born in calamity and die in peace

声 shēng　一 十 吉 吉 吉 吉 声

(聲　一 十 吉 吉 吉 吉 声 声 声 殸 殸 殸 殸 殸 殸 聲 聲 聲)

释义 Meaning

名词 n.

sound; voice: 我听不清楚，请你大声一点儿。I can't hear you, please speak up!

词语 Words and Phrases

声称	shēngchēng	profess; claim; assert
声调	shēngdiào	tones (of Chinese syllables)
声明	shēngmíng	① declare; announce ② statement; declaration
声势	shēngshì	impetus; momentum
声讨	shēngtǎo	denounce; condemn
声响	shēngxiǎng	sound; noise
声音	shēngyīn	sound; voice
声誉	shēngyù	reputation; fame

| 声援 | shēngyuán | express support for |
| 声张 | shēngzhāng | make public; disclose |

熟语 Idioms

声东击西	shēng dōng jī xī	feint in the east and attack in the west
声泪俱下	shēng lèi jù xià	shed tears while speaking; in a tearful voice
声名狼藉	shēng míng láng jí	disrepute; be held in ill repute
声色俱厉	shēng sè jù lì	stern both in voice and in countenance
声嘶力竭	shēng sī lì jié	shout oneself hoarse

胜 shèng 丿 刀 月 月 厈 胪 肸 胖 胜

(勝 丿 刀 月 月 肝 胪 胪 胪 胪 睎 脎 滕 勝)

释义 Meaning

动词 v.

1. win: 东方队已经连胜了十场比赛。The Oriental (Team) has won ten games in a row. 反义词 antonym: 败

2. surpass; be superior to: 我看她胜过你十倍。I think she is ten times better than you.

词语 Words and Phrases

胜败	shèngbài	victory or defeat; success or failure
胜负	shèngfù	victory or defeat; success or failure
胜利	shènglì	① victory; triumph ② successfully; triumphantly
胜任	shèngrèn	competent; well qualified
胜仗	shèngzhàng	victorious battle; victory

熟语 Idioms

| 胜败乃兵家常事 | shèng bài nǎi bīng jiā cháng shì | defeats or victories are ordinary things to a general; it is a way of life |
| 胜不骄，败不馁 | shèng bù jiāo, bài bù něi | not made dizzy with success, nor be discouraged by failure; take it as it is |

省 shěng 　一　ⸯ　⺌　少　少　省　省　省　省

释义 Meaning

（一）动词 v.

1. save; economize: 她用省下的钱帮助农村的孩子上学。She helps the village children to go to school with her savings.

2. omit; leave out: 这个词不能省掉。This term cannot be omitted.

（二）名词 n.

province: 我出生在山东省。I was born in Shandong Province.

词语 Words and Phrases

省城	shěngchéng	provincial capital
省得	shěngdé	so as to save; so as to avoid
省份	shěngfèn	province
省会	shěnghuì	provincial capital
省力	shěnglì	save labuor; save effort;
省略	shěnglüè	leave out; omit
省钱	shěngqián	save money; be economical
省事	shěngshì	save trouble; simplify matters
省心	shěngxīn	save worry

熟语 Idioms

省吃俭用　　shěng chī jiǎn yòng　skimp and save; eat sparingly and spend frugally

剩 shèng

一 二 干 干 干 乖 乖 乖 乖
乘 乘 剩

释义 Meaning

动词 v.

surplus; remnant; leave over: 桌上的剩菜总是父亲吃了。
Father always polishes off whatever is left on the table at the end of a meal.

词语 Words and Phrases

剩下　　shèngxià　　be left over; remain
剩余　　shèngyú　　surplus; remainder

师 shī

丨 刂 广 广 师 师

（師 丿 亻 亻 亻 自 自 自 師 師 師）

释义 Meaning

名词 n.

1. teacher; master: 师生之间应该互相尊重，互相理解。
Teachers and students should respect and understand each other.
2. a person skilled in a certain profession: 她弟弟是位工程师。Her brother is an engineer.
3. division: 那时我正在第十一步兵师服役。I was in the 11th infantry division at that time.

词语 Words and Phrases

师法　　shīfǎ　　model on; imitate

师范	shīfàn	teacher-training; pedagogical
师傅	shīfù	master
师生	shīshēng	teacher and student
师徒	shītú	master and apprentice
师长	shīzhǎng	① teacher ② division commander
师资	shīzī	teaching qualification

诗 shī ` 讠 讠 计 诗 诗 诗 诗

(詩 ` ˊ ˊ ˊ 言 言 言 言 計 計 詩

詩 詩)

释义 Meaning

名词 n.

poem; poetry; verse: 李白的诗连小孩都会背。Even a child can recite some poems by Li Bai.

词语 Words and Phrases

诗词	shīcí	*shi* and *ci* , two types of traditional Chinese poetry
诗歌	shīgē	poems and songs; poetry
诗句	shījù	verse; line
诗人	shīrén	poet
诗意	shīyì	poetic quality or flavor; romantic scenes

熟语 Idioms

| 诗情画意 | shī qíng huà yì | artistic charm |

湿 shī ` ˋ 氵 氵 氵 沪 沪 沪 湿 湿

湿 湿

(濕 ` ˋ 氵 氵 氵 沪 沪 沪 湿 湿 湿

湿 濕 濕 濕 濕 濕)

释义 Meaning

形容词 a.

wet; damp; humid: 穿湿衣服，你会着凉的。 If you wear damp clothes, you will probably catch cold. 反义词 antonym: 干

词语 Words and Phrases

湿度	shīdù	humidity
湿淋淋	shīlínlín	dripping wet; drenched
湿润	shīrùn	moist
湿透	shītòu	wet through; drenched

十 shí   二 十

释义 Meaning

数词 num.

ten: 我一天学十个汉字。 I learn ten Chinese characters everyday.

词语 Words and Phrases

十二月	shí'èryuè	December
十分	shífēn	very; fully; utterly; extremely
十一月	shíyīyuè	November
十月	shíyuè	October
十字架	shízìjià	Cross
十字路口	shízìlùkǒu	crossroad
十足	shízú	① 100 percent ② fully

熟语 Idioms

| 十八般武艺 | shíbā bān wǔyì | skills in using 18 kinds of weapons; skillful and well qualified |

十恶不赦	shí è bú shè	unpardonable crime; guilty beyond forgiveness
十拿九稳	shí ná jiǔ wěn	90 percent sure; ten to one
十年树木，百年树人	shí nián shù mù, bǎi nián shù rén	it takes ten years to grow a tree, but a hundred years to bring up a generation of people; a long and meaningful venture
十全十美	shí quán shí měi	be perfect in every respect
十万八千里	shí wàn bā qiān lǐ	a distance of one hundred and eight thousand *li* ; far far away
十万火急	shí wàn huǒ jí	desperately urgent; extremely urgent
十有八九	shí yǒu bā jiǔ	in eight or nine cases out of ten; in all probability
十指连心	shí zhǐ lián xīn	the nerves of the fingertips are linked to the heart; well related

石 shí　　二 丆 厂 石 石

释义 Meaning

名词 n.

stone; rock: 广场上树立着英雄的石像。A stone statue of the hero stands in the square.

词语 Words and Phrases

石碑	shíbēi	stone tablet; stone monument
石雕	shídiāo	① carved stone ② stone carving
石膏	shígāo	gypsum; plaster stone
石灰	shíhuī	lime
石匠	shíjiàng	stone mason
石刻	shíkè	① carved stone ② stone inscription

石棉	shímián	asbestors
石墨	shímò	graphite
石器	shíqì	neolithic (age); stone artifact;
石头	shítou	stone; rock
石英	shíyīng	quartz
石油	shíyóu	petroleum; oil
石子	shízi	cobblestone; pebble

熟语 Idioms

| 石沉大海 | shí chén dà hǎi | like a stone dropped into the sea; have no response |
| 石破天惊 | shí pò tiān jīng | earth-shattering and heaven-battering; remarkably original and forceful |

时 shí ｜ 冂 日 日 旷 时 时

(時 ｜ 冂 日 日 旷 旷 旷 旷 時 時)

释义 Meaning

名词 n.

1. time; times; days: 工作忙时就顾不上家了。I can't take much care of my family when I'm busy with my work.

2. fixed time; due time: 我们一定按时把信件送到。We will definitely send the letter there before the deadline.

词语 Words and Phrases

时不时	shíbùshí	often
时差	shíchā	time difference
时代	shídài	① times; era; epoch ② a peorid in one's life
时光	shíguāng	time

时候	shíhou	① (the duration of) time ② (a point in) time; moment
时机	shíjī	opportunity; an opportune moment
时间	shíjiān	time; hour
时刻	shíkè	① time; moment ② always; constantly
时髦	shímáo	fashionable; in vogue
时期	shíqī	period
时时	shíshí	often; constantly
时事	shíshì	current affairs; current events
时速	shísù	speed per hour
时针	shízhēn	hour hand (of a clock)
时钟	shízhōng	clock
时装	shízhuāng	fashionable dress

熟语 Idioms

时不我待	shí bù wǒ dài	time stays for no man
时过境迁	shí guò jìng qiān	circumstances change with the passage of time
时来运转	shí lái yùn zhuǎn	fortune is smiling; time has moved in one's favor

识 shí ` 讠 讥 识 识 识 识

(識 ` ˋ ˊ ˈ 言 言 言 訁 訁 訁 訁 訁 訅 訛 識 識 識 識)

释义 Meaning

动词 v.

know; recognize: 我受教育是从识字开始的。I started my education by learning charecters.

词语 Words and Phrases

| 识别 | shíbié | discriminate; distinguish; discern |

识货	shíhuò	know all about the goods; be able to tell good from bad
识破	shípò	see through; penetrate
识字	shízì	learn to read: become literate

熟语 Idioms

| 识大体，
顾大局 | shí dàtǐ,
gù dà jú | keep the whole situation in mind |
| 识时务者
为俊杰 | shí shí wù zhě
wéi jùn jié | those who suit their actions to the time of day are wise |

拾 shí 二 丁 扌 扩 扒 护 拎 拾 拾

释义 Meaning

动词 v.

pick up (from ground); collect: 小时候我们一起上山拾柴。We collected firewood on the hill together when we were young. 反义词 antonym: 丢，扔

词语 Words and Phrases

拾荒	shíhuāng	glean and collect scraps
拾取	shíqǔ	pick up; collect
拾遗	shíyí	① appropriate lost property ② make good omissions

熟语 Idioms

| 拾金不昧 | shí jīn bú mèi | not to pocket the money one has picked up |
| 拾人牙慧 | shí rén yá huì | pick up phrases from sb. and pass them off as one's own; plagiarism |

食 shí ノ 人 人 今 今 今 食 食 食

释义 Meaning

（一）动词 v.

eat: 不劳动者不得食。He who does not work, neither shall he eat.

（二）名词 n.

1. meal: 北方人喜欢吃面食。Northerners like foods made of wheat.

2. eclipse: 日食是一种有趣的天文现象。Solar eclipse is an interesting astronomical phenomenon.

词语 Words and Phrases

食品	shípǐn	food; foodstuff; provision
食宿	shísù	board and lodging
食堂	shítáng	dining room; canteen
食糖	shítáng	sugar
食物	shíwù	food; eatables
食言	shíyán	break one's promise; go back on one's word
食盐	shíyán	salt
食用	shíyòng	edible
食油	shíyóu	edible oil; cooking oil
食欲	shíyù	appetite
食指	shízhǐ	forefinger; index finger

熟语 Idioms

食不甘味	shí bù gān wèi	eat without relish; be in deep sorrow or anxiety
食不果腹	shí bù guǒ fù	not to have enough food to eat
食不厌精	shí bú yàn jīng	one does not object to the finest food
食古不化	shí gǔ bú huà	swallow ancient learning

without digesting it; be pedantic

| 食之无味，
弃之可惜 | shí zhī wú wèi
qì zhī kěxī | be hardly worth eating but not bad enough to throw away; something necessary but not highly treasured |

史 shǐ   丶   丆   口   史   史

释义 Meaning

名词 n.

history: 他专门研究宗教史。He is specialized in the study of the history of religion.

词语 Words and Phrases

史籍	shǐjí	historical records; history
史迹	shǐjì	historical site and relics
史料	shǐliào	historical data; historical materials
史诗	shǐshī	epic
史实	shǐshí	historical facts
史书	shǐshū	historical records; history
史学	shǐxué	the study of history; historiography

熟语 Idioms

| 史无前例 | shǐ wú qián lì | without parallel in history; unprecedented in history |

使 shǐ   丿   亻   仁   仨   佢   佢   使   使

释义 Meaning

动词 v.

1. use; apply: 大家劲往一处使，齐心把事情办好。Everyone makes efforts towards the same goal to fulfill the task.

2. make; cause; enable: 虚心使人进步，骄傲使人落后。
Modesty helps one to go forward, conceit makes one lag
behind.

词语 Words and Phrases

使出	shǐchū	ues; exert
使得	shǐdé	make; cause; render
使馆	shǐguǎn	diplomatic mission; embassy
使节	shǐjié	diplomatic envoy
使劲	shǐjìn	exert all one's strength
使命	shǐmìng	mission
使用	shǐyòng	use; make use of; employ; apply
使者	shǐzhě	messenger; envoy

熟语 Idioms

使性子	shǐ xìngzi	lose one's temper; get angry
使眼色	shǐ yǎnsè	tip sb. the wink; wink

始 shǐ   ㄥ ㄥ ㄥ ㄥ ㄥ ㄥ 始 始

释义 Meaning

（一）动词 v.

begin; start: 我们的交往始于去年秋天。Our intercourse
began last fall.

（二）名词 n.

beginning; start: 无论做什么事，都要有始有终。Whatever
you do, you should do it to the end. 反义词 antonym: 终

词语 Words and Phrases

始末	shǐmò	from the beginning until the end; the whole story
始终	shǐzhōng	from beginning to end; all along; throughout

熟语 Idioms

始终不渝	shǐzhōng bú yú	be unchanged from beginning to end; unswerving
始终如一	shǐzhōng rú yī	be consistent from beginning to end; persistent

世 shì 　 一　十　廿　廿　世

释义 Meaning

名词 n.

1. lifetime; generation: 我做人一世清白，对得起任何人。 I have lived a decent life, doing dirt to no one.

2. world; era: 那一幕情景恍如隔世。 I felt that it was a scene from another world.

词语 Words and Phrases

世代	shìdài	for generations; from generation to generation
世纪	shìjì	century
世界	shìjiè	world
世界语	shìjièyǔ	Esperanto
世面	shìmiàn	wordly aspects of society
世人	shìrén	common people
世上	shìshàng	in the world; on earth
世俗	shìsú	① common customs ② worldly; secular
世态	shìtài	the way of the world
世袭	shìxí	hereditary

熟语 Idioms

世风日下	shìfēng rì xià	moral standards degenerate continuously
世上无难事，	shìshàng wú nán shì,	nothing in the world is difficult to a man with a

只怕	zhǐ pà	will
有心人	yǒuxīnrén	
世态炎凉	shìtài yánliáng	snobbishness of human relationships
世外桃源	shì wài táoyuán	a paradise

市 shì 　丶 亠 广 亣 市

释义 Meaning

名词 n.

1. market: 今年的花市是最热闹的。This year's flower market is the busiest one ever.

2. city; municipality: 市中心有一个大公园。There is a big park at the center of the city.

词语 Words and Phrases

市场	shìchǎng	marketplace; market
市郊	shìjiāo	suburb; outskirts
市面	shìmiàn	market condition; business
市民	shìmín	residents of a city; townspeople
市区	shìqū	urban district; city proper
市容	shìróng	the appearrance of a city
市长	shìzhǎng	mayor

式 shì 　二 三 亍 弌 式 式

释义 Meaning

名词 n.

1. type; style; model: 这家商店卖西式点心。This shop sells Western-style pastry.

2. ceremony; ritual: 开幕式下午三点举行。The opening ceremony is going to be held at 3 p.m.

3. formula: 你能帮我解一下这个算式吗？Can you solve

this arithmetic formula for me?

词语 Words and Phrases

| 式样 | shìyàng | style; type; model |
| 式子 | shìzi | formula |

事 shì　　一　厂　厂　厇　写　写　写　事

释义 Meaning

名词 n.

1. matter; affair; thing; business: 我还有件事要问你呢。
   There's another thing I want to ask you about.
2. trouble; accident: 这孩子总在外面惹事。The child often goes out and makes trouble.

词语 Words and Phrases

事故	shìgù	accident; mishap
事后	shìhòu	after the event; afterwards
事迹	shìjì	deed; achievement
事假	shìjià	leave of absence; compassionate leave
事件	shìjiàn	incident; event
事理	shìlǐ	reason; logic
事例	shìlì	example; instance
事前	shìqián	before the event; in advance; beforehand
事情	shìqíng	affair; matter; thing; business
事实	shìshí	fact
事态	shìtài	state of affairs; situation
事务	shìwù	① work; routine ② general affairs
事物	shìwù	thing; object
事先	shìxiān	in advance; beforehand; prior
事业	shìyè	cause; undertaking; career

熟语 Idioms

事半功倍	shì bàn gōng bèi	get double the result with half the effort
事倍功半	shì bèi gōng bàn	get half the result with double the effort
事不关己，高高挂起	shì bù guān jǐ, gāogāo guà qǐ	let things drift if they do not affect one personally
事不宜迟	shì bù yí chí	one must lose no time in doing it; delays are dangerous
事出有因	shì chū yǒu yīn	everything has its seed; there is good reason for it
事到临头	shì dào líntóu	when the situation becomes critical; at the last moment
事后诸葛亮	shìhòu zhūgé liàng	be wise after the event; afterwit
事与愿违	shì yǔ yuàn wéi	things turn out contrary to one's expectation

试 shì ` 讠 讠 讠 讠 讠 试 试

(試 ` ⺊ ⺀ ⺀ 言 言 言 言 言 訂 訂 試 試)

释义 Meaning

动词 v.

try; test; attempt: 让我试一下。Let me have a try.

词语 Words and Phrases

试点	shìdiǎn	make experiments; conduct tests at selected points
试管	shìguǎn	test tube
试卷	shìjuàn	examination paper; test paper

试探	shìtàn	sound out; feel out; probe; explore
试题	shìtí	examination question; test question
试图	shìtú	attempt; try
试行	shìxíng	try out
试验	shìyàn	trial; experiment; test
试用	shìyòng	on trial; try out; on probation
试运行	shìyùnxíng	pilot run; test run
试制	shìzhì	trial-produce; trial-manufacture

室 shì 丶 丶 宀 宀 宀 室 室 室 室

释义 Meaning

名词 n.

room: 我住2105室。My room number is 2105.

词语 Words and Phrases

室内	shìnèi	indoor; interior
室外	shìwài	outdoor; outside
办公室	bàngōngshì	office
地下室	dìxiàshì	basement; cellar
更衣室	gēngyīshì	changing room; locker room
皇室	huángshì	imperial family
会客室	huìkèshì	reception room
科室	kēshì	administrative or technical offices
起居室	qǐjūshì	living room
温室	wēnshì	hothouse; greenhouse; glasshouse
卧室	wòshì	bedroom
浴室	yùshì	bathroom; shower room

是 shì 丨 冂 日 日 旦 旱 昂 昰 是

释义 Meaning

（一）动词 v.

1. be: 我是中国人。I am Chinese.

2. be; exist: 大楼前面是花园。There is a garden in front of the building.

3. be···, but: 这东西是旧了，可还能用。Yes, it is old, but it can still be used.

4. yes; right: 是的，我是中国人。Yes, I am Chinese.

（二）副词 adv.

certainly; really: 这件衬衫是很漂亮。This shirt really is beautiful.

词语 Words and Phrases

| 是非 | shìfēi | ① right and wrong ② quarrel; dispute |
| 是否 | shìfǒu | whether or not; whether; if |

熟语 Idioms

是非颠倒	shìfēi diāndǎo	confound right and wrong
是非曲直	shìfēi qūzhí	rights and wrongs; truth and falsehood; merits and demerits
是非之地	shìfēi zhī dì	a place where one is apt to get into trouble
是可忍，孰不可忍	shì kě rěn, shú bù kě rěn	if this can be endured, what else can't?

收 shōu ㇖ ㇙ ㇙ ㇙ 收 收

释义 Meaning

动词 v.

1. receive; accept: 她收到很多生日礼物。She received a lot of birthday gifts.

2. collect; gather: 快把地上的玩具收起来。Gather up all

the toys scatterd on the ground at once.

词语 Words and Phrases

收藏	shōucáng	collect; store up
收场	shōuchǎng	① wind up; end up; stop ② ending; denouement
收成	shōuchéng	harvest; crop
收到	shōudào	receive; obtain
收费	shōufèi	collect fees; charge
收复	shōufù	recover; recapture
收割	shōugē	reap; harvest
收工	shōugōng	stop work for the day; knock off; pack up
收购	shōugòu	purchase; buy
收回	shōuhuí	① take back; regain ② withdraw
收获	shōuhuò	harvest; gains; results
收集	shōují	collect; gather
收件人	shōujiànrén	addressee; consignee
收缴	shōujiǎo	take over; capture
收据	shōujù	receipt
收款人	shōukuǎnrén	payee
收敛	shōuliǎn	① weaken or disappear ② restrain oneself
收留	shōuliú	take sb. in; have sb. in one's care
收拢	shōulǒng	draw sth. in
收录	shōulù	① include ② listen in and take down; record
收罗	shōuluó	collect; gather; enlist
收买	shōumǎi	① purchase; buy in ② buy over; bribe
收盘	shōupán	closing quotation (on the exchange, etc.)
收入	shōurù	① income; revenue; earnings ② take in; include

收拾	shōushi	① put in order; tidy ② get things ready; pack up
收缩	shōusuō	① contract; shrink ② concentrate one's forces; draw back
收条	shōutiáo	receipt
收听	shōutīng	listen to
收尾	shōuwěi	wind up; ending
收效	shōuxiào	yield results; produce effects; bear fruit
收养	shōuyǎng	take in and bring up; adopt
收益	shōuyì	income; profit; earnings; gains
收音机	shōuyīnjī	radio set; wireless set
收支	shōuzhī	revenue and expenditure; income and expanses

手 shǒu 一 二 三 手

释义 Meaning

名词 n.

1. hand: 他手里拿着一本书。He has a book in his hand.

2. a person doing or good at a certain job: 开车我还是个新手。I'm a new driver.

词语 Words and Phrases

手背	shǒubèi	the back of the hand
手臂	shǒubì	arm
手表	shǒubiǎo	wrist watch
手册	shǒucè	handbook; manual
手电筒	shǒudiàntǒng	electric torch; flashlight
手段	shǒuduàn	① means; medium; measure; method ② trick; artifice
手法	shǒufǎ	① results; produce; technique ② trick; gimmick

手风琴	shǒufēngqín	accordion
手稿	shǒugǎo	original manuscript
手工	shǒugōng	① handwork ② manual; by hand
手脚	shǒujiǎo	movement of hands or feet
手绢	shǒujuàn	handkerchief
手帕	shǒupà	handkerchief
手气	shǒuqì	luck at gambling, card playing, etc.
手枪	shǒuqiāng	pistol
手势	shǒushì	gesture; sign; signal
手术	shǒushù	surgical operation
手套	shǒutào	gloves; mittens
手提	shǒutí	portable
手头	shǒutóu	① right beside one; on hand; at hand ② one's financial condition at the moment
手腕	shǒuwàn	① wrist ② artifice; finesse; stratagem; social skill
手下	shǒuxià	under the leadership of; under
手心	shǒuxīn	① the palm of the hand ② control
手艺	shǒuyì	craftsmanship; handicraft; trade
手语	shǒuyǔ	sign language
手掌	shǒuzhǎng	palm
手杖	shǒuzhàng	walking stick; stick
手指	shǒuzhǐ	finger
手指甲	shǒuzhǐjiǎ	finger nail
手纸	shǒuzhǐ	toilet paper
手足	shǒuzú	brothers

熟语 Idioms

手不释卷	shǒu bú shì juàn	always have a book in one's hand; be very studious

手到病除	shǒu dào bìng chú	illness departs at a touch of the hand; sickness retires at one's touch
手忙脚乱	shǒu máng jiǎo luàn	act with confusion; in a frantic rush; in a great bustle
手无寸铁	shǒu wú cùn tiě	bare-handed; unarmed
手无缚鸡之力	shǒu wú fù jī zhī lì	lack the strength to truss up a chicken; physically weak
手舞足蹈	shǒu wǔ zú dǎo	wave one's arms and stamp one's feet in joy
手下留情	shǒuxià liú qíng	hold one's hands; be lenient
手足无措	shǒuzú wú cuò	all in a fluster; be at a loss what to do

守 shǒu 丶 丶 宀 宀 守 守

释义 Meaning

动词 v.

1. guard; defend: 你在这儿守门，不要让任何人出去。 You keep the door here, don't let anybody go out. 反义词 antonym: 攻

2. observe; serve; abide to: 你不用担心，他是很守信用的。Don't worry, he is always as good as his word.

词语 Words and Phrases

守财奴	shǒucáinú	miser
守法	shǒufǎ	abide by the law; keep the law
守寡	shǒuguǎ	remain a widow; live in widowhood
守候	shǒuhòu	① wait for; expect ② keep watch
守旧	shǒujiù	adhere to past practices; be conservative

守军	shǒujūn	defending troops; defenders
守门	shǒumén	① be on duty at the door or gate ② goal keeper (soccer)
守卫	shǒuwèi	guard; defend
守信	shǒuxìn	keep one's word; abide by one's word
守则	shǒuzé	rules; regulations

熟语 Idioms

| 守口如瓶 | shǒu kǒu rú píng | keep one's mouth shut; breathe not a single word |
| 守株待兔 | shǒu zhū dài tù | stand by a stump waiting for more hares to come and dash themselves against it; trust to chance naively |

受 shòu 一 ⼂ ⺈ ⺈ ⻥ ⺈ 受 受

释义 Meaning

动词 v.

1. recieve; accept: 他受过高等教育。He has received a higher eduation.

2. suffer; be subjected to: 这样做会使国家经济受损失的。This will cause the country to suffer economic losses.

3. endure; bear: 他的脾气真够受的。His temper is hard to put up with.

词语 Words and Phrases

受害	shòuhài	suffer injury; fall victim
受累	shòulèi	be put to much trouble; be inconvenienced
受益	shòuyì	profit by; benefit from
承受	chéngshòu	endure; bear
感受	gǎnshòu	feel; experience

| 接受 | jiēshòu | accept |
| 享受 | xiǎngshòu | enjoy; enjoyment |

熟语 Idioms

| 自作自受 | zì zuò zì shòu | reap the fruits of one's action |

授 shòu 一 十 扌 扩 扩 扩 扩 扩 扩 授

释义 Meaning

动词 v.

award; confer; vest: 国家授他以英雄称号。The nation conferred upon him the title of being a hero.

词语 Words and Phrases

授课	shòukè	give lesssons
授奖	shòujiǎng	award a prize
授予	shòuyǔ	award; confer
传授	chuánshòu	pass on (knowledge, skill, etc.); teach
函授	hánshòu	give a correspondence course
教授	jiàoshòu	professor; teach

瘦 shòu 丶 亠 广 广 广 广 疒 疒 疒 疒 疒 痹 瘦 瘦

释义 Meaning

形容词 a.

1. thin; emaciated: 他比原来瘦了很多。He was much thinner than before. 反义词：胖

2. lean: 我要买瘦一点的肉。I want to buy some leaner meat. 反义词：肥

3. tight: 这件衣服我穿有点瘦。This clothing is a bit tight

for me. 反义词：肥

词语 Words and Phrases

瘦长	shòucháng	long and thin; tall and thin
瘦弱	shòuruò	thin and weak
瘦小	shòuxiǎo	thin and small
消瘦	xiāoshòu	become emaciated

熟语 Idioms

面黄肌瘦	miàn huáng jī shòu	pale and emaciated

书 shū ⁻ 乛 书 书

(書 ⁻ ⁻ ⁻ ⁻ 聿 聿 書 書 書 書)

释义 Meaning

名词 n.

1. book: 这是一本经济方面的书。This is a book on economics.
2. letter: 我正在写一封申请书。I am writing an application letter.

词语 Words and Phrases

书包	shūbāo	schoolbag
书本	shūběn	book
书店	shūdiàn	bookstore
书法	shūfǎ	calligraphy
书房	shūfáng	study
书籍	shūjí	books; works
书签	shūqiān	bookmark
书信	shūxìn	letter; written message
读书	dúshū	study; attend school
家书	jiāshū	a letter from home

| 念书 | niànshū | study; read |
| 证书 | zhèngshū | certificate |

叔 shū ㇕ ㇒ ㇔ ㇓ ㇓ ㇓ ㇔ 叔

释义 Meaning

名词 n.

father's younger brother; uncle: 他是我的三叔。He is my third uncle.

词语 Words and Phrases

叔父	shūfù	uncle; father's younger brother
叔叔	shūshu	uncle
大叔	dàshū	a form of address for a man about one's father's age

输 shū 一 ㇒ 车 车 车 轮 轮 轮 轮 轮 轮 轮 输

(輸 一 厂 ㇆ ㇆ 百 車 車 車 軠 軠 輸 輸 輸 輸 輸)

释义 Meaning

动词 v.

lose; be beaten: 这场篮球比赛，我们队输了。Our team lost this basketball game. 反义词：赢

词语 Words and Phrases

输出	shūchū	export; output
输入	shūrù	import; input
输送	shūsòng	carry; convey
输血	shūxiě	blood transfusion
输赢	shūyíng	lose or win

认输	rènshū	admit defeat; give up
运输	yùnshū	transport

熟 shú

丶 亠 广 亠 声 亯 亨 享 郭 孰
孰 孰 孰 熟 熟

释义 Meaning

形容词 a.

1. ripe: 桃子熟了。The peaches are ripe.

2. done; cooked: 米饭已经熟了。The rice is done.
   反义词：生

3. familiar: 这首歌听起来很熟。This song sounds familiar.
   反义词：生

4. skilled; experienced: 这个舞我练得很熟。I have learned this dance thoroughly.

5. deeply: 孩子睡熟了。The child was in a deep sleep.

词语 Words and Phrases

熟练	shúliàn	skilled; practised
熟人	shúrén	acquaintance; friend
熟识	shúshí	be well acquainted with
熟食	shúshí	prepared food; cooked food
熟悉	shúxī	know sth. or sb. well
熟知	shúzhī	know very well
成熟	chéngshú	ripe; mature
面熟	miànshú	look familiar

熟语 Idioms

熟能生巧	shúnéng shēng qiǎo	practice makes proficiency
熟视无睹	shú shì wú dǔ	pretending not to notice something

| 轻车熟路 | qīng chē shú lù | drive in a light car on a familiar road; make easy progress from experience |

术 shù 一 十 才 木 术

(術 ′ ′ イ 彳 彳 犳 犳 犲 犲 犲 犲 術)

释义 Meaning

名词 n.

art; technique: 他的医术很高明。He has excellent medical skills.

词语 Words and Phrases

术语	shùyǔ	technical terms
技术	jìshù	technology
美术	měishù	the fine arts
魔术	móshù	magic; conjuring
权术	quánshù	political trickery
手术	shǒushù	surgical operation
武术	wǔshù	Chinese martial arts
学术	xuéshù	learning; academic studies
艺术	yìshù	art
战术	zhànshù	military tactics

熟语 Idioms

| 不学无术 | bù xué wú shù | have neither learning nor skill |

束 shù 一 丆 百 百 审 束 束

释义 Meaning

（一）量词 measure w.

bundle; bunch: 他送我一束鲜花。He gave me a bundle of

flowers.

（二）动词 v.

bind; tie: 他腰上束着皮带。He wears a belt round his waist.

词语 Words and Phrases

束缚	shùfù	tie; bind up
束手	shùshǒu	have one's hands tied; be helpless
管束	guǎnshù	restrain; control
拘束	jūshù	constrained; ill at ease
约束	yuēshù	keep within bounds; restrain

熟语 Idioms

束手无策	shù shǒu wú cè	fold one's hands without knowing what to do; feel quite helpless
束之高阁	shù zhī gāo gé	bundle sh. up and put on the shelf; not to pay attention

树 shù 一 十 オ 木 杧 权 杈 树 树

（樹 一 十 オ 木 杧 杧 桂 桂 桔 桔 桔 桔 槌 槌 樹 樹）

释义 Meaning

（一）名词 n.

tree: 这是一棵苹果树。This is an apple tree.

（二）动词 v.

1. plant; cultivate: 俗话说，十年树木，百年树人。As the saying goes, it takes ten years to grow trees, but a hundred years to nurture people.

2. set up; establish: 我们应该树正气，压歪风。We should uphold healthy tendencies and suppress evil trends.

词语 Words and Phrases

树敌	shùdí	make an enemy of sb.
树干	shùgàn	tree trunk
树立	shùlì	set up; establish
树林	shùlín	woods; grove
树木	shùmù	trees
树枝	shùzhī	branch; twig
果树	guǒshù	fruit tree
建树	jiànshù	make a contribution

熟语 Idioms

树大招风	shù dà zhāo fēng	a big tree blocks the wind; a person in a high position is likely to attract envy
树倒猢狲散	shù dǎo hú sūn sàn	when the tree falls the monkeys scatter; rats leave a sinking ship

数₁ shǔ

数 shǔ ` ˇ ⺍ ⺣ ⺦ 米 ⺧ 娄 娄 娄 娄 数 数

（數 ｜ 冂 ⺆ ⺆ ⺕ ⺕ 冉 曲 婁 婁 婁 婁 數 數）

释义 Meaning

动词 v.

1. count: 两岁的小孩可以从一数到二十。A child of two can count from one to twenty.

2. be reckoned as exceptionally (good, bad, etc.): 全国数这个城市人口最多。This city is the most populated city in the country.

词语 Words and Phrases

数得着	shǔdézháo	be reckoned as outstanding, important, etc.
数落	shǔluo	(in oral speech) rebuke; reprove
数数	shǔshù	count

熟语 Idioms

数一数二	shǔ yī shǔ èr	be counted as one of the very best

数₂ shù 丶 ⺀ ⺰ ⺦ ⺦ ⺦ 娄 娄 娄 娄 娄 数 数

(數 丶 冂 冉 冉 冉 冉 昌 曲 婁 婁 婁 婁 婁 數 數**)**

释义 Meaning

名词 n.

1. number; figure: 这是个五位数。This is a five-figure number.
2. several; few: 参加比赛的有数百人。Several hundred people took part in the competition.

词语 Words and Phrases

数量	shùliàng	quantity
数目	shùmù	amount; number
数学	shùxué	mathematics
数位	shùwèi	numeral; figure
分数	fēnshù	mark; grade
无数	wúshù	innumerable; countless
总数	zǒngshù	sum total

熟语 Idioms

数以万计	shù yǐ wàn jì	be counted as tens of thousands
不计其数	bú jì qí shù	beyond count; innumerable

刷 shuā ⁻ ⁻ 尸 尸 月 吊 刷 刷

释义 Meaning

（一）名词 n.

brush: 我要买一把油漆刷。I want to buy a paintbrush.

（二）动词 v.

1. brush; scrub: 他在刷鞋子。He is polishing the shoes.

2. paste up: 墙还没刷好。The wall has not been whitewashed yet.

词语 Words and Phrases

刷洗	shuāxǐ	scrub
刷新	shuāxīn	① renovate; refurbish ② break (a record, etc.)
刷牙	shuāyá	brush one's teeth
刷子	shuāzi	brush; scrub

双 shuāng ㄱ 又 邓 双

(雙 ′ 亻 亻 亻 亻 仹 佳 隹 倠 倠 倠 倠 倠 倠 倠 雙 雙)

释义 Meaning

（一）量词 measure w.

pair: 这双鞋好看吗？Is this pair of shoes nice?

（二）形容词 a.

two; both: 他事业爱情双丰收。He did well both in work

and love.

词语 Words and Phrases

双胞胎	shuāngbāotāi	twins
双层	shuāngcéng	double-deck; having two layers
双方	shuāngfāng	both sides; the two parties
双号	shuānghào	even numbers (of tickets, seats, etc.)
双亲	shuāngqīn	(both) parents
双手	shuāngshǒu	both hands
双数	shuāngshù	even numbers
双双	shuāngshuāng	in pairs
双职工	shuāngzhígōng	working couple

熟语 Idioms

双管齐下	shuāng guǎn qí xià	paint a picture with two brushes at the same time; double the efficiency

谁 shuí ` 讠 讠 讠 讠 讠 讠 谁 谁

（誰 ` 二 亠 言 言 言 言 訂 訂 訂 訐 訅 誰 誰）

释义 Meaning

代词 pron.

1. who: 你找谁？Who are you looking for?
2. someone; anyone: 谁爱去，谁就去。Whoever wants to go can go.

水 shuǐ 亅 刁 水 水

释义 Meaning

名词 n.

water: 请给我倒杯水。Please pour me a cup of water.

词语 Words and Phrases

水产	shuǐchǎn	aquatic product
水分	shuǐfèn	moisture content; exaggeration
水果	shuǐguǒ	fruit
水流	shuǐliú	flow; current
水陆	shuǐlù	land and water
水平	shuǐpíng	level; standard
水乡	shuǐxiāng	a region of rivers and lakes
水运	shuǐyùn	water transport
水准	shuǐzhǔn	level; standard
降水	jiàngshuǐ	precipitation

熟语 Idioms

水到渠成	shuǐ dào qú chéng	where water flows, a channel is completed; success will come when conditions are ripe
水滴石穿	shuǐ dī shí chuān	drops of water outwear the stone; constant effort brings success
水乳交融	shuǐ rǔ jiāo róng	mix milk with water; in complete harmony

睡 shuì　丨　丨丨　丨丨　丨丨　丨丨　丨厂　丨厂　丨开　丨开　睡 睡 睡 睡

释义 Meaning

动词 v.

sleep: 他一觉睡到天亮。It was daylight when he woke up.

词语 Words and Phrases

睡觉	shuìjiào	sleep
睡梦	shuìmèng	sleep; slumber
睡眠	shuìmián	sleep

睡醒	shuìxǐng	wake up
睡衣	shuìyī	night clothes; pajamas
睡意	shuìyì	sleepiness; drowsiness
入睡	rùshuì	go to sleep; fall asleep

顺 shùn 丿 丿 川 厂 厂 厂 顺 顺 顺

(順 丿 丿 川 厂 厂 厂 順 順 順 順 順 順)

释义 Meaning

（一）形容词 a.

smooth, without a hitch: 这几年他一直很顺。His life has been very smooth these few years.

（二）动词 v.

1. along; in the same direction as: 顺着这条路走到头，就是银行。Walk along this road till the end, you will find the bank.

2. obey; yield to: 不能事事顺着孩子。We can't obey the children's wish in every thing.

3. suitable; agreeable: 最近他的表现很不顺我的意。What he has done lately does not meet my expectations

4. arrange; put in order: 我的思路很乱，要顺一顺。My train of thought is very confused, so I need to organize it.

词语 Words and Phrases

顺便	shùnbiàn	conveniently; in passing
顺从	shùncóng	be obedient to; submit to
顺风	shùnfēng	have a tail wind
顺口	shùnkòu	say offhandedly; read smoothly
顺利	shùnlì	smoothly; successfully

顺路	shùnlù	on the way; direct route
顺水	shùnshuǐ	downstream
顺心	shùnxīn	satisfactory
顺序	shùnxù	order; sequence
孝顺	xiàoshùn	show filial obedience

熟语 Idioms

顺理成章	shùn lǐ chéng zhāng	to write well, you must follow a logical train of thought
顺水推舟	shùn shuǐ tuī zhōu	drift with the current; follow the line of least resistance
顺藤摸瓜	shùn téng mō guā	look for the melon by following the vine; search for sb. or sth. by following the clues
一帆风顺	yì fān fēng shùn	plain sailing; very smoothly

说 shuō `ˋ 讠 讠ˋ 讠ˊ 讠ˊ 讱 讱 讱 说

（説 `ˋ ˊ ˊ 言 言 言 訁 訁ˊ 訁ˊ 訁ˊ
訁 訁 説）

释义 Meaning

动词 v.

1. speak; say: 请你慢点儿说。Please speak more slowly.

2. explain: 我一说，他就明白了。He understood me after my explanation.

3. scold: 爸爸说了我一顿。My father gave me a scolding.

词语 Words and Phrases

| 说不定 | shuōbúdìng | perhaps; maybe |
| 说不上 | shuōbúshàng | ① cannot say; cannot tell ② not |

worth mentioning

说法	shuōfǎ	way of saying a thing; statement; version
说服	shuōfú	persuade; convince
说话	shuōhuà	speak; talk
说明	shuōmíng	① explain; illustrate ② explanation; directions
说笑	shuōxiào	chatting and laughing
传说	chuánshuō	it is said; legend
据说	jùshuō	allegedly; they say
难说	nánshuō	hard to say
学说	xuéshuō	theory; doctrine

熟语 Idioms

| 说来话长 | shuō lái huà cháng | it's a long story |
| 说一不二 | shuō yī bú èr | be true to one's words; play the tyrant |

私 sī　　一　二　千　禾　禾　私　私

释义 Meaning

形容词 a.

private: 我不了解他的私生活。I don't know his private life.

词语 Words and Phrases

私交	sījiāo	personal friendship
私立	sīlì	privately run
私人	sīrén	private; personal
私事	sīshì	private affairs
私下	sīxià	in secret; in private
私心	sīxīn	selfish motives; selfishness
私有	sīyǒu	privately owned

私自	sīzì	secretly; without permission
无私	wúsī	unselfish
隐私	yǐnsī	privacy
自私	zìsī	selfish

熟语 Idioms

| 大公无私 | dà gōng wúsī | selfless; perfectly impartial |

死 sǐ   二 厂 歹 歹 歼 死

释义 Meaning

（一）动词 v.

die: 这棵树死了。This tree has died. 反义词：活

（二）副词 adv.

1. extremely; to death: 我热死了。I am terribly hot.

2. firmly; resolutely: 他死不服输。He resolutely denies defeat.

（三）形容词 a.

1. fixed; inflexible: 他读书很死。He studies very mechanically. 反义词：活

2. impassable; closed: 别往前走了，这是一条死胡同。Don't go ahead, this is a blind alley.

3. deadly; implacable: 他们俩是死对头。They two are sworn enemies.

词语 Words and Phrases

死板	sǐbǎn	rigid; inflexible
死党	sǐdǎng	sworn brothers
死路	sǐlù	the road to destruction; blind alley
死亡	sǐwáng	death; doom
死心	sǐxīn	drop the idea forever
生死	shēngsǐ	life and death

熟语 Idioms

死得其所	sǐ dé qí suǒ	die a worthy death
死记硬背	sǐ jì yìng bèi	learn by rote
死里逃生	sǐ lǐ táo shēng	have a narrow escape
死去活来	sǐ qù huó lái	hovering between death and life

四 sì 丨 冂 四 四 四

释义 Meaning

数词 numeral

four: 我家有四口人。There are four people in my family.

词语 Words and Phrases

四处	sìchù	all around; everywhere
四季	sìjì	the four seasons
四面	sìmiàn	(on) four sides
四声	sìshēng	the four tones of Chinese pronunciation of a character
四月	sìyuè	April
四周	sìzhōu	all around

熟语 Idioms

四分五裂	sì fēn wǔ liè	be scattered and disunited; badly split
四面楚歌	sìmiàn chǔ gē	be hemmed in by enemy troops; be completely isolated
四平八稳	sì píng bā wěn	steady and sure; not to take even a minor risk
四通八达	sì tōng bā dá	in all directions; communication lines reaching far and wide

似 sì 丿 亻 亻 似 似 似

释义 Meaning

动词 v.

1. like; similar: 骄阳似火。The sun was scorching hot.

2. seem; appear: 我们俩似曾相识。We two seem to have met before.

3. than: 他的病一天好过一天。His illness is getting better day by day.

词语 Words and Phrases

似乎	sìhū	it seems; as if
类似	lèisì	similar; analogous
胜似	shèngsì	be better than; surpass
相似	xiāngsì	be alike; resemble
似的	sìde	be similar to

熟语 Idioms

似是而非　sì shì ér fēi　　appears right but actually wrong

松₁ sōng 　二　十　扌　朩　朳　朳　松　松

（鬆　一　厂　严　严　镸　镸　镸　髟　髟　髟　髟　髟　髟　髟　鬏　鬏　鬏）

释义 Meaning

（一）形容词 a.

1. loose; slack: 这里的土很松。The soil here is very loose.
反义词：紧

2. not hard up: 最近他手头比较松。He has been quite better off recently. 反义词：紧

（二）动词 v.

relax; relieve: 现在我可以松一口气了。Now I can have

a breathing spell.

词语 Words and Phrases

松弛	sōngchí	flabby; lax
松口	sōngkǒu	relax one's bite and release what is held; be less intransigent
松气	sōngqì	relax one's effort
松软	sōngruǎn	soft; spongy
松散	sōngsǎn	relax; take ease
松鼠	sōngshǔ	squirrel
松树	sōngshù	pine tree
松懈	sōngxiè	slacken; slack
放松	fàngsōng	relax; slacken
轻松	qīngsōng	light; relaxed

松₂ sōng ⼀ ⼗ ⼨ ⼨ ⼯ ⼨ 松 松

释义 Meaning

名词 n.

the name of pine tree: 庙前有一棵千年古松。There grows an old pine tree of a thousand years in front of the temple.

送 sòng ⼀ ⼀ ⼀ ⼀ 兰 关 关 关 送 送

释义 Meaning

动词 v.

1. give as a gift: 他送我一件礼物。He gave me a gift.

2. deliver; carry: 我要去给他送一封信。I am going to deliver a letter to him.

3. see sb. off or out: 我要去机场送姐姐。I am going to the airport to see my elder sister off.

词语 Words and Phrases

送别	sòngbié	see sb. off
送货	sònghuò	deliver goods
送礼	sònglǐ	present sb. a gift
送信儿	sòngxìnr	send word; go and tell
送行	sòngxíng	give sb. a send-off party
发送	fāsòng	transimit by radio; dispatch (letters, etc.)
欢送	huānsòng	see off; send off
目送	mùsòng	follow sb. with one's eyes; watch sb. go
赠送	zèngsòng	present (as a gift)

酸 suān 一 厂 厂 厅 丙 西 西 酉 酉 酉 酉 酸 酸 酸 酸

释义 Meaning

形容词 a.

1. sour: 这橘子很酸。The tangerine is very sour.

2. grieved; sick at heart: 他鼻子一酸，流下了眼泪。His nose smarted and he began to weep.

3. tingle; ache: 我觉得腰很酸。I have a pain on the back.

词语 Words and Phrases

酸楚	suānchǔ	grieved; distressed
酸奶	suānnǎi	yoghurt; sour milk
酸痛	suāntòng	ache
酸味	suānwèi	tart flavour
酸枣	suānzǎo	wild jujube
寒酸	hánsuān	miserable and shabby
辛酸	xīnsuān	sad; bitter

算 suàn ／ ／ ／ ／ ／ ／ 竹 竹 竹 管 管 管 管 算 算

释义 Meaning

动词 v.

1. calculate; compute: 我要算一下旅行的费用。I will calculate the cost of the journey.

2. include; count: 算你在内，一共十个人。There are ten people including you.

3. count as; consider: 这次考试很难，七十分已经算很不错了。The examnation was very difficult, to get a mark of seventy was considered fairly good.

4. count; carry weight: 世界上的事不应该由两个国家说了算。One or two powers should not have the final say on world affairs.

词语 Words and Phrases

演算法	yǎnsuànfǎ	a logarithm
算命	suànmìng	fortune-telling
算是	suànshì	at last
算术	suànshù	arithmetic
算数	suànshù	count; stand
打算	dǎsuàn	plan; intend
失算	shīsuàn	miscalculate; be injudicious
总算	zǒngsuàn	at long last; finally
算了	suànle	let it be; let it pass

虽 suī ˋ 冂 冂 尸 吕 吕 虽 虽 虽

(雖 ˋ 冂 冂 尸 吕 吕 虽 虽 虽 雖 雖 雖 雖 雖 雖 雖)

释义 Meaning

连词 conj.

though; even if: 他年纪虽小，但很懂事。Although he is young, he is very sensible.

词语 Words and Phrases

虽然　　suīrán　　though; although
虽说　　suīshuō　　though

岁 suì ｜ ｜ ｜ ｌ ｐ 岁 岁

(歲 ｜ ｜ ｌ ｌ ｌ ｐ 芦 芦 芦 芦 蔗 歲 歲 歲）

释义 Meaning

名词 n.

1. year (of age): 他今年三十二岁。He is thirty-two years old this year.

2. year: 辞旧岁，迎新年。Ring out the Old Year and ring in the New.

词语 Words and Phrases

岁末　　suìmò　　the end of the year
岁首　　suìshǒu　　the beginning of the year
岁数　　suìshù　　age; years
岁月　　suìyuè　　years
年岁　　niánsuì　　age; years

碎 suì ｜ ｜ ｌ ｌ 石 石 矿 矿 矿 矿 碎 碎 碎

释义 Meaning

形容词 a.

1. smashed; broken: 鸡蛋都碎了。All the eggs were smashed.
2. gabby: 少说两句，嘴别太碎。Speak little, don't be so garrulous.

词语 Words and Phrases

碎嘴子	suìzuǐzi	a garrulous person
粉碎	fěnsuì	broken to pieces; smash
破碎	pòsuì	tattered; broken
琐碎	suǒsuì	trifling; trivial

熟语 Idioms

宁为玉碎，不为瓦全	nìng wéi yùsuì, bù wéi wǎquán	rather be a shattered vessel of jade than an unbroken piece of pottery; better to die with honor than survive with guilt

所 suǒ ⎯ 厂 斤 斤 斤 所 所 所

释义 Meaning

(一) 名词 n.

institute: 他在一家研究所上班。He is working in a research institute.

(二) 量词 measure w.

used for a school, hospital, house, etc.: 我家附近有所中学。There is a middle school near my home.

(三) 代词 pron.

1. used before a verb, and the verb should be followed by the word which accepts the action: 我被他的精神所感动。I was moved by his spirit.
2. used before a verb, and the verb is followed by "者" or

"的" which stands for the things that accept the action: 这就是我所知道的。This is all that I know.

词语 Words and Phrases

所长	suǒcháng	what one is good at; one's forte
所得	suǒdé	income; gains
所谓	suǒwèi	so-called; what is called
所以	suǒyǐ	so; therefore
所有	suǒyǒu	all; possessions; possess
所在	suǒzài	place; location
场所	chángsuǒ	place; arena
处所	chùsuǒ	location
住所	zhùsuǒ	residence; domicile

熟语 Idioms

所向披靡	suǒ xiàng pī mǐ	(of troops) sweep away all obstacles

他 tā 　ノ　亻　仁　仲　他

释义 Meaning

代词 pron.

1. he: 他是教师。He is a teacher.

2. be used in a general sense: 一个人如果没有朋友，他将在孤独中度过一生。Whoever has no friends will spend his life in loneliness.

词语 Words and Phrases

他们	tāmen	they
他人	tārén	another person; others
他日	tārì	some day; later on
他乡	tāxiāng	a place far away from home
吉他	jítā	guitar
其他	qítā	other; else

她 tā　　ㄥ　ㄥ　ㄥ　如　她

释义 Meaning

代词 pron.

　she; her: 她和她父母住在一起。She lives with her parents.

词语 Words and Phrases

　她们　　　　tāmen　　　　(used for females) they; them

它 tā　　、　、　宀　宀　它

释义 Meaning

代词 pron.

　it: 这只狗很凶，别碰它。This dog is very fierce, don't
　bother it.

词语 Words and Phrases

　它们　　　　tāmen　　　　they (refers to things except people)

台₁ tāi　　ㄥ　ㄥ　台　台　台

anything shaped like a platform, stage, etc.: 我的写字台放
在窗边。My writing desk is placed beside the window.

台₂ tái　　ㄥ　ㄥ　台　台　台

（臺　一　士　吉　吉　吉　吉　声　声　喜　喜　喜
　壹　臺　臺）

释义 Meaning

(一) 名词 n.

1. stage; terrace: 他激动地走上了台去领奖。In great
   excitement, he walked on to the stage to receive the award.
2. broadcasting station: 你知道中央电视台在哪儿吗？Do
   you know where the Central Television Station is located?

（二）量词 measure w.

used for a machine, performance, etc.: 我有两台电脑。I have two computers.

词语 Words and Phrases

台词	táicí	actor's lines
台灯	táidēng	desk lamp
台风	táifēng	typhoon; manner on stage
台阶	táijiē	a flight of steps; stage
台球	táiqiú	billiards
台湾	táiwān	Taiwan
电台	diàntái	broadcasting station
柜台	guìtái	counter
后台	hòutái	backstage; backstage supporter
舞台	wǔtái	arena; stage

抬 tái　　二 十 扌 扩 护 拌 抬 抬

释义 Meaning

动词 v.

lift; carry: 你帮我把桌子抬出去，好吗？Can you help me carry the table outside?

词语 Words and Phrases

抬杠	táigàng	argue for the sake of arguing
抬举	táijǔ	praise or promote sb. to show favour; favour sb.
抬头	táitóu	raise one's head; look up; rise

太 tài　　二 プ 大 太

释义 Meaning

副词 adv.

1. excessively; too: 天气太热了。It's too hot!

2. extremely (used in praise): 真是太感谢你了！I'm really grateful to you!

3. very (used in a negative sentence): 上司对他的工作不太满意。His boss was not very satisfied with his work.

词语 Words and Phrases

太公	tàigōng	great-grandfather
太后	tàihòu	mother of an emperor
太空	tàikōng	outer space
太极拳	tàijíquán	a kind of martial arts called *taichi*
太平	tàipíng	peace and tranquility
太平洋	tàipíngyáng	the Pacific Ocean
太太	tàitai	madam; the mistress of a household
太阳	tàiyáng	the sun; sunshine
太子	tàizǐ	crown prince

谈 tán

（谈 `丶亠亠言言言言言諮諮諮諮諮谈）

释义 Meaning

（一）动词 v.

　　talk; chat: 他们谈了一个下午。They've talked for a whole afternoon.

（二）名词 n.

　　what is said or talked about: 他的话纯属无稽之谈。What he said was sheer nonsense.

词语 Words and Phrases

谈话	tánhuà	conversation; talk
谈论	tánlùn	discuss; talk about
谈判	tánpàn	negotiations; talks

谈天	tántiān	chat
谈心	tánxīn	heart-to-heart talk
交谈	jiāotán	talk with each other
美谈	měitán	a story passed on with approval
奇谈	qítán	strange tale
洽谈	qiàtán	chat; engage in chit-chat

熟语 Idioms

谈虎色变	tán hǔ sè biàn	turn pale at the mention of a tiger; be easily scared
谈笑风声	tán xiào fēng shēng	talk in a happy manner
高谈阔论	gāotán kuò lùn	talk in a lofty strain; harangue

汤 tāng ` ` 氵 氻 汤 汤

（湯 ` ` 氵 氵 氵 氵 氵 湡 湡 湯 湯 湯）

释义 Meaning

名词 n.

soup; broth: 喝一碗汤吧。Please have a bowl of soup.

词语 Words and Phrases

汤包	tāngbāo	steamed dumplings filled with minced meat and gravy
汤匙	tāngchí	soup spoon
汤面	tāngmiàn	noodles in soup
汤勺	tāngsháo	soup ladle
汤药	tāngyào	a decoction of medicinal ingredients
汤圆	tāngyuán	stuffed dumplings made of glutinous rice flour served in soup

糖 táng ` ` ` ` 丷 半 米 米 米 籵 籵 籵

粝 粝 糒 糒 糖 糖

释义 Meaning

名词 n.

1. sugar: 做菜有时要放一点糖。A little sugar is needed in cooking sometimes.
2. sweets; candy: 他给了孩子一颗糖。He gave the child a piece of candy.

词语 Words and Phrases

糖醋	tángcù	sugar and vinegar; sweet and sour
糖果	tángguǒ	sweets; candy
糖水	tángshuǐ	syrup; a kind of Cantonese desert
白糖	báitáng	refined sugar
冰糖	bīngtáng	crystal sugar
砂糖	shātáng	granulated sugar
蔗糖	zhètáng	cane sugar

躺 tǎng ′ ⺆ 勹 勹 勹 身 身 身′ 身′ 身″ 躯″ 躳 躳 躺 躺

释义 Meaning

动词 v.

lie; recline: 他躺在床上。He is lying in bed.

词语 Words and Phrases

躺倒	tǎngdǎo	lie down
躺椅	tǎngyǐ	deck chair
躺下	tǎngxià	lie down

掏 tāo 一 十 扌 扩 扪 扪 扪 掏 掏 掏

释义 Meaning

动词 v.

1. draw out; pull out: 他口袋里掏出一盒烟。He drew a box of cigarettes out of his pocket.
2. steal from sb.'s pocket: 他的钱包被人掏了。He had his wallet stolen by a pickpocket.

词语 Words and Phrases

掏腰包	tāo yāo bāo	pay out of one's own pocket; pick sb.'s pocket

逃 táo ノ ノ ジ 丬 儿 北 兆 兆 逃 逃

释义 Meaning

动词 v.

run away; escape; flee: 一只猴子从动物园里逃了出来。A monkey escaped from the zoo.

词语 Words and Phrases

逃避	táobì	escape; evade; shirk
逃兵	táobīng	army deserter; deserter
逃荒	táohuāng	flee from famine
逃命	táomìng	run for one's life
逃难	táonàn	flee from a calamity; be a refugee
逃跑	táopǎo	run away; flee; take flight
逃生	táoshēng	flee for one's life; escape with one's life
逃税	táoshuì	evade tax; tax evasion
逃脱	táotuō	succeed in escaping; make good one's escape; get clear of
逃亡	táowáng	become a fugitive; flee from home; go into exile
逃学	táoxué	play truant; cut class
逃走	táozǒu	run away; flee; take flight

熟语 Idioms

逃之夭夭　　táo zhī yāo yāo　　decamp; slip away

讨 tǎo 　 丶 讠 讠 计 讨

(討 丶 亠 亠 言 言 言 言 言 討 討)

释义 Meaning

动词 v.

1. demand; ask for: 我去跟老张讨点墨汁。I'm going to ask Lao Zhang for some Chinese ink.
2. marry: 他三十岁了还没讨上老婆。He is 30 years old already, but hasn't yet found a wife.
3. incur; invite: 这小女孩真讨人喜欢！What a cute little girl!

词语 Words and Phrases

讨伐	tǎofá	send a punitive expedition against
讨饭	tǎofàn	beg for food; be a beggar
讨好	tǎohǎo	① ingratiate oneself with; fawn on ② be rewarded with a fruitful result
讨教	tǎojiào	ask for advice
讨论	tǎolùn	discuss; talk over
讨巧	tǎoqiǎo	act artfully to get what one wants; choose the easy way out
讨厌	tǎoyàn	① disagreeable; disgusting ② hard to handle; nasty ③ dislike; loathe
讨债	tǎozhài	demand repayment of a loan

熟语 Idioms

讨价还价　　tǎo jià huán jià　　bargain; chaffer

套 tào 　 二 广 广 夳 夲 夲 奎 套 套 套

释义 Meaning

（一）名词 n.

1. cover; sleeve; sheath: 椅子套都已经磨破了。 The slip-cover of the chair is already worn out.

2. convention; formula: 说来说去都是老一套。 What has been repeated again and again is the same old stuff.

（二）动词 v.

1. cover with; slip on: 外边冷，套上件毛衣再出去。 It's cold outside, slip on a sweater before you go out.

2. coax a secret out of sb.: 他不停地拿话套她。 He tricked her into telling the truth all the time.

（三）量词 measure w.

set; suit; suite: 他今天穿了一套新军装。 He is wearing a new suit of military dress today.

词语 Words and Phrases

套车	tàochē	harness an animal to a cart
套购	tàogòu	fraudulently purchase
套话	tàohuà	polite, conventional verbal exchanges
套间	tàojiān	apartment; flat
套衫	tàoshān	pullover
套用	tàoyòng	apply mechanically; use indiscriminately
套子	tàozi	sheath; case; cover

特 tè ′ ⹇ 牛 牛 牜 牜 牜 牜 特 特

释义 Meaning

副词 adv.

1. special; particular; unusual: 我今天特别高兴。 I am particularly joyful today.

2. for a special purpose; specially: 听说你病了，我特来看看你。 I heard you were sick, so I came specially to see you.

词语 Words and Phrases

特别	tèbié	① out of the ordinary; special ② particularly; especially
特产	tèchǎn	special local product; specialty
特长	tècháng	what one is skilled in; strong point
特此	tècǐ	hereby
特地	tèdì	for a special purpose; specially
特点	tèdiǎn	characteristic; distinguishing feature; peculiarity
特定	tèdìng	① specially appointed; specially designated ② given; specified
特惠	tèhuì	indulgence
特级	tèjí	special grade; superfine
特急	tèjí	extra urgent
特技	tèjì	① stunt; trick ② special effects
特价	tèjià	special offer; bargain price
特快	tèkuài	express
特权	tèquán	privilege; prerogative
特色	tèsè	characteristic; distinguishing feature
特使	tèshǐ	special envoy
特殊	tèshū	special; particular; peculiar; exceptional
特务	tèwù	special agent; spy
特效	tèxiào	specially effect
特性	tèxìng	specific property
特有	tèyǒu	peculiar; characteristic
特约	tèyuē	engaged by special arrangement
特征	tèzhēng	characteristic; feature; trait

特种　　　tèzhǒng　　　special type; particular kind

疼 téng　　`　亠　广　疒　疒　疒　疒　疼　疼　疼

释义 Meaning

动词 v.

1. ache; pain; sore: 我胃疼得厉害。I have a severe stomachache.
2. love dearly; be fond of: 奶奶最疼小孙子。Granny dotes on her little grandson.

词语 Words and Phrases

疼爱　　　téng'ài　　　be very fond of; love dearly

疼痛　　　téngtòng　　　pain; ache; soreness

踢 tī　　丨　冂　口　𠯻　𠯻　𧾷　𧾷　𧾷　𧾷　𧾷　𧾷　𧾷　跔　踢　踢

释义 Meaning

动词 v.

kick: 这场比赛他踢进了三个球。He kicked three goals in this match.

词语 Words and Phrases

踢踏舞　　　tī tā wǔ　　　step dance; tap dance

熟语 Idioms

踢皮球　　　tī píqiú　　　① play children's football ② pass the buck

提 tí　　一　十　扌　扌　护　护　护　捍　捍　捍　捍　提

释义 Meaning

动词 v.

1. carry in one's hand: 他正提着水桶往家走。He is on his way home carrying a bucket in his hand.
2. lift; raise; promote: 汽油已经提价三次了。The price of petrol has been raised three times already.
3. put forward; bring up; raise: 我们提了不少意见和建议。We made a lot of comments and suggestions.
4. mention; refer to: 别再提那件事了。Don't bring that up again.

词语 Words and Phrases

提案	tí'àn	motion; proposal; draft resolution
提拔	tíbá	promote
提包	tíbāo	handbag; shopping bag
提倡	tíchàng	advocate; promote; encourage; recommend
提成	tíchéng	deduct a percentage (from a sum of money)
提出	tíchū	put forward; advance; pose; raise
提法	tífǎ	the way sth. is put; formulation; wording
提纲	tígāng	outline
提高	tígāo	raise; heighten; increase; improve
提供	tígōng	provide; supply; offer
提货	tíhuò	pick up goods; take delivery of goods
提交	tíjiāo	submit to; refer to
提炼	tíliàn	extract and purify; refine
提名	tímíng	nominate
提起	tíqǐ	① mention; speak of ② raise; arouse; brace up

提前	tíqián	① shift to an earlier date; move up ② in advance; ahead of time
提亲	tíqīn	a match-making; talk about marriage
提琴	tíqín	musical instruments of the violin family
提取	tíqǔ	① draw; pick up ② extract; abstract
提神	tíshén	refresh oneself; give oneself a lift
提升	tíshēng	promote; advance
提示	tíshì	point out; prompt
提问	tíwèn	put question to; quiz
提醒	tíxǐng	remind; warn
提要	tíyào	summary; abstract; epitome; synopsis
提议	tíyì	① propose; suggest ② proposal; motion
提早	tízǎo	shift to an earlier time; be earlier than planned or expected

熟语 Idioms

| 提纲挈领 | tí gāng qiè lǐng | bring out the most essential points |
| 提心吊胆 | tí xīn diào dǎn | have one's heart in one's mouth; be filled with anxiety |

题 tí

丨 冂 日 日 旦 早 早 昰 是 是 旲 旲 题 题 题

(題

丨 冂 日 日 旦 早 早 昰 是 是 旲 題 題 題 題 題 題)

释义 Meaning

名词 n.

topic; subject; title; problem: 你知道第三题的答案吗？

Do you know the answer of the third question?

词语 Words and Phrases

题材	tícái	subject matter; theme
题词	tící	① write an inscription ② inscription
题名	tímíng	① autograph ② title; subject
题目	tímù	① title; subject; topic ② exercise problems; examination questions
题字	tízì	inscription; autograph

体 tǐ　　ノ　亻　仁　什　伫　休　体

(體　丨　冂　甲　冊　冎　凸　骨　骨　骨　骨

骨　骨　骨　骨　骨　骨　骨　骨　骨　骨　體)

释义 Meaning

名词 n.

1. body; part of the body: 这条船的船体是用水泥造的。
   The body of this boat is made of cement.

2. state of the substance; form; type: 零度以下，水就变成固体了。Water becomes solid when the temperature drops below zero.

词语 Words and Phrases

体裁	tǐcái	types or forms of literature
体操	tǐcāo	gymnastics
体罚	tǐfá	physical punishment; corporal punishment
体格	tǐgé	physique; build
体会	tǐhuì	know from experience; realize
体积	tǐjī	volume; bulk
体力	tǐlì	physical strength; physical power

体谅	tǐliàng	show understanding and sympathy for; make allowances for
体面	tǐmiàn	① dignity; face ② honourable; creditable; respectable
体魄	tǐpò	physique
体态	tǐtài	posture; carriage
体贴	tǐtiē	show consideration for; give every care to
体温	tǐwēn	bodily temperature
体系	tǐxì	system; setup
体现	tǐxiàn	embody; incarnate; reflect; give expression to
体型	tǐxíng	type of build or figure
体验	tǐyàn	learn through one's personal experience
体育	tǐyù	physical culture; physical training; sports
体制	tǐzhì	system of organization; system
体质	tǐzhì	physique; constitution
体重	tǐzhòng	weight

熟语 Idioms

体无完肤	tǐ wú wán fū	① have cuts and bruises all over the body ② be refuted down to the last point

替 tì

一 二 扌 孝 夫一 夫二 扶 扶 扶 替 替 替

释义 Meaning

(一) 动词 v.

take the place of; replace; substitute for: 你歇会儿，我来替你。Have a rest, I'll take over.

（二）介词 prep.

for; on behalf of: 你也替我买一本词典吧。Please buy a dictionary for me as well.

词语 Words and Phrases

替代	tìdài	substitute for; replace; supersede
替换	tìhuàn	replace; substitute for; take the place of
替身	tìshēn	substitute; replacement; stand-in

熟语 Idioms

替死鬼	tìsǐguǐ	scapegoat; fall guy
替罪羊	tìzuìyáng	scapegoat

天tiān　二 三 于 天

释义 Meaning

名词 n.

1. sky; heaven: 白云在蓝天上飘浮。The white clouds are floating in the blue sky.
2. day: 我过两天跟你联系。I'll make contact with you after a few days.
3. time; a period of time in a day: 天不早了，我该走了。It's getting late, I have to go now.
4. weather: 天要下雨了。It's going to rain.

词语 Words and Phrases

天边	tiānbiān	horizon; the ends of the earth
天才	tiāncái	① talent; genius; gifted ② man of genius
天窗	tiānchuāng	skylight
天地	tiāndì	① heaven and earth; universe; world ② field of activity; scope of operation
天鹅	tiān'é	swan

天井	tiānjǐng	small yard; courtyard
天空	tiānkōng	the sky; the heavens
天蓝	tiānlán	sky blue; azure
天理	tiānlǐ	justice
天平	tiānpíng	balance; scales
天气	tiānqì	weather
天然	tiānrán	natural
天生	tiānshēng	born; inborn; inherent; innate
天使	tiānshǐ	angel
天堂	tiāntáng	paradise; heaven
天体	tiāntǐ	celestical body
天天	tiāntiān	every day; daily
天文	tiānwén	astronomy
天下	tiānxià	① land under heaven; world ② rule; domination
天线	tiānxiàn	aerial; antenna
天性	tiānxìng	natural instincts; nature
天涯	tiānyá	the end of the world; the remotest corner of the earth
天灾	tiānzāi	natural disaster
天真	tiānzhēn	innocent; artless; naive
天子	tiānzǐ	the emperor; the Son of Heaven

熟语 Idioms

天崩地裂	tiān bēng dì liè	heaven falling and earth cracking; violent (political or social) upheavals
天不怕，地不怕	tiān bú pà, dì bú pà	defy heaven and earth; fear nothing at all
天长地久	tiān cháng dì jiǔ	as long as the heaven and earth endure; everlasting and unchanging

天赐良机	tiān cì liáng jī	a godsend chance
天翻地覆	tiān fān dì fù	the sky and the earth turning upside down; earth-shaking
天各一方	tiān gè yì fāng	living in a different corner of the world; separated
天寒地冻	tiān hán dì dòng	the weather is cold and the ground is frozen
天花乱坠	tiān huā luàn zhuì	as if it were raining flowers; in extravagant terms
天昏地暗	tiān hūn dì àn	a murky heaven over a dark earth; gloomy above and dark below
天经地义	tiān jīng dì yì	according to the principles of heaven and earth; perfectly justified
天罗地网	tiān luó dì wǎng	an escape-proof net
天马行空	tiān mǎ xíng kōng	a heavenly steed soaring across the skies; a powerful and unconstrained style
天南海北	tiān nán hǎi běi	① all over the country ② rambling
天壤之别	tiān rǎng zhī bié	a whale of a difference; poles apart
天网恢恢	tiān wǎng huī huī	the net of Heaven has large meshes, but it lets nothing through; God comes with leaden feet, but strikes with iron hands
天无绝人之路	tiān wú jué rén zhī lù	Heaven never let people down so long he preserves
天下乌鸦一般黑	tiān xià wū yā yì bān hēi	all crows are black in colour; some people are bad all over the world
天旋地转	tiān xuán dì zhuàn	the sky and earth are spinning round; very dizzy

天有不	tiān yǒu bú	a blustering night, a fair
测风云	cè fēng yún	day; sth. unexpected may
		happen any time
天之骄子	tiān zhī jiāo zǐ	God's favored one; an un-
		usually blessed person
天诛地灭	tiān zhū dì miè	be destroyed by heaven
		and earth; God forbid

添 tiān 　`丶丶氵氵氵氵氵添添添添

释义 Meaning

动词 v.

add; increase; have more: 给你们添麻烦了，真不好意
思。Sorry to have troubled you.

词语 Words and Phrases

| 添加 | tiānjiā | add to; increase |
| 添置 | tiānzhì | add to one's possessions; acquire |

熟语 Idioms

| 添油加醋 | tiān yóu jiā cù | add color and emphasis to (a narration); play up |
| 添砖加瓦 | tiān zhuān jiā wǎ | add bricks and tiles; do what little one can to help |

甜 tián 　一二千千舌舌舌甜甜甜甜

释义 Meaning

形容词 a.

1. sweet; honeyed: 蜂蜜是甜的。Honey is sweet.
2. sound: 昨晚我睡得很甜。I had a sound sleep last night.

词语 Words and Phrases

甜菜	tiáncài	beet
甜美	tiánměi	① sweet; luscious ② pleasant; refreshing
甜蜜	tiánmì	sweet; happy
甜食	tiánshí	sweet food; sweetmeats
甜头	tiántou	① sweet taste; pleasant flavor ② good; benefit

熟语 Idioms

| 甜酸苦辣 | tián suān kǔ là | sweet and bitter experience of life |
| 甜言蜜语 | tián yán mì yǔ | sweet words and honeyed phrases; fine-sounding words |

填 tián   一 十 土 圹 圹 圹 坊 埴 埴 填 填 埴 填

释义 Meaning

动词 v.

1. fill up; stuff: 他们用土把坑填平了。They filled the pit with earth.

2. fill in; write: 别把日期填错了。Don't fill in the wrong date.

词语 Words and Phrases

填表	tián biǎo	fill in a form
填补	tiánbǔ	fill
填空	tiánkòng	fill a vacant position; fill in the blanks
填写	tiánxiě	fill in; write

挑₁ tiāo   一 十 扌 扒 扒 扒 挑 挑 挑

释义 Meaning

动词 v.

1. pick; select; choose: 我给你挑了个红的。I picked a red one for you.

2. carry on the shoulder with a pole; shoulder: 她每天去河边挑水。She goes to the river and carrys water every day.

词语 Words and Phrases

挑刺儿	tiāocìr	find fault; pick holes
挑错	tiāocuò	find fault; pick flaws
挑剔	tiāotī	nitpick; be hypercritical; be fastidious
挑选	tiāoxuǎn	choose; select; pick out
挑子	tiāozi	carrying pole with its load; load carried on a shoulder pole

熟语 Idioms

挑肥拣瘦	tiāo féi jiǎn shòu	pick the fat or choose the lean; be fastidious in choosing
挑三拣四	tiāo sān jiǎn sì	pick this and choose that; be choosy

挑₂ tiǎo 一 十 扌 扌 扌 扌 挑 挑 挑

释义 Meaning

动词 v.

1. push sth. up with a pole or stick; poke: 她挑开门帘走了进去。She raised the door curtain and went in.

2. stir up; instigate: 这事是他挑起来的。It was he who stired up the trouble.

词语 Words and Phrases

挑拨	tiǎobō	instigate; incite; sow discord
挑动	tiǎodòng	provoke; stir up; incite

挑逗	tiǎodòu	provoke; tease; tantalize
挑起	tiǎoqǐ	provoke; stir up; instigate
挑衅	tiǎoxìn	provoke
挑战	tiǎozhàn	throw down the gauntlet; challenge to battle; challenge to a contest

条 tiáo　ノ　ク　々　冬　冬　条　条

(條　ノ　亻　亻　伫　伫　佟　佟　修　條　條)

释义 Meaning

（一）名词 n.

1. twig; strip; slip; a long narrow piece: 拖把是用布条扎成的。The mop is made of strips of cloth.

2. item; article: 这项条约的正文共八条。The main body of the treaty consists of eight articles.

（二）量词 measure w.

a pair of; a bar of; a carton of: 她送给我一条领带。She gave me a tie.

词语 Words and Phrases

条幅	tiáofú	a vertically-hung scroll
条件	tiáojiàn	① condition; term; factor ② requirement; prerequisite; qualification
条理	tiáolǐ	proper arrangement or presentation; orderliness
条例	tiáolì	regulations; rules; ordinances
条目	tiáomù	① clauses and subclauses ② entry
条文	tiáowén	article; clause
条约	tiáoyuē	treaty; pact
条子	tiáozi	① strip ② a brief informal note

熟语 Idioms

条条框框	tiáotiáo-kuāngkuāng	rules and regulations; conventions and taboos

跳 tiào

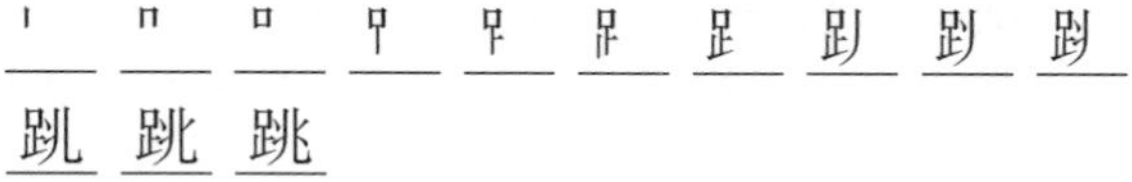

释义 Meaning

动词 v.

1. jump; leap; spring: 他从篱笆上跳了过去。He jumped over the fence.
2. skip; make omissions: 我们从第三课跳到第五课。We jumped from lesson three to lesson five.

词语 Words and Phrases

跳板	tiàobǎn	① gangplank ② springboard
跳槽	tiàocáo	abandon one position in favor of another; change jobs
跳动	tiàodòng	move up and down; beat; pulsate
跳高	tiàogāo	high jump
跳级	tiàojí	skip a grade
跳棋	tiàoqí	Chinese checkers
跳伞	tiàosǎn	parachute; bail out
跳水	tiàoshuǐ	dive
跳舞	tiàowǔ	dance
跳远	tiàoyuǎn	long jump; broad jump
跳跃	tiàoyuè	jump; leap; bound

熟语 Idioms

跳梁小丑	tiàoliáng xiǎochǒu	a buffoon who performs antics; a little rascal

贴 tiē

(贴 丨 冂 冃 冃 目 貝 貝 貼 貼 貼 贴
贴)

释义 Meaning

动词 v.

1. paste; stick; glue: 别忘了贴邮票！Don't forget to stick on the stamp!

2. keep close to; nestle closely to: 孩子紧紧贴在妈妈身边。The child was nestling closely to his mother.

词语 Words and Phrases

贴补	tiēbǔ	subsidize; help out financially
贴金	tiējīn	cover with gold leaf; prettify; touch up
贴近	tiējìn	press close to; nestle up against
贴切	tiēqiè	apt; suitable; appropriate; proper
贴身	tiēshēn	next to the skin; sth. very close
贴现	tiēxiàn	discount
贴心	tiēxīn	intimate; close

铁 tiě 丿 𠂉 𠂉 𠂉 钅 钅 钅 铲 铗 铁

(鐵 丿 𠂉 𠂉 𠂉 牟 牟 牟 金 金 釒 釒
釒 鈝 鈝 鐽 鐽 鐼 鐼 鐵 鐵 鐵)

释义 Meaning

名词 n.

1. iron: 男孩子们在小道上滚铁环。Boys were playing with hoops on the path.

2. hard or strong as iron; indisputable; unalterable: 铁的事实是无法抵赖的。The ironclad evidence is undeniable.

词语 Words and Phrases

铁窗	tiěchuāng	a window with iron grating; prison bars; prison
铁匠	tiějiàng	blacksmith; ironsmith
铁路	tiělù	railway; railroad
铁门	tiěmén	iron gate
铁桶	tiětǒng	metal pail; metal bucket
铁腕	tiěwàn	iron hand
铁锈	tiěxiù	rust
铁证	tiězhèng	ironclad proof; inrefutable evidence

熟语 Idioms

铁壁铜墙	tiě bì tóng qiáng	iron wall and brass partitions; impregnable fortress
铁杵磨成针	tiě chǔ mó chéng zhēn	an iron pestle can be ground down to a needle; perseverance will prevail
铁面无私	tiě miàn wú sī	integrity and justice
铁石心肠	tiě shí xīncháng	has a heart of stone; be flint-hearted
铁树开花	tiěshù kāi huā	the *ti* tree bursting into blossom; sth. seldom seen or hardly possible

厅 tīng 　一 厂 厅 厅

（廳　一 二 广 广 广 庁 庁 庁 厈 厈 厈 厈 厈 厈 厈 庿 庿 厰 厰 厰 厰 廳 廳 廳）

释义 Meaning

名词 n.

1. hall: 休息厅里挤满了人。The lounge was crowded with

people.

2. office; department: 我父亲在省教育厅工作。My father works at the education department of the provincial government.

听 tīng

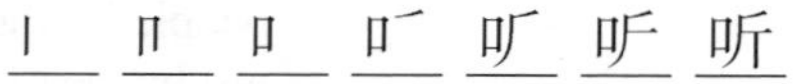

(聽

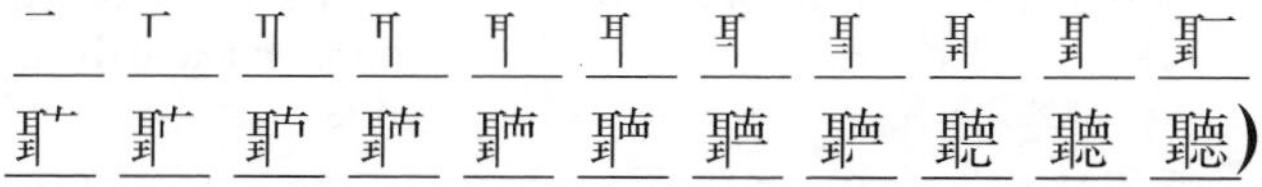

)

释义 Meaning

(一) 动词 v.

1. listen; hear: 你能听到我的声音吗？Can you hear me?
2. obey; heed: 我劝他别去，可他不听。I advised him not to go, but he wouldn’t listen.

(二) 量词 measure w.

tin; can: 他买了三听猪肉罐头。He bought three tins of pork.

词语 Words and Phrases

听从	tīngcóng	obey; heed; comply with
听话	tīnghuà	heed what an elder or superior says; be obedient
听见	tīngjiàn	hear
听课	tīngkè	attend a lecture; sit in on a class
听力	tīnglì	① hearing ② listening comprehension
听凭	tīngpíng	allow; let
听任	tīngrèn	allow; let
听说	tīngshuō	be told; hear of
听信	tīngxìn	① wait for information ② believe what one hears

| 听诊器 | tīngzhěnqì | stethoscope |
| 听众 | tīngzhòng | audience; listeners |

熟语 Idioms

听其言，观其行	tīng qí yán, guān qí xíng	hear what a man says and see how he acts; judge people by their deeds, not just by their words
听其自然	tīng qí zìrán	let things take their own course; leave the matter as it is
听天由命	tīng tiān yóu mìng	abide by the will of Heaven; trust to chance
听之任之	tīng zhī rèn zhī	let sth. go unchecked; let sb. have his own way

停 tíng ノ 亻 亻 亻 广 亻 亻 亻 亻 亻 停

释义 Meaning

动词 v.

1. stop; cease; halt: 雨不停地下了三天。 It kept on raining for three days.

2. stop over; stay; be parked: 你把车停在哪儿了？ Where did you park the car?

词语 Words and Phrases

停泊	tíngbó	anchor; come to an anchor; berth
停产	tíngchǎn	stop production
停车	tíngchē	① stop; pull up ② park
停电	tíngdiàn	cut off power; power failure
停顿	tíngdùn	① stop; halt ② pause
停放	tíngfàng	park; place
停火	tínghuǒ	cease fire

停靠	tíngkào	stop; berth
停课	tíngkè	suspend classes
停战	tíngzhàn	cease-fire; armistice; truce
停止	tíngzhǐ	stop; cease; halt; suspend; call off

挺 tǐng　一　丁　扌　扩　扩　托　挺　挺　挺

释义 Meaning

（一）动词 v.

straighten up; stick out: 把背挺直喽。Straighten up your back!

（二）副词 adv.

very; rather: 这故事挺有趣的。The story is quite interesting indeed.

词语 Words and Phrases

挺拔	tǐngbá	tall and straight; forceful
挺举	tǐngjǔ	clean and jerk
挺立	tǐnglì	stand upright; stand firm
挺身	tǐngshēn	straighten one's back; come out boldly
挺住	tǐngzhù	endure; stand; hold out; in support of sb.

通 tōng　一　マ　广　疒　疒　甬　甬　甬　通　通

释义 Meaning

（一）动词 v.

1. lead to; through; open: 这条路通中央广场。This road leads to the central square.

2. notify; tell: 我晚上跟你通电话。I'll call you up tonight.

3. know; understand: 他精通英语和法语。He knows English and French very well.

(二) 名词 n.

expert; authority: 我要成为一个中国通。I want to be a Sinologue.

词语 Words and Phrases

通报	tōngbào	① circulate a notice ② bulletin; journal
通病	tōngbìng	common failing; common mistake
通常	tōngcháng	general; usual; normal
通畅	tōngchàng	unobstructed; easy and smoothly
通车	tōngchē	be open to fraffic
通道	tōngdào	thoroughfare; passageway
通风	tōngfēng	① ventilated; airy ② divulge information; tip-off
通告	tōnggào	① give public notice; announce ② announcement; circular
通过	tōngguò	① pass through; get past ② adopt; carry ③ by means of; by way of
通话	tōnghuà	communicate by telephone; converse; talk with sb.
通融	tōngróng	make an exception in sb.'s favor
通顺	tōngshùn	clear and coherent; smooth
通俗	tōngsú	popular; common
通宵	tōngxiāo	all night; throughout the night
通晓	tōngxiǎo	thoroughly understand; be proficient in
通心粉	tōngxīnfěn	macaroni
通信	tōngxìn	communicate by letter; correspond
通行	tōngxíng	① pass through ② current; general
通讯	tōngxùn	① communication ② news report; news dispatch
通用	tōngyòng	in common use; current; general
通知	tōngzhī	① notify; inform; let know ② notice; circular; notification

熟语 Idioms

| 通情达理 | tōng qíng dá lǐ | stand to reason; reasonable |

同 tóng 丨 冂 冂 冃 同 同

释义 Meaning

（一）动词 v.

be the same as; together: 我们两个人同岁。The two of us are the same age.

（二）介词 prep.

with: 我同你商量个事。I have something to disscuss with you.

（三）连词 conj.

and; with: 她同父母一起住。She lives with her parents.

词语 Words and Phrases

同伴	tóngbàn	companion
同胞	tóngbāo	born of the same parents; fellow countryman; compatriot
同行	tóngháng	of the same trade or occupation
同情	tóngqíng	sympathize with; show sympathy for
同时	tóngshí	① at the same time; meanwhile ② moreover; besides
同事	tóngshì	colleague; fellow worker
同乡	tóngxiāng	a person from the same village, town or province
同心	tóngxīn	with one heart
同行	tóngxíng	travel together
同学	tóngxué	fellow student; schoolmate
同样	tóngyàng	same; equal; similar
同意	tóngyì	agree; consent; approve

| 同志 | tóngzhì | comrade; partner in a gay or lesbian communtiy |

熟语 Idioms

同病相怜	tóng bìng xiāng lián	those who have the same ailment sympathize with each other; misery loves company
同仇敌忾	tóng chóu díkài	share a bitter hatred of the enemy
同床异梦	tóngchuángyìmèng	share the same bed but dream different dreams
同甘共苦	tóng gān gòng kǔ	share comfort and hardship; through thick and thin
同归于尽	tóng guī yú jìn	die with; end up in common ruin
同呼吸，共命运	tóng hū xī, gòng mìng yùn	breathe the same air and share the same fate
同流合污	tóng liú hé wū	associate with an evil person; go along with sb. in his evil deeds
同室操戈	tóng shì cāo gē	family members drawing swords on each other
同心协力	tóng xīn xié lì	be of one mind; unite in a concerted effort

痛 tòng 　丶　二　广　广　疒　疒　疒　疒　痌　痌　痌　痛

释义 Meaning

（一）名词 n.

pain; ache: 我嗓子痛。I have a sore throat.

（二）副词 adv.

bitterly; deeply; extremely: 我把他痛骂了一顿。I scolded

him severely.

词语 Words and Phrases

痛打	tòngdǎ	beat badly
痛恨	tònghèn	hate bitterly; utterly detest
痛哭	tòngkū	cry bitterly; wail
痛苦	tòngkǔ	pain; suffering; agony
痛快	tòngkuài	① very happy; delighted ② to one's great satisfaction ③ forthright; straightforward
痛心	tòngxīn	pained; distressed; grieved
痛痒	tòngyǎng	sufferings; importance

熟语 Idioms

痛不欲生	tòng bú yù shēng	grieve to the extent of wishing to die
痛改前非	tòng gǎi qián fēi	reform earnestly one's misdeeds; thoroughly rectify one's errors
痛心疾首	tòng xīn jí shǒu	be very distressed about; with bitter hatred

偷 tōu　ノ 亻 亻 亽 亽 偷 偷 偷 偷 偷 偷

释义 Meaning

（一）动词 v.

steal; pilfer; make off with: 我的钱包被偷了。My purse was stolen.

（二）副词 adv.

secretly; on the sly: 他躲在门后偷听。He was eavesdropping behind the door.

词语 Words and Phrases

偷盗	tōudào	steal; pilfer
偷窃	tōuqiè	steal; pilfer
偷税	tōushuì	evade taxes
偷听	tōutīng	eavesdrop; bug; tap
偷偷	tōutōu	stealthily; secretly; covertly

熟语 Idioms

偷工减料	tōu gōng jiǎn liào	cheat in work and materials
偷鸡不着 蚀把米	tōu jī bù zháo shí bǎ mǐ	try to steal a chicken only to end up losing the rice; go for wool and come back shorn
偷梁换柱	tōu liáng huàn zhù	steal the beams and pillars and replace them with rotten timber; fraudulent

头 tóu　` ` ⺮ 头 头

（頭 一 一 一 一 一 一 豆 豆 豆 豇 頭 頭 頭 頭 頭 頭）

释义 Meaning

（一）名词 n.

1. head: 他头上戴着帽子。He is wearing a cap on his head.

2. top; beginning; end: 我在走廊的西头等你。I'll wait for you at the west end of the corridor.

3. head; chief; boss: 我们的头很聪明。Our boss is a clever man.

4. first: 这是我头一次来中国。This is my first time to come to China.

（二）量词 measure w.

(for cattles): 他家养了一百头羊。He raised 100 sheep.

（三）后缀 suff.

(noun suffix): 我从来没有动过这种念头。I have never had such ideas.

词语 Words and Phrases

头发	tóufà	hair
头昏	tóuhūn	dizzy; giddy
头脑	tóunǎo	① brain; mind ② main threads; clue
头疼	tóuténg	headache
头痛	tóutòng	headache
头衔	tóuxián	title
头像	tóuxiàng	head sculpture; head portrait
头绪	tóuxù	main threads; essential part
头晕	tóuyūn	dizzy; giddy
头子	tóuzi	chieftain; chief; boss

熟语 Idioms

头破血流	tóu pò xuè liú	head broken and bleeding; be badly battered
头痛医头，脚痛医脚	tóu tòng yī tóu, jiǎo tòng yī jiǎo	treat the head when the head aches, treat the foot when the foot hurts; defensive stopgap measure
头头是道	tóu tóu shì dào	clear and logical; coherent and cogent
头重脚轻	tóu zhòng jiǎo qīng	weighed down and top-heavy

投 tóu　　一　十　扌　扩　护　投　投

释义 Meaning

动词 v.

throw; fling; hurl: 他把篮球投进了篮圈。He shot the basketball right through the hoop.

词语 Words and Phrases

投保	tóubǎo	insure
投标	tóubiāo	submit a tender; enter a bid
投产	tóuchǎn	go into operation; put into production
投递	tóudì	deliver
投放	tóufàng	① throw in; put in ② put money into circulation; put goods on the market
投稿	tóugǎo	submit a piece of writing for publication; contribute
投机	tóujī	① congenial; agreeable ② speculate
投靠	tóukào	go and seek refuge with sb.
投票	tóupiào	vote; cast a vote
投入	tóurù	in; throw in
投身	tóushēn	throw oneself into
投降	tóuxiáng	surrender; capitulate
投资	tóuzī	invest; investment

熟语 Idioms

投笔从戎	tóu bǐ cóng róng	cast aside the pen to join the army
投其所好	tóu qí suǒ hào	cater to sb's pleasure
投石问路	tóu shí wèn lù	throw a stone to clear the road
投桃报李	tóu táo bào lǐ	give a plum in return for a peach; return present for present

透 tòu   一 二 千 禾 禾 秀 秀 秀 诱 透

释义 Meaning

动词 v.

1. penetrate; pass through; seep through: 阳光透过窗户照进来。Sunlight came in through the windows.

2. appear; show: 我先给你透个信儿。I will tip you off in advance.

3. in a penetrating way; thoroughly; fully: 苹果熟透了。The apples are thoroughly ripe.

词语 Words and Phrases

透彻	tòuchè	penetrating; thorough; incisive
透顶	tòudǐng	thoroughly; downright; through and through
透露	tòulù	divulge; leak; reveal
透明	tòumíng	transparent
透气	tòuqì	① ventilate ② breathe freely
透视	tòushì	① perspective ② fluoroscopy
透支	tòuzhī	overdraw; draw one's salary in advance

图 tú 丨 冂 冂 冈 冈 图 图 图

（圖 丨 冂 冂 冂 冋 冒 冒 圂 圂 圖 圖 圖 圖）

释义 Meaning

（一）名词 n.

picture; drawing; chart; map: 他一边说一边画着示意图。He is drawing a sketch map as he explains.

（二）动词 v.

seek; pursue: 他这么做既不图名，又不图利。He did all of this for neither fame nor gain.

词语 Words and Phrases

图案	tú'àn	pattern; design
图表	túbiǎo	chart; diagram; graph
图画	túhuà	drawing; picture; painting
图谋	túmóu	plot; scheme; conspire
图片	túpiàn	picture; photograph
图书	túshū	books
图书馆	túshūguǎn	library
图腾	túténg	totem
图像	túxiàng	picture; image
图章	túzhāng	seal; stamp
图纸	túzhǐ	blueprint; drawing

熟语 Idioms

图财害命	tú cái hài mìng	murder for money
图穷匕首见	tú qióng bǐ shǒu xiàn	when the map was unrolled, the dagger was revealed; the real intention is revealed at the end of an unrolled scroll

土 tǔ　 一 十 土

释义 Meaning

（一）名词 n.

soil; earth: 他鞋上都是土。There is dirt all over his shoes.

（二）形容词 a.

1. local; native: 我给你带来一些家乡的土产。I brought you some local products from my hometown.

2. indigenous; unrefined: 各地都有一些有效的治病土方。You can find effective folk herbal prescriptions

everywhere.

词语 Words and Phrases

土产	tǔchǎn	local product
土地	tǔdì	① land; soil; ground ② territory
土豆	tǔdòu	potato
土方	tǔfāng	① traditional cure; folk prescription ② earth work ③ cubic meter of earth
土匪	tǔfěi	bandit; brigand
土话	tǔhuà	local, colloquial expressions; local dialect
土壤	tǔrǎng	soil
土著	tǔzhùrén	original inhabitants; natives; aborigines

熟语 Idioms

土崩瓦解	tǔ bēng wǎ jiě	collapse like a house of cards; disintegrate; fall to pieces
土豪劣绅	tǔ háo liè shēn	local bullies and bad gentry
土生土长	tǔ shēng tǔ zhǎng	born and brought up in one's native land
土头土脑	tǔ tóu tǔ nǎo	stupid and not refine; rustic

吐₁ tǔ 丨 丨一 丨一 叶一 叶 吐

释义 Meaning

动词 v.

spit; pour out: 不要随地吐痰。Don't spit in public.

词语 Words and Phrases

| 吐露 | tǔlù | reveal; tell |

熟语 Idioms

| 吐故纳新 | tǔ gù nà xīn | exhale the old and inhale the new |

吐₂ tù ｜ 口 口 口一 吐 吐

释义 Meaning

动词 v.

vomit; throw up; spit: 我觉得恶心想吐。I feel like vomiting.

团 tuán ｜ 冂 冂 团 团 团

(團 ｜ 冂 冂 冂 冋 冋 冒 匷 匷 匷 匷 團 團 團)

释义 Meaning

名词 n.

1. round; sth. shaped like a ball: 女孩长着一张团脸。The girl has a round face.
2. group; society; organization: 我们代表团一行共八个人。Our delegation consists of eight members.
3. regiment: 这一仗我们消灭了敌人三个团。We wiped out three enemy regiments in this battle.

词语 Words and Phrases

团结	tuánjiē	unite; rally
团聚	tuánjù	reunite
团体	tuántǐ	organization; group; team
团团	tuántuán	round and round; all round
团圆	tuányuán	reunion
团长	tuánzhǎng	① head of a delegation ② regimental commander
团子	tuánzi	dumpling

推 tuī 　 一 十 扌 扩 扎 扩 扩 拌 拄 推 推

释义 Meaning

动词 v.

1. push; shove; advance: 他推开门走了出去。He pushed the door open and went out.

2. push away; shirk; shift: 都是你的错，不要把责任推给别人。It is all your fault, don't try to shift the responsibility on to others.

词语 Words and Phrases

推测	tuīcè	infer; conjecture; guess
推迟	tuīchí	put off; postpone; defer
推崇	tuīchóng	hold in esteem; praise highly
推辞	tuīcí	decline
推动	tuīdòng	push forward; promote; give impetus to
推翻	tuīfān	① overshrow; overturn ② repudiate; cancel; reverse
推广	tuīguǎng	popularize; spread; extend; disseminate
推荐	tuījiàn	recommend
推举	tuījǔ	① elect; choose ② clean and press
推理	tuīlǐ	inference; reasoning
推敲	tuīqiāo	weigh; deliberate
推让	tuīràng	decline
推销	tuīxiāo	promote sales; market; peddle
推卸	tuīxiè	shirk
推行	tuīxíng	carry out; pursue; practice
推选	tuīxuǎn	elect; choose

熟语 Idioms

推波助澜	tuī bō zhù lán	help intensify the billows and waves; increase trouble
推陈出新	tuī chén chū xīn	weed out the old to let the new emerge
推三阻四	tuī sān zǔ sì	decline with all sorts of excuses; give the run-around
推心置腹	tuī xīn zhì fù	repose full confidence in sb.; heart to heart

腿 tuǐ ⺆ ⺆ ⺆ 月 月 月 月 肚 肶 腿 腿 腿 腿

释义 Meaning

名词 n.

1. leg: 他摔断了腿。He fell and broke his leg.

2. a leglike support: 他头撞在桌腿上了。He bumped his head against a leg of the table.

词语 Words and Phrases

腿脚	tuǐjiǎo	legs and feet; ability to walk

退 tuì ⺆ ⺕ ⺕ 艮 艮 艮 退 退 退

释义 Meaning

动词 v.

1. move back; retreat: 他往后退了几步。He stepped back a few paces.

2. decline; recede: 潮水退了。The tide has receded.

3. return; give back: 他要把昨天买的电视机退了。He wants to return the TV set he bought yesterday.

词语 Words and Phrases

退避	tuìbì	withdraw and keep off; keep out of the way
退步	tuìbù	lag behind; retrogress
退潮	tuìcháo	ebb tide
退出	tuìchū	withdraw from; secede; quit
退化	tuìhuà	degeneration; degenerate; deteriorate; retrograde
退还	tuìhuán	return
退回	tuìhuí	① return; send back ② go back
退货	tuìhuò	return of goods; returned purchase
退路	tuìlù	① route of retreat ② room for maneuver; leeway
退让	tuìràng	make a concession; yield; give in
退烧	tuìshāo	bring down a fever
退缩	tuìsuō	shrink back; flinch
退位	tuìwèi	give up the throne; abdicate
退伍	tuìwǔ	discharge
退休	tuìxiū	retire
退学	tuìxué	leave school; discontinue one's schooling

熟语 Idioms

退避三舍	tuìbì sān shě	give way to sb. to avoid a conflict
退而求其次	tuì ér qiú qí cì	seek what is less attractive than one's original objective; second best

拖 tuō 一 十 扌 扩 扩 拧 拧 拖

释义 Meaning

动词 v.

1. pull; drag; haul: 拖轮拖着几条小船。The tugboat was towing some small boats.
2. delay; drag on; procrastinate: 这事不能再拖下去了。This work can not be dragged on any more.

词语 Words and Phrases

拖把	tuōbǎ	mop
拖车	tuōchē	trailer
拖船	tuōchuán	tugboat; towboat
拖拉	tuōlā	dilatory; slow; sluggish
拖拉机	tuōlājī	tractor
拖累	tuōlèi	① encumber; be a burden on ② implicate; involve
拖欠	tuōqiàn	be behind in payment; be in arrears
拖沓	tuōtà	dilatory; sluggish; laggard
拖鞋	tuōxié	slippers
拖延	tuōyán	delay; put off; procrastinate

熟语 Idioms

拖泥带水	tuō ní dài shuǐ	be dragged through mud; messy; sloppily
拖时间	tuō shíjiān	stall for time; delay on purpose

脱 tuō 丿 丿 月 月 凡 凡 凡 胪 胪 胪 脱

释义 Meaning

动词 v.

1. take off; cast off: 他脱下大衣，把它挂在衣架上。He took off the overcoat and hung it on the clothes hanger.

2. shed; come off; escape from: 他头发都脱光了。He has lost all his hair.

词语 Words and Phrases

脱发	tuōfà	trichomadesis
脱钩	tuōgōu	unhook; unpegged
脱轨	tuōguǐ	derail
脱节	tuōjié	come apart; be disjointed; be out of line with
脱离	tuōlí	separate oneself from; break away from; be divorced from
脱落	tuōluò	drop; fall off; come off
脱身	tuōshēng	get away; get free; extricate oneself
脱俗	tuōsú	free from vulgarity; refined
脱逃	tuōtáo	run away; escape; flee
脱险	tuōxiǎn	be out of danger; escape danger
脱销	tuōxiāo	out of stock; sold out
脱脂	tuōzhī	de-fat; degrease; fat free

熟语 Idioms

脱口而出	tuō kǒu ér chū	speak by impulse; blurt out
脱胎换骨	tuō tāi huàn gǔ	cast off one's old self; re-mold oneself thoroughly
脱颖而出	tuō yǐng ér chū	fully display one's talents among a group

袜 wà ` ⺀ ⻊ ⻊ ⻊ ⻊ ⻊ 衬 袜 袜

(襪 ` ⺀ ⻊ ⻊ ⻊ ⻊ ⻊ 襪 襪 襪 襪 襪 襪 襪 襪 襪 襪 襪 襪)

释义 Meaning

名词 n.

sock; stockings; hose: 圣诞礼物是放在你袜子里的。The Christmas present is put in your sock.

词语 Words and Phrases

袜子	wàzi	socks; stockings; hose
短袜	duǎnwà	socks
长袜	chángwà	stockings
连裤袜	liánkùwà	panty hose; tights

歪 wāi

释义 Meaning

（一）形容词 a.

1. askew; inclined: 这个字写歪了。This word was written askew. 反义词 antonym: 正

2. devious; underhand 你这套歪理到哪儿也行不通。Your false reasoning can't work anywhere.

（二）动词 v.

tilt: 他一歪头，把球顶进了球门。With a tilt of his head, he head-baffed the ball into the goal.

词语 Words and Phrases

歪道	wāidào	evil ways; depraved life
歪曲	wāiqū	distort, misrepresent; twist

熟语 Idioms

歪风邪气	wāi fēng xié qì	a gust of evil wind; bad tendency
歪门邪道	wāi mén xié dào	crooked means; dishonest methods

外 wài　　ノ　ク　タ　列　外

释义 Meaning

名词 n.

1. outer; outward; outside: 他在外面等你呢。He is waiting for you outside. 反义词 antonym: 里

2. external: 他在国外工作了十年。He has worked aboard for ten years. 反义词 antonym: 内

3. foreign: 这个大学没有外文系。There is no foreign languages department in this university.

4. (relatives) of one's mother, sisters or daughters: 我外祖母是英国人。My grandmother is from England.

词语 Words and Phrases

外币	wàibì	foreign currency
外地	wàidì	parts of the country other than where one is
外国	wàiguó	foreign country
外交	wàijiāo	diplomacy
外面	wàimiàn	outward appearance; exterior
外婆	wàipó	(maternal) grandmother
外孙	wàisūn	daughter's son; grandson
外孙女	wàisūnnǚ	granddaughter; daughter's daughter
外语	wàiyǔ	foreign language
外祖父	wàizǔfù	maternal grandfather
外祖母	wàizǔmǔ	maternal grandmother; grandmother on mother's side
中外	zhōngwài	China and outside China
此外	cǐwài	besides; in addition; moreover

熟语 Idioms

外强中干	wài qiáng zhōng gān	strong in appearance but weak in reality

| 置之度外 | zhì zhī dù wài | not take into account; leave out of consideration |

弯 wān 丶 亠 亣 亣 亦 峦 弯 弯 弯

(彎 丶 亠 亠 訁 言 言 言 绉 绉 绉 绉 绉 绉 緯 緯 緯 緯 緯 緯 緯 緯 緯 緯 彎)

释义 Meaning

(一)名词 n.

1. turn; curve: 一直走，拐一个弯儿就到了。You can get there by going straight and turning the corner.

2. bend: 这根管子有个弯儿。There is a bend on this pipe.

(二)形容词 a.

1. curved; tortuous: 弯弯的月牙儿挂在夜空。A crescent moon hung in the night sky. 反义词 antonym: 直

2. bend; flex: 累累的果实把树枝都压弯了。The fruit growing in close clusters weighed the branches down.

(三)动词 v.

bend: 他弯着腰刷牙。He bent over to brush his teeth.

词语 Words and Phrases

弯路	wānlù	winding course; crooked road; tortuous path
弯曲	wānqū	winding; meandering
转弯	zhuǎnwān	go round curves; turn a corner

熟语 Idioms

| 拐弯抹角 | guǎi wān mò jiǎo | talk in a roundabout way |

完 wán 丶 宀 宀 字 字 宇 完

释义 Meaning

动词 v.

1. exhaust; finish; use up: 复印纸用完了。The duplicating paper was used up.

2. complete; be over; be through: 我的话完了，你说吧。I am through speaking, it's your turn to speak.

词语 Words and Phrases

完成	wánchéng	complete; accomplish; fulfil
完蛋	wándàn	(colloquial) be finished; be doomed; be done for
完好	wánhǎo	intact; whole; in good condition
完美	wánměi	perfect; consummate
完全	wánquán	complete; whole
完事	wánshì	finish; get though; come to an end
完整	wánzhěng	complete; integrated; intact

熟语 Idioms

完璧归赵	wán bì guī zhào	return something to its owner intact
完美无缺	wán měi wú quē	flawless; in good shape

玩 wán 一 二 干 王 王 王 玎 玩

动词 v.

1. have fun: 他昨天去度假村玩了一天。He spent yesterday relaxing at a vacation resort.

2. play: 男孩子喜欢玩足球。Boys like to play football.

3. joke: 他是说着玩的，你别当真。He was only joking, you mustn't take it seriously.

词语 Words and Phrases

玩具	wánjù	toy
玩弄	wánlòng	play with dally with

玩赏	wánshǎng	enjoy; find pleasure in; appreciate
玩耍	wánshuǎ	play; have fun; amuse oneself
玩笑	wánxiào	joke; jest
古玩	gǔwán	antique
游玩	yóuwán	amuse oneself; go sight-seeing

熟语 Idioms

| 玩火自焚 | wán huǒ zì fén | whoever plays with fire gets burnt |
| 玩世不恭 | wán shì bù gōng | be cynical; live in defiance of convention |

晚 wǎn ｜ ｜｜ ｜｜ ｜｜ ｜｜ ｜｜ ｜｜ ｜｜ ｜｜ 晚
晚

释义 Meaning

（一）名词 n.

evening; night

1. 昨晚你去哪儿了？Where did you go last night? 反义词 antonym: 早

2. 我妈妈从早到晚忙个不停。My mother is busy from morning till night.

（二）形容词 a.

late; far on in time

1. 对不起，我来晚了。Sorry, I am late. 反义词 antonym: 早

2. 火车晚到了几分钟。The train arrived here several minutes late.

词语 Words and Phrases

| 晚安 | wǎn'ān | good night |
| 晚饭 | wǎnfàn | supper |

晚会	wǎnhuì	everning party
晚婚	wǎnhūn	marry at a mature age; late marriage
晚年	wǎnnián	old age
晚上	wǎnshàng	(in the) evening; (at) night
傍晚	bàngwǎn	at dusk
夜晚	yèwǎn	night

熟语 Idioms

大器晚成　　dà qì wǎn chéng　　talent matures slowly

碗 wǎn　一　丆　仴　石　石　石　矿　矿　矿　矿
矿　砳　碗

释义 Meaning

名词 n.

bowl: 小姐，给我一碗面条儿。Miss, give me a bowl of noodle.

词语 Words and Phrases

碗橱	wǎnchú	cupboard
饭碗	fànwǎn	rice bowl; job
铁饭碗	tiě fànwǎn	iron rice bowl; a secure job
砸饭碗	zá fànwǎn	lose one's job

万 wàn　一　丁　万

(萬　一　艹　艹　芢　芇　苫　苗　茵　萬　萬
萬)

释义 Meaning

（一）形容词 a.

a very great number; myriad

1. 祝你万事如意。Wish you all the very best.

2. 万紫千红总是春。It is spring when all the flowers are blooming.

（二）副词 adv.

absolutely; by all means: 万没想到会在这里遇见你。I never expected that I could meet you here.

词语 Words and Phrases

万分	wànfēn	very much; extremely
万能	wànnéng	omnipotent
万万	wànwàn	absolutely; wholly
万一	wànyī	just in case; if by any chance
万众	wànzhòng	millions of people; the multitude
千万	qiānwàn	ten million; be sure

熟语 Idioms

万水千山	wàn shuǐ qiān shān	ten thousand mountains and rivers; long and arduous journey
万无一失	wàn wú yì shī	no chance of an error
千真万确	qiān zhēn wàn què	absolutely true; as sure as fate

网 wǎng 丨 冂 冂 冈 冈 网

（網 ⺃ ⺃ ⺃ ⺃ ⺃ ⺃ ⺃ 紉 紉 網 網 網 網 網）

释义 Meaning

（一）名词 n.

1. net: 渔民们在撒网打鱼。The fishermen are netting fish.

2. network: 破坏了敌人的通信网。The enemy's communication network was destroyed.

词语 Words and Phrases

网点	wǎngdiǎn	microdot; the point on a network
网络	wǎngluò	network
网球	wǎngqiú	tennis ball
法网	fǎwǎng	the net of justice
落网	luòwǎng	fall into the net; be caught; be captured
情网	qíngwǎng	love net, deeply in love

熟语 Idioms

| 一网打尽 | yì wǎng dǎ jìn | catch all in a dragnet; make a clean sweep of |
| 天罗地网 | tiān luó dì wǎng | a gigantic net; an invisible net preventing escape |

往 wǎng ′ ′ 彳 彳 彳 彳 往 往

释义 Meaning

动词 v

1. go: 南来北往的火车都要经过这里。All trains have to pass through here. 反义词 antonym: 来
2. in the direction of; toward: 你往南，他往北，你们俩不同路。You are going southwards; he is going northwards. You two don't go the same way.

词语 Words and Phrases

往常	wǎngcháng	habitually in the past; as one used to do formerly
往来	wǎnglái	contact; dealings; intercourse
往往	wǎngwǎng	often; frequently; more often than not
往事	wǎngshì	past events; the past
交往	jiāowǎng	association; contact; associate with; be in contact with
向往	xiàngwǎng	yearn for; look forward to; be attracted toward

熟语 Idioms

既往不咎	jì wǎng bú jiù	forgive sb.'s past wrong doing; let bygones be bygones
一往无前	yì wǎng wú qián	press forward with indomitable will
礼尚往来	lǐ shàng wǎng lái	courtesy demands reciprocity

忘 wàng　　丶 亠 亡 产 忘 忘 忘

释义 Meaning

动词 v.

forget; escape one's memory

1. 喝水不忘掘井人。When you drink water, think of its source. 反义词 antonym: 记

2. 这件事我一辈子也忘不了。I will never forget this matter as long as I live.

词语 Words and Phrases

忘掉	wàngdiào	forget; let slip from one's mind
忘记	wàngjì	forget; slip from one's memory
忘却	wàngquè	forget
忘我	wàngwǒ	oblivious of oneself; selfless
健忘	jiànwàng	forgetful; having a bad memory; have a poor memory
难忘	nánwàng	unforgettable; memorable
遗忘	yíwàng	forget

熟语 Idioms

| 忘恩负义 | wàng ēn fù yì | lack any sense of gratitude; bite the hand that feeds |
| 得意忘形 | dé yì wàng xíng | get dizzy with success; have one's head turned by success |

| 念念不忘 | niàn niàn bú wàng | bear in mind constantly |

望 wàng

丶 亠 亡 亅 切 刞 刞 刞 望
望 望

释义 Meaning

动词 v.

1. gaze into the distance; look over: 你望着我，我望着你，两个人都笑了起来。We are looking at each other and begin to laugh.

2. hope; expect: 望你早日恢复健康。I hope you can recover soon.

3. hopeful: 今年丰收有望了。There is much hope for a bountiful harvest this year.

词语 Words and Phrases

绝望	juéwàng	hopelessness; despair; give up all hope
看望	kànwàng	call on; visit
渴望	kě wàng	long for; yearn
名望	míngwàng	reputation
失望	shī wàng	disappoint
探望	tànwàng	call on; visit
希望	xī wàng	hope; expect; look forward to
愿望	yuànwàng	wish; will

熟语 Idioms

望尘莫及	wàng chén mòjí	be too far behind to catch up
望梅止渴	wàng méi zhǐ kě	look at plums to quench thirst; dreams can help even without the real thing
大失所望	dà shī suǒ wàng	to one's great disappointment

为 wéi 　丶 丿 为 为

(為 一 亠 宀 宀 宀 宀 严 严 严 爲 爲 爲)

释义 Meaning

动词 v.

1. regard as; take for: 你太极拳打得太好了，我要拜你为师。He is very skilled at *Taiji* boxing. I want to take him as my teacher.

2. act as; serve as: 大家选他为出席全国科学大会的代表。He was elected as a representative to attend the national science conference.

3. become: 变沙漠为良田。Turn the desert into arable land.

（二）介词 prep.

by: 这种艺术形式渐渐为广大观众所接受。Little by little this artistic form is being accepted by the general audience.

词语 Words and Phrases

为难	wéinán	feel embarrassed; feel awkward
为人	wéirén	behave; conduct oneself
为止	wéizhǐ	up to; till
成为	chéngwéi	become
认为	rènwéi	think; consider; hold; deem
行为	xíngwéi	behaviour
以为	yǐ wéi	think; believe; consider
因为	yīnwèi	because

熟语 Idioms

为所欲为	wéi suǒ yù wéi	do as one pleases; do whatever one likes
一言为定	yì yán wéi dìng	that's settled then

| 事在人为 | shì zài rén wéi | it all depends on human effort |

围 wéi ｜ 冂 冂 冃 帀 丙 围

（圍 ｜ 冂 冂 冃 帀 帀 丙 帀 帀 圍 圍 圍）

释义 Meaning

动词 v.

1. enclose; surround: 孩子们围着她，请她签名。The children gathered round her, asking for her signature.
2. round: 她头上围着一条花头巾。A coloured scarf is round her neck.

词语 Words and Phrases

围巾	wéijīn	scarf
围棋	wéiqí	*go*
围墙	wéiqiáng	enclosing wall; enclosure
围绕	wéirào	around; round; centre on; revolve round
包围	bāowéi	surround; encircle
范围	fànwéi	scope; range; limits
周围	zhōuwéi	around

熟语 Idioms

| 围魏救赵 | wéi wèi jiù zhào | besiege Wei to rescue Zhao—relieve the besieged by besieging the base of the besiegers |

卫 wèi ㄱ 卫 卫

（衛 ´ ⼻ ⼻ ⼻ 彳 彳 彳 彳 律 律 律 衛 衛 衛 衛）

释义 Meaning

动词 v.

defend; guard; protect: 保家卫国，人人有责。It is everybody's duty to protect our homes and defend our country.

词语 Words and Phrases

卫兵	wèibīng	guard; bodyguard
卫生	wèishēng	hygiene; sanitation
卫生间	wèishēngjiān	toilet; restroom
卫生纸	wèishēngzhǐ	toilet paper
卫星	wèixīng	satellite
警卫	jǐngwèi	(security) guard
门卫	ménwèi	entrance guard; gateman; doorman
守卫	shǒuwèi	guard; defend

熟语 Idioms

精卫填海	jīng wèi tián hǎi	the mythical bird *Jingwei* trying to fill up the sea with pebbles; pledge oneself not to give up and charge on until a job has been accomplished

位 wèi 丿 亻 亻 仁 仁 位 位

释义 Meaning

（一）名词 n.

1. place; location: 把这项工作放在第一位。Put this job in the first priority.

2. place; figure; digit: 计算到小数点后五位。Calculate to five decimal places.

（二）量词 measure w.

1. 家里来了一位年长的客人。An old guest came to my home.

2. 我的话说完了，谢谢各位。My speech is over, thanks you!

词语 Words and Phrases

位于	wèiyú	be located; be situated; lie
位置	wèizhi	seat; place; site; location
单位	dānwèi	unit
地位	dìwèi	status
岗位	gǎngwèi	post; station
学位	xuéwèi	academic degree
职位	zhíwèi	position; post
诸位	zhūwèi	everyone

熟语 Idioms

尸位素餐	shī wèi sù cān	hold down a job without doing a stroke of work

味 wèi 丨 丨丨 丨丨 丨丨 丨二 吀 吀 味

释义 Meaning

名词 n.

1. taste; flavour: 我不喜欢没有甜味的水果。I don't like fruits without any sweet taste.

2. smell; odor: 这个牌子的香水香味很好闻。This brand of perfume smells good.

3. game (as food): 哥哥捉到了一只野兔，今天我们有野味吃了。Brother caught a hare, so today we have food to eat.

词语 Words and Phrases

味道	wèidào	taste
味精	wèijīng	monosodium glutamate; food flavouring
味觉	wèijué	sense of taste

风味	fēngwèi	flavour
口味	kǒuwèi	a person's taste; flavour; taste of food
气味	qìwèi	smell; odor; flavour
趣味	qùwèi	interest
一味	yíwèi	blindly; simply
滋味	zīwèi	taste; flavour

熟语 Idioms

| 臭味相投 | chòu wèi xiāng tóu | meeting of dirty minds |
| 津津有味 | jīn jīn yǒu wèi | with enormous gusto; with zest of relish |

喂 wèi ｜ ｜ ｜ ｜ ｜￢ ｜￢ ｜￢ ｜ 喂 喂 喂 喂

释义 Meaning

（一）叹词 int.

int. hello; hey

1. 喂，你的东西掉了。Hi, you dropped sth.

2. 喂！喂！你是北京大学中文系吗？Hello, hello, is this the Chinese Language Department of Beijing University?

（二）动词 v.

feed; raise; keep

1. 孩子饿了，你快给他喂饭吧。The child is starving. You had better feed him soon.

2. 家里喂着几只鸡，所以天天有蛋吃。The family raises several chickens, so they can eat fresh eggs everyday.

词语 Words and Phrases

喂奶	wèinǎi	breast-feed; suckle
喂食	wèishí	feed
喂养	wèiyǎng	feed; raise

温 wēn ` `丶 氵 氵 沪 沪 沪 沪 沪 沪 温 温

温 温

释义 Meaning

（一）形容词 adj.

tepid: 这水是温的，再热一下吧。The water is tepid, please heat it up.

（二）动词 v.

warm up: 黄酒要温一温才好喝。Millet wine tastes best warm.

词语 Words and Phrases

温度	wēndù	tmperature
温和	wēnhé	mild; moderate
温暖	wēnnuǎn	warm
温泉	wēnquán	hotspring
温柔	wēnróu	gentle and soft
保温	bǎowēn	keep warm; insulate
高温	gāowēn	high temperature
降温	jiàngwēn	lower the temperature
气温	qìwēn	air temperature; atmospheric temperature
体温	tǐwēn	body temperature

熟语 Idioms

温故知新	wēn gù zhī xīn	review what has been learned and learn something new
重温旧梦	chóng wēn jiù mèng	relive an old dream; relive an old experience

文 wén ` 亠 亣 文

释义 Meaning

名词 n.

1. language: 这本书是什么文的？ Which language is this book written in?

2. liberal arts: 他在大学里是学文的。He was in liberal arts in the university.

3. article; essay: 他在一篇短文中提到这件事。He mentioned this matter in a short essay.

词语 Words and Phrases

文化	wénhuà	culture
文件	wénjiàn	documents; papers; file
文明	wénmíng	civilization
文物	wénwù	cultural relic; historical relic
文学	wénxué	literature
文章	wénzhāng	essay; article
文字	wénzì	characters; script; writing
课文	kèwén	text
外文	wàiwén	foreign language
中文	zhōngwén	Chinese

熟语 Idioms

文房四宝	wén fáng sì bǎo	the four treasures of the study (referring to writing brush, ink, ink stone and paper)
文质彬彬	wén zhì bīn bīn	with elegant manners

稳 wěn　一 二 千 禾 禾 利 秒 秒 秒 稳
稳 稳 稳 稳

(稳 一 二 千 千 禾 禾 禾 秆 秆 秆 秆 稈 稈 稈 稈 稽 稽 稽 稳 稳)

释义 Meaning

形容词 adj.

1. steady; firm: 别着急，等车停稳了再下。 Don't hurry. Get off after the car comes to a complete stop.

2. reliable: 她做事很稳。 She is steady and reliable in doing things.

3. sure; certain: 这场比赛中国队稳赢。 The Chinese team is certain to win the game.

词语 Words and Phrases

稳定	wěndìng	stable; steady
稳固	wěngù	firm; stable
稳重	wěnzhòng	steady; staid; sedate
平稳	píngwěn	smooth and steady; smooth; stable

熟语 Idioms

稳操胜券	wěn cāo shèng quàn	be surely to win
十拿九稳	shí ná jiǔ wěn	90 percent sure; be very sure

问 wèn 丶 冂 门 问 问 问

(問 丨 冂 冂 冃 冃 門 門 門 門 問 問)

释义 Meaning

动词 v.

1. ask; inquire: 学生们问了很多问题。 The students asked many questions. 反义词 antonym: 答

2. ask after; inquire after: 她在信里问起你。 She asks after you in her letter.

3. say hello to: 请向你爸爸妈妈问个好。Please say hello to your parents.

词语 Words and Phrases

问号	wènhào	question mark
问候	wènhòu	send one's respects (regards) to
问题	wèntí	question; problem
反问	fǎnwèn	ask (a question) in reply; rhetorical question
访问	fǎngwèn	visit; call on
慰问	wèiwèn	express sympathy and solicitude for
学问	xuéwèn	learning; knowledge; scholarship

熟语 Idioms

| 问道于盲 | wèn dào yú máng | ask a blind man the way; seek advice from an ignorant person |
| 入境问俗 | rù jìng wèn sú | on entering a country, inquire about its customs |

我 wǒ ⼂ ⼆ 千 手 扰 我 我

释义 Meaning

代词 pron.

1. I or me: 你去，我也去。If you go, I will go too.

2. we or us: 最近几年，我国的经济增长得很快。For the past several years, the economy of our country has been growing very fast.

3. (use coordinately with 你 in parallel structures) one; anyone: 大家你一言我一语，讨论得可热烈了。There was an animated discussion at the meeting.

词语 Words and Phrases

| 我们 | wǒmen | we |

| 忘我 | wàngwǒ | oblivious of oneself; selfless |
| 自我 | zìwǒ | self; oneself |

熟语 Idioms

| 我行我素 | wǒ xíng wǒ sù | go one's own way; follow one's usual way of doing things no matter what others say |
| 你死我活 | nǐ sǐ wǒ huó | life-and-death; mortal |

握 wò 一 十 扌 扩 扩 扩 护 挥 挥 握 握 握

释义 Meaning

动词 v.

hold; grasp: 两个人的手紧紧地握在一起。The two hold each other's hands tightly.

词语 Words and Phrases

握别	wòbié	shake hands at parting; part
握拳	wòquán	make a fist; clench one's fist
握手	wòshǒu	shake hands; clasp hands
把握	bǎwò	grasp; hold; assurance; certainty
掌握	zhǎngwò	grasp; master; know well

熟语 Idioms

| 握手言欢 | wò shǒu yán huān | become reconciled with sb. |

无 wú 一 二 于 无

（無 ノ ハ 乍 乍 年 無 無 無 無 無 無 無）

释义 Meaning

动词 v.

1. nothing; none: 他们父子俩白手起家，从无到有，现在已经经营一个千人大公司了。The father and son built up their fortune from nothing. Now they are running a big company with a thousand employees. 反义词 antonym: 有

2. regardless of; no matter whether, what, etc: 事无大小，都有人负责。Everything, big and small, is properly taken care of.

词语 Words and Phrases

无耻	wúchǐ	shameless; brazen; impudent
无法	wúfǎ	unable; incapable
无关	wúguān	have nothing to do with; be unconcerned
无理	wúlǐ	unreasonable; unjustifiable
无论	wúlùn	no matter what; how
无情	wúqíng	merciless; ruthless; heartless
无数	wúshù	innumerable; countless
无心	wúxīn	not be in the mood for; not intentionally; not willingly

熟语 Idioms

无法无天	wú fǎ wú tiān	lawless; run wild
无能为力	wú néng wéi lì	unable to do anything about something
无中生有	wú zhōng shēng yǒu	sheer fabrication; groundless

五 wǔ 二 丁 五 五

释义 Meaning

数词 num.

Five: 我只有五块钱了。I only have five yuan (left).

词语 Words and Phrases

五官	wǔguān	the five sense organs; facial features
五月	wǔyuè	May
五味	wǔwèi	the five flavours
五指	wǔzhǐ	the five fingers
五洲	wǔzhōu	five continents

熟语 Idioms

五光十色	wǔ guāng shí sè	multicoloured; of various colours
五湖四海	wǔ hú sì hǎi	all corners of the country
五花八门	wǔ huā bā mén	a great variety of; omnifarious
四分五裂	sì fēn wǔ liè	fall apart; be all split up; disintegrate

午wǔ ノ 厂 仁 午

释义 Meaning

名词 n.

noon: 午后下了一场大雨,现在凉快多了。There was a heavy rain after noon. Now it is nice and cool.

词语 Words and Phrases

午餐	wǔcān	lunch; midday meal
午饭	wǔfàn	lunch
午觉	wǔjiào	noon break; midday rest; noontime rest
午睡	wǔshuì	afternoon nap; noontime snooze

午夜	wǔyè	midnight
上午	shàngwǔ	morning
下午	xiàwǔ	afternoon
中午	zhōngwǔ	noon

舞 wǔ ╱ ╭ ╰ ╭ ╭ ╭ 舞 舞 舞 舞 舞 舞 舞 舞

释义 Meaning

(一)名词 n.

dance: 她给我们表演了一个新疆舞。She performed a Xinjiang dance for us.

(二)动词 v.

dance with sth. in one's hands: 他每天早上要舞一回剑。He does a sword dance every morning.

词语 Words and Phrases

舞伴	wǔbàn	dancing partner
舞场	wǔchǎng	dance hall; ballroom
舞蹈	wǔdǎo	dance
舞会	wǔhuì	dance; ball; dance party
舞厅	wǔtīng	ballroom; dance hall
伴舞	bànwǔ	be a dancing partner
歌舞	gēwǔ	singing and dance
跳舞	tiào wǔ	dance

熟语 Idioms

| 手舞足蹈 | shǒu wǔ zú dǎo | gesticulate with hands and feet |
| 龙飞凤舞 | lóng fēi fèng wǔ | like dragons flying and phoenixes dancing; lively and vigorous in calligraphy |

物 wù　　ノ　ト　牛　牛　牛　物　物　物

释义 Meaning

名词 n.

thing; matter: 中国人口众多，地大物博。China has a large population, vast territory and abundant resources.

词语 Words and Phrases

物价	wùjià	(commodity) prices
物理	wùlǐ	physics
物品	wùpǐn	article; goods
物质	wùzhì	matter; substance; material
财物	cáiwù	property; belongings
动物	dòngwù	animal
废物	fèiwù	trash; waste material
礼物	lǐwù	gift; present
食物	shíwù	food
事物	shìwù	thing; object
植物	zhíwù	plants

熟语 Idioms

物极必反	wù jí bì fǎn	when pushed to extreme, things will react in the opposite direction
玩物丧志	wán wù sàng zhì	riding a hobby saps one's will; play through life and have no serious ambition

误 wù　　丶　讠　讠　讵　误　误　误　误

(誤　丶　二　亖　言　言　言　誤　誤　誤　誤　誤　誤　誤)

释义 Meaning

(一)形容词 adj.

mistake; error: 这是误传，你不要相信。This is a misleading rumour. You shouldn't believe it.

(二)动词 v.

hinder; impede: 你这样教学生，不是误人子弟吗！You are leading young people astray by teaching students in this way!

词语 Words and Phrases

误点	wùdiǎn	late; overdue; behind schedule
误会	wùhuì	misunderstand
误解	wùjiě	misread; misunderstand
误伤	wùshāng	accidentally injure
误事	wùshì	cause delay in work or business; hold things up
错误	cuòwù	mistake
耽误	dānwù	delay; hold up

熟语 Idioms

一误再误	yí wù zài wù	make things worse by repeated delays, one mistake begets another

雾 wù　一 厂 户 币 承 乘 乘 乘 雫 雯 雯 雯 雾

(霧 一 厂 户 币 承 乘 乘 乘 乘 雫 雫 雫 雾 霏 霏 霧 霧 **)**

释义 Meaning

名词 n.

fog: 今天雾很大，你别开车了。Today there's a heavy

fog. You had better not drive the car.

词语 Words and Phrases

雾气	wùqì	mist; vapor
迷雾	míwù	dense fog
烟雾	yānwù	smog; fog

熟语 Idioms

| 雾里看花 | wù lǐ kàn huā | appreciate flowers in a dense fog; not really sure of what one sees |

西 xī 二 丆 丙 西 西 西

释义 Meaning

名词 n.

1. west: 你往东，我往西，咱们分头找。You go eastwards and I will go westwards. We can search seperately. 反义词 antonym: 东。

2. occidental; western: 走，今天我请客，请你吃西餐。Let's go. It is my treat today. I will invite you for a western-style dinner.

词语 Words and Phrases

西方	xīfāng	the West
西风	xīfēng	west wind; westerly wind
西服	xīfú	western-style clothes; suit
西瓜	xīguā	watermelon
西欧	xī'ōu	Western Europe
西式	xīshì	western style
西药	xīyào	western medicine
西医	xīyī	western medicine
西装	xīzhuāng	suit; western-style clothes

熟语 Idioms

日薄西山	rì báo xī shān	the sun is setting beyond the western hills
声东击西	shēng dōng jī xī	announce on the east and strike at the west; a strategy to distract the attention of the enemy

吸 xī   丨 丨丨 丨丨 丨丬 吸 吸

释义 Meaning

动词 v.

1. inhale; breathe in: 屋里太闷，我出去吸点新鲜空气。 The room is too stuffy. I have to go out for a breath of fresh air.

2. absorb; suck up: 这种纸一点也不吸水。 This kind of paper can't absorb water at all.

词语 Words and Phrases

吸毒	xīdú	take illicit drugs
吸取	xīqǔ	absorb; draw; assimilate;
吸收	xīshōu	absorb; suck up; assimilate; imbibe
吸烟	xīyān	smoke
吸引	xīyǐn	attract; draw; fascinate
呼吸	hūxī	breathe; respire

习 xí   丁 习 习

(習 ﹁ ﹁ ﹃ ﹃﹁ ﹃﹁ ﹃﹃ ﹃﹃ 習 習 習 習)

释义 Meaning

（一）动词 v.

practise; exercise; review: 古语说："学而时习之。"这句话说得非常对。 The ancient saying, "study and review often" is absolutely right.

（二）名词 n.

habit; custom; usual practice: 吸毒是一种恶习。Taking addictive drugs is a kind of bad habit.

词语 Words and Phrases

习惯	xíguàn	habit; be accustomed to
习俗	xísú	custom; convention
习题	xítí	exercises (in school work)
复习	fùxí	review; brush up
练习	liànxí	exercise
学习	xuéxí	study; learn
预习	yùxí	preview
自习	zìxí	study by oneself in scheduled time or free time

熟语 Idioms

| 习以为常 | xí yǐ wéi cháng | be accustomed to something |

席 xí ` 亠 广 广 庐 庐 庐 庐 庐 席

释义 Meaning

名词 n.

seat; place: 请坐来宾席。Please sit in one of the guest seats.

词语 Words and Phrases

出席	chūxí	be present (at a meeting; social gathering, etc.)
酒席	jiǔxí	banquet; feast
缺席	quēxí	absent (from a meeting, etc.)
退席	tuì xí	leave a meeting or a banquet
宴席	yànxí	banquet; feast
主席	zhǔxí	chairman

熟语 Idioms

席不暇暖	xí bù xiá nuǎn	have no time to sit long enough to warm the seat; constantly on the go
座无虚席	zuò wú xū xí	no empty seat; full house

洗 xǐ　丶 丶 氵 氵 汇 汼 洗 洗 洗

释义 Meaning

动词 v.

wash

1. 把这些衣服拿到洗衣店去洗。Take these clothes to the laundry for washing.
2. 给孩子洗洗脸。Wash the child's face.

词语 Words and Phrases

洗手间	xǐshǒujiān	toilet; lavatory; washroom
洗澡	xǐzǎo	have a bath
干洗	gānxǐ	dry-clean

熟语 Idioms

洗心革面	xǐ xīn gé miàn	change one's heart and face; reform oneself totally
一贫如洗	yì pín rú xǐ	as poor as a church mouse; penniless

喜 xǐ　一 十 吉 吉 吉 吉 吉 吉 壴 壴 喜 喜

释义 Meaning

动词 v.

1. happy; delighted; pleased: 她笑在脸上，喜在心里。
   She is with a smile on her face and joy in her heart.

2. a welcome fall of seasonable snow: 干旱已久的西北地区喜降大雪。There was a welcome fall of seasonable snow in the drought-plagued northwest.

词语 Words and Phrases

喜爱	xǐ'ài	like; love; be fond of; be keen on
喜欢	xǐhuān	like
喜酒	xǐjiǔ	drinks offered to guests at wedding; wedding-feast
喜事	xǐshì	ahappy event; wedding
喜讯	xǐxùn	happy news; good news; glad tidings
恭喜	gōngxǐ	congratulate

熟语 Idioms

喜出望外	xǐ chū wàng wài	be pleasantly surprised
皆大欢喜	jiē dà huān xǐ	everybody is happy; to the satisfaction of all

戏 xì　フ　又　戈　戏　戏　戏

(戲　'　卜　ト　广　户　卢　虍　卢　虍　虍　虍
虍　虘　虘　戯　戲　戲)

释义 Meaning

名词 n.

play; drama; show: 这场戏演得很精彩。It was a wonderful performance.

词语 Words and Phrases

戏剧	xìjù	play; drama; theatre
戏迷	xìmí	theatre fan
戏曲	xìqǔ	traditional opera
戏院	xìyuàn	theatre

唱戏	chàng xì	sing and act in a traditional opera
演戏	yǎn xì	put on a play; act in a play
游戏	yóuxì	play a game

熟语 Idioms

| 逢场作戏 | féng chǎng zuò xì | have occasional recreation; join in the spirit of the occasion; not serious |
| 视同儿戏 | shì tóng ér xì | treat (a serious matter) as a trifle; trifle with |

细 xì 　ㄥ ㄥ ㄥ 纟 纲 纲 细 细

(細 　ㄥ ㄥ ㄥ ㄥ ㄥ ㄥ 糹 絧 絧 細 細)

释义 Meaning

形容词 adj.

1. thin; slender: 她把眉毛画得又细又长。 She penciled her eyebrows thin and long. 反义词 antonym: 粗

2. careful; meticulous; detailed: 她这个人心很细。 She is a careful woman.

词语 Words and Phrases

细菌	xìjūn	germ; bacterium
细小	xìxiǎo	very small; tiny; fine; trivial
细心	xìxīn	careful; attentive
细致	xìzhì	careful; meticulous
粗细	cūxì	size
详细	xiángxì	detailed; minute
仔细	zǐxì	careful; attentive

熟语 Idioms

| 细水长流 | xì shuǐ cháng liú | small but steady stream; do something little by little without a break |

| 精打细算 | jīng dǎ xì suàn | careful calculation and strict budgeting; well planned |

下 xià   一 丁 下

释义 Meaning

（一）名词 n.

1. down; downward: 你往下看，就可以看到了。Keep on reading you will see it then. 反义词 antonym: 上

2. Indicating scope, state, condition, etc: 在老师的帮助下，他进步很快。With the help of the teacher, he made great progress.

3. next (in time or order); latter: 下个星期要考试了。There will be a test next week.

（二）动词 v.

1. get off (a conveyance); alight: 还有一站我们该下车了。We should get off after one more stop.

2. (of rain, snow, etc.) come down; fall: 大雨下了一天一夜才停。The heavy rain lasted for a full day and night before stopping.

词语 Words and Phrases

下班	xià bān	go off work
下边	xiàbiān	below; under; underneath
下课	xiàkè	end the lesson; class is over
下面	xiàmiàn	below; under; underneath
下午	xiàwǔ	afternoon
地下	dìxià	underground
以下	yǐxià	as follows

熟语 Idioms

| 下不为例 | xià bù wéi lì | this behavior must not be |

repeated; never do it again

七上八下　　　qī shàng bā xià　　be agitated; be perturbed

吓 xià　｜ Ⅱ Ⅱ 厂 叮 吓

（嚇　｜ Ⅱ Ⅱ 厂 吐 吐 呀 听 听 听 听
吓 听 听 嚇 嚇 嚇 嚇）

释义 Meaning

动词 v.

1. frighten; intimidate: 小心点，别吓着孩子。Be careful not to frighten the child.

2. scare: 这种困难吓不倒我们。Difficulties like this don't scare us.

词语 Words and Phrases

吓唬	xiàhu	frighten; scare; intimidate
吓人	xiàrén	be frightening
惊吓	jīngxià	frighten; scare

熟语 Idioms

杀鸡吓猴	shā jī xià hóu	kill the chicken to scare the monkey; punish someone as a warning to others

夏 xià　二 一 厂 厅 百 百 頁 戸 夏 夏

释义 Meaning

名词 n.

summer: 春去夏来，一年过去了。Summer comes as spring goes and one year is gone.

词语 Words and Phrases

夏季	xiàjì	summer
夏粮	xiàliáng	summer gain crops

夏令	xiàlìng	summertime
夏收	xiàshōu	summer-harvest
夏天	xiàtiān	summer
夏装	xiàzhuāng	summer clothing
初夏	chūxià	early summer
华夏	huáxià	archaic name for China
盛夏	shèngxià	the height of summer; midsummer

先 xiān ノ ⺊ ⺦ ⺦ 牛 先

释义 Meaning

（一）副词 adv.

at first; before: 你先怎么不告诉我？Why didn't you tell me in the first place?

（二）副词 adv.

earlier; before sb. else: 今天我比你先到。Today I arrived earlier than you did. 反义词 antonym: 后

词语 Words and Phrases

先后	xiānhòu	one after another; first and second
先进	xiānjìn	advanced
先前	xiānqián	before; previously
先生	xiānsheng	teacher; Mister (Mr.); sir; gentleman; husband
领先	lǐngxiān	be in the lead; lead; precede; be in front of
事先	shìxiān	in advance
首先	shǒuxiān	at first
祖先	zǔxiān	ancestor

熟语 Idioms

| 先见之明 | xiān jiàn zhī míng | preconception; foresight |

先下手为强　xiān xià shǒu wéi qiáng　take the initiative is to gain the upper hand

鲜 xiān ノ ╱ 亻 刍 刍 角 鱼 鱼 魚 魚 魚 魚 魰 鲜

（鲜 ノ ╱ 亻 刍 刍 角 鱼 鱼 鱼 鱼 鱼 魚 鯗 鲜 鯗 鮮 鲜**）**

释义 Meaning

形容词 a.

1. fresh: 下班以后带一公斤鲜肉回来。Bring a kilogram of fresh pork home after work.

2. bright-coloured; bright: 这块布颜色太鲜了。The colour of this piece of cloth is too bright.

3. (of salty dishes or soup) delicious; tasty: 这汤的味道鲜极了。The soup tastes delicious!

词语 Words and Phrases

鲜果	xiānguǒ	fresh fruit
鲜红	xiānhóng	bright-red; scarlet
鲜花	xiānhuā	fresh flowers
鲜美	xiānměi	delicious; fresh and pleasing
鲜明	xiānmíng	bright; clear-cut; distinctive
海鲜	hǎixiān	sea food
新鲜	xīnxiān	fresh

熟语 Idioms

屡见不鲜　lǚ jiàn bù xiān　common occurrence; nothing special

县 xiàn 丨 冂 日 且 且 县 县

(縣 丨 冂 冃 冃 目 且 具 具 县 県 県 県 県 県 県 縣**)**

释义 Meaning

名词 n.

county: 以前上海有十个县，现在很多县都改为区了。Shanghai had ten counties previously. Now most of those counties have been reorganized into districts.

词语 Words and Phrases

县城	xiànchéng	county seat; county town
县份	xiànfèn	county
县志	xiànzhì	general records of a county; county annals

线 xiàn ㄥ ㄠ ㄠ 纟 纟 纟 线 线 线

(綫 ㄥ ㄠ ㄠ 幺 幺 糸 紅 紋 綫 綫 綫 綫 綫 綫**)**

释义 Meaning

（一）名词 n.

1. thread: 做衣服离不开针和线。The thread and needle are indispensable to tailoring.

2. route; line: 沪宁线上发生了交通事故。A traffic accident happened on the Shanghai-Nanjing railway line.

3. Demarcation line; boundary: 他越过了国境线。He crossed the country's border.

（二）量词 measure.

word (used with numeral before abstract things, indicating very little): 他感到还有一线希望。He realized that he had still had a ray of hope.

词语 Words and Phrases

线路	xiànlù	line; circuit
线条	xiàntiáo	line
光线	guāngxiàn	light; ray

乡 xiāng   ⺈ 纟 乡

(鄉 ⺈ 纟 乡 乡 纟 纟 纟 纟 纟 鄉 鄉)

释义 Meaning

名词 n.

1. native place; home village or town: 他回乡探亲了。He returned to his home village to visit his relatives.

2. countryside; village: 县里的干部常常下乡调查。The cadres in this county often go to the countryside for investigation.

词语 Words and Phrases

乡村	xiāngcūn	village
乡亲	xiāngqīn	fellow villager or townsman
乡土	xiāngtǔ	native soil
乡下	xiāngxià	countryside; village
故乡	gùxiāng	native place
家乡	jiāxiāng	home town
老乡	lǎoxiāng	fellow-townsman; from the same village
同乡	tóngxiāng	a person from the same village or town

熟语 Idioms

入乡随俗	rù xiāng suí sú	when in Rome do as the Romans do
背井离乡	bèi jǐng lí xiāng	leave one's native place (esp. against one's will)

相 xiāng   一 十 才 木 朾 朾 柑 相 相

释义 Meaning

副词 adv.

1. each other; one another: 两个人相爱已经很久了。They two have been in love with each other for a long time.

2. be away from: 上海和南京相距数百里。Shanghai is several hundred miles from Nanjing.

词语 Words and Phrases

相比	xiāngbǐ	compare with
相称	xiāngchèn	match; suit; be commensurate to
相处	xiāngchǔ	get along with; live together
相当	xiāngdāng	match; balance; correspond to; be equivalent to
相反	xiāngfǎn	opposite; contrary; adverse; reverse
相互	xiānghù	mutual; reciprocal; each other
相同	xiāngtóng	identical; the same; alike
相信	xiāngxìn	believe in; be convinced of; have faith in
互相	hùxiāng	each other

熟语 Idioms

相安无事	xiāng ān wú shì	live peacefully with each other
相敬如宾	xiāng jìng rú bīn	treat each other with respect

香 xiāng   一 二 千 チ 禾 禾 香 香 香

释义 Meaning

形容词 adj.

1. fragrant; sweet-smelling: 这花儿真香。This flower smells very fragrant. 反义词 antonym: 臭

2. (of sleep) sound: 他睡得正香。He is sleeping soundly.

3. With relish; with good appetite: 我这几天吃东西不香。
   I have had no appetite these past few days.

词语 Words and Phrases

香肠	xiāngcháng	sausage
香蕉	xiāngjiāo	banana
香水	xiāngshuǐ	perfume
香烟	xiāngyān	cigarette
清香	qīngxiāng	delicate fragrance; faint scent
口香糖	kǒuxiāngtáng	chewing gum

熟语 Idioms

古色古香	gǔ sè gǔ xiāng	ancient colour and ancient odor; of classic motif
鸟语花香	niǎo yǔ huā xiāng	singing birds and fragrant flowers; characterizing a fine spring day

箱 xiāng

丿 ㄏ ㄌ ㄌ ㄌ ㄌ ㄌ ㄌ ㄌ
ㄌ ㄌ ㄌ 箱 箱 箱 箱

释义 Meaning

名词 n.

chest; case: 这箱是书，那箱是衣服。This case is for books,
and that is for clothes.

词语 Words and Phrases

箱子	xiāngzi	case; chest; box; trunk
冰箱	bīngxiāng	refrigerator; freezer; icebox
皮箱	píxiāng	leather suitcase
信箱	xìnxiāng	mail-box
油箱	yóuxiāng	fuel tank
保险箱	bǎoxiǎnxiāng	safe; safe deposit box

| 电冰箱 | diànbīngxiāng | (electric) refrigerator; fridge; freezer |
| 集装箱 | jízhuāngxiāng | (shipping) container |

熟语 Idioms

| 翻箱倒柜 | fān xiāng dǎo guì | rummage through chests and cupboards |

响 xiǎng

丨 丨丨 丨丨 丨丨′ 叮′ 叭′ 叭 响 响

(響

生 生 纟 纟 纟′ 纟′ 纟′ 纟 纟 纟3 鄉

鄉 鄉 鄉 鄉 響 響 響 響 響)

释义 Meaning

（一）动词 v.

make a sound; sound; ring: 全场响起了暴风雨般的掌声。
A storm of applause broke out in the hall.

（二）形容词 a.

noisy; loud: 他说话声音真响。He speaks so loud.

词语 Words and Phrases

响亮	xiǎngliàng	loud and clear
响声	xiǎngshēng	sound; noise
响应	xiǎngyīng	respond; answer
影响	yǐngxiǎng	influence
交响乐	jiāoxiǎngyuè	symphony; symphonic music

熟语 Idioms

| 响彻云霄 | xiǎng chè yún xiāo | resound to the skies |
| 不同凡响 | bù tóng fán xiǎng | outstanding; out of the ordinary; out of the common run |

想 xiǎng

一 十 才 木 朾 相 相 相 相

相 想 想 想

释义 Meaning

（一）动词 v.

1. think; ponder: 她想出来一个好办法。She has thought out a good idea.

2. suppose; reckon; consider: 我想她今天不会来。I don't think she will be coming today.

3. miss; remember with longing: 你走了，我会想你的。After you have left, I will be missing you.

（二）助动词 a.v.

want to; would like to; feel like (doing sth.): 许多外国朋友都想了解中国。Many foreign friends want to know more about China.

词语 Words and Phrases

想法	xiǎngfǎ	idea; opinion; what one has in mind
想来	xiǎnglái	it may be assumed that; presumably
想念	xiǎngniàn	long to see again; miss; remember with longing
想象	xiǎngxiàn	imagine; fancy; visualize
理想	lǐxiǎng	ideal
思想	sīxiǎng	thought

熟语 Idioms

想入非非	xiǎng rù fēi fēi	have day dreams
胡思乱想	hú sī luàn xiǎng	go off into wild flights of fancy

向 xiàng   ㇒ 丨 冂 向 向 向

释义 Meaning

（一）介词 prep.

1. towards: 向南一直走就到火车站了。Go straight south-wards to get to the railway station.

2. in the direction of: 你的女儿文学学得很好，应该向
   这方面发展。Your daughter is good at literature. She
   ought to develop her ability in that direction.

3. to: 我要向你讲几句心里话。I want to tell you something which has been on my mind.

（二）动词 v.

take sb.'s part; side with; be partial to: 你别老向着她。
You don't always side with her.

词语 Words and Phrases

向导	xiàngdǎo	guide
向来	xiànglái	always; all along
向往	xiàngwǎng	yearn for; look forward to; be attracted toward
向阳	xiàngyáng	exposes to the sun; sunny
方向	fāngxiàng	direction
一向	yíxiàng	consistenly; all along
志向	zhìxiàng	aspiration; ideal; ambition

熟语 Idioms

| 所向无敌 | suǒ xiàng wú dí | find no match wherever one goes; irresistible |
| 晕头转向 | yūn tóu zhuǎn xiàng | confused and disoriented |

象 xiàng ノ ⺈ ⺈ ⺈ 乌 多 争 身 豸 豸 象

释义 Meaning

名词 n.

elephant: 这只象是从印度来的。This elephant is from India.

词语 Words and Phrases

| 象棋 | xiàngqí | (Chinese) chess |

象征	xiàngzhēng	symbolize; signify; stand for
对象	duìxiàng	target; object
好象	hǎoxiàng	seem
气象	qìxiàng	meteorological phenomena
图象	túxiàng	picture; image
现象	xiànxiàng	phenomenon; appearance (of things)
想象	xiǎngxiàng	imagine; fancy; visualize
形象	xíngxiàng	image; form; figure
印象	yìnxiàng	impression

熟语 Idioms

| 万象更新 | wàn xiàng gēng xīn | everything takes on a completely new look |
| 盲人摸象 | máng rén mō xiàng | like the blind trying to size up the elephant |

像 xiàng ノ 亻 亻 亻 伫 伫 伫 傍 傍 傍 像 像 像

释义 Meaning

动词 v.

1. be like; resemble; take after: 妹妹长得很像姐姐。The two sisters are very much alike.

2. look as if; seem: 像要下雨了。It looks like going to rain.

3. such as; like: 像苹果、香蕉、桔子，都是我爱吃的水果。Fruits such as apple, banana and orange are all favorites of mine.

词语 Words and Phrases

像样	xiàngyàng	up to the mark; presentable; decent
画像	huàxiàng	portrait; portrayal
人像	rénxiàng	portrait; image; figure
塑像	sùxiàng	statue

小 xiǎo 丿 小 小

释义 Meaning

形容词 adj.

1. young: 我比你小一岁。I am one year younger than you are. 反义词 antonym: 大

2. the last in order of seniority: 这位是老王的小儿子。This is the youngest son of Mr. Wang.

词语 Words and Phrases

小便	xiǎobiàn	urinate; pass water; make water
小吃	xiǎochī	snack; refreshments
小孩儿	xiǎoháir	child
小伙子	xiǎohuǒzi	youngster; lad; young fellow
小姐	xiǎojiě	Miss; a young lady
小朋友	xiǎopéngyǒu	children; child
小时	xiǎoshí	hour
小说	xiǎoshuō	novel
小偷	xiǎotōu	petty thief; sneak thief; pilferer
小心	xiǎoxīn	take care; be careful; be cautious
小学	xiǎoxué	elementary school; primary school

熟语 Idioms

小题大做	xiǎo tí dà zuò	a storm in a teacup; much ado about nothing
大材小用	dà cái xiǎo yòng	use talented people for trivial tasks; put fine timber to petty use

校 xiào 二 十 ナ 木 木 杧 杧 杧 校 校

释义 Meaning

名词 n.

school: 全校同学都要参加运动会。All students of the

school should take part in the sports meeting.

词语 Words and Phrases

校服	xiàofú	school uniform
校规	xiàoguī	school regulations
校庆	xiàoqìng	founding anniversary of a school or a college;
校友	xiàoyǒu	alumnus; alumna
校园	xiàoyuán	campus; school yard
校长	xiàozhǎng	president; headmaster
高校	gāoxiào	college; university
母校	mǔxiào	one's old school; Alma Mater
学校	xuéxiào	school
夜校	yèxiào	night school; evening school

笑 xiào ノ ト ト ペ 竹 竹 竺 竺 竺 笑

释义 Meaning

动词 v.

1. smile; laugh: 他刚说完，大家都笑了起来。He had just finished his speech when everyone began to laugh.

2. ridicule; laugh at: 我刚学跳舞，你别笑我。I just begin to learn dancing. Don't laugh at me.

词语 Words and Phrases

笑话	xiàohuà	joke; jest; laugh at; ridicule
笑脸	xiàoliǎn	smiling face
笑嘻嘻	xiàoxīxī	grinning; smiling broadly
好笑	hǎoxiào	funny; laughable; ridiculous
欢笑	huānxiào	laugh heartily
说笑	shuōxiào	chatting and laughing
玩笑	wánxiào	joke
微笑	wēixiào	smile

开玩笑　　kāi wánxiào　make fun of; joke; crack a joke

熟语 Idioms

笑里藏刀	xiào lǐ cáng dāo	conceal dirty tricks in one's smile; a smile of treachery
眉开眼笑	méi kāi yǎn xiào	be all smiles; beam with joy

些 xiē　　　丨　卜　止　止　此　此　些　些

释义 Meaning

量词 measure w.

1. some; a few: 我去买些东西，马上回来。I'm going to buy something. I'll be right back.

2. a little more; a little: 你快些走，要来不及了。Hurry up, there is not enough time.

词语 Words and Phrases

好些	hǎoxiē	quite a lot; a good deal of
哪些	nǎxiē	which; who; what
那些	nàxiē	those
一些	yìxiē	some
有些	yǒuxiē	some; somewhat; rather
这些	zhèxiē	these
那么些	nàme xiē	so many; so much
这么些	zhème xiē	so many; so much

鞋 xié　　一　十　卄　廿　芇　艹　昔　莒　革　革　革　靬　鞋　鞋　鞋

释义 Meaning

名词 n.

shoes: 他来不及穿鞋就跑出去了。He didn't have enough

time to put on shoes, but ran out at once.

词语 Words and Phrases

鞋带儿	xiédàir	shoelace; shoestring
鞋油	xiéyóu	shoe polish; shoe scream
鞋子	xiézi	shoes
布鞋	bùxié	cloth shoes
凉鞋	liángxié	sandals
棉鞋	miánxié	cotton-padded shoes
皮鞋	píxié	leather shoes
拖鞋	tuōxié	slippers
雨鞋	yǔxié	rain shoes; rain boots

斜 xié ノ 人 亼 亼 仒 余 余 余 斜 斜

释义 Meaning

形容词 adj.

1. tilt: 这座塔有点儿斜。This tower is a little tilted.

2. recline: 他斜躺在沙发上。He reclined on a sofa.

词语 Words and Phrases

斜路	xiélù	uphill path
歪斜	wāixié	crooked; askew; aslant

写 xiě 丶 冖 写 写

(寫 丶 宀 宕 宕 宕 宕 宕 寫 寫 寫 寫 寫 寫)

释义 Meaning

动词 v.

1. write: 他每天写一百个字。He writes one hundred char-

acters everyday.

2. compose: 她写的诗没人看。No one reads her poems.

3. write (as an author, report, etc.): 这本小说写的人物都很可爱。The characters in this novel are all likable.

词语 Words and Phrases

写法	xiěfǎ	style of writing; way of writing characters
写作	xiězuò	writing
编写	biānxiě	compile; edit
描写	miáoxiě	describe; depict
默写	mòxiě	write from memory
听写	tīngxiě	dictate

熟语 Idioms

| 轻描淡写 | qīng miáo dàn xiě | touch on lightly; mention casually; describe with a delicate touch |

谢 xiè ` 讠 讠 讠 讠 诮 诮 诮 诮 诮 诮 谢 谢

（**謝** ` 亠 亠 亠 言 言 言 言 言 訃 訃 訃 訃 訃 謝 謝）

释义 Meaning

动词 v.

1. thank: 这点儿小事不用谢了。Needless to say thank you for this trifle.

2. (of flowers, leaves) wither: 花谢了。The flowers withered.

词语 Words and Phrases

| 谢绝 | xièjué | refuse; decline |
| 谢幕 | xièmù | answer a curtain call |

谢谢	xièxie	thanks; thank you
谢意	xièyì	gratitude; thankfulness
多谢	duōxiè	thanks a lot; many thanks
感谢	gǎnxiè	thank
致谢	zhìxiè	express one's thank

熟语 Idioms

| 谢天谢地 | xiè tiān xiè dì | thank heaven; thanks a lot |
| 新陈代谢 | xīn chén dài xiè | metabolism; the new superseding the old |

心 xīn　　丶　忄　心　心

释义 Meaning

名词 n.

1. heart; mind: 你的心是好的，但是事情办得不好。You meant well but you didn't handle the job well.
2. feeling; intention: 他人在这儿，心不在。He himself is here, but his thoughts are elsewhere.

词语 Words and Phrases

心爱	xīn'ài	love; treasure
心肠	xīncháng	heart; intention
心烦	xīnfán	be vexed; be perturbed
心急	xīnjí	impatient; short-tempered
心里	xīnlǐ	psychology; mentality
心情	xīnqíng	frame of mind; state of mind
心事	xīnshì	aload on one's mind
心疼	xīnténg	love dearly
心脏	xīnzàng	the heart

熟语 Idioms

| 心口如一 | xīn kǒu rú yī | say what one thinks |
| 心有余而 | xīn yǒu yú ér | be willing but unable |

力不足　　　lì bù zú

新 xīn　　丶　ˊ　ˋ　亠　产　立　辛　辛　亲　亲
新　新　新

释义 Meaning

形容词 adj.

1. brand new; unused: 她买了一件新衣服。She bought a piece of new clothing. 反义词 antonym: 旧

2. newly; freshly; recently: 班里来了一位新同学。A new student came to the class. 反义词 antonym: 老

3. new: 他是我新认识的朋友。He's a new friend of mine.

词语 Words and Phrases

新房	xīnfáng	bridal-chamber
新居	xīnjū	new home; new residence
新年	xīnnián	new year
新式	xīnshì	new style; modern
新闻	xīnwén	news
新鲜	xīnxiān	fresh
重新	chóngxīn	again; anew; afresh

熟语 Idioms

喜新厌旧	xǐ xīn yàn jiù	love the new and loathe the old; abandon the old for the new
吐故纳新	tǔ gù nà xīn	get rid of the stale and take in the fresh

信 xìn　　ノ　亻　亻　信　信　信　信　信

释义 Meaning

（一）名词 n.

1. letter; mail: 今天我收到两封信。Today I received two

letters.

2. message; word; information: 你到了美国给我来个信儿。 Please send me word after you arrive in the U.S.

（二）动词 v.

1. believe: 你别信他的话。 You mustn't believe anything he says.

2. believe in; profess faith in: 我不信鬼，怕什么！ I don't believe in ghosts. What's to be scared of!

词语 Words and Phrases

信封	xìnfēng	envelope
信号	xìnhào	signal
信任	xìnrèn	trust; have confidence in
信息	xìnxī	information
信箱	xìnxiāng	mail-box
信心	xìnxīn	confidence
信用卡	xìnyòngkǎ	credit card

熟语 Idioms

| 信口开河 | xìn kǒu kāi hé | wag one's tongue too freely |
| 背信弃义 | bèi xìn qì yì | break faith with sb. |

兴 xīng 丶 丷 丷 兴 兴 兴

（興 ´ 「 「 「 「 阝 阝 阝 阝 阝 阝 阝 阝 阝 阩 興 興）

释义 Meaning

动词 v.

1. prevail; be come popular: 前几年兴长发，现在又兴短发了。 Long hair has prevailed over the past few years.

Now short hair is becoming popular again.

2. (often used in the negative) permit; allow: 要讲道理，不 兴打人。 Please reason with people. It is not permissible to beat others.

词语 Words and Phrases

兴办	xīngbàn	initiate; set up
兴奋	xīngfèn	be excited
兴许	xīngxǔ	perhaps
新兴	xīnxīng	new and developing; burgeoning
振兴	zhènxīng	develop vigorously; promote

熟语 Idioms

| 兴风作浪 | xīng fēng zuò làng | stir up trouble; make trouble |
| 望洋兴叹 | wàng yáng xīng tàn | lament one's littleness before a vast ocean |

星 xīng   丶 冂 冂 日 尸 尸 甲 星 星

释义 Meaning

名词 n.

1. star: 天上有多少颗星？ How many stars are there in the sky?

2. bit; particle: 菜里见不到一点儿油星。 There is not a drop of fat in the dish.

词语 Words and Phrases

星期	xīngqī	week
星期六	xīngqī liù	Saturday
星期二	xīngqī 'èr	Tuesday
星期日	xīngqī rì	Sunday
星期三	xīngqī 'sān	Wednesday
星期四	xīngqī sì	Thursday

星期五	xīngqī wǔ	Friday
星期一	xīngqī yī	Monday
星球	xīngqiú	celestial (heavenly) body; star
星星	xīngxing	star
火星	huǒxīng	Mars
明星	míngxīng	star (movie)
卫星	wèixīng	satellite

熟语 Idioms

星火燎原	xīng huǒ liáo yuán	a single spark can start a prairie fire
寥若晨星	liáo ruò chén xīng	as sparse as the morning stars

行 xíng ㇒ ㇒ 彳 彳 行 行

释义 Meaning

(一) 动词 v.

1. do; perform: 你这个办法行不通。Your way won't work.

2. be all right; will do: 经理，你看这么办行不行？Manager, is this method acceptable?

(二) 形容词 adj.

capable; competent: 他真行，三天就把文章写出来了。He is really something. He has finished writing his article in three days.

词语 Words and Phrases

行动	xíngdòng	move about; get about; act; take action
行李	xínglǐ	luggage
行人	xíngrén	pedestrian
行为	xíngwéi	action; behavior; conduct
不行	bùxíng	no way
步行	bùxíng	go on foot; walk

进行	jìnxíng	proceed
举行	jǔxíng	hold; perform
流行	liúxíng	prevalent; popular; in vogue; fashionable
旅行	lǚxíng	travel
实行	shíxíng	put into practice; carry out; practise; implement
送行	sòngxíng	see off

熟语 Idioms

| 行成于思 | xíng chéng yú sī | a deed is accomplished based on an idea |
| 身体力行 | shēn tǐ lì xíng | earnestly practises what one advocates |

形 xíng　一　二　于　开　开　形　形

释义 Meaning

名词 n.

shape; form: 门窗都是方形的。The doors and windows are all square.

词语 Words and Phrases

形成	xíngchéng	form; take shape; take form
形容	xíngróng	describe
形式	xíngshì	form; shape
形势	xíngshì	situation; circumstance; condition; state of affairs
形象	xíngxiàng	figure; image; form
形状	xíngzhuàng	shape
体形	tǐxíng	shape (of a person's body)
无形	wúxíng	intangible

熟语 Idioms

| 形形色色 | xíng xíng sè sè | of all forms and shades |

| 形影不离 | xíng yǐng bù lí | inseparable; follow each other as body and shadow |

醒 xǐng 二 厂 厂 丙 西 西 酉 酊 酊 酊 酊 酊 酊 醒 醒 醒

释义 Meaning

动词 v.

1. wake up; be awake: 快醒醒，都七点了。 Wake up! It is already 7 O'clock.

2. regain consciousness; sober up; come to: 病人醒过来了。 The patient came to consciousness. 反义词 antonym: 昏

词语 Words and Phrases

醒目	xǐng mù	be striking to the eye; conspicuous
醒悟	xǐng wù	come to realize (or see) the truth, one's error, etc.; wake up to reality
惊醒	jīngxǐng	wake up with a start
清醒	qīngxǐng	regain consciousness
苏醒	sūxǐng	revive
提醒	tíxǐng	remind

熟语 Idioms

| 如梦初醒 | rú mèng chū xǐng | as if awakening from a dream; become enlightened suddenly |

姓 xìng 乚 女 女 女 姓 姓 姓 姓

释义 Meaning

动词 v.

surname: 他姓张，不姓王。 His surname is Zhang, not Wang.

词语 Words and Phrases

| 姓名 | xìngmíng | name |

百姓	bǎixìng	common people; ordinary people; civilians
复姓	fùxìng	compound surname
同姓	tóngxìng	same surname
老百姓	lǎobǎixìng	common people; folks

熟语 Idioms

| 隐姓埋名 | yǐn xìng mái míng | conceal one's identity; keep one's identity hidden |

幸 xìng 二 十 士 立 立 幸 幸 幸

释义 Meaning

形容词 a.

fortunate: 今天得以相见, 真是三生有幸。It is really most fortunate for me to meet you today.

语词 Words and Phrases

幸福	xìngfú	happiness; well-being
幸好	xìnghǎo	fortunately; luckily
幸会	xìnghuì	(a rather formal greeting) very pleased to meet you
幸亏	xìngkuī	fortunately; luckily
幸运	xìngyùn	good fortune; good luck
幸运儿	xìngyùn'ér	fortune's favorite; lucky fellow
不幸	búxìng	unfortunately
侥幸	jiǎoxìng	lucky; by luck;
荣幸	róngxìng	be honoured
万幸	wànxìng	very lucky; be very fortunate; by sheer luck

熟语 Idioms

| 幸灾乐祸 | xìng zāi lè huò | gloat over others' misfortune |

三生有幸　　　sān shēng yǒu xìng　consider oneself most fortunate (to make sb's acquaintance, etc.)

性 xìng 　ˊ　ˋ　忄　忄　忄　忄　性　性

释义 Meaning

（一）名词 n.

gender: 他有很多女性朋友。He has many female friends.

（二）尾词 suff.

A suffix designating a specified quality, property, scope, etc: 这部电影艺术性很强。This movie has high artistic quality.

词语 Words and Phrases

性别	xìngbié	sexual differentiation; sex; sexual distinction; gender
性格	xìnggé	nature; disposition
性急	xìngjí	impatient; short-tempered; quick-tempered
性命	xìngmìng	life
性质	xìngzhì	quality; nature; character
本性	běnxìng	natural instincts (or character, disposition)
个性	gèxìng	individual character; individuality;
记性	jìxìng	memory
男性	nánxìng	male
时间性	shíjiānxìng	seasonality; timeliness; topicality
思想性	sīxiǎngxìng	ideological content (or level)
一次性	yícìxìng	once only (without a second time)

熟语 Idioms

性命交关	xìng mìng jiāo guān	(a matter) of life and death;

| 习与性成 | xí yǔ xìng chéng | habit becomes second nature |

兄 xiōng 　丨　冂　口　尸　兄

释义 Meaning

名词 n.

brother: 兄妹二人办了一家公司。 The brother and sister ran a company.

词语 Words and Phrases

兄弟	xiōngdì	brothers
兄弟	xiōngdi	younger brother; a familiar form of address for a man younger than oneself
兄长	xiōngzhǎng	elder brother
弟兄	dìxiōng	brother
父兄	fùxiōng	father and elder brothers; head of family
师兄	shīxiōng	senior (male) fellow apprentice

熟语 Idioms

| 称兄道弟 | chēng xiōng dào dì | address each other in great familiarity |
| 难兄难弟 | nàn xiōng nàn dì | two of a kind; two just alike |

胸 xiōng 　丿　刀　月　月　肐　肐　肑　胸　胸　胸

释义 Meaning

名词 n.

chest; breast: 这几天我胸有点儿疼。 These few days I have got a bit of a pain in my chest.

词语 Words and Phrases

| 胸怀 | xiōnghuái | mind; heart |

| 胸膛 | xiōngtáng | chest |
| 心胸 | xīnxiōng | breath of mind; aspiration; ambition |

熟语 Idioms

| 胸无点墨 | xiōng wú diǎn mò | have little learning; utterly uneducated |
| 胸有成竹 | xiōng yǒu chéng zhú | have definite ideas to meet a situation; well prepared |

熊 xióng ノ ム ㇀ 台 育 育 育 能 能 能 能 熊 熊

释义 Meaning

名词 n.

bear: 他在树林里看到了一只大熊。He saw a big bear in the forest.

词语 Words and Phrases

| 熊猫 | xióngmāo | panda |

熟语 Idioms

| 熊腰虎背 | xióng yāo hǔ bèi | have a back like a tiger's and a waist like a bear's; tough and stocky; strong |

休 xiū ノ 亻 仁 什 休 休

释义 Meaning

动词 v.

1. stop; cease: 不要为这点儿小事争论不休。Don't argue over this trifle ceaselessly.

2. rest: 他身体不好，休了一个月假。He is not in good health. He took a month's sick leave.

词语 Words and Phrases

| 休会 | xiūhuì | adjourn |

休假	xiūjià	have a holiday or vacation
休息	xiūxī	have a rest
休养	xiūyǎng	recuperate; convalesce
公休	gōngxiū	general holiday; official holiday
离休	líxiū	(of veteran cadres) retire
退休	tuìxiū	retire

熟语 Idioms

休戚相关	xiū qī xiāng guān	joys and sorrows interconnected; of close concern to each other
无尽无休	wú jìn wú xiū	incessant; endless
一不做， 二不休	yī bú zuò, èr bù xiū	carry it through, whatever the consequences; in for a penny, in for a pound

修 xiū ⟨丿 亻 亻 亻 俨 攸 修 修 修⟩

释义 Meaning

动词 v.

1. repair: 自行车坏了，要去修一修。The bike is broken. It has to be taken for repairs.
2. build; construct: 这里新修了一条铁路。There is a newly built railway here.

词语 Words and Phrases

修订	xiūdìng	revise
修复	xiūfù	repair; restore; renovate
修改	xiūgǎi	revise; modify; amend; alter
修建	xiūjiàn	build; construct; erect
修养	xiūyǎng	accomplishment; training; mastery
修正	xiūzhèng	revise; amend; correct
修筑	xiūzhù	build; construct; put up
进修	jìnxiū	engage in advanced studies

| 选修 | xuǎnxiū | take as an elective course |
| 装修 | zhuāngxiū | fit up (a house, etc.); rennovate |

熟语 Idioms

| 修旧利废 | xiū jiù lì fèi | repair and utilize old and discarded things |
| 不修边幅 | bù xiū biān fú | does not care about our's appearance |

秀 xiù　一　二　千　禾　禾　秀　秀

释义 Meaning

形容词 adj.

elegant; beautiful: 这里山清水秀，景色十分迷人。Here are green hills and clear waters, with a picturesque scenery.

词语 Words and Phrases

秀丽	xiùlì	beautiful; handsome; pretty
秀气	xiùqi	delicate; elegant; fine
清秀	qīngxiù	delicate and pretty
优秀	yōuxiù	excellent

熟语 Idioms

秀色可餐	xiùsè kě cān	be a feast to the eyes (usu. said of a very attractive woman, or of a beautiful scenery)
秀外慧中	xiù wài huì zhōng	beautiful and intelligent
苗而不秀	miáo ér bú xiù	put forth shoots but fail to flower; show great potentials but fail to bear fruit

需 xū　一　一　一　一　一　一　一　一　一　一　一　一　一　一

释义 Meaning

动词 v.

need: 只需一把火, 就能把它从洞里赶出来。If we only had a torch of fire, we could drive it (that thing) from the cave.

词语 Words and Phrases

需求	xūqiú	requirement; demand
需要	xūyào	need; want; require; demand
必需	bìxū	essential; indispensable
急需	jíxū	be badly in need of; urgent needed

熟语 Idioms

不时之需	bù shí zhī xū	a need which may arise any time in the future

许 xǔ 　`　讠　讠　讠　许　许

(許　`　亠　亠　亖　言　言　言　計　許　許　許)

释义 Meaning

(一) 动词 v.

permit; allow: 这个工作三天一定要完成，不许拖延。This job has to be done in three days, delay is not permitted.

(二) 副词 adv.

perhaps: 他今天没来，许是生病了。He didn't come today. Perhaps he was ill.

词语 Words and Phrases

许多	xǔduō	many; much; a great deal of; a lot of
许久	xǔjiǔ	for a long time; for ages
许可	xǔkě	permit; allow
或许	huòxǔ	perhaps
少许	shǎoxǔ	a few; a little

也许	yěxǔ	perhaps; maybe
允许	yǔnxǔ	allow; permit
准许	zhǔnxǔ	permit; allow

熟语 Idioms

封官许愿　fēng guān xǔ yuàn　offer official posts and make lavish promises

宣 xuān 　丶　丶　宀　宀　宀　宦　宦　宣　宣

释义 Meaning

动词 v.

declare: 他们不宣而战，我们只好奉陪到底了。They opened hostilities without declaring war. We had to take up the fight to the finish.

词语 Words and Phrases

宣布	xuānbù	declare; proclaim; announce
宣称	xuānchēng	assert; declare; profess
宣传	xuānchuán	conduct propaganda; propagate; disseminate; give publicity to
宣读	xuāndú	read out (in public)
宣告	xuāngào	declare; proclaim
宣誓	xuānshì	take (or swear) an oath
宣言	xuānyán	declaration; manifesto
宣扬	xuānyáng	publicize; propagate; advocate

熟语 Idioms

心照不宣　xīn zhào bú xuān　have a tacit mutual understanding

选 xuǎn 　丿　广　牛　生　失　先　先　选　选

(選 ㄱ ㄱ ㅂ ㅂ ㅂ ㅂ ㅂ 毕 毕 毕 罪

罪 罪 選 選)

释义 Meaning

动词 v.

1. select; choose; pick: 那个女孩子被导演选上了。That girl was choosen by the director.

2. elect: 我们选他当班长。We elected him our monitor.

词语 Words and Phrases

选举	xuǎnjǔ	elect
选手	xuǎnshǒu	an athlete selected for a sport game
选修	xuǎnxiū	take as an elective course
选择	xuǎnzé	select; choose; opt for
挑选	tiāoxuǎn	pick out; choose; select

学 xué 丶 丷 ⺌ ⺌ 兴 学 学 学

(學 ´ ⺁ ㇠ ㇠ ㇠ ㇠ ㇠ 闶 闶 闶 闶

闶 與 學 學 學)

释义 Meaning

动词 v.

1. study; learn: 他哥哥在美国学电脑。His brother is majoring in computer science in the US.

2. imitate; mimic: 孩子学他爸爸走路的样子。The child imitates his father's way of walking.

词语 Words and Phrases

学费	xuéfèi	fee; tuition
学科	xuékē	a branch of learning; studies
学年	xuénián	school (or academic) year

学期	xuéqī	semester
学生	xuéshēng	student
学时	xuéshí	class hour; period
学术	xuéshù	academic learning
学位	xuéwèi	academic degree; degree
学问	xuéwèn	academic learning
学习	xuéxí	study; learn
学校	xuéxiào	school
学院	xuéyuàn	college
大学	dàxué	university
汉学	hànxué	sinology
教学	jiàoxué	teaching education
开学	kāi xué	school opens; term begins
留学	liú xué	study abroad
上学	shàng xué	go to school
同学	tóngxué	classmate
文学	wénxué	literature
小学	xiǎoxué	primary school
中学	zhōngxué	junior or senior high school
自学	zìxué	study on one's own; self-study

熟语 Idioms

学而不厌	xué ér bú yàn	insatiable in learning
学以致用	xué yǐ zhì yòng	make study serve practical purpose
不学无术	bù xué wú shù	have neither learning nor skill

雪 xuě　一 厂 戸 雨 雨 雨 雨 雪 雪 雪

释义 Meaning

名词 n.

snow: 昨天晚上下了一场大雪。Last night there was a heavy fall of snow.

词语 Words and Phrases

雪白	xuěbái	snow white
雪花	xuěhuā	snowflake
雪亮	xuěliàng	bright as snow; shiny; clear
雪山	xuěshān	a snow-capped mountain
滑雪	huá xuě	ski

熟语 Idioms

雪上加霜	xuě shàng jiā shuāng	add frost to snow; one disaster after another
雪中送炭	xuě zhōng sòng tàn	send coal during snowing winter; provide timely help

血 xuè ′ ｒ 白 血 血 血

释义 Meaning

名词 n.

energetic and high-spirited: 他是个血性汉子,受不了半点虚假。He is a courageous and upright man who cannot stand any hypocrisy.

词语 Words and Phrases

血管	xuèguǎn	blood vessel
血汗	xuèhàn	blood and sweat; sweat and toil
血型	xuèxíng	blood group; blood type
血压	xuèyā	blood pressure
血液	xuèyè	(human) blood
心血	xīnxuè	painstaking care (or effort)

熟语 Idioms

血气方刚	xuèqì fāng gāng	the hot blood of youth
血肉相连	xuè ròu xiāng lián	be inseparably linked to each other
呕心沥血	ǒu xīn lì xuè	shed one's heart's blood; take infinite pains for (a cause)

训 xùn ` 讠 训 训 训

(訓 ` ˊ ˊ ˊ 言 言 言 訓 訓 訓)

释义 Meaning

动词 v.

give sb. a lecture; admonish: 父亲把孩子训了一顿。The father gave his child a lecture.

词语 Words and Phrases

训练	xùnliàn	train; drill
教训	jiàoxùn	lesson; moral; chide; teach sb. a lesson
培训	péixùn	train (personnel)

讯 xùn ` 讠 讯 讯 讯

(訊 ` ˊ ˊ ˊ 言 言 言 訊 訊 訊)

释义 Meaning

名词 n.

information; news; message: 消防队闻讯赶到火灾现场。The fire brigade was informed and got to the scene where fire broke out.

词语 Words and Phrases

讯问	xùnwèn	interrogate; question

电讯	diànxùn	(telegraphic) dispatch; telecommunication
简讯	jiǎnxùn	news in brief
通讯	tōngxùn	communication; news report; news dispatch
问讯	wènxùn	inquire; ask
音讯	yīnxùn	mail; message; news

压 yā　二 厂 厃 圧 压 压

(壓 二 厂 厂 厍 厍 厍 厍 厢 厢 厢 厎
厎 厭 厭 壓 壓 壓)

释义 Meaning
动词 v.

1. press; push down; hold down; weigh down: 大雪把树枝压弯了。A heavy fall of snow weighed the branches down.

2. overwhelm; overpower; prevail over: 多大的困难都没把他压倒。Difficulty can't overwhelm him.

词语 Words and Phrases

压力	yālì	pressure
压迫	yāpò	oppress; repress
压缩	yāsuō	compress
压抑	yāyì	constrain; inhibit; depress
压制	yāzhì	pressing
电压	diànyā	voltage
气压	qìyā	atmospheric pressure
血压	xuèyā	blood pressure

牙 yá　二 三 牙 牙

释义 Meaning

名词 n.

tooth: 他刚拔了个牙齿，还不能吃饭。He has just had a tooth pulled. He still can't eat.

词语 Words and Phrases

牙齿	yáchǐ	tooth
牙膏	yágāo	toothpaste
牙签儿	yáqiānr	toothpick
牙刷	yáshuā	toothbrush

熟语 Idioms

虎口拔牙	hǔ kǒu bá yá	pull a tooth from the tiger's mouth; dare the greatest danger
以眼还眼，以牙还牙	yǐ yǎn huán yǎn, yǐ yá huán yá	an eye for an eye and a tooth for a tooth

延 yán   一 丁 干 正 延 延

释义 Meaning

动词 v.

postpone: 假期向后延了。The holiday has been postponed.

词语 Words and Phrases

延长	yáncháng	lengthen; prolong; extend
延迟	yánchí	delay; defer; postpone
延期	yánqī	postpone; defer; put off
延缓	yánhuǎn	continue; go on; last
拖延	tuōyán	delay; put off; procrastinate

熟语 Idioms

延年益寿	yán nián yì shòu	promote longevity; extend one's life
苟延残喘	gǒu yán cán chuǎn	be on one's last legs

严 yán 一 丁 下 兀 兀 亚 严

(嚴 ` 冖 冖 冖 严 严 严 严 严 严 严
严 严 严 严 严 严 严 嚴)

释义 Meaning

形容词 adj.

1. tight: 他嘴严，从来不乱说。He is tight-mouthed, and never talks nonsense. 反义词 antonym: 松

2. strict; severe: 老师对学生要求很严。The teacher is very strict with students. 反义词 antonym: 宽

词语 Words and Phrases

严格	yángé	strict; rigorous; rigid; stringent
严寒	yánhán	severe cold; bitter cold
严禁	yánjìn	strictly forbid (or prohibit)
严峻	yánjùn	stern; severe; rigorous; grim
严厉	yánlì	stern; severe
严密	yánmì	tight; close
严肃	yánsù	serious; solemn; earnest
严重	yánzhòng	serious; grave; critical

熟语 Idioms

严阵以待	yán zhèn yǐ dài	stand readily in battle
义正词严	yì zhèng cí yán	speak sternly with justice

言 yán ` 亠 亖 言 言 言 言

释义 Meaning

名词 n.

speech; word: 大家你一言我一语，展开了热烈的讨论。
Everyone spoke out in a lively discussion.

词语 Words and Phrases

言论	yánlùn	opinion on public affairs; expression of one's political views
言行	yánxíng	words and deeds
言语	yányǔ	speak; talk; answer
方言	fāngyán	(regional) dialect
谎言	huǎngyán	lie
诺言	nuòyán	promise
谣言	yáoyán	words bandied from mouth to mouth; hearsay; rumor
语言	yǔyán	language

熟语 Idioms

言必信，行必果	yán bì xìn, xíng bì guǒ	be true in word and resolute in deed
言过其实	yán guò qí shí	overstate; talk big
言行不一	yán xíng bù yī	the deeds do not match the words
言者无罪，闻者足戒	yán zhě wú zuì, wén zhě zú jiè	not to blame the one who speaks out but heed what you hear

沿 yán ` ` 氵 氵 氵 沿 沿 沿

释义 Meaning

介词 prep.

along

1. 船沿着海岸航行。The ship is sailing along the coast.

2. 沿河边种了一排柳树。A line of willows is planted along the river-bank.

词语 Words and Phrases

沿岸	yán'àn	along the bank or coast
沿海	yánhǎi	along the coast

| 沿途 | yántú | on the way |
| 沿线 | yánxiàn | along the line (i.e. a railway, highway, air or shipping line) |

研 yán　二 丁 亻 石 石 矴 矴 矴 研

释义 Meaning

动词 v.

grind; pestle: 墨研好了，快来写吧。The ink is ready. Come to write soon.

词语 Words and Phrases

研究	yánjiū	study; research
研究生	yánjiūshēng	graduate (student); researcher
研究员	yánjiūyuán	research fellow
研讨	yántǎo	deliberate; study and discuss
科研	kēyán	scientific research
钻研	zuānyán	study intensively; dig into
教研室	jiàoyánshì	teaching and research section

盐 yán　一 十 土 圤 扑 扑 卦 盐 盐 盐

（鹽 一 丆 王 乎 乎 臣 臥 臣 臣 臣 臣

臨 臨 臨 臨 臨 臨 臨 臨 臨 臨 臨

鹽 鹽）

释义 Meaning

名词 n.

salt: 他喜欢吃淡的，菜里少放点儿盐。He likes to eat light foods. You had better put less salt in the dishes.

词语 Words and Phrases

| 盐湖 | yánhú | salt lake |

食盐　　shíyán　　table salt

颜 yán

名 ` 亠 亠 产 立 产 产 彦 彦 彦 彦 彦 颜 颜 颜

(顔 ` 亠 亠 产 立 产 产 彦 彦 彦 彦 顔 顔 顔 顔 顔 顔)

释义 Meaning

名词 n.

appearance; looks: 她说起话来总是和颜悦色。She is always with a kind and pleasant countenance when she speaks.

词语 Words and Phrases

颜料　　yánliào　　pigment; colouring
颜色　　yánsè　　colour
容颜　　róngyán　　appearance; looks

熟语 Idioms

和颜悦色　　hé yán yuè sè　　friendly and accessible
五颜六色　　wǔ yán liù sè　　colourful
喜笑颜开　　xǐ xiào yán kāi　　light up with pleasure
鹤发童颜　　hè fà tóng yán　　white hair and ruddy complexion; healthy in old age

眼 yǎn

丨 刂 刂 目 目 目 目 目 眼 眼

释义 Meaning

名词 n.

1. eye: 那个人一喳眼瞎了。That man was blind in one eye.

2. look; glance: 我一眼就认出是她。I recognized her at first glance.

3. a small hole; aperture: 她用针在纸上扎了很多眼儿。She pierced many holes on the paper with a needle.

词语 Words and Phrases

眼光	yǎnguāng	eye; sight; foresight
眼睛	yǎnjīng	eye
眼镜	yǎnjìng	glasses
眼看	yǎnkàn	soon; in a moment
眼泪	yǎnlèi	tears
眼力	yǎnlì	eyesight; vision
眼前	yǎnqián	before one's eyes, now
眼色	yǎnsè	a hint given with the eyes
眼神	yǎnshén	expression in one's eyes
眼下	yǎnxià	at the moment; at present; nowadays
亲眼	qīnyǎn	with one's own eyes
心眼儿	xīnyǎnr	heart; mind

熟语 Idioms

眼高手低	yǎn gāo shǒu dī	have high ambition but little talent
眼明手快	yǎn míng shǒu kuài	sharp and quick

演 yǎn 　丶　丶　氵　氵　氵　汛　汿　汿　渀　渀　演　演　演　演

释义 Meaning

动词 v.

act; perform; put on: 这位演员在电影里常常演坏人。This actor often plays the evildoer in movies.

词语 Words and Phrases

演变	yǎnbiàn	develop; evolve
演唱	yǎnchàng	sing (in a performance)
演出	yǎnchū	perform; show; put on a show
演讲	yǎnjiǎng	give a lecture; make a speech
演说	yǎnshuō	deliver a speech
演算	yǎnsuàn	perform mathematical calculations
演习	yǎnxí	manoeuvre; exercise; drill
演奏	yǎnzòu	give an instrumental performance
表演	biǎoyǎn	act; perform
导演	dǎoyǎn	director
开演	kāiyǎn	the performance starts

厌 yàn ⼀ 厂 厂 厌 厌 厌

(厭 ⼀ 厂 厂 厭 厭 厭 厭 厭 厭 厭 厭 厭 厭 厭)

释义 Meaning

动词 v.

be fed up with; be bored with; be tired of: 天天这个菜，我吃厌了。I am sick of eating this dish everyday.

词语 Words and Phrases

厌烦	yànfán	be sick of; fed up with
厌恶	yànwù	detest; abhor; abominate; be disgusted with
讨厌	tǎoyàn	disagreeable; disgusting

熟语 Idioms

| 不厌其烦 | bú yàn qí fán | not mind taking the trouble |
| 百读不厌 | bǎi dú bú yàn | be worth reading a hundred times |

验 yàn 丁 马 马 马 马 马 马 马 马 验 验

（驗 一 厂 Ϝ Ϝ Ϝ 馬 馬 馬 馬 馬 馬
驗 驗 驗 驗 驗 驗 驗 驗 驗 驗 驗
驗 ）

释义 Meaning

动词 v.

examine; check; test: 护照验完了，可以走了。The checking of your passport has been completed, you can go now.

词语 Words and Phrases

验看	yànkàn	examine; inspect
验收	yànshōu	check and accept; check before acceptance
验证	yànzhèng	verify
测验	cèyàn	examination; test
经验	jīngyàn	experience
考验	kǎoyàn	test; trial
实验	shíyàn	experiment
试验	shìyàn	experiment
体验	tǐyàn	learn from practice

扬 yáng 一 十 扌 扚 扬 扬

（揚 一 十 扌 扌 护 护 护 捛 捛 揚
揚 ）

释义 Meaning

动词 v.

raise (or kick up) a dust: 汽车开过，扬起许多尘土。The car passed by and raised a lot of dust.

词语 Words and Phrases

表扬	biǎoyáng	praise
发扬	fāyáng	carry on (or forward); champion
宣扬	xuānyáng	publicize; propagate
赞扬	zànyáng	praise

熟语 Idioms

扬长避短	yáng cháng bì duǎn	show one's advantage and avoid one's disadvantage
扬眉吐气	yáng méi tǔ qì	with one's chin up; feel proud and elated
趾高气扬	zhǐ gāo qì yáng	strut about and give oneself airs

羊 yáng 丶 丷 兰 兰 兰 羊

释义 Meaning

名词 n.

sheep: 他数了数，少了一只羊。He counted the sheep and came up one short.

词语 Words and Phrases

羊毛	yángmáo	sheep's wool; wool; fleece
羊肉	yángròu	mutton

熟语 Idioms

羊肠鸟道	yángcháng niǎo dào	a zigzag path
羊质虎皮	yáng zhì hǔ pí	a sheep in a tiger's skin; outwardly strong, inwardly weak
顺手牵羊	shùn shǒu qiān yáng	lead off a goat in passing; pick up sth. on the way (steal something)

阳 yáng ﻆ 阝 阝 阳 阳 阳

(陽 ⁊ ⻖ ⻖ ⻖ ⻖ ⻖ ⻖ ⻖ 阳 阳 陽)

释义 Meaning

名词 n.

the sun: 向阳的地方花草长得好。The place facing south is good for flowers and grass.

词语 Words and Phrases

阳光	yángguāng	sunlight; sunshine
阳历	yánglì	solar calendar
阳台	yángtái	balcony or veranda
太阳	tàiyáng	the sun

熟语 Idioms

| 阳春白雪 | yáng chūn báixuě | highbrow tune |
| 阳奉阴违 | yáng fèng yīn wéi | outwardly obey orders but secretly ignore them |

养 yǎng ` ⸴ 丷 兰 兰 关 美 美 养

(養 ` ⸴ 丷 兰 兰 关 关 关 耮 耮 耮 耮 養 養)

释义 Meaning

动词 v.

1. support; provide for: 他从小失去父母，是叔叔把他养大的。He lost his parents when he was a child and was brought up by his uncle.

2. raise; keep; grow: 他的爱好是养花。His hobby is to plant flowers.

3. rest; convalesce; heal: 他的病养了一段时间，已经好了。He took a good rest and already recovered from his illness.

4. cultivate; form; acquire: 他从小养成了爱劳动的习惯。He cultivated good habits of working hard when he was a child.

词语 Words and Phrases

养活	yǎnghuó	support; feed
养老院	yǎnglǎoyuàn	nursing home
养料	yǎngliào	nourishment
养育	yǎngyù	bring up; rear
培养	péiyǎng	train; nurture
休养	xiūyǎng	recuperate; convalesce
营养	yíngyǎng	nutrition

熟语 Idioms

养精蓄锐	yǎng jīng xù ruì	build up strength and store up energy
养尊处优	yǎng zūn chǔ yōu	lead a comfortable and wellfed life
娇生惯养	jiāoshēngguànyǎng	have been delicately brought up

样 yàng 一 十 才 木 术 栏 栏 栏 栏 样

(樣 一 十 才 木 术 栏 栏 栏 栏 样 样 様 様 樣)

释义 Meaning

（一）名词 n.

appearance; shape: 上海一年一个样。Shanghai varies its look every year.

（二）量词 measure w.

kind; type: 桌上放着四样点心，三样水果。There are four kinds of pastries and three kinds of fruits on the table.

词语 Words and Phrases

样式	yàngshì	pattern; type; style; form
样子	yàngzi	appearance; shape
那样	nàyàng	such; so
式样	shìyàng	style
同样	tóngyàng	same
一样	yíyàng	same
怎样	zěnyàng	how; what; why
这样	zhèyàng	so; such
怎么样	zěnmeyàng	how; what
不怎么样	bùzěnmeyàng	so so

熟语 Idioms

依样画葫芦	yī yàng huà húlu	copy mechanically
一模一样	yì mú yí yàng	exactly alike; as like as two peas

腰 yāo 丿 刀 刀 月 厂 厂 厂 腭 腭 腭 腭 腰 腰 腰

释义 Meaning

名词 n.

waist: 他弯着腰在找什么东西。He bent over to look for sth.

词语 Words and Phrases

腰包	yāobāo	purse; pocket
腰带	yāodài	belt; girdle

熟语 Idioms

腰缠万贯	yāo chán wàn guàn	be loaded; be very rich
点头哈腰	diǎn tóu hā yāo	bow unctuously

虎背熊腰	hǔ bèi xióng yāo	have a back like a tiger's and a waist like a bear's; tough and stocky appearance

邀 yāo

′ ⼴ ⼴ ⽩ ⽩ ⽩ ⾃ ⾃ ⾝ ⾝
⾝ ⾝ ⾝ ⾝ 激 邀

释义 Meaning

动词 v.

invite: 应邀出席的还有大使夫人。The wife of the ambassador was also invited to appear.

词语 Words and Phrases

邀请	yāoqǐng	invite
特邀	tèyāo	specially invited
应邀	yīngyāo	at sb's invitation; on invitation

摇 yáo

⼆ ⼗ ⼿ 扩 扩 扩 扩 扩 扩 抵
择 捤 摇

释义 Meaning

动词 v.

shake; wave: 他什么也不说，只是摇头。He said nothing, but shook his head.

词语 Words and Phrases

摇摆	yáobǎi	sway; swing; rock; vacillate
摇晃	yáohuàng	rock; sway; shake
遥控	yáokòng	remote control
动摇	dòngyáo	shake; vacillate; waver

熟语 Idioms

摇头晃脑	yáo tóu huǎng nǎo	wag one's head; look pleased with oneself

| 摇摇欲坠 | yáo yáo yù zhuì | tottering; crumbling; on the verge of collapse |

咬 yǎo ⏐ ⏐⏐ ⏐⏐ ⏐⏐` ⼝ ⼝ ⼝ ⼝ 咬

释义 Meaning

动词 v.

1. bite; snap at: 昨天晚上我被蚊子咬了几个大包。 Last night I was bitten a lot by the mosquitoes.

2. chew: 这种面包太硬了，老人咬不动。This kind of bread is too tough to chew for the aged.

熟语 Idioms

| 咬牙切齿 | yǎo yá qiè chǐ | clench one's teeth in bitter hatred or anger |

药 yào 一 十 艹 艻 艻 芴 莇 药 药

(藥 一 十 艹 艹 产 苷 苷 苷 苗 萌 蓢 薜 蕐 蕐 藭 蕐 蕐 藥)

释义 Meaning

名词 n.

medicine: 这种药效果不错。This kind of medicine has good effect.

词语 Words and Phrases

药店	yàodiàn	drugstore; chemist's shop
药片	yàopiàn	(medicinal) tablet
西药	xīyào	Western medicine
中药	zhōngyào	Chinese medicine

熟语 Idioms

| 不可救药 | bù kě jiù yào | incurable; hopeless |
| 换汤不换药 | huàn tāng bú huàn yào | old wine in new bottle |

要 yào 一 厂 厂 厂 两 两 要 要 要

释义 Meaning

（一）助动词 auxiliary verb

1. want to; wish to: 他要学游泳。He wants to learn swimming.

2. shall; will; be going to: 天要下雨了。It will begin raining soon.

（二）动词 v.

1. want; desire: 你要啤酒还是可口可乐？Would you like beer or coke?

2. ask for: 我去跟医生要点儿止痛片。I will ask for some asprin from the doctor.

（三）连词 conj.

if; suppose; in case: 明天要下雨，我就不去了。If it rains tomorrow, I will not go.

词语 Words and Phrases

要不	yàobù	otherwise; or else; or
要不然	yàobùrán	otherwise
要不是	yàobúshì	if it were not for; but for
要点	yàodiǎn	main point; essentials; gist
要好	yàohǎo	be on good terms
要紧	yàojǐn	important; essential
要么	yàome	or; either...or...
要命	yàomìng	drive sb. to his death
要是	yàoshì	if; suppose
不要	búyào	won't
快要	kuàiyào	will be doing
只要	zhǐyào	as long as
重要	zhòngyào	important

主要　　　zhǔyào　　　main

熟语 Idioms

要言不烦　　yào yán bù fán　　brief and to the point

简明扼要　　jiǎn míng è'yào　　brief and to the point; concise

也 yě ㇆ 十 也

释义 Meaning

副词 adv.

1. also; too: 风停了，雨也住了。The wind stopped. The rain stopped, too.
2. both... and; either...or: 他也会开车，也会修车。He can both drive and repair a car.
3. whether... or: 你去我也去，你不去我也去。I will go whether you go or not.
4. still; yet: 你不说，我也知道。You don't have to tell me. I know already.
5. used for emphasis, often before a negative expression: 连孩子也能回答这个问题。Even a child can answer this question.

词语 Words and Phrases

也许　　　yěxǔ　　　perhaps; maybe

熟语 Idioms

空空如也　　kōng kōng rú yě　　absolutely empty

业 yè 丨 丬 业 业 业

(業 丿 丬 丬 业 业 业 业 当 当 当 業 業 業)

释义 Meaning

名词 n.

词语 Words and Phrases

业务	yèwù	business
业余	yèyú	after-hours; amateurish
毕业	bì yè	graduate
工业	gōngyè	industry
就业	jiù yè	obtain employment
农业	nóngyè	agriculture
企业	qǐyè	enterprise
商业	shāngyè	commerce
失业	shīyè	lose one's job; be out of work; be un-employed
事业	shìyè	cause; undertaking; career
营业	yíngyè	do business
职业	zhíyè	career; profession
专业	zhuānyè	profession; professional
作业	zuòyè	homework; work

熟语 Idioms

业精于勤	yè jīng yú qín	mastery of work comes from diligent application
安居乐业	ān jū lè yè	live and work in peace and contentment
兢兢业业	jīng jīng yè yè	cautious and conscientious

叶 yè   丨   刂   叮   叮一   叶

(葉 一 艹 艹 芇 芇 苹 苹 葦 葦 葦 葦

葉**)**

释义 Meaning

名词 n.

leaf: 这是一棵只长叶不开花的树。This is not a flowering tree. It will grow leaves, but will not blossom.

词语 Words and Phrases

叶子	yèzi	leaf
茶叶	cháyè	tea

熟语 Idioms

叶落归根	yè luò guī gēn	the leaves fall back to their root; a person residing elsewhere finally returns to his native land at old age
粗枝大叶	cū zhī dà yè	crude and careless; sloppy
添枝加叶	tiān zhī jiā yè	add colour and emphasis to (a narration)

页 yè　二 二 广 页 页 页

(頁 二 二 广 页 百 百 百 頁 頁)

释义 Meaning

名词 n.

page: 这本书有五百八十页。This book has five hundred and eighty pages.

词语 Words and Phrases

页码	yèmǎ	page number
画页	huàyè	page with illustrations

夜 yè　丶 二 广 广 疒 夜 夜 夜

释义 Meaning

名词 n.

night: 这件事三天三夜也讲不完。 反义词 antonym: 日或昼。 It would take days to tell it all.

词语 Words and Phrases

夜班	yèbān	night shift
夜间	yèjiān	at night
夜里	yèlǐ	in the night
夜晚	yèwǎn	night
夜宵	yèxiāo	snack (or refreshments) taken at night
半夜	bànyè	midnight
日夜	rìyè	day and night; round the clock
午夜	wǔyè	midnight

熟语 Idioms

夜长梦多	yè cháng mèng duō	a long night brings many dreams; delay brings danger
夜以继日	yè yǐ jì rì	night and day
深更半夜	shēn gēng bàn yè	at the deadth of night

一yī　　二

释义 Meaning

（一）数词 num.

1. one: 北京我去过一次。 I have been to Beijing once.

2. used in the middle of a duplicated verb: 让我看一看。 Let me have a look.

3. whole; all; throughout: 我打了场球，出了一身汗。 I played a game of (basket) ball and was sweating all over.

4. same: 你说的跟他说的不是一回事。 What you said is not the same as what he said.

5. used before a verb or a verbal measure to indicate an action to be followed by a result: 他一脚把球踢进了球门。He shot the ball into the goal with one kick.

（二）副词 adv.

1. single; alone; only one: 他一猜就猜中了这个谜语。He got the answer to the riddle on his first guess.

2. used before a verb or an adjective, indicating the suddenness or thoroughness of an action or a change in the situation: 早上起来一看，外边雪下得很厚了。When I got up, I looked out and found a thick layer of snow outside.

词语 Words and Phrases

一半	yíbàn	half
一定	yídìng	fixed; certainly
一共	yígòng	in all; altogether
一会儿	yíhuìr	a little while
一块儿	yíkuàir	at the same place; together
一切	yíqiè	all
一下儿	yíxiàr	one time; once
一下子	yíxiàzi	in a short while
一样	yíyàng	same
一般	yìbān	general
一点儿	yìdiǎnr	a bit; a little
一起	yìqǐ	in the same place; together
一些	yìxiē	some; a number of
一直	yìzhí	straight; all along

熟语 Idioms

一寸光阴 一寸金	yí cùn guāngyīn yí cùn jīn	Every second counts; time is precious
一路平安	yí lù píng'ān	a pleasant journey

| 一无所有 | yì wú suǒ yǒu | penniless; have nothing at all |
| 不管三七
二十一 | bù guǎn sān qī
èr shí yī | casting all caution to the winds |

衣 yī 丶 亠 宀 衣 衣 衣

释义 Meaning

名词 n.

clothes: 在那里，常常可以见到衣不蔽体的孩子。 One can often see children dressed in rags there.

衣服	yīfu	clothes
衣裳	yīshang	clothing; clothes
大衣	dàyī	overcoat
毛衣	máoyī	sweater
内衣	nèiyī	underwear
睡衣	shuìyī	pyjamas; nightclothes
外衣	wàiyī	coat; jacket; outer clothing

熟语 Idioms

| 衣冠禽兽 | yī guān qín shòu | a beast in human dress |
| 量体裁衣 | liáng tǐ cái yī | cut the garment according to the figure; act according to actual circumstances |

医 yī 一 厂 匚 匸 至 至 医

（醫 一 厂 匚 匸 至 至 医 医 医 医 医 医 医 医 医 殹 殹 醫 醫 醫 醫 醫 ）

释义 Meaning

（一）名词 n.

medical science: 我想学医。 I want to study medicine.

(二) 动词 v.

cure; treat: 医生医好了他的病。 The doctor cured him of his illness.

词语 Words and Phrases

医疗	yīliáo	medicial treatment
医生	yīshēng	doctor
医院	yīyuàn	hospital
医治	yīzhì	cure; treat; heal
西医	xīyī	Western medicine
中医	zhōngyī	Chinese medicine

熟语 Idioms

| 头痛医头，
脚痛医脚 | tóutòng yī tóu,
jiǎo tòng yī jiǎo | treat the head when the head aches, treat the foot when the foot hurts; treat the symptoms but not the cause |

依yī ノ 亻 亻 仁 仁 依 依 依

释义 Meaning

动词 v.

comply with; listen to; yield to: 你的主意好，就依你。 Yours is a good idea. Let's just go with it.

词语 Words and Phrases

依旧	yījiù	as before; still
依据	yījù	according to; in the light of
依靠	yīkào	rely on; depend on
依然	yīrán	still; as before
依照	yīzhào	according to; in accordance with

熟语 Idioms

| 依然如故 | yī rán rú gù | remain unchanged |

依依不舍　　　yī yī bù shě　　　　unwilling to part with

宜 yí　　`　宀　宀　宀　官　官　宜

释义 Meaning

形容词 a.

suitable; appropriate: 中国也有少儿不宜的电影。China also has films that are unsuitable for children.

词语 Words and Phrases

便宜　　biányi　　　cheap

适宜　　shìyí　　　suitable; appropriate; favuorable

熟语 Idioms

权宜之计　　quányí zhī jì　　　an expedient measure

不合时宜　　bùhé shíyí　　　be out of keeping with the times

姨 yí　　乚　女　女　妒　妒　妒　娉　姨

释义 Meaning

名词 n.

aunt: 二姨去了美国，三姨去了日本。Mother's second sister went to the US, her third sister went to Japan.

词语 Words and Phrases

姨父　　yífu　　　uncle (husband of mother's sister)

姨母　　yímǔ　　　aunt (mother's sister)

阿姨　　āyí　　　aunt; a form of address for a woman of one's parents' generation

小姨子　　xiǎoyízi　　　wife's younger sister

移 yí　　一　二　千　千　禾　禾　秒　秒　移　移　移

释义 Meaning

动词 v.

move; remove: 把这花儿移到大花盆里去。Move this flower to the big flowerpot.

词语 Words and Phrases

移动	yídòng	move; shift
移民	yímín	migrate; emigrate or immigrate
移植	yízhí	transplant
迁移	qiānyí	move; remove; migrate

熟语 Idioms

移风易俗	yí fēng yì sú	transform established traditions and practices
移山倒海	yí shān dǎo hǎi	move mountains and drain seas; transform nature

已 yǐ　　　乛 コ 已

释义 Meaning

副词 adv.

already: 中国已和一百多个国家建立了外交关系。China has already established diplomatic relations with more than a hundred countries.

词语 Words and Phrases

已经	yǐjīng	already
早已	zǎoyǐ	long ago; for a long time

熟语 Idioms

木已成舟	mù yǐ chéng zhōu	the wood is already made into a boat; what is done cannot be undone
迫不得已	pò bù dé yǐ	have no alternative (but to)

以 yǐ　　 丨ㄥ 丨ㄥ 以 以

释义 Meaning

（一）介词 prep.

1. as: 我以老朋友的身份劝你不要这样做。As an old friend of yours, I advise you not to do this.

2. take as; regard as: 我们以这样的英雄而自豪。We are proud to be associated with such a hero.

（二）连词 conj.

in order to; so as to: 青年人应该努力学习，以适应建设祖国的需要。Young people should study hard to meet the need of building up their country.

词语 Words and Phrases

以便	yǐbiàn	so that; in order to
以后	yǐhòu	later; afterwards
以及	yǐjí	as well as; along with
以来	yǐlái	since
以内	yǐnèi	within; less than
以前	yǐqián	before; formerly
以上	yǐshàng	more than; over; above
以外	yǐwài	beyond; outside; other than
以为	yǐwéi	think; believe; consider
以下	yǐxià	below; under
以至	yǐzhì	down to; up to
以致	yǐzhì	so that; with the result that; as a result
可以	kěyǐ	can; may
所以	suǒyǐ	so

熟语 Idioms

以毒攻毒	yǐ dú gōng dú	use poison as an antidote

to poison

以理服人　　yǐ lǐ fú rén　　persuade somebody through reasoning

以眼还眼，　yǐ yǎn huán yǎn,　an eye for an eye, a tooth
以牙还牙　　yǐ yá huán yá　　for a tooth

椅 yǐ　　一 十 才 术 术 栌 栌 栌 梏 梏 椅 梏 椅

释义 Meaning

名词 n.

chair: 房子刚盖好，桌椅板凳还没买呢。The house has just been built. Tables, chairs and benches haven't been bought yet.

椅子　　yǐzi　　chair

义 yì　　丶 丷 义

(義 丶 丷 兰 兰 羊 羊 羊 差 差 羕 義 義 義)

释义 Meaning

名词 n.

justice; righteousness: 你对我不仁，就别怪我对你不义。If you treat me wthout consideration, don't blame me for treating you unfairly.

词语 Words and Phrases

义务　　yìwù　　duty; obligation

意义　　yìyì　　meaning

主义　　zhǔyì　　doctrine; -ism

熟语 Idioms

| 义不容辞 | yì bù róng cí | be incumbent on; be duty-bound to |
| 忘恩负义 | wàng ēn fù yì | devoid of gratitude |

艺 yì   一 十 艹 艺

(藝 一 十 艹 艹 艹 莎 莎 菸 菇 菇 菇 菇 藪 蓻 蓻 藝 藝 藝)

释义 Meaning

名词 n.

art: 六岁开始拜师学艺。(He) began to study art with a master when (he) was just six years old.

词语 Words and Phrases

艺术	yìshù	art
艺术品	yìshùpǐn	work of art
文艺	wényì	literature and art

熟语 Idioms

| 多才多艺 | duō cái duō yì | versatile; gifted in many ways |

议 yì   ` 讠 讠 议 议

(議 ` 亠 亠 亖 言 言 言 計 計 譁 譁 譁 譁 譁 譁 議 議 議)

释义 Meaning

动词 v.

discuss: 这件事大家先议一议。Let's discuss this matter first.

词语 Words and Phrases

议案	yì'àn	proposal; motion
议会	yìhuì	parliament; congress; legislative assembly
议论	yìlùn	discuss
会议	huìyì	meeting
建议	jiànyì	propose; suggest; recommend
提议	tíyì	propose; suggest

熟语 Idioms

| 不可思议 | bù kě sī yì | inconceivable; unimaginable |
| 街谈巷议 | jiē tán xiàng yì | street gossip; the talk of the town |

译 yì   丶 讠 讠 讠 讠 讠 译

(譯   丶 亠 亠 言 言 言 言 言 言 言
言 言 言 言 言 言 言 言 譯)

释义 Meaning

动词 v.

translate: 这本外国名著译得好。 This foreign masterpiece was translated well.

词语 Words and Phrases

译文	yìwén	translated text; translation
译音	yìyīn	transliteration
译员	yìyuán	interpreter
译者	yìzhě	translator
翻译	fānyì	translation

易 yì   丨 冂 日 日 日 易 易 易

释义 Meaning

形容词 a.

easy: 这种方法简便易行。This method is easy and feasible.

反义词 antonym: 难

词语 Words and Phrases

贸易	màoyì	trade
轻易	qīngyì	easily
容易	róngyì	easy
好容易	hǎoróngyì	very easy

熟语 Idioms

易如反掌	yì rú fǎn zhǎng	as easy as turning over one's hand
谈何容易	tán hé róng yì	easier said than done

意 yì ⎯ 丶 亠 立 产 音 音 音 音 音 意 意 意

释义 Meaning

名词 n.

meaning: 他说话吞吞吐吐，词不达意，一定有什么问题。He muttered and mumbled, the words failed to convey the idea. There must be something wrong.

词语 Words and Phrases

意见	yì jiàn	idea; view
意料	yìliào	anticipate; expect
意识	yìshí	consciousness; awareness
意思	yìsī	meaning; idea
意图	yìtú	intention; intent
意外	yìwài	unexpected; unforeseen
意味着	yìwèizhe	signify; mean; imply

意义	yìyì	meaning; sense
意志	yìzhì	will; will power; determination
故意	gùyì	deliberately
乐意	lèyì	be pleased to
满意	mǎnyì	satisfied
情意	qíngyì	tender regards; affection; goodwill
生意	shēngyì	business
特意	tèyì	specially; for a special purpose
同意	tóngyì	agree
谢意	xièyì	gratitude; thankfulness
愿意	yuàn yì	be willing; be ready
主意	zhǔyì	idea
注意	zhùyì	pay attention to

熟语 Idioms

得意忘形	dé yì wàng xíng	grow dizzy with success
心满意足	xīn mǎn yì zú	be perfectly content
三心二意	sān xīn èr yì	be of two minds; shilly-shally

因 yīn　丨 冂 冃 冈 因 因

释义 Meaning

(一)名词 n.

cause: 这件事的前因后果就是这样。The entire process of this event is like this.

(二)连词 conj.

because: 会议因故改期。The date of the meeting was changed due to unforeseen circumstances.

词语 Words and Phrases

| 因此 | yīncǐ | so; therefore; for this reason; consequently |

因而	yīn'ér	thus; as a result; therefore
因素	yīnsù	factor; element
因为	yīnwèi	because
原因	yuányīn	reason

熟语 Idioms

| 因小失大 | yīn xiǎo shī dà | lose the big for the small |
| 因噎废食 | yīn yē fèi shí | stop eating altogether on account of a hiccup |

阴 yīn ⺈ ⻖ 阝 阴 阴 阴

（陰 ⺈ ⻖ 阝 阺 阹 阼 陰 陰 陰 陰）

释义 Meaning

形容词 a.

overcast: 天阴了。 It was overcast. 反义词 antonym: 晴

词语 Words and Phrases

阴暗	yīn'àn	dark; gloomy
阴谋	yīnmóu	conspire; plot; scheme
阴天	yīntiān	an overcast sky
光阴	guāngyīn	time

熟语 Idioms

阴错阳差	yīn cuò yáng chā	a mistake or error due to a strange combination of circumstances
阴谋诡计	yīn móu guǐ jì	schemes and intrigues
阳奉阴违	yáng fèng yīn wéi	overtly agree but covertly oppose

音 yīn ` 亠 立 立 产 产 音 音 音

释义 Meaning

名词 n.

1. pronunciation: 这个音你没有发准。You didn't pronounce this syllable correctly.

2. News; tidings: 我等你的回音。I'm waiting for your reply.

3. pronounce: "区"字作姓时音"欧"。When "*Qu*" is used as a surname, it is pronounced as "*Ou*".

词语 Words and Phrases

音乐	yīnyuè	music
音乐会	yīnyuèhuì	concert
音响	yīnxiǎng	sound; acoustics
发音	fāyīn	pronounciation
声音	shēngyīn	sound
噪音	zàoyīn	noise

银 yín ノ ㇒ ㇒ ㇒ 钅 钅 钅 钅 银 银 银

(银 ノ 𠂊 ㇒ ㇒ 𠂤 𠂤 金 金 钅 钅 钅 钅 钅 银**)**

释义 Meaning

名词 n.

silver: 他送给我一把银壶。He gave me a silver pot.

词语 Words and Phrases

银行	yínháng	bank
银幕	yínmù	(motion-picture) screen

引 yǐn ㇆ ㇆ 弓 引

释义 Meaning

动词 v.

1. lead; guide: 把水引到山上去。Divert the water to the mountain top.

2. quote; cite: 文章开头引了一段古人的话。At the beginning of the article, an old saying was quoted.

3. cause; make: 他这句话引得大家都笑了。His remark set everybody laughing.

词语 Words and Phrases

引导	yǐndǎo	guide; lead
引进	yǐnjìn	recommend (a person)
引起	yǐnqǐ	give rise to; lead to; set off
引入	yǐnrù	lead into; draw into
引用	yǐnyòng	quote; cite
引诱	yǐnyòu	lure; entice; seduce
吸引	xīyǐn	attract

熟语 Idioms

引狼入室	yǐn láng rù shì	invite a dangerous person into one's house
引人注目	yǐn rén zhù mù	attrack attention; conspicuous

印 yìn   ˊ 匚 互 臼 印

释义 Meaning

动词 v.

print: 这本小说印了一百万册。A million copies of this novel have been printed.

词语 Words and Phrases

印染	yìnrǎn	printing and dyeing (of textiles)

印刷	yìnshuā	printing
印象	yìnxiàng	impression
打印	dǎyìn	put a seal on; mimeograph
复印	fùyìn	duplicate; xerox; photocopy

熟语 Idioms

| 心心相印 | xīn xīn xiāng yìn | have mutual affinity |
| 一步一个脚印 | yí bù yígè jiǎoyìn | every step leaves its print; work steadily and make solid progress |

应 yīng `丶 亠 广 广 应 应 应`

(應 `丶 亠 广 广 广 广 广 广 庐 庐 庐 雁 雁 雁 應 應 應`)

释义 Meaning

（一）动词 v.

answer; respond: 我叫了他半天，他才应了一声。I called him for quite a long time before he answered.

（二）助动词 aux. v.

should; ought to: 保护动物是每个人应尽的责任。Protecting animals is the responsibility that everyone should have.

词语 Words and Phrases

| 应当 | yīngdāng | ought to; should |
| 应该 | yīnggāi | should; ought to |

英 yīng `一 艹 艹 艹 苎 苎 英 英`

释义 Meaning

名词 n.

hero: 明日召开群英大会。Tomorrow will be a gathering of heroes.

词语 Words and Phrases

英镑	yīngbàng	pound sterling
英俊	yīngjùn	handsome
英明	yīngmíng	wise; brilliant
英雄	yīngxióng	hero
英勇	yīngyǒng	heroic; valiant; brave; gallant
英语	yīngyǔ	English

迎 yíng   ´ ㇄ 匚 卬 卬 迎 迎

释义 Meaning

动词 v.

1. welcome; greet: 爆竹声中迎来了新的一年。The sound of fireworks rang in the new year.

2. down the wind; with the wind: 一面面旗子迎风飘扬。Many flags fluttered in the breeze.

词语 Words and Phrases

迎接	yíngjiē	meet; welcome; greet
迎面	yíngmiàn	head-on; in one's face
欢迎	huānyíng	welcome

熟语 Idioms

迎刃而解	yíng rèn ér jiě	bamboo splits all the way down as soon as it touches the knife's edge; be easily solved
迎头赶上	yíngtóu gǎn shàng	try hard to catch up

赢 yíng   ˋ 亠 亡 亡 亡 亡 扄 扄 扄 扄 扄 扄 扄 赢 赢 赢 赢

(赢 ` 亠 亠 亠 亩 亩 亩 亩 亩 亩 亩 亩
亩 亩 亩 亩 亩 赢 赢 赢 赢**)**

释义 Meaning

动词 v.

1. win; beat: 这场比赛红队赢了。The red team won this match. 反义词 antonym: 输
2. gain (profit): 他赢了二十块钱。He won twenty *Yuan*.

词语 Words and Phrases

赢得　　　yíngdé　　　win; gain

影 yǐng ｜ 冂 冃 日 旦 早 晃 景 景 景 景 景 影 影 影

释义 Meaning

名词 n.

shadow: 一会儿工夫，他消失得无影无踪。He disappeared completely in a moment.

词语 Words and Phrases

影片　　　yǐngpiān　　movie; film
影响　　　yǐngxiǎng　　influence; effect
影子　　　yǐngzi　　　shadow; reflection
电影　　　diànyǐng　　movie

熟语 Idioms

捕风捉影　　*bǔ fēng zhuō yǐng*　　chase the wind and clutch at shadows; make groundless judgements

立竿见影　　*lì gān jiàn yǐng*　　set up a pole and you see its shadow; get instant results

硬yìng

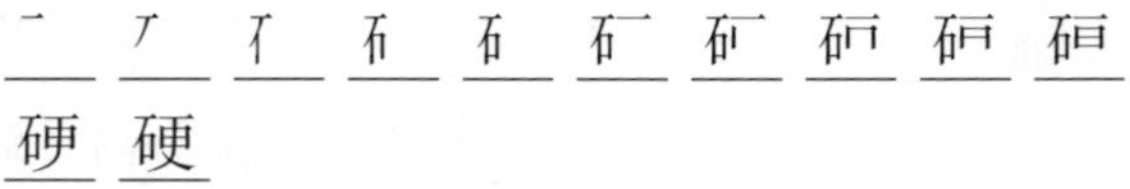

释义 Meaning

(一) 形容词 a.

1. hard; stiff: 这种木头很硬。This kind of wood is hard.
   反义词 antonym: 软
2. dauntless; unyielding: 硬汉子也会流眼泪。A man of iron still will shed his tears.

(二) 副词 adv.

1. insist on doing sth: 不让他去，他硬要去。We did not want to let him go, but he insisted on going.
2. manage to do sth. with difficulty: 他硬压住心头怒火。He choked down his anger.

词语 Words and Phrases

硬币	yìngbì	coin
硬件	yìngjiàn	hardware
生硬	shēngyìng	stiff; rigid

熟语 Idioms

硬着头皮	yìng zhe tóupí	put a bold face on it; force oneself to do sth. against one's will
欺软怕硬	qī ruǎn pà yìng	bully the weak and fear the strong

拥yōng

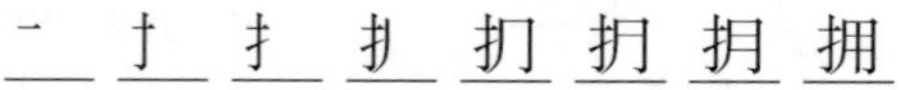

(擁 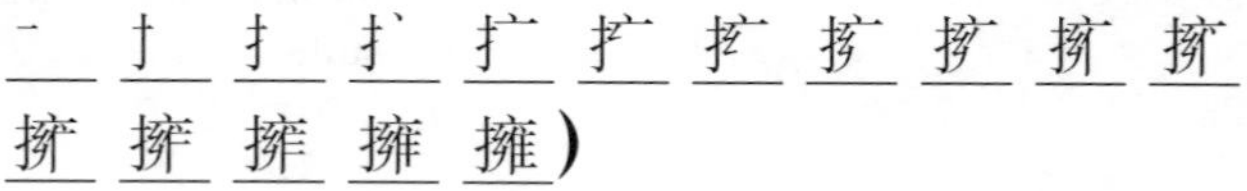 **)**

释义 Meaning

动词 v.

1. gather around; wrap around: 观众拥着体操冠军，要求签名。The audience crowded around the gymnastics champion, asking for his autograph.

2. crowd; throng: 大家拥上前去看热闹。People crowded forward to watch the fun.

词语 Words and Phrases

拥抱	yōngbào	embrace; hug; hold in one's arms
拥护	yōnghù	support; uphold
拥挤	yōngjǐ	be crowded; be packed
拥有	yōngyǒu	posses; have; own

永 yǒng `丶 亅 永 永 永`

释义 Meaning

副词 adv.

forever: 他是个永不向困难低头的人。He is a person who never bows to difficulties.

词语 Words and Phrases

永久	yǒngjiǔ	permanent; perpetual; everlasting
永远	yǒngyuǎn	always; forever; ever

熟语 Idioms

永垂不朽	yǒng chuí bù xiǔ	immortal

泳 yǒng `丶 丶 氵 汈 汋 汃 泳 泳`

释义 Meaning

动词 v.

swim: 这个游泳池的泳道有点儿窄。The lane of this swimming pool is a little bit narrow.

词语 Words and Phrases

游泳	yóuyǒng	swim

勇 yǒng ⟍ ⟍ ⼴ ⿸ ⿸ ⿸ ⿸ 勇 勇

释义 Meaning

形容词 a.

courageous: 这场拳击比赛，穿红裤的运动员越战越勇。
The boxer in red trunks became more amd more aggressive as
the match progressed.

词语 Words and Phrases

勇敢	yǒnggǎn	brave; courageous
勇气	yǒngqì	courage; nerve
勇士	yǒngshì	a brave and strong man; gladiator; warrior

熟语 Idioms

勇往直前	yǒng wǎng zhí qián	stride bravely forward
自告奋勇	zì gào fèn yǒng	offer to undertake (a difficult or dangerous task)

用 yòng

释义 Meaning

动词 v.

1. use: 你会不会用筷子？Can you use chopsticks?
2. need: 这句话还用解释吗？Does this sentence need any
   explanation?

词语 Words and Phrases

用不着	yòngbuzháo	no need
用处	yòngchù	use; good
用法	yòngfǎ	use; usage

用功	yònggōng	hardwork
用户	yònghù	consumer; user
用具	yòngjù	utensil; apparatus; appliance
用途	yòngtú	use
用心	yòngxīn	motive; intention
用意	yòngyì	intention; purpose
不用	búyòng	no need
公用	gōngyòng	for public use
利用	lìyòng	make use of
使用	shǐyòng	use; employ; apply
信用	xìnyòng	trustworthiness; credit
作用	zuòyòng	act on; affect; influence

熟语 Idioms

别有用心	bié yǒu yòng xīn	have ulterior motives
大材小用	dà cái xiǎo yòng	large material put to small use; one's talent wasted on a petty job

优 yōu ノ 亻 仁 仕 优 优

(優 ノ 亻 亻 亻 庌 伄 伂 僡 僡 僡 僡 僡 僡 僡 僡 優 優)

释义 Meaning

形容词 a.

excellent: 广告中说："一旦录用，待遇从优。"The advertisement says, "Once hired, excellent pay and terms of service will be given".

词语 Words and Phrases

优点	yōudiǎn	merit; strong (or good) point; virtue
优惠	yōuhuì	preferential; favourable

优良	yōuliáng	fine; good
优美	yōuměi	graceful; fine; exquisite
优胜	yōushèng	winning; superior
优势	yōushì	superiority; preponderance
优先	yōuxiān	have priority; take precedence
优秀	yōuxiù	outstanding; excellent; splendid; fine
优异	yōuyì	excellent; outstanding
优越	yōuyuè	superior; advantageous
优质	yōuzhì	high (or top) quality; high grade

熟语 Idioms

| 养尊处优 | yǎng zūn chǔ yōu | enjoy high position and live in comfort |

由 yóu　丨　冂　日　由　由

释义 Meaning

介词 prep.

1. (done) by sb: 这个问题由他们解决。Leave this problem to them.

2. because of; due to: 病人由感冒引起了肺炎。The pneumonia came from catching a cold.

3. by; through; via 他们由北京出发，经过日本到美国。 They traveled from Beijing, through Japan to the US.

词语 Words and Phrases

由于	yóuyú	because of
理由	lǐyóu	reason
自由	zìyóu	freedom

熟语 Idioms

| 由此可见 | yóu cǐ kě jiàn | thus it can be seen; from this it can be seen |

| 由浅入深 | yóu qiǎn rù shēn | from the shallow to the deep; from the superficial to the profound |

油 yóu 丶 丶 氵 汀 汩 泪 油 油

释义 Meaning

（一）名词 n.

oil; fat: 这个菜油放得太多了。There is too much oil in this dish.

（二）形容词 a.

oily; greasy: 这种点心太油，我不想吃。This kind of snack is too greasy. I don't want to eat it.

词语 Words and Phrases

油画	yóuhuà	oil painting
油漆	yóuqī	paint
油田	yóutián	oilfield

熟语 Idioms

| 油腔滑调 | yóu qiāng huá diào | talk persuasively but not necessarily reliably |
| 火上加油 | huǒ shàng jiā yóu | add fuel to the flames; make an already difficult situation worse |

游 yóu 丶 丶 氵 汁 汸 汸 浒 游 游 游 游

释义 Meaning

动词 v.

1. swim: 鱼在水里游来游去。The fish is swimming in the water.
2. travel; tour: 今天游长城，明天参观故宫。Today we

are scheduled to visit the Great Wall. Tomorrow is the Imperial Palace.

词语 Words and Phrases

游客	yóukè	visitor; tourist
游览	yóulǎn	go sight-seeing; tour; visit
游人	yóurén	visitor
游玩	yóuwán	amuse oneself; play
游戏	yóuxì	game
游行	yóuxíng	parade; march; demonstration
游泳	yóuyǒng	swim
游泳池	yóuyǒngchí	swimming pool
导游	dǎoyóu	tour-guide
郊游	jiāoyóu	outing; excursion

熟语 Idioms

游手好闲	yóu shǒu hào xián	loaf; idle away one's time

友 yǒu　　二 ナ 方 友

释义 Meaning

名词 n.

这几天他忙着探亲访友，没时间陪我。

He has been busy with visiting relatives and friends these a few days. He doesn't have time to accompany me.

词语 Words and Phrases

友爱	yǒu'ài	friendly; affection; fraternal love
友好	yǒuhǎo	close friend; friend
友情	yǒuqíng	friendly sentiments; friendship
友人	yǒurén	friend
友谊	yǒuyì	friendship
朋友	péngyou	friend

| 亲友 | qīnyǒu | relatives and friends |
| 小朋友 | xiǎo péng you | child, children |

熟语 Idioms

| 酒肉朋友 | jiǔ ròu péng yǒu | friends only for wining and dining together |
| 良师益友 | liáng shī yì yǒu | good teacher and helpful friend |

有 yǒu   一 ナ オ 冇 有 有

释义 Meaning

动词 v.

1. have; possess: 我有新的《汉英词典》。I have a new Chinese English Dictionary.

2. used in making an estimate or a comparison: 他有他哥哥那么高。He is as tall as his brother. 反义词 antonym: 没有

3. used to express the idea of having plenty of: 他是个有学问的人。He is quite a scholar.

4. used to indicate sth. appearing or occurring: 他有病了。He is ill.

5. there is; exist: 屋子里有很多人。There are many people in the room. 反义词 antonym: 没有

词语 Words and Phrases

有的	yǒude	some
有的是	yǒudeshì	have plenty of
有关	yǒuguān	be related to
有机	yǒujī	organic
有利	yǒulì	advantageous
有名	yǒumíng	famous
有趣	yǒuqù	interesting

有时	yǒushí	sometimes
有时候	yǒushíhou	sometimes
有限	yǒuxiàn	limited
有效	yǒuxiào	effective
有（一）些	yǒu(yì)xiē	somewhat; rather
有些	yǒuxiē	some
有（一）点儿	yǒu(yì)diǎnr	somewhat; a bit
有意	yǒuyì	purposely
有意思	yǒu yìsī	significant
有益	yǒuyì	profitable; beneficial
有用	yǒuyòng	useful

熟语 Idioms

有的放矢	yǒu dì fàng shǐ	shoot with a definite target in view; on purpose
有目共睹	yǒu mù gòng dǔ	be obvious to all
有声有色	yǒu shēng yǒu sè	full of sound and colour; looks like neal

又 yòu   乛 又

释义 Meaning

副词 adv.

1. (used for an actual action) again: 他拿着信看了又看。 He took the letter and read it over and over again.

2. (reduplicated, with verbs or adjectives) both...and; not only... but also: 这儿的东西又好又便宜。 Things here are both of good quality and cheap.

3. used, sometimes in pairs, to indicate contrary actions or ideas: 她又想去，又不想去，拿不定注意。 She couldn't make up her mind whether to go or not.

4. also; in addition: 天很黑，又下着雨，路更难走了。

On top of it being dark it was raining, which made the journey even tougher.

右 yòu　一 ナ ナ 右 右

释义 Meaning

名词 n.

the right side: 你一直走，在前面的马路向右拐，就到了。To get there, go straight to the corner and then turn to the right. 反义词 antonym: 左

词语 Words and Phrases

右边	yòubiān	the right side
右面	yòumiàn	the right side
右手	yòushǒu	the right hand
左右	zuǒyòu	about; the left and right sides
右派	yòupài	right wing

于 yú　一 二 于

释义 Meaning

介词 prep.

1. (indicating time or place) in; on; at: 她生于1973年。She was born in 1973.

2. with regard to; concerning; to: 场上的形势于中国队有利。The situation is advantageous to the Chinese team.

3. indicating comparison: 学校演电影每周不少于一次。The school shows movies no less than once every week.

词语 Words and Phrases

于是	yúshì	thereupon; hence; consequently
等于	děngyú	equal to
限于	xiànyú	be limited to

| 由于 | yóuyú | owing to; thanks to; as a result of |
| 终于 | zhōngyú | finally; at last |

熟语 Idioms

| 轻于鸿毛 | qīng yú hóngmáo | as light as a goose feather; sth. not important |
| 无动于衷 | wú dòng yú zhōng | aloof and indifferent |

余 yú ╱ ㄟ ㅅ ⼆ 仝 余 余

(餘 ╱ ㄟ ㅅ ⼂ ⼂ ⼂ 食 食 食 飠 飠 飠 飠 餰 餘)

释义 Meaning

（一）动词 v.

surplus; spare; remaining: 买完东西，还余十多块钱。After shopping, there is a balance of more than ten *Yuan*.

（二）名词 n.

beyond; after: 他常常利用工作之余，教孩子们画画。He often makes use of the time after work to teach the children painting.

（三）数词 num.

more than; odd; over: 这个学校学生有一万余人。There are more than ten thousand students in this school.

鱼 yú ╱ ㄜ ⼓ 甪 甶 鱼 鱼 鱼

(魚 ╱ ㄜ ⼓ 甪 甶 鱼 鱼 魚 魚 魚 魚)

释义 Meaning

名词 n.

fish: 今天我买了一条你爱吃的鱼。Today I bought your favorite fish.

与 yǔ　　二　与　与

(與　　一　厂　戶　戶　戶　戶　臼　臼　臼　臼　與
　與　與)

释义 Meaning

（一）介词 prep.

used to introduce the recipient of an action: 我们要有勇气
与困难作斗争。We should be courageous to strive to over-
come difficulties.

（二）连词 conj.

(used to indicate involvement, relationship, etc.) with: 我与
他们没有任何关系。I have nothing to do with them.

词语 Words and Phrases

与其　　yǔqí　　　　　would rather...than

熟语 Idioms

与人为善　　yǔ rén wéi shàn　　　be with the intention of
helping others

事与愿违　　shì yǔ yuàn wéi　　　something doesn't turn
out the way one wishes

雨 yǔ　　二　厂　厅　帀　雨　雨　雨

释义 Meaning

名词 n.

rain: 外面下雨了。It's raining outside.

词语 Words and Phrases

雨伞　　yǔsǎn　　　umbrella

雨水　　yǔshuǐ　　　rainwater; rainfall; rain

雨衣　　yǔyī　　　　raincoat

大雨　　dàyǔ　　　　heavy rain

| 雷雨 | léiyǔ | thunderstorm |

熟语 Idioms

| 雨后春笋 | yǔ hòu chūnsǔn | spring up like mushrooms |
| 风雨无阻 | fēngyǔ wú zǔ | neither wind nor rain can stop [it] |

语 yǔ ` 讠 讠 讠 讠 语 语 语 语

（語 ` ⸏ ⸋ ⸌ 言 言 言 言 訂 語 語 語 語 語）

释义 Meaning

名词 n.

speak; say: 会上大家你一言我一语，讨论得很热烈。 Everyone spoke out at the meeting. There was an animated discussion.

词语 Words and Phrases

语调	yǔdiào	intonation
语法	yǔfǎ	grammar
语气	yǔqì	tone
语文	yǔwén	Chinese; language class
语言	yǔyán	language
语音	yǔyīn	speech sounds; pronunciation
成语	chéngyǔ	set phrase
词语	cíyǔ	word
汉语	hànyǔ	Chinese language
口语	kǒuyǔ	colloquial language
母语	mǔyǔ	native language; mother tongue
熟语	shúyǔ	idiom; Idioms
外语	wàiyǔ	foreign language

熟语 Idioms

语重心长	yǔ zhòng xīn cháng	speak sincerely and earnestly
三言两语	sān yán liǎng yǔ	in a few words
甜言蜜语	tián yán mì yǔ	honey-tongued; soft voice; convincing (with an evil purpose)

玉 yù   一 二 三 干 王 玉

释义 Meaning

名词 n.

jade: 他脖子上挂着一块玉。A piece of jade hangs at his neck.

词语 Words and Phrases

玉米	yùmǐ	maize; Indian corn; corn

熟语 Idioms

玉不琢，不成器	yù bù zhuó, bù chéng qì	if jade is not cut and polished, it won't be made into anything valuable; jade requires chiseling as man needs training and discipline
抛砖引玉	pāo zhuān yǐn yù	cast brick to attract jade; a polite expression which means that one will give one's opinions to elicit other's valuable comments

育 yù   ` 一 亠 云 云 产 育 育 育

释义 Meaning

动词 v.

现在是封山育林的季节。Now it is the season for closing

mountain regions in order to allow forest propagation.

词语 Words and Phrases

教育	jiàoyù	education
体育	tǐyù	physical

预 yù ⸯ ⸜ ⸚ 予 予 予 预 预 预 预

(預 ⸯ ⸜ ⸚ 予 予 予 预 預 預 預 預 預 預)

释义 Meaning

副词 adv.

明天要试验了，我预祝你马到成功。Tomorrow it will be a test. I congratulate you in advance on an immediate victory.

词语 Words and Phrases

预报	yùbào	forecast
预备	yùbèi	prepare
预订	yùdìng	subscribe; book; place an order
预防	yùfáng	prevent; take precautions against
预告	yùgào	announce in advance
预习	yùxí	preview
预先	yùxiān	in advance; beforehand
预约	yùyuē	make an appointment
预祝	yùzhù	congratulate beforehand

遇 yù ⎸ ⎅ 日 日 尸 月 禺 禺 禺 遇 遇 遇

释义 Meaning

动词 v.

1. encounter: 他在工作中遇到了很多问题。He encountered many problems in his job.
2. meet: 昨天我在马路上遇见了一个熟人。I met an acquaintance in the street yesterday.

词语 Words and Phrases

待遇	dàiyù	treatment
机遇	jīyù	opportunity
巧遇	qiǎoyù	unexpected encounter

熟语 Idioms

十年九不遇	shí nián jiǔ bú yù	not occur once in ten years; be very rare

元 yuán 二 三 テ 元

释义 Meaning

量词 measure w.

monetary unit of China, equal to 10 *jiao* or 100 *fen* : 这件衣服八十八元。This piece of clothing costs eighty-eight *Yuan*.

词语 Words and Phrases

元旦	yuándàn	New Year's Day
元首	yuánshǒu	head of state
元素	yuánsù	element
元宵	yuánxiāo	the night of the fifteenth of the first lunar month
公元	gōngyuán	the Christian era

员 yuán 丿 冂 冂 尸 呂 呂 员

(員 丿 冂 冂 尸 冎 咼 咼 咼 員 員)

释义 Meaning

（一）名词 n.

member: 他把狗也看作家庭中的一员。He regarded his dog as a member of his family.

（二）尾词 suff.

a person engaged in some field of activity: 她当了三年售货员。She worked as a shop assistant for three years.

词语 Words and Phrases

员工	yuángōng	staff; personnel
病员	bìngyuán	one on the sick list; patient
官员	guānyuán	government official
教员	jiàoyuán	teacher
人员	rényuán	personnel; stuff
学员	xuéyuán	student; student of a college or training school
译员	yìyuán	interpreter
职员	zhíyuán	office worker; staff member
服务员	fúwùyuán	attendant; steward waiter

园 yuán 丨 冂 冋 冃 户 园 园

（園 丨 冂 冋 門 門 門 門 門 圊 園 園
園 園 **）**

释义 Meaning

名词 n.

an area of land for growing plants: 山前面是一片果园。There is an orchard in front of the mountain.

词语 Words and Phrases

园林	yuánlín	landscape garden; park

园子	yuánzi	land for growing plants
公园	gōngyuán	park
花园	huāyuán	garden
动物园	dòngwùyuán	zoo
幼儿园	yòu'éryuán	nursing school; kindergarten
植物园	zhíwùyuán	botanical garden

原 yuán 　二 厂 厂 厂 厒 厈 盾 原 原 原

释义 Meaning

形容词 a.

original; primary: 公司开办时，原有人数十多个，两年以后已有一百多个了。When the company was founded, there were originally just over ten people. Two years later, there are already more than a hundred people.

词语 Words and Phrases

原来	yuánlái	former; originally
平原	píngyuán	plain
原理	yuánlǐ	maxim; principle; tenet
原谅	yuánliàng	excuse; forgive; pardon
原料	yuánliào	raw material
原始	yuánshǐ	original; firsthand; primeval; primitive
原先	yuánxiān	primary; former
原因	yuányīn	reason; cause
原则	yuánzé	principle
原子	yuánzǐ	atom
原子弹	yuánzǐdàn	atomic bomb
原子能	yuánzǐnéng	atomic energy
草原	cǎoyuán	grassland; prairie
高原	gāoyuán	plateau; highland; tableland

熟语 Idioms

原封不动	yuánfēng bú dòng	be kept intact; maintain unchanged in its original state

圆 yuán 丨 冂 冂 冂 冃 冃 冃 厠 圆 圆

(圆 丨 冂 冂 冂 冃 冃 冃 冃 冃 冒 圓 圓 圓 圓 **)**

释义 Meaning

（一）形容词 a.

round: 中秋节的月亮圆又亮。During the Mid-autumn Festival the moon is both round and bright.

（二）名词 n.

monetary unit of China, equal to 10 *jiao* or 100 *fen*: 人民币一圆等于十角。One *Yuan* in RMB is equal to ten *jiao*.

词语 Words and Phrases

圆满	yuánmǎn	satisfatory
圆形	yuánxíng	round
圆珠笔	yuánzhūbǐ	ball-point pen
汤圆	tāngyuán	boiled rice dumpling; stuffed dumpling made partly or wholly of glutinous rice flour served in soup
团圆	tuányuán	reunion

熟语 Idioms

破镜重圆	pò jìng chóng yuán	a broken mirror was made; a reunion of a couple after long separation

远 yuǎn 一 二 于 元 元 远 远

(遠 一 十 土 吉 吉 吉 吉 吉 京 袁 袁 遠 遠)

释义 Meaning

形容词 a.

1. far away (in time or space): 我家离火车站很远。My home is far away from the railway station. 反义词 antonym: 近
2. by far; far and away: 他是冠军，我跟他差得远了。He is the champion. I am far behind him.

词语 Words and Phrases

远大	yuǎndà	long-range; broad; ambitious
远方	yuǎnfāng	distant place
远景	yuǎnjǐng	long perspective
深远	shēnyuǎn	profound and lasting
永远	yǒngyuǎn	forever

熟语 Idioms

远水不救近火	yuǎn shuǐ bú jiù jìn huǒ	water afar cannot put off fire nearby; future remedy cannot meet present urgency
舍近求远	shě jìn qiú yuǎn	cast near and seek from distant; unreasonable

院 yuàn 了 阝 阝 阝 阡 阡 阼 院 院

释义 Meaning

名词 n.

college; academy; institute: 我院教职工一百零二人。There are one hundred and two staff members in our college.

词语 Words and Phrases

院长	yuànzhǎng	dean
院子	yuànzi	courtyard

剧院	jùyuàn	theater
学院	xuéyuàn	college; academy; institute
医院	yīyuàn	hospital
电影院	diànyǐngyuàn	movie house; cinema; movie; motion-picture theatre

愿 yuàn 一 厂 厂 厂 匚 盾 盾 原 原 原 原 愿 愿 愿

(願 一 厂 厂 厂 斤 斤 盾 原 原 原 原 原 願 願 願 願 願 願)

释义 Meaning

（一）动词 v.

hope; wish; desire: 愿你早日成功！Hope you succeed soon.

（二）助动词 a.v.

be willing; be ready: 愿去杭州的，每人交三百块钱。
Those who are willing to go to Hangzhou should each pay three hundred *Yuan*.

词语 Words and Phrases

愿望	yuànwàng	desire; wish; aspiration
愿意	yuànyì	will; want; wish
宁愿	níngyuàn	would rather; better
心愿	xīnyuàn	cherished desire; aspiration; dream; wish
志愿	zhìyuàn	aspiration; volunteer
自愿	zìyuàn	voluntary of one's own accord

熟语 Idioms

| 如愿以偿 | rú yuàn yǐ cháng | have one's wishes fulfilled |
| 心甘情愿 | xīngān qíngyuàn | willingly |

约 yuē ˊ ˊ ˊ ˊ 约 约

(約 ˊ ˊ ˊ ˊ 糸 糸 糸 約 約)

释义 Meaning

（一）动词 v.

1. ask or invite in advance: 他约我到他家做客。He asked me to be a guest in his family.

2. make an appointment; arrange: 今天去杭州是我们上星期就约好的。Our engagement to go to Hangzhou today was set last week.

（二）副词 adv.

about; around; approximately: 他们父子俩谈了约有两个钟头。The father and son talked for about two hours.

词语 Words and Phrases

约会	yuēhuì	appointment; engagement; date
约束	yuēshù	bind; restrain; control; restrict
大约	dàyuē	about; probably
节约	jiéyuē	economy
失约	shīyuē	fail to keep an appointment
条约	tiáoyuē	treaty

熟语 Idioms

约定俗成	yuē dìng sú chéng	accepted through common practice; sanctioned by popular usage

月 yuè ⌿ 丿 月 月

释义 Meaning

名词 n.

1. moon: 一弯新月挂在夜空。The crescent moon hangs

in the sky.

2. month: 他来香港已有一个月了。He has already been in Hongkong for a month.

词语 Words and Phrases

月饼	yuèbǐng	moon cake (esp. for the Mid-Autumn Festival)
月份	yuèfèn	month
月光	yuèguāng	moonlight
月亮	yuèliang	moon
月球	yuèqiú	moon (as a planet)
年月	niányuè	days
岁月	suìyuè	years

熟语 Idioms

月下老人	yuè xià lǎorén	matchmaker
长年累月	cháng nián lěi yuè	year in and year out; year after year

越 yuè　一　十　土　キ　キ　走　走　赴　赵　越　越　越

释义 Meaning

（一）动词 v.

get over; jump over: 他们跨过平原，越过高山，向西部挺进。They crossed the plain, and went over the high mountain, marching toward the West.

（二）副词 adv.

the more...the more: 这首歌我越听越爱听。The more I listened to this song, the more I was attracted to it.

词语 Words and Phrases

越…越… yuè...yuè...　the more...the more...

越冬	yuèdōng	live through the winter
越过	yuè guò	cross; surmount; surplus
越来越	yuèláiyuè	more and more
超越	chāoyuè	exceed; surmount; overstep
优越	yōuyuè	superior; advantageous over

云 yún 一 二 云 云

(雲 一 一 一 一 雨 雨 雨 雨 雨 雲 雲 雲 雲)

释义 Meaning

名词 n.

cloud: 天上一点云也没有。There is not the least bit of cloud in the sky.

词语 Words and Phrases

| 云彩 | yúncǎi | clouds |
| 风云 | fēngyún | wind and cloud; a stormy or unstable situation; a memorable event |

熟语 Idioms

| 云消雾散 | yún xiāo wù sǎn | when the clouds part, one sees the sun |
| 平步青云 | píng bù qīng yún | rapid promotion; have a meteoric rise |

运 yùn 一 二 云 云 运 运 运

(運 一 一 一 一 一 一 一 一 宜 軍 軍 運 運)

释义 Meaning

动词 v.

carry; transport; ship

1. 这些蔬菜全部运到香港。These vegetables are all to be shipped to Hongkong.

2. 这么多行李我一个人运不了。I can't carry so much luggage all by myself.

词语 Words and Phrases

运动	yùndòng	sports
运动会	yùndònghuì	sports meeting
运动员	yùndòngyuán	athlete
运气	yùnqì	luck
运输	yùnshū	transport
运送	yùnsòng	transport; ship; convey
运行	yùnxíng	move; be in motion
运用	yùnyòng	utilize; wield; apply; put to use
运转	yùnzhuǎn	revolve; turn round
搬运	bānyùn	carry; transport
命运	mìngyùn	destiny; fate; lot
幸运	xìngyùn	good fortune; chance

熟语 Idioms

运筹帷幄	yùnchóu wéiwò	devise strategies within the command quarter; well planned

扎 zā ＿ 十 扌 扎

释义 Meaning

动词 v.

1. prick; run or stick (a needle, etc.): 她不小心扎了手指。She was so careless that she pricked her finger.

2. plunge into; get into: 他连衣服也没脱，扎进水里把孩子救了起来。Without even shedding his clothing, he plunged into the water and saved the child.

词语 Words and Phrases

扎实	zāshi	sturdy; strong

杂zá 丿 九 九 杂 杂 杂

（雜 ` 宀 广 广 亣 亣 卒 卒 亲 亲 亲 雜 雜 雜 雜 雜 雜 雜）

释义 Meaning

形容词 a.

miscellaneous; sundry; mixed: 今天事情太杂，必须安排好。There are too many miscellaneous tasks to do today. I must arrange them well.

词语 Words and Phrases

杂技	zájì	acrobatics
杂乱	záluàn	be mixed and disorderly; in a jumble
杂文	záwén	essay
杂志	zázhì	magazine
杂质	zázhì	foreign substance
复杂	fùzá	complicated

熟语 Idioms

杂乱无章	záluàn wú zhāng	in a mess; in disorder
杂七杂八	zá qī zá bā	odds and ends of things; all mixed together
龙蛇混杂	lóng shé hùnzá	snake and dragon mix together; good and bad people mixed up

灾 zāi   丶 ⼂ 宀 宀 宀 灾 灾

(災   ⼂ ⼅ ⼼ ⼿ ⼿ 災 災)

释义 Meaning

名词 n.

1. calamity; disaster: 那一年长江中下游洪水成灾。The middle and lower reaches of the Yangtse River flooded in that year.

2. personal misfortune; adversity: 我没病没灾，日子过得很好。I am in good health and good fortune. I lead a happy life.

词语 Words and Phrases

灾害	zāihài	plague; calamity; disaster
灾荒	zāihuāng	famine due to crop failures
灾难	zāinàn	calamity; catastrophe; disaster; suffering

熟语 Idioms

天灾人祸	tiānzāi rénhuò	natural and man made calamities
幸灾乐祸	xìngzāi lè huò	take pleasure in other's misfortune

再 zài   二 丆 厅 襾 再 再

释义 Meaning

副词 adv.

1. (for an action yet to take place or contemplated) again: 请你再说一遍。Please say it again.

2. used to indicate the continuing of a situation in conditional or suppositional clauses: 吃完饭再干一会儿就可以结

束了。After dinner, keep on working for a while. Then you can finish your job.

3. (for a delayed action, preceded by an expression of time or condition) then; only then: 我跟他商量以后再决定。I will decide after discussing with him.

4. (used before adjectives) more; -er: 再多一点儿就好了。If there is a little bit more, it will be just right.

词语 Words and Phrases

再见	zàijiàn	good-bye
再三	zàisān	over and over again
再说	zàishuō	besides; what's more; say again; hold over; put off until some time later

熟语 Idioms

再接再厉	zài jiē zài lì	make sustained and redoubled efforts

在 zài   二 ナ 犬 存 存 在

释义 Meaning

（一）动词 v.

1. be at; in or on (a place): 我先生不在家。My husband was not at home.

2. exist; be alive: 你小学毕业时的照片还在吗？Do you still keep your elementary school graduation photos?

（二）介词 prep.

at, in, or on (a place or time): 他在电脑公司工作。He works at a computer company.

（三）副词 adv.

(used to indicate action in progress): 我去的时候，她在做饭。She was cooking when I went there.

词语 Words and Phrases

在场	zàichǎng	witness; be present on the scene
在乎	zàihū	care about; take to heart
在意	zàiyì	take notice of; pay attention to; take to heart; care about
在于	zàiyú	rest with; depend on
在座	zàizuò	be present

熟语 Idioms

| 在所不辞 | zài suǒ bù cí | never to shirk one's responsibilities |

脏 zāng 丿 刀 月 月 月` 扩 扩 胪 脏 脏

(髒 丨 冂 冃 冃 凨 骨 骨 骨 骨 骨 骨
骨 骨 骨 髊 髊 髊 髒 髒 髒 髒)

释义 Meaning

形容词 a.

dirty: 这些衣服都是脏的，要洗一洗。These clothes are all dirty. They need to be washed. 反义词 antonym: 干淨 clean

早 zǎo 丨 冂 日 日 旦 早

释义 Meaning

(一) 名词 n.

(early) morning: 我妈妈从早到晚忙个不停。My mother is busy from morning to evening. 反义词 antonym: 晚

(二) 形容词 a.

1. long ago; as early as; for a long time: 这件事我们早就商量好了。We came to an agreement on this matter long ago.

2. early; in advance; beforehand: 明天你早点儿来。Tomorrow you had better come earlier. 反义词 antonym: 晚

词语 Words and Phrases

早晨	zǎochén	morning
早点	zǎodiǎn	(light) breakfast
早饭	zǎofàn	breakfast
早日	zǎorì	at an early date
早期	zǎoqī	early stage
早上	zǎoshàng	earrly morning
早晚	zǎowǎn	morning and evening; sooner or later
早先	zǎoxiān	previously; in the past
早已	zǎoyǐ	long ago

熟语 Idioms

起早贪黑	qǐ zǎo tān hēi	start work early and knock off late

造 zào   ′ ㇒ ㇏ 生 牛 告 告 告 浩 造

释义 Meaning

动词 v.

make; build; create: 这个船厂造了一条世界上最大的船。This shipyard built the biggest ship in the world.

词语 Words and Phrases

造反	zàofǎn	rebel; revolt
造价	zàojià	cost (of building or manufacture)
造句	zàojù	sentence-making
造型	zàoxíng	model; mold
创造	chuàngzào	create
改造	gǎizào	reform; change
建造	jiànzào	build; construct; make

人造	rénzào	artificial; man-made
伪造	wěizào	forge; falsify; counterfeit; fabricate
制造	zhìzào	manufacture; make

熟语 Idioms

| 造谣惑众 | zào yáo huò zhòng | spread rumors to deceive people |
| 粗制滥造 | cū zhì làn zào | manufacture sth in a rough and slipshod way |

择 zé 　一 丁 扌 扩 护 拦 捽 择

(擇 　一 丁 扌 扩 扩 扩 扩 押 押 押 押 擇 擇 擇 擇 擇)

释义 Meaning

动词 v.

choose; select: 他已经到了饥不择食的地步，这么难吃的东西，他一下子就吃了个精光。He was hungry enough to eat almost anything with pleasure, he even finished eating the unsavory stuff in just a few moments.

词语 Words and Phrases

| 选择 | xuǎnzé | choose; select |

责 zé 　一 二 キ 圭 責 青 责 责

(責 　一 二 キ 圭 青 青 青 責 責 責 責)

释义 Meaning

名词 n.

duty; responsibility: 爱护花草人人有责。It is everybody's duty to take good care of flowers and grasses.

词语 Words and Phrases

责备	zébèi	reproach; blame; reprimand
责怪	zéguài	blame
责任	zérèn	duty; responsibility
责任制	zérènzhì	system of job responsibility
负责	fùzé	be responsible for; be in charge of
指责	zhǐzé	charge; denounce; reprove

熟语 Idioms

责无旁贷	zé wú páng dài	duty-bound

怎 zěn ⟍ ⟍ ⟋ ⟋ 乍 乍 怎 怎 怎

释义 Meaning

代词 pron.

Why; how: 你怎不早说呀？Why didn't you say so earlier?

词语 Words and Phrases

怎么	zěnme	how; what; however; somewhat; how could
怎么样	zěnmeyàng	how
怎么着	zěnmezhāo	what about; why
怎样	zěnyàng	how

曾₁ zēng ⟍ ⟍ ⟋ 兯 兯 兯 兯 兯 曾 曾 曾

释义 Meaning

形容词 adj.

relationship between great-grandchildren and great grand parents: 他的曾祖父是留法博士。His great-grandfather earned a Ph.D. in France.

词语 Words and Phrases

曾孙	zēngsūn	great-grandson
曾孙女	zēngsūnnǚ	great-granddaughter
曾祖	zēngzǔ	(paternal) great-grandfather
曾祖母	zēngzǔmǔ	(paternal) great-grandmother

曾₂ céng ` ⹁ ⼍ ⼧ ⼧ ⼧ ⼧ ⼩ 曽 曽 曽 曾

释义 Meaning

副词 adv.

ever: 她曾到过非洲。She has been to Africa.

词语 Words and Phrases

| 曾经 | céngjīng | once; in the past |

增 zēng 一 十 土 圠 圠 圹 圹 圹 圹 圹 圹 増 增 增 增

释义 Meaning

动词 v.

increase; add: 今年工厂的产量猛增。The factory's output increased sharply this year.

词语 Words and Phrases

增产	zēngchǎn	boost production; increase output
增加	zēngjiā	increase; swell; improve; expand; wax
增进	zēngjìn	promote; enhance
增强	zēngqiǎng	strengthen; enhance
增设	zēngshè	put up; expand
增添	zēngtiān	add
增援	zēngyuán	reinforce

增长　　zēngzhǎng　increase; swell; grow; rise

熟语 Idioms

与日俱增　　yǔ rì jù zēng　　　grow with each passing day

摘 zhāi

一　十　扌　扩　扩　扩　扩　扩　拍　拍
拍　捇　摘　摘

释义 Meaning

动词 v.

1. pick; pluck; take off: 他从果园里摘了很多苹果带回来。He brought back many apples picked from the trees in the orchard.

2. select; make extracts from: 老师从那本小说中摘了一段话念给学生们听。The teacher extracted a paragraph from that novel and read it to the students.

词语 Words and Phrases

摘要　　zhāiyào　　make a summary; roundup; abstract

窄 zhǎi

丶　丷　宀　宀　空　空　空　窄　窄　窄

释义 Meaning

形容词 a.

narrow: 前面是一条老街，很窄，汽车开不进去。There is an old street ahead. It is so narrow that cars can't enter.

词语 Words and Phrases

狭窄　　xiázhǎi　　narrow

熟语 Idioms

冤家路窄　　yuānjiā lù zhǎi　　opponents often meet

站 zhàn

丶　亠　产　立　立　立丨　立丨　站　站　站

释义 Meaning

（一）动词 v.

1. stand; take a stand: 请大家坐着，不要站起来。Please be seated. Don't stand up.
2. stop; halt: 红灯亮了，车全站住了。When the red light is on, all the cars stop.

（二）名词 n.

station; stop: 我去火车站接一位朋友。I am going to meet one of my friends at the railway station.

词语 Words and Phrases

站立	zhànlì	stand; be on one's feet
车站	chēzhàn	stop; station

张 zhāng ` ` ⺈ ⼸ ⼸ ⼸ ⼸ 张 张

（張 ` ` ⺈ ⼸ ⼸ ⼸ ⼸ ⼸ ⼸ ⼸ ⼸ 張）

释义 Meaning

（一）动词 v.

open; spread; stretch: 她张大了嘴，气得一句话也说不出来。She opened her mouth wide, but she was so angry that she couldn't say anything.

（二）量词 measure w.

这个房间只能放两张床。This room can only accommodate two beds.

词语 Words and Phrases

张望	zhāngwàng	peep (through a crack, etc.)
慌张	huāngzhāng	helter-skelter; flurried; flustered
紧张	jǐnzhāng	nervous; tense; tight

| 夸张 | kuāzhāng | exaggerate; overstate |
| 主张 | zhǔzhāng | take up the responsibility for making a decision; advocate; maintain; view; opinion |

熟语 Idioms

张冠李戴	zhāng guān lǐ dài	put Zhang's hat on Li's head; attribute something to the wrong person
张口结舌	zhāng kǒu jié shé	gaping and speechless; tongue-tied
纲举目张	gāng jǔ mù zhāng	once the key link is grasped, everything falls into place

涨 zhǎng ` ㇏ 丶 氵 汃 汈 沙 浐 浐 涨 涨

(漲 ` ㇏ 丶 氵 汃 汈 沙 浐 泙 泙 浘 涱 涱 漲)

释义 Meaning

动词 v.

(of water, prices, etc.) rise; go up: 你买的股票涨了没有？
Is your stock rising? 反义词：跌

词语 Words and Phrases

| 涨价 | zhǎngjià | rise in price |
| 上涨 | shàngzhǎng | rise; go up |

熟语 Idioms

| 水涨船高 | shuǐ zhǎng chuán gāo | when the water rises, the boat floats; one's achievement does not owe to efforts but to one's luck |

掌 zhǎng ⎯ ⎯ ⎯ ⎯ ⎯ ⎯ ⎯ ⎯ ⎯
⎯ ⎯ ⎯

释义 Meaning

名词 n.

palm: 听了他的话，大家都拍掌叫好。After his words, we all clapped hands and shouted "Bravo!".

词语 Words and Phrases

掌管	zhǎngguǎn	be in charge of
掌声	zhǎngshēng	clapping; applause
掌握	zhǎngwò	possess; master; know well
鼓掌	gǔzhǎng	clap one's hands; applaud
手掌	shǒuzhǎng	palm

熟语 Idioms

掌上明珠	zhǎng shàng míngzhū	a pearl in the palm; usually refers to a beloved daughter
了如指掌	liǎo rú zhǐ zhǎng	know as one knows his fingers; understand well
易如反掌	yì rú fǎn zhǎng	as easy as turning over one's hands

丈 zhàng ⎯ ⎯ ⎯

释义 Meaning

量词 measure w.

一丈宽的河，你能跳过去吗？How can you jump over a river that is one *zhang* wide?

词语 Words and Phrases

丈夫	zhàngfu	husband

熟语 Idioms

| 一落千丈 | yí luò qiān zhàng | drop many metres in one fall; suffer a disastrous decline |

招 zhāo 一 十 扌 扝 扨 招 招 招

释义 Meaning

动词 v.

1. beckon: 你看，他在向我们招手呢！Look, he is beckoning to us!
2. provoke; tease: 这孩子爱哭，别招他。He is a crybaby. Don't tease him.

词语 Words and Phrases

招待	zhāodài	entertainment; server
招待会	zhāodàihuì	party; reception
招聘	zhāopìn	give public notice of a vacancy to be filled; recruit and employ through advertisement and examination
招生	zhāoshēng	enroll new students
招收	zhāoshōu	recruit
招手	zhāoshǒu	beckon

熟语 Idioms

| 招摇撞骗 | zhāo yáo zhuàng piàn | swindle by impersonating somebody |
| 不打自招 | bù dǎ zì zhāo | confess without being pressed |

找 zhǎo 一 十 扌 扝 找 找 找

释义 Meaning

动词 v.

1. try to find; seek; look for: 钱包丢了，还能找得到？

My purse was lost. Can it still be found?

2. give; change: 一共六十块，这是一百块，找您四十块。It costs sixty *yuan* in all. This is a hundred *yuan* note, I will give you forty *yuan* as the change.

词语 Words and Phrases

寻找　　xún zhǎo　　seek

熟语 Idioms

骑牛找马　　qí niú zhǎo mǎ　　hold on to one job while seeking a better one

照 zhào 丨 丨 刀 刀 日 刀 刀 昭 昭 昭 照 照 照

释义 Meaning

(一) 动词 v.

1. shine; illuminate; light up: 我一觉醒来，阳光已经照在窗子上了。When I woke up, the sunlight was already shining on the windows.

2. reflect; mirror: 你照一照镜子，看看脸上有什么东西。You had better look in the mirror to see what is on your face.

3. take a picture (or photograpy); photograph; film; shoot: 这张相片照得很好。This photo was well taken.

(二) 介词 prep.

1. in the direction of; towards: 你照这个方向一直走，就可以到那儿。If you keep going in this direction, you will get there.

2. according to; in accordance with: 照我看，他今天不会来了。If you ask me, he won't come today.

词语 Words and Phrases

照常	zhàocháng	as usual
照相机	zhàoxiàngjī	camera
照顾	zhàogù	give consideration to; take care of; (of a customer) patronize
照样	zhàoyàng	after a pattern or model; all the same
照会	zhàohuì	present (or deliver, address) a note to (a government)
照耀	zhàoyào	shine
照例	zhàolì	as a rule
照应	zhàoyìng	see after; coordinate
照料	zhàoliào	take care of
按照	ànzhào	according to
照明	zhàomíng	illumination
护照	hùzhào	passport
照片	zhàopiàn	photograph
拍照	pāizhào	take a picture (photograph)
照相	zhàoxiàng	take a picture (或 photograph)

熟语 Idioms

肝胆相照	gān dǎn xiāng zhào	devotion and trust between close friends

折 zhé 一 十 扌 扩 扩 折 折

释义 Meaning

动词 v.

1. break; snap: 老人摔了一跤，折断了膝盖骨。The old man stumbled and broke his kneecap.

2. turn back; change direction: 他刚走不远又折回来了。He just left for a while and then turned back again.

3. fold: 她把信折好，装在信封里。She folded the letter

and put it into the envelope.

词语 Words and Phrases

折合	zhéhé	convert into
折磨	zhémó	torment; rack; torture
骨折	gǔzhé	fracture
曲折	qūzhé	bending; zig-zag; tortuous; winding
转折	zhuǎnzhé	a turn in the course of events

这 zhè 　丶　亠　方　文　这　这　这

(這 丶　亠　亠　言　言　言　言　言　這)

释义 Meaning

代词 pron.

1. this: 这本词典是在哪儿买的？ Where did you buy this dictionary?

2. now: 我这才知道运动的好处。 Now I know the advantage of sports.

词语 Words and Phrases

这边	zhèbiān	this side; here
这个	zhège	this; such
这会儿	zhèhuìr	at the moment
这里	zhèlǐ	here
这么	zhème	so; like that; this way
这么着	zhèmezhe	like this; so; this way
这儿	zhèr	here
这些	zhèxiē	these
这样	zhèyàng	such
这样一来	zhèyàng yìlái	if so

针 zhēn 　丿　㇏　㇏　㇏　钅　钅　针

(針 ⼂ ⼈ ⼈ ⼈ ⾦ ⾦ ⾦ ⾦ ⾦ 針)

释义 Meaning

名词 n.

1. needle: 我这儿有针也有线，你拿去用吧。Here you are, the needle and thread.

2. stitch: 这儿开线了，我给你缝几针吧。The sew is parting here. Let me put a few stitches for you.

3. injection; shot: 你发烧了，要吃药，还要打针。You have a fever. You have to take some medicine and have an injection.

词语 Words and Phrases

针对	zhēnduì	direct; counter; be aimed at
针灸	zhēnjiǔ	acupuncture

熟语 Idioms

针锋相对	zhēn fēng xiāng duì	tit for tat; measure for measure; two sides of argument match point by point
一针见血	yì zhēn jiàn xiě	pinpoint; straight from the shoulder
海底捞针	hǎi dǐ lāo zhēn	fish for a needle in the ocean; strive for the impossible
见缝插针	jiàn fèng chā zhēn	stick in a pin wherever there's room; make use of every bit of time or space

真 zhēn ⼀ ⼇ ⼴ ⼗ ⼮ ⼱ ⼲ 直 真 真

释义 Meaning

（一）形容词 a.

real; true; genuine: 这幅张大千的画是真的。This is a

genuine painting by Zhang Daqian. 反义词 antonym: 假

（二）副词 adv.

really; truly; indeed: 时间过得真快。How time fies!

词语 Words and Phrases

真诚	zhēnchéng	true; genuine; sincere
真理	zhēnlǐ	truth
真实	zhēnshí	truth; true; real; genuine; authentic
真是	zhēnshì	indeed; certainly
真相	zhēnxiàng	truth
真心	zhēnxīn	bona fides; honest; sincere
真正	zhēnzhèng	true; really
传真	chuánzhēn	fax
认真	rènzhēn	take to heart; conscientious
天真	tiānzhēn	nature; freedom; innocent; naive

熟语 Idioms

真金不怕火炼	zhēn jīn bú pà huǒ liàn	true gold fears no fire; a person of integrity can stand tests
真相大白	zhēnxiàng dà bái	the whole truth has come out
弄假成真	nòng jiǎ chéng zhēn	what was make-believe has become reality

阵 zhèn 𠃌 阝 阝 阵 阵 阵

（陣 𠃌 阝 阝 阝 阝 阝 阝 陣）

释义 Meaning

（一）量词 measure w.

short period; spell: 今天下了好几阵雨。Today it rained several times.

（二）名词 n.

position; front: 只一个回合，他就败下阵来。He lost the field in just one round.

词语 Words and Phrases

阵地	zhèndì	position; battlefield; bastion; terrain
阵容	zhènróng	battle array; lineup
阵线	zhènxiàn	front; alignment
阵营	zhènyíng	a group of people who pursue a common interest; camp

熟语 Idioms

| 临阵磨枪 | lín zhèn mó qiāng | sharpen one's spear only before going into battle; unprepared |

争 zhēng ╱ ╱ ╯ ╯ ╯ 争

释义 Meaning

动词 v.

1. argue; dispute: 为这个问题大家争得面红耳赤。They argued over this issue until everyone was red with anger.
2. contend; vie; strive: 讨论会上，大家争着发言。Everyone at the seminar was competing for the floor.

词语 Words and Phrases

争吵	zhēngchǎo	quarrel
争端	zhēngduān	dispute
争夺	zhēngduó	contend
争论	zhēnglùn	controversy; argue; contend; skirmish
争气	zhēngqì	try to make a good showing
争取	zhēngqǔ	strive for
争议	zhēngyì	dispute
斗争	dòuzhēng	fight; war; strife; struggle

| 竞争 | jìngzhēng | competition |
| 战争 | zhànzhēng | war |

熟语 Idioms

争分夺秒	zhēng fēn duó miǎo	against time
争先恐后	zhēng xiān kǒng hòu	rush off to the front; strive to be the first and fear to lag behind
与世无争	yǔ shì wú zhēng	bear no ill will against anybody; contended

整 zhěng

一 厂 厂 戸 申 束 束 束' 束'
敕' 敕 敕 敕 整 整 整

释义 Meaning

形容词 a.

full; whole; complete; entire: 现在是十二点整。Now it is twelve o'clock sharp. 反义词 antonym: 零

词语 Words and Phrases

整顿	zhěngdùn	consolidate; rectify
整风	zhěngfēng	rectify the incorrect styles of work (political term.)
整个	zhěnggè	complete; entire; full; total; all
整洁	zhěngjié	neat; trim
整理	zhěnglǐ	arrange; put in order
整齐	zhěngqí	tidy; neat; put in order
整数	zhěngshù	integer (integral, whole) number
整体	zhěngtǐ	entirety; whole; total
整天	zhěngtiān	the whole day; all day; all day long
整整	zhěngzhěng	whole
调整	tiáozhěng	adjust; regulate
完整	wánzhěng	complete

熟语 Idioms

重整旗鼓　　chóng zhěng qí gǔ　rally one's forces (after a defeat)

正 zhèng 　一　丁　下　下　正　正

释义 Meaning

（一）副词 adv.

just (doing sth.); just now: 他们正开会，你一会儿再找他吧！They are having a meeting now. You had better look for him later.

（二）形容词 a.

straight; upright: 这幅画挂得不正。This picture is not hung straight. 反义词 antonym: 歪

词语 Words and Phrases

正常	zhèngcháng	normal
正当	zhèngdāng	just when; proper; rightful
正规	zhèngguī	regular; standard
正好	zhènghǎo	just in time; just right; just enough
正经	zhèngjīng	decent; respectable
正面	zhèngmiàn	front; the right side; positive
正巧	zhèngqiǎo	happen to; chance to
正确	zhèngquè	correct; right; proper
正式	zhèngshì	formal
正义	zhèngyì	justice; just
正在	zhèngzài	in process of; in course of
反正	fǎnzhèng	anyhow
改正	gǎizhèng	put right; correct
公正	gōngzhèng	just; fair-minded; equitable
真正	zhēnzhèng	real

熟语 Idioms

正中下怀	zhèngzhòngxiàhuái	just to one intention; fit in exactly with one wishes
名正言顺	míng zhèng yán shùn	with right titles and proper words; be appropriated to the occasion
一本正经	yì běn zhèng jīng	put on an air of serious manner
改邪归正	gǎi xié guī zhèng	give up evil ways and return to the right; abandon evil and do good

证 zhèng `　讠　讠　证　证　证　证

（證 `　亠　ソ　ゴ　言　言　言　訁　訃　訐　訐　証　証　証　証　證　證　證　證）.

释义 Meaning

名词 n.

certificate; card: 你没有出入证，不能进去。You don't have an entrance permit. You are not allowed to enter.

词语 Words and Phrases

证件	zhèngjiàn	paper; certificate; credential
证据	zhèngjù	evidence; proof; testimony
证明	zhèngmíng	demonstrate; certificate
证实	zhèngshí	affirm; demonstrate; confirm; verify
证书	zhèngshū	certificate
保证	bǎozhèng	guarantee
公证	gōngzhèng	notarization
签证	qiānzhèng	visa

熟语 Idioms

铁证如山　　tiě zhèng rú shān　　irrefutable evidence; iron-clad proof

政 zhèng　一　丁　下　下　正　正　正　政　政

释义 Meaning

名词 n.

1. political view: 怎么对待不同政见的人？How to treat a person holding different political views?
2. politics: 发动群众参政议政。Mobilize the masses to participate in government and discuss political affairs.

词语 Words and Phrases

政变	zhèngbiàn	coup
政策	zhèngcè	policy
政党	zhèngdǎng	party
政府	zhèngfǔ	government
政权	zhèngquán	state political power; organs of state power
政治	zhèngzhì	politics; political affairs
财政	cáizhèng	public finance
内政	nèizhèng	internal (or domestic) affairs
邮政	yóuzhèng	postal service

熟语 Idioms

精兵简政　　jīng bīng jiǎn zhèng　　better troops and simpler administration

支 zhī　一　十　支　支

释义 Meaning

（一）动词 v.

1. prop up; put up: 他用两手支着头正在想什么。He rested

his head in both hands thinking.

2. support; sustain; bear: 他肚子疼得支不住了，我们就把他送到了医院。He could not bear the stomachache. We sent him to the hospital at once.

（二）量词 measure w.

(for long, thin, inflexible objects): 他一天抽二十几支香烟。He smokes more than twenty cigarettes every day.

词语 Words and Phrases

支撑	zhīchēng	prop up; sustain; support; keep out; ward off
支援	zhīyuán	assist; support; supply; sustain; holdout; bear; prop up
支出	zhīchū	pay out; expenditure
支付	zhīfù	pay
支配	zhīpèi	arrange; allocate; budget; control; dominate; guide
支票	zhīpiào	cheque
支持	zhīchí	support
支柱	zhīzhù	support; bolster; pillar; prop; mainstay

熟语 Idioms

支离破碎	zhī lí pòsuì	disconnected; fragmented
独木难支	dú mù nán zhī	a single stick cannot support the entire scaffold

知 zhī ノ ト ヒ 午 矢 知 知 知

释义 Meaning

动词 v.

know: 这话不知是谁说的。It is unknown who said this.

词语 Words and Phrases

知道	zhīdào	know

知觉	zhījué	consciousness; perception; know; understand; comprehend
知识	zhīshi	knowledge
知识份子	zhīshí fèn zi	intellectual
通知	tōngzhī	notify; inform; give notice; notice; circular; notification

熟语 Idioms

知己知彼	zhī jǐ zhī bǐ	know the enemy and know oneself
知难而进	zhī nán ér jìn	press forward in the face of difficulties
知其一，不知其二	zhī qí yī, bù zhī qí èr	know only superficially
知无不言，言无不尽	zhī wú bù yán, yán wú bú jìn	say all one knows and say it without reservation
尽人皆知	jìn rén jiē zhī	be known to all

直 zhí   二 十 丁 古 直 直 直 直

释义 Meaning

(一) 动词 v.

straighten: 她笑得直不起腰来。She doubled up with laughter.

(二) 形容词 a.

straight: 这条马路又宽又直。This road is wide and straight.

(三) 副词 adv.

1. till; until: 那个会议直到晚上一点才结束。That meeting was not over until one o'clock in the morning.

2. continuously: 我在后面直喊他，他就是听不见。I kept calling him from behind. He just couldn't hear me.

词语 Words and Phrases

| 直播 | zhíbō | direct seeding; direct broadcast; on air |

直达	zhídá	through; nonstop
直到	zhídào	directly arrive; until; up to
直接	zhíjiē	direct; immediate
直径	zhíjìng	diameter
直线	zhíxiàn	straight line
直至	zhízhì	till
笔直	bǐzhí	perfectly straight
简直	jiǎnzhí	simply; at all
一直	yìzhí	straight; continuously; always; all along; all the way

熟语 Idioms

| 直截了当 | zhíjié-liǎodàng | without preamble; outspoken |
| 直言不讳 | zhí yán bú huì | call a spade a spade; talk straight |

值 zhí　ノ　亻　仁　仁　亡　伓　佶　值　值　值

释义 Meaning

动词 v.

be worth: 这套茶具值多少钱？How much is this tea set worth?

词语 Words and Phrases

值班	zhíbān	be on duty
值得	zhídé	deserve; be worth
贬值	biǎnzhí	devaluation; depreciation; devaluate; depreciate
产值	chǎnzhí	output value
价值	jiàzhí	value; worth

熟语 Idioms

| 价值连城 | jiàzhí lián chéng | worth several cities; invaluable |

职 zhí   一 厂 ォ 耳 耳 耳 耶 职 职 职 职

(職   一 厂 ォ 耳 耳 耳 取 取 取 职 职 职 耶 聆 聆 職 職 職)

释义 Meaning

名词 n.

duty; job

词语 Words and Phrases

职称	zhí chēng	the title of a technical or professional post (such as engineer, professor, lecturer, academician, etc.)
职工	zhígōng	staff and workers
职务	zhíwù	post; duties; job
职员	zhíyuán	office worker; staff member
辞职	cízhí	resign; hand in (send in) one's resignation
兼职	jiānzhí	part-time job; moonlight; hold two or more posts concurrently; concurrent post

植 zhí   一 十 ォ 木 杧 柿 柿 植 植 植 植 植

释义 Meaning

动词 v.

plant; grow: 植树造林，可以造福子孙后代。Tree planting and afforestation can be beneficial to our offspring.

词语 Words and Phrases

植物	zhíwù	plant

| 种植 | zhòngzhí | grow; plant; cultivate |

止 zhǐ 丨 ㅏ 止 止

释义 Meaning

动词 v.

1. stop: 眼泪止不住地往下流。(She) could not stop the tears from trickling down.

2. to; till: 参观时间自上午八时起至下午五时止。Visiting hours are from eight o'clock in the morning to five o'clock in the afternoon.

词语 Words and Phrases

不止	bùzhǐ	more than; without end
防止	fángzhǐ	prevent; avert; hinder; guard against; protect against
禁止	jìnzhǐ	prohibit
停止	tíngzhǐ	stop; cease; halt; pause; bring an end to; end up; fetch up; leave off
阻止	zǔzhǐ	stop; hinder; hold back; prevent

熟语 Idioms

| 望梅止渴 | wàng méi zhǐ kě | quench one's thirst by thinking of plums; it is a superficial substitute |
| 适可而止 | shì kě ér zhǐ | stop before going too far; never overdo sth.; stop where you reach the limit |

只₁ zhǐ 丨 冂 口 只 只

(祇 丶 冫 礻 礻 礻 礻 祇 祇)

释义 Meaning

副词 adv.

only; just; merely

1. 我的钱包里只剩下七块钱。There is only 7 *Yuan* left in my purse.
2. 家里只我一个人。I am the only one home right now.

词语 Words and Phrases

只得	zhǐdé	be obliged to; have to; have no alternative but to
只顾	zhǐgù	merely; simply; be absorbed in
只管	zhǐguǎn	merely;
只好	zhǐhǎo	be forced to; have to; the only alternative is to
只能	zhǐnéng	only
只是	zhǐshì	merely; simply; only; but then; however
只要	zhǐyào	so long as
只有	zhǐyǒu	only; alone
不只	bùzhǐ	not only

熟语 Idioms

只许州官放火，不许百姓点灯	zhǐ xǔ zhōuguān fàng huǒ, bù xǔ bǎi xìng diǎn dēng	the magistrate is allowed to burn down houses, while the common people are forbidden even to light lamps; the privileged can get away with anything while ordinary people have no freedom at all

只₂ zhī 丨 冂 口 只 只

(隻 丿 亻 亻 亻 亻 亻 隹 隹 隻 **)**

释义 Meaning

量词 measure w.

1. 她家里养了两只兔子。She kept two rabbits in her family.
2. 湖上有一只小船。There is a small boat on the lake.

纸zhǐ ㇉ ㄠ ㄠ ㄠ 纟 红 纸 纸

(紙 ㇉ ㄠ ㄠ ㄠ ㄠ 糹 糽 紅 紙 紙)

释义 Meaning

名词 n.

paper: 你有没有纸？给我一张。Do you have any paper? Give me a piece.

词语 Idioms

纸张	zhǐzhāng	paper
报纸	bàozhǐ	newspaper
信纸	xìnzhǐ	letterpaper

指zhǐ 二 丁 扌 扩 护 挃 指 指 指

释义 Meaning

动词 v.

point at; point to

1. 时针正指着十二点。The hour hand points to twelve.
2. 老师指着黑板上的字，让学生念。The teacher is pointing to the characters on the blackboard and letting the students read aloud.

词语 Words and Phrases

指标	zhǐbiāo	target; index; quota
指出	zhǐchū	indicate; point out
指导	zhǐdǎo	guide; direct

指点	zhǐdiǎn	give advice (directions); show how to do sth.
指定	zhǐdìng	designate
指挥	zhǐhuī	command; conduct; commander
指令	zhǐlìng	instruct; order; instruction
指明	zhǐmíng	indicate
指南针	zhǐnánzhēn	compass
指示	zhǐshì	point out; instruct; instructions
指望	zhǐwàng	count on; look for help; look to
指引	zhǐyǐn	aim; guide; point at way

熟语 Idioms

指手划脚	zhǐ shǒu huà jiǎo	gesticulate; to interfere by pointing
首屈一指	shǒu qū yì zhǐ	come first on the list; be second to none

至 zhì   一 丁 丏 玄 至 至

释义 Meaning

介词 prep.

to until: 营业时间自早上九时至晚上十时。Business hours are from nine o'clock in the morning to ten o'clock in the evening.

词语 Words and Phrases

至多	zhìduō	at (the) most
至今	zhìjīn	up to now; to this day; so far
至少	zhìshǎo	least
至于	zhìyú	as for; as to; as for; go so far as to
甚至	shènzhì	even
以至	yǐzhì	down to; up to; so that...; to such an extent as to

熟语 Idioms

至理名言	zhìlǐ-míngyán	a golden saying; famous dictum
无微不至	wú wēi bú zhì	in every possible way; meticulously

志 zhì　　一　十　士　产　志　志　志

释义 Meaning

名词 n.

aspiration; ideal; ambition: 他立志做一名教师。He made up his mind to be a teacher.

词语 Words and Phrases

志气	zhìqì	aspiration; ambition
志愿	zhìyuàn	aspiration; volunteer
标志	biāozhì	sign; mark
同志	tóngzhì	comrade; colleagues (in a political party); homosexual partner
意志	yìzhì	will

熟语 Idioms

志同道合	zhì tóng dào hé	cherish the same ideals and follow the same route; be in the same camp
专心致志	zhuān xīn zhì zhì	devote oneself to; set one's heart on

制 zhì　　′　′′　′′′　′′′′　′′′′′　′′′′′′　制　制

(製　′　′′　′′′　′′′′　′′′′′　′′′′′′　製　製　製　製　製 製 製)

释义 Meaning

动词 v.

1. make: 她们正忙着缝制一面大旗。They are busy with sewing a big flag.

2. system: 我们是全民所有制企业。We are a publicly-owned enterprise.

词语 Words and Phrases

制裁	zhìcái	sanction; punish
制定	zhìdìng	lay down; draw up; draft; formulate
制订	zhìdìng	work out; formulate
制度	zhìdù	system; institution
制服	zhìfú	subdue; bring under control; uniform
制品	zhìpǐn	goods; products
制约	zhìyuē	restrict; govern
制造	zhìzào	manufacture; make
制止	zhìzhǐ	check; curb; prevent; stop
制作	zhìzuò	make; manufacture
法制	fǎzhì	legal system
体制	tǐzhì	system of organization; system
限制	xiànzhì	confine; restrict; limit; quota system
学制	xuézhì	educational (or school) system; arrangements for schooling; length of schooling

熟语 Idioms

先发制人	xiān fā zhì rén	gain the initiative by striking the first blow

治 zhì   丶 丶 氵 氵 氵 氵 治 治

释义 Meaning

动词 v.

cure; treat (a disease): 他的病还能治好吗？Can his illness still be cured?

词语 Words and Phrases

治安	zhì'ān	public order; public security
治理	zhìlǐ	administer; govern; manage; rule; bring under control; put in order
治疗	zhìliáo	treat
防治	fángzhì	prevention and cure
统治	tǒngzhì	control; rule; dominate
政治	zhèngzhì	politics

熟语 Idioms

治病救人	zhì bìng jiù rén	cure the sickness to save the patient; criticize a person only in order to help him

质 zhì   一 厂 厂 厂 厌 厌 质 质

(質   一 厂 厂 斤 斤 斦 斦 斦 斦 斦 質 質 質 質 質)

释义 Meaning

名词 n.

1. nature; character: 不同的事物有不同的本质。Different things differ in nature.

2. quality: 产品的质和量都不能忽视。We cannot neglect the quality and the quantity of the products.

词语 Words and Phrases

质变	zhìbiàn	qualitative change

质量	zhìliàng	quality; mass
质朴	zhìpǔ	unpretentious; plain; unaffected, be simple and unadorned
本质	běnzhì	nature; essence
品质	pǐnzhì	character; quality
气质	qìzhì	temperament; disposition
人质	rénzhì	pawn; hostage
物质	wùzhì	objective reality; matter; substance
性质	xìngzhì	quality; nature; character

熟语 Idioms

| 文质彬彬 | wén zhì bīnbīn | gentle; balance of outward grace and solid worth; combination of elegance and plainness |

中 zhōng 丨 口 口 中

释义 Meaning

名词 n.

1. China: 桂林是闻名中外的旅游胜地。Guilin is a well-known resort all over China and the world.

2. in; among; amidst: 你的话我牢记心中。I keep your words firmly in my mind.

词语 Words and Phrases

中部	zhōngbù	central section; middle
中餐	zhōngcān	Chinese meal; Chinese food
中等	zhōngděng	medium; middling; moderate
中断	zhōngduàn	interrupt; discontinue; suspend; come to stop; break down (off)
中间	zhōngjiān	centre; middle; between; among
中立	zhōnglì	neutral; independent
中年	zhōngnián	middle age; medium term

中秋	zhōngqiū	mid-autumn
中途	zhōngtú	halfway; midway
中文	zhōngwén	the Chinese language
中午	zhōngwǔ	noon; midday
中心	zhōngxīn	centre; heart; middle; nucleus
中型	zhōngxíng	medium-sized; middle-sized
中学	zhōngxué	middle school
中旬	zhōngxún	the middle ten days of a month
中央	zhōngyāng	centre; central authorities
中药	zhōngyào	traditional Chinese medicine
中医	zhōngyī	traditional Chinese medical science; doctor of traditional Chinese medicine
当中	dāngzhōng	in the middle; in the centre; among
集中	jízhōng	concentrate; centralize; converge; sum up; bring together; centre on
其中	qízhōng	among; in (which)
心中	xīnzhōng	in the heart; at heart; in mind

熟语 Idioms

| 无中生有 | wúzhōngshēngyǒu | out of thin air; sheer fabrication |
| 雪中送炭 | xuě zhōng sòng tàn | help in one's hour of need |

终 zhōng ⟍ ⟨ ⟨ ⟨ ⟨ ⟨ ⟨ 终

（终 ⟍ ⟨ ⟨ ⟨ ⟨ ⟨ ⟨ ⟨ ⟨ ⟨ 終）

释义 Meaning

（一）名词 n.

end; finish: 最后还是以失败告终。Ultimately it still ended in failure. 反义词 antonym: 始

（二）副词 adv.

eventually; after all; in the end: 美好的理想终将实现。

The glorious ideal will come true in the end.

词语 Words and Phrases

终点	zhōngdiǎn	terminus; final stop
终究	zhōngjiū	after all
终年	zhōngnián	perennially
终身	zhōngshēn	life; lifelong; all one's life
终于	zhōngyú	finally; after all
终止	zhōngzhǐ	stop; conclude; close
始终	shǐzhōng	from beginning to end

熟语 Idioms

终身大事	zhōngshēn dà shì	an important event in one's life (usu. referring to marriage)
有始有终	yǒu shǐ yǒu zhōng	carry something through to the end; have a good beginning as well as a good end

钟 zhōng ノ ト ヒ ヒ 乍 钅 钅 钔 钔 钟

（鐘 ノ ト ヒ ヒ 午 午 金 金 金 釒 釒 釒 釒 鈩 鈶 鈶 鐈 鐈 鐘 鐘 鐘）

释义 Meaning

名词 n.

1. bell: 教堂敲钟了。The church is sounding the bell.

2. clock: 墙上挂着一个钟。A clock is hanging on the wall.

3. time as measured in hours and minutes: 京剧开演还有十分钟。There is ten minutes left before the Beijing opera starts.

词语 Words and Phrases

钟表	zhōngbiǎo	clocks and watches
钟点	zhōngdiǎn	hour; time
钟头	zhōngtóu	hour

种₁ zhǒng 一 二 千 千 禾 利 和 和 种

(種 一 二 千 千 禾 秆 秆 秆 秆 稆 稆 種 種 種)

释义 Meaning

（一）名词 n.

seed: 这是麦种，不能拿走。 This is the seed of wheat. You can't take it away.

（二）量词 measure w.

这种颜色的衣服我不喜欢。 I don't like clothes of this colour.

词语 Words and Phrases

种类	zhǒnglèi	kind; sort; type
种子	zhǒngzi	seed
种族	zhǒngzú	stock; race; ethnic group
品种	pǐnzhǒng	breed; variety
种种	zhǒngzhǒng	a variety of

种₂ zhòng 一 二 千 千 禾 利 和 和 种

释义 Meaning

动词 v.

plant; grow: 马路两旁种了很多树。 Many trees grow on both sides of the road.

词语 Words and Phrases

种植	zhòngzhí	plant; grow

熟语 Idioms

| 种瓜得瓜，种豆得豆 | zhòng guā dé guā, zhòng dòu dé dòu | as a man sows, so he shall reap |

众 zhòng ノ 人 个 外 分 众

(眾 ′ ｀ 宀 宀 宀 血 罒 罒 罗 眾 眾)

释义 Meaning

(一)形容词 a.

many; numerous: 俗话说，"众人拾柴火焰高"，只要大家一齐努力，一定会成功。The saying goes, "when everybody adds fuel the flames rise high, the more people, the more strength".

(二)名词 n.

crowd; multitude: 代表们十分关心民众的疾苦。The representatives are very concerned about the difficulties of the people's livelihood.

词语 Words and Phrases

众多	zhòngduō	multitudinous; many; numerous
众人	zhòngrén	multitude; everybody; common people
大众	dàzhòng	the masses
观众	guānzhòng	audience
群众	qúnzhòng	the masses
听众	tīngzhòng	audience

熟语 Idioms

| 众人拾柴火焰高 | zhòngrén shí chái huǒ yàn gāo | the fire burns high when people add wood to it; the more people, the greater strength |

| 万众一心 | wàn zhòng yī xīn | all of one heart and one mind |
| 寡不敌众 | guǎ bù dí zhòng | the few cannot withstand the many; a small force cannot hold back a large opposing force |

重₁ zhòng 一 二 亠 亣 亣 亩 亩 重 重

释义 Meaning

形容词 a.

1. weight: 这条鱼有五公斤重。This fish weighs five kilogram.
2. heavy: 这只箱子很重。This case is very heavy. 反义词 antonym: 轻
3. serious: 他的病很重。He was seriously ill.

词语 Words and Phrases

重大	zhòngdà	great; big; important; major
重点	zhòngdiǎn	stress; main point; focal point; important point; emphasize
重量	zhòngliàng	weight
重视	zhòngshì	mind; treasure; value; pay great attention to; think highly of
重心	zhòngxīn	centre of gravity; core
重要	zhòngyào	important
比重	bǐzhòng	specific gravity; in proportion
超重	chāozhòng	overload; overweight
体重	tǐzhòng	body weight
严重	yánzhòng	serious; grave; critical

熟语 Idioms

| 头重脚轻 | tóu zhòng jiǎo qīng | top-heavy; be weighed down |
| 举足轻重 | jǔ zú qīng zhòng | hold the balance |

重₂ chóng 一 二 亠 亇 亓 盲 重 重 重

释义 Meaning

（一）副词 adv.

again; once more: 你写错了，重写一遍。You wrote it wrong, write it over again.

（二）动词 v.

repeat; duplicate: 他们俩买书买重了。They have bought two copies of the same book by mistake.

词语 Words and Phrases

重重	chóngchóng	layer upon layer; ring upon ring
重迭	chóngdié	one on top of another; overlapping
重复	chóngfù	repeat; duplicate
重新	chóngxīn	again; anew; afresh

熟语 Idioms

重蹈覆辙	chóng dǎo fù zhé	follow the same catastrophic steps

周 zhōu 丿 冂 冂 冃 冄 周 周 周

释义 Meaning

名词 n.

1. week: 下周我们要考试了。We will have a test next week.
2. circumference; periphery; circuit: 运动员绕场一周，向观众们致意。The athletes made a circuit of the arena to extend greetings to the audience.

词语 Words and Phrases

周到	zhōudào	considerate; thoughtful; be attentive and satisfactory
周密	zhōumì	thorough; careful
周末	zhōumò	weekend

周年	zhōunián	anniversary
周期	zhōuqī	period; cycle
周围	zhōuwéi	round
周折	zhōuzhé	setback; twists and turns
四周	sìzhōu	surrounding

熟语 Idioms

| 周而复始 | zhōu ér fù shǐ | go round and begin again |
| 众所周知 | zhòng suǒ zhōu zhī | as all know; it is known to all |

珠 zhū   一 二 三 王 王 珏 珔 珒 玨 珠 珠

释义 Meaning

名词 n.

pearl: 孩子的脸上挂着泪珠呢！Teardrops are still shining on the children's faces.

词语 Words and Phrases

| 珠子 | zhūzi | pearl; bead; a thing resembling pearl or bead |

熟语 Idioms

| 鱼目混珠 | yú mù hùn zhū | regard eyeball of a fish as a pearl; confuse the genuine with the fictitious |
| 掌上明珠 | zhǎng shàng míng zhū | a pearl in the palm; a beloved daughter |

猪 zhū   丿 犭 犭 狘 狘 狫 猪 猪 猪 猪 猪

释义 Meaning

名词 n.

pig: 他家养了一头猪。His family kept a pig.

竹 zhú ノ ト 仁 仁 竹 竹

释义 Meaning

名词 n.

bamboo: 熊猫是喜欢吃竹的动物。The pandas like to eat bamboo.

词语 Words and Phrases

竹笋	zhúsǔn	bamboo shoot
竹子	zhúzi	bamboo
爆竹	bàozhú	firecracker

熟语 Idioms

| 势如破竹 | shì rú pò zhú | smash into the enemy territory like splitting a bamboo |
| 胸有成竹 | xiōng yǒu chéng zhú | to have a well-thought-out plan beforehand; have a card up one's sleeves |

主 zhǔ 丶 亠 三 主 主

释义 Meaning

名词 n.

1. 宾主互送礼物。The guest and the host exchanged gifts. 反义词 antonym: 宾

2. 主队以三比二取胜。The home team won 3 : 2. 反义词 antonym: 客

词语 Words and Phrases

主办	zhǔbàn	direct; undertake; sponsor
主持	zhǔchí	take charge of; take care of; manage; direct
主动	zhǔdòng	initiative; actively
主观	zhǔguān	subjective

主力	zhǔlì	main forces; main strength of an army
主权	zhǔquán	sovereignty; sovereign right
主人	zhǔrén	host; hostess; master; mistress
主任	zhǔrèn	director head; chairman
主席	zhǔxí	chairman; president; host at a dinner
主要	zhǔyào	main; chief; principal; major; leading; essential; primary; first
主义	zhǔyì	-ism
主意	zhǔyì	definite view; one's own judgment; idea; thought
主张	zhǔzhāng	advocate; maintain; stand for
民主	mínzhǔ	democracy

熟语 Idioms

| 反客为主 | fǎn kè wéi zhǔ | reverse the positions of the host and the guest; turn from a guest into a host |
| 六神无主 | liù shén wú zhǔ | all six vital organs failing to function; in a state of confusion |

住 zhù ╱ 亻 亻 广 仁 住 住

释义 Meaning

动词 v.

1. live; reside; stay: 你住在什么地方？Where do you live?
2. stop; cease: 雨住了。The rain has stopped.
3. (used before a verb) firmly; to a stop: 他的电话号码我没记住。I didn't remember his telephone number.

词语 Words and Phrases

住房	zhùfáng	housing
住所	zhùsuǒ	dwelling place; residence; domicile
住院	zhùyuàn	be hospitalized

| 住宅 | zhùzhái | residence; dwelling; house; domicile |
| 居住 | jūzhù | live |

熟语 Idioms

| 衣食住行 | yī shí zhù xíng | clothing, food, shelter and means of transportation |

助 zhù ┃ ┃┃ ┃┃ ┃┃ ┃┃ ┃┃ 助

释义 Meaning

动词 v.

help: 他们俩成了互学互助的好朋友。They have become good friends who can help and learn from each other.

词语 Words and Phrases

助长	zhùzhǎng	encourage; fatten; abet; foster
助理	zhùlǐ	assistant; deputy
助手	zhùshǒu	assistant; deputy
帮助	bāngzhù	help
援助	yuánzhù	help; support; aid

熟语 Idioms

| 助人为乐 | zhù rén wéi lè | find pleasure in helping others |
| 爱莫能助 | ài mò néng zhù | would be glad to help but cannot |

注 zhù 丶 丶 氵 氵 汁 汁 注 注

释义 Meaning

动词 v.

pour; fill

词语 Words and Phrases

| 注册 | zhùcè | enroll; register |
| 注解 | zhùjiě | annotate; explain with notes |

注目	zhùmù	gaze at; fix one's eyes on; noticeable
注射	zhùshè	inject; injection
注释	zhùshì	note; footnote; annotation; annotate; explain with notes
注视	zhùshì	gaze at; look attentively at; watch with concern
注意	zhùyì	pay attention to; attend to; take notice of; be careful; look out
注重	zhùzhòng	lay stress on; pay attention to; attach importance to
关注	guānzhù	concern

熟语 Idioms

孤注一掷	gū zhù yí zhì	risk everything in a single venture; put all one's eggs in one basket
引人注目	yǐn rén zhùmù	noticeable; conspicuous; strike the eye; spectecular
全神贯注	quán shén guàn zhù	be absorbed in

祝 zhù　　`ㄱ　ㄱ　ㄱ　ㄱ　ㄱ　ㄱ　ㄱ　祝

释义 Meaning

动词 v.

express good wishes; wish

1. 祝你生日快乐！Happy birthday to you!
2. 祝你一路顺风！Have a nice trip!

词语 Words and Phrases

祝福	zhùfú	blessing; benediction
祝贺	zhùhè	congratulate; congratulation
祝愿	zhùyuàn	wish
庆祝	qìngzhù	celebrate

著 zhù   一 十 艹 艹 芏 芏 荖 荖 著 著 著

释义 Meaning

(一) 动词 v.

write: 鲁迅著《阿Q正传》。*The True Story of Ah Q* was written by Lu Xun.

(二) 名词 n.

book; work: 这本小说是世界名著。This novel is a well-known world classic.

词语 Words and Phrases

著名	zhùmíng	famous; celebrated
著作	zhùzuò	write; work; book; writings
名著	míngzhù	famous book
显著	xiǎnzhù	notable; striking; marked; outstanding; remarkable
专著	zhuānzhù	treatise; specialized publication

抓 zhuā   一 十 扌 扩 扩 抓 抓

释义 Meaning

动词 v.

1. grab; seize; clutch: 他抓起帽子就往外走。He grabbed his cap and made for the door.

2. take charge of; be responsible for: 这位员工是抓后勤工作的。That worker is in charge of logistic services.

词语 Words and Phrases

抓紧	zhuā jǐn	firmly grasp; pay close attention to

专 zhuān   一 二 专 专

(專　一　厂　厃　冇　亩　申　車　重　重　専　専)

释义 Meaning

形容词 a.

special: 这位医生专治眼病。The doctor is an eye specialist.

词语 Words and Phrases

专长	zhuāncháng	speciality; special skill or knowledge
专程	zhuānchéng	special trip
专家	zhuānjiā	expert; specialist
专科	zhuānkē	specialized subject; training school
专利	zhuānlì	patent
专门	zhuānmén	single household; specially; special; specialized
专人	zhuānrén	specially-assigned person
专题	zhuāntí	special subject; special topic
专心	zhuānxīn	be absorbed; concentrate one's attention
专业	zhuānyè	special field of study; profession
专用	zhuānyòng	for a special purpose
专政	zhuānzhèng	dictatorship; autocratic
专制	zhuānzhì	autocracy; autocratic

熟语 Idioms

| 专心致志 | zhuān xīn zhì zhì | concentrate on; apply one's mind on |

转₁ zhuǎn　一　土　车　车　轩　轩　转　转

(轉　一　厂　厅　爭　百　亘　車　軒　軒　軒　軒　軒　軒　軒　軒　軒　轉　轉)

释义 Meaning

动词 v.

1. turn; shift; change: 明天上午有小雨，下午阴转晴。 Tomorrow morning it will drizzle, then would change from overcast to clear in the afternoon.

2. pass on; transfer: 请把这封信转给他。Please pass the letter on to him.

词语 Words and Phrases

转变	zhuǎnbiàn	change; transform
转播	zhuǎnbō	relay a radio or TV broadcast; rebroadcast
转达	zhuǎndá	pass on; convey; mediate
转动	zhuǎndòng	turn; move; turn round
转告	zhuǎngào	pass on word; communicate
转化	zhuǎnhuà	inversion
转换	zhuǎnhuàn	change; transform
转交	zhuǎnjiāo	pass on; transmit
转让	zhuǎnràng	transfer the possession of; make over
转入	zhuǎnrù	change over to; shift to; switch to
转弯	zhuǎn wān	turn a corner; make a turn
转向	zhuǎnxiàng	change direction; change one's politcal stand; go over to
转折	zhuǎnzhé	a turn in the course of events; transition
好转	hǎozhuǎn	take a turn for the better; improve

熟语 Idioms

转弯抹角	zhuǎn wān mò jiǎo	speak in a roundabout way; smooth operation

转₂ zhuàn 　一　土　午　车　车　车　转　转

(轉 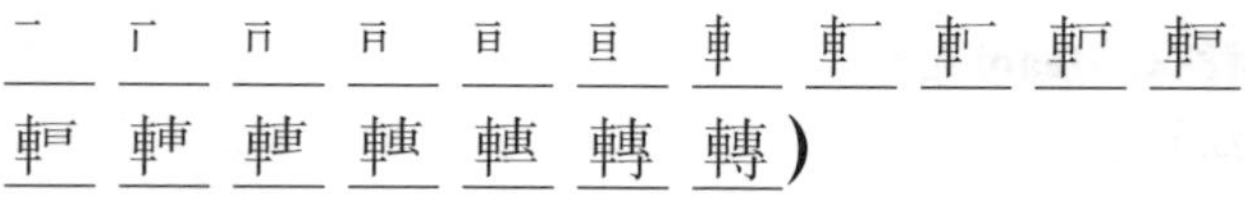)

释义 Meaning

动词 v.

1. turn; revolve; rotate: 地球绕着太阳转。The earth revolves round the sun.
2. take a short walk; go for a stroll: 我到街上转转，顺便带点儿菜回来。I will take a short walk in the street, and bring some vegetables home in passing.

装 zhuāng

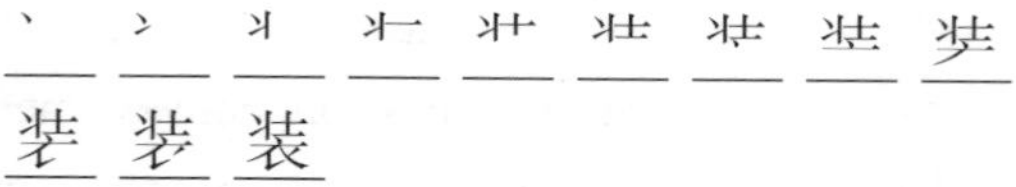

(裝 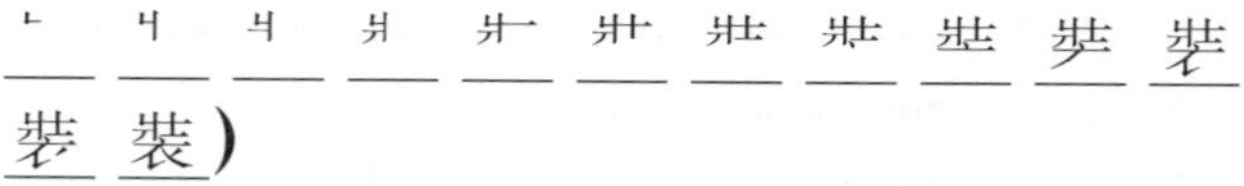)

释义 Meaning

动词 v.

1. install; fit; assemble: 机器已经装好了。The machine has been assembled.
2. load; pack; hold: 家具都装上了汽车。The furniture was loaded on the bus.

词语 Words and Phrases

装备	zhuāngbèi	equip; fit out; equipment
装配	zhuāngpèi	assemble; fit together
装饰	zhuāngshì	decorate; dress up; embellish; trim decoration; ornament
装卸	zhuāngxiè	load and unload; assemble and disassemble
装置	zhuāngzhì	installation; unit device; install; fit

安装	ānzhuāng	install; fix
服装	fúzhuāng	dress; clothing
假装	jiǎzhuāng	pretend; disguise; dissimulate; feign; make believe; make to believe
武装	wǔzhuāng	arm; military equipment; battle outfit

熟语 Idioms

装腔作势	zhuāng qiāng zuò shì	assume airs of importance; strike an attitude

撞 zhuàng ⟋ 扌 扌 扌 扩 扩 扩 护 护 护 掊 撞 撞 撞 撞

释义 Meaning

动词 v.

bump against; run into; strike; collide: 老人不小心撞上了汽车。 The old man bumped into the car carelessly.

词语 Words and Phrases

撞车	zhuàngchē	collision
撞见	zhuàngjiàn	meet or discover by chance

熟语 Idioms

当一天和尚撞一天钟	dāng yì tiān hé shang zhuàng yì tiān zhōng	do as little as possible, take a passive attitude towards one's work
横冲直撞	héng chōng zhí zhuàng	push one's way by shoving or bumping; dash around madly

追 zhuī ⟋ 冖 冖 冖 自 自 自 追 追

释义 Meaning

动词 v.

1. chase (or run) after; pursue: 他刚走，现在去追，还追

得上。He has just left. If you run after him now, you can still catch up with him.

2. court (a woman); woo: 两个小伙子都在追这个姑娘。Two boys are both courting this girl.

词语 Words and Phrases

追查	zhuīchá	investigate and trace; find out
追悼	zhuīdào	mourn over a person's death
追赶	zhuīgǎn	quicken one's pace to catch up; pursue
追究	zhuījiū	look into; find out; investigate (police)
追求	zhuīqiú	seek; pursue; woo; court; chase
追问	zhuīwèn	question closely; make a detailed inquiry

熟语 Idioms

急起直追　jí qǐ zhí zhuī　　rouse oneself to catch up

准 zhǔn　丶　冫　冫　冫　冫　冫　汁　汁　准　准

（準　丶　冫　冫　冫　汁　汁　汸　洚　准　准　准　準）

释义 Meaning

（一）形容词 a.

accurate; exact: 他发音不准。His pronounciation is not accurate.

（二）动词 v.

1. allow; grant: 老师准了我三天假。The teacher has granted me three days off.

2. permit: 这里不准随便进入。People are not allowed to randomly enter here.

词语 Words and Phrases

准备	zhǔnbèi	prepare; get ready; intend; plan
准确	zhǔnquè	exact; accurate; precise
准时	zhǔnshí	punctuality; punctual; on time; on schedule
准许	zhǔnxǔ	permit; allow
标准	biāozhǔn	standard
批准	pīzhǔn	authorize; ratify; approve

捉 zhuō 一 丁 扌 扌 扩 护 护 捉 捉 捉

释义 Meaning

动词 v.

catch; capture: 他在公共汽车上捉住了一个小偷。He seized a pickpocket on the bus.

词语 Words and Phrases

捉弄	zhuōnòng	tease; make fun of; embarrass

熟语 Idioms

捉襟见肘	zhuō jīn jiàn zhǒu	so poor that one cannot afford to be adequately dressed to cover the body and the elbow at the same time; not enough resources to cover all needs.

桌 zhuō 丨 𠂆 广 卢 卢 卓 卓 卓 桌 桌

释义 Meaning

名词 n.

table; desk: 妈妈准备了一桌菜，可是客人还没来。Mother has prepared a table of dishes, but the guests haven't come yet.

词语 Words and Phrases

桌子	zhuōzi	desk; table

着 zhuó ` ⺀ ⺌ ⺝ 兰 差 羊 着 着 着 着

释义 Meaning

动词 v.

1. Land; touch down: 飞机着陆了，大家松了口气。The plane landed. Eveybody gave a sigh of relief.
2. 他身着蓝色运动服，看上去非常精神。He looks very energetic, wearing a suit of blue sportswear.

词语 Words and Phrases

着手	zhuóshǒu	put one's hand to; set about
着想	zhuóxiǎng	consider; think about
着重	zhuózhòng	stress; emphasize
沉着	chénzhuó	steady and thoughtful
衣着	yīzhuó	clothing

资 zī ` ⺀ ⺈ 冫 次 次 咨 资 资
(資 ` ⺀ ⺈ 冫 次 咨 咨 資 資 資 資)

释义 Meaning

名词 n.

capital: 他们合资购买了一部拖拉机。They pooled their capital and bought a tractor.

词语 Words and Phrases

资本	zībǐn	capital; what is capitalized on; sth. used to one's own advantage; equity

资本家	zīběnjiā	capitalist
资本主义	zīběnzhǔyì	capitalism
资产	zīchǎn	property; capital fund; capital; equity
资产阶级	zīchǎnjiējí	bourgeoisie; the capitalist class
资格	zīgé	qualification; seniority
资金	zījīn	fund; financial resource
资料	zīliào	means; data; material
资源	zīyuán	resources
资助	zīzhù	aid financially; subsidize; support
工资	gōngzī	salary; wages; pay
投资	tóuzī	invest; capital investment; money invested
外资	wàizī	foreign capital
物资	wùzī	goods and materials

子 zǐ 　 一 了 子

释义 Meaning

名词 n.

son; child: 他有两个孩子，一子一女。He has two children, a son and a daughter.

词语 Words and Phrases

子弹	zǐdàn	bullet
子弟	zǐdì	son and younger brother; children
子女	zǐnǚ	sons and daughters; children
子孙	zǐsūn	children and grandchildren; descendants; offspring; posterity
父子	fùzǐ	father and son

熟语 Idioms

妻离子散	qī lí zǐ sàn	broken family
花花公子	huā huā gōngzǐ	playboy; coxcomb; pleasure monger

字 zì　　`丶` `丷` `宀` `字` `宁` `字`

释义 Meaning

名词 n.

1. word; character: 这本书有五十万字。This book has fifty thousand characters.
2. pronunciation (of a word or charater): 他说话字字清楚。He pronounces every word clearly.

词语 Words and Phrases

字典	zìdiǎn	dictionary
字母	zìmǔ	alphabet
打字	dǎzì	type
汉字	hànzì	Chinese characters
名字	míngzì	name
数字	shùzì	number
文字	wénzì	writing
错别字	cuòbiézì	wrongly written or mispronounced words
繁体字	fántǐzì	the original complex form of Chinese characters
简体字	jiǎntǐzì	simplified Chinese characters

熟语 Idioms

识文断字　　shí wén duàn zì　　literate; be able to read

自 zì　　`丿` `亻` `自` `自` `自` `自`

释义 Meaning

（一）介词 prep.

from; since: 热烈欢迎来自各国的朋友。Warmly welcome friends from different countries.

(二) 副词 adv.

certainly; of course; naturally: 他来问我，我自有话回答。

If he come to ask me, I will certainly have words to answer.

词语 Words and Phrases

自从	zìcóng	since
自动	zìdòng	automatic; voluntarily; of one's own accord
自费	zìfèi	at one's own expense
自豪	zìháo	pride; be proud of
自己	zìjǐ	oneself; self; own; one's own
自觉	zìjué	conscious; aware; awakened; subjective
自来水	zìláishuǐ	running water; piped water; tap water
自满	zìmǎn	complacent; self-satisfied
自然	zìrán	nature; natural
自身	zìshēn	self; oneself; personally; in person
自私	zìsī	selfish; self-centered; egotistic
自我	zìwǒ	self; oneself; ego
自信	zìxìn	self-confidence; be sure of oneself; believe in oneself
自行车	zìxíngchē	bicycle; bike
自学	zìxué	study independently; teach oneself
自由	zìyóu	free; freedom; liberty
自愿	zìyuàn	voluntary; of one's own accord
自治	zìzhì	autonomy; self-government
自治区	zìzhìqū	autonomous region
自主	zìzhǔ	act on one's own; decide for oneself; keep the initiative in one's own hand; stand on one's own feet

熟语 Idioms

自力更生	zì lì gēng shēng	rely on one's own efforts

自始至终	zì shǐ zhì zhōng	from first to last; from beginning to end
自相矛盾	zì xiāng máo dùn	self contradictory; contradict oneself
自言自语	zì yán zì yǔ	talk to oneself; speak to oneself; soliloquize

总 zǒng ` ` ⺆ ⺍ ⺌ ⺈ 兰 总 总

（總 ⺥ ⺃ ⺃ ⺃ 纟 纟 纟 纠 纳 緃 絤 緫 緫 緫 緫 總）

释义 Meaning

（一）动词 v.

assemble; put together; sum up: 把两笔帐总到一块儿。 Put these two accounts into one.

（二）形容词 a.

general; overall; total: 总的情况对我们非常有利。The overall situation is very favorable to us.

（三）副词 adv.

anyway; after all; eventually: 不要着急，问题总会解决的。Don't worry, the problem will be settled sooner or later.

词语 Words and Phrases

总得	zǒngděi	must; have to; be bound
总共	zǒnggòng	in all; altogether; sum up; in the aggregate
总计	zǒngjì	amount to; total; add up to; grand total
总结	zǒngjié	sum up; summarize; summary; summing-up
总理	zǒnglǐ	premier; chancellor
总是	zǒngshì	always
总数	zǒngshù	total; sum total

总算	zǒngsuàn	at long last; finally
总统	zǒngtǒng	president; the chief executive
总之	zǒngzhī	in a word; in short; in brief

熟语 Idioms

| 总而言之 | zǒng ér yán zhī | in short; in a word; in brief |

走 zǒu 　二　十　土　キ　キ　走　走

释义 Meaning

动词 v.

1. walk; go: 八个月的孩子已经会走了。A baby of eight months old can already walk.
2. run; move: 我的表不走了。My watch has stopped.
3. leave; go away: 明天她要走了，你不去送送她？ Tomorrow she will leave. Won't you go to see her off?
4. through; from: 咱们走这个门出去吧。Let's go out through this door.

词语 Words and Phrases

走访	zǒufǎng	interview; have an interview with; pay a visit to; go and see
走后门儿	zǒuhòuménr	get in by the "back door"; get sth. done through personal connection and influence
走廊	zǒuláng	corridor; passage; passageway
走私	zǒusī	smuggle; have extra-marital affairs
走弯路	zǒu wānlù	roundabout way; detour
走向	zǒuxiàng	move towards; head for; turn into; march to; be in transition to
奔走	bēnzǒu	rush about; hasten; run
赶走	gǎnzǒu	stave off; vote out; dislodge; dive away
逃走	táozǒu	run; flee

行走   xíngzǒu   walk; go on foot

熟语 Idioms

走马看花   zǒu mǎ kàn huā   observe the flowers from horseback; superficial understanding

走投无路   zǒu tóu wú lù   find oneself cornered; find no way out

租 zū   一　二　千　千　禾　利　和　租　租　租

释义 Meaning

动词 v.

rent: 她在学校附近租了一间房。She rented a room near the school.

词语 Words and Phrases

租金   zūjīn   rent; rental; rent payable by lessee to lessor

出租   chūzū   rent

房租   fángzū   rent (for a house, flat, etc.)

足 zú   丨　口　口　무　무　무　足

释义 Meaning

（一）名词 n.

foot; leg

（二）形容词 a.

1. enough; ample; sufficient: 吃饱了，喝足了。I have drunk and eaten to my satisfaction.

（三）副词 adv.

fully; as much as

1. 她哥哥足有一米九高。Her brother is fully 1.9 meters tall.

2. 我们足足等了一个钟头，她也没来。We spent fully an hour waiting for her and she still didn't come.

词语 Words and Phrases

足够	zúgòu	enough; ample; sufficient
足球	zúqiú	football; soccer; association football
足以	zúyǐ	enough; sufficient
充足	chōngzú	sufficient; abundant; adequate
满足	mǎnzú	satisfied

熟语 Idioms

丰衣足食	fēng yī zú shí	be well-fed and well-clothed; have ample food and clothing
画蛇添足	huà shé tiān zú	draw a snake by adding feet to it; ruin the effect by adding sth. superfluous
心满意足	xīn mǎn yì zú	content; be perfectly satisfied

族 zú   ` ﹃ 于 方 方 方 方 族 族 族 族

释义 Meaning

名词 n.

race; nationality: 他们都是维吾尔族。They are all ethnic Uygur nationality.

词语 Words and Phrases

汉族	hànzú	Han nationality
家族	jiāzú	house; clan; family
民族	mínzú	naitonality
少数民族	shǎoshùmínzú	minority

组 zǔ   ﹄ ﹂ 纟 纠 纽 纽 组 组

(組 ㄥ ㄠ ㄠ 幺 幺 糸 糸 紅 組 組 組 組)

释义 Meaning

（一）动词 v.

organize; form: 十个人组成一个小队。Ten persons form a group.

（二）名词 n.

group: 五十个人分成五个组。Fifty persons are divided into five groups.

词语 Words and Phrases

组合	zǔhé	make up; compose; constitute; association; combination
组长	zǔzhǎng	chief of a group
组织	zǔzhī	organize; structure; form; organization; organized system
词组	cízǔ	phrase
小组	xiǎozǔ	group; team

祖zǔ ` ㇕ 礻 礻 礻 礽 祖 祖 祖

释义 Meaning

名词 n.

originator: 他祖籍是福建厦门。His ancestral family home is Xiamen in Fujian province.

词语 Words and Phrases

祖父	zǔfù	grandfather
祖国	zǔguó	one's native country; motherland; mother country; fatherland; homeland
祖母	zǔmǔ	paternal grandmother
祖先	zǔxiān	ancestry; ancestors; forefather

嘴 zuǐ

丨 丨丨 丨丨 丨丨丨 丨丨卜 丨丨卜 丨卜 丨卜 丨卜 丨卜
丨卜 丨卜 嘴 嘴 嘴 嘴

释义 Meaning

名词 n.

mouth: 不认识没关系，有嘴就可以问。It doesn't matter if you don't know it, just ask.

词语 Words and Phrases

嘴巴	zuǐbā	mouth
嘴唇	zuǐchún	lip
插嘴	chāzuǐ	cut in; get a word in edgewise; be able to enter the conversation; interrupt
吵嘴	chǎozuǐ	quarrel
亲嘴	qīnzuǐ	kiss

熟语 Idioms

驴唇不对马嘴	lúchún bú duì mǎzuǐ	be beside the point; far-fetched answer or reasoning

最 zuì

丨 冂 冂 日 旦 旦 旱 旱 旱 最
最 最

释义 Meaning

副词 adv.

(used before an adjective or a verb) most; -est

1. 她有三个女儿，小女儿最漂亮。She has three daughters. The youngest one is the most beautiful.
2. 妈妈最了解自己的女儿。Mother understands her daughter best.

词语 Words and Phrases

最初	zuìchū	initial; first; original; the very beginning

最好	zuìhǎo	best; the first rate
最后	zuìhòu	final; last; ultimate; utmost
最近	zuìjìn	recently; lately

醉 zuì

二 丁 丌 丙 西 西 酉 酉 酉` 酉宀 酉宀 酉宀 酉宀 醉 醉

释义 Meaning

动词 v.

drunk; intoxicated; tipsy: 他喝醉了，不能让他再喝了。
He is tipsy. Don't let him drink any more.

尊 zūn

` ` 丷 广 广 芮 西 西 酋 酋 尊 尊

释义 Meaning

动词 v.

respect; venerate; honour: 尊老爱幼是她的好品德。Respecting the aged and caring for the children are her virtues.

词语 Words and Phrases

尊敬	zūnjìng	respect; venerate; revere; esteem
尊严	zūnyán	dignity; honour
尊重	zūnzhòng	respect; esteem; honor; value
自尊	zìzūn	self-respect; self-esteem

熟语 Idioms

| 妄自尊大 | wàng zì zūn dà | self-conceited; play the peacock |

遵 zūn

` ` 丷 广 广 芮 西 西 酋 酋 尊 尊 尊 遵 遵

释义 Meaning

动词 v.

abide by; obey; observe; follow: 遵上级之命，即刻办理此事。Act at once per the supervisor's instruction.

词语 Words and Phrases

遵守	zūnshǒu	abide by; observe; keep; comply with; obey (rules, laws, orders)
遵循	zūnxún	follow; abide by; comply with
遵照	zūnzhào	act in accordance with; obey

昨 zuó 丨 丨丨 日 日 昨 昨 昨 昨

释义 Meaning

名词 n.

night: 昨晚工作到十二点。Last night (I) worked till twelve o'clock.

词语 Words and Phrases

昨天	zuótiān	yesterday

左 zuǒ 二 ナ ナ 左 左

释义 Meaning

名词 n.

the left (side): 你一直走，往左拐，再走三四分钟就可以到那儿了。Go straight and turn to the left. After walking for three to four minutes, you will arrive there. 反义词：右

词语 Words and Phrases

左边	zuǒbiān	the left side
左右	zuǒyòu	the left and right sides; nearby; at hand; at one's side; courtier; attendant

熟语 Idioms

| 左右逢源 | zuǒ yòu féng yuán | all water runs to one's mill; everything goes well with one |

作 zuò ノ 亻 亻 仁 仁 作 作

释义 Meaning

动词 v.

1. compose: 他作的曲子非常好听。The song which he composed is very pleasant.
2. give sb. a report: 校长给学生作了一个报告。The principal gave the students a report.

词语 Words and Phrases

作案	zuò'àn	commit a crime or an offence
作法	zuòfǎ	way of doing or making a thing; method of work; practice
作废	zuòfèi	become invalid; discard as useless; be nullified; cancel; make null and void
作风	zuòfēng	style; style of work; way
作家	zuòjiā	writer
作品	zuòpǐn	works; composition
作为	zuòwéi	what one does; conduct; deed; action; achievement; accomplishment; regard as; take for; look on as; as
作文	zuòwén	write a composition; composition
作物	zuòwù	crop
作业	zuòyè	school assignment; homework; task
作用	zuòyòng	act on; affect; influence
作战	zuòzhàn	operation; combat; fight; conduct operation; do battle; war
作者	zuòzhě	author; writer

作主	zuòzhǔ	decide; take the responsibility for a decision
创作	chuàngzuò	create; produce; write; creation
动作	dòngzuò	action
工作	gōngzuò	work; job
合作	hézuò	cooperate; work together; collaborate
写作	xiězuò	write; compose; written work
著作	zhùzuò	write; works; book; writings

熟语 Idioms

自作聪明	zì zuò cōngmíng	act on the strength of one's own imagined cleverness
大有作为	dà yǒu zuòwéi	there is plenty of scope for one's talents
兴风作浪	xīng fēng zuò làng	stir up trouble; make waves

坐 zuò ノ 人 从 丛 坐 坐

释义 Meaning

动词 v.

1. sit: 请里边坐。Please be seated inside.
2. travel by or on (any conveyance except those which one straddles): 我坐船去日本。I went to Japan by ship.

词语 Words and Phrases

| 坐班 | zuòbān | work at one's office during office time |

熟语 Idioms

坐井观天	zuò jǐng guān tiān	see the sky from the bottom of a well; have a very narrow view of something
坐立不安	zuò lì bù ān	feel uneasy and restless whether sitting or standing
坐享其成	zuò xiǎng qí chéng	sit idle and enjoy the fruits of other's work; gains without pains

座 zuò ` 亠 广 广 庐 庐 座 座 座

释义 Meaning

量词 measure w.

(for mountains, buildings, and other similar immovable objects)

1. 他家后面有两座山。There are two mountains behind his house.
2. 这儿原来是一座古城。Originally this was an ancient city.

词语 Words and Phrases

座儿	zuòr	seat
座谈	zuòtán	have an informal discussion
座位	zuòwèi	seat; place
座右铭	zuòyòumíng	motto; maxim
茶座	cházuò	tea house; seats in a teahouse or tea garden
讲座	jiǎngzuò	a course of lectures

做 zuò 丿 亻 仁 什 仕 估 估 估 估 做 做

释义 Meaning

动词 v.

1. do; make; produce: 用这些木头做一张桌子。Use the wood to make a desk.
2. write; compose: 文章做好了。The article has been finished.
3. do; act; engage in: 他在广州做买卖。He does business in Guangzhou.

4. become; be: 做父亲的不能这样对待自己的孩子。As a father, you can't treat your child like this.

词语 Words and Phrases

做法	zuòfǎ	way of doing or making things; behavior
做工	zuògōng	do manual work; workmanship
做客	zuòkè	be a guest
做梦	zuòmèng	have a dream; dream
叫做	jiàozuò	be called; be known as

熟语 Idioms

白日做梦	báirì zuò mèng	daydream
小题大做	xiǎo tí dà zuò	a storm in a tea cup

Appendix 1

The *Hanyu Pinyin* (Romanization) System

(1) List of Initial Consonants（聲母表）

b	p	m	f	d	t	n	l
玻	坡	摸	佛	得	特	訥	勒
g	k	h		j	q	x	
哥	科	喝		基	欺	希	
zh	ch	sh	r	z	c	s	
知	蚩	詩	日	資	雌	思	

(2) List of Compound Vowels（韻母表）

		i	衣	u	烏	ü	迂
a	啊	ia	呀	ua	蛙		
o	喔			uo	窩		
e	鵝	ie	耶			üe	約
ai	哀			uai	歪		
ei	欸			uei	威		
ao	熬	iao	腰				
ou	歐	iou	憂				
an	安	ian	烟	uan	彎	üan	冤
en	恩	in	因	uen	溫	ün	暈
ang	昂	iang	央	uang	汪		
eng	亨	ing	英	ueng	翁		
ong	轟	iong	雍				

Appendix 2

Rules of the Stroke-order of Chinese Characters
汉字笔顺规则表

笔顺规则 Stroke-order Rules	例字 Examples	笔画顺序 Stroke Orders
先横后竖 "heng" precedes "shu"	十	一 十
	下	一 丁 下
先撇后捺 "pie" precedes "na"	人	丿 人
	天	一 天 天
从上到下 from up to bottom	言	亠 言 言
	喜	士 吉 壴 喜
从左到右 from left to right	做	亻 估 做
	洲	氵 氵 汈 洲 洲
从外到内 from outside to inside	同	冂 同
	月	刀 月
先里头后封口 inside precedes the sealing stroke	田	冂 田 田
	固	冂 固 固
先中间后两边 middle precedes the two sides	小	亅 小 小
	水	亅 刁 水
先右上后左下 the top right-hand corner precedes the bottom left-hand corner	边	力 边
	远	二 元 远
右上方的「点」最后写 leave "dian" in the top right-hand corner for the last	我	扌 我 我
	找	扌 找 找

Appendix 3

China's Nationalities
中国各民族

阿昌族	Achang	回族	Hui	羌族	Qiang
白族	Baizu	景颇族	Jingpo	俄罗斯族	Russ
布朗族	Blang	基诺族	Jino	撒拉族	Salar
保安族	Bonan	哈萨克族	Kazak	畲族	She
布依族	Bouyei	柯尔克孜族	Kirgiz	水族	Sui
朝鲜族	Chaoxian	拉祜族	Lahu	塔吉克族	Tajik
傣族	Dai	珞巴族	Lhoba	塔塔尔族	Tatar
达斡尔族	Daur	傈僳族	Lisu	土族	Tu
德昂族	De'ang	黎族	Li	土家族	Tujia
独龙族	Derung	满族	Man	维吾尔族	Uygur
东乡族	Dongxiang	毛南族	Maonan	乌孜别克族	Uzbek
侗族	Dong	苗族	Miao	佤族	Va
鄂温克族	Ewenki	门巴族	Monba	锡伯族	Xibe
高山族	Gaoshan	蒙古族	Mongol	瑶族	Yao
仡佬族	Gelao	仫佬族	Mulam	彝族	Yi
京族	Gin	纳西族	Naxi	裕固族	Yugur
汉族	Han	怒族	Nu	藏族	Zang
哈尼族	Hani	鄂伦春族	Oroqen	壮族	Zhuang
赫哲族	Hezhen	普米族	Primi		

Appendix 4

The Twenty-four Solar Terms
二十四节气表

Solar Terms 节气名(日期)	Equivalent Signs of the Zodiac 相当于黄道十二宫的位置
立春 the Beginning of Spring (Feb. 3, 4 or 5)	宝瓶宫 Aquarius
雨水 Rain Water (Feb. 18, 19 or 20)	双鱼宫 Pisces
惊蛰 the Waking of Insects (Mar. 5, 6 or 7)	双鱼宫 Pisces
春分 the Spring Equinox (Mar. 20, 21 or 22)	白羊宫 Aries
清明 Pure Brightness (Apr. 4, 5 or 6)	白羊宫 Aries
谷雨 Grain Rain (Apr. 19, 20 or 21)	金牛宫 Taurus
立夏 the Beginning of Summer (May 5, 6 or 7)	金牛宫 Taurus
小满 Grain Full (May 20, 21 or 22)	双子宫 Gemini
芒种 Grain in Ear (June 5, 6 or 7)	双子宫 Gemini
夏至 the Summer Solstice (June 21 or 22)	巨蟹宫 Cancer
小暑 Slight Heat (July 6, 7 or 8)	巨蟹宫 Cancer
大暑 Great Heat (July 22, 23 or 24)	狮子宫 Leo
立秋 the Beginning of Autumn (Aug. 7, 8 or 9)	狮子宫 Leo
处暑 the Limit of Heat (Aug. 22, 23 or 24)	室女宫 Virgo
白露 White Dew (Sep. 7, 8 or 9)	室女宫 Virgo
秋分 the Autumnal Equinox (Sep. 22, 23 or 24)	天秤宫 Libra
寒露 Cold Dew (Oct. 8 or 9)	天秤宫 Libra
霜降 Frost's Descent (Oct. 23 or 24)	天蝎宫 Scorpio
立冬 the Beginning of Winter (Nov. 7 or 8)	天蝎宫 Scorpio
小雪 Slight Snow (Nov. 22 or 23)	人马宫 Sagittarius
大雪 Great Snow (Dec. 6, 7 or 8)	人马宫 Sagittarius
冬至 the Winter Solstice (Dec. 21, 22 or 23)	摩羯宫 Capricorn
小寒 Slight Cold (Jan. 5, 6 or 7)	摩羯宫 Capricorn
大寒 Great Cold (Jan. 20 or 21)	宝瓶宫 Aquarius

Appendix 5

A Chronology of Chinese Dynasties
中国朝代年表

五帝　（公元前约26世纪初至公元前2070年）　The Five Rulers

夏　（公元前2070年至公元前1600年）　The Xia Dynasty

商　（公元前1600年至公元前1046年）　The Shang Dynasty

周　（公元前1046年至公元前256年）　The Zhou Dynasty

   西周　（公元前1046年至公元前771年）　The Western Zhou Dynasty

   东周　（公元前770年至公元前256年）　The Eastern Zhou Dynasty

秦　（公元前221年至公元前206年）　The Qin Dynasty

汉　（公元前206年至公元220年）　The Han Dynasty

   西汉　（公元前206年至公元23年）　The Western Han Dynasty

   东汉　（25年至220年）　The Eastern Han Dynasty

三国　（220年至280年）　The Three Kingdoms

   魏　（220年至265年）　The Wei Dynasty

   蜀汉　（221年至263年）　The Shu Han Dynasty

   吴　（222年至280年）　The Wu Dynasty

晋　（265年至420年）　The Jin Dynasty

   西晋　（265年至316年）　The Western Jin Dynasty

   东晋　（317年至420年）　The Eastern Jin Dynasty

十六国　（304年至439年）　The Sixteen Kingdoms

南北朝　（420年至589年）　Northern and Southern Dynasties

   南朝　Southern Dynasties

      宋　（420年至479年）　The Song Dynasty

      齐　（479年至502年）　The Qi Dynasty

      梁　（502年至557年）　The Liang Dynasty

      陈　（557年至589年）　The Chen Dynasty

   北朝　Northern Dynasties

      北魏　（386年至534年）　The Northern Wei Dynasty

东魏　（534年至550年）　The Eastern Wei Dynasty

北齐　（550年至577年）　The Northern Qi Dynasty

西魏　（535年至556年）　The Western Wei Dynasty

北周　（557年至581年）　The Northern Zhou Dynasty

隋　（581年至618年）　The Sui Dynasty

唐　（618年至907年）　The Tang Dynasty

五代十国　（907年至979年）　Five Dynasties and Ten Kingdoms

五代　（907年至960年）　Five Dynasties

后梁　（907年至923年）　The Posterior Liang Dynasty

后唐　（923年至936年）　The Posterior Tang Dynasty

后晋　（936年至946年）　The Posterior Jin Dynasty

后汉　（947年至950年）　The Posterior Han Dynasty

后周　（951年至960年）　The Posterior Zhou Dynasty

十国　（902年至979年）　The Ten Kingdoms

宋　（960年至1279年）　The Song Dynasty

北宋　（960年至1127年）　The Northern Song Dynasty

南宋　（1127年至1279年）　The Southern Song Dynasty

辽　（907年至1125年）　The Liao Dynasty

西夏　（1038年至1227年）　The Western Xia Dynasty

金　（1115年至1234年）　The Jin Dynasty

元　（1279年至1368年）　The Yuan Dynasty

明　（1368年至1644年）　The Ming Dynasty

清　（1644年至1911年）　The Qing Dynasty

Appendix 6

Names of Notable Places

Provinces, Autonomous Regions, Municipalities and Special Administration Regions
中国各省、自治区、直辖市和特别行政区

Names （名称）		Classification （区分）	Abbreviation （简称）	Capital （省会或首府）
安徽	Anhui	省	皖 Wan	合肥 Hefei
北京	Beijing	市	京 Jing	
重庆	Chongqing	市	渝 Yu	
福建	Fujian	省	闽 Min	福州 Fuzhou
甘肃	Gansu	省	甘、陇 Gan, Long	兰州 Lanzhou
广东	Guangdong	省	粤 Yue	广州 Guangzhou
广西	Guangxi	壮族自治区	桂 Gui	南宁 Nanning
贵州	Guizhou	省	贵、黔 Gui, Qian	贵阳 Guiyang
海南	Hainan	省	琼 Qiong	海口 Haikou
河北	Hebei	省	冀 Ji	石家庄 Shijiazhuang
黑龙江	Heilongjiang	省	黑 Hei	哈尔滨 Harbin
河南	Henan	省	豫 Yu	郑州 Zhengzhou
香港	Hong Kong	特别行政区	港 Gang	
湖北	Hubei	省	鄂 E	武汉 Wuhan
湖南	Hunan	省	湘 Xiang	长沙 Changsha
江西	Jiangxi	省	赣 Gan	南昌 Nanchang
江苏	Jiangsu	省	苏 Su	南京 Nanjing
吉林	Jilin	省	吉 Ji	长春 Changchun
辽宁	Liaoning	省	辽 Liao	沈阳 Shenyang
澳门	Macao	特别行政区	澳 Ao	
内蒙古	Neimenggu	自治区	内蒙古 Neimenggu	呼和浩特 Hohhot
宁夏	Ningxia	回族自治区	宁 Ning	银川 Yinchuan
青海	Qinghai	省	青 Qing	西宁 Xining
陕西	Shaanxi	省	陕、秦 Shan, Qin	西安 Xi'an
山东	Shandong	省	鲁 Lu	济南 Jinan

Names （名称）		Classification （区分）	Abbreviation （简称）	Capital （省会或首府）
上海	Shanghai	市	沪、申 Hu, Shen	
山西	Shanxi	省	晋 Jin	太原 Taiyuan
四川	Sichuan	省	川、蜀 Chuan, Shu	成都 Chengdu
台湾	Taiwan	省	台 Tai	台北 Taibei
天津	Tianjin	市	津 Jin	
新疆	Xinjiang	维吾尔族自治区	新 Xin	乌鲁木齐 Urumqi
西藏	Xizang	自治区	藏 Zang	拉萨 Lhasa
云南	Yunnan	省	云、滇 Yun, Dian	昆明 Kunming
浙江	Zhejiang	省	浙 Zhe	杭州 Hangzhou